THE OXFORD HANDBOOK OF

OFFSHORING AND GLOBAL EMPLOYMENT

THE OXFORD HANDBOOK OF

OFFSHORING AND GLOBAL EMPLOYMENT

Edited by

ASHOK BARDHAN, DWIGHT M. JAFFEE

and

CYNTHIA A. KROLL

OXFORD
UNIVERSITY PRESS

OXFORD
UNIVERSITY PRESS

Oxford University Press is a department of the University of Oxford.
It furthers the University's objective of excellence in research, scholarship,
and education by publishing worldwide.

Oxford New York
Auckland Cape Town Dar es Salaam Hong Kong Karachi
Kuala Lumpur Madrid Melbourne Mexico City Nairobi
New Delhi Shanghai Taipei Toronto

With offices in
Argentina Austria Brazil Chile Czech Republic France Greece
Guatemala Hungary Italy Japan Poland Portugal Singapore
South Korea Switzerland Thailand Turkey Ukraine Vietnam

Published in the United States of America by
Oxford University Press
198 Madison Avenue, New York, NY 10016

Library of Congress Cataloging-in-Publication Data

The Oxford handbook of offshoring and global employment / edited by
Ashok Bardhan, Dwight M. Jaffee, and Cynthia A. Kroll.
p. cm. — (Oxford handbooks)
Includes bibliographical references and index.
ISBN 978-0-19-976590-4 (cloth : alk. paper) 1. Offshore outsourcing.
2. Labor market. I. Bardhan, Ashok Deo, 1957– II. Kroll, Cynthia A.
III. Jaffee, Dwight M., 1943–
HD2365.O99 2013
331.12—dc23
2012038210

ISBN 978-0-19-976590-4

1 3 5 7 9 8 6 4 2
Printed in the United States of America
on acid-free paper

Contents

SECTION IB SMALL, DEVELOPED, AND OPEN ECONOMIES

SECTION II OTHER DEVELOPED COUNTRIES

SECTION III THE BRIC COUNTRIES

Acknowledgments

We would like to thank the Policy Advisory Board of the Fisher Center for Real Estate and Urban Economics as well as the Haas School of Business, University of California Berkeley, which provided support for preparing this book. We would like to acknowledge comments and suggestions from Pranab Bardhan, Claire Brown, Farok Contractor, Samir Dutt, Robert Edelstein, Michael Reich, AnnaLee Saxenian, Tim Sturgeon, Branko Urosevic, Pravin Varaiya, and Richard Walker. Tyler Fach, student assistant at the Fisher Center for Real Estate and Urban Economics collected background material and acted as chief herder—ensuring that authors received and returned materials in a timely manner. The Industry Studies Association list serve was a useful forum in the early stages of the book as we shaped our topic and identified authors. We would also like to thank the Oxford University Press, especially Catherine Rae, Terry Vaughn, and Cathryn Vaulman, as well as their production team at Newgen Knowledge Works in India headed by Sreejith Viswanathan. Given the subject matter of the book, we were interested to participate in a fully global process of production. Of course this volume would not have been possible without the participation of the numerous contributing authors whose work appears on the following pages.

List of Contributors

Jyrki Ali-Yrkkö is head of unit at the Research Institute of the Finnish Economy (ETLA).

Miriam Altman is distinguished research director at the Human Sciences Research Council in South Africa.

Penny Bamber is research associate at the Center on Globalization Governance & Competitiveness, Duke University.

Ashok Bardhan is senior research associate at the Fisher Center for Real Estate and Urban Economics, Haas School of Business, University of California, Berkeley.

Frank Barry is professor of international business and development at the School of Business, Trinity College, Dublin.

William J. Baumol is the Harold Price professor of entrepreneurship and in the Stern School of Business at New York University; he is also senior economist and professor emeritus in the Department of Economics at Princeton University.

Bob Bell Jr. is a PhD candidate at University of California at Berkeley's School of Information where he focuses on the emergence and internationalization of African IT-enabled services sectors.

Adele Bergin is a research officer at the Economic and Social Research Institute and an adjunct lecturer in economics at Trinity College, Dublin.

Thomas Bernhardt is a PhD candidate in economics at the New School for Social Research.

Fabien Besson is trade economist in the Trade and Investment Department of the French directorate-general of the treasury and associated researcher of the Centre d'Economie de la Sorbonne (University Paris 1, Panthéon-Sorbonne).

Thomas Bredgaard is associate professor at the Centre for Labour Market Research, Department of Political Science, Aalborg University in Denmark.

Rosario Crinò is assistant professor of economics at CEMFI.

Arthur Daemmrich is assistant professor at Harvard Business School and visiting professor at the China Europe International Business School (CEIBS) in Shanghai.

Gouranga Gopal Das is professor of economics at the Department of Economics, Hanyang University, South Korea.

Matthias Deschryvere is research scientist at the innovation studies unit of VTT Technical Research Centre of Finland.

Cédric Durand is associate professor in economics in Paris 13 and member of the CEPN (CNRS, University Paris 13).

Cai Fang is director of the Institute of Population and Labor Economics, Chinese Academy of Social Sciences and serves as the member of the Standing Committee of the 11th National People's Congress.

Karina Fernandez-Stark is a senior research analyst at the Center on Globalization, Governance & Competitiveness, Duke University.

Gary Gereffi is professor, Department of Sociology, and director, Center on Globalization, Governance & Competitiveness, Duke University.

Naj Ghosheh is research officer at the International Labour Organization on working and employment conditions as well as labour and company law issues.

Paulo Roberto Gião was a visiting PhD student at Judge Business School, University of Cambridge, and received his PhD from University of São Paulo.

Ralph E. Gomory is research professor in the Stern School of Business at New York University; he is the former president of the Alfred P. Sloan Foundation and the former head of IBM's Research Division.

Hongyul Han is professor of economics at the Department of Economics, Hanyang University, South Korea, since 1995 and senior research fellow at the Center for International Economic Studies.

Daniel Horgos is research associate at the Department of Economics and Social Sciences, Helmut Schmidt University, Hamburg.

Banri Ito is associate professor of economics, Senshu University, and fellow (adjunct) at the Research Institute of Economy, Trade and Industry.

Dwight M. Jaffee is the Willis H. Booth Professor of Banking and Finance at the Haas School of Business, University of California, Berkeley, where he is the faculty director of the school's masters in financial engineering program and a cochair of the Fisher Center for Real Estate and Urban Economics.

Julia Kotlarsky is professor of technology and global sourcing at Aston Business School, Aston University, United Kingdom.

Cynthia A. Kroll is senior regional economist and executive director for staff research at the Fisher Center for Real Estate and Urban Economics, University of California, Berkeley.

Ekaterina Kuraksina is an analyst for the Man Group plc.

Natalia Levina is an Associate Professor at the Information, Operations, and Management Sciences Department at the Stern School of Business, New York University.

Jon C. Messenger is senior research officer at the ILO, with the lead responsibility for its program on working time and work organization.

William Milberg is professor and chair of economics at the New School for Social Research and a fellow at the New School's Schwartz Center for Economic Policy Analysis.

Sébastien Miroudot is senior trade policy analyst in the Trade in Services Division of the OECD Trade and Agriculture Directorate.

Moacir de Miranda Oliveira Júnior is an associate professor of strategy and international business at the Business Administration Department, University of São Paulo.

Balaji Parthasarathy is the ICICI associate professor at the International Institute of Information Technology, Bangalore, India.

Enrique Dussel Peters is a professor at the Graduate School of Economics, Universidad Nacional Autónoma de México (UNAM) and consultant for several Mexican and international institutions.

Yasuyuki Todo is professor, Department of International Studies, Graduate School of Frontier Sciences, University of Tokyo, and faculty fellow, the Research Institute of Economy, Trade and Industry.

Eiichi Tomiura is dean, College of Economics, and professor of economics at the Graduate School of Social Sciences, Yokohama National University, and faculty fellow, the Research Institute of Economy, Trade and Industry, Japan.

Désirée van Gorp is professor of international business strategy and associate dean of degree programs, Nyenrode Business Universiteit, the Netherlands.

Desirée van Welsum is an economist at The Conference Board (USA). This work was undertaken prior to her appointment at The Conference Board.

Ryuhei Wakasugi is professor at the Center for Economic Growth Strategy, Yokohama National University and Institute of Economic Research, Kyoto University, and program director of the Research Institute of Economy, Trade and Industry, Japan

Meiyan Wang is a professor at the Institute of Population and Labor Economics, Chinese Academy of Social Sciences.

Deborah Winkler is a consultant at the World Bank International Trade Department and research associate with the Schwartz Center for Economic Policy Analysis at the New School for Social Research.

Du Yang is a professor at the Institute of Population and Labor Economics, chief of the Division of Labor and Human Capital, and deputy director at the Research Center for Human Resources, Chinese Academy of Social Sciences.

Qu Yue is an associate professor in the Institute of Population and Labor Economics, Chinese Academy of Social Sciences.

Christopher Ziguras is associate professor of international studies at RMIT University in Melbourne, Australia.

Editors' Note

How global economic integration and technological change impact job creation in countries around the world is a matter of acute interest for policy makers and scholars. We began our study of globalization and offshoring in the mid-1990s. The offshoring of manufacturing had accelerated and changing telecommunications technology was just beginning to enable global trade of many services activities previously thought to be firmly in the local or domestic sphere. The global labor market for many occupations and activities initially seemed a one-way migration of jobs from developed to developing economies, but it soon became evident that a more complex mix of effects and impacts was under way in both sets of countries. Data limitations and even conceptual issues related to measuring services trade and trade in intermediate goods made analysis of employment effects challenging. However, over the past decade, a rich body of literature has emerged that has effectively confronted this challenge. The collection of essays in this book pulls together work of some of the most eminent scholars and thinkers in the field as well as some "emerging" experts. The work is unique on two counts: first, it looks at both sides of the offshoring divide—from the point of view of countries that have offshored jobs, as well as the perspective of countries in the developing world that have been at the receiving end; and second, many of the chapters also deal with the impact of the global economic crisis, which brought all these issues into sharper focus.

SECTION IA

GLOBALIZATION AND EMPLOYMENT IN THE DEVELOPED WORLD

CHAPTER 1

The Global Lessons of Offshoring

ASHOK BARDHAN, DWIGHT JAFFEE,
AND CYNTHIA KROLL

Over recent decades, the issue of globalization has generated animated debate and discussion among policymakers, academics, and affected citizens alike. In the aftermath of the Great Recession of 2008 and the continuing tepid recovery in the global economy, the topic has acquired a renewed urgency and edge. The offshore migration of jobs, first from manufacturing and later from services, has led to a contentious debate over the costs and benefits of globalization. In the developed economies, there is growing concern over the prospects for job creation, competitiveness, and future standards of living. At the same time, developing countries and the hitherto fast-growing emerging economies are feeling increasingly insecure about the sustainability of their recent economic boom. While many emerging countries have been significant beneficiaries of the offshoring phenomenon, they increasingly face their own social and economic problems, in some cases arising out of the very success story of their economic growth. There are widespread challenges from growing inequality, uneven economic development, widening rural–urban divide, and educational, infrastructural and institutional constraints. These concerns are an understandable response as long as it remains unclear to what extent the "winners" will share the dividends of globalization to achieve broader social goals.

Technological change, the other iconic phenomenon of our times, has been closely intertwined with the impacts of globalization. Technological advances have been a major driver of economic growth. At the same time, they have had a disruptive effect, particularly when seen as the source of job losses. Indeed, the costs to those losing their jobs may be virtually the same whether the actual causative factor is offshoring or domestic technological change.

How globalization and technological change interact to impact employment, the key politico-economic variable of interest globally, is the central purpose and objective of this book. Two other defining characteristics of this volume, that set it apart from other edited books on global economic integration, are its global reach and its timing and context in the aftermath of the global economic crisis. We have brought together an extraordinary collection of academics, policymakers, and thinkers, who have authored country-specific chapters from both developed and developing parts of the world, representing a geographically and structurally diverse set of countries. The chapters also illustrate the wide variety of research methods and analytical perspectives that may be used to shed light on different aspects of globalization and employment. Drawing from multiple disciplines, multiple locations, and a wide array of employment experiences with globalization and offshoring, the collection presents a kaleidoscope of experiences in the globalized economy, demonstrating the opportunities and pitfalls that stem from global linkages.

Offshoring, Globalization, and the Research Questions Addressed

Many of the chapters in this book structure their analysis around the core concept of global offshoring. Some chapters apply a narrow concept of offshoring, defining it as a process whereby the production of a good or service that was earlier being carried out domestically in an industrialized country, say the United States, is now transferred to a developing country, say China, with the primary objective of importing the product or service back into the United States. Other chapters, however, employ and elaborate on somewhat more flexible variations of offshoring that may include, for example, foreign direct investment carried out for the purpose of serving foreign markets. The more flexible definitions underscore the more nuanced, multilateral, linkages between a variety of different economies at different stages of development and the more complex nature of global value chains.

While considerable research has been carried out on the impact of offshoring and other types of globalization on employment in the industrialized economies, the chapters in this book address additional topics that need further attention:

- The analysis of the impact on developing and emerging economies that host offshore activity remains in an early stage.
- Issues with regard to services offshoring have received limited attention, especially due to data limitations.
- The manufacturing–services dichotomy has yet to be factored in properly in the globalization debate.
- The incentives for globalization and offshoring—organizational, transactions costs related, firm-strategic, and others—remain in need of further clarification.
- The impacts of globalization on firm structure and behavior are still being worked out.
- Finally, the impact of the Great Recession of 2008 on the course and magnitude of global economic integration and on offshoring remains an open topic.

The impact on employment and wages is a key topic in many of the chapters. These discussions raise a wide range of related questions, including the following:

- Do different types of offshoring and global linkages have different consequences for employment?
- What happens to the skills mix of employment in the process of globalization, for both the developed and developing economy participants?
- What role do labor-market institutions and regulations play?
- Does the interaction between the education sector and labor market modify the impact of globalization?

Most chapters have been authored by academics, practitioners, and policymakers located in the countries studied. Thus, we have the China chapter written from the point of view of Chinese economists, the case study of Brazil is written by academics from Brazil, and so forth. We believe this provides a unique perspective on globalization based on the special vantage point of each country.

The book emphasizes the effects of globalization on both manufacturing and services sectors as well as across occupations. Indeed, some chapters examine service occupations within manufacturing sectors. Since these chapters have been written during a time of uncertainty in the global economy, as nations struggle to emerge from a period of crisis, they also address the importance of factors related to the business cycle in the country's globalization experience.

Given the United States' position as a center of the offshoring phenomenon, the discussions provide deep insights into the lessons of this stage of globalization for this country. Most importantly, the book allows policymakers and academics in the United States to learn about the employment impact of offshoring from the experiences with globalization of a wide range of diverse economies. In this introductory chapter, we summarize the contributions of the authors to the literature and identify some of the implications for the United States.

Book Scope, Organization, and Content

The chapters in the book employ a variety of approaches and concepts related to globalization and offshoring. For example, Gomory and Baumol frame their discussion as a conceptual and theoretical analysis of trade, comparative advantage, and their effects on employment, while Fernandez-Stark, Bamber, and Gereffi build their discussion of Latin America on the conceptual framework of global value chains, and Bernhardt and Milberg focus on the connection between socioeconomic outcomes and international economic performance. Other authors focus on a narrower definition of offshoring. Horgos discusses alternative indices used for offshoring, while Besson, Durand, and Miroudot, as well as Das and Han, point to the shortcomings of relying on an imported input measure alone, which fails to capture the possibility of offshoring final assembly. Other authors select a specific segment of activity in a sector; for example, the offshoring of research and development by Finnish firms is the focus in the chapter by Deschryvere and Ali-Yrkkö.

Research methodologies and approaches range from analysis that is predominantly theoretical and conceptual to empirical studies applying descriptive statistics or detailed econometric analysis, or both. Some studies take a cross-country approach while others provide a cross-industry analysis within a given country. The analyses include both industrywide surveys and qualitative descriptions based on in-depth interviews and case studies. There is a normative–positive split, with some studies providing statistical analysis of the effect on employment and wages, others focusing on business-oriented assessments of a country's potential for offshore linkages, while still others take an explicitly policy perspective.

The book covers a significant part of the developed and developing world. Countries included in the volume are shown in Table 1.1, with general economic characteristics as of 2010 (unless otherwise noted). Economies were chosen to provide a wide range in size, from Kenya and Ireland to the two largest—the United States and China. Population ranges from under 5 million (Ireland) to over a billion (India and China). A vast diversity of incomes per capita and inequality levels is also represented, as are levels of openness of economies. With this degree of variation among countries, the book provides a comprehensive look at how globalization, technological change, and economic development have evolved in different locations, the range of effects on different types of economies and on employment levels, and the lessons that are available for economic policy at this present stage in the global economy.

We divide the book into sections, by level of economic development and country size, informed by geographic clustering. Thus we have the United States and large western European countries forming the first part of section I. Section I then continues with smaller developed countries, such as Denmark, Finland, and the Netherlands. Section II includes developed countries with complex multilateral linkages (Japan, Korea, Ireland, and Australia), some of which have experience with both sides of offshoring transactions. Section III has the four BRIC countries, Brazil, Russia, India, and China, the last two having played a defining role in offshoring and globalization debates. Finally, section IV presents chapters on a range of developing countries from three different continents, starting with two chapters that carry out cross-country comparisons among the developing countries.

Section Ia: Globalization and Employment in the Developed World

In chapter 2, Gomory and Baumol extend the earlier debate between Samuelson (2004) and Bhagwati, Panagaria, and Srinivasan (2004), as well as their own earlier work (Gomory and Baumol 1998 and 2000), to present a conceptual discussion of changing

Table 1.1 Comparative economic and social data (2010 unless otherwise indicated)

Country	GDP ($ billion, PPP*)	Population	Per capita income or GDP per capita ($)	Gini coefficient	GDP rate of growth %	Exports ($ billion)	Imports ($ billion)	Exports/GDP	Imports/GDP	Export Share/ Import Share
Australia	882.4	21,766,711	41,000	30.5 (2006)	2.7	210.9	195.2	.24	.22	1.080
Brazil	2,172	203,429,773	10,800	53.9 (2009)	7.5	201.9	181.7	.09	.08	1.111
Chile	257.9	16,888,760	15,400	52.1 (2009)	5.3	71.03	55.17	.28	.21	1.287
China	10,090	1,336,718,015	7,600	41.5 (2007)	10.3	1,581	1,327	.16	.13	1.191
Denmark	201.7	5,529,888	36,600	29 (2007)	2.1	96.58	87.44	.48	.43	1.105
Finland	186	5,259,250	35,400	26.8 (2008)	3.1	69.4	64.96	.37	.35	1.068
France	2,145	65,312,249	33,100	32.7 (2008)	1.5	517.3	590.5	.24	.28	0.876
Germany	2,940	81,471,834	35,700	27 (2006)	3.5	1,303	1,099	.44	.37	1.186
India	4,060	1,189,172,906	3,500	36.8 (2004)	10.4	225.4	359	.06	.09	0.628
Ireland	172.3	4,670,976	37,300	29.3 (2009)	-1	111.3	61.98	.65	.36	1.796
Japan	4,310	126,475,664	34,000	37.6 (2008)	3.9	765.2	639.1	.18	.15	1.197
Kenya	66.03	41,070,934	1,600	42.5 (2008)	5	4.984	10.63	.08	.16	0.469
S. Korea	1,459	48,754,657	30,000	31.4 (2009)	6.1	464.3	422.4	.32	.29	1.099
Mexico	1,567	113,724,226	13,900	51.7 (2008)	5.5	298.5	306	.19	.20	0.975
Netherlands	676.9	16,847,007	40,300	30.9 (2007)	1.7	485.9	429	.72	.63	1.133
Philippines	351.4	101,833,938	3,500	45.8 (2006)	7.3	50.72	61.07	.14	.17	0.831
Russia	2,223	138,739,892	15,900	42.2 (2009)	4	400.1	248.7	.18	.11	1.609
S. Africa	524	49,004,031	10,700	65 (2005)	2.8	85.83	81.86	.16	.16	1.048
UK	2,173	62,698,362	34,800	34 (2005)	1.3	410.3	561.6	.19	.26	0.731
USA	14,660	313,232,044	47,200	45 (2007)	2.8	1,289	1,936	.09	.13	0.666

Source: CIA, *The World Fact Book*, https://www.cia.gov/library/publications/the-world-factbook/rankorder/rankorderguide.html.
* Purchasing Power Parity.

comparative advantage between an advanced and a rapidly developing economy. They highlight circumstances under which increased trade is not always beneficial to both parties. They outline various cases where changing conditions in one of the countries may lead to asymmetric benefits from trade. One possibility is that enhanced productivity in a trading partner may be harmful to the home country. This arises in their analysis from a dominant/dominated trade relationship between two countries that is beneficial to the dominating and harmful to the dominated country. The dominant position may be reached either by circumstances or by strategy (e.g., by pursuing a deliberate policy of subsidies, currency manipulation, and so on), while there are policy strategies regarding a diversified industrial base that can minimize the degree of domination that occurs. They conclude that in order to maintain prosperity, countries like the United States must go beyond a focus on education and innovation and find means of keeping segments of manufacturing of innovative products within the United States. Rather than tariffs, they suggest an export/import certificate scheme similar to carbon permits that will help balance trade.

Several authors address a diverse set of questions focused on globalization and the major European countries. In chapter 3, Crino takes advantage of a data set recently released by Eurostat that includes data on services imports by industry. He analyzes the effects of services offshoring on employment and wages in nine European Union countries across twenty different industries, over the period from the mid-1990s to the mid-2000s. A key finding is that the aggregate effects on employment are small and weakly positive overall, largely driven by business services. The effects are positive, but weakly significant, for all countries studied except France, Italy, and the Netherlands, and negative and significant consistently for France alone. He finds a complementary relationship between services offshoring and high-end employment and with no negative effects on skill groups at any of three levels. According to his results, "service offshoring may make labor demand more elastic, especially for low skilled workers in countries with weak labor market regulations."

Winkler (chapter 4) looks specifically at services offshoring, but within German manufacturing sectors. She finds that services offshoring within German manufacturing increased by an average of 5.6 percent annually between 1995 and 2004, but that the level of services offshoring is still quite small (0.85 percent in 2004, compared to 24.9 percent for total imported intermediate inputs, i.e., manufacturing offshoring). Winkler finds a negative relationship between the level of services offshoring and relative demand for white-collar workers in manufacturing, measured as their wage share in a sector's total wage bill. Interpreting the results, Winkler concludes that services offshoring may have reduced demand for white-collar workers in Germany by between 0.10 and 0.16 percentage points over the period 1995–2004, within the thirty-five manufacturing industries studied, and by perhaps as much as 0.22 percent if outlier sectors are excluded.

Daniel Horgos's analysis (chapter 5) also centers on Germany, but concentrates on the sector bias of labor-market effects of offshoring within the manufacturing sector. He argues that relative wages of high-skilled labor increase if offshoring takes place in the relatively high-skill intensive industry, while low-skilled labor receives a wage premium if offshoring takes place in the relatively low-skill intensive industry. Since high-skill sectors are more likely to offshore high-skill work, while low-skill sectors are most likely to offshore low-skill work, evidently this offshoring raises the wages of remaining workers in the skill category. As a result, offshoring low-skill work in low-skill industries will reduce the wage gap between high- and low-skilled workers, while the opposite effect occurs for offshoring of high-skilled work from high-skill industries. Like Crino, Horgos finds that labor market institutions (flexibility of wage adjustment and hiring and firing regulations) will also affect the degree and direction of employment effects.

The case of the other large continental European economy is analyzed by Besson, Durand, and Miroudot (chapter 6), who provide much more detail on France than does Crino's overview chapter on Europe and confirm the overall negative results of offshoring on French employment (using either measures based on imported inputs or on overall imports in consumption to capture the effects of final-assembly offshoring). When value added is examined, they find that the effects of offshoring may be positive, suggesting the possibility of a changing composition of skills accompanying job losses. While all manufacturing sectors in France have experienced increased offshoring over the past two decades, and many have experienced job losses accompanying this trend, there are some that have experienced job gains along with extensive offshoring. Services in general have experienced less offshoring than have manufacturing sectors, with a wider range of sectors experiencing employment gains. For France, they say, the substitution effect has been stronger than the scale effect. They find there are some sectors where offshoring is associated with a decrease in the labor share and an increase in the income of shareholders, while in some other sectors offshoring has allowed firms to increaseproductivity due to greater and more effective participation in global value chains."

Section Ib. Small, Developed, and Open Economies

Daemmrich and Bredgaard (chapter 7) examine the role that Denmark's institutional structure, including strong social welfare policies, has played in developing an economic niche for the country in an increasingly globalized world. They note that Denmark is a small open economy that has embraced international trade and outsourcing while at the same time funding world-class education, continuous upgrading of workplace skills, and comprehensive welfare programs. These "flexicurity" policies, according to the authors, have been key to building complementarities between a generous welfare state, a competitive labor market, and integration with the global economy. With the backing of unemployment, health, and other social insurance, as well as a broad set of social welfare programs, including retraining and retirement benefits, both workers and entrepreneurs can take risks in the emergent knowledge economy. Similarly, small and midsize Danish firms can afford to pioneer global market niche strategies to avoid direct competition with low-wage workers in developing countries. Critically, a century-long history of collective bargaining between employers and unions has given the country an established structure within which to cooperatively negotiate the consequences of globalizing production chains and a global labor force. Unions did not oppose job offshoring for some industries and occupations, as long as the change was accompanied by worker retraining and hiring opportunities elsewhere. Nevertheless, events in the most recent decade have challenged this national consensus from several directions. While cultural conflicts with immigrant communities have led to moves towards tighter controls on immigration, the dislocation caused by the financial crisis has led to new union demands in the face of declining unemployment benefits, and fiscal stress has threatened retraining programs.

Deschryvere and Ali-Yrkkö (chapter 8) use surveys of Finnish firms to test hypotheses regarding the offshoring of R&D. The authors find that for the 2001 to 2006 period, of firms (with fifty or more employees) conducting research and development, about 10 percent offshored R&D work. The organizational structure and channel of offshoring varied, with 5 percent doing captive offshoring and 6 percent resorting to offshore outsourcing. In contrast, 17 percent outsourced R&D domestically. They found that captive offshoring was significantly associated with employment decreases (for the 2006 to 2008 period), while outsourced offshoring had a positive association with employment change. The relationships appeared to be stronger for manufacturing firms than for services firms, but it is conceded that this may have been due to the small number of services firms in the sample.

Van Gorp and van Welsum (chapter 9) focus on the implications of services offshoring for a small, open European economy, in their case the Netherlands. They emphasize that services trade is very active in Europe and that much of this trade occurs among European countries. For the smaller countries in particular, offshoring provides access to a range of services and skills that are not available within the country. The Netherlands is one of the top three offshoring countries in the OECD. In the view of the authors, the image of offshoring as the transfer of low wage work to developing countries is an inaccurate simplification, and that in fact, the destination country may have relatively small wage differences and high education levels vis-à-vis the home country. They argue that the response to offshoring cannot be cost competition, as cost advantages are often short lived, even for developing countries. Instead they argue for a focus on the creation of sustainable comparative local advantages.

Section II: Other Developed Countries

This section includes case studies of other developed countries, namely Japan, Korea, Ireland, and Australia. They are separated here for geographic and for structural reasons. In some cases, "offshoring" is multilateral, in the sense that a country may both import and export intermediate goods and services in a complex and nuanced region-wide supply chain.

Tomiura, Ito, and Wakasugi (chapter 10) show a steady rise in outward foreign direct investment (FDI) for Japan, a large increase in the ratio of intermediate imports to value added, and a doubling of the ratio of offshore production to total sales among Japanese manufacturing firms. Their firm level data reveal some specific characteristics of offshoring firms:

- The number of firms active in resorting to offshore sourcing is much smaller than that active in domestic sourcing;
- Offshoring, as the sourcing of specialized intermediate products and services, excluding purchases of standardized intermediates, is overwhelmingly to China;
- Offshoring of service tasks and offshoring by small firms remain inactive;
- Offshore outsourcing firms are substantially more productive, capital-intensive, and larger than domestic firms but less so compared with firms setting up captive units in China.
- R&D is the only category in which the share offshored to the United States and Europe exceeds that offshored to China and it is the task most likely to be offshored to company-owned subsidiaries.
- Final-assembly and customer service are also more likely to be conducted by company subsidiaries, while most other tasks are more likely to be conducted at arm's length outsourced foreign firms.

Todo (chapter 11) also studies Japan, reporting on the offshoring aspects of small and medium-sized Japanese manufacturing firms, drawn from a data set comprising responses to two surveys, from 2006 and 2009. The author analyzes offshoring both from the perspective of a narrow definition, where the imported product is consumed in Japan, and a broader definition that includes international contracting. In his sample, less than 3 percent of firms are engaged in offshoring based on a broad definition and less than 1 percent based on the narrower definition, much lower than for the larger firms, as reported by Tomiura, Ito, and Wakasugi in chapter 10. Todo finds that offshoring is more likely to occur among firms with CEOs who have international experience and an outlook with a longer time horizon. Firm age, employment size, and previous exporting experience also influence the decision to offshore. The statistical analyses do not show a consistent impact of offshoring on employment levels, but to the extent that a significant relationship appears, it tends to be positive. Todo also concludes that offshoring is associated with a higher share of workers with college education. Combining his findings with those of other studies, he concludes that:

- Services offshoring is lagging behind goods offshoring in Japan, to a greater extent than in other developed countries;
- Goods offshoring has a positive impact on productivity, while services offshoring does not appear to impact productivity;
- Offshoring does not appear to reduce domestic employment, but may have a large effect on skill upgrading.

Das and Han (chapter 12), in describing trade in intermediate inputs between Korea and China, focus on the potential of a "tripartite regional production network" involving Japan as well, reflecting the relative economic development of the three partners. They note that this set of relationships is illustrative of a broader set of global value chain production relationships that involve many other East Asian countries. As China's economy has grown and globalized, its imports from East Asian countries and Korea have increased, especially of electronic intermediate goods, while at the same time it exports labor-intensive manufactured products. Korean manufacturing has developed as part of a triangle, with China as an assembly site, located between the production of higher-end technical inputs in Korea (by Korean or foreign companies) and the export of final goods to consumers worldwide. While Korea's early moves into China were cost related, later offshore investments in China expanded to include plants serving the growing Chinese market. The authors point to differential employment and wage effects from Korea's production sharing with Japan on the one hand (which shifted demand away from Korean tertiary workers) and China on the other (which shifted demand towards tertiary and away from secondary workers). They also highlight a number of factors encouraging this production relationship, including cultural affinity, geographic proximity, and the large size of the labor force in China that is available to replace the aging labor force in Korea.

Barry and Bergin (chapter 13) discuss the unique situation for Ireland among the European countries in this volume, better known as a destination for offshoring rather than a typical developed-country source of offshoring. Barry and Bergin focus on a range of FDIs in Ireland and the types of activities and jobs these have generated. Their chapter provides case studies of three of the most important FDI-intensive manufacturing sectors—ICT, pharmaceuticals, and medical devices—and two of the substantially foreign-owned internationally traded services segments—software and IT, and international financial services. As an English-speaking country, located between the United States and the rest of Europe, Ireland presented attractive opportunities as an export platform for US firms, with its EU membership giving the United States access to a much larger market than Ireland alone could have offered. The authors document the shift away from manufacturing to services activities, both within manufacturing firms (including marketing, information technology, and R&D related) and across a range of sectors from tourism to finance. Barry and Bergin also highlight policy issues, such as efforts to improve the country's education base, the support of institutions specifically focused on global business (such as IDA-Ireland and the International Financial Services Center), and the application of relatively low and stable tax rates. They describe how Ireland's inward FDI sectors have fared over the course of the global financial crisis: while office machinery fared poorly, the country's relative competitive advantage in pharmaceuticals and chemicals, as well as in computer and information services, helped counterbalance negative trends in other sectors.

Ziguras (chapter 14) highlights a different aspect of services globalization, the export of education services from a developed country, Australia, to a wide range of developing and emerging countries, primarily in Asia. Australia's geographic location has given the country a unique position in relation to the growing Asian economies. Major offshore programs began in Singapore, Malaysia, and Hong Kong—locations with a common British colonial history. Over 600,000 foreign students are enrolled in higher-education programs in Australia and an additional 150,000 are in offshore Australian programs, the two together accounting for more than one-fourth of all higher-education students enrolled in Australia. At US$16.2 billion in 2009–10, education expenditures by international students are the country's third most valuable export, behind only coal and iron ore. Ziguras points out that in the case of Australian institutions, the purpose of offshore sites is not to bring an enriched educational experience to Australian students (in contrast to a number of American university foreign programs aimed at US students) but to bring Australian programs to foreign students in their home countries, with the possibility of their later completing higher-education programs in Australia. The case of Australia highlights the increasingly global nature of services and the complex linkages and delivery modes.

Section III: The BRIC (Brazil, Russia, India, and China) Countries

Each BRIC-country chapter highlights unique attributes of that country's global economic position. In contrast to a number of other chapters in this book, which refer to China's role in the global value chain network, the article by Cai, Du, Wang, and Qu (chapter 15) argues that China's growth in the last decade has not been primarily due to trade, but has been primarily driven by growth in internal demand, and not exports or inward FDI. Using a shift-share approach, they conclude that the export-driven portion of growth in manufacturing was smaller than that due to the domestic portion. Wage growth has occurred for urban workers and migrants alike and for workers across sectors—agricultural, manufacturing, construction, and others. The authors assert that the "flying geese" pattern of development, where, as a country's economy becomes more developed and costly in terms of doing business worldwide, production activities are spun off to neighboring countries, will be internalized in China; that is, this pattern will occur domestically rather than across borders. The rising wages in the hinterland relative to the coastal cities are evidence of this, although the authors expect a wage differential to continue to exist. Nevertheless, this shift is not simply export production moving inland to cheaper labor markets, but it reflects a shift to production for the growing domestic market, with higher value-added production now increasingly occurring inland.

Parthasarathy (chapter 16) stresses the history of offshoring in information and communications technology (ICT) in illustrating the complex employment consequences in the offshore service-providing country (India). Technological changes and a series of complementary developments, such as developed countries looking to offshore services work as a means of cutting costs during periods of slumping demand for software products, helped India capitalize on the emerging opportunities in this sphere. Expansion of large offshore businesses in developing countries also led to growth in demand for a myriad of new products, leading to the move of innovation activities to India. Using case studies of Infosys and Cisco Systems, Parthasarathy emphasizes the nuanced nature of the effects of offshoring on labor markets and employment opportunities, with implications for both high- and low-skilled workers and for advanced and emerging economies. Infosys, for example, by 2010, had established sixty-three global development and delivery centers, with fewer than half in India. These included centers in customer areas, as well as "near shoring" centers that served customers in countries of the same geographic region (in South America and East Europe). The author concludes that offshoring to places like India is being driven by the emergence of new markets and the need for spatial proximity to meet growing new demand. Thus, the rationale for offshoring is no longer limited to either comparative advantage or to technological changes and is leading to multiple spatial outcomes.

Gião and de Miranda Oliveira Júnior (chapter 17) focus their paper on the complex range of activities of multinational corporations (MNCs) in Brazil. The chapter highlights the relationship between the MNC and domestic opportunities, as captive (intra-firm) offshoring by the MNCs to Brazil may be followed by domestic outsourcing by these subsidiaries of foreign MNCs to domestic Brazilian firms. The chapter concentrates on the distinction between strategic and nonstrategic offshoring activities. While offshoring is often characterized as an effort to find lower costs for routine activities, the authors' research finds that strategic activities are a significant component of captive offshore activity. They also note that the subsidiaries surveyed internalized both high and low value-added functions, while at the same time outsourcing similar functions as well, thus demonstrating a business model in which internal and external environments were complementary. Survey responses from 145 MNC subsidiaries reveal that many activities that the authors define as "strategic" (and that many other authors call high-end), such as R&D, innovation, and product development, are likely to be performed internally within offshore subsidiaries, and training for many of the strategic jobs tends to occur within the firm.

Kotlarsky, Levina, and Kuraksina, in the concluding chapter in this section (chapter 18), examine why Russia has not managed to expand its offshore services on the scale of India, China, or Brazil, as well as what the outlook is for the industry in Russia going forward. In evaluating the factors that contribute to the growth of offshore business worldwide, the authors find that wages and infrastructure costs may make Russia less competitive than other BRIC countries. Technical skills are a strong element of Russia's offshore services, but the authors warn that there is evidence the education system is not maintaining the same level of technical excellence as was inherited from the Soviet period. The largest Russian IT offshoring companies illustrate the emerging transnational nature of IT business, with some "Russian" companies using primarily Russian technical workers but headquartered in the United States or Eastern Europe. The majority of Russian offshore IT service providers are small to mid-sized niche players offering skilled and creative rather than low-cost routine work. FDI from US and Canadian firms is an integral driver of this sector, and most of the offshore customers are North American, although Western Europe is of growing importance. Following a SWOT analysis,[1] the authors conclude that the typical depiction of Russia in competition with other BRIC countries is not very accurate but that the major competitive threats for niche markets are SMEs from Central European nations.

Section IV: Other Parts of the Developing World

This section opens with two broad chapters that look at the employment effects and socioeconomic experience of developing countries with globalization and offshoring.

Ghosheh and Messenger (chapter 19) focus specifically on the discussion of offshoring of business services (whether captive or outsourced) from developed to developing countries and discuss considerations underlying the job-quality issues of business process outsourcing (BPO) employment. The chapter describes various aspects of the offshore relationship that can affect job quality, including salary, work load, hours, scheduling, job stability and security, workplace health and safety, and employee initiative and discretion. Research across developing countries in general has found that many BPO offshore jobs are of higher quality than the country's other, existing alternatives but that there is a wide variation in job quality, partly associated with the type of work and the structural relationship with the client for whom the work is performed. Back-office workers were found to have better working conditions than call-center workers, while MNC subsidiary (captive) jobs were typically of higher quality than outsourced ones. Other issues have also become important, such as the balance of work and family life (as many of the workers are women, entering the labor force for the first time), whether there is adequate skilled labor supply to sustain growth in the industry, and what spillover benefits, if any, might accrue to the country's wider economy. Authors also provide policy recommendations for policymakers and organizations to develop and implement practices at both the national and the workplace level that could result in better-quality jobs and working environment in this fast-growing industry.

Bernhardt and Milberg (chapter 20) conduct a study of four sectors—apparel, horticulture, mobile phones, and tourism—over the period 1990–2009 in a number of developing countries and examine the extent to which the internationalization of production has improved living standards in those developing countries that attracted significant offshoring activity. The authors connect industrial/economic upgrading to "social upgrading," with economic upgrading defined as a combination of growth in export market shares and export unit values and social upgrading defined as a combination of increases in sectoral employment and real wages. Facing data limitations, the authors nevertheless are able to illustrate the wide degree of variation in how expansion or contraction of a country's role in a global value chain may affect employment and wage levels. Both horticulture and apparel have seen an apparently simultaneous economic and social upgrading, implying wide spillovers and societal benefits. All four developing countries with sizeable global market shares (China, South Korea, Mexico, and Malaysia) had economic upgrading in mobile telecom, but appeared as likely to have social downgrading as upgrading in this sector. Tourism, where their sample included China, Turkey, and Thailand, in contrast, showed social upgrading in most countries, whether or not the country had experienced economic upgrading. Using alternative measures to aggregate the trends, the number of countries with both economic and social upgrading is reduced significantly. While recognizing the serious data limitations of the exercise, the authors use the results to question the assumption that there is a direct connection between productivity growth and trade performance on the one hand and economic prosperity in terms of employment levels and wages on the other. They note that industrial upgrading is a necessary but not sufficient condition for social upgrading. That is, economic upgrading does not automatically translate into progress on the social front. Instead the relation between the two is likely contingent on the specific institutions, regulations, and governance structures in place in the different countries and industries.

Fernandez-Stark, Bamber, and Gereffi (chapter 21) provide a broad overview of the trajectory of services offshoring in Latin America. Using a global value chain framework, they underline the importance of foreign direct investment in building an offshore services industry in many different parts of the region. The industry has largely depended on a customer base in the United States and Spain. Offshore service provision by Latin American countries has typically started with low-end services, but Chile, for example, which began with a strong entry into the call-center business has transitioned to higher-value services, including a successful segment in mining-related engineering offshoring. Peru, on the other hand, has continued to compete for lower-end services employment, drawing some of the early call-center business from Chile. While captive centers play a significant role in building the offshore services sector, global service providers are also active in Latin America, including several from India that opened offices originally to serve the local country but then expanded operations to serve a broader global area. As some of the early manufacturing offshoring began to shift from Brazil and Mexico towards China, the multinational companies shifted work from manufacturing to services for both local and offshore customers. Over time, a hierarchy of places has developed, with the higher-value jobs and services developing in the more advanced countries and larger cities, and call-center and other low-value offshore services moving to secondary cities and smaller countries. The switch, however, has not been job neutral. High-end offshore activity has produced relatively fewer jobs than at the lower end, and niche markets like specific engineering occupations have proved more volatile in terms of output and employment in response to economic shifts than have the lower end offshore activities.

Dussel Peters (chapter 22) describes the effects of Mexico's export-oriented industrialization strategy, which replaced the previous import substitution approach. The author argues that since the implementation of an export-oriented approach, GDP growth in Mexico has lagged behind much of Latin America. The country has maintained a trade surplus with the United States, but has had growing deficits with the European Union and Asia. Since the 1990s, manufacturing's share of exports has far exceeded that of oil (which accounted for 80 percent of Mexico's exports in the early 1980s). The majority of exports from Mexico, however, originated as temporary imports that are exported, resulting in an economy that depends on "import-oriented industrialization" to drive export growth. Because of this uncertain value-addition, the manufacturing share of GDP and of employment has dropped since the late 1980s. The yarn-textile-garment (YTG) value added chain illustrates the effects of the policy on the manufacturing sector. Although exports grew from 1995 to 2000, almost half the jobs have been lost since 2000, in part as a result of competition with Asian producers. Mexico's share of US YTG imports fell from 13 percent in 1999 to 5 percent in 2009, while China's share of US imports grew from 12 percent to 40 percent. Rather than moving up the value chain, or expanding local production through "social learning," manufacturing has become polarized, concentrated in a smaller number of firms, and increasingly dependent on imports.

Bell (chapter 23), by framing a case study of Kenya in the context of cluster development, illustrates the entrepreneurial aspects of offshore IT-enabled services. Bell describes the role of the early players, highlighting the individuals and firms that initiated BPO and call-center work in Kenya. The early stages of offshoring in Kenya relied on individual entrepreneurs who saw the opportunity to build a global customer base for services that could be delivered from Kenya. As these businesses developed, they spurred the need for broader institutional and infrastructure support. Bell emphasizes the role that national and international organizations as well as private bodies played in contributing to the infrastructure required by the IT industry. Kenya illustrates many of the limitations faced by small developing countries trying to leverage offshoring for economic development. Key impediments have included the size and skill set of the workforce, infrastructure availability and quality, "relational infrastructure" such as business linkages for offshore work, and financing (including start-up funding). The connection of Kenya to undersea fiber optic cables in 2009 did not bring the anticipated expansion of offshore work, indicating that other impediments were of equal or greater importance. Equally important have been policy issues, incentives, the political climate, and security perceptions. Domestic and near-sourcing IT operations face challenges somewhat different from offshoring challenges and are largely centered on building trust, identifying clients, and developing a reputation for being able to provide needed capacity. Nevertheless, the cluster development that began for BPO and call-center offshoring shows potential to become the basis for building a domestic industry.

Altman (chapter 24) examines the potential for BPO development in South Africa by comparing the country's attributes with the successful offshore service sectors that have developed in India and the Philippines. Altman places South Africa's interest in offshore services as being driven by the needs of economic development, and in the broader context of the increasing importance of services as an employment sector in the South African economy. BPO would offer job development opportunities across a range of skills and for a diverse set of customers that are very much needed in view of the very high rates of unemployment, especially for the younger workforce. There is a bifurcated labor force, with a large proportion of the black population having only recently started benefiting from universal education. At the same time, the country possesses a sophisticated and highly trained workforce in many types of business services. The need for increased employment has led to government policy encouraging BPO activity in the form of call centers, but with less attention as yet paid to higher-end sectors where the country has significant advantages, such as the finance sector. Large multinational providers (including several from India) have located in South Africa to provide services to customers in South Africa as well as to other parts of the continent. At the same time, South Africa outsources a significant amount of IT and other services work to India. Altman highlights the experience of India and the Philippines as a contrast to South Africa and points to the sector's potential to offer employment opportunities at a wide range of skill levels, allowing for skill upgrading of the labor force.

Insights, Future Directions, Ongoing Questions

This collection of essays by leading academics, policymakers, and researchers provides many insights on globalization, offshoring, and technological change and their impact on employment. Some implications stand out. First, although globalization has had a profound impact on the structure and location of specific industries, the overall impact on a country may be much more measured, especially if viewed over a relatively short time period. Second, the level, intensity, and actual direction of effects can vary widely among countries, even within the same economic "grouping" (advanced, emerging, developing). The effects are highly conflated with local factors: the history of economic development of each country is path dependent, and the cause–effect linkage so difficult to tease out, that any attempt to extract precise policies is fraught with difficulties, especially if globalization is very broadly defined.

Some of the other issues raised, policies probed, and questions discussed include:

- The findings of different empirical studies are often the result of applying different definitions and measures of offshoring. (For example, should imports of just intermediate inputs be taken into account or should it include imports of final assembly?)
- How are data issues concerning captive units to be taken into account? How may FDI for foreign sales be differentiated from that for offshoring purposes?
- Interactive effects are important; globalization involves simultaneous and complex impacts on many economic variables and is affected by them in turn.
- While many studies address findings at an individual industry or occupation level, spillover and multiplier effects beyond industry and occupational clusters are clearly important.

- While global labor arbitrage will continue to shape production location and wage structure, domestic demand remains a major driver of development for many countries. This is particularly true of most large countries, such as the United States, India, and Brazil. Indeed, the China chapter focuses on the sources of domestic demand and their role in the country's economic growth, confirming an old adage that local domestic market integration remains more important than global economic integration.
- Distance, national borders, jurisdictions, and currencies all matter. An efficiently globalized economy must also be well integrated locally and internally. In Mexico, initial success in international trade led it to bypass opportunities for developing and targeting local demand.
- Intrafirm trade in intermediate inputs is significant in overall trade, especially in high-tech goods. Intrafirm imports of intermediate goods and services by firms based in developed countries—that is, captive offshoring—have been important as well.
- Although a key organizing principle of the book has been to cluster chapters according to general perceptions of countries as advanced, emerging, or developing, there are highly developed sectors in emerging economies.There are also relatively advanced economies that take the role of an intermediate offshore host (such as Ireland), and there are countries (like South Africa) with dual economies, with some developed sectors, while the others struggle in the early stages of development. Offshoring, therefore, is not a simple one-way street.
- Several chapters point to the importance of networks, historical experience and memory, and the hysteresis factor. Countries that were at an early stage of offshoring when the crisis occurred were likely to find opportunities curtailed, while countries with established networks not only rode out the storm but even thrived.
- Infrastructural, regulatory, and institutional support can help an infant offshoring industry, expanding the application of the traditional infant industry argument.
- In the host country, long-term supportive policies, such as investment in education at all levels and the development of secondary and tertiary urban centers, may help make growth of this sector sustainable and allow the country to move up the value chain.
- Many developed countries, including large ones such as Japan and Germany, have retained and developed a high-end manufacturing sector in niche markets, thanks to judicious support from regulatory, institutional, financial, retraining, and educational resources.

Both developing and developed countries face the problem of mitigating the pain of adjustment from the changes wrought by globalization. The interplay of trade and technology has created "gainers" and "losers" in both sets of countries, leaving policymakers grappling with an overarching challenge to ensure that the benefits of the global specialization of labor can be channeled and harnessed for job creation and larger social and development goals. The trick is to compensate the "losers" from the overall net gains in a way that is not detrimental to efficiency, innovation, and future competitiveness.

Is There a Lesson to Be Drawn for the United States?

Lastly, we consider whether there are any lessons for policymaking in the United States, the center of the offshoring phenomenon. How do these chapters inform the US debate, which has been going on for over a decade? A number of US-based economists have been carrying out both theoretical and empirical work on the implications of offshoring/outsourcing for both manufacturing and services. Indeed, most of the initial empirical work on the impact of offshoring on manufacturing, as well as on services, focused on the US experience. Feenstra and Hanson (1996), Grossman and Helpman (2002), and Harrison and Macmillan (2011), among others, have written extensively on the causes, structure and jobs/wages impact of outsourcing and offshoring in manufacturing. Mann (2003) stresses the positive effect on productivity growth. Bardhan and Kroll (2003), Blinder (2006), Jaffee (2004), Dossani and Kenney (2006), Kirkegaard (2004), and Jensen and Kletzer (2005) have written on the labor market impact of services offshoring. Bardhan and Jaffee (2005) and Ernst (2006) point out the factors behind the emerging new wave of R&D offshoring from developed countries to China, India, and Russia, including the diminishing cost-effectiveness of innovative activity in developed countries, the need to "design to market" in developing countries, and the availability of low-cost scientific labor.

Three broad trends and issues inform the position of the US economy vis-à-vis the global economic situation and future competitiveness:

- Is the US offshoring of manufacturing, services, and R&D activity to cheaper locales abroad irreversible?
- Is the US shift into services similarly irreversible?
- Is innovation the only dependable and sustainable avenue for job creation?

It is the interaction of these three defining attributes of the US economy that set the stage and background for policymaking.

While offshoring may have adversely affected employment and increased inequality, it has also played a significant role in boosting productivity and helping US firms and sectors restructure. The massive hollowing-out of manufacturing has, however, raised a number of questions. Does manufacturing matter, and if yes, can it be brought back? And if manufacturing can be recovered, will it be through new manufacturing sectors, such as 3-D customized printing, which fuse customized craftsmanship and manufacturing, and bypass the "economies of scale" issue, which has been so well exploited by the emerging economies?

The fact that the US economy and most other developed economies are primarily services-based poses unique and unprecedented challenges to their national economic policies. Most of the services that are not offshoreable are precisely those where productivity growth is intrinsically slow (e.g., personal services) or sometimes not even desirable (arts, creative fields), which means that they become relatively costlier, condemning advanced economies to even higher cost structures in future. Many of these nonoffshoreable occupations operate in winner-take-all markets, leading to large disparities in incomes within the same occupation, in addition to rising inequalities across occupations. Furthermore, the competitive advantage of many developed countries in services does not necessarily lead to export-driven job creation, since the exports of services, such as consulting, legal, technical services, and so on, frequently lead to establishment of offices abroad and, as a consequence, local hiring. The delivery mode, lack of scalability, cultural specificity, and home-bias further hinder job creation through services exports. Analysis, as well as policy formulation, is complicated by what might be termed the "goods content of services and the services content of goods."

While some services do not require any tangible manufactured goods for their delivery, most others, such as medical care, software, and finance, do. Manufacturing and services are therefore inseparable; it is difficult to be competitive in manufacturing-dependent services without commensurate quality in supporting tangible goods. Of course, the latter could be manufactured abroad and imported, but that raises a strategic issue. Many sectors are of heightened importance relative to their weight in the economy, because they participate in the early stages of the sequential value chain (e.g., primary, resource sectors, such as oil), as well as due to the fact that many early stage inputs have few substitutes. Importing these from abroad may then give hold-up power to foreign firms and nations, a fact of clear strategic importance.

There is increasing recognition that the current competitiveness challenge differs significantly from its predecessors. This is not the 1980s threat of Japanese competition. Countries such as China and India, whose sectors and occupations are competing with the United States, enjoy the multiple attributes of low wages, large absolute numbers of skilled labor, a rapid approach to the technological frontier (with even the possibility of technological leapfrogging in some sectors), and a savvy consumer class of early adopters of new products and technologies.

For innovation to be the panacea for all ills of the US economy two questions must be answered. First, how can innovation be promoted? And second, how can it be ensured that it will lead to significant job creation? The latter question is linked both to the location and origin of innovation and to its economic appropriation. It also requires better coordination and harmonization between the higher-education sphere and the demands of the labor market (Bardhan, Hicks, and Jaffee 2012).

As Gomory and Baumol point out, traditional comparative advantage may no longer be determined by relative resource endowments, and international trade may no longer provide unequivocal welfare gains. The global distribution of jobs will likely be contested, with the contest covering a broad swath of industries and occupations across many countries. Ultimately, it may require concerted international effort to reconcile the four guiding elements of the global economy of our time—free markets, globalization, nation states as the unit of policymaking, and governments that respond to the demands of their citizens.

Note

1. SWOT is a commonly used strategic planning method of analysis that examines "strengths, weaknesses, opportunities, and threats."

References

Bardhan, A., D. Hicks, and D. Jaffee. 2013. "How Responsive is Higher Education? The Linkages between Higher Education and the Labor Market." *Applied Economics* 45 (10): 1239–1256.

Bardhan, A., and D. M. Jaffee. 2005. "Innovation, R&D and Offshoring." Fisher Center for Real Estate & Urban Economics Research Report (October).

Bardhan, A., and C. Kroll. 2003. "The New Wave of Outsourcing." Fisher Center for Real Estate & Urban Economics Research Report (October).

Bhagwati, J., A. Panagariya, and T. N. Srinivasan. 2004. "The Muddles over Outsourcing." *Journal of Economic Perspectives* 18 (4): 93–114.

Blinder, A. 2009. "How Many US Jobs Might be Offshorable?" *World Economics* 10 (2) (April–June): 41–78.

Dossani, R., and M. Kenney. 2006. "The Next Wave of Globalization: Relocating Service Provision to India." *World Development* 35 (5): 772–791.

Ernst, D. 2006. "Innovation Offshoring: Asia's Emerging Role in Global Innovation Networks." Honolulu: East-West Center.

Feenstra, R. C., and G. H. Hanson. 1996. "Globalization, Outsourcing, and Wage Inequality." *American Economic Review* 86 (2): 240–245.

Gomory, R. E., and W. J. Baumol. 1998. *National Trade Conflicts Caused by Productivity Changes.* http://pages.stern.nyu.edu/~rgomory/academic_papers/82_national.pdf [accessed December 6, 2012].

———. 2000. *Global Trade and Conflicting National Interests.* Cambridge, MA: MIT Press.

Grossman, G. M., and E. Helpman. 2002. "Outsourcing in a Global Economy." NBER Working Paper, no. 8728. Cambridge, MA: National Bureau of Economic Research.

Harrison, A. E., and M. S. McMillan. 2006. "Outsourcing Jobs? Multinationals and US Employment." NBER Working Paper no. 12372. Cambridge, MA: National Bureau of Economic Research.

Jaffee, D. 2004. "Globalization, Offshoring, and Economic Convergence: A Synthesis." Conference Understanding Global Outsourcing, Stern School of Business, December 10, 2004.

Jensen, J. B., and L. G. Kletzer. 2005. "Tradable Services: Understanding the Scope and Impact of Services Outsourcing." Working Paper 05–9m. Washington, DC: Peterson Institute for International Economics.

Kirkegaard, J. 2004. "Outsourcing: Stains on the White Collar?" Working Paper. Washington, DC: Peterson Institute for International Economics.

Mann, C. L. 2003. "Globalization of IT Services and White-collar Jobs: The Next Wave of Productivity Growth." Policy Brief 03-11. Washington, DC: Peterson Institute of International Economics.

Markusen, J. 2005. "Modeling the Offshoring of White-Collar Services: From Comparative Advantage to the New Theories of Trade and FDI." NBER Working Paper, no. 11827. Cambridge, MA: National Bureau of Economic Research.

Samuelson, P. A. 2004. "Where Ricardo and Mill Rebut and Confirm Arguments of Mainstream Economists Supporting Globalization." *Journal of Economic Perspectives* 18 (3): 135–146.

CHAPTER 2

On Technical Progress and the Gains and Losses from Outsourcing

RALPH E. GOMORY[1] AND WILLIAM J. BAUMOL[2]

Introduction

Today, comparative advantage in trade between two countries is no longer determined primarily by the happenstance of the distribution of natural resources between the trading partners. This change does not call for fundamental revision of Ricardo's comparative advantage analysis, but it does bring out more emphatically some attributes and implications of the analysis that are often misunderstood (though Ricardo himself was sufficiently astute to avoid these misapprehensions). In particular, in this chapter we will show the following are particularly significant possibilities in the contemporary world and its trading activities.

(1) Enhanced productivity in the industries of a trading partner can be harmful to the home country. Although the effect of such development can be beneficial to both countries when the partner's productive activities are initially primitive and inefficient, beyond some degree of success in the catch-up process it becomes damaging to the welfare of the home country.
(2) There is a dominant and dominated relationship possible between two trading countries, a relationship that is beneficial for the dominant economy and damaging to the dominated one.
(3) A country can attain a dominant position without intervention if the trading partner is in a properly undeveloped state by the happenstance of history or other fortuitous circumstances. But the development lag also can be imposed by

its trading partner's mercantilist activities, if they succeed in destroying foreign industries.

(4) There is an inherent conflict of interest not only between a nation in a dominant trade position and its relatively advanced trading partner, but also between that dominant partner and the combined interests of a hypothesized two-country world.

(5) While a country cannot gain a dominant position just by enhancing the productivity of its industries, it can avoid a dominated position and assure a beneficial outcome for itself and the world, on balance, by developing a sufficient subset of its own industries and not allowing them to be destroyed.

MISCONCEPTIONS ON COMPARATIVE ADVANTAGE

Many of the misconceptions related to our subject stem from imputing to the powerful principle of comparative advantage alleged implications that simply do not flow from Ricardo's analysis.

Perfect specialization. To a considerable degree, these misunderstandings are attributable to the failure to take into account the role of demand, relative and absolute, for the traded commodities at issue. Let us note some of the ways in which this omission affects the discussion.

First, we will observe that the "law" of comparative advantage does not imply that in a regime governed by the principle, there will be full specialization, with each country serving as the sole producer of its own set of exported commodities. Of course, simple observation confirms that reality displays nothing even approximating such an outcome. But the elementary textbooks persist in providing such artificial illustrations, using two producing parties and two commodities. The usual parable postulates that one of the two traders (Ricardo's England) is less efficient in producing each of these two commodities, A and B, but is more inefficient in producing B. If one producer makes only good A, while the other supplier (Ricardo's Portugal) makes only good B, both will gain by trading.

So far so good, but suppose that the demand for good B (e.g., wine) is minuscule and that for good A (e.g., cloth) is relatively abundant. The world demand for wine from Ricardo's Portugal is limited by fear of inebriation, while the cold winters elicit an enormous cloth market. Then, surely, Portugal will end up producing *both* commodities, and specialization will no longer be the state of affairs.[3] A moment's thought surely will confirm that there is nothing surprising about this observation. This, in turn, leads to a possibility that is less obvious.

***Mutual* gains.** Expository discussions of comparative advantage theory assert, or at least imply, that in a world market so constituted, the gains from trade of two countries engaged in that activity must be mutual—that is, each participant must share in the benefits and, presumably, derive a share that is not negligible. But this too surely is affected by the relative strength of the demand for the two products being traded.

However, even this more modest conclusion does not hold everywhere. Indeed, it does not normally hold at all in Ricardo's cloth–wine parable. Remember that production in this two-good case is strictly linear. Suppose, then, that demand is such as to lead Portugal to produce both wine and cloth. Then, in equilibrium, the ratio of the prices must equal the ratio of their marginal costs to Portugal and, by linearity, also be equal to the ratio of their average costs.

A moment's thought then readily confirms that whatever gains Portugal obtains from its trade with England, it would gain exactly equally by producing both items for itself in a state of autarky. Thus, Portugal gains nothing by engaging in trade!

Mutual benefits from enhancement of productivity in one country. That conclusion, in itself, admittedly entails a very special case and is of interest only in its warning that the standard conclusions in the comparative advantage arena may not be correct. But a related and more significant conclusion that productivity improvements in one country can actually harm its trading partner already has been noted by eminent analysts. For instance, this was pointed out by Professor J. R. Hicks in his inaugural address at Oxford University (Hicks 1953), by the present authors in Gomory and Baumol (2000)—which contains a significant part of the reasoning that is the basis for this chapter, and most recently in Samuelson (2004).

Diagramatic representation

This analysis is easily formalized and summarized in a version that is derived directly from the standard mathematization of the Ricardian model. (A mathematical representation of that model is given in appendix 1 of this chapter.) From this, the equilibrium solution with any given vector of parameter values can be obtained. Each such solution yields for each of the trading countries, among other things, the national incomes of each country (in a simplified world composed of two countries that trade with one another), the price of each commodity, the quantity produced, and the equilibrium magnitude of exports and imports. From these numbers, one can easily and directly compute the national incomes of the two countries, Y_1 and Y_2, and from the utility functions included in the model we can calculate the total utility, U_i ($i = 1, 2, w$), thereby obtained by each country and the world. It also is convenient to formulate another variable, $Z_i = Y_i/(Y_1 + Y_2)$, which gives the share of country i in world income.

The single equilibrium just described can be represented by three points on a simple graph (see Figure 2.1), with Z_1 on the horizontal axis indicating for any given equilibrium the division of incomes between the two countries. For that value of Z_1, the corresponding three points indicate respectively the utility levels, U_1, U_2, and U_w, achieved with that share of world income by Country 1, Country 2, and the world in total.[4]

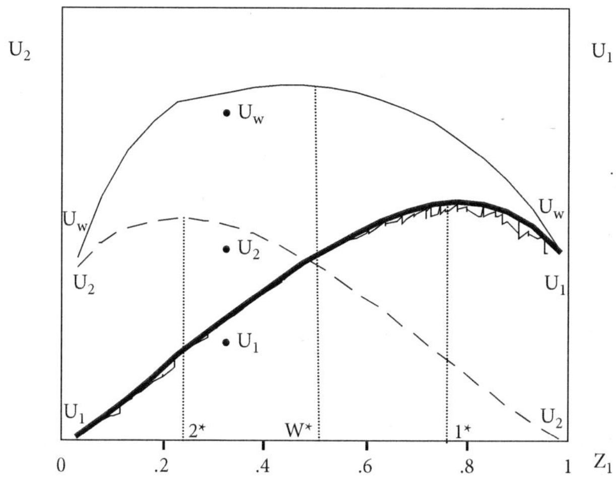

FIGURE 2.1 Graph of utility and share.

By varying the productivity levels for the different products in the two countries, we obtain different equilibria, represented by different sets of the three points in Figure 2.1. Since the production of workers in any of the industries is bounded above by what can be produced using the best current technology, the quantities of the various goods that can be produced are all bounded from above. It follows immediately that the utilities of the two countries also must be bounded from above. So all possible equilibrium points will be bounded from above by three upper boundary curves—one for each country and one for the world. In Figure 2.1, these are labeled U_wU_w, U_1U_1, and U_2U_2, respectively.

It is plausible that the outcomes generally should look like the one in Figure 2.1.[5] We expect the curves to be roughly hill-shaped, with the world curve (U_wU_w) having its peak between those of the two countries. While careful calculation via the model shows that the boundary curves for models with only a small number of traded commodities are rather jagged,[6] intuition leads us to expect the curves to approximate those rounded shapes, and this is confirmed by calculation. The value of Z_1 on the horizontal axis gives Country 1's share of world income. It is implausible that the world will be at its most prosperous when one country produces almost every product (as is true at $Z_1 = 0$ or $Z_1 = 1$), so that the world curve will attain its summit, W*, more toward the middle of the graph.

Next, we note that 1*, the summit point of Country 1, will always lie to the right of the world summit, W*, while the reverse will always be true for the summit of Country 2. That is, at 1*, Country 1 will be better off than it would be at the level of Z_1 that is optimal for the world, and Country 2 will have suffered a substantial loss of utility. An intuitive explanation is straightforward. As we move to the right from W*, toward point 1*, we can think of the change as one in which the world output pie has shrunk (i.e., the world utility boundary has declined). But Country 1, by obtaining a larger slice of this smaller pie, still benefits until this trade-off goes too far. In that situation, Country 2 evidently obtains a *smaller share of a smaller pie*. Hence, self-interest will drive Country 1 to try to move to the right of W*, at the expense of Country 2, and the reverse is evidently desired by Country 2. In short, each country wants to improve its payoff by acquiring a share of the world's industries that is greater than that which is best for the world as a whole.[7] (See appendix 3 for more discussion of the shape of the boundary curves.)

We can think of the country that succeeds in this tug-of-war as the country that has achieved dominance, and we can consider the other nation to be the dominated country. We use this labeling later in this chapter, where we note that each country hopes to be the one that is dominant, achieving this desired state through enhancement of its productivity levels in some of the commodities it seeks to export, rather than importing them—as it did in the past.

For two countries with labor forces of equal size, dominance is obtained by producing considerably more of the world's value than the trading partner. This means that the dominant country is the producer in a set of industries, S_1, for which the total world demand is large, while the trading partner is the producer in a set of industries, S_2, for which the total world demand is small. This desirable state for the dominant country can be brought about if it has some insurmountable natural advantage in all the industries of S_1, or, as is more likely in the modern world, if it has acquired state-of-the-art abilities in the industries of S_1 that its trading partner does not have.

This state of affairs can be established easily if the trading partner has never developed these industries. It also can be created through the use of mercantilist practices, such as subsidies or currency manipulation, which destroy the trading partner's S_1 industries.

Outsourcing: How It Can Benefit the Outsourcer's Firms and Harm the Home Country's Inhabitants

We have just seen how a trading country can benefit at the expense of the general welfare of society by acquiring industries from other countries. In this process, Country A gains not only at the expense of Country B, its trading partner, but also via a decline in welfare in the world economy, generally. Now let us look at this story in more detail, bringing outsourcing explicitly into the picture. In addition to simply losing its value-added in a particular industry through the loss of that industry to a trading partner, a country can lose value added in the industry through outsourcing, while retaining all or part of the production of the final product. To make the story more suggestive, let us deal with two countries that we will call "India" and the "United States." We begin our story with an "India" of former years, when it had a very limited cadre of trained engineers and technicians among its population. Because their employment opportunities were very limited, their wages were very low. Suddenly there is a change in regime in that country, and the opportunities for education in the sciences and engineering expand markedly, offering some gain in income for those who graduate from these new programs. However, those wages are still very low, compared to those in the "United States" for people with similar capabilities.

At this point, managements in "American" firms realize that investment in "India" offers profitable prospects. Laboratory work, industrial design, and other such activities can be carried out there by trained and capable individuals whose wages, though significantly higher than before, are still significantly lower than those in the "United States." The sequel is obvious. Wherever they can be done profitably, these activities in the "United States" will be threatened with outsourcing to "India."

The benefits to the large "American" firms, which thereby have their outputs produced more cheaply, are obvious. They can sell their products at lower prices that attract larger sales volumes or they can choose to cut their prices only modestly and, thereby, yield greater profit margins than before.

The plausible implications for wages in the two countries are also fairly obvious. As usual, the pressure of competition upon two suppliers of a given product is also clear: The wage levels will be driven toward equality, reducing them in the "United States" and raising them in "India." These wage changes then will extend to other industries in the two countries. For instance, increased demand for labor in the activities outsourced to "India" will put upward pressure on the wages of workers with comparable skills, working on other "Indian"-produced outputs for both domestic consumption and export.

Other consequences are not so simple. For example, if the outsourcing occurs during a relatively prosperous period in the "United States," no decline in the level of employment will necessarily result there. Wages will be driven downward, but jobs will not dry up. Still, that is no blessing for the labor force. In a period of recession and unemployment, outsourcing can indeed exacerbate the shortage of jobs.

There is a second, less obvious consequence for the well-being of the "American" public. True, as often argued, consumers in the "United States" will benefit from the decreased prices of the outsourced commodities. But there are other products that the "United States" had been importing from "India" before the outsourcing began. With "Indian" wages rising generally, the prices of those other "Indian" manufactures also will move upward. Systematic analysis, such as that provided in Gomory and Baumol (1998), shows that as more and more activities are transferred from the "United States" to an initially impoverished "India," both will benefit initially, but eventually—when the status of "India" has improved sufficiently—the net effect of the further transfer of industries from the "United States" to "India" will be a fall in the economic well-being in the former and a rise in that of the latter. This in fact is the message from the shape of the curves in Figure 2.1.

Toward Generalization: Dominant and Dominated Economies versus the Intermediate World Ideal

We already have mentioned the concept of dominating and dominated economies, and it is not difficult to conclude that in the real world, at least until recently, the economy of the actual India was dominated by that of the United States. Indeed, this characterization of their relative positions doubtless continues to be valid today. But it is equally clear that India and other emerging economies (e.g., China, Brazil, etc.) hope to move in the direction of dominance, though the fields in which they seek to advance differ from country to country.

In addition, we already have noted that, analytically speaking, we can think of the acquisition of industries by one country, at the expense of the country in which those industries formerly were located, as the archetypical instrument by which the formerly dominated country can strengthen its dominance over its trading partners. We also have seen (1) that there is an intermediate distribution of industries between two such countries at which the welfare of their combined populations is maximized, but that (2) each country will be motivated to seek to acquire more than this ubiquitously optimal share of industries because this gain in industries will increase the wealth of the gaining country, at the expense of the country that loses its industries. That is, the gains of the former will be exceeded by the losses imposed upon its trading partner.

In such a world in which economies are not driven by eleemosynary ambitions and charitable aims, each country can be expected to act in a way that is expected to bring gains to itself, at the expense of its trading partner. However, purely profit-driven outsourcing is a threat to a home country's well-being that works in the opposite direction. That is, outsourcing from dominant Country A to dominated Country B facilitates realization of the latter's ambition to transform itself from dominated toward dominator. As Country A does so, on the initiative of its firms with an international presence, those firms clearly will have the opportunity to profit, but at the expense of the welfare of the inhabitants of their home country.

Innovation and Enhanced Education as Remedies?

In searching for the cure for America's unbalanced trade, many observers place their faith in Silicon Valley and other centers of innovation. They note that past technological progress, with its origins in the United States, constituted a successful defense against imported products supplied by "cheap foreign labor." Based on this, they conclude that the cure for today's and tomorrow's problems stemming from the current conditions of trade entails increasing the number of students who specialize in subjects useful for furthering innovation, such as engineering and physics. The sequel to this, it is believed, will be acceleration in the appearance of new products and other innovations in the United States, which, in turn, will provide more jobs and better wages.

There is evidently some substance to these contentions, but matters are not quite so simple. As we will argue next, these views fail to account adequately for important factors that influence trade, such as demand, the varying productivity performance of different economic sectors, and more recently the outsourcing of jobs. Most notably, this viewpoint devotes inadequate attention to the role of domestic demand for labor in the relevant sectors of the economy.

Does the United States need to educate more engineers and applied scientists? First, let us consider the education component of the argument that the training of more engineers and scientists will lead to more innovation and, thereby, spur economic growth. It is undoubtedly true that the spectacular innovative performance of the United States played an important role in its balance of payments in the period after the Second World War and even in the pre-Depression 1920s, when, as today, it also was widely noted that the US economy faced the rivalry of "cheap foreign labor."[8]

The United States seemingly had no shortage of engineers and scientists in these earlier periods, and we may do well to question the need for more now. Some evidence of the answer to this question is, in fact, readily available. The market, working via the supply–demand mechanism, surely does its bit to indicate which occupations are in need of more workers—an item in short supply will dependably be one whose price is relatively high. However, a comparison of the earnings of engineers and physicists with those of doctors, lawyers, and business executives surely indicates that the market for engineers and physicists does not seem to be driven by severe current shortage. True, 2009 data from the United States Bureau of Labor Statistics suggest that the average engineer actually earns a little bit more than the average business manager and that the average physicist makes a little bit more than the average lawyer. But if we compare the average of engineers' and physicists' average hourly wages with the average of doctors,' lawyers,' and business managers' average hourly wages, we find that the latter are demonstrably higher than the former (US Bureau of Labor Statistics, 2009). In short, there appears to be a good market for the services of those who lead the innovation process, but surely no evidence of a desperate shortage of engineers and applied scientists.

Will continued innovative performance ensure good jobs and high wages? The recent performance of the Chinese economy indicates that rapid growth can occur in the absence of spectacular invention. Indeed, that country, which arguably was the world's leader of invention during Europe's Middle Ages, until very recently apparently devoted little effort to inventive activity. Ironically, the general population of China benefited little from that earlier outpouring of domestic invention. Only today, with an economy driven by manufacturing, is its growth rate outpacing much of the world.

As China's case hints, if an economy is to have good jobs and high wages, more than rapid innovation growth is required. But rather, *a substantial share of the subsequent manufacturing process entailed in supply of the innovative product must remain in the innovator country*. For example, the United States, though not the sole inventor of the automobile, was the creator of the inexpensive version of the vehicle that first attracted an abundant consumer market. Just as important, the United States was also the creator of the mass-production methods that made continuation of the automobile's affordability possible.

Thus, the number of jobs provided by the invention process itself is usually minuscule, relative to those that are offered by the manufacturing sector when a particular innovation is produced for mass consumption. This remains true, despite the fact that there is persistently growing labor productivity in the manufacturing sector. Today, the United States continues to be a leader in the invention process, but much of the manufacturing of its inventions is now outsourced to other countries, where reasonably skilled labor is available at prices far lower than in the United States.

A second and distinct observation follows from this. Americans continue to be large-scale consumers of manufactured goods—from automobiles to television sets and computers. If we do not make these products ourselves, we must trade for them. However since most trade—and, notably, most of America's imbalance in trade—is in manufactured goods, we are unlikely to be able to shift our negative balance toward a surplus solely by increasing our positive trade balance in services. Thus, unless they improve their country's manufacturing performance, Americans eventually will have to curtail their consumption of manufactured goods sharply, or else continue to go deeper into debt with America's trading partners. This process surely will not be allowed to go on indefinitely.

It follows from these considerations that continued good performance in the innovation process is not to be spurned. However, innovation by itself, without the retaining the resulting manufacturing, may not be enough to propel continued prosperity in the United States and other developed (i.e., dominant) nations.

Toward remedies

As the prior discussion makes clear, the United States must consider changes in its trade policy if it is to balance its imports and exports and ensure continued economic growth. As the discussion above has shown, in order to avoid being dominated a country must continue to produce a considerable portion of the world's traded goods. But what changes to the United States' trade position to produce such a balance are possible?

We will not recapitulate in any detail the well-known arguments against tariffs—that they may balance trade, but retaliatory tariffs are then likely to cause that rebalance to entail a lower economic level for both trading partners. Instead, we will focus on other possible courses of action that merit further investigation. For instance, the United States may wish to provide incentives for the domestic production of domestic inventions. As part of this, it may be advantageous to offer government support for early investment in innovative ventures and for training in the requisite technical and production skills required to manufacture both innovative traditional products in more productive ways.

There is also good reason to search for innovative new solutions to the ongoing US trade imbalance. For example, the United States should not reject out of hand Warren Buffett's proposal (Buffett 2003) to make use of the market mechanism for this purpose. An approach similar to carbon emissions entailing the use of tradable permits, which already has demonstrated considerable effectiveness, may prove helpful here. Such a scheme might award exporters saleable certificates that authorize the holder to import products with a market value that does not exceed that of the exports represented by the certificates. The certificates could be traded among importers and exporters on a market, much like those used for the trading of carbon emissions allowances.

This approach already has proven itself reasonably effective and viable in the arena of environmental protection, and it seems reasonable to expect that it would perform effectively in balancing US trade. Surely it would ensure a reduction, if not the complete elimination, of trade imbalances and would provide automatic incentives for domestic manufacturers to avoid the added cost of purchasing import licensing certificates for components produced by outsourcing. Moreover, if such an import–export certificates market is sufficiently competitive, the added result will be a set of imports and exports that most effectively fits in with the demands of the consuming public in the United States.

In addition, when compared with tariffs, this approach has the peculiar distinction of succeeding in its mission of balancing trade, even if our trading partners adopt retaliatory import certificate programs. Should any trading partners choose to retaliate by adopting ordinary tariffs to restrict imports from the United States, that also would help, rather than hinder, this program by automatically lowering that country's exports to the United States and, thereby, rebalancing trade. Thus, the incentive structure and likely consequences of such an import–export certificate scheme are radically different from those of a program of tariffs.

Concluding comment

Obviously there are other ways in which a country can protect itself from the damaging effects of a formerly dominated trading partner's progress toward a dominant position. For example, as we already have argued elsewhere (Gomory and Baumol 2011), a dominated country's entrance into industries in which it was formerly not capable of operating need not be seriously damaging to its trade partner. Intuitively, this result rests upon the fact that when both countries are able to supply and sell an identical product in a competitive world market, their prices must be the same—leaving consumers in each country the choice between the two sources.

This hints at the range of possibilities and the avenues open to a formerly dominant economy to preserve its prosperity. The central point of this chapter is to reiterate the importance of the issue discussed in this paper for the well-being of already dominant economies akin to that of the United States. It also is urgently important that we study the means by which other countries, such as China, can emerge from poverty without doing so at the expense of already prosperous economies and their people.

Clearly the most desirable outcome is a world in which both countries have a high standard of living. That can be attained, but it requires that the already developed country continue to be effective in enough industries to prevent its standard of living from being eroded by the emergence of the newly developed trading partner. This is represented by the middle of the hilltop, shown in Figure 2.1. It is not as advantageous for the developed country as a trade partner that can be exploited, but it makes for a more stable world in which both trading partners spur each other on and develop more rapidly because the total resources and capabilities of the world are enhanced beyond those that were available in the previous, unbalanced situation.

Notes

1. Leonard N. Stern School of Business, New York University, New York, NY 10012, USA; Tel. +1 212 998 0399
2. Berkley Center for Entrepreneurship and Innovation, Leonard N. Stern School of Business, New York University, New York, NY 10012, USA; Tel. +1 212 998 8943
3. This common-sense observation is confirmed by direct calculation using the equations in appendix 1.
4. Here it is important to clarify a few matters regarding utility versus national income. If we consider a single equilibrium, it is natural to compare various bundles of goods by comparing their priced value. The result of the comparison is not affected by the choice of the monetary unit, as the value of two bundles of goods would be affected equally by change. However, in this article we are constantly comparing what a country obtains at different equilibria and, therefore, we encounter the well-known problem of the "numeraire."

   We have chosen to compare the bundles of goods a country obtains at the various equilibria by their utility, specifically Cobb–Douglas utility—the utility whose maximization produces the (Cobb–Douglas) demand that we use in our model. If we had chosen to use the priced value of the goods a country produces as a measure, we could take, for example, the goods the country consumes in autarky with fully developed industries and then compare the cost of that bundle at current equilibrium prices with the current national income. As with the consumer price index, different choices of a comparison bundle generally will produce different results. We have done calculations with this approach and have obtained diagrams that exhibit exactly the same features as Figure 2.1.

   This is what we would expect, since we can show that for any chosen Z_1 (share of national income), there are a finite number of dominating equilibria—all clustered near the upper regional utility boundary. For any equilibrium having that Z_1, one of the cluster will provide the same or a greater amount of every good. So whatever measure is chosen, the maximizing equilibrium for Z_1 will be one of that cluster, and the maximizing boundary with that choice of measure will be close to that obtained by utility.
5. A fuller treatment of this is available in Gomory and Baumol (2000), and an even more rigorous treatment can be found in Gomory and Baumol (1998).
6. In Figure 2.1 the light, jagged line for Country 1 is the exact boundary in an eleven-industry model. The data for that model are listed in appendix 2. The other curves in Figure 2.1 are smoothed upper bounds.
7. Here we should bear in mind that, in general, the more productive equilibria are higher up in Figure 2.1, while the less productive ones are located lower down in the diagram. For any equilibrium, p, for industries in which both countries can increase their productivities, there will be equilibria directly above p in the diagram that deliver as much or more of every good as p does. So, the Pareto optimal equilibria have the property that in every industry one or the other country is at its maximal productivity. These Pareto optimal equilibria can be shown to form a band that lies below and has the shape of the upper boundary. We have

discussed this as the "region of maximal productivity" in our earlier work (Gomory and Baumol 1998; Gomory and Baumol 2000: 102–103).

8. It may be noted, as a fact suggesting how much matters can change, that during these earlier years the standard joke was that products of questionable quality always bore the label "Made in Japan."
9. This is the usual problem of the "numeraire."

References

Buffett, W. 2003. "America's Growing Trade Deficit Is Selling the Nation out from under Us." *Fortune*, November 10. http://money.cnn.com/magazines/fortune/fortune_archive/2003/11/10/352872/index.htm.

Gomory, R. 1994. "A Ricardo Model with Economies of Scale." *Journal of Economic Theory* 62 (2): 394–419.

Gomory, R., and W. J. Baumol. 1998. "National Trade Conflicts Caused by Productivity Changes: The Analysis with Full Proofs." C. V. Starr Economic Research Report, no. 98-36, New York University. http://pages.stern.nyu.edu/~rgomory/academic_papers/81_National_Trade.pdf.

Gomory, R., and W. J. Baumol. 2000. *Global Trade and Conflicting National Interests*, Cambridge, MA: MIT Press.

Gomory, R., and W. J. Baumol. 2011. "Ricardo Revisited: Sino-American Trade and Economic Conflict." Policy Paper, New America Foundation, http://growth.newamerica.net/sites/newamerica.net/files/policydocs/Ricardo%20Revisited%203-25.pdf.

Hicks, J. R. 1953. "An Inaugural Lecture." *Oxford Economic Papers* 5: 117–135.

Samuelson, P. A. 2004. "Where Ricardo and Mill Rebut and Confirm Arguments of Mainstream Economists Supporting Globalization." *Journal of Economic Perspectives* 18 (3): 135–146.

US Bureau of Labor Statistics. 2009. "Hourly Mean Earnings." *National Compensation Survey*, http://data.bls.gov.

Appendix 1: Equilibrium equations

Notation

In our standard Ricardian model there are two countries and n industries. The quantity $q_{i,j}$ of good i produced in Country j is determined by linear production function $e_{i,j}\, l_{i,j}$ with $l_{i,j}$ denoting the amount of labor employed in Country j in producing good i. The size of labor force for each country is L_j. Country j's *consumption* of good i is denoted by $y_{i,j}$ and its *production* of good i by $q_{i,j}$. Country j's production *share* or *market share* of world output of good i is represented by $x_{i,j} = q_{i,j}/(q_{i,1} + q_{i,2})$, so that the vector $x = (x_{i,j})$ describes the pattern of production.

Each of the two countries participating in trade has a given utility function of Cobb–Douglas form with demand parameters $d_{i,j}$.

The price of good i, p_i, and w_j, the wage in Country j, and Y_j the national income of Country j are all expressed in monetary units. The standard equilibrium equations given below are homogenous in these variables. This means that if we choose a different monetary unit thus replacing any set of p_i, w_j, and Y_j values at an equilibrium by kp_i, kw_j, and kY_j, these values too would satisfy the equilibrium conditions while leaving all the non-pecuniary variables such as $q_{i,j}$ and $l_{i,j}$ unchanged.[9] We eliminate this ambiguity by choosing at each equilibrium the monetary unit, the MU, that that makes the total world income $Y_1 + Y_2 = 1$ MU. The national incomes with this normalization we will refer to as Z_1 and Z_2. We will then have at each equilibrium uniquely determined pecuniary values and the uniquely determined national income, expressed in MU units, satisfy $Z_1 + Z_2 = 1$.

Equilibrium conditions

For any given vector of productivity parameters $\varepsilon = \{e_{i,j}\}$ there is a stable equilibrium giving a national income Z_j and a utility U_j for each country.

The first equilibrium condition stares that national income or consumption Z_j in Country j must equal the total value of the goods produced in Country j. With a Cobb-Douglas utility each country spends $d_{i,j}Z_j$ on good i, so total world expenditure on the ith good is $(d_{i,1}Z_1 + d_{i,2}Z_2)$. Since the fraction produced in each country is $x_{i,j}$ the balance of the value of production and consumption requires for each country:

$$\sum_i x_{i,j}(d_{i,1}Z_1 + d_{i,2}Z_2) = Z_j. \qquad (1.1)$$

Second, we have a zero-profit condition. World expenditure on Country j's output of good i all goes into the wages of the labor $l_{i,j}$ employed in that industry, so:

$$w_j l_{i,j} = x_{i,j}(d_{i,1}Z_1 + d_{i,1}Z_2) \tag{1.2}$$

Third, is the full-employment requirement for each country. This is expressed as the condition that the wage rate times the country's total labor force equals national income (the wage rate condition):

$$w_1 L_1 = Z_1, \qquad w_2 L_2 = Z_2 \tag{1.3}$$

Fourth, we have the requirement that, for each good the value of the output of good i at the equilibrium price p_i equals the total amount consumers are willing to spend on it

$$p_i(q_{i,1} + q_{i,2}) = d_{i,1}Z_1 + d_{i,2}Z_2 \quad \text{or} \quad p_i q_{i,j} = w_j l_{i,j} \tag{1.4}$$

where the second form of (Equation 1.4) follows directly from the first by multiplying through by $x_{i,j} = q_{i,j}/(q_{i,1} + q_{i,2})$ and using (Equation 1.2).

Finally, we have the conditions that require that in each industry production, or equivalently market share, is always assigned to the producer or producers with the lowest unit cost. For example, if in industry i $w_1/e_{i,1} < w_2/e_{i,2}$, then $x_{i,1} = 1$ and $x_{i,2} = 0$. More generally:

$$\begin{aligned}&\text{if Country 1 unit cost } (w_1/e_{i,1}) < (w_2/e_{i,2}) \text{ then } x_{i,1} = 1 \text{ and } x_{i,2} = 0\\&\text{if Country 1 unit cost } (w_1/e_{i,1}) > (w_2/e_{i,2}) \text{ then } x_{i,1} = 0 \text{ and } x_{i,2} = 1\\&\text{if unit costs are equal } (w_1/e_{i,1}) = (w_2/e_{i,2}) \text{ any } x_{i,1} + x_{i,2} = 1 \text{ is allowed.}\end{aligned} \tag{1.5}$$

It is, of course, the actual producer's unit cost that determines the price p_i. The conditions (Equation 1.5) include the familiar comparative-advantage criterion.

Note that because of (Equation 1.1) the equilibrium conditions include balanced trade.

Appendix 2: Data for Figure 2.1

Both countries' labor forces are of size 1. L[1] = L[2] = 1.

Productivities of the two countries are given below.

e[1] = {0.97, 0.92, 0.72, 0.94, 0.84, 0.52, 0.73, 0.77, 0.53, 0.91, 0.89}

e[2] = {0.52, 0.61, 0.91, 0.92, 0.84, 0.97, 0.83, 0.92, 0.31, 0.83, 0.72}

Demands of the two countries (approximated to three decimal places) are given below.

d[1] = {0.033, 0.14, 0.073, 0.1, 0.153, 0.047, 0.053, 0.067, 0.133, 0.087, 0.113}

d[2] = {0.081, 0.081, 0.169, 0.113, 0.177, 0.032, 0.048, 0.105, 0.056, 0.097, 0.040}

Appendix 3: Explaining the Characteristic Regional Shape

In this appendix we offer a brief summary of the reasons why the calculations of equilibria always result in regions of equilibria with the characteristic shape shown in Figure 2.1. While the full reasoning takes up a good deal of space in Gomory and Baumol (1998), we will try to give the essentials behind that reasoning here.

Calculating the Boundary: A Linear Programming Problem

The height of the boundary curve for Country 1 at a given Z_1 value represents the upper bound of the utilities that Country 1 can obtain at any of the equilibria having that Z_1. In other words, if we can find a calculation that maximizes utility, subject to the constraint that we deal only with equilibria whose value is Z_1, and we then repeat that calculation for each Z_1, we will get the utility value represented by the Country 1 boundary curve.

Two helpful facts simplify computing these boundaries.

First: We do not need to deal in this calculation with all the equilibrium properties listed in appendix 1, but only with Equation 1.1, which asserts that the value of a country's production must match the value of its consumption.

Second: We do not need to deal directly with Cobb–Douglas utility in doing the maximization. Rather we use a simplified version of it, called "linearized utility," introduced in Gomory (1994), which gives the same value as Cobb–Douglas utility at all equilibria but is linear in the production variables $x_{i,j}$.

These two facts turn the problem of maximizing utility over all equilibria with a given Z_1 into a much simpler problem: the problem of maximizing an objective function that is linear in the production variables $x_{i,j}$, subject only to the constraint (Equation 1.1) for the given Z_1. However, the constraint (1.1) is also linear in the production variables $x_{i,j}$. The problem of finding the boundary, therefore, can be recognized as an ordinary linear programming problem.

In fact, it is the simplest form of linear programming problem, the so-called "knapsack" problem. In the usual knapsack problem we have an assortment of object having given values and given weights. The problem is to find the choice of objects that can be put into the knapsack without exceeding the weight limit. In our boundary problem the objects we put into the knapsack are industries whose production is assigned to Country 1, and the weight limit is the specified national income, Z_1. Country 1 cannot have an assignment of industries that exceeds its Z_1, and the corresponding constraint holds for Country 2.

The classical level

If both countries are fully developed (i.e., $e_{i,j} = e^{max}_{i,j}$), the equilibrium that results is called "the classical equilibrium." We refer to the Z_1 value of the classical equilibrium as the classical level, Z_C.

We show in Gomory and Baumol (1998) what is intuitively plausible in any case—that Country 1 cannot get a larger share of world output (i.e., a $Z_1 > Z_C$) by its own efforts. It is, after all, already fully developed at Z_C. To obtain an equilibrium with $Z_1 > Z_C$, Country 1 must acquire industries in which its trading partner is not fully developed; Country 1 would not be the cheaper producer in these industries if its trading partner were fully developed.

On the other hand, for Z_1 values less than Z_C there are enough industries in which Country 1 is the cheaper producer so that if they were all assigned to Country 1, it would have a total production that would exceed Z_1. So the problem for Country 1 is to choose the subset of these industries that maximize utility.

The derivative of the boundary curve in a special case

If the countries are of equal size ($L_1 = L_2$) and have the same demand structure ($d_{i,1} = d_{i,2}$), the boundary equilibria (those with highest utility) will always be obtained by simply assigning industries to Country 1 in the order of Country 1's (fully developed) comparative advantage, until the limit Z_1 is reached. This is a very simple way to solve the maximization problem and obtain the boundary curve.

In this case the derivative of the boundary dU_1/dZ_1 is given by

$$\frac{1}{U_1}\frac{dU_1}{dZ_1} = \frac{1}{Z_1} + \mathrm{In}\frac{e^{max}_{i,1}\,Z_2}{e^{max}_{i,2}\,Z_1} = \frac{1}{Z_1} + \mathrm{In}\frac{e^{max}_{i,1}\,W_2}{e^{max}_{i,2}\,W_1} \tag{3.1}$$

where the index i designates the last industry that was assigned in whole or in part to Country 1 and caused it to reach the limit Z_1.

The term $1/Z_1$ on the right is always positive and reflects the fact that with increasing Z_1, Country 1's share of the output of every industry is $d_{i,1}Z_1$, which grows with Z_1.

The next term reflects the impact of the industry that is currently being moved from Country 2 to Country 1. If $Z_1 < Z_C$ this will still be an industry in which Country 1 is the cheaper producer, (i.e., $e^{max}_{i,1}/w_1 > e^{max}_{i,2}/w_2$) and the term inside the logarithm in (Equation 3.1) will be greater than 1, so that this term will be positive.

Since both terms on the right are positive, the move underway will have a positive impact on the utility of Country 1. So, for all Z_1 values that are $< Z_C$, the derivative of utility will be positive and the boundary curve will be sloping upward.

However, for $Z_1 > Z_C$, Country 1 is acquiring industries in which it would not be the cheaper producer if its trading partner were fully developed. Therefore the logarithm term will be negative and will start to counteract the positive effect of the term $1/Z_1$. Eventually, as $1/Z_1$ grows smaller with increasing Z_1 and the second term becomes more negative with decreasing comparative advantage, the total on the right will turn negative and the boundary curve will have negative slope and will turn downward. This is, in fact, the behavior we see in Figure 2.1.

THE DERIVATIVE OF THE BOUNDARY CURVE IN THE GENERAL CASE

It is still possible to obtain the derivative of the boundary in the general case without solving the linear programming problem. This is explained in Gomory and Baumol (1998). The result is

$$\frac{1}{U_1}\frac{dU_1}{dZ_1} = (1-\gamma(x))\left\{\frac{1}{Z_1} + \frac{d_{i,1}}{TD_i}\ln\frac{e_{i,1}\,L_1\,Z_2}{e_{i,2}\,L_2\,Z_1}\right\} \tag{3.2}$$

Despite the apparent increased complexity the derivative in the general case has the same qualitative features as the special case, described above.

The first term in parentheses is always positive, as $\gamma(x)$ is a measure of the asymmetry of the demands and cannot exceed 1. So the sign of the derivative is always determined by the bracket term.

Within the bracket, $1/Z_1$ is always positive, and as $TD_i = (d_{i,1} Z_1 + d_{i,2} Z_2)$ is the total worldwide demand for the ith product, it too is positive. The sign of the logarithm term again is determined by which country is the cheaper producer in the industry that is shifting. As before, the logarithm term is positive for $Z_1 < Z_C$ and increasingly negative for $Z_1 > Z_C$.

So, in general, the boundary curve for Country 1 ascends up to Z_C and continues upward until the gain from increasing world share for Country 1 is outweighed by the decreasing effect on world output, which is caused by Country 1 being the producer in many industries in which it is not the (potentially) best producer. At this point, the curve turns downward.

This is all a direct consequence of the equations of equilibrium.

CHAPTER 3

Service Offshoring and Labor Demand in Europe*

ROSARIO CRINÒ+

1 Introduction

Over the last decade, technological progress has sharply reduced the cost of trading services internationally (Freund and Weinhold 2002; Head et al. 2009). This has allowed firms to transfer an increasing number of service activities to foreign locations (UNCTAD 2004; OECD 2007b). The labor-market implications of this new phenomenon, which is known as *service offshoring*, have become an important concern in many industrialized countries. Notwithstanding the increasing attention by media and politicians (see, in particular, Bhagwati et al. 2004; Amiti and Wei 2005; Trefler 2005; and Mankiw and Swagel 2006), data constraints have complicated econometric research until now. In this chapter, we aim to shed new light on the labor market implications of service offshoring, by providing novel and extensive empirical evidence on how it affects the demand for labor in Western European countries. To make the terminology clear, we will define service offshoring as the foreign relocation of service activities, via foreign direct investment or arm's length contracts with unaffiliated parties (Helpman 2006).

We study two main channels through which service offshoring may affect labor demand. First, service offshoring may induce a parallel shift in the demand schedule. Second, it may change, and possibly increase, its slope (wage elasticity). The first effect may occur because imported services usually interact with domestic labor, either substituting for or complementing it in the production process. Service offshoring may thus induce firms to reoptimize their employment decisions, thereby changing the level of domestic employment, ceteris paribus (Amiti and Wei 2005, 2006). Furthermore, service offshoring may affect firms' productivity and scale of operations, with an additional impact on the employment level (Olsen 2006; Crinò 2008; Daveri and Jona-Lasinio 2008; Görg et al. 2008; Amiti and Wei 2009; Hijzen et al. 2010; Görg and Hanley 2011).

The second effect may instead occur because service offshoring increases the flexibility with which firms can potentially substitute domestic workers with foreign inputs (see, e.g., Hijzen and Swaim 2010; and Senses 2010). A higher elasticity, in turn, implies a greater volatility of wages and employment in response to economic shocks, a lower bargaining power of workers, and a larger incidence of non-wage labor costs on employees (Rodrik 1997). In principle, this effect requires the simple "threat" of offshoring; it does not necessarily require also a large current impact on the employment level. These two channels may thus offer complementary explanations for why concerns about service offshoring are mounting in Western Europe.

To investigate these issues empirically, we use novel and comparable data for nine members of the European Union (EU) over the last decade. For each country, we have information on twenty industries, which span both the manufacturing and the services sector. Following previous work by Amiti and Wei (2005, 2006, 2009), we measure service offshoring as the share of imported private services in the industry's total purchases of intermediate inputs. To construct this indicator, we use the import matrices recently released by Eurostat (ESA 95 Supply, Use and Input-Output tables), which contain official information on the imports of different services in each industry. The use of import matrices allows us to relax the assumptions that would be necessary to construct the indicator using input–output tables and economy-wide service imports, as done in most of the existing literature (see Feenstra and Jensen 2009 for a discussion on this point). In addition, the import matrices allow us to build disaggregate indicators for specific types of imported services, and this enables us to explore heterogeneity in the effects of service offshoring across different activities. We complement these data with industry-level information on employment, hours worked, wages, skills, and other characteristics of the production technology, drawn from the EUKLEMS database (O'Mahony and Timmer 2009).

To study how service offshoring affects the location and elasticity of labor demand, we estimate both conditional (on output) and unconditional labor demand functions, augmented by our proxies for service offshoring (Feenstra and Hanson 1996, 1999, 2003; Amiti and Wei 2005, 2006; Crinò 2010b, 2012). The conditional demand functions describe the employment effects of service offshoring at constant levels of output; instead, the unconditional demand models also capture the indirect effect of service offshoring passing through changes in the scale of operations. Hence, this framework makes the analysis of the first issue fairly straightforward. Following Hamermesh (1993), we choose a log-linear representation for both demand models. With this formulation, the analysis of the second issue becomes straightforward as well: the effects of service offshoring on labor demand elasticity can in fact be gauged by simply adding to the model an interaction term between log wages and service offshoring.

We start by analyzing the effects of service offshoring on the location of labor demand, making use of the entire sample of countries. The results show that the effects are small and, if anything, weakly positive. We then investigate whether the effects differ across types of services, countries, and skill groups of workers. We find that the aggregate results are almost entirely driven by offshoring of business services, the largest category in Europe; financial, computer, and R&D service offshoring have instead negligible impacts on the employment level. We also detect some heterogeneity in the sign of the effects across countries; however, the economic magnitude of the impacts is always small. Finally, we do not find negative effects on any of three skill groups of workers; rather, our results suggest imported services to complement domestic workers of higher skills.

In the last part of the chapter, we turn to the effects on labor demand elasticity. We first discuss the aggregate results obtained on the pooled sample of countries. They suggest service offshoring to make labor demand more elastic; however, the economic magnitude of the effect is found to be small also in this case. Next, we study the individual countries separately and find heterogeneity in the sign of the effect across them. Building on recent work by Hasan et al. (2007) and Hijzen and Swaim (2010), we explore one potential explanation for such heterogeneity: differences in labor market regulations across countries. In countries with weak regulations, in fact, labor demand may be adjusted more flexibly by firms, and the effect of service offshoring may end up being larger as a result. We thus reestimate the models separately on two subsamples of countries characterized respectively by strict and weak employment-protection legislation (EPL). Consistent with this argument, we find that service offshoring raises labor demand elasticity only in countries with weak regulations and that the effect is almost entirely borne by unskilled workers.

The remainder of the chapter is organized as follows. Section 2 briefly reviews the evidence on service offshoring and labor demand. Section 3 describes the data set and provides stylized facts on service offshoring and labor demand in Western Europe. Section 4 introduces the empirical models. Section 5 presents and discusses the results. Finally, section 6 briefly concludes.

2 Related literature

This section contains a brief review of the evidence on service offshoring and labor demand in developed countries. Due to space constraints, and given the empirical nature of the chapter, we do not cover the theoretical studies on service offshoring. Those studies deal with the effects on productivity, wages, and welfare more in general. The interested reader can refer to Bhagwati et al. (2004), Samuelson (2004), Deardorff (2005), Markusen (2005), Antràs et al. (2006), Baldwin (2006), Markusen and Strand (2008), Grossman and Rossi-Hansberg (2008), Baldwin and Robert-Nicoud (2010), and Rodriguez Clare (2010). The reader can also refer to Feenstra and Hanson (2003), Hijzen (2005), Crinò (2009), and Feenstra (2010) for more detailed and comprehensive surveys of the theoretical and empirical literature on service offshoring.

A first set of empirical studies have tried to quantify the number of service jobs potentially at risk from offshoring in the industrialized countries. To this purpose, these studies have computed how many workers are currently employed in service occupations with "tradability" characteristics. Among other attributes, these occupations require little face-to-face contact with final consumers, depend substantially on information and communication technologies, and consist of routine tasks (Autor et al. 2003; Levy and Murname 2004; Blinder 2006). The main message of these studies is that the fraction of jobs potentially at risk of being offshored is large. The available evidence suggests, in fact, that between one-fifth and one-fourth of domestic employment in the United States, the EU, and other developed countries, is in tradable occupations. Hence, a substantial share of workers in the industrialized world are facing the potential risk of being offshored in the near future. See, in particular, Bhardan and Kroll (2003), Dossani and Kenney (2004), Garner (2004), Van Welsum and Reif (2005), Van Welsum and Vickery (2005), Jensen and Kletzer (2005, 2008), Blinder (2006, 2009), Kroll (2007), Moncarz et al. (2008), Blinder and Krueger (2009), and Kletzer (2009).

The high number of jobs potentially at risk of relocation should certainly induce us not to overlook the service offshoring phenomenon. At the same time, however, further empirical evidence suggests that the actual impact of service offshoring on the employment levels has so far been small in many industrialized countries. Three pieces of evidence support this consideration.

First, looking at the subset of firms that have laid off workers during the first half of the past decade, offshoring has accounted for only 2–4 percent of the job separations in the United States (Bhagwati et al. 2004; Mankiw and Swagel 2006) and for similar shares in the EU and Japan (Kirkegaard 2007).

Second, employment in tradable occupations has increased (rather than decreased) in the United States over the last decade and growth has been particularly pronounced in more skilled and higher-wage occupations (Mann 2003; Kirkegaard 2004; Jensen and Kletzer 2005; Moncarz et al. 2008).

Third, the existing econometric studies show that the effects of service offshoring on total employment have generally been small until now. In some cases, the effects have even been found to be weakly positive, suggesting that service offshoring may have actually increased total employment slightly by boosting productivity and expanding the scale of firms' operations. See Amiti and Wei (2006), Blinder and Krueger (2009), and Liu and Trefler (2011) for the United States; Amiti and Wei (2005) and Hijzen et al. (2011) for the United Kingdom; Hijzen and Swaim (2007) and OECD (2007a, 2007b) for OECD countries; Görg and Hanley (2005) for Ireland; Jensen et al. (2006) for Denmark; Crinò (2010a) and Falzoni and Tajoli (2011) for Italy.

A related, but smaller, number of contributions have investigated the effects of service offshoring on the skill and occupational composition of labor demand. By and large, these studies show that service offshoring shifts the composition of labor demand in favor of more skilled workers. The effect reflects the fact that imported services complement with high skilled domestic labor, and may sometimes also substitute for less skilled domestic labor. See Geishecker and Görg (forthcoming) for the United Kingdom and Crinò (2010a, 2012) for Italy and other European countries. In addition, recent evidence for the United States shows that service offshoring also changes the occupational composition of labor demand at given skill level. In particular, controlling for the level of education, service offshoring penalizes occupations with stronger tradability attributes and favors less tradable jobs (Crinò, 2010b).

The studies mentioned so far are closely related to the first part of this chapter, which investigates the effects of service offshoring on the location of labor demand. The chapter contributes to this literature by providing novel and extensive empirical evidence for a large and representative set of Western European countries. In addition, thanks to the richness of the available data, the chapter can investigate several sources of heterogeneity in the effects of service offshoring, most of which have remained largely unexplored in the empirical literature. In particular, along with the effects on different skill groups of workers, the chapter studies the implications of service offshoring for individual countries and explores heterogeneity in the effects across types of offshored services.

A further contribution of the chapter is to study how service offshoring affects the wage elasticity of labor demand. To the best of our knowledge, none of the existing contributions have dealt with this issue. Several studies exist, instead, on the effects of trade liberalization and globalization more in general. According to Rodrik (1997), these phenomena may make labor demand more elastic, mostly by raising product market competition. Yet, the available evidence is inconclusive; see, among others, Greenaway et al. (1999), Slaughter (2001), Barba Navaretti et al. (2003), Barba Navaretti and Venables (2004), Bruno et al. (2004), Hasan et al. (2007), Görg et al. (2009), and Hakkala et al. (2010). A few other studies have specifically dealt with the effects of material offshoring. They have found some evidence that material offshoring contributes to making labor demand more elastic. Material offshoring mostly works by allowing countries to access new and cheaper inputs, which enlarge the possibilities for firms to substitute domestic labor. The effect has been found both in the United States (Senses 2010) and in other OECD countries (OECD 2007a). In this latter case, it has been found to be stronger in economies with weak labor-market regulations, where firms have greater flexibility to adjust their mix of domestic and foreign inputs (Hijzen and Swaim 2010).

3 Data and stylized facts

In this section, we first describe the data and the main variables used in the empirical analysis. Then, we provide stylized facts on service offshoring and labor demand in Western Europe.

3.1 Data and variables

The empirical analysis is based on two samples of countries. The first comprises seven Western European economies and spans the period 1995–2006. The second includes nine Western European countries and covers the years 1995, 2000, and 2005. The structure of the two samples is dictated by the availability of import matrices, which are used to construct the service offshoring indicators as explained below. Overall, the two samples are largely representative of the EU. According to population figures from Eurostat, for instance, in 2005 the nine countries in the second sample accounted for about 60 percent of the population in the twenty-seven members of the EU (EU27). For each country, both samples include information on twenty industries, classified according to the "Classification of Economic Activities in the European Community" (NACE Rev. 1). Out of these industries, thirteen are in the manufacturing sector and seven in the services sector. The list of countries and industries is reported in Table 3.1. Note that the twenty industries account for more than 60 percent of each country's private sector employment in the year 2005.

The main variables used in the empirical analysis come from EUKLEMS, a large data set issued by eighteen European institutions within the Sixth EU Framework Program (O'Mahony and Timmer 2009). In particular, EUKLEMS provides us with industry-level information, comparable across countries, on the following variables: total number of

Table 3.1 Composition and coverage of the estimation samples

Industries

NACE	Description	NACE	Description
15, 16	Food, beverages, tobacco	30–33	Electrical, optical equipment
17–19	Textiles, leather, footwear	34, 35	Transport equipment
20	Wood and cork	36, 37	Manufacturing, nec
21, 22	Pulp, paper, printing, publishing	50	Wholesale and retail, motor vehicles
23	Coke, refined petroleum and nuclear fuel	51	Wholesale, except motor vehicles
24	Chemicals	52	Retail, except motor vehicles
25	Rubber and plastics	60–63	Transportation and storage
26	Other nonmetallic mineral products	64	Post and telecommunication
27, 28	Basic metals and fabricated metal products	70	Real estate
29	Machinery, n.e.c.	71–74	Other business activities

Country	Sample	% of private-sector employment in the twenty industries (2005)
Belgium	nine-country sample	75.0
Denmark	both	77.0
Finland	both	78.0
France	both	76.0
Germany	both	79.0
Italy	both	74.0
Netherlands	both	78.0
Spain	both	64.0
Sweden	nine-country sample	80.0

Source: EUKLEMS.

employees (L); total number of hours worked (H); yearly and hourly wages (W); hours worked and hourly wages for workers with at least a bachelor's degree (high skilled, HS), for workers with either upper secondary or vocational education (medium skilled, MS), and for workers with no formal qualification (low skilled, LS); gross output (Y) and output prices (P^Y); average prices of intermediate inputs (P^I) and disaggregate prices of material (P^M), service (P^S) and energy inputs (P^E); capital stock (K) and, for some countries, capital prices (P^K). To pool the data meaningfully across countries, we express the nominal figures in purchasing power parity, using the deflators provided by EUKLEMS. Moreover, we convert in euros the data for Sweden and Denmark, using exchange rates from the *International Financial Statistics* published by the International Monetary Fund.

Following Amiti and Wei (2005, 2006, 2009), we proxy for service offshoring using the share of imported private services in total input purchases. The underlying idea is the following: the output of offshored services has to be imported into Western Europe to enter the production process with other inputs; hence, this indicator will be higher the greater the intensity of service offshoring. The typical problem encountered by previous studies in constructing this proxy is the lack, or limited disaggregation, of service import data at the industry level. To sidestep this problem, Amiti and Wei (2005, 2006, 2009) have proposed estimating these figures by combining input–output tables with data on service imports at the economy-wide level. In recent years, however, the national statistical institutes and Eurostat have released detailed import matrices containing official data on service imports in individual industries. We make use of these matrices to construct the indicators of service offshoring employed in this chapter.[1]

As shown in Table 3.2, the import matrices are obtained from Eurostat for all countries except Italy and Spain, for which they are gathered from the national statistical institutes. The same table also shows that, for all countries except Belgium and Sweden, the import matrices are available for most of the years between 1995 and 2006; for Belgium and Sweden, the import matrices are instead available only for 1995, 2000, and 2005. Accordingly, the seven-country sample spans the entire period 1995–2006, with values for the missing years being linearly interpolated.[2] Instead, the nine-country sample covers only the years 1995, 2000, and 2005, and always uses official data.

Table 3.2 Import matrices

Country	Availability	Source
Belgium	1995, 2000, 2005	Eurostat
Denmark	1995, 2000–2006	Eurostat
Finland	1995–2006	Eurostat
France	1995, 1997, 1999–2006	Eurostat
Germany	1995, 2000–2006	Eurostat
Italy	1995–2006	National Statistical Institute
Netherlands	1995–2002, 2004–2006	Eurostat
Spain	1995–1997, 1999, 2000, 2002–2006	National Statistical Institute
Sweden	1995, 2000, 2005	Eurostat

For each industry in the two samples, the import matrices report the value of imports of four types of services: financial and insurance services, computer services, research and development services, and other business services. Let M_{cit}^{s} denote imports of service *s* by industry *i* in country *c* at time *t*. Summing up these figures across the four services, we obtain the time series of total service imports at the industry level, $IMPS_{cit}$:

$$IMPS_{cit} = \sum_{s=1}^{4} M_{cit}^{s}$$

Finally, to construct the main proxy for service offshoring (*SOS*) we normalize *IMPS* by the value of total input purchases (*NE*). These latter data come from the use matrices of the input–output accounts of each country. Formally,

$$SOS_{cit} = \frac{IMPS_{cit}}{NE_{cit}} \tag{1}$$

Using inputs as the denominator of equation (1) makes the offshoring proxy comparable with previous studies, in particular Amiti and Wei (2005, 2006, 2009). This normalization, however, may be sensitive to the substitution between imported and domestically purchased services; it may also lead us to underestimate the change in service offshoring when the imported services substitute for those produced in-house, as in this case *IMPS* and *NE* increase by the same amount.[3] We therefore check that the main results are robust with respect to changes in the normalization by using industry output as an alternative denominator of equation (1), as in previous work by Hijzen et al. (2005) and Crinò (2012). The corresponding proxy for service offshoring is called *SOS_Y*.

In order to investigate whether the effects of service offshoring are heterogeneous across types of services, we decompose the proxy in equation (1) into four disaggregate indicators, which correspond to the four services mentioned before. In particular, we construct the following variables:

$$SOS_{cit}^{FIN} = \frac{M_{cit}^{FIN}}{NE_{cit}},\quad SOS_{cit}^{R\&D} = \frac{M_{cit}^{R\&D}}{NE_{cit}},\quad SOS_{cit}^{COMP} = \frac{M_{cit}^{COMP}}{NE_{cit}},\quad SOS_{cit}^{OTHBUS} = \frac{M_{cit}^{OTHBUS}}{NE_{cit}} \tag{2}$$

where the superscripts *FIN*, *R&D*, *COMP*, and *OTHBUS* stand for, respectively, financial and insurance, research and development, computer, and other business services.

For comparison, we also construct an equivalent proxy for material offshoring (MOS), by using the information on imported material inputs contained in the import matrices. This indicator includes imports of all material inputs and thus captures a broad concept of offshoring (Feenstra and Hanson 1999, 2003).

3.2 Stylized facts

Table 3.3 reports information on the levels and changes in the service offshoring indicators for the seven-country sample, the nine-country sample, and each economy separately. For comparison, the table also reports the same information for the material offshoring indicator. Note that service offshoring is still a limited phenomenon in Western Europe, although its importance is growing over time. In particular, service imports account for about 2 percent of input purchases on average and have increased by 1 percentage point (p.p.), or 64 percent, between 1995 and 2006. The largest increases have occurred in the Netherlands, Sweden, and Denmark (about 1.7 p.p.), followed by Spain (1.5 p.p.), Germany, Finland, and Belgium (approximately 0.7 p.p.). Consistent with previous studies, such as OECD (2007b), our data also show that service offshoring is still lower than material offshoring and that the latter has increased as well over time. In particular, material imports account for about 20 percent of input purchases on average and have grown by 2 p.p., or 10 percent, between 1995 and 2006.

Looking at the disaggregate indicators of service offshoring reported in Table 3.3, a clear fact emerges: the bulk of service offshoring in Western Europe consists of imports of business services. These services account for 1.3 percent of total input purchases on average, approximately two-thirds of overall service offshoring. Across countries, the share of business services in total input purchases ranges between 0.4 percent in Sweden and 2.2 percent in the Netherlands. Business services have also driven the growth in overall service offshoring, as they have increased by about 0.4 p.p. since 1995. The largest increases have taken place in Denmark and Spain (approximately 1 p.p.); in Sweden, instead, the share of business services in total input purchases has declined by 1.2 p.p. The remaining services generally constitute a smaller share of overall service offshoring. In particular, they account for about 0.2 percent of total input purchases on average. An interesting exception is represented by R&D services in Sweden, which account for about 2 percent of total input purchases in that country.

Table 3.4 provides details on the geographical origin of service imports in Western Europe. In particular, the table reports intra- and extra-EU27 import shares constructed using data from Eurostat. Because the geographical data are available only for a few recent years and the information on individual service categories only for some countries, the table is constructed for the year 2007 and the group "All services" refers to total service imports. The table clearly shows that most service imports come from other European economies, especially from other EU27 countries. Note, in fact, that more than 60 percent of imports originate within the EU27 and that those coming from outside mainly originate in other European countries. North America and Asia account for smaller, albeit nonnegligible shares (12 and 9 percent respectively). The picture is similar across types of services, although the share of North America is substantially higher for R&D and computer services. In addition, the picture is similar across the individual countries, with the exception of Swedish imports of R&D services, which mostly come from North America.

Next, we describe some key features of the behavior of labor demand in Western Europe. In brief, over the period under scrutiny total employment and hours worked

Table 3.3 Offshoring indicators

	Mean	Δ 95–06		Mean	Δ 95–05		Mean	Δ 95–05		Mean	Δ 95–06		Mean	Δ 95–06		Mean	Δ 95–06	
	%	p.p.	%	%	p.p.	%	%	p.p.	%	%	p.p.	%	%	p.p.	%	%	p.p.	%
	7-Country Sample			*9-Country Sample*			*Belgium*			*Denmark*			*Finland*			*France*		
SOS	1.9	0.9	64.3	2.1	1.0	62.6	2.5	0.6	26.6	1.8	1.8	255.4	2.5	0.8	28.4	1.2	-0.1	-8.8
SOS^{OTHBUS}	1.3	0.5	50.3	1.3	0.3	30.2	1.6	0.4	33.5	1.1	1.0	167.6	1.9	0.1	5.1	0.8	0.2	25.8
SOS^{COMP}	0.1	0.1	332.4	0.1	0.1	172.1	0.3	0.0	-7.7	0.3	0.3	580.1	0.1	0.3	990.0	0.0	0.0	160.6
SOS^{FIN}	0.3	0.1	41.8	0.3	0.1	27.0	0.3	0.1	31.6	0.4	0.3	441.0	0.2	-0.2	-63.4	0.3	-0.4	-68.3
$SOS^{R\&D}$	0.2	0.2	130.1	0.4	0.5	304.4	0.3	0.0	18.1	0.1	0.2	-	0.3	0.5	266.5	0.1	0.1	64.7
MOS	19.9	2.0	10.4	21.2	0.7	3.5	29.7	-0.5	-1.7	26.8	2.0	7.7	20.2	2.4	12.3	15.7	2.8	19.7

	Mean	Δ 95–06		Mean	Δ 95–06		Mean	Δ 95–06		Mean	Δ 95–06		Mean	Δ 95–05	
	%	p.p.	%	%	p.p.	%	%	p.p.	%	%	p.p.	%	%	p.p.	%
	Germany			*Italy*			*Netherlands*			*Spain*			*Sweden*		
SOS	1.0	0.8	185.9	1.4	0.3	24.1	3.5	1.6	59.9	2.0	1.5	118.3	2.9	1.7	95.1
SOS^{OTHBUS}	0.5	0.4	141.1	0.9	0.4	46.6	2.2	0.4	22.9	1.8	1.3	123.7	0.4	-1.2	-100.0
SOS^{COMP}	0.2	0.2	345.0	0.1	0.1	351.8	0.1	0.0	58.1	0.0	0.0	-82.5	0.2	0.2	155.2
SOS^{FIN}	0.1	0.1	864.9	0.3	-0.1	-35.4	0.5	0.7	574.3	0.2	0.1	165.5	0.3	-0.2	-43.2
$SOS^{R\&D}$	0.2	0.1	104.6	0.1	0.0	-9.6	0.7	0.4	75.6	0.1	0.0	60.7	2.0	2.9	1742.4
MOS	15.8	2.9	20.1	15.9	2.7	17.3	26.6	-3.5	-11.9	18.0	4.7	29.6	20.9	0.3	1.6

Author's calculations based on Eurostat and the statistical offices of Italy and Spain. See Table 3.2 for the availability of import matrices used to construct the offshoring indicators. The seven-country sample spans the period 1995–2006. The nine-country sample covers the years 1995, 2000, and 2005.

Table 3.4 Geographical origin of service imports

	Intra-EU27	Extra-EU27	*of which:* Other Europe	North America	Latin America	Asia	Africa	Oceania	Intra-EU27	Extra-EU27	*of which:* Other Europe	North America	Latin America	Asia	Africa	Oceania
	All Countries								*Belgium*							
All services	60.3	39.7	12.8	11.8	1.7	9.3	3.6	0.4	71.5	28.5	10.1	8.4	0.9	5.3	3.6	0.3
Other business services	65.1	34.9	10.4	14.1	0.8	7.3	2.0	0.5	75.2	24.8	8.1	12.2	0.8	3.0	0.6	0.2
Computer	65.5	34.5	7.3	18.5	0.3	7.5	0.6	0.3	80.0	20.0	2.7	12.3	0.3	3.6	0.9	0.1
Finance and insurance	64.7	35.3	18.3	10.5	0.6	5.0	0.5	0.2	75.1	24.9	9.7	9.0	0.8	4.4	0.6	0.4
Research and development	53.0	47.0	8.5	27.1	0.8	9.0	0.9	0.7	42.2	57.8	4.0	46.5	0.6	6.0	0.4	0.2
	Denmark								*Finland*							
All services	54.9	45.1	9.6	14.3	2.7	13.4	4.1	0.9	64.0	36.0	13.8	11.7	0.7	8.4	0.4	1.0
Other business services	68.6	31.4	12.2	12.5	1.0	5.0	0.5	0.3	-	-	-	-	-	-	-	-
Computer	67.9	32.1	14.2	11.4	0.2	6.0	0.3	0.1	68.0	32.0	6.6	14.2	0.3	9.6	1.1	0.2
Finance and insurance	66.7	33.3	7.9	16.9	4.5	3.7	0.2	0.1	-	-	-	-	-	-	-	-
Research and development	63.0	37.0	16.1	15.3	0.7	3.6	0.4	1.0	56.4	43.6	26.2	-	-	17.3	0.0	-
	France								*Germany*							
All services	52.0	48.0	12.6	12.0	2.8	11.4	8.5	0.7	58.0	42.0	15.3	12.6	0.0	11.6	2.5	0.0
Other business services	59.8	40.2	10.7	17.7	0.9	7.3	3.2	0.5	59.0	41.0	12.1	16.3	1.1	9.9	1.0	0.6
Computer	61.4	38.6	3.2	29.4	0.3	5.2	0.5	0.0	56.7	43.3	9.3	22.8	0.6	10.1	0.3	0.2
Finance and insurance	53.7	46.3	24.3	12.3	1.8	6.4	1.0	0.5	59.7	40.3	24.4	10.2	0.2	5.1	0.1	0.2
Research and development	56.9	43.1	10.4	20.9	0.9	7.4	2.9	0.6	59.3	40.7	6.4	24.7	1.0	7.6	0.5	0.4

(*Continued*)

Table 3.4 (Continued)

	Intra-EU27	Extra-EU27	*of which:* Other Europe	North America	Latin America	Asia	Africa	Oceania	Intra-EU27	Extra-EU27	*of which:* Other Europe	North America	Latin America	Asia	Africa	Oceania
	Italy								*Netherlands*							
All services	62.5	37.5	13.7	8.8	2.4	7.7	4.3	0.6	61.3	38.7	10.9	13.7	2.4	9.1	2.0	0.7
Other business services	71.3	28.7	10.5	7.8	0.7	4.5	4.9	0.3	68.4	31.6	8.2	13.8	0.0	7.9	1.2	0.5
Computer	82.4	17.6	4.1	10.3	0.1	2.4	0.1	0.6	71.0	29.0	4.9	13.1	-	8.8	1.5	0.6
Finance and insurance	83.1	16.9	8.0	6.3	0.3	1.7	0.7	0.0	64.8	35.2	13.1	11.9	-	8.9	1.2	0.2
Research and development	75.0	25.0	10.1	11.5	0.0	3.4	0.0	0.0	53.7	46.3	2.1	26.8	-	16.8	0.4	0.1
	Spain								*Sweden*							
All services	67.1	32.9	9.4	10.4	4.4	5.5	2.9	0.3	62.0	38.0	15.2	14.9	0.6	5.9	0.7	0.8
Other business services	-	-	-	-	-	-	-	-	65.4	34.6	8.9	15.8	0.9	7.4	1.3	0.3
Computer	-	-	-	-	-	-	-	-	69.6	30.4	9.2	17.8	0.2	2.8	0.1	0.3
Finance and insurance	-	-	-	-	-	-	-	-	45.7	54.3	30.0	19.0	0.3	4.3	0.5	0.3
Research and development	-	-	-	-	-	-	-	-	35.9	64.1	3.9	49.7	1.6	6.4	0.7	1.9

Reported figures are the share of each region (indicated in columns) in the total imports of each service category (indicated in rows). *All services* includes imports of all types of services. *Extra-EU27* is computed as total imports minus intra-EU27 imports. *Other Europe* is computed as Extra-EU27 imports minus the sum of imports from the other regions. Data refer to the year 2007. Source: Eurostat.

have slightly increased in our samples, by about 14 and 8 percent respectively. The increase has taken place in all countries except Germany, where total employment has risen but hours worked have remained almost constant. Medium-skilled workers make the lion's share (66 percent) of total hours worked in the last year of the samples, whereas high- and low-skilled workers account for 13 and 21 percent respectively. (The picture is similar across the individual countries.) Over time, the skill composition of labor demand has shifted in favor of more educated workers: the number of hours worked by low-skilled employees has declined everywhere (except in Germany), whereas hours worked by medium- and high-skilled employees have always increased. Finally, a comparison of labor demand elasticities estimated for two subperiods—pre- and post-2001—shows that labor demand has flattened out over time: on average, the absolute value of the elasticity has increased by about 50 percent, from 0.2 to 0.3. The elasticity has increased everywhere except in Italy, the Netherlands, and Sweden.

To sum up, these stylized facts show that the incidence of service offshoring in Western Europe has increased since the mid-1990s, although the phenomenon is still limited in size compared to the offshoring of production stages. There is no evidence of large drops in employment and hours worked over the same time period: if anything, employment and hours worked have moderately increased in all countries. At the same time, the composition of employment has shifted in favor of more skilled workers and labor demand has become more elastic.

While many factors could have been responsible for these changes in the labor market, the aim of this chapter is to shed some light on the possible role of service offshoring. As a first step in that direction, we briefly summarize the results of a simple reduced-form approach, in which we correlate the change in service offshoring between the endpoints of our sample with the changes in a number of proxies for the location, skill composition, and elasticity of labor demand. This exercise yields several interesting results. First, the correlation between changes in employment and service offshoring is weakly positive in all but three countries (France, Italy, and the Netherlands). Second, this positive correlation is driven by offshoring of business services; for the remaining service categories, changes in offshoring and employment are virtually uncorrelated. Third, the correlation between changes in hours worked and service offshoring is positive for all groups of workers, but is stronger for those with higher skills. Finally, the growth in service offshoring has been to some extent related with the observed increase in labor demand elasticity; in particular, labor demand elasticity has grown more in country-industry pairs where service offshoring has increased faster than the sample median. In the next sections, we use a more structural approach to investigate these issues in more detail.

4 Empirical Models

Following previous studies (in particular Amiti and Wei 2005, 2006), we estimate log-linear labor demand functions augmented by service offshoring. In particular, our main specifications read as follows (country, industry, and time subscripts are omitted to clarify notation):

$$\ln L = \beta_0 + \beta_W \ln W + \sum_{r\in\{M,S,E\}} \beta_r \ln P^r + \beta_Y \ln Y + \beta_K \ln K + \sum_{z\in Z} \beta_z z \tag{3}$$

and

$$\ln L = \beta_0 + \beta_W \ln W + \sum_{r\in\{M,S,E\}} \beta_r \ln P^r + \beta_{P^Y} \ln P^Y + \beta_K \ln K + \sum_{z\in Z} \beta_z z \tag{4}$$

where z denotes a number of shift-factors, including service offshoring, and the parameter β_W measures the wage elasticity of labor demand.[4] Note that if $\beta_{SOS} > 0\ (<0)$, an increase in service offshoring shifts the demand function outward (inward) and thus raises (lowers) employment, ceteris paribus. Importantly, because equation (3)—the conditional demand function—depends on output, the effects of service offshoring estimated from it do not account for changes in the scale of operations. The latter are instead captured by the effects estimated from equation (4)—the unconditional demand function—in which the output level is replaced by the output price.[5]

These models can be immediately extended to study the effects of service offshoring (or any other shift-factor) on the wage elasticity of labor demand. In particular, following previous studies (e.g., Bruno et al. 2004), this can be done by adding interaction terms between log wages and service offshoring (or any other shift-factor). Hence, the models modify as follows:

$$\ln L = \beta_0 + \beta_W \ln W + \sum_{r\in\{M,S,E\}} \beta_r \ln P^r + \beta_Y \ln Y + \beta_K \ln K + \sum_{z\in Z} \beta_z z + \sum_{z\in Z} \beta_{W,z} \ln W \cdot z \tag{5}$$

and

$$\ln L = \beta_0 + \beta_W \ln W + \sum_{r\in\{M,S,E\}} \beta_r \ln P^r + \beta_{P^Y} \ln P^Y + \beta_K \ln K + \sum_{z\in Z} \beta_z z + \sum_{z\in Z} \beta_{W,z} \ln W \cdot z \tag{6}$$

Note that if $\beta_{W,SOS} > 0\ (<0)$, an increase in service offshoring makes labor demand less (more) elastic. Offshoring mainly affects labor demand elasticity by expanding the flexibility with which firms can potentially substitute domestic labor with foreign inputs (Senses 2010). Moreover, the elasticity estimates may be seriously biased by shocks to product demand if industry output is not controlled for (Hasan et al. 2007). For these reasons, when studying the effects of service offshoring on labor demand elasticity, we focus only on equation (5) and discard the unconditional demand function in equation (6).

5 Results

This section presents the empirical results. We first investigate the effects of service offshoring on the location of labor demand. Then, we turn to the effects on the elasticity.

5.1 The effects of service offshoring on the location of labor demand

We start by discussing the baseline estimates of equations (3) and (4). Then we explore heterogeneity in the effects of service offshoring across types of services, individual countries, and skill groups of workers.

5.1.1 *Baseline estimates*

The baseline estimates of equations (3) and (4) are reported in Table 3.5; both models include country-industry and year effects, which account, respectively, for unobserved heterogeneity at the country-industry level and for macroeconomic shocks common to all countries and industries. Columns (1)–(8) report the results obtained on the seven-country sample, columns (9)–(10) those obtained on the nine-country sample. For each sample, the table shows estimates of the conditional labor demand function (columns (1)–(4) and (9)) and of the unconditional labor demand function (columns (5)–(8) and (10)). For each function, the estimates obtained on the seven-country sample encompass four specifications, which differ in the choice of intermediate input prices and controls for capital. In what follows, we first explain these differences in detail and comment on the coefficients on the technology variables. Then we discuss the coefficient on the main variable of interest, service offshoring.

Columns (1) and (5) estimate the benchmark models presented in section 4. As expected, the coefficient on log wage is negative and significant, suggesting that labor demand is downward sloping. The wage elasticity of labor demand ranges between −0.1 and −0.2, in line with existing estimates (see Hamermesh 1993). The coefficients on log output and log capital are both positive, implying that larger scale of production and greater capital investment increase the use of labor. As for intermediate inputs, only the coefficient on log energy prices is statistically significant; its negative sign suggests energy to be a complement for labor in production. Columns (2) and (6) replace the prices of energy, materials, and services with the log average price of intermediate inputs. This makes the specifications similar to those used in previous work, for example by Hasan et al. (2007) and Hijzen and Swaim (2010). The coefficient on intermediate input prices is not very precisely estimated, while those on wages, capital, and output remain largely unchanged.

Columns (3) and (7) exclude intermediate inputs altogether, as in Amiti and Wei (2005, 2006). The implicit assumption is that the price of intermediates is a function of time and thus gets absorbed by the year dummies. Apart from a slight increase in the absolute value of the wage elasticity, there is no noteworthy change in the previous

Table 3.5 The effect of service offshoring on labor demand: baseline specifications

	Seven-country sample								Nine-country sample	
	Conditional Demand Functions				Unconditional Demand Functions				Cond. Demand	Uncond. Demand
	3 Interm. Inputs	Ov. Interm. Inp.	No Interm. Inputs	Price of Capital	3 Interm. Inputs	Ov. Interm. Inp.	No Interm. Inputs	Price of Capital	3 Interm. Inputs	3 Interm. Inputs
	(1)	(2)	(3)	(4)	(5)	(6)	(7)	(8)	(9)	(10)
lnW	-0.199***	-0.174**	-0.210***	-0.176*	-0.083*	-0.083*	-0.098**	-0.101	-0.263***	-0.200***
	[0.075]	[0.077]	[0.078]	[0.096]	[0.043]	[0.045]	[0.050]	[0.075]	[0.055]	[0.045]
lnP^M	0.121			0.143*	0.049			0.115	0.161**	0.149***
	[0.078]			[0.077]	[0.066]			[0.079]	[0.073]	[0.057]
lnP^S	-0.018			-0.040	0.008			-0.070	-0.034	-0.047
	[0.056]			[0.062]	[0.051]			[0.062]	[0.056]	[0.049]
lnP^E	-0.102**			-0.131**	-0.092*			-0.089	-0.159***	-0.142***
	[0.047]			[0.057]	[0.052]			[0.067]	[0.047]	[0.051]
lnP^I		0.155*				-0.112				
		[0.085]				[0.211]				
lnY	0.326***	0.323***	0.307***	0.466***					0.340***	
	[0.085]	[0.080]	[0.085]	[0.097]					[0.070]	
lnP^Y					0.169**	0.250	0.141*	-0.057		0.021
					[0.085]	[0.211]	[0.085]	[0.109]		[0.072]
lnK	0.437***	0.474***	0.464***		0.639***	0.646***	0.652***		0.412***	0.572***
	[0.074]	[0.073]	[0.072]		[0.067]	[0.068]	[0.067]		[0.063]	[0.064]
lnP^K				0.507**				0.876***		
				[0.234]				[0.241]		
SOS	0.009**	0.008*	0.007*	0.010**	0.011**	0.010**	0.010**	0.014**	0.013***	0.017***
	[0.004]	[0.004]	[0.004]	[0.005]	[0.005]	[0.004]	[0.004]	[0.006]	[0.005]	[0.006]
Obs.	1679	1680	1680	1439	1679	1680	1680	1439	540	540
R-squared	0.52	0.52	0.51	0.45	0.45	0.44	0.44	0.26	0.53	0.44

The dependent variable is the log number of employees. All specifications control for country-industry and year effects. The specifications estimated on the 7-country sample also include a dummy equal to 1 for the interpolated observations. Standard errors are corrected for clustering at the country-industry level. ***, **, *: indicates significance at the 1, 5, and 10 percent level respectively. See also notes to previous tables.

results. A similar picture emerges from columns (4) and (8), in which the capital stock is replaced by the log capital price; the wage elasticity is however imprecisely estimated in the unconditional demand model. Finally, the estimates obtained on the nine-country sample (columns (9) and (10)) are similar to those obtained on the seven-country sample. In addition, they deliver a significant coefficient on the log price of material inputs; its positive sign suggests these inputs to substitute for labor in production.

Having shown that the results for the technology variables are robust across different models, we now turn to the coefficient on service offshoring. Note that, independent of the specification and estimation sample, the coefficient on *SOS* is weakly positive. The point estimates are larger for the unconditional demand functions, suggesting that service offshoring may induce some positive scale effects that end up raising labor demand. However, the size of the effect is generally small: a 1 p.p. increase in service offshoring (which corresponds to the actual change in *SOS* during the sample period) is associated with a 1 percent increase in domestic employment.

The above results are robust across a number of sensitivity checks, which we briefly summarize below. First, the main evidence is preserved when the model is extended to account for other factors usually studied in the empirical literature. These include: (1) technological progress (as proxied by the price of software, the price of information and communication technology, an index of TFP growth, the ICT share of total capital compensation, and a full set of country-industry-specific time trends); (2) other aspects of globalization (material offshoring, import penetration, trade openness, service inshoring, inward and outward foreign direct investment, and international immigration); (3) union coverage; and (4) other time-varying factors that cannot be precisely measured or are unobserved (as captured by full sets of country-time and industry-time dummies). Second, the results are qualitatively similar under alternative empirical approaches and estimation methods. In particular, when: (1) hours worked and hourly wages are used in place of total employment and yearly wages; (2) *SOS* is replaced by *SOS_Y*; (3) the model is estimated in first differences (with and without including country-industry fixed-effects); (4) the first lag of all regressors is added to the specification; (5) the model is estimated in long differences (five-year and eleven-year); (6) dynamic panel data models are estimated by either GMM (Arellano and Bond 1991) or bias-corrected least-square-dummy-variables (Bun and Kiviet 2003; Bruno 2005a, 2005b); (7) the potential endogeneity of service offshoring is tackled by means of instrumental variables, using lags of all regressors as instruments.

To summarize, the results of this section suggest that service offshoring has not induced any large loss of domestic employment in Western Europe. It may have actually increased employment slightly through positive scale effects. This evidence is largely consistent with some of the studies reviewed in section 2. Next, we explore potential heterogeneity across types of services, individual countries, and workers of different skill levels.

5.1.2 *Heterogeneity*

We start by reestimating equations (3) and (4) using the four disaggregate indicators of service offshoring in place of *SOS*. We find that the estimated coefficients are similar to those on *SOS* for business services, whereas they are very small and imprecisely estimated for the remaining categories. These results imply that the aggregate findings discussed before are to a large extent driven by offshoring of business services, which constitutes the bulk of service offshoring in Western Europe. Offshoring of other service categories has instead negligible effects on labor demand.

Next, we estimate the baseline specification of equations (3) and (4) individually on each country in order to unveil potential heterogeneity in the effects of service offshoring across the nine economies. The results are reported in Table 3.6. The estimated coefficients are positive in half of the countries and negative in the remaining cases. However, the point estimates are often imprecise and generally small in absolute value. Overall, this suggests the effects of service offshoring to be moderate also in the individual countries, which is broadly consistent with the aggregate evidence discussed before and with some of the existing empirical studies.

Finally, we discuss the effects on workers with different educational levels. To this purpose, we estimate equations (3) and (4) separately on high-, medium-, and low-skilled employees. There are two main differences between these models and the benchmark specifications presented in section 4. First, the dependent variables are hours worked by each skill group rather than total employment. Second, the yearly wage is replaced by the hourly wages of the three skill groups. Table 3.7 reports the results. Interestingly, the coefficients on service offshoring are small and weakly positive for all educational groups, suggesting that the aggregate results discussed before

Table 3.6 The effect of service offshoring on labor demand: individual countries

	Conditional Demand Functions								
	Belgium	Denmark	Finland	France	Germany	Italy	Netherlands	Spain	Sweden
SOS	0.039*	0.032***	0.011	-0.079***	0.033	-0.047*	-0.005	0.004	-0.007
	[0.019]	[0.010]	[0.007]	[0.026]	[0.034]	[0.024]	[0.006]	[0.003]	[0.008]
Obs.	60	240	239	240	240	240	240	240	60
R-squared	0.52	0.71	0.53	0.70	0.66	0.37	0.71	0.80	0.83
	Unconditional Demand Functions								
	Belgium	Denmark	Finland	France	Germany	Italy	Netherlands	Spain	Sweden
SOS	0.031	0.052***	0.011	-0.137***	0.023	-0.018	-0.006	-0.005*	-0.002
	[0.021]	[0.014]	[0.008]	[0.030]	[0.035]	[0.034]	[0.007]	[0.003]	[0.010]
Obs.	60	240	239	240	240	240	240	240	60
R-squared	0.51	0.60	0.51	0.66	0.62	0.41	0.63	0.86	0.80

The dependent variable is the log number of employees. The specifications include the same regressors as in columns (1) and (5) of Table 3.5. Only the coefficients on service offshoring are reported. Standard errors are corrected for clustering at the industry level. ***, **, *: indicates significance at the 1, 5, and 10% level respectively. See also notes to previous tables.

Table 3.7 The effect of service offshoring on labor demand: estimates by skill group

	Conditional Demand Functions									
	Seven-country sample									Nine-country sample
	Baseline	SOS_Y	Price of software	Material offshoring	Service inshoring	Union density	Country-time and industry-time effects	Eleven-year differences	IV	Baseline
	(1)	(2)	(3)	(4)	(5)	(6)	(7)	(8)	(9)	(10)
High Skilled Labor										
SOS	0.013**		0.012*	0.013**	0.013**	0.015***	0.009	0.026**	0.053***	0.013*
	[0.006]		[0.006]	[0.006]	[0.006]	[0.005]	[0.005]	[0.011]	[0.018]	[0.007]
SOS_Y		0.020**								
		[0.010]								
R-squared	0.56	0.56	0.56	0.56	0.56	0.59	0.74	0.39	0.06	0.65
Medium Skilled Labor										
SOS	0.010		0.008	0.011	0.009	0.011	0.006	0.021*	0.020*	0.006
	[0.007]		[0.007]	[0.007]	[0.007]	[0.007]	[0.004]	[0.012]	[0.011]	[0.007]
SOS_Y		0.005								
		[0.009]								
R-squared	0.45	0.44	0.50	0.45	0.46	0.45	0.82	0.47	0.23	0.45
Low-skilled labor										
SOS	0.012		0.010	0.012	0.011	0.011	0.005	0.012	-0.024	0.006
	[0.008]		[0.007]	[0.007]	[0.007]	[0.007]	[0.004]	[0.015]	[0.017]	[0.009]
SOS_Y		0.004								
		[0.010]								
R-squared	0.63	0.63	0.61	0.63	0.64	0.64	0.86	0.46	0.53	0.68
Obs.	1675	1675	1435	1675	1675	1675	1675	135	1115	540

(Continued)

Table 3.7 (Continued)

	Unconditional Demand Functions									
	Seven-country sample									Nine-country sample
	Baseline	SOS_Y	Price of Software	Material Offshoring	Service Inshoring	Union Density	Country-Time and Industry-Time Effects	11-Year Differences	IV	Baseline
	(1)	(2)	(3)	(4)	(5)	(6)	(7)	(8)	(9)	(10)
High-skilled labor										
SOS	0.018*** [0.005]		0.017*** [0.005]	0.016*** [0.005]	0.017*** [0.005]	0.019*** [0.004]	0.011** [0.005]	0.036*** [0.010]	0.050*** [0.014]	0.020*** [0.007]
SOS_Y		0.029*** [0.007]								
R-squared	0.55	0.55	0.55	0.55	0.55	0.57	0.73	0.35	0.18	0.63
Medium-skilled labor										
SOS	0.015*** [0.006]		0.014** [0.006]	0.015*** [0.006]	0.015*** [0.005]	0.016*** [0.006]	0.008* [0.004]	0.037*** [0.011]	0.029*** [0.009]	0.017** [0.007]
SOS_Y		0.017 [0.011]								
R-squared	0.46	0.45	0.50	0.46	0.47	0.46	0.80	0.51	0.09	0.44
Low-skilled labor										
SOS	0.016** [0.007]		0.015** [0.007]	0.015** [0.007]	0.015** [0.007]	0.014** [0.007]	0.005 [0.005]	0.023 [0.015]	-0.008 [0.017]	0.012 [0.009]
SOS_Y		0.012 [0.012]								
R-squared	0.62	0.61	0.59	0.62	0.62	0.63	0.85	0.45	0.60	0.65
Obs.	1675	1675	1435	1675	1675	1675	1675	135	1115	540

The dependent variable is the log number of hours worked by each skill group. Standard errors are corrected for clustering at the country-industry level. In columns (3)–(6), the baseline specification is extended to include the following controls: *price of software* (sourced from EUKLEMS); *material offshoring* (share of imported material inputs in total input purchases, sourced from Eurostat); *service inshoring* (service exports over GDP, sourced from the World Development Indicators); *union density* (union members' share of population, sourced from OECD and the WDI). In column (7), the time dummies are replaced by full sets of country-time and industry-time effects. In column (8), the baseline specification is estimated in 11-year differences. In column (9), all explanatory variables are instrumented using their third and fourth lags. Only the coefficients on service offshoring are reported. ***, **, *: indicates significance at the 1, 5, and 10 percent level respectively. See also notes to previous tables.

generally apply to workers of different skill levels. Moreover, the estimated effects tend to be larger, and more precise, for more skilled workers. Consistent with previous work by Crinò (2012), this suggests imported services to complement especially with high domestic skills.

A large number of studies use a different approach to investigate whether the effects of offshoring are heterogeneous across workers with different skill levels. Specifically, they estimate a system of variable-cost share equations by seemingly unrelated regressions or iterated three-stage least squares. These studies include Morrison and Siegel (2001), Falk and Koebel (2001, 2002), Ekholm and Hakkala (2005), Hijzen et al. (2005), Becker et al. (2009), and Crinò (2012). In our case, the results obtained with this approach are broadly consistent with those reported in Table 3.7. In particular, for none of the groups is the coefficient on service offshoring significantly negative. Moreover, the coefficient on *SOS* tends to be larger and more precise for more skilled workers.

5.2 The effects of service offshoring on labor demand elasticity

The previous section shows that service offshoring exerts small effects on the level of labor demand in Western Europe. This section investigates a different channel through which service offshoring may affect domestic workers, namely by changing, and possibly increasing, the wage elasticity of labor demand. As mentioned in the introduction, service offshoring may make labor demand more elastic by expanding the flexibility with which firms can potentially substitute domestic workers with foreign inputs (Hijzen and Swaim 2010; Senses 2010). A greater elasticity, in turn, implies a higher volatility of wages and employment in response to economic shocks, a lower bargaining power of workers, and a larger incidence of non-wage labor costs on employees (Rodrik 1997). Importantly, the simple threat of service offshoring may be sufficient to flatten out labor demand. Hence, this effect is not incompatible a priori with the small changes in the employment levels induced by service offshoring until now, which we have documented in the previous section.

In order to study this issue, we start by estimating equation (5) on the whole sample of countries. The results are in Table 3.8. Starting from the baseline specification in column (1), note that the coefficient on the interaction between service offshoring and log wages is negative and precisely estimated. This result is generally robust across the remaining specifications. In particular, it remains qualitatively unchanged when normalizing imported services by industry output (column (2)), when accounting for concomitant factors related to technical change, globalization, and union density (columns (3)–(7)), when using hours worked instead of total employment (column (8)), and when estimating the model in long differences or by Instrumental Variables (columns (9)–(10)). Overall, this suggests that service offshoring may make labor demand more elastic. Nevertheless, the effect is not large in economic terms. The point estimates imply, in fact, that a 1 p.p. increase in *SOS* raises the absolute value of the wage elasticity by approximately 0.01.

Table 3.8 The effect of service offshoring on labor demand elasticity

	Seven-country sample										Nine-country sample
	Baseline	SOS_Y	Price of software	Material offshoring	Service inshoring	Union density	Country-time and industry-time effects	Hours worked	Eleven-year differences	IV	Baseline
	(1)	(2)	(3)	(4)	(5)	(6)	(7)	(8)	(9)	(10)	(11)
lnW	-0.178**	-0.184**	-0.132*	-0.211**	-0.199**	-0.134	-0.077**	-0.174**	-0.257***	-0.239**	-0.264***
	[0.075]	[0.075]	[0.075]	[0.098]	[0.087]	[0.101]	[0.034]	[0.084]	[0.095]	[0.101]	[0.057]
lnP^{M}	0.114	0.107	0.101	0.122	0.109	0.110	0.094	0.118	0.248	0.212	0.160**
	[0.076]	[0.076]	[0.077]	[0.077]	[0.079]	[0.077]	[0.067]	[0.078]	[0.156]	[0.216]	[0.073]
lnP^{S}	-0.004	-0.006	-0.040	-0.008	-0.026	-0.001	-0.087	-0.027	-0.076	0.147	-0.034
	[0.055]	[0.056]	[0.055]	[0.055]	[0.057]	[0.056]	[0.055]	[0.058]	[0.087]	[0.097]	[0.057]
lnP^{E}	-0.108**	-0.098**	-0.053	-0.114**	-0.069	-0.098**	0.047	-0.067	-0.204***	-0.099	-0.159***
	[0.046]	[0.046]	[0.055]	[0.046]	[0.053]	[0.044]	[0.055]	[0.046]	[0.076]	[0.087]	[0.047]
lnY	0.339***	0.336***	0.306***	0.341***	0.312***	0.342***	0.345***	0.306***	0.415***	0.573***	0.340***
	[0.083]	[0.085]	[0.088]	[0.083]	[0.082]	[0.082]	[0.078]	[0.087]	[0.103]	[0.148]	[0.069]
lnK	0.427***	0.428***	0.375***	0.420***	0.445***	0.423***	0.095	0.447***	0.416***	0.303**	0.413***
	[0.072]	[0.075]	[0.074]	[0.074]	[0.072]	[0.077]	[0.062]	[0.077]	[0.089]	[0.119]	[0.065]
SOS	0.104**		0.135***	0.111***	0.154***	0.111***	0.086***	0.122***	0.149***	0.085	0.009
	[0.041]		[0.044]	[0.042]	[0.046]	[0.042]	[0.029]	[0.046]	[0.048]	[0.066]	[0.043]
SOS*lnW	-0.009**		-0.012***	-0.010**	-0.014***	-0.010**	-0.008***	-0.010**	-0.012***	-0.007	0.000
	[0.004]		[0.004]	[0.004]	[0.004]	[0.004]	[0.003]	[0.004]	[0.004]	[0.006]	[0.004]
SOS_Y		0.128*									
		[0.075]									
SOS_Y*lnW		-0.011									
		[0.007]									
lnP^{SOFT}			1.489*								
			[0.857]								

$lnP^{SOFT}*lnW$			-0.125								
			[0.083]								
MOS				-0.014							
				[0.018]							
MOS*lnW				0.001							
				[0.002]							
INSH					-0.060*						
					[0.035]						
INSH*lnW					0.006						
					[0.004]						
UNDENS						0.014					
						[0.013]					
UNDENS*lnW						-0.001					
						[0.002]					
Obs.	1679	1679	1439	1679	1679	1679	1679	1679	139	1119	540
R-squared	0.53	0.52	0.54	0.53	0.54	0.53	0.82	0.50	0.60	0.42	0.53

The dependent variable is the log number of employees, except in column (8) where it is the log number of hours worked. Standard errors are corrected for clustering at the country-industry level. ***, **, *: indicates significance at the 1, 5, and 10 percent level respectively. See also notes to previous tables.

Also in this case, the effects of service offshoring are heterogeneous across countries. In particular, when equation (5) is estimated individually on each economy, the coefficient on the interaction term is negative in five countries (Denmark, Finland, Germany, Italy, and Sweden) and positive in the remaining four. Recent work by Hasan et al. (2007) and Hijzen and Swaim (2010) suggests that such heterogeneity may be linked to differences in labor-market regulations across countries. In particular, in countries with weak regulations, firms may have greater flexibility to adjust their mix of domestic and foreign inputs and the effects of service offshoring may end up being larger as a result.

To investigate this source of heterogeneity, we have reestimated the baseline specification on two subsamples of countries, with strict and weak labor-market regulations respectively. Countries with strict regulations are those for which the index of EPL constructed by Nickell (2006) is above the sample median. Consistent with our expectations and with previous findings by Hasan et al. (2007) and Hijzen and Swaim (2010), we found that the interaction between log wages and service offshoring is significantly negative only in the subsample of countries with weak EPL, where firms may have greater flexibility to substitute domestic labor with foreign inputs.

Table 3.9 The effect of service offshoring on labor demand elasticity: estimates by skill group

	Strict EPL			Weak EPL		
	High-skilled labor	Medium-skilled labor	Low-skilled labor	High-skilled labor	Medium-skilled labor	Low-skilled labor
$\ln W^{HS}$	0.183	-0.104	-0.095	-0.903***	-0.206*	-0.147
	[0.176]	[0.094]	[0.144]	[0.116]	[0.105]	[0.121]
$\ln W^{MS}$	-0.651**	-0.348**	0.281	0.756***	0.514**	-0.489
	[0.294]	[0.169]	[0.267]	[0.233]	[0.237]	[0.355]
$\ln W^{LS}$	0.019	-0.011	0.106	-0.028	-0.463*	0.206
	[0.047]	[0.014]	[0.073]	[0.222]	[0.250]	[0.311]
SOS	0.029	-0.101***	-0.220*	0.077*	-0.006	-0.116***
	[0.089]	[0.037]	[0.123]	[0.042]	[0.037]	[0.044]
$SOS*\ln W^{HS}$	0.088	0.031	0.110*	0.003	0.017	0.086
	[0.056]	[0.029]	[0.057]	[0.046]	[0.058]	[0.074]
$SOS*\ln W^{MS}$	-0.088	-0.025	-0.063	-0.051	0.017	0.182*
	[0.085]	[0.035]	[0.113]	[0.071]	[0.073]	[0.095]
$SOS*\ln W^{LS}$	-0.021	0.018	-0.003	0.023	-0.033	-0.250***
	[0.040]	[0.018]	[0.058]	[0.042]	[0.043]	[0.050]
Obs.	716	716	716	959	959	959
R-squared	0.59	0.46	0.79	0.71	0.59	0.61

Results are based on the seven-country sample. The dependent variable is the log number of hours worked by each skill group. Only the coefficients on log wages, service offshoring and their interactions are reported. Standard errors are corrected for clustering at the country-industry level.***, **, *: indicates significance at the 1, 5, and 10 percent level respectively. See also notes to previous tables.

Finally, in Table 3.9 we estimate the model separately for the three skill groups of workers, using the seven-country sample to save space and maximize degrees of freedom. The estimates show that, in countries with strict EPL, service offshoring does not raise the elasticity of labor demand for any skill group. In countries with weak EPL, instead, service offshoring exerts no effect on workers with high and medium skill levels, but raises the elasticity of labor demand for low skilled workers.

6 Conclusion

This chapter studied the effects of service offshoring on the location and elasticity of labor demand, using novel and comparable data for nine Western European countries between 1995 and 2006. The empirical results showed that, in the aggregate, service offshoring exerts small, and possibly weakly positive, effects on the level of labor demand. These effects are mostly driven by offshoring of business services, whereas offshoring of other services has negligible impacts on labor demand. Some heterogeneity exists across countries, but the economic magnitude of the effect of service offshoring is always small. Finally, skilled workers are more likely to complement imported services than unskilled workers; however, neither for this latter group of employees are the effects of service offshoring significantly negative.

As for the second topic, the results show that service offshoring makes labor demand more elastic. Nevertheless, the economic magnitude of this effect is also small. Interestingly, the effect depends on the strictness of labor-market regulations in each country. In particular, the elasticity of labor demand rises with service offshoring only in countries with weak regulations, and this effect is mostly borne by low-skilled workers.

Taken together, these findings support the main message from previous studies, according to which the "fear of service offshoring" (Amiti and Wei 2005) is probably exaggerated. At the same time, however, they suggest that specific types of government policies may help alleviate this fear and mitigate the adjustment costs faced by some groups of workers. In particular, improved access to on-the-job training and higher education may help low-educated and poorly qualified individuals upgrade their skills and thereby make them more complementary with imported services (OECD 2005). Similarly, EPL may reduce the negative effects of service offshoring on the wage elasticity of labor demand, especially for low-skilled workers.

The main caveat of these results is the potential endogeneity of service offshoring in labor demand models. Endogeneity may have two origins. First, as a result of the business cycle or unobserved shocks, labor demand and service offshoring may change simultaneously, and this may inflate the positive correlation between the two variables. Second, industries experiencing faster employment growth may resort more heavily to service offshoring. This may give rise to reverse causality which, again, may inflate the estimated coefficient on service offshoring. Our large set of control variables should take care of the first issue, whereas the instrumental variables regressions should partially accommodate the second. One of the main challenges of the most recent empirical literature is to find exogenous instruments for offshoring, which would crucially help solve both problems (see, most notably, Autor et al. 2011; Hummels et al. 2011).

In conclusion, we mention a possible avenue for future research related to this chapter. Service offshoring may have different implications for individual employees, depending on their educational level and other characteristics, such as gender, race, occupation, labor-market experience, and geographical mobility. The chapter does not study these factors due to its focus on more aggregate effects. Nevertheless, the studies on service offshoring based on microlevel data are still very limited. Among them are the recent works by Blinder and Krueger (2009) and Liu and Trefler (2011) for the United States, and by Hijzen et al. (2011) and Geishecker and Görg (forthcoming) for the United Kingdom. The increasing availability of worker-level data sets will offer a great opportunity to expand the number and geographic coverage of these studies, thereby improving our understanding of the labor-market implications of service offshoring in developed countries.

Notes

*. This chapter has greatly benefitted from the comments of the editors and anonymous reviewers. All results mentioned in the text but not reported can be found in the working paper version of the chapter, available at https://sites.google.com/site/crinoecon. Research for this chapter was partially funded by the European Community's Seventh Framework Programme (Project INGINEUS, Grant Agreement No. 225368, www.ingineus.eu).
+. Address: CEMFI.Casado del Alisal 5, 28014 Madrid, Spain. E-mail: crino@cemfi.es.

1. The import matrices are part of the input–output accounts of each country. They adopt a common industrial classification (the "European System of Accounts," ESA 95) and are thus comparable across economies.
2. In order to make sure that the empirical results are not driven by the interpolation, all specifications estimated on this sample include a dummy equal to 1 for the interpolated observations.
3. See Castellani et al. (2011) for further discussion on the properties of offshoring indices.
4. The shift factors z are not expressed in logarithms, because most of them are measured in percentages.
5. Note that we do not impose price homogeneity of degree zero on the demand functions. Because this property is generally rejected by our data, imposing it would exacerbate bias due to measurement error (Clark and Freeman 1980).

References

Amiti, M., and S.-J. Wei. 2005. "Fear of Service Outsourcing: Is It Justified?" *Economic Policy* 20: 308–347.

——. 2006. "Service Offshoring, Productivity, and Employment: Evidence from the United States." Discussion Paper N. 5475, London: Centre for Economic Policy Research.

——. 2009. "Service Offshoring and Productivity: Evidence from the US." *World Economy* 32: 203–220.

Antràs, P., L. Garicano, and E. Rossi-Hansberg. 2006. "Offshoring in a Knowledge Economy." *Quarterly Journal of Economics* 121: 31–77.

Arellano, M., and S. Bond. 1991. "Some Tests of Specification for Panel Data: Monte Carlo Evidence and an Application to Employment Equations." *Review of Economic Studies* 58: 277–297.

Autor, D. H., D. Dorn, and G. H. Hanson. 2011. "The China Syndrome: Local Labor Market Effects of Import Competition in the United States." Mimeograph, University of California San Diego.

Autor, D. H., F. Levy, and R. J. Murname. 2003. "The Skill Content of Recent Technological Change: An Empirical Exploration." *Quarterly Journal of Economics* 118: 1279–1333.

Baldwin, R. (2006). "Globalization: The Great Unbundling(s)," Mimeograph, Graduate Institute of International Studies, Geneva.

Baldwin, R., and F. Robert-Nicoud. 2010. "Trade-in-goods and trade-in-tasks: An Integrating Framework." Working Paper, no. 15882. Cambridge, MA: National Bureau of Economic Research.

Barba Navaretti, G., D. Checchi, and A. Turrini. 2003. "Adjusting Labor Demand: Multinational Versus National Firms: A Cross-European Analysis." *Journal of the European Economic Association* 1: 709–719.

Barba Navaretti, G., and A. J. Venables. 2004. *Multinational Firms in the World Economy*. Princeton: Princeton University Press.

Bardhan, A. D., and C. Kroll. 2003. "The New Wave of Outsourcing." Working Paper, no. 1103. Fisher Center for Real Estate and Urban Economics, University of California Berkeley.

Becker, S. O., K. Ekholm, and M. Muendler. 2009. "Offshoring and the Onshore Composition of Tasks and Skills." Discussion Paper N. 7391. London: Centre for Economic Policy Research.

Bhagwati, J., A. Panagariya, and T. N. Srinivasan. 2004. "The Muddles over Outsourcing." *Journal of Economic Perspectives* 18: 93–114.

Blinder, A. S. 2006. "Offshoring: The Next Industrial Revolution?" *Foreign Affairs* 85: 113–128.

———. 2009. "How Many U.S. Jobs Might Be Offshorable?" *World Economics* 10: 41–78.

Blinder, A. S., and A. B. Krueger. 2009. "Alternative Measures of Offshorability: A Survey Approach." Working Paper, no. 15287. Cambridge, MA: National Bureau of Economic Research.

Bruno, G. S. F. 2005a "Approximating the Bias of the LSDV Estimator for Dynamic Unbalanced Panel Data Models." *Economics Letters* 87: 361–366.

———. 2005b. "Estimation and Inference in Dynamic Unbalanced Panel-Data Models with a Small Number of Individuals." *Stata Journal* 5: 473–500.

Bruno, G. S. F., A. M. Falzoni, and R. Helg. 2004. "Measuring the Effect of Globalization on Labour Demand Elasticity: An Empirical Application to OECD Countries." Working Paper, no. 153. Milan: CESPRI-Bocconi University.

Bun, M. J. G., and J. F. Kiviet. 2003. "On the Diminishing Returns of Higher Order Terms in Asymptotic Expansions of Bias." *Economics Letters* 79: 145–152.

Castellani, D., L. De Benedictis, and D. Horgos. 2011. "Can We Really Trust Offshoring Indices?" Working Paper, no. 114. Hamburg: Helmut Schmidt University.

Clark, K. B., and R. B. Freeman. (1980). "How Elastic is the Demand for Labor?" *Review of Economics and Statistics* 62: 509–520.

Crinò, R. 2008. "Service Offshoring and Productivity in Western Europe," *Economics Bulletin* 6: 1–8.

———. 2009. "Offshoring, Multinationals and Labor Market: A Review of the Empirical Literature." *Journal of Economic Surveys* 23: 197–249.

———. 2010a. "Employment Effects of Service Offshoring: Evidence from Matched Firms." *Economics Letters* 107: 253–256.

———. 2010b. "Service Offshoring and White-Collar Employment." *Review of Economic Studies* 77: 595–632.

———. 2012. "Service Offshoring and the Skill Composition of Labour Demand." *Oxford Bulletin of Economics and Statistics* 74: 20–57.

Daveri, F., and C. Jona-Lasinio. 2008. "Off-shoring and Productivity Growth in the Italian Manufacturing Industries." *CESifo Economic Studies* 54: 414–450.

Deardorff, A. V. 2005. "A Trade Theorist's Take on Skilled-Labor Outsourcing." *International Review of Economics and Finance* 14: 259–271.

Dossani, R., and M. Kenney. 2004. "The Next Wave of Globalization? Exploring the Relocation of Service Provision to India." Working Paper, no. 156. Asia Pacific Research Center, Stanford University.

Ekholm, K., and K. N. Hakkala. 2005. "The Effect of Offshoring on Labor Demand: Evidence from Sweden." Working Paper, no. 5648. London: Centre for Economic Policy Research.

Falk, M., and B. M. Koebel. 2001. "A Dynamic Heterogeneous Labour Demand Model for German Manufacturing." *Applied Economics* 33: 339–348.

———. 2002. "Outsourcing, Imports and Labour Demand." *Scandinavian Journal of Economics* 104: 567–586.

Falzoni, A., and L. Tajoli. 2011. "Offshoring and the Skill Composition of Employment in the Italian Manufacturing Industries." *Rivista di Politica Economica*, 101: 121–153.

Feenstra, R. C. 2010. *Offshoring in the Global Economy: Microeconomic Structure and Macroeconomic Implications (Ohlin Lectures)*. Cambridge, MA, and London: MIT Press.

Feenstra, R. C., and G. H. Hanson. 1996. "Globalization, Outsourcing, and Wage Inequality." *American Economic Review* 86: 240–245.

———. 1999. "The Impact of Outsourcing and High-Technology Capital on Wages: Estimates for the United States, 1979–1990." *Quarterly Journal of Economics* 114: 907–940.

———. 2003. "Global Production Sharing and Rising Inequality: A Survey of Trade and Wages." In *Handbook of International Trade*, edited by E. K. Choi and R. J. Harrigan, 146–185. Oxford: Basil Blackwell.

Feenstra, R. C., and J. B. Jensen. 2009. "Evaluating Estimates of Materials Offshoring from U.S. Manufacturing." In *Measurement Issues Arising from the Growth of Globalization*, edited by S. N. Houseman and K. F. Ryder, 359–378. Washington, DC: W. E. Upjohn Institute for Employment Research and National Academy of Public Administration.

Freund, C., and Weinhold, D. 2002. "The Internet and International Trade in Services." *American Economic Review Papers and Proceedings* 92: 236–240.

Garner, A. C. 2004. "Offshoring in the Service Sector: Economic Impact and Policy Issues." *Federal Reserve Bank of Kansas City Economic Review* 3: 5–37.

Geishecker, I., and G. Görg. Forthcoming. "Service Offshoring and Wages: Evidence from Micro Data." *Oxford Economic Papers*, forthcoming, DOI Number: 10.1093/oep/gpr055.

Görg, H., and A. Hanley. 2005. "Labour Demand Effects of International Outsourcing: Evidence from Plant-Level Data." *International Review of Economics and Finance* 14: 365–376.

———. 2011. "Services Outsourcing and Innovation: An Empirical Investigation." *Economic Inquiry* 49: 321–333.

Görg, H., A. Hanley, and E. Strobl. 2008. "Productivity Effects of International Outsourcing: Evidence from Plant-Level Data." *Canadian Journal of Economics* 41: 670–688.

Görg, H., E. Strobl, and F. Walsh. 2009. "Multinational Companies, Backward Linkages and Labour Demand Elasticities." *Canadian Journal of Economics* 42: 332–348.

Greenaway, D., R. C. Hine, and P. Wright. 1999. "An Empirical Assessment of the Impact of Trade on Employment in the United Kingdom." *European Journal of Political Economy* 15: 485–500.

Grossman, G. M., and E. Rossi-Hansberg. 2008. "Trading Tasks: A Simple Theory of Offshoring." *American Economic Review* 98: 1978–1997.

Hakkala, K. N., F. Heyman, and F. Sjöholm. 2010. "Multinationals, Skills, and Wage Elasticities." *Review of World Economics* 146: 263–280.

Hamermesh, D. S. 1993. *Labor Demand*, Princeton and Chichester, UK: Princeton University Press.

Hasan, R., D. Mitra, and K. V. Ramaswamy. 2007. "Trade Reforms, Labor Regulations, and Labor Demand Elasticities: Empirical Evidence from India." *Review of Economics and Statistics* 89: 466–481.

Head, K., T. Mayer, and J. Ries. 2009. "How Remote is the Offshoring Threat?" *European Economic Review* 53: 429–444.

Helpman, E. 2006. "Trade, FDI, and the Organization of Firms." *Journal of Economic Literature* 44: 580–630.

Hijzen, A. 2005. "A Bird's Eye View of International Outsourcing: Data, Measurement and Labour Demand Effects." *Economie Internationale* 104: 45–63.

Hijzen, A., H. Görg, and R. C. Hine. 2005. "International Outsourcing and the Skill Structure of Labour Demand in the United Kingdom." *Economic Journal* 115: 860–878.

Hijzen, A., T. Inui, and Y. Todo. 2010. "Does Offshoring Pay? Firm-Level Evidence from Japan." *Economic Inquiry* 48: 880–895.

Hijzen, A., M. Pisu, R. Upward, and P. Wright. 2011. "Employment, Job Turnover, and Trade in Producer Services: UK Firm-Level Evidence." *Canadian Journal of Economics* 44: 1020–1043.

Hijzen, A., and P. Swaim. 2007. "Does Offshoring Reduce Industry Employment?" *National Institute Economic Review* 201: 86–96.

———. 2010. "Offshoring, Labour Market Institutions and the Elasticity of Labour Demand." *European Economic Review* 54: 1016–1034.

Hummels, D., R. Jørgensen, J. R. Munch, and C. Xiang. 2011. "The Wage Effects of Offshoring: Evidence from Danish Matched Worker-Firm Data." Working Paper, no. 17496. Cambridge, MA: National Bureau of Economic Research.

Jensen, P. D., J. F. Kirkegaard, and N. S. Laugesen. 2006. "Offshoring in Europe: Evidence of a Two-Way Street from Denmark." Working Paper, no. 06-03. Washington, DC: Peterson Institute for International Economics.

Jensen, J. B. and L. Kletzer. 2005. "Tradeable Services: Understanding the Scope and Impact of Services Offshoring." In *Offshoring White-Collar Work: The Issues and the Implications*, edited by L. Brainard and S. M. Collins, 73–133. Washington, DC: Brookings Trade Forum.

———. 2008. "Measuring Tradeable Services and the Task Content of Offshorable Services Jobs." In *Labor in the New Economy*, edited by K. Abraham, M. Harper, and J. Spletzer, 309–335. Chicago: University of Chicago Press.

Kirkegaard, J. F. 2004. "Outsourcing: Stains on the White-Collar?" Working Paper. Washington, DC: Peterson Institute for International Economics.

———. 2007. "Offshoring, Outsourcing, and Production Relocation: Labor Market Effects in the OECD Countries and Developing Asia." Working Paper, no. 07-02. Washington, DC: Peterson Institute for International Economics.

Kletzer, L. 2009. "Understanding the Domestic Labor Market Impact of Offshore Services Outsourcing: Measurement Issues." Mimeograph. University of California Santa Cruz.

Kroll, C. 2007. "Globalization of Services and White-Collar Work: Implications for Firms, Employment and Wages." Paper prepared for the conference "Globalization Comes Home," University of California Berkeley, February.

Levy, F., and R. J. Murname. 2004. *The New Division of Labor: How Computers are Creating the Next Job Market*. Princeton: Princeton University Press.

Liu, R., and D. Trefler. 2011. "A Sorted Tale of Globalization: White Collar Jobs and the Rise of Service Offshoring." Working Paper, no. 17559. Cambridge, MA: National Bureau of Economic Research.

Mankiw, G. N., and P. Swagel. 2006. "The Politics and Economics of Offshore Outsourcing." *Journal of Monetary Economics* 53: 1027–1056.

Mann, C. L. 2003. "Globalization of IT Services and White-Collar Jobs: The Next Wave of Productivity Growth." Policy Brief, no. 03-11. Washington, DC: Peterson Institute for International Economics.

Markusen, J. 2005. "Modeling the Offshoring of White-Collar Services: From Comparative Advantage to the New Theories of Trade and FDI." In *Offshoring White-Collar Work: The Issues and the Implications*, edited by L. Brainard and S. M. Collins, 1–34. Washington, DC: Brookings Trade Forum.

Markusen, J., and B. Strand. 2008. "Offshoring of Business Services in Small Open Economies: Toward a General-Equilibrium Modeling Approach." *Journal of Industry, Competition and Trade* 8: 231–246.

Moncarz, R. J., M. G. Wolf, and B. Wright. 2008. "Service-Providing Occupations, Offshoring, and the Labor Market." *Monthly Labor Review* 131: 71–86.

Morrison, C., and D. Siegel. 2001. "The Impacts of Technology, Trade and Outsourcing on Employment and Labor Composition." *Scandinavian Journal of Economics* 103: 241–264.

Nickell, W. 2006. "The CEP-OECD Institutions Data Set (1960–2004)." CEP Discussion Paper N. 759. Centre for Economic Performance, London School of Economics and Political Science.

Olsen, K. B. 2006. "Productivity Impacts of Offshoring and Outsourcing: A Review." Working Paper, no. 2006/1. Directorate for Science, Technology and Industry (STI). Paris and Washington, DC: OECD.

O'Mahony, M., and M. P. Timmer. 2009. "Output, Input and Productivity Measures at the Industry Level: The EU KLEMS Database." *Economic Journal* 119: F374–F403.

OECD (Organisation for Economic Co-operation and Development). 2005. "Trade-Adjustment Costs in OECD Labour Markets: A Mountain or a Molehill?" In *OECD Employment Outlook*. Paris and Washington, DC: OECD.

———. 2007a. *OECD Employment Outlook*. Paris and Washington, DC: OECD.

———. 2007b. *Offshoring and Employment: Trends and Impacts*. Paris and Washington, DC: OECD.

Rodriguez Clare, A. 2010. "Offshoring in a Ricardian World." *American Economic Journal: Macroeconomics* 2: 227–258.

Rodrik, D. 1997. *Has Globalization Gone Too Far?* Washington, DC: Institute for International Economics.

Samuelson, P. A. 2004. "Where Ricardo and Mill Rebut and Confirm Arguments of Mainstream Economists Supporting Globalization." *Journal of Economic Perspectives* 18: 135–146.

Senses, M. Z. 2010. "The Effects of Offshoring on the Elasticity of Labor Demand." *Journal of International Economics* 81: 89–98.

Slaughter, M. J. 2001. "International Trade and Labor-Demand Elasticities." *Journal of International Economics* 54: 27–56.

Trefler, D. 2005. "Offshoring: Threats and Opportunities." In *Offshoring White-Collar Work: The Issues and the Implications*, edited by L. Brainard and S. M. Collins, 35–73. Washington, DC: Brookings Trade Forum.

United Nations Conference on Trade and Development. 2004. *World Investment Report: The Shift Towards Services*. New York and Geneva: UNCTAD (UNCTAD).

Van Welsum, D. and Reif, X. (2005). "Potential Offshoring: Evidence from Selected OECD Countries." In *Offshoring White-Collar Work: The Issues and the Implications*, edited by L. Brainard and S. M. Collins, 165–202. Washington, DC: Brookings Trade Forum.

Van Welsum, D. and Vickery, G. (2005). "Potential Off-Shoring of ICT-Intensive Occupations." In *Enhancing the Performance of the Services Sector*, 179–204. Paris and Washington, DC: OECD.

CHAPTER 4

Services Offshoring and the Relative Demand for White-collar Workers in German Manufacturing

DEBORAH WINKLER[1]

1 Introduction

1.1 Offshoring and heterogeneous labor

Intensifying globalization processes have coincided with low economic growth rates and high unemployment in Germany, especially in the 1990s. Globalization in the economic sense comprises the transnational movement of production factors, goods, and services, which is reflected in a higher integration of international goods, money, and capital markets. Trade and investment flows in particular have increased, which often leads to the one-sided conclusion that growing globalization causes negative labor-market effects. In Germany, the discussion of offshoring-induced labor-market effects has gained momentum in recent years. Opponents of globalization equate German outward foreign direct investment with German job losses, whereas many economists praise the removal of barriers to foreign trade and investment based on an expectation of increased economic efficiency. This chapter is concerned with the effect of services offshoring on the relative demand for white-collar workers in German manufacturing sectors.

A number of developments have contributed to a growing awareness of offshoring and its actual and potential labor-market effects in Germany and other industrialized countries. First, the growing availability of skilled labor at a lower wage level abroad has fostered the offshoring discussion. In the case of Germany, the geographical and cultural proximity of the new Central and Eastern European countries that joined the European Union has contributed to a growing fear of offshoring, since many of these countries dispose of a large, cheaper, and often German-speaking talent pool. A second change is that the scope of activities being offshored has expanded to high-skill jobs, while in the 1990s, cost-oriented offshoring focused on low-skill activities. Third, employment-related topics, such as the debate on minimum wages, are often associated with potential job relocations. Fourth, economic slowdown like the recent global economic crisis may encourage domestic firms to cut costs by moving jobs offshore. And fifth, offshoring is related to Germany's shortage of skilled specialists in certain sectors. Besides migration, offshoring constitutes the only short-term solution for domestic firms to respond to a shortage of human capital.

This chapter differentiates between different types of labor. Labor can be classified, for example, according to its skill level. In Germany and in other industrialized countries, less-skilled workers face a higher risk of unemployment or wage cuts compared to their high-skilled counterparts. The development of German qualification-specific unemployment rates is shown in Figure 4.1. Three skill levels, namely workers with primary, secondary, and tertiary education, are taken into account. Obviously, workers with tertiary education—the highest educational attainment—had the lowest risk of unemployment, with stable unemployment rates of around 4 percent between 1991 and 2004.

Workers with secondary education, that is, vocational education and training, faced a slightly higher unemployment rate of 5.6 percent in 1991, which rose steadily to 9.9

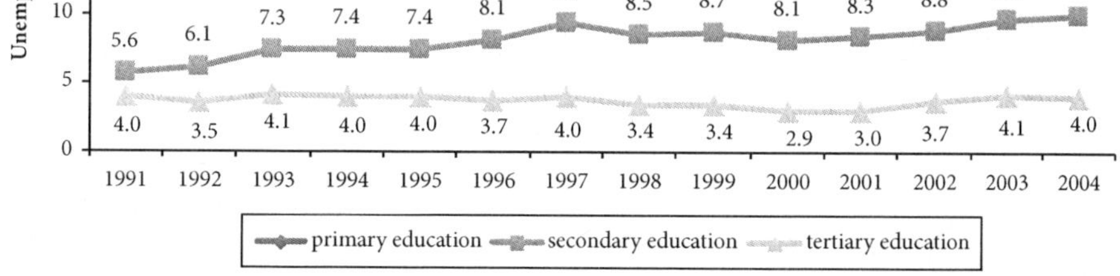

FIGURE 4.1 Skill-specific unemployment rates in Germany, 1991–2004.

Source: Based on Winkler (2009: 11).

Note: Unemployment rates are calculated as a percentage of civilian labor force (without apprentices) of same skills. Workers without any information on educational attainment according to the micro-census are proportionally distributed to all skill levels. Primary education = workers without vocational qualification. Secondary education = workers with vocational education and training. Tertiary education = workers with a master's (and other university degrees) or bachelor's degree.

percent in 2004. In other words, their unemployment rate increased by 4.3 percentage points over the period, or by on average 4.5 percent per year. Workers with primary education, the lowest educational attainment, do not possess any vocational education. In 1991, their unemployment rate averaged 14.5 percent and climbed to 24.6 percent in 2004. This represents an increase of more than 10 percentage points over the period, or an average annual growth rate of 4.1 percent.

While researchers generally do not question the higher jobless rate among less-skilled workers in industrialized countries, they haven't found a consensus on the underlying causes. The debate centers on an argument between two main causes: trade versus technology. While empirical studies often denied that international trade had harmed less-skilled workers in the 1980s, newer studies provided evidence for a higher trade-induced risk for less-skilled workers during the 1990s. Despite this evidence, economists continued to favor skill-biased technological progress as the main explanation for the higher jobless rate among less-skilled workers, since the relative appreciation of human capital was observed more strongly within than between industries.

Under the assumption of downward wage rigidities, however, the intraindustrial appreciation of human capital does not preclude the results of standard trade theory, whereby less-qualified labor is systematically squeezed out of the labor market (Geishecker 2002). According to this reasoning, international trade can still be considered a possible explanation for the appreciation of high-skilled labor. Feenstra and Hanson (2001) also argue for international trade as the main driver behind the appreciation of high-skilled labor:

> The argument against trade is based, in part, on a misreading of the data. Stable trade to GDP ratios, an apparent increase in the relative price of skill-intensive goods, and employment shifts towards skilled workers that occur mainly within, rather than between, industries are all cited as evidence that trade cannot have contributed to rising [...] inequality. This line of reasoning emphasizes trade in final goods and ignores the globalization of production and recent dramatic increases in trade in intermediate inputs. (Feenstra and Hanson 2001: 46)

Advocates of the skill-biased technological progress base their arguments primarily on trade in final goods, neglecting that the globalization of production has resulted in growing international trade flows in intermediate goods. Like skill-biased technological progress, imported intermediates or offshoring could lead to intrasectoral rather than inter-sectoral appreciation of human capital. The sourcing of intermediate inputs from labor-abundant low-wage countries would result in an intraindustrial shift towards skilled labor, as activities with lower skill intensities are more likely produced abroad (Winkler 2009). However, offshoring depends not only on a sector's skill intensity, but also on its structure and the offshorability of certain activities. Besides trade and technological progress, the insufficient skill adaptation of labor supply, increased labor participation of women, institutional changes, and a decreasing relevance of manufacturing industries are factors that contribute to the worsening employment and income situation of less-skilled labor (Rukwid 2007).

1.2 Is services offshoring different?

Why should researchers and policy makers be concerned with the effects of services offshoring on the relative demand for skilled labor, when higher skills seem to be correlated with a lower risk of unemployment in industrialized countries? Several indicators suggest that services offshoring differs from goods offshoring in various aspects. First, services offshoring has grown in terms of both quantity and quality. Only one and a half decades ago, most services were considered nontradable, but the emergence and development of new information and communication technologies (ICTs) has made many services internationally tradable and, thus, vulnerable to international relocation. In the United States, for example, Bardhan and Kroll (2003) estimate that 11 percent of all jobs in 2001 were at risk of services offshoring. Blinder (2007) estimates an even higher potential offshorability of thirty to forty million services jobs, which corresponds to 22 to 29 percent of the US workforce in 2004.

Second, while goods offshoring traditionally targets less-skilled labor in industrialized countries, many offshorable services include medium-skill tasks, such as financial and accounting services, standardized programming work, routine data analysis and processing or back-office services such as ticketing and billing, and high-skill services, which encompass, for instance, research and development, design services, architectural drawings, new software development, animation, medical testing or analysis, and technology systems design (UNCTAD 2004). Imported service inputs are therefore more likely to substitute for medium- and high-skilled labor. Interestingly, Autor (2010) suggests that job opportunities in the United States fell only for middle-wage, middle-skill jobs since the last 1980s, while high-skill, high-wage and low-skill, low-wage employment expanded, which he relates, among other factors, to offshoring of middle-skill "routine" services. And third, offshoring of services appears to be much faster and less costly compared to offshoring of manufactured inputs, as neither large factory buildings nor assembly lines are required (Winkler 2009).

At the same time, several other developments at the unilateral, regional, and multilateral level have further accelerated the process of services offshoring. First, the talent pool in low and middle-income countries, such as India, China or Eastern Europe including Russia, has dramatically increased over the past twenty years. Public and private investment in human resources seems to have fostered the growing availability of skilled labor in these countries, but the excess supply of human capital (for example, engineering and technology graduates) and the "brain drain" of skilled workers to industrialized countries combined with a subsequent return to their home country have also been identified as major drivers. Second, the presence of multinational companies in developing countries has fostered the development and growth of domestic software industries due to positive spillover effects from foreign direct investment. Third, unilateral liberalization of service industries in developing countries, especially constant privatization, competition, and independent regulation, enabled the transformation from protectionist to open market economies in the last one to two decades. Finally, regional—and to a lesser extent multilateral—liberalization of trade in services are further important factors that have supported this development (Winkler 2009).

Services offshoring in general comprises all kinds of foreign services activities of a multinational company that are aimed at supporting its production. The motives behind an offshoring decision can be mainly market-oriented, cost-oriented, or procurement-oriented. Services offshoring is expected to have the potential for harming employment when formerly home-produced services are relocated for cost reasons and reimported to the country of origin. Therefore, my special definition of services offshoring focuses on cost-oriented motives:

> Services offshoring in the narrower sense designates the provision of service inputs from a foreign supplier that are produced abroad mainly for cost reasons and re-imported to the home country. The foreign purchase either happens externally, via an independent supplier (offshore outsourcing), or internally within the multinational company (captive offshoring). (Winkler 2009: 28)

This chapter is structured as follows: Section 2 gives an overview of relevant theoretical and empirical studies focusing on the effect of offshoring on heterogeneous labor. In section 3, I explain how services offshoring intensity is measured and show its development in German manufacturing. Section 4 focuses on the effect of services offshoring on the relative demand for white-collar workers in German manufacturing. I first introduce the theoretical and empirical model, followed by a data description, the presentation of the regression results and their discussion. Section 5 concludes.

2 Offshoring and Skilled Labor in the Literature

2.1 Econometric studies

The relative demand for heterogeneous labor in econometric studies is captured by the cost share of specific labor in the sector's total wage bill wL, where w denotes the wage rate and L labor input. If we consider high-skilled labor L_{HS} as specific labor input, its cost share is defined as $S_{HS} = w_{HS}L_{HS}/wL$. The cost share S_{HS} can be interpreted in a twofold way. First, it reflects the relative demand for high-skilled labor L_{HS}. Second, it also reflects the relative wage w_{HS} of high-skilled labor. If n is the number of specific labor inputs, $n-1$ cost shares are linearly independent. In the case of two specific labor inputs, for example, high-skilled and less-skilled labor, the cost share of less-skilled labor is defined as $S_{LS} = 1 - S_{HS}$.

Table 4.1 gives an overview of econometric studies measuring the effect of offshoring on the relative demand for high-skilled labor. The table is based on the literature overview of Crinò (2009) and includes own revisions and updates. While

Table 4.1 Literature overview

Source	Country	Unit of Analysis	Years	Measure of Offshoring	Effect
Offshoring and the relative demand for skilled labor in studies with two labor inputs					
Feenstra and Hanson (1996)	US	435 mfg. ind.	1977–1993	imported material inputs (broad)/output	+
Anderton and Brenton (1999)	UK	11 textiles and non-electr. machinery ind.	1970–1986	imports from low-income countries/output	+
Feenstra and Hanson (1999)	US	447 mfg. ind.	1979–1990	imported material inputs (narrow and broad)/total nonenergy inputs	+
Hansson (2000)	Sweden	34 mfg. ind.	1970–1993	imports from non-OECD countries/domestic demand	+
Slaughter (2000)	US	32 mfg. ind.	1977–1994	affiliate employment/total employment	no ev.
Anderton et al. (2002)	Sweden	41 mfg. ind.	1975–1993	imports from low-income countries/output	+
Head and Ries (2002)	Japan	1,070 mfg. MNCs	1965–1989	affiliate employment/total MNCs' employment	+
Strauss-Kahn (2004)	France	50 mfg. ind.	1977–1993	imported material inputs (narrow and broad)/output	+
Egger and Egger (2005)	Austria	20 mfg. ind.	1990–1998	imported material inputs (narrow)	+
Hansson (2005)	Sweden	73 mfg. MNCs	1990–1997	affiliate employment in non-OECD countries/total MNCs' employment	+
Helg and Tajoli (2005)	Italy	13 mfg. ind.	1988–1996	outward processing trade imports/output	+
	Germany	20 mfg. ind.	1993–1997	outward processing trade imports/output	no ev.
Hsieh and Woo (2005)	Hong Kong	54 mfg. ind.	1971–1996	(i) imports from China/consumption, (ii) imported intermediates from China/consumption	+
Lorentowicz et al. (2005)	Austria	15 mfg. ind.	1995–2002	imported material inputs (narrow)/value added	–
	Poland	23 mfg. ind.	1994–2002	(i) foreign fixed assets/domestic fixed assets, (ii) number of foreign firms/number of domestic firms	+
Geishecker (2006)	Germany	23 mfg. ind.	1991–2000	imported material inputs from CEECs (narrow and broad)/output	+
Minondo and Rubert (2006)	Spain	12 mfg. ind.	1986–1994	imported material inputs (narrow and broad)/total nonenergy inputs	+
Yan (2006)	Canada	81 mfg. ind.	1981–1996	imported intermediates (broad)	+
Becker et al. (2009)	Germany	1,266 mfg. and serv. plants in 490 MNCs	1998–2001	affiliate employment/total MNCs' employment	+

(Continued)

Table 4.1 (Continued)

Source	Country	Unit of Analysis	Years	Measure of Offshoring	Effect
Winkler (2009)	Germany	28 mfg. ind.	1991–2000	imported services inputs (broad)/total nonenergy inputs	+
				imported material inputs (broad)/total nonenergy inputs	+
		35 mfg. ind.	1995–2004	imported services inputs (broad)/total nonenergy inputs	–
				imported material inputs (broad)/total non-energy inputs	no ev.
Offshoring and the relative demand for the highest skill category in studies with more than two labor inputs					
Morrison Paul and Siegel (2001)	US	450 mfg. ind.	1959–1989	imports/output	+
Falk and Koebel (2002)	Germany	26 mfg. ind.	1978–1990	imported material inputs	no ev.
Hijzen et al. (2005)	UK	50 mfg. ind.	1982–1996	imported material inputs (narrow)/value added	+
Ekholm and Hakkala (2006)	Sweden	20 mfg. ind.	1995–2000	imported material inputs (narrow and broad)/output	+
Crinò (2010)	USA	144 mfg. and serv. ind.	1997–2006	imported services inputs (broad)/total nonenergy inputs	+
Crinò (2011)	9 EU	20 mfg. and serv. ind./13 mfg. ind.	1990–2004	imported services inputs (broad)/total nonenergy inputs	+

Source: Crinò (2009) and own revisions and updates.
Note: CEECs = Central and Eastern European countries, EU = European Union, MNC = multinational corporation, OECD = Organisation for Economic Co-operation and Development, UK = United Kingdom, US = United States.

many studies were originally concerned with the impact of offshoring on the relative demand for less-skilled labor, the effects for high-skilled labor can be easily derived thanks to the symmetric nature of these estimations in the case of two labor inputs. In the case of more than two labor inputs, I report only the effect of offshoring on the highest skill level.

The majority of studies focus on the effect of goods offshoring in manufacturing industries and find a positive effect on the relative demand for high-skilled workers (Feenstra and Hanson 1996, 1999, and Morrison Paul and Siegel 2001 for the United States; Anderton and Brenton 1999, and Hijzen et al. 2005 for the United Kingdom; Hansson 2000, Anderton et al. 2002, Ekholm and Hakkala 2006 for Sweden; Strauss-Kahn 2004 for France; Egger and Egger 2005 for Austria; Helg and Tajoli 2005 for Italy; Hsieh and Woo 2005 for Hong Kong; Lorentowicz et al. 2005 for Poland; Geishecker 2006 and Winkler 2009 for Germany; Minondo and Rubert 2006 for Spain; and Yan 2006 for Canada). Only a few comparable studies cannot confirm these results (Falk and Koebel 2002 and Helg and Tajoli 2005 for Germany) or even find evidence that goods offshoring lowers the relative demand for skilled labor (Lorentowicz et al. 2005 for Austria).

These studies above measure offshoring as imports or imported inputs, mostly as a percentage of total nonenergy inputs, output, value added, or consumption, but in a few cases also as a standalone variable. Authors often distinguish between a narrow and broad measure of offshoring, the first referring to imports from the same industry and the latter referring to imports from more or all industries. Other studies focus on the effects of captive offshoring and define offshoring as the ratio of foreign affiliates' employment to the multinational company's total employment. While Slaughter (2000) finds no influence of captive offshoring on the relative demand for skilled workers for the United States, Hansson (2005) and Becker et al. (2009) confirm a positive impact for Sweden and Germany, respectively. Only one study to my knowledge focuses on the effects of captive offshoring in an emerging country, confirming that offshoring benefits high-skilled labor in Poland (Lorentowicz et al. 2005). This study uses different definitions of captive offshoring, namely the ratio of foreign to domestic assets and the number of foreign relative to domestic firms. Some of the studies mentioned above focus on offshoring from specific low-income regions or countries (Hansson 2000, 2005; Anderton et al. 2002; Hsieh and Woo 2005; Geishecker 2006).

Only four studies incorporate services offshoring into their analysis. Crinò (2010) confirms the positive influence of services offshoring on the relative demand for high-skilled workers in manufacturing and services industries for the United States. Crinò (2012) also finds positive effects of services offshoring for nine Western European countries when they are combined and at the individual country level for Austria, France, Germany, the Netherlands, and the United Kingdom. While Winkler (2009) also confirms a positive effect in German manufacturing for the period 1991–2000, she finds weak evidence for a reversed effect for the period 1995–2004 where services offshoring lowered the relative demand for high-skilled workers.

Researchers and policy makers should generally be cautious when assessing the effects of offshoring for the following reasons. First, most studies cover older periods and, thus, do not necessarily reflect recent offshoring developments. Of all studies listed above, only Crinò (2010 and 2012) and Winkler (2009) incorporate the 2000s in their analysis. Second, most studies rely on proxy measures of offshoring. This is due to the fact that many countries do not publish disaggregated input–output tables for imported and domestically purchased inputs, but only—if at all—aggregated input matrices. Empirical research for the United States, for instance, has relied entirely on a proxy-based measure of offshoring, using what the OECD refers to as the "proportionality assumption." That is, every sector is assumed to import inputs of each service in the same proportion as its economy-wide use of that input. The assumption was introduced by Feenstra and Hanson (1996, 1999) and has been adopted in all major studies. For a discussion of the potential bias in the "proportionality assumption" used in the measurement of offshoring, see Winkler and Milberg (2012).

This study contributes to the growing body of research on the labor market effects of offshoring in several ways. First, I measure the effect of services offshoring on the relative demand for skilled labor, which still constitutes a gap in the empirical literature. Second, my analysis covers the years 1995 to 2004, reflecting the relevant ICT-period and the increase in the offshorability of services. My study is closest to the study by Crinò (2012) with regard to these two points. Third, my calculations of German offshoring intensities are based on published German import matrices, which represent a direct measure for the share of imported inputs.[2] Finally, I extend the analysis of Winkler (2009) and control for the potential endogeneity of offshoring and other variables by using static and dynamic instrumental variables estimators. Egger and Egger (2003), for example, show that relative labor demand regressions can be biased when offshoring is treated as an exogenous variable.

2.2 A model of trade in skilled tasks

The widely cited Grossman and Rossi-Hansberg publication (2008) studies the labor-market effects of offshoring—modeled as "trade in tasks"—in a Heckscher–Ohlin framework. Allowing for heterogeneous labor, these intermediate inputs can be produced by two factors of production: less-skilled or high-skilled labor.[3] There are two countries, home and foreign, and there are two goods, a skill-intensive and a low-skill-intensive good. The domestic country exports one of the two goods (for example, the skill-intensive good) and imports the other good. Both sectors are assumed to be perfectly competitive. The authors consider a scenario where the home country offshores skill-intensive tasks to a foreign country. Wages of high-skilled workers in this case are still lower for similar tasks in the foreign country due to technology lags.

A rise of offshorability, that is, falling offshoring costs, can affect wages of high-skilled workers at home through three channels: the productivity, relative-price, and labor-supply effect (see Figure 4.2). While offshoring first reduces the demand for high-skilled labor at home because foreign workers substitute for domestic workers, a positive productivity effect occurs because lower unit costs due to offshoring act as an incentive for both sectors to expand, more so for the high-skill-intensive than for the low-skill-intensive sector. This results in a growing demand for high-skilled labor and rising high-skill wages. The relative-price effect refers to changes in output composition (at initial prices) due to offshoring, since the two sectors have an incentive to expand. In our scenario, the relative-price effect lowers high-skill wages, since an expansion of the high-skill sector reduces its terms of trade. This leads to rising wages of the relatively scarce factor less-skilled labor, while wages of high-skilled labor fall. However, the relative-price effect holds only if the country is large and affects world prices.

Finally, the labor-supply effect refers to the substitution of foreign for domestic high-skilled labor due to offshoring, making redundant some high-skilled workers who previously produced these tasks. This creates imbalances between labor supply and labor demand (at primary factor prices), output levels, and techniques of production, depending on the extent of offshoring. Changing factor supplies have no influence on factor prices in a Heckscher–Ohlin framework with imperfect specialization, that is, if both goods are produced in the country. However, assuming perfect specialization in one good only, the labor-supply effect in our scenario leads to an increase in high-skilled labor worldwide at a given level of less-skilled labor in the domestic country, which may increase the wages of less-skilled labor. Overall, one could consider the case where negative relative-price and labor-supply effects offset the productivity gains of high-skilled labor. The model implies full employment, that is, offshoring affects labor markets solely through wage adjustments. Assuming labor-market rigidities (for example, minimum wages) that counteract perfect price flexibility, layoffs instead of wage reductions are possible in the short run.

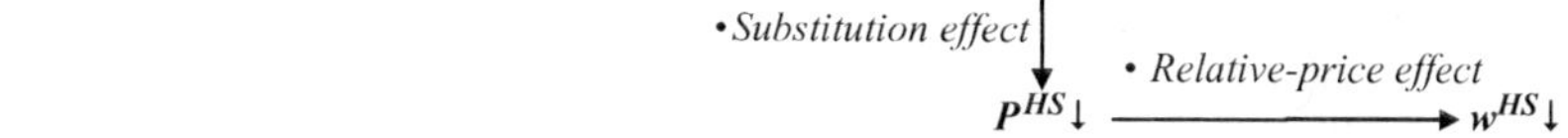

FIGURE 4.2 Offshoring of skill-intensive tasks and the relative wage effects for skilled labor.

Source: Grossman and Rossi-Hansberg (2008).

NB: LD^{HS} = domestic demand for high-skilled labor, $LS^{HS,W}$ = worldwide supply of high-skilled labor, w^{HS} = domestic wage rate of high-skilled labor, YS^{HS} = domestic supply of high-skill-intensive good.

3 Measuring Services Offshoring Intensities

3.1 Sectoral offshoring intensities in manufacturing

The calculation of sectoral offshoring intensities is based on revised input-output data from the German Federal Statistical Office covering the period 1995–2004 and thus reflecting the relevant ICT-period. German input-output tables originally comprise seventy-one sectors and due to their symmetry also seventy-one inputs. The calculation of offshoring intensities considers all material inputs plus seven selected service inputs (see appendix 1). I drop primary inputs and the secondary inputs "mining" and "quarrying," as they generally do not represent offshoring inputs.

Services offshoring is expected to have the potential for harming employment when formerly home-produced services are relocated for cost reasons and reimported to the country of origin. Since the underlying motive for an offshoring decision is unknown using input–output data, I focus on service inputs where offshoring for cost reasons is likely. The selection of seven out of twenty-seven service inputs includes tradable business activities in the broader sense according to the aggregation of Kalmbach et al. (2005). I exclude "wholesale, trade, and commission, excluding motor vehicles" services from the original definition, as they do not represent typical offshoring services. Abramovsky et al. (2004), for instance, classify them among nonbusiness services. Consumer-related and social services are also not considered, since the former do not represent typical offshoring services and the latter are not tradable. Business activities comprise "other business activities" in a narrower sense, as well as the following six inputs: post and telecommunications; financial mediation (except insurance and pension funding); activities related to financial mediation; rental of machinery and equipment; computer and related activities; research and development.

The services offshoring intensity OSS_{ist} measures the share of imported inputs of service *s* out of all non-energy inputs used by sector *i* at time *t*:

$$OSS_{ist} = \frac{(imported\ inputs\ of\ service\ s\ used\ by\ sector\ i)_t}{(total\ non\text{-}energy\ inputs\ used\ by\ sector\ i)_t} \qquad (1)$$

The denominator includes all thirty-six nonenergy manufacturing inputs plus the seven service inputs selected above.

The services offshoring intensity OSS_{it} for sector *i* at time *t* is calculated by summing OSS_{ist} over all seven service inputs *s*:

$$OSS_{it} = \sum_s OSS_{ist} \qquad (2)$$

My empirical analysis in this chapter is restricted to the manufacturing sector due to the lack of occupational-specific wage and worker data in the services sectors. Figure 4.3 shows average sectoral services offshoring intensities for 1995 and 2004 in German manufacturing.[4] Services offshoring intensities have increased in almost all manufacturing industries except for leather, consumer electronics, medical instruments, and motor

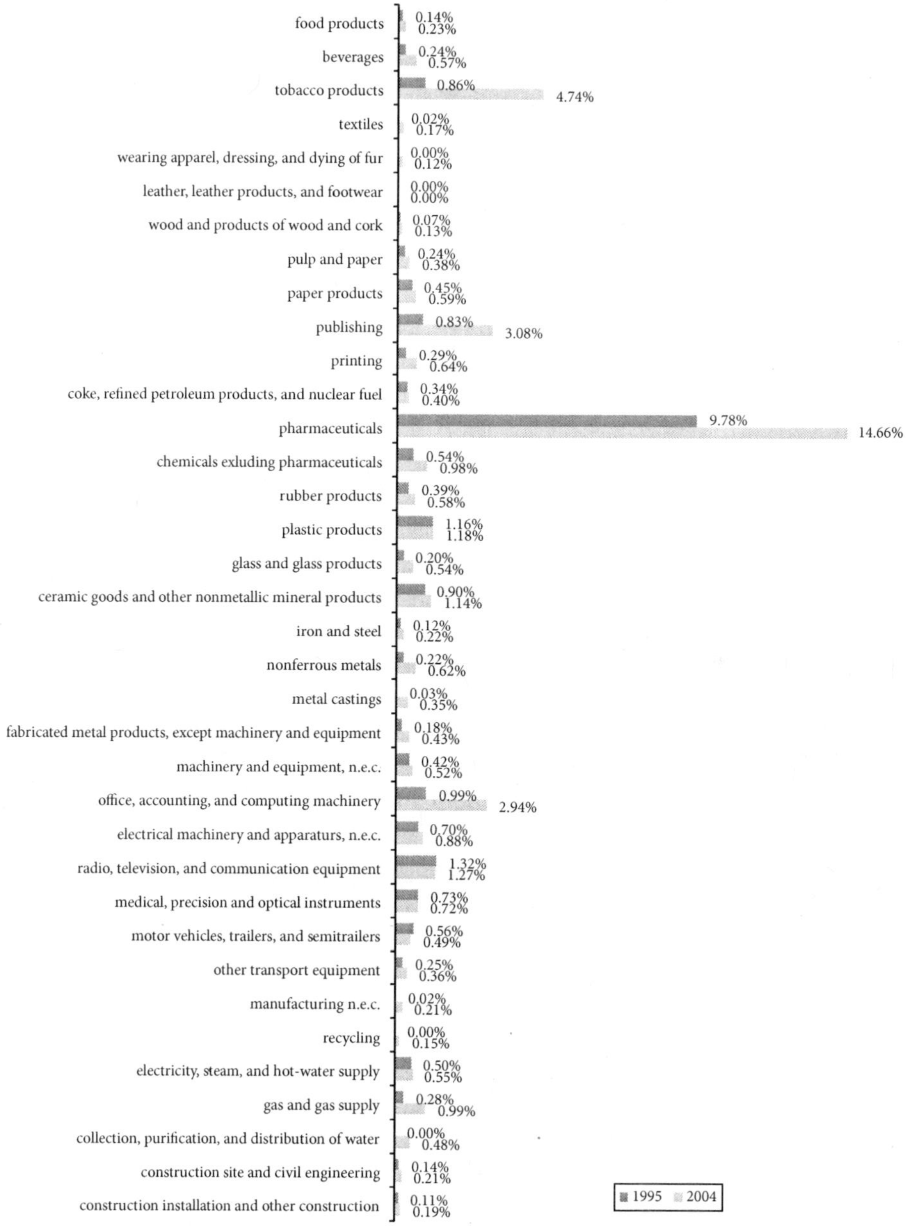

FIGURE 4.3 Sectoral services offshoring intensities in manufacturing sectors, 1995 versus 2004.
Source: Own calculations. Data: German Federal Statistical Office, revised input-output tables, 1995–2004.

vehicles. They are highest in pharmaceuticals, tobacco, publishing and office, accounting, and computing machinery.

3.2 Overall offshoring intensities in manufacturing

The average services offshoring intensity OSS_t at time t across all sectors and services is obtained by aggregating the respective OSS_{it}, weighted by total sectoral nonenergy inputs INP:

$$OSS_t = \sum_i OSS_{it} \cdot (INP_{it} / INP_t), \tag{3}$$

where

$$INP_t = \sum_i INP_{it}{}^5 \tag{4}$$

I take the sum of total sectoral nonenergy inputs across all thirty-six manufacturing industries for the calculation of offshoring intensities. Goods offshoring intensities OSG_t are calculated analogously.

The definition of offshoring intensities suffers from two related shortcomings. First, the measures underestimate the actual offshoring values, since the import prices of these services are generally lower than their purchase prices. Second, total nonenergy inputs include only purchased inputs but do not include self-produced inputs used by a given sector i (Amiti and Wei 2005).

Figure 4.4 shows the development of average offshoring intensities in German manufacturing industries. Between 1995 and 2004, services offshoring intensities in

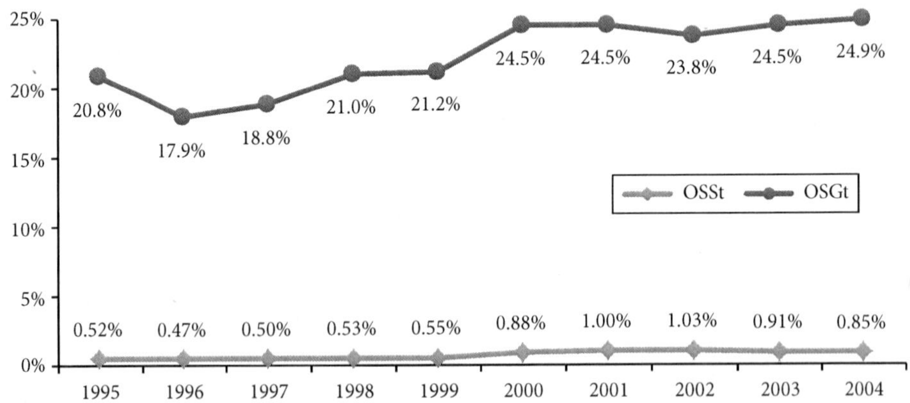

FIGURE 4.4 Offshoring intensities in German manufacturing, 1995–2004.

Source: Own calculations. Data: German Federal Statistical Office, revised input–output tables, 1995–2004.

manufacturing grew by on average 5.6 percent per year from 0.52 percent to 0.85 percent. Goods offshoring intensities increased by on average 2.0 percent per annum from 20.8 percent in 1995 to 24.9 percent in 2004. While services offshoring grew at a higher rate compared to goods offshoring, goods offshoring intensities are still clearly higher in terms of levels. We can conclude that services offshoring intensities have grown considerably in most German manufacturing industries, but the offshoring levels for services are still relatively low.

4 Empirical analysis

4.1 Theoretical and empirical model

A variable unit cost function CV is specified following Geishecker (2006):

$$CV = CV(Y, w_{HS}, w_{LS}, K/Y, T) \tag{5}$$

where Y denotes the output and w_{HS} and w_{LS} are the exogenous wages for the variable input factors high-skilled labor L_{HS} and less-skilled labor L_{LS}. Capital is considered a quasi-fixed input factor in the form of capital intensity K/Y.[6] The technology shifter $T = T(OSS, OSG, RD/Y)$ is defined as a function of services and goods offshoring OSS and OSG and research and development (R&D) intensity.

Using the transcendental logarithmic (translog) form[7] of the variable unit cost function as introduced by Brown and Christensen (1981) and applying Shephard's Lemma[8], the following factor demand function can be derived:

$$\begin{aligned} S_{HS,it} = \alpha_{HS} + \zeta_Y \ln Y_{it} + \gamma_w \ln \frac{w_{LS,it}}{w_{HS,it}} + \zeta_K \ln(K/Y)_{it} \\ + \theta_{OSS} OSS_{it} + \theta_{OSG} OSG_{it} + \theta_{RD} (RD/Y)_{it} + D_i + D_t + \varepsilon_{it} \end{aligned} \tag{6}$$

where i designates the sector dimension, t the time dimension, D_t fixed year effects, D_i fixed sector effects, and ε_{it} a random error term.

S_{HS} is the cost share of L_{HS} in variable costs CV. Since w_{HS} and w_{LS} are the only variable costs, CV is determined by the sum of the products of the variable factor costs with their respective factors, $CV = w_{HS} L_{HS} + w_{HS} L_{HS} = wL$, where w designates the average wage per labor input L, regardless of the qualification. A decrease of S_{HS} can reflect both a fall in L_{HS} and/or a fall in w_{HS}, which implies a rise in S_{LS} and thus an increase in L_{LS} and/or in w_{LS}. Hence, the composite term $S_{HS} = w_{HS} L_{HS}/wL$ can be considered the relative demand for high-skilled labor.

The coefficient sign of output, ζ_Y, is not unambiguously predictable. An increase in Y normally leads to a higher overall wage bill and therefore to larger variable costs CV. If the cost increase is equally distributed between less-skilled and high-skilled labor, there should be no influence on S_{HS}. If the wage bill of less-skilled labor increases more than proportionally, for example, due to better bargaining power, this results in a higher L_{LS} and/or w_{LS}, and S_{HS} is expected to fall ($\zeta_Y < 0$).

One expects a lower cost share of L_{HS} in variable costs CV and thus a lower S_{HS} when relative wages for less-skilled labor as part of CV rise ($\gamma_w < 0$). An increase in the capital coefficient is predicted to increase S_{HS}, since capital can be considered a substitute for less-skilled labor rather than for high-skilled labor ($\zeta_K > 0$). The influence of OSS, OSG and R&D intensity on S_{HS} is not easily predictable, as offshoring could be a substitute for high-skilled ($\theta_{OSS} < 0$, $\theta_{OSG} < 0$, and $\theta_{RD} < 0$) or less-skilled labor ($\theta_{OSS} > 0$, $\theta_{OSG} > 0$, and $\theta_{RD} > 0$).

4.2 Data

S_{HS} and the calculation of relative wages require skill-specific wage and employment data by sector. I follow the standard approach associating skilled labor with white-collar workers and less-skilled labor with blue collar workers.[9] I retrieved the data from the German Federal Statistical Office ("Monthly reports for firms: wage bill and payroll for blue- and white-collar workers"). As S_{HS} corresponds to the share of high-skilled workers in the total wage bill by sector, the numerator consists of the payroll of white-collar workers, while the denominator covers the total wage bill for all workers (i.e. white-collar and blue-collar workers). I divide the occupational-specific wage bill and payroll by the number of blue-collar and white-collar workers, respectively, to obtain occupational-specific wages. My regression analysis covers only manufacturing industries due to the lack of occupational-specific wage and employment data in services industries. I include all manufacturing industries listed in Figure 4.3 except for construction installation and other construction because of unavailable occupational-specific wage and employment data in this sector.

I used input–output data at current prices to calculate offshoring intensities OSS and OSG. Since offshoring intensities are ratios, deflation of the numerator and the denominator is not necessary. German input-output tables are disaggregated to seventy-one industries following the three-digit and, for some industries, the four-digit NACE Rev. 1.1 classification from the German Federal Statistical Office (revised input–output tables 1995 to 2004, Series 18, No. 2). My econometric analysis is restricted to the period 1995–2004 because of limited data availability of comparable input–output data (available only from 1995 onwards) and occupational-specific data (available only up to 2004).

Capital stock K is matched using the sectoral net capital stock at 2000 prices from the German Federal Statistical Office. I prefer net capital stock over gross capital stock, as the first accounts for depreciation, which is advantageous for at least two reasons. First, depreciation reflects physical deterioration and efficiency losses, and second, different

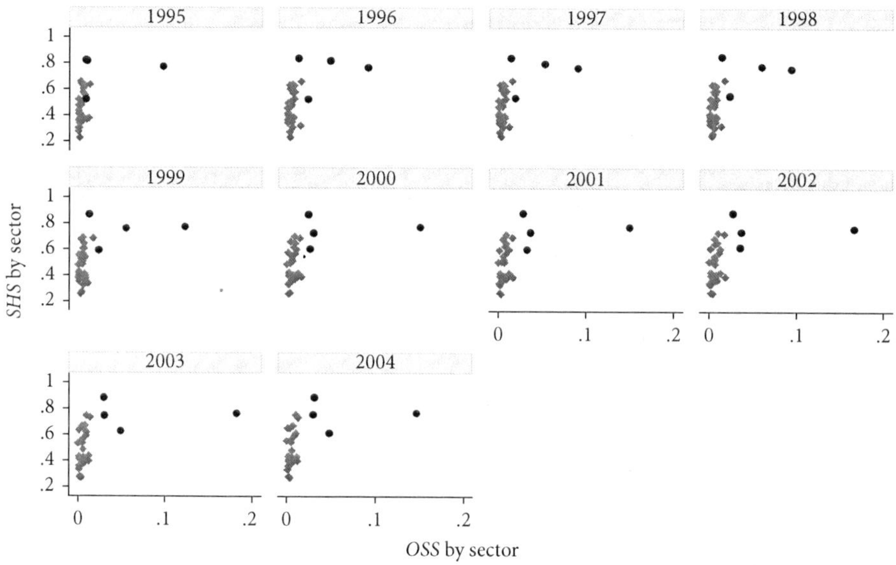

FIGURE 4.5 *OSS* versus *SHS* by manufacturing sector, 1995–2004.

Source: Own calculations. Data: German Federal Statistical Office. NB: Circles designate the following outliers: tobacco; pharmaceuticals; publishing; and office, accounting, and computing machinery.

rates of depreciation are applied to different types of capital (Hijzen et al. 2005). Other authors, such as Falk and Koebel (2002), Strauss-Kahn (2004), or Geishecker (2006), also use net capital stocks when measuring labor demand equations. I split capital stock into equipment and buildings, as their effects can be different. I then calculate capital intensity dividing capital stock *K* by gross output *Y*.

I derived gross output *Y* from the input-output tables and calculate real output using sectoral producer price indices from the German Federal Statistical Office. Finally, I obtained R&D expenditures from the OECD STAN Industrial Database (ANBERD, R&D Expenditure in Industry (ISIC Rev. 3), vol. 2006 release 01). I cumulate R&D expenditures over the period 1995–2004 to obtain a measure of R&D stocks and divide R&D stocks by gross output to calculate R&D intensities.

4.3 Regression results

The following panel regression analysis measures the impact of services offshoring on the relative demand for skilled labor, defined as the share of white-collar workers in the total wage bill of sectors, in German manufacturing for the period 1995–2004. The summary statistics can be found in appendix 2. All estimations produce standard errors robust to heteroscedasticity (Huber–White sandwich estimators) and control for fixed sector effects D_i, that is, shocks that are industry-specific and time-invariant, as well as fixed year effects D_t, that is, shocks that are year-specific and are expected to affect all industries equally.

I run the regressions on two sector samples: (1) a full sample including thirty-five manufacturing industries[10] and (2) a reduced sector sample excluding outliers. Figure 4.5 plots sectoral services offshoring intensities and the relative demand for skilled labor for all thirty-five manufacturing industries by year. The following four outliers, marked as circles in the scatterplots, can be easily detected: tobacco; pharmaceuticals; publishing; and office, accounting, and computing machinery. These four industries not only show the highest services offshoring intensities (see Figure 4.3), but are also characterized by a high relative demand for white-collar workers, which will upward-bias the estimation results. The summary statistics for the reduced sample can be found in appendix 3.

In a first step, I use the consistent fixed-effects estimator. The results are shown in columns (1) to (4) of Table 4.2. Columns (1) and (2) report the results for all industries, and columns (3) and (4) for the reduced sample. Finally, I include sectoral import shares as an additional control variables to every other specification, since the effect of offshoring intensities might be overestimated when correlated variables are omitted (Amiti and Wei 2009).

Output has a negative effect on the relative demand for white-collar workers. That is, an increase in output benefits the wage bill for blue-collar workers in a sector's total wage bill, because the demand or wage rate for blue-collar workers rises. As expected, a higher relative wage of blue-collar workers has a negative impact on the wage share of white-collar workers. A higher intensity of equipment increases the relative demand for white-collar workers, which is only significant in the whole sector sample. Surprisingly, services offshoring has a negative effect on the relative demand for white-collar workers across all specifications, and the coefficient is twice as large when outliers are excluded. R&D intensity has only a positive effect in the reduced sample without controlling for import shares. The latter increases the relative demand for white-collar workers in the reduced sector sample.

It is plausible that inputs, that is, services and goods offshoring and import share, and the relative demand for labor are simultaneously determined (Egger and Egger 2003). Analogously, occupational-specific wages and the relative demand for labor are probably simultaneously determined. I therefore treat relative wages, services and goods offshoring, and import shares as endogenous variables and use the first two lags of each endogenous variable as instruments. In columns (4) to (8) I apply the instrumental variables two-stage least squares (IV 2SLS) fixed effects estimator to control for potential endogeneity of relative wages, services and goods offshoring, and import shares. The previous results can be confirmed. Moreover, a higher capital stock of buildings now shows a significantly negative effect on the wage share of white-collar workers. One explanation might be that (factory) buildings for blue-collar workers are larger and/or more likely a firm's own property, while buildings for white-collar workers tend to be smaller and/or more often rented.

A different approach to address the endogeneity of relative wages, offshoring intensity and import share is to use the difference and system generalized method of moments (GMM) estimators. These estimators include the lagged value of the

Table 4.2 Regression results, fixed effects and IV 2SLS fixed effects estimators, 1995–2004

Dependent variable: $S_{HS,t}$

	Fixed Effects Estimator				IV 2SLS Fixed Effects Estimator			
	All industries		Without outliers		All industries		Without outliers	
	(1)	(2)	(3)	(4)	(5)	(6)	(7)	(8)
$\ln Y_t$	-0.0540***	-0.0511***	-0.0318***	-0.0126*	-0.0394***	-0.0373**	-0.0189**	0.0189
	(0.000)	(0.000)	(0.000)	(0.084)	(0.000)	(0.041)	(0.017)	(0.125)
$\ln(w_{LS}/w_{HS})_t$	-0.1273***	-0.1305***	-0.1748***	-0.2068***	-0.1008*	-0.1143**	-0.1580	-0.2455**
	(0.003)	(0.004)	(0.000)	(0.000)	(0.059)	(0.047)	(0.167)	(0.013)
$\ln(K^{equip})_t$	0.0735***	0.0809***	0.0129	0.0166	0.0762***	0.0828***	0.0482**	0.0421*
	(0.001)	(0.000)	(0.562)	(0.415)	(0.001)	(0.000)	(0.035)	(0.070)
$\ln(K^{build})_t$	-0.0329	-0.0323	-0.0072	0.0129	-0.0467**	-0.0526**	-0.0441**	-0.0163
	(0.113)	(0.121)	(0.732)	(0.509)	(0.034)	(0.017)	(0.044)	(0.498)
OSS_t	-0.2763*	-0.2995*	-0.7421**	-0.5622*	-0.3720*	-0.4834*	-1.4115**	-1.3103**
	(0.065)	(0.062)	(0.037)	(0.094)	(0.057)	(0.080)	(0.017)	(0.026)
OSG_t	-0.0139	-0.0113	-0.0047	-0.0297	-0.0375	-0.0119	-0.0517	-0.0688
	(0.567)	(0.660)	(0.870)	(0.224)	(0.327)	(0.718)	(0.266)	(0.125)
$(RD/Y)_t$	0.0214	0.0034	0.0849***	0.0334	0.0296	0.0149	0.0766**	0.0263
	(0.297)	(0.889)	(0.001)	(0.132)	(0.187)	(0.732)	(0.019)	(0.294)
$(IM/Y)_t$		0.0273		0.1009***		0.0260		0.1718***
		(0.227)		(0.000)		(0.692)		(0.000)
Fixed sector effects	Yes	Yes	Yes	Yes	Yes	Yes	Yes	Yes
Fixed year effects	Yes	Yes	Yes	Yes	Yes	Yes	Yes	Yes
First stage results:								
Shea Partial R-squared:								
$\ln(w_{LS}/w_{HS})_t$					0.4806	0.4828	0.2726	0.2655
OSS_t					0.5616	0.5529	0.5516	0.5514
OSG_t					0.2464	0.2838	0.3009	0.3035
$(IM/Y)_t$						0.1453		0.3875
Hansen J statistic					$X^2(3) = 0.27$	$X^2(4) = 0.27$	$X^2(3) = 0.20$	$X^2(4) = 0.73$
P-value								
Observations	349	349	309	309	279	279	247	247
No. of industries	35	35	31	31	35	35	31	31
R-squared (within)	0.56	0.57	0.59	0.66	0.51	0.52	0.55	0.56

Source: Own calculations. $p^* < 0.1$, $p^{**} < 0.05$, $p^{***} < 0.01$ (p-values in parentheses).

dependent variable on the right-hand side which makes the model dynamic. I treat relative wages, offshoring, and import share as predetermined rather than endogenous variables.[11] Columns (1) to (4) of Table 4.3 report the results for the dynamic difference GMM estimator which uses the lagged levels of the dependent and the predetermined variables, and the differences of the strictly exogenous variables as instruments (Arellano and Bond 1991). Note that the difference signs (for example, $\Delta \ln OSS_t$) are not reported in Table 4.3 for space reasons. Most of the previous results can be confirmed in the dynamic model. Most importantly, services offshoring has a negative effect on the relative demand for white-collar workers. Moreover, the wage share of white-collar workers is strongly correlated with the wage share of white-collar workers in the previous period.

Since the Arellano-Bond estimator has recently been shown to suffer from the problem of lagged levels being weak instruments in the first differenced equation, I also apply the system GMM estimator (Arellano and Bover 1995; Blundell and Bond 1998; Roodman 2009). Predetermined and endogenous variables in levels are instrumented with suitable lags of their own first differences. Due to the small sample size, I specify that the estimator should create one instrument for each variable and lag distance, rather than one for each time period, variable, and lag distance (collapsed instruments). This allows us to avoid the bias that arises as the number of instruments approaches the number of observations (Roodman 2009).

Columns (5) to (8) report the results for the dynamic system GMM estimator. The results are less significant, especially in the full sample. Output and relative wages still show a negative influence. Capital stock of buildings now turns positive. Services offshoring has a negative effect on the relative demand for white-collar workers only in the full sample including import share (column (2)). The reduced significance might be explained by the lagged dependent variable which explains a large share of the contemporaneous wage share of white-collar workers, especially in columns (5) and (6).

Overall, my findings suggest that services offshoring reduced the relative demand for white-collar workers over the period 1995–2004. These results are robust across several sector samples and estimation methodologies. In the following the results are interpreted focusing on specifications only that control for import share. The coefficients of services offshoring range between −0.30 (Table 4.2, column (2)) and −0.48 (Table 4.2, column (6)) in the full sector sample. In the reduced sector sample, the coefficient sizes of services offshoring are larger and range between −0.56 (Table 4.1, column (4)) and −1.31 (Table 4.2, column (8)).

Between 1995 and 2004, services offshoring grew by 0.33 percentage points in the full manufacturing sample from 0.55 percent to 0.88 percent. Holding all other variables constant, this implies that services offshoring reduced the relative demand for white-collar workers in Germany by between −0.10 and −0.16 percentage points over the period. When outliers are dropped services offshoring increased by 0.168 percentage points from 0.40 percent to 0.56 percent. This implies that services offshoring reduced the wage share of white-collar workers in the reduced manufacturing sample

Table 4.3 Regression results, dynamic difference and system GMM estimators, 1995–2004

Dependent variable: $S_{HS,t}$

	Dynamic Difference GMM Estimator				Dynamic System GMM Estimator			
	All industries		Without outliers		All industries		Without outliers	
	(1)	(2)	(3)	(4)	(5)	(6)	(7)	(8)
$S_{HS,t-1}$	0.6407***	0.6300***	0.8488***	0.7988***	1.0891***	1.0778***	0.8691***	0.9328***
	(0.000)	(0.000)	(0.000)	(0.000)	(0.000)	(0.000)	(0.000)	(0.000)
$\ln Y_t$	-0.0275***	-0.0285***	-0.0440***	-0.0204	0.0044	0.0050	-0.0196***	-0.0113**
	(0.002)	(0.007)	(0.003)	(0.140)	(0.385)	(0.256)	(0.004)	(0.016)
$\ln(w_{LS}/w_{HS})_t$	-0.0645	-0.0729	-0.0305	-0.1636*	0.0091	0.0107	-0.2186***	-0.1777***
	(0.373)	(0.234)	(0.724)	(0.096)	(0.733)	(0.691)	(0.000)	(0.000)
$\ln(K^{equip})_t$	0.0377**	0.0311	0.0436*	0.0368*	-0.0052	-0.0080	0.0095	0.0008
	(0.032)	(0.118)	(0.066)	(0.054)	(0.357)	(0.104)	(0.192)	(0.911)
$\ln(K^{build})_t$	-0.0534***	-0.0558**	-0.0388	-0.0309	-0.0008	0.0001	0.0192***	0.0150***
	(0.009)	(0.017)	(0.114)	(0.174)	(0.819)	(0.963)	(0.001)	(0.000)
OSS_t	-0.3001**	-0.3576***	-0.2762	-0.7625*	-0.2466	-0.3018*	0.5671	0.3493
	(0.043)	(0.005)	(0.581)	(0.060)	(0.104)	(0.076)	(0.257)	(0.270)
OSG_t	0.0080	0.0045	0.0169	0.0236	0.0054	0.0023	-0.0119	-0.0185
	(0.715)	(0.817)	(0.478)	(0.249)	(0.771)	(0.870)	(0.560)	(0.262)
$(RD/Y)_t$	0.0255**	0.0430***	0.0249	0.0246*	-0.0058	0.0022	-0.0063	-0.0043
	(0.047)	(0.001)	(0.174)	(0.074)	(0.639)	(0.762)	0.602)	(0.659)
$(IM/Y)_t$		-0.0112		0.0382**		-0.0050		-0.0103
		(0.509)		(0.038)		(0.432)		(0.419)
Fixed sector effects	Yes	Yes	Yes	Yes	Yes	Yes	Yes	Yes
Fixed year effects	Yes	Yes	Yes	Yes	Yes	Yes	Yes	Yes
Hansen J statistic P-value	$p > X^2 = 0.98$	$p > X^2 = 1.00$	$p > X^2 = 1.00$	$p > X^2 = 1.00$	$p > X^2 = 1.00$	$p > X^2 = 1.00$	$p > X^2 = 0.98$	$p > X^2 = 1.00$
H_0: no 2nd order autocorrelation	$p > z=0.59$	$p > z = 0.55$	$p > z = 0.99$	$p>z=0.85$	$p > z = 0.18$	$p > z = 0.27$	$p > z = 0.75$	$p > z = 0.84$
Observations	280	280	248	248	315	315	279	279
No. of industries	35	35	31	31	35	35	31	31

Source: Own calculations. $p^* < 0.1$, $p^{**} < 0.05$, $p^{***} < 0.01$ (p-values in parentheses).

by between −0.09 and −0.22 percentage points. Interestingly, these results are in line with the Grossman and Rossi-Hansberg (2008) model showing that offshoring of skill-intensive tasks can lead to the case where negative relative-price and labor-supply effects offset the productivity gains of high-skilled labor.

4.4 Discussion of results

My results differ from the results by Crinò (2012) who finds that services offshoring increases the relative demand for medium- and high-skilled labor not only across nine Western European countries, but also for Germany alone. The author suggests the skill-complementarity argument as the underlying mechanism where skill-intensive foreign services and domestic skills are complements and not substitutes. What explains these contradicting results? Crinò's study includes 13 manufacturing and seven services industries over the period 1990–2004, while my study focuses on services offshoring in over 30 manufacturing industries covering the period 1995–2004. However, Crinò (2012) also reports the results for the nine European countries combined in the manufacturing industries alone, which confirm that services offshoring leads to a higher relative demand for skilled workers.[12]

Besides industry-selection and time period, two other important differences are found in the measures of our variables of interest, namely skill-levels and services offshoring.[13] Crinò (2012) captures skill levels in terms of educational level, differentiating between high-skilled workers with a bachelor's degree or higher, medium-skilled workers with either upper secondary or vocational education, and less-skilled workers with no formal qualification, which represents an advantage of his study. I follow the standard way of operationalizing skilled and less-skilled workers associating skilled with white-collar workers and less-skilled with blue-collar workers. It is safe to assume that there is a high correlation between medium- and high-skilled workers (with at least upper secondary or vocational education) and white-collar workers. As a consequence, the different ways in capturing skill levels should not translate in opposing effects on the relative demand for skilled labor.

The most important difference lies in the definition of services offshoring. Crinò (2012) approximates imported service inputs at the industry level by multiplying country-wide imports of a specific service, which are available for all years, with the industry-specific average import share of this service input, which is based on import matrices for 1995 and 2000 and averaged out across these two years. While this definition of offshoring solves the problem of the "proportionality assumption," where every sector is assumed to import inputs of each service in the same proportion as its economy-wide use of that input, it has the disadvantage of assuming an identical sectoral import share for a service input across the whole period 1990–2004. Increases in imported service inputs are therefore only a result of growing economy-wide services imports, but not of a higher sectoral import share of such imports.

As additional robustness checks, Crinò (2012) runs the regressions for 1995 and 2000 only, the two years where import matrices are available. He also applies the 1995 import share for the period 1990–1999 and the 2000 import share for the period 2000–2004 to allow for some industry variability. His main results for the nine Western European countries combined, however, do not change.[14] My study has the advantage of using German import matrices which are available for all years over the period 1995–2004 and represent a direct, and thus better, measure for the share of imported inputs. While it is difficult to assess which of the factors described above led to the contradicting results, the outcomes are definitely sensitive to the measures of services offshoring and, to a lesser extent, skill levels.

5 Concluding Remarks

The new offshorability of services has raised the public awareness of the labor-market effects of services offshoring in industrialized countries. The majority of econometric studies conclude that goods offshoring increases the relative demand for white-collar workers. In the case of services offshoring this finding has been challenged, as many offshorable services are medium- to high-skill intensive. As a result, services offshoring is more likely to substitute for white-collar workers in industrialized countries, while goods offshoring typically targets the tasks of blue-collar workers. In this chapter, I estimated the effect of services offshoring on the relative demand for white-collar workers in German manufacturing.

My measure of services offshoring represents the proportion of imported service inputs in total nonenergy inputs used in domestic production. Between 1995 and 2004, services offshoring intensities increased in almost all manufacturing industries. Overall services offshoring intensities in manufacturing industries grew by on average 5.6 percent per year from 0.52 percent to 0.85 percent. While services offshoring grew at a larger rate compared to goods offshoring, goods offshoring intensities are still clearly higher in terms of levels.

My regression results for the period 1995–2004 show that services offshoring reduced the relative demand for white-collar workers in Germany by between −0.10 and −0.16 percentage points in thirty-five manufacturing industries, holding all other variables constant. Dropping outliers, the relative demand for white-collar workers declined by −0.09 to −0.22 percentage points due to services offshoring. Interestingly, these results are in line with the Grossman and Rossi-Hansberg (2008) model showing that offshoring of skill-intensive tasks can lead to the case where negative relative-price and labor-supply effects offset the productivity gains of high-skilled labor.

I then discussed my results in light of Crinò's (2012) recent study on this topic which finds that services offshoring increased the relative demand for medium- and high-skilled workers in nine European countries combined and in Germany alone. I identified several factors that might have led to these contradicting results. Most importantly, our measures of the two variables of interest—offshoring and the relative demand for skills—differ. I followed the standard way of operationalizing skilled and less-skilled workers associating skilled with white-collar workers and less-skilled with blue-collar workers, while Crinò (2012) differentiates between three different educational levels. On the other hand, my study uses a direct measure for services offshoring, while Crinò (2012) relies on a proxy measure.

Economic policy conclusions depend on reliable econometric results, including credible measures of offshoring and skill levels. Most available studies, however, show weaknesses in at least one of these measures. Policymakers should therefore be cautious about drawing policy conclusions from estimates using proxy-based measures of offshoring and should not necessarily associate white-collar workers with skilled jobs only. Given my results, I would urge that policymakers seek to improve data availability on imported intermediates as well as labor and wages by education levels, especially in countries where the labor-market effects of offshoring are subject of considerable policy debate.

Notes

1. World Bank, 1818 H St NW, Washington DC 20433. Correspondence should be addressed to dwinkler2@worldbank.org. The author would like to thank the editors for valuable comments. The views expressed in this chapter are those of the author and should not be attributed to the World Bank, its executive directors, or the countries they represent.
2. The value of imported material inputs in German input–output tables by sector is based on German trade statistics, while the value of imported services inputs is obtained from German balance of payments statistics. With a few exceptions the German Federal Statistical Office applies the same assumptions on the usage of imported versus domestically purchased intermediates. All inputs are classified into 3,000 different product categories, 900 of which can be uniquely attributed to one single sector. The distribution of the remaining inputs is derived from estimates and imputation, based on various additional data sources and information.
3. For a discussion of the different channels through which offshoring can affect overall labor demand, see for example, Milberg and Winkler (2010) and Winkler (2010).
4. While comparable German input-output tables are currently available up to 2007, sectoral data on the wage share of white-collar workers are only available up to 2004 which restricts my econometric analysis to the period 1995–2004.
5. Amiti and Wei (2005, 2009) use sectoral outputs as weights. Using total nonenergy inputs instead of output results in a more accurate overall offshoring intensity, as it directly refers to the denominator of the offshoring measure.
6. If one considers a partial state equilibrium as introduced by Brown and Christensen (1981), the assumption of quasi-fixed input factors relaxes the assumption of full static equilibrium. Only the variable factor inputs are in the state equilibrium.
7. The translog cost function in the empirical work on trade and the demand for heterogeneous labor was first introduced by Berman et al. (1994) and applied by most studies listed in Table 4.1.
8. According to Shephard's Lemma (1953), factor demand is determined by the first partial derivative of the cost function with respect to the corresponding factor price, regardless of the kind of production function.
9. This assumption might not always be appropriate, since blue-collar workers can have a high technical skill level. This might apply even more strongly to the German case where vocational education plays a major role.
10. Although the sector construction installation and other construction is missing, we refer to the 35 manufacturing sectors as the "full sample."
11. Predetermined variables assume that $E[x_{ir}\varepsilon_{it}] \neq 0$ for $r < t$, but $E[x_{ir}\varepsilon_{it}] = 0$ for all $r \geq t$. Thus, idiosyncratic shocks ε_{it} in t have an influence on subsequent x_{it}.

12. Country-level results are not reported for manufacturing industries alone.
13. The econometric approach and variable selection could be further explanations for the differences.
14. Country-level results are not reported using these alternative measures of services offshoring.

References

Abramovsky, L., R. Griffith, and M. Sako. 2004. "Offshoring of Business Services and its Impact on the UK Economy." Advanced Institute of Management Research, London Business School, (November).

Amiti, M., and S.-J. Wei. 2005. "Fear of Service Outsourcing: Is it justified?" *Economic Policy* 20 (42): 308–347.

——. 2009. "Service Offshoring and Productivity: Evidence from the US." *World Economy* 32 (2): 203–220.

Anderton, R., and P. Brenton. 1999. "Outsourcing and low-skilled workers in the UK," *Bulletin of Economic Research* 51 (4): 267–285.

Anderton, R., P. Brenton, and E. Oscarsson. 2002. "What's trade got to do with it? Relative demand for skills," *Review of World Economics* 138 (4): 629–651.

Arellano, M., and S. Bond. 1991. "Some Tests of Specification for Panel Data: Monte Carlo Evidence and an Application to Employment Equations." *Review of Economic Studies* 58 (2): 277–297.

Arellano, M., and O. Bover. 1995. "Another Look at the Instrumental-Variable Estimation of Error-Components Models." *Journal of Econometrics* 68 (1): 29–52.

Autor, D. 2010. "Polarization of Job Opportunities in the U.S. Labor Market: Implications for Employment and Earnings." (April). Washington, DC: Center for American Progress and Hamilton Project/Brookings Institution.

Bardhan, A., and C. Kroll. 2003. "The New Wave of Outsourcing." Fisher Center for Real Estate & Urban Economics Research Report Series, No. 1103 (November).

Becker, S., K. Ekholm, and M. Muendler. 2009. "Offshoring and the Onshore Composition of Tasks and Skills." CEPR Discussion Paper, No. 7391 (August).

Blinder, A. 2007. "How many U.S. jobs might be offshorable?" CEPS Working Paper No. 142 (March), Princeton University.

Blundell, R., and S. Bond. 1998. "Initial Conditions and Moment Restrictions in Dynamic Panel Data Models." *Journal of Econometrics*, 87(1): 115–137.

Blundell, R., and S. Bond. 1998. "Initial Conditions and Moment Restrictions in Dynamic Panel Data Models." *Journal of Econometrics* 87 (1): 115–137.

Brown, R., and L. Christensen. 1981. "Estimating elasticities of substitution in a model of partial static equilibrium: an application to US agriculture, 1947–1974." In *Modeling and Measuring Natural Resource Substitution*, edited by E. Berndt and B. Field, 209–229. Cambridge, MA: MIT Press.

Crinò, R. 2009. "Offshoring, Multinationals and Labor Market: A Review of the Empirical Literature." *Journal of Economic Surveys* 23 (2): 197–249.

——. 2010. "Service Offshoring and White-Collar Employment," *Review of Economic Studies* 77 (2): 595–632.

——. 2012. "Service Offshoring and the Skill Composition of Labour Demand." *Oxford Bulletin of Economics and Statistics* 74 (1): 20–57.

Egger, H., and P. Egger. 2003. "Outsourcing and Skill-specific Employment in a Small Economy: Austria and the Fall of the Iron Curtain." *Oxford Economic Papers* 55 (4): 625–643.

———. 2005. "Labor market effects of outsourcing under industrial interdependence." *International Review of Economics and Finance* 14 (3): 349–363.

Ekholm, K., and K. Hakkala. 2006. "The Effect of Offshoring on Labour Demand: Evidence from Sweden." CEPR Discussion Paper, No. 5648 (April).

Falk, M., and B. Koebel. 2002. "Outsourcing, Imports and Labour Demand." *Scandinavian Journal of Economics* 104 (4): 567–586.

Feenstra, R. C., and G. H. Hanson. 1996. "Globalization, Outsourcing, and Wage Inequality." *American Economic Review* 86 (2): 240–245.

———. 1999. "The Impact of Outsourcing and High-Technology Capital on Wages: Estimates for the United States, 1979–1990." *Quarterly Journal of Economics* 114 (3): 907–940.

———. 2001. "Global Production Sharing and Rising Inequality: A Survey of Trade and Wages." NBER Working Paper, No. 8372 (July).

Geishecker, I. 2002. "Outsourcing and the Demand for Low-skilled Labour in German Manufacturing: New Evidence." DIW Discussion Paper, No. 313 (November).

Geishecker, I. 2006. "Does Outsourcing to Central and Eastern Europe Really Threaten Manual Workers' Jobs in Germany?" *World Economy* 29 (5): 559–583.

Grossman, G., and E. Rossi-Hansberg. 2008. "Trading Tasks: A Simple Theory of Offshoring." *American Economic Review* 98 (5): 1978–1997.

Hansson, P. 2000. "Relative Demand for Skills in Swedish Manufacturing: Technology or Trade?" *Review of International Economics* 8 (3): 533–555.

———. 2005. "Skill Upgrading and Production Transfer within Swedish Multinationals." *Scandinavian Journal of Economics* 107 (4): 673–692.

Head, K., and J. Ries. 2002. "Offshore Production and Skill Upgrading by Japanese Manufacturing Firms." *Journal of International Economics* 58 (1): 81–105.

Helg, R., and L. Tajoli. 2005. "Patterns of International Fragmentation of Production and the Relative Demand for Labor." *North American Journal of Economics and Finance* 16 (2): 233–254.

Hijzen, A., H. Görg, and R. C. Hine. 2005. "International Outsourcing and the Skill Structure of Labour Demand in the United Kingdom." *Economic Journal*, 115 (506): 860–878.

Hsieh, C., and K. Woo. 2005. "The Impact of Outsourcing to China on Hong Kong's Labor Market." *American Economic Review* 95 (5): 1673–1687.

Kalmbach, P., R. Franke, K. Knottenbauer, and H. Krämer. 2005. *Die Interdependenz von Industrie und Dienstleistungen, Zur Dynamik eines komplexen Beziehungsgeflechts.* Berlin: Edition Sigma.

Lorentowicz, A., D. Marin, and A. Raubold. 2005. "Is Human Capital Losing from Outsourcing? Evidence for Austria and Poland." Discussion Paper 5344. London: Centre for Economic Policy Research.

Milberg, W., and D. Winkler. 2010. "Financialisation and the Dynamics of Offshoring in the USA." *Cambridge Journal of Economics* 34 (2): 275–293.

Minondo, A., and G. Rubert. 2006. "The Effect of Outsourcing on the Demand for Skills in the Spanish Manufacturing Industry." *Applied Economics Letters* 13 (9): 599–604.

Morrison Paul, C., and D. Siegel. 2001. "The Impacts of Technology, Trade and Outsourcing on Employment and Labor Composition." *Scandinavian Journal of Economics* 103 (2): 241–264.

Roodman, D. 2009. "How to do xtabond2: An Introduction to Difference and System GMM in Stata." *Stata Journal* 9 (1): 86–136.

Rukwid, R. 2007. "Arbeitslosigkeit und Lohnspreizung, Empirische Befunde zur Arbeitsmarktsituation gering Qualifizierter in Deutschland." Schriftenreihe des Promotionsschwerpunks Globalisierung und Beschäftigung, no. 24.

Shephard, R. 1953. *Cost and Production Functions*, Princeton: Princeton University Press.

Slaughter, M. 2000. "Production Transfer within Multinational Enterprises and American Wages." *Journal of International Economics* 50 (2): 449–472.

Strauss-Kahn, V. 2004. "The Role of Globalization in the Within-industry Shift away from Unskilled Workers in France." In *Challenges to Globalization: Analyzing the Economics*, edited by R. E. Baldwin and L. A. Winters, 209–231. Chicago: University of Chicago Press.

UNCTAD (United Nations Conference on Trade and Development). 2004. "The Shift towards Services." World Investment Report 2004. New York and Geneva: UNCTAD.

Winkler, D. 2009. *Services Offshoring and its Impact on the Labor Market, Theoretical Insights, Empirical Evidence, and Economic Policy Recommendations for Germany*. Contributions to Economics Series. Heidelberg: Springer.

———. 2010. "Services Offshoring and Its Impact on Productivity and Employment: Evidence from Germany, 1995–2006." *World Economy* 33 (12): 1672–1701.

Winkler, D., and W. Milberg. 2012. "Bias in the 'Proportionality Assumption' Used in the Measurement of Offshoring." *World Economics* 13(4): 39–59.

Yan, B. 2006. "Demand for Skills in Canada: The Role of Foreign Outsourcing." *Canadian Journal of Economics* 39 (1): 53–67.

APPENDIX 4.A1

MATERIAL AND SERVICE INPUTS

	Material inputs (36)
1	Food products
2	Beverages
3	Tobacco products
4	Textiles
5	Wearing apparel, dressing, and dying of fur
6	Leather, leather products, and footwear
7	Wood and products of wood and cork
8	Pulp and paper
9	Paper products
10	Publishing
11	Printing
12	Coke, refined petroleum products, and nuclear fuel
13	Pharmaceuticals
14	Chemicals excluding pharmaceuticals
15	Rubber products
16	Plastic products
17	Glass and glass products
18	Ceramic goods and other nonmetallic mineral products
19	Iron and steel
20	Nonferrous
21	Metal castings
22	Fabricated metal products, except machinery and equipment
23	Machinery and equipment, n.e.c.
24	Office, accounting, and computing machinery
25	Electrical machinery and apparatus, n.e.c.
26	Radio, television, and communication equipment
27	Medical, precision, and optical instruments
28	Motor vehicles, trailers, and semitrailers
29	Other transport equipment
30	Manufacturing, n.e.c.
31	Recycling
32	Electricity, steam, and hot water supply
33	Gas and gas supply
34	Collection, purification, and distribution of water
35	Construction site and civil engineering
36	Construction installation and other construction
	Service inputs (7)
37	Post and telecommunications
38	Financial intermediation except insurance and pension funding
39	Activities related to financial intermediation

40	Renting of machinery and equipment
41	Computer and related activities
42	Research and development
43	Other business activities

Source: Input-output tables, German Federal Statistical Office. NB: "n.e.c." = not elsewhere classified.

APPENDIX 2

SUMMARY STATISTICS, FULL SAMPLE, 1995–2004

Variable	Obs	Mean	Std. Dev.	Min	Max
$S_{HS,t}$	350	0.4933857	0.1514533	0.2260212	0.890725
$\ln Y_t$	350	10.07449	1.076324	7.352441	12.43005
$\ln(w_{LS}/w_{HS})_t$	349	-0.4624667	0.1264865	-0.7398468	-0.2013674
$\ln(K^{equip})_t$	350	1.937718	1.085065	-0.6733446	4.016563
$\ln(K^{build})_t$	350	1.566056	1.170758	-0.7339692	4.669084
OSS_t	350	0.0106258	0.0228435	0	0.1826894
OSG_t	350	0.2409564	0.1467992	0.0257271	0.7015968
$\ln(RD/Y)_t$	350	0.1798713	0.3477556	0.0014828	1.858215
$(IM/Y)_t$	350	0.4547136	0.5120559	0	2.703693

APPENDIX 3

SUMMARY STATISTICS, REDUCED SAMPLE, 1995–2004

Variable	Obs	Mean	Std. Dev.	Min	Max
$S_{HS,t}$	310	0.4606796	0.1226524	0.2260212	0.7579198
$\ln Y_t$	310	10.15242	1.090486	7.352441	12.43005
$\ln(w_{LS}/w_{HS})_t$	309	-0.4545415	0.1212069	-0.7296743	-0.2013674
$\ln(K^{equip})_t$	310	1.999285	1.108848	-0.6733446	4.016563
$\ln(K^{build})_t$	310	1.676254	1.165276	-0.7133499	4.669084
OSS_t	310	0.0050002	0.0038407	0	0.0182527
OSG_t	310	0.2462013	0.1444714	0.0257271	0.7015968
$\ln(RD/Y)_t$	310	0.1294651	0.2488153	0.0014828	1.319764
$(IM/Y)_t$	310	0.4199458	0.4508996	0	2.17187

NB: The reduced sample excludes the following outliers: tobacco; pharmaceuticals; publishing; and office, accounting, and computing machinery.

CHAPTER 5

THE SECTOR BIAS OF OFFSHORING

Empirical Importance for Labor-market Implications

DANIEL HORGOS

1 INTRODUCTION

For several years, offshoring (as the process of importing intermediate products from abroad) has been an important topic in political and social discussion, and in economic research as well. The main fears that people in industrialized economies associate with offshoring activities are, depending on the respective labor-market institutions, either a decrease in wages or an increase in unemployment. Since industrialized economies are traditionally assumed to offshore low-skill intensive parts of production, concerns arise mostly for the low skilled.[1] The argumentation follows the line of the so-called factor bias of offshoring, presented by several contributions of Feenstra and Hanson (1996a, 1996b, 1999): If an economy relocates its relatively low-skill-intensive parts of production abroad, relative demand for low-skilled labor decreases. This induces a downward pressure on the relative wage of the low skilled. In relative terms, this effect is beneficial for the high skilled but harmful for low-skilled workers and leads to welfare-reducing effects in general equilibrium.

These causalities differ when shifting the focus toward more disaggregated industry levels or, in more formal terms, when distinguishing between the skill intensity of different industries. Then, as Arndt (1997, 1998a, 1998b) showed, a sector bias of offshoring occurs: If offshoring takes place in an industry, production costs of this industry decrease. This induces an additional gain and, if we consider a small economy facing given world prices, enables a wage premium. Depending on the relative skill intensity of the industry, the wage premium flows either to the low skilled (if offshoring takes place in the relative low-skill-intensive industry) or to the high skilled (if offshoring takes place in the relative high-skill-intensive industry). Therefore, by contrast to the factor bias of offshoring, the sector bias allows for situations where low-skilled labor may benefit from offshoring activities in receiving a wage premium. In general equilibrium, this decreases the welfare-reducing effects of offshoring.

Regarding the empirical literature on offshoring, most contributions investigate the factor bias. Feenstra and Hanson (1996a, 1996b, 1999) showed, for example, that offshoring increased the relative wages of the high skilled in the US manufacturing industry. Regarding the manufacturing sector in France, Strauss-Kahn (2003) showed that offshoring decreases the share of unskilled workers in employment. Hijzen et al. (2005) examined the effects of offshoring within the manufacturing sector in the United Kingdom and showed that offshoring reduces demand for low-skilled labor. Since these contributions examine offshoring on more aggregated industry levels, they are not able to focus on the sector bias. In order to investigate the sector bias, analysis has to examine more disaggregated industry levels. In this regard, only a few contributions provide empirical evidence.

Based on a microeconometric analysis, Geishecker and Görg (2005, 2008) showed for the German economy that offshoring significantly reduces the real wage of low-skilled workers employed in low-skill-intensive industries. Effects for low-skilled workers in high-skill-intensive industries, by contrast, are not as significant. On the other hand, high-skilled workers significantly gain from offshoring only if they are employed in high-skill-intensive industries. Hijzen (2007) investigated the implications of offshoring on factor prices in the United Kingdom. While illuminating that technological change is the predominant force behind the change in relative wages, he showed that labor-market effects of offshoring are significant and he mentioned the importance of the sector bias for the latter. Horgos (2011b) investigated the sector bias of offshoring for Germany. Distinguishing between the industries' skill intensity, results showed that the wage gap between high- and low-skilled workers increases if offshoring takes place in relative high-skill-intensive industries. By contrast, the wage gap decreases if offshoring takes place in relative low-skill-intensive industries.

When empirically investigating the sector bias of offshoring, crucial challenges emerge. First, since there are only a few contributions investigating the sector bias of offshoring theoretically, empirical analyses do often not base their regressions on clearly stated testable hypotheses. Thus, results are often not directly comparable, either with respect to those of other empirical studies or with respect to theoretical contributions. Second, when investigating the effects of offshoring at the industry level, the problem that offshoring is not directly observable emerges. Therefore, different indices have been developed to proxy offshoring activities. Depending on which index is used, results vary dramatically. And, third, as implications of offshoring are assumed to differ with respect to different labor-market institutions, the picture gets additionally blurred.

This chapter provides an overview of the sector bias of offshoring, focusing on the empirical importance for labor-market effects. In order to provide a closer look on the economic mechanism, section 2 starts by summarizing the main theoretical findings of the sector bias of offshoring and provides empirically testable hypotheses concerning labor-market implications. Section 3 addresses measurement problems. It discusses the problems arising when offshoring needs to be proxied at the industry level. Different indices that are used to measure offshoring activities are presented and examined with respect to their quality. Section 4 presents empirical results for Germany that illuminate the existence of the sector bias of offshoring. Section 5 discusses the empirical results from an exhaustive perspective, also taking different labor-market institutions into account. Section 6 concludes by summarizing the main results and addressing possible lines for further research. Relevant issues for policy makers are extracted as well.

Several conclusions can be drawn from this chapter: (1) When examining labor-market effects of offshoring empirically, it is of high importance which index is used to proxy offshoring activities. (2) The sector bias is an important feature characterizing labor-market effects of offshoring. Hence, the industry where offshoring takes place is of crucial importance. (3) When discussing employment effects of offshoring, it is also important to consider the labor-market institutions in force. Employment effects are, for example, strongly dependent on how flexibly wages are allowed to adjust.

2 THE SECTOR BIAS OF OFFSHORING: A BRIEF SUMMARY

As mentioned in the introduction, contributions investigating the sector bias of offshoring theoretically are relative rare. This section provides a short overview of the sector bias of offshoring. It focuses on labor-market implications and describes how offshoring affects wages, labor-unit requirements, and employment.

The sector bias of offshoring was first presented by Arndt (1997, 1998a, 1998b). Motivated by the work of Feenstra and Hanson (1996a, 1996b), Arndt investigated how the implications of offshoring may change when focusing on more disaggregated industry levels. Using a traditional 2×2 HO framework, Arndt analyzed offshoring activities in the same way as skill-biased technological progress was normally modeled, as examined in Jones (1965). He depicted the implications of offshoring within a Pearce–Lerner diagram and argued as follows: If offshoring takes place in the relative low-skill-intensive industry, the industry needs fewer workers to produce one unit of output. Since the economy is assumed to be small and thus, given world prices, unit costs of this industry decrease. This leads producers to increase output since the price of the good does not change. With the increase in output, the relative demand of low-skilled labor increases, inducing an upward pressure on relative wages of the low skilled.

It is important to note that implications for relative wages do not depend on the skill intensity of the production block that gets relocated, but on the skill intensity of the industry where offshoring takes place. Thus, if offshoring takes place in the relative low-skill-intensive industry, relative wages of the low skilled increase, whether the industry relocates its relative low- or its relative high-skill-intensive part of production.

If, by contrast, offshoring takes place in the relative high-skill-intensive industry, relative wages of the high skilled increase also in both scenarios: if the industry relocates its low-or its high-skill-intensive production block. This is the main difference to the factor bias of offshoring, where the relative skill intensity of the relocated production block matters, not the skill intensity of the industry. One important assumption that the Arndt model makes to achieve this result is to put the focus on a small open economy. With prices remaining unchanged, changes in demand will be absorbed by the world market. While foreign procurement decreases overall costs in the offshoring industry, whereas the relative price of the commodity remains unchanged, producers will want to increase output. In doing so, they raise relative demand for the factor intensively used in this industry. Therefore, it is the increase in productivity that puts pressure on the respective wages, not the change in the industry's production structure.[2] Proposition 1 summarizes the effects of the sector bias of offshoring on relative wages.

Proposition 1: *If offshoring takes place in the relative high-skill-intensive industry, relative wages of the high skilled increase. By contrast, relative wages of the low skilled increase if offshoring takes place in the relative low-skill-intensive industry.*

Concerning the effects on the industries' skill ratio (captured by the industries' labor-unit requirements) and the industries' employment structure, results are not as clear cut as with respect to the effects on wages. As Arndt (1997, 1998a, 1998b) mentioned, results are unambiguous with respect to relative wages, however, concerning the effects on relative labor-unit requirements, results are ambiguous in two of four possible cases: if the relative low-skill-intensive industry relocates its high-skill-intensive fragment, or if the relative high-skill-intensive industry relocates its low-skill-intensive production block.

As formally shown in Horgos (2011a), the reason for these ambiguities is that, for the implications on the industries' skill composition and employment, the direct offshoring effect is accompanied by a secondary effect, resulting from the change in relative wages. If the elasticity of substitution between low- and high-skilled labor exceeds a critical value, results on relative labor-unit requirements and on employment are unambiguously supporting the sector bias of offshoring. The critical value of the elasticity of substitution lies in each case beneath unity. Thus, assuming, for example, Cobb–Douglas elasticities, unambiguous results can be achieved. Proposition 2 summarizes the effects of the sector bias of offshoring on the industries' labor-unit requirements and the industries' employment structure.

Proposition 2: *Assuming Cobb–Douglas elasticities of substitution, unambiguous results can also be achieved for labor-unit requirements and employment. If offshoring takes place in the relative low-skill-intensive industry, the industry shifts production toward more high-skill-intensive tasks. By contrast, if offshoring takes place in the relative high-skill-intensive industry, relative labor-unit requirements of the low skilled increase. Concerning implications on employment and output, the industry where offshoring takes place expands output and employment as well. The industry that holds to its integrated production process reduces output and employment.*

3 Measurement problems: the use of different indices

This section addresses difficulties that arise when empirically measuring offshoring activities at the industry level. Since it is not able to observe offshoring activities of industries, different indices have been developed as proxies. While some of these indices are common in use, their definition, their measurement quality, and their property when being used in econometric analyses differ notably. This section provides an overview of different indices used in the offshoring literature. It first examines the design of the different indices, shows how descriptive results differ when the indices are used to measure offshoring activities, and discusses the quality of the indices in proxying offshoring.

3.1 Design of the indices

Indices that proxy offshoring activities are often calculated on base of input–output tables and are thus not able to provide information at the level of the firm. Therefore, it is not possible to distinguish between the imported intermediates produced in-house or bought from external suppliers. Horgos (2009) investigated measurement differences of different indices in detail and showed that it is possible to distinguish between four different groups of indices:

(1) imported intermediates relative to total imports (IITM);
(2) imported intermediates relative to total inputs (IITI);
(3) imported intermediates relative to production (e.g., gross output) (IIGO);
(4) imported intermediates (estimated) relative to production (VS).[3]

All these indices relate imported inputs (either observed or estimated) to some form of denominator. Concerning index 1, imported inputs to total imports, a crucial informational problem arises: While input–output tables provide information on imported inputs used by a specific industry, total imports are provided as aggregated number at the commodity level. Index 1 thus combines information at the level of industries with information at the level of commodities. Since total imports contain, for example, also goods for consumption, the two numbers can (but may not) diverge. This problem may become significant if the index is calculated for more disaggregated industry levels or for changes over time. Most of the contributions that used this index considered this problem (intuitively) and calculated the index only for one point of time and for more aggregated industry levels. However, while using total imports as denominator, the index controls for variations in trade flows, that may be needed in some specific cases.[4]

Since index 2 relates values within the industry (imported inputs to total inputs), it avoids the problem mentioned for index 1. Thus, the index is a very direct form of measuring offshoring activities but it does not control for the industries' level of production. The index can be seen as an industry's import penetration of inputs.[5]

Index 3 additionally controls for the production level of the industries. As with index 2, index 3 relates comparable within industry values.[6]

With respect to the design, index 4 is similar to index 3, however, it does not use the imported inputs observed but some estimated numbers of imported inputs as numerator. An estimation can, for example, be the relation of the industry's imports to the industry's domestic use of inputs. The big advantage of this index is that it does not require input–output tables as data source. The index relates also within industry components and captures the industries' production level as well. The quality of this index in proxying offshoring activity depends crucially on which estimator is used for the imported inputs component. If imported inputs are estimated well, the index should lead to results similar to index 3 and exhibit a similar quality.[7]

3.2 Descriptive statistics: measuring offshoring activities

After addressing the design of the indices, this section illuminates their differences when being used to measure offshoring activities descriptively. As data, input-output tables for Germany are used (provided by the German Federal Statistical Office). In order to focus on the sector bias, it is important to move analysis to more disaggregated industry levels. Therefore, offshoring is measured for the manufacturing industry, and for low- and high-skill-intensive industries of the manufacturing sector separately. To distinguish between low- and high-skill-intensive industries, I refer to a cluster analysis done by Geishecker and Görg (2005).[8]

A first overview can be seen in Figure 5.1; Table 5.1 presents the numbers.

As the figure and the table show, index 2, 3 and 4 exhibit similar tendencies. Measured with these three indices, offshoring in Germany increased over the considered time period, for high-skill-intensive industries and for low-skill-intensive industries as well. The increase is more pronounced in high-skill-intensive industries. From 1991 to 2000, index 2 measures an increase of offshoring activities in high-skill-intensive industries of 24 percent. Index 3 measures this number as 25 percent. Index 4, which estimates the imported-inputs component, differs slightly. It shows the same tendency, however, but it distinguishes more concretely between low- and high-skill-intensive industries. The emerging pattern shows a more volatile picture of offshoring. While the index measures an increase of 6 percent in low-skill-intensive industries, offshoring activity in high-skill-intensive industries increased by 47 percent.[9]

Index 1, which relates imported inputs to total imports and, as already mentioned, which is characterized by crucial dimensional problems, shows a very different picture. The overall levels of offshoring activities are very high, around 45 to 60 percent. This explains the large numbers presented by Yeats (2001). It does not, however, indicate a high level of offshoring activities in general, but a high proportion of offshoring in trade flows (measured as total imports here). With respect to the development of the index,

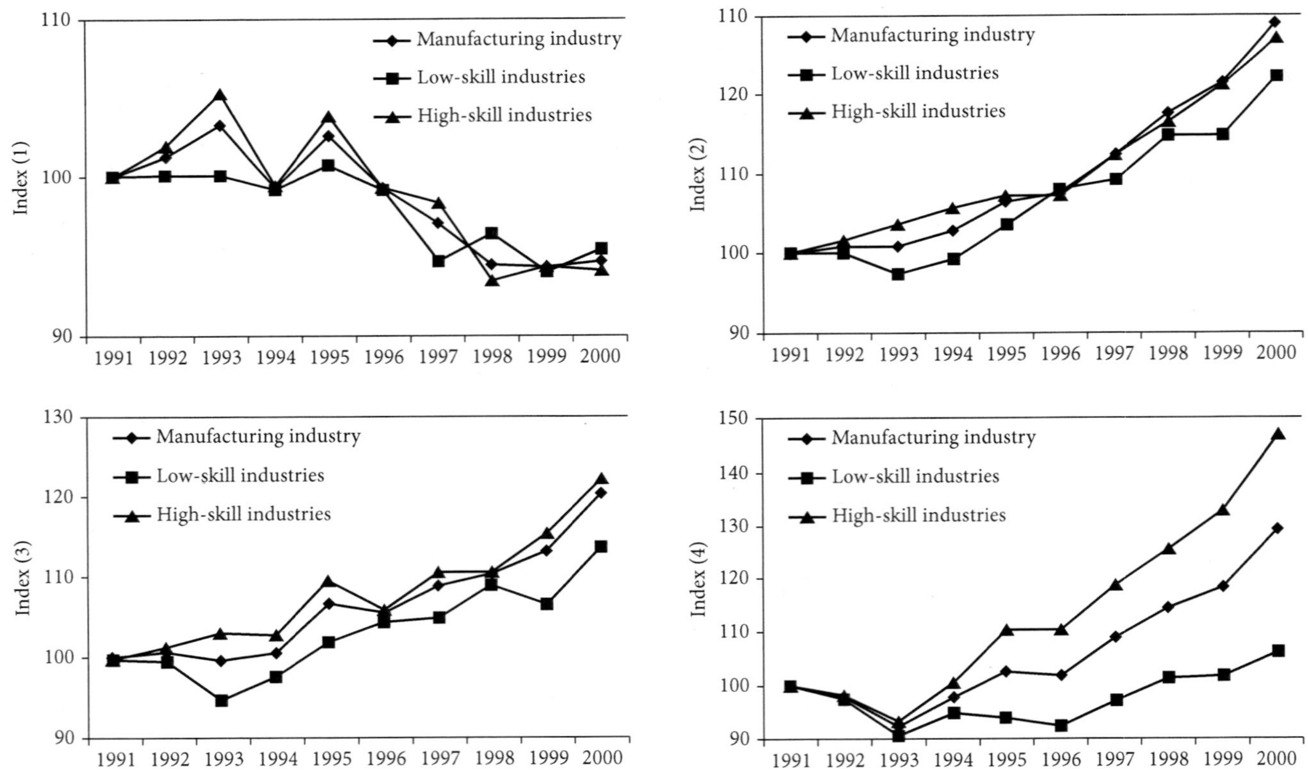

FIGURE 5.1 Descriptive statistics: offshoring in Germany.

Table 5.1 Level and percentage change of offshoring in Germany

	index 1	index 2	index 3	index 4
	52 (1991)	24 (1991)	12 (1991)	11 (1991)
Manufacturing industry	48 (2000)	29 (2000)	14 (2000)	15 (2000)
	-7 (Δ)	20 (Δ)	19 (Δ)	29 (Δ)
	61 (1991)	25 (1991)	13 (1991)	13 (1991)
Low-skill industries	56 (2000)	28 (2000)	14 (2000)	14 (2000)
	-7 (Δ)	14 (Δ)	11 (Δ)	6 (Δ)
	46 (1991)	24 (1991)	11 (1991)	10 (1991)
High-skill industries	44 (2000)	29 (2000)	14 (2000)	15 (2000)
	-4 (Δ)	24 (Δ)	25 (Δ)	47 (Δ)

Data Source: Input output tables from German Federal Statistical Office; All numbers in percent.
Δ denotes the percentage change from 1991 to 2000.

offshoring activities decrease, which is in sharp contrast to the picture presented with the other indices. This decreasing tendency can be interpreted as a decrease in the fraction of offshoring in general trade flows, which may explain the findings in Chen et al. (2005): It is possible for this index to decrease even if the offshoring activity of an industry increases.

However, most empirical contributions investigating offshoring in developed economies show an increase in offshoring activities. This descriptive evidence is based on the use of indices 2, 3, and 4. Index 1 is, if ever, used only to calculate the level of offshoring at one specific point of time, but not over a time period.

3.3 Do the indices really proxy offshoring activities?

Hummels et al. (2001), Strauss-Kahn (2003), and Horgos (2009) present shift-share analyses in order to investigate the quality of offshoring indices. This section discusses the core findings of their analyses. Shift-share analysis is an easy statistical tool to examine if the indices really capture offshoring activities or if there are other forces driving the main part of the indices' variance. With shift-share analysis it is possible to extract these different forces. The increase of an index can be due to an increase in offshoring activities. However, considering the design of the indices, an increase may also result from structural changes (e.g., a change in the industries' output relative to aggregate production of the economy). Thus, an index may increase even if the offshoring component of the index has not changed, or has even declined. With shift-share analysis we are able to break down the indices' variance and to clearly distinguish the offshoring part from a structural component. Therefore, we apply

$$\Delta O^z = \Delta \sum_{j=1}^{n} \theta_j F_j = \sum_{j=1}^{n} \overline{\theta}_j \Delta F_j + \sum_{j=1}^{n} \Delta \theta_j \overline{F}_j \qquad (1)$$

with ΔO as the absolute change in offshoring index z (z = IITM, IITI, IIGO, VS), θ capturing the structural and F the offshoring component of the index in industry j. A bar indicates that this component remains unchanged. This is essential in order to extract the intrinsic variation of the other component. Table 5.2 presents results of the shift-share analysis for the four indices.

The table summarizes results presented in Horgos (2009). The data source is, as above, Germany for the time period 1991–2000. Results are presented in four different rows: "within" shows the variation of the industries' offshoring activity as it focuses on the change in imported inputs, holding the structural component constant ($\sum_{j=1}^{n} \bar{\theta}_j \Delta F_j$). Row "between" captures the structural component of the indices' variation ($\sum_{j=1}^{n} \Delta\theta_j \bar{F}_j$).[10] Row "total" presents the absolute change of the index ($\Delta \sum_{j=1}^{n} \theta_j F_j$). The row "within / total" calculates the contribution of offshoring activities of an industry to the total variation of the index. Thus, it may be used as an indicator of the quality of an index, with numbers around 100 percent denoting very good quality.[11]

Regarding index 1, "within / total" numbers are mostly far away from the level of 100 percent. Thus, offshoring is not the main component driving the variation of this index. Instead, the change in the index is largely due to structural changes (in this particular case, general trade flows). Thus, index 1 can be seen as an index of lower quality in proxying offshoring activities. The above-mentioned dimensional problems may

Table 5.2 Quality of the offshoring indices: a shift-share analysis

	index 1	index 2	index 3	index 4
	Manufacturing Industry			
Within	-0.0241	0.0533	0.0212	0.0326
Between	-0.0126	-0.0058	0.0002	0.0004
Total	-0.0367	0.0475	0.0214	0.0330
Within/Total	66%	112%	99%	99%
	High Skill Intensive Industries			
Within	0.0016	0.0571	0.0257	0.0463
Between	-0.0195	-0.0009	0.0016	0.0024
Total	-0.0179	0.0562	0.0273	0.0487
Within/Total	-9%	102%	94%	95%
	Low Skill Intensive Industries			
Within	-0.0720	0.0475	0.0138	0.0100
Between	0.0287	-0.0124	-0.0001	-0.0018
Total	-0.0433	0.0351	0.0137	0.0082
Within/Total	166%	135%	101%	122%

Source: Horgos (2009).

explain this result partly. The three other indices are all of very high quality. The variation of the indices is mainly driven by offshoring activities (that is numbers in the row "within / total" around 100 percent). Index 2 slightly underestimates offshoring activities (with numbers mostly above 100 percent). Castellani et al. (2011) present results of an extensive empirical analysis estimating the quality of offshoring indices throughout Europe. They differentiate between business service, service, and material offshoring and consider different industry aggregates. Their results show that, especially for business service and service offshoring, structural shifts drive a large part of the variation of the indices over time. Considering material offshoring, by contrast, offshoring indices provide a less blurred picture.

4 Empirical Evidence for the Sector Bias

After discussing problems that arise with the use of indices to measure offshoring activities, this section illuminates the empirical existence of the sector bias of offshoring in Germany. Thereby, the focus is set on labor-market implications, in particular effects on relative wages.[12]

Geishecker and Görg (2005) provided the first empirical analysis for wage effects of offshoring in the German economy that is conducted at more disaggregated industry levels. Using index 3, they present a descriptive picture of the level and the development of offshoring in Germany for the years 1991–2000. Regarding the German manufacturing industry as a whole, offshoring increased over the considered time period, while the strongest increase was measured for 1996–2000. The novelty of their econometrical examination was that they estimated the effects of offshoring not only for low- and high-skill-intensive industries, but for different skill groups within these industries as well. As endogenous variables they considered real wages for low-skilled and high-skilled labor (both in the low-skill-intensive and high-skill-intensive industries). Within a panel-data analysis, they focused on an industry's offshoring activity as the main exogenous variable.[13] Table 5.3 summarizes their main findings.

Table 5.3 Implications of offshoring on real wages

	skill-intensive industries		low-skill-intensive industries	
	high skilled	low skilled	high skilled	low skilled
offshoring (index 3)	.0277*** (2.92)	-.0096 (-1.41)	-.0871 (1.30)	-.0360** (2.49)

Source: Geishecker and Görg (2005); endogenous variable: real wages; several micro- and macroeconomic control variables are not presented in the table; t-Statisctics in parantheses; **/*** significant at 5/1 percent.

As the table shows, offshoring has a significant positive effect on real wages of high-skilled workers if they are employed in high-skill-intensive industries. By contrast, for high-skilled workers employed in low-skill-intensive industries, there is no such obviously significant effect. On the other hand, offshoring significantly decreases real wages of the low skilled only if they are employed in low-skill-intensive industries. There is no such significant effect for low-skilled workers employed in relative high-skill-intensive industries. Beside these first results for offshoring effects on more disaggregated industry levels, Geishecker and Görg additionally provide useful information for the industry structure in Germany. They conduct a cluster analysis in order to distinguish between low- and high-skill-intensive industries of the German manufacturing sector, which is a very important and useful result for further analysis.

Horgos (2011b) focused more directly on the sector bias of offshoring in estimating the effects of offshoring on the wage gap between low- and high-skilled labor. He proxied offshoring activities with index 4 and followed the same high- and low-skill-intensive industry structure as presented in Geishecker and Görg (2005). Regarding descriptive statistics, he presented results for offshoring in the whole German economy, the manufacturing sector, the service sector, as well as high- and low-skill-intensive industries of the manufacturing sector. Additionally, he provided numbers for the low-skill-intensive industry offshoring its low-skill-intensive parts, its high-skill-intensive parts, and also both scenarios for the high-skill-intensive industry. Offshoring activity in the German service sector is in line with numbers presented in Amiti and Wei (2005a, 2005b) for the United States and the United Kingdom. While offshoring in the service sector is still at a low level (5 percent in 2000), it increases at very high rates (40 percent from 1991 to 2000).[14] Interesting results also emerge for the different, more disaggregated offshoring scenarios. While the low-skill-intensive industries offshore mostly relative low-skill-intensive parts of production, high-skill-intensive industries offshore mostly relative high-skill-intensive parts. Descriptive results for the manufacturing industry, and the high- and low-skill-intensive industries of the manufacturing sector are in line with results presented, for example, by Geishecker and Görg (2005): While offshoring in Germany fluctuated slightly between 1991 and 1995, it increased strongly between 1995 and 2000. Offshoring in the high-skill-intensive industries increased stronger than offshoring in the low-skill-intensive industries.

In order to investigate labor-market implications of the sector bias of offshoring, Horgos applied a panel-data analysis and regressed the wage gap between high- and low-skilled workers on the industries offshoring activity and additional macroeconomic control variables.[15] Table 5.4 summarizes the results.

Results presented in Table 5.4 directly support the sector bias of offshoring in Germany, as pointed out in section 2. Considering several control variables (which are not presented in the table), offshoring does not significantly affect the wage gap between high- and low-skilled workers in the more aggregated manufacturing sector. This is in line with what we would have expected, since the significant but diverse effects in the disaggregated low- and high-skill-intensive industries level out in the aggregate.

Table 5.4 Implications of offshoring on the wage gap

	Manufacturing Industry	Low-Skill Industries	High-Skill Industries
offshoring (index 4)	-8.3 (-0.80)	-24.6*** (-4.58)	19.4* (2.02)

Source: Horgos (2011b); endogenous variable: wage differential between high and low-skilled workers; several macroeconomic control variables are not presented in the table; t-Statistics in parentheses; */*** significant at 10/1 percent.

Regarding the low-skill-intensive industries of the German manufacturing sector, offshoring decreases the wage gap, statistically significant at the level of 1 percent. By contrast, if offshoring takes place in the relative high-skill-intensive industries, the wage gap between high- and low-skilled workers increases, significant at the level of 10 percent. This supports directly the sector bias of offshoring: Since offshoring takes place in relative low-skill-intensive industries, relative wages of the low skilled increase. Therefore, the wage gap between high- and low-skilled workers decreases. If offshoring takes place in relative high-skill intensive industries, relative wages of the high skilled increase, and the wage gap increases too.[16]

5 Discussion

Summarizing the results so far, the last sections showed that the sector bias of offshoring is an important feature characterizing labor-market effects in developed economies. Additionally to the factor bias, which focuses on the skill intensity of the relocated production fragment, the industry where offshoring takes place (that is, the focus of the sector bias) is of crucial importance as well.

Most contributions, empirical and theoretical ones, investigate implications on wages, whereas contributions examining implications on employment are relative rare. Furthermore it is interesting to note that empirical evidence on the effects of offshoring on relative wages is achieved with data for European economies. As Geishecker and Görg (2005) or Horgos (2011b), for example, showed, offshoring affects wages (in absolute as well as in relative terms) even in an economy like Germany, where labor markets are partially characterized by low-skilled wage rigidity. An interesting question would therefore be, whether the respective labor-market institution (such as minimum wages, fair or flexible wage set ups) would alter the expected offshoring effects. This would provide the possibility of studying changes in occupation or employment rates in addition to the effects on factor prices. Some offshoring contributions that investigate these issues are, for example, Skaksen (2004), Koskela and Stenbacka (2007), or Egger and Kreickemeier (2008).

However, what would employment effects look like when considering rigid labor markets within the sector bias of offshoring? As we know from the previous sections, the industry where offshoring takes place is of crucial importance. If offshoring takes place in the relative low-skill-intensive industries, relative wages of the low skilled increase. Relative wages of the high skilled, by contrast, increase if offshoring takes place in relative high-skill-intensive industries. Thus, considering that labor-market frictions are mostly applied to avoid low-skilled wages to decrease, they would not be binding if offshoring takes place in low-skill intensive industries. By contrast, offshoring in high-skill intensive industries induces a downward pressure on low-skill wages: a case where low-skill wage rigidity would be binding.

This argumentation was adopted by Horgos (2012). He provided a theoretical framework and supporting empirical evidence on how labor-market effects of the sector bias of offshoring would change if the labor market were characterized by low-skilled wage rigidity. The theoretical model directly compares labor-market implications of offshoring within a flexible wage benchmark model with the effects arising within a rigid labor-market set-up (modeling low-skilled wage rigidity, as in Brecher 1974a, 1974b). As the results show, the implications differ fundamentally between the flexible and the minimum-wage approach. When offshoring takes place in the relative high–skill-intensive industry, relative wages of the high skilled still increase, however, not as strongly as in the flexible-wage scenario. In order to keep production positive and to maintain the minimum cost level, the relatively low-skill-intensive industry has to reduce output. This additional reduction in output forces the industry to set low-skilled labor free. Since not all of these workers can be absorbed by the expanding relative high–skill-intensive industry, offshoring increases unemployment of the low skilled. These theoretical findings are supported by an empirical exercise. Applying a logit model to analyze German microeconomic panel data, results show that the probability for low-skilled labor to be unemployed increases dramatically in extent and significance if offshoring takes place in industries characterized by low-skilled wage rigidity. If industries are characterized by a more flexible labor-market institution, by contrast, offshoring has no significant effect on employment of the low skilled.

6 Conclusion

This chapter investigates the sector bias of offshoring and illuminates its empirical importance for labor-market implications. Since most contributions that examine labor-market effects of offshoring focus on the factor bias, the sector bias achieved only minor attention. In order to illuminate the importance of the sector bias of offshoring, this chapter started by providing its economic mechanism in a nutshell. Concerning effects on relative wages, the sector bias shows that relative wages of the low skilled increase if offshoring takes place in the relative low-skill-intensive industry. If offshoring takes place in the relative high-skill-intensive industry, relative wages of the low skilled decrease. After describing the basic causalities, the empirical examination started by addressing problems when measuring offshoring activities at the industry level. Therefore, section 3 introduced different indices that are used as offshoring proxies, presented results when these indices are used as descriptive statistics, and discussed the quality of the indices in really capturing offshoring activities. Afterwards, the chapter presented econometric results that support the sector bias of offshoring for the German economy and discussed alterations with respect to labor market frictions.

Because the sector bias of offshoring is identified as an important feature characterizing labor-market implications on the industry level, it is important to notice its key findings also from a more aggregated, political-economy perspective. The sector bias allows for situations, in which low-skilled labor may benefit from offshore sourcing: If offshoring takes place in low-skill-intensive industries. Thus, as Arndt (1997) mentioned: "concerns about the welfare-reducing implications of offshore sourcing appear to be greatly exaggerated" (77).

Several limitations of theoretical as well as empirical contributions on the sector bias of offshoring provide interesting lines for possible future research. As mentioned in section 2, one of the core assumptions in most of the sector bias models is to set the focus on a small open economy that takes world prices as given. This, however, neglects an examination of the demand side of the models. Most contributions, also empirical ones, accept this assumption and exclude implications resulting from a growth in demand in response to lower prices. For future research, it would be interesting to consider possible price changes and the demand side of the model as well. Further interesting research questions could emerge when examining effects on employment, output, or the industries' skill composition. Since implications for the industries skill composition are driven by different forces (more direct offshoring effects, but also effects resulting from the change in factor prices), they are more complex and not as easy to assess then implications on relative wages. It would also be of interest how the sector bias could be seen from an insourcing economy point of view.

Notes

1. Even if more recent contributions show that high-skill intensive parts of production are "offshorable" as well. See, for example, the discussion by Blinder (2007) and Baldwin (2009).
2. Several contributions discussed and extended the effects of the factor or the sector bias of offshoring. See, for example, Deardorff (2001a, 2001b), who illuminated the importance of the factor intensity of the production blocks that are exported. Egger and Falkinger (2003) considered different equilibrium situations and determined the dominance of the factor or the sector bias of offshoring. A dynamic product cycle view on the wage effects of offshoring was adopted by Sayek and Sener (2006). Kohler (2009) examined differences between the sector bias model and the literature examining the task trade model of

Grossman and Rossi-Hansberg (2008), showing inter alia how the sector bias of offshoring can be reconciled with the task-trade framework.

3. For a formal definition of these indices, as presented in Horgos (2009), see Appendix 1.
4. The index is used, for example, by Yeats (2001), Egger and Egger (2002, 2003), Egger (2003), and Chen et al. (2005). While Egger (2003) and Egger and Egger (2003) use the IITM index only to measure the level of offshoring, they calculate the IIGO index to investigate the dynamics of offshoring activities.
5. The index is used, for example, by Feenstra and Hanson (1996b), Amiti and Wei (2004), Bardhan and Kroll (2003), or Calmfors et al. (2005).
6. The index is used, for example, by Egger and Egger (2003) and Geishecker and Görg (2005).
7. Campa and Goldberg (1997), Feenstra (1998), Strauss-Kahn (2003), or Horgos (2011b) are contributions that use this kind of index.
8. The results of the cluster analysis in Geishecker and Görg (2005) are presented in Appendix 2.
9. For a more detailed analysis of the level and development of offshoring in Germany see also Geishecker and Görg (2005) (for separated industries) or Horgos (2009) (for the whole economy and the service sector as well).
10. Note that the structural component needs to differ with respect to the definition of the index used. While we use the industries' output to economy wide production as the structural component for the IIGO and the VS index, used inputs to total imports is used as the structural component for the IITM index. For the IITI index, we relate total inputs of industry j to total inputs of the whole economy.
11. When following the argumentation as in Hummels et al. (2001), Strauss-Kahn (2003), or Horgos (2009), an index would be of high quality if its variation is mainly driven by offshoring or, in other words, if the contribution of the change in imported inputs to the total change of the index is around 100 percent. However, quality may also be defined in another manner: It may, for example, be warrantable to capture the structural change of the industries as well. In this contribution, however, I follow the argumentation of the above-mentioned authors.
12. A descriptive overview of the level and development of wages of high- and low-skilled workers in Germany is provided in Appendix 3.
13. Since the endogenous variable in the regression is individual real wage, Geishecker and Görg controlled for observable individual characteristics (age, marital status, number of children, geographic region, tenure, occupational category, size and ownership of the firm, educational dummies) and the output of the industry where the individual is employed as well.
14. It is, however, very important to differ between offshoring implications in the service sector and service offshoring instead. Investigating service offshoring is an interesting and important topic and of high interest in economic research, however, beyond the scope of this contribution. For an exhaustive investigation of service offshoring in Germany see, for example, Winkler (2010) or Crinò (2009) for an interesting survey.
15. In order to control for time-varying industry characteristics, Horgos included the output of the industries as well as their high-skill labor utilization.
16. Horgos (2011b) also presents results using a narrow version of index 4, that considers only those inputs that are imported from the same two-digit-nace industry as where they are used. Results are in line with the results when using the wide version of the index.

References

Amiti, M., and S.-J. Wei. 2005a. "Fear of Service Outsourcing: Is it Justified?" *Economic Policy* 20 (42): 308–347.

———. 2005b. "Service Offshoring, Productivity, and Employment: Evidence from the United States." IMF Working Paper WP/05/238.

Arndt, S. W. 1997. "Globalization in the Open Economy." *North American Journal of Economics and Finance* 8 (1): 71–79.

———. 1998a. "Globalization and the Gains from Trade." In *Trade, growth, and economic policy in open economies: Essays in honor of Hans-Jürgen Vosgerau*, edited by K.-J. Koch and K. Jaeger, 3–12. Berlin: Springer.

———. 1998b. "Super-specialization and the Gains from Trade." *Contemporary Economic Policy* 16: 480–485.

Baldwin, R. 2009. "How Many Jobs are Onshorable? Re-interpreting the Blinder Numbers in the Light of New Trade Theory." June 15, www.voxeu.org/index.php?q=node/3659.

Bardhan, A. D., and C. A. Kroll. 2003. *The New Wave of Outsourcing. Fischer Center for real Estate and Urban Economics Research Report Series No. 1103*, University of California, Berkeley. http://escholarship.org/uc/item/02f8z392.

Blinder, A. S. 2007. "How many U.S. Jobs Might Be Offshorable?" CEPS Working Paper No. 142, 1–45.

Brecher, R. A. 1974a. "Minimum Wage Rates and the Pure Theory of International Trade." *Quarterly Journal of Economics* 88 (1): 98–116.

———. 1974b. "Optimal Commercial Policy for a Minimum-wage Economy." *Journal of International Economics* 4: 139–149.

Calmfors, L., et al. 2005. "Outsourcing." In *Report on the European Economy*, European Economic Advisory Group, 39–50. Munich: Ifo Institute for Economic Research.

Campa, J. and L. S. Goldberg. 1997. "The evolving external orientation of manufacturing industries: Evidence from four countries." NBER Working Paper, no. 5919. Cambridge, MA: National Bureau of Economic Research.

Castellani, D., L. De Benedictis, and D. Horgos. 2011. "Can We Really Trust Offshoring Indices?" *Structural Change and Economic Dynamics* 2012, DOI: 10.1016/j.strueco.2012.10.001.

Chen, H. M. Kondratowicz, and K.-M. Yi. 2005. "Vertical Specialization and Three Facts about U.S. International Trade." *North American Journal of Economics and Finance* 16: 33–59.

Crinò, R. 2009. "Offshoring, Multinationals and Labor Market: A Review of the Empirical Literature." *Journal of Economic Surveys* 23 (2): 197–249.

Deardorff, A. V. 2001a. "Fragmentation across Cones." In *Fragmentation: New Production Patterns in the World Economy*, edited by S. W. Arndt and H. Kierzkowski, 35–51. New York: Oxford University Press.

———. 2001b. "Fragmentation in Simple Trade Models." *North American Journal of Economics and Finance* 12: 121–137.

Egger, H. 2003. "Outsourcing in a Global World." PhD Diss., University of Zürich.

Egger, H., and P. Egger. 2002. "How International Outsourcing Drives up Eastern European Wages." *Weltwirtschaftliches Archiv* 138: 83–96.

———. 2003. "On market concentration and international outsourcing." *Applied Economics Quarterly* 49: 49–64.

Egger, H., and J. Falkinger. 2003. "The Distributional Effects of International Outsourcing in a 2 x 2 Production Model." *North American Journal of Economics and Finance* 14, 189–206.

Egger, H., and U. Kreickemeier. 2008. "International Fragmentation: Boon or Bane for Domestic Employment?" *European Economic Review* 52: 116–132.

Feenstra, R. C. 1998. "Integration of Trade and Disintegration of Production in the Global Economy." *Journal of Economic Perspectives* 12 (4): 31–50.

Feenstra, R. C., and G. H. Hanson. 1996a. "Foreign investment, outsourcing, and relative wages." In *The Political Economy of Trade Policy: Essays in Honor of Jagdish Bhagwati*, edited by R. C. Feenstra, G. M. Grossman, and D. A. Irwin, 89–127. Cambridge, MA: MIT Press.

———. 1996b. "Globalization, Outsourcing, and Wage Inequality." *American Economic Review* 86 (2): 240–245.

———. 1999. "The Impact of Outsourcing and High-technology Capital on Wage Estimates for the United States, 1979–1990." *Quarterly Journal of Economics* 114 (3): 907–940.

Geishecker, I. and H. Görg. 2005. "Do Unskilled Workers always Lose from Fragmentation?" *North American Journal of Economics and Finance* 16: 81–92.

———. 2008. Winners and losers: a micro-level analysis of international outsourcing and wages. *Canadian Journal of Economics* 41 (1): 243–270.

Grossman, G. M., and E. Rossi-Hansberg. 2008. "Trading Tasks: A Simple Theory of Offshoring." *American Economic Review* 98 (5): 1978–1997.

Hijzen, A. 2007. "International Outsourcing, Technological Change, and Wage Inequality." *Review of International Economics* 15 (1): 188–205.

Hijzen, A., H. Görg, and R. C. Hine. 2005. "International Outsourcing and the Skill Sstructure of Labour Demand in the United Kingdom." *Economic Journal* 115 (506): 860–878.

Horgos, D. 2009. "Labor Market Effects of International Outsourcing: How Measurement Matters." *International Review of Economics and Finance* 18, 611–623.

———. 2011a. "The Elasticity of Substitution and the Sector Bias of International Outsourcing." *Economics Research International*, Article 491278.

———. 2011b. "International Outsourcing and the Sector Bias: New Empirical Evidence." *Review of international Economics* 19 (2), 232–244.

———. 2012. "International Outsourcing and Wage Rigidity." *Global Economy Journal* 12 (2), Article 1.

Hummels, D., J. Ishii, and K.-M. Yi. 2001. "The Nature and Growth of Vertical Specialization in World Trade." *Journal of International Economics* 54, 75–96.

Jones, R. W. 1965. "The Structure of Simple General Equilibrium Models." *Journal of Political Economy* 73 (6), 557–572.

Kohler, W. 2009. "Offshoring: Why Stories Differ?" In *The EU and Emerging Markets*, edited by G. Tondl, 17–49. Vienna: Springer.

Koskela, E., and R. Stenbacka. 2007. "Equilibrium Unemployment with Outsourcing and Wage Solidarity under Labour Market Imperfections." CESifo Working Paper No. 1988.

Sayek, S., and F. Sener. 2006. "Outsourcing and Wage Inequality in a Dynamic Product Cycle Model." *Review of Development Economics* 10: 1–19.

Skaksen, J. R. 2004. "International Outsourcing when Labor Markets Are Unionized." *Canadian Journal of Economics* 37 (1): 78–94.

Strauss-Kahn, V. 2003. "The Role of Globalization in the Within-industry Shift away from Unskilled Workers in France." NBER Working Paper, no. 9716. Cambridge, MA: National Bureau of Economic Research.

Winkler, D. 2010. "Services Offshoring and its Impact on Productivity and Employment: Evidence from Germany." *World Economy* 33 (12): 1672–1701.

Yeats, A. J. 2001. "Just How Big Is Global Production Sharing?" In *Fragmentation: New Production Patterns in the World Economy*, edited by S. W. Arndt and H. Kierzkowski, 108–143. New York: Oxford University Press.

APPENDIX 1

A Formal Definition of Offshoring Indices

Horgos (2009) examined the definition of different offshoring indices in greater detail. The indices presented in this contribution can be assigned to the indices in Horgos (2009) as follows:

$$\text{Index (1)} = \frac{\sum_{j=1}^{n}\sum_{w=1}^{z} i_{wj}}{\sum_{w=1}^{z} m_w} (\equiv \text{IITM})$$

$$\text{Index (2)} = \frac{\sum_{j=1}^{n}\sum_{w=1}^{z} i_{wj}}{\sum_{w=1}^{z}\sum_{w=1}^{z} q_{wj}} (\equiv \text{IITI})$$

$$\text{Index (3)} = \frac{\sum_{j=1}^{n}\sum_{w=1}^{z} i_{wj}}{\sum_{j=1}^{n} o_j} (\equiv \text{IIGO})$$

$$\text{Index (4)} = \sum_{j=1}^{n}\sum_{w=1}^{z} \frac{f_w \cdot q_{wj}}{p_j} (\equiv \text{VS})$$

with i_{wj} as imported inputs from industry w (w = 1,..., z) used in industry j (j = 1,..., n), q_{wj} as total inputs, m_w as total imports of intermediate w, o_j as gross output, p_j as production, and f_w as an estimator of the degree of internationality.

APPENDIX 2

Cluster Analysis to Distinguish Between Low- and High-skill-intensive Industries

Geishecker and Görg (2005) provided results from a cluster analysis in order to differ between relative low and relative high-skill intensive industries of the manufacturing sector in Germany. Table 5.A1 presents these results for the two-digit NACE aggregation level.

Table 5.A1 Classification of high- and low-skill-intensive industries

	Industry	NACE
Low-Skill Industries	Food products and beverages/tobacco	15
	Textiles	17
	Wearing apparel	18
	Tanning, dressing of leather	19
	Wood products, except furniture	20
	Pups, paper and paper products	21
	Coke, refined petroleum	23
	Rubber and plastic products	25
	Other non metallic mineral products	26
	Fabricated metal products	28
	Furniture; manufacturing n.e.c.	36
High-Skill Industries	Publishing, printing and reproduction	22
	Chemicals and chemical products	24
	Basic metals	27
	Machinery and equipment	29
	Office machinery and computer	30
	Electrical machinery and apparatus	31
	Radio, television and communication	32
	Medical, precision and optical instrum.	33
	Motor vehicles, trailer	34
	Other transport equipment	35

Source: Geishecker and Görg (2005).

Appendix 3

Descriptive Statistics on Wages for High- and Low-skilled Workers

In order to get an impression of the development of high and low skilled wages, different figures are provided in this appendix. Figures 5.A1 and 5.A2 depict the development of relative high to low skilled wages Germany. As examples, "food products and beverages/tobacco," "wood products, except furniture," "rubber and plastic products," and "other non metallic mineral products" are chosen as relative low skill intensive industries (NACE15, NACE20, NACE25, and NACE26). "Machinery and equipment," "electrical machinery and apparatus," "medical, precision and optical instrum.," and "motor vehicles, trailer" are chosen as examples for high skill intensive industries (NACE29, NACE31, NACE33, NACE34).

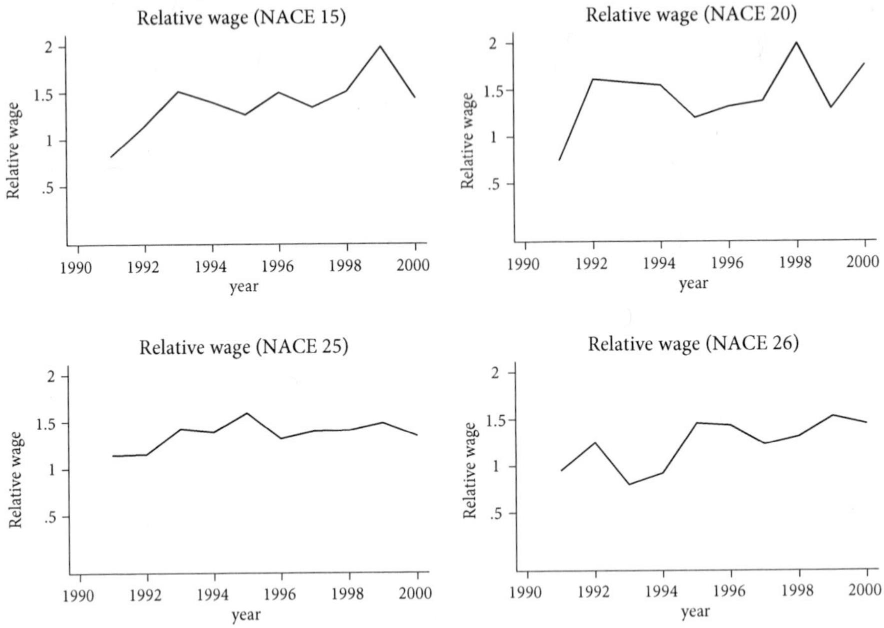

FIGURE 5.A1 Relative wages in low-skill intensive industries.

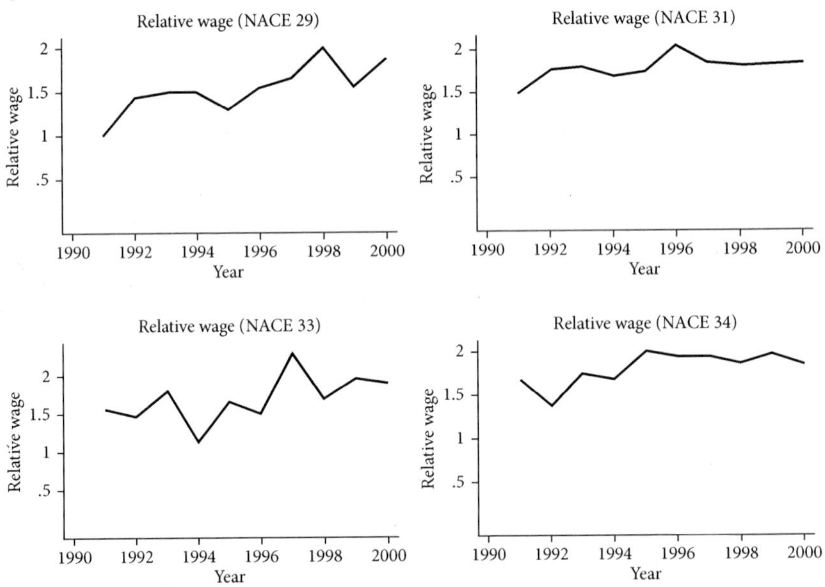

FIGURE 5.A2 Relative wages in high-skill intensive industries.

The development of average real wages for low and high skilled workers in these industries in Germany is shown in Figures 5.A3 and 5.A4.

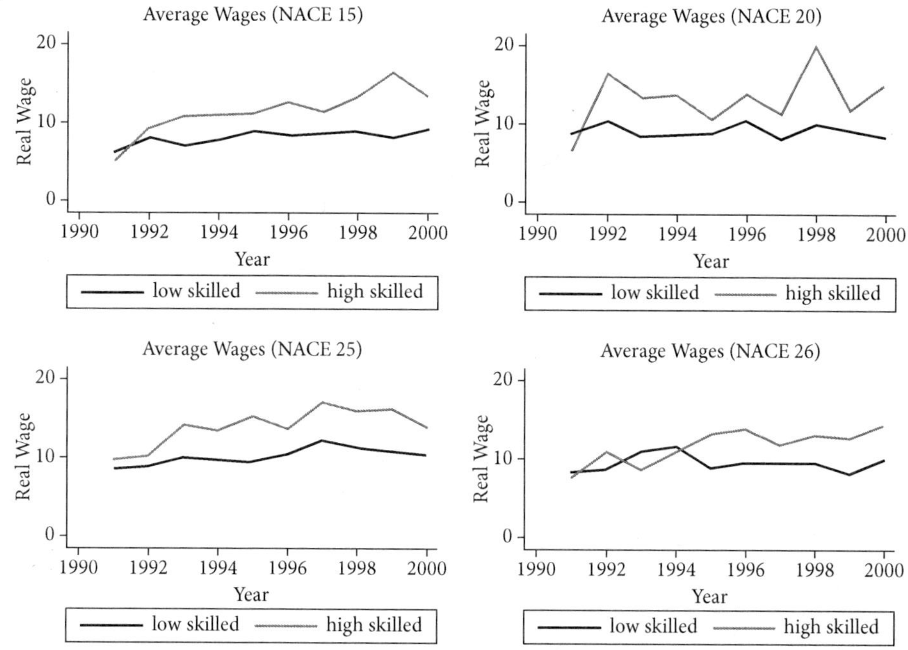

FIGURE 5.A3 Average wages in low-skill intensive industries.

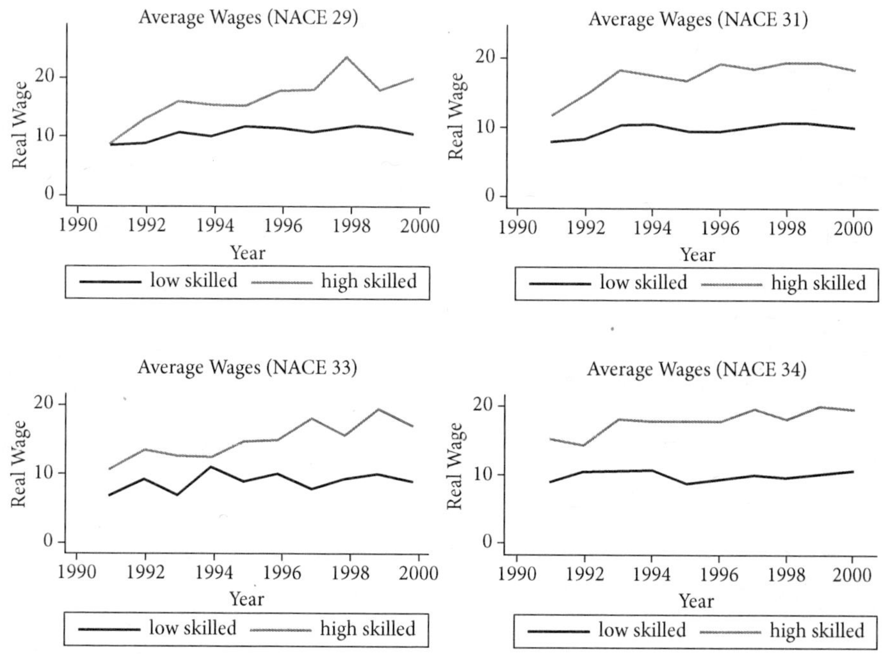

FIGURE 5.A4 Average wages in high-skill intensive industries.

CHAPTER 6

How Much Does Offshoring Matter?

Evolution of Imports and their Relation to Profits, Labor, and Firms' Strategies in France, 1990–2009

FABIEN BESSON, CÉDRIC DURAND, AND SÉBASTIEN MIROUDOT

1 Introduction

This chapter assesses the evolution of offshoring and its socioeconomic impact in France over the period 1990–2009. The relationship between offshoring and employment is analyzed and we explore the links between globalization and financialization and their consequences for labor.

Offshoring may affect labor (employment and wages) through various channels and with ambiguous effects. Some authors (for example Cohen 2006; Amiti and Wei 2005; Mankiw and Swagel 2006) argue that the direct effects on employment are pretty limited and that they are more than compensated by the gains from international trade in terms of lower prices and new outlets. Winkler and Milberg (2009) mention four links between offshoring dynamics and labor demand: the direct substitution effect and the productivity effect reduce labor demand for a given unit of output; however, the mark-up effect—which rises profits and potentially investment, productivity and output—and the scale effect—resulting from a higher demand for cheaper products—should lead to stronger labor demand. An important leakage in this virtuous circle comes from the possibility that the rise of profits does not lead to higher investment and stronger labor demand. Indeed, European countries and the United States have experienced an accumulation slowdown as firms favor dividends and stock buybacks (Stockhammer 2004; Orhangazi 2008).

In developed economies, international offshoring may allow firms to satisfy profitability claims made by financial markets. Offshoring would, therefore, contribute to a fall in the labor share of national income, as suggested in some empirical studies (Milberg and Winkler 2010a, 2010b; IMF 2007; Guscina 2006). Three mechanisms are involved. First, an increase in competition in end-products oligopolistic markets prevents firms from raising final goods prices but leaves them with the possibility of reducing inputs prices through effective management of the global value chain and a favorable market power position (Milberg 2008). Second, as offshoring shrinks the scope of productive activities and investments of firms, it favors higher returns of earnings to shareholders. Such an evolution is consistent with a shift of management behavior from "retain and reinvest" towards "downsize and distribute" (Lazonick and O'Sullivan 2000). Third, offshoring contributes to reducing the domestic cost of labor at the sectoral level or the labor share at the macro level. Indeed, "divide and rule" by transnational corporations plus a "race to the bottom" resulting from greater global labor expansion and a level playing field competition between various socio-productive systems may reduce workers bargaining power (Peoples and Sugden 2000; Glyn 2007; Freeman 2007). However, because of the destructive effect of increased competition on inputs and finished-products markets, the impact of offshoring on profitability should be heterogeneous: positive for companies and/or sectors that source cheaper inputs abroad or outsource abroad, but negative for local providers who suffer increased competition.

Moreover, because of the aforementioned deterioration of labor's position and skill-biased technological change, lower social standards and underemployment tend to diffuse in the whole economy at the expense of low-skilled workers (Petit 2010; Goos et al. 2009). In OECD countries, offshoring is thus associated with wages and employment polarization between low-skilled and high-skilled workers. But semi-skilled and high-skilled workers appears to be more vulnerable also as offshoring evolves from manufacturing to services (Bardhan and Kroll 2003; Crinò 2010; Besson and Durand 2006; Lipsey 2006) and towards more and more complex activities (Geishecker 2008; Winkler 2009), including R&D activities (Bardhan and Jaffee 2005).

Our work explores to what extent the general mechanisms described above are relevant for the French case. We focus on the issue of employment and the distribution of value-added between labor compensation and profits, going beyond macro evidence to investigate the variety of industry dynamics. While we are aware of their importance in the offshoring debate, we have decided not to focus on skills and wage inequalities issues. Section 2 presents the state of the literature on offshoring in France and section 3 describes our data and our methodology. Section 4 assesses at the macro level the evolution of offshoring in France during the two past decades and offers preliminary findings of firms' behavior in the context of the 2008–2009 financial crisis. Section 5 then proposes an econometric analysis of the relationship between offshoring, employment, and the share of labor in value-added. As aggregate results are often inconclusive, section 6 provides a more detailed outlook at the industry level. Section 7 summarizes our results and points out the policy implications of the analysis in the context of slow recovery and uncertainties on the economic prospects of high-income economies such as France.

2 Literature

The academic literature on offshoring in France is quite limited, especially in terms of empirical quantification (see Table 6.1 below for an overview). For example, recent research (Demmou 2010) does not allow isolating the impact of the phenomenon; while analyzing the causes of French deindustrialization on the period 1980–2007, it points out foreign competition as one among other domestic factors explaining the loss of manufacturing jobs.

Most of the quantitative studies focus on the impact of international competition on employment and differ in many ways, especially in their empirical strategy and the construction of their sample (for a comprehensive survey, see Daudin and Levasseur 2005). The assumption is that the French labor market is more regulated than others, explaining why firms are keener on adjusting quantities (employment) rather than prices (wages).

Two studies quantifying the impact of offshoring on the French labor market should be mentioned. Based on firms' restructuring announcements since 2002, the first one, carried out by the European Monitoring Centre on Change (EMCC 2006), concludes that offshoring job losses account for 4.6 percent of French employment losses. However, the EMCC may underestimate the impact of offshoring because the study takes into account only firms with at least 250 workers and a minimal destruction of 100 jobs.

The second study on the impact of offshoring in France is a research by Aubert and Sillard (2005), which is based on firms and groups data. It has been actualized by the French National Institute of Statistics and Economic Studies (INSEE) in 2007 (Barlet et al. 2007). Their work proposes an original definition of offshoring based on two cumulative criteria: (1) there is a significant decrease of employment in the firm for a short period of time (a decrease of at least 25 percent[1] of the initial level of employment in a period of three consecutive years) or the definitive closure of an establishment; and (2) there is a significant increase of imports for the same kind of goods by this firm. According to this methodology, offshoring would explain between 10 and 20 percent of the industrial job losses between 1995 and 2001. More precisely, 95,000 manufacturing jobs have been lost in France and offshored to foreign countries, that is to say 13,500 on average per year. This number has increased in the subsequent period, with a yearly average of offshored jobs amounting to 14,975 for the period 2000–2003.

This work also points out that developed countries are hosting a majority of offshored French jobs—around 53 percent (the main destination countries are: Spain, 16 percent; Italy, 15 percent; and Germany, 14 percent—i.e., EU neighbors—followed by the United States, 13 percent) suggesting that offshoring is related to the general restructuring of multinational firms rather than to strategies focused on the reduction of labor costs. Regarding developing countries, China is without surprise the main receiving economy, accounting for 30 percent of the jobs offshored (Eastern European countries, 19 percent, and North African countries,[2] 16 percent).

Table 6.1 Overview of the literature quantifying the impact of offshoring in France

Reference	Results	Methodology	Sectors
SESSI (Mathieu 1997)	1.9% of industrial production in 1993 (from 0.2% [printing, mineral products, mechanics] to 10.9% [clothing, leather])	Direct imports from emerging and low wages countries compared to domestic production	Manufacturing industry, firms with at least 20 workers
Boulhol (2004: 174)	0.15% of industrial employment in average by year between 1970 and 2002	Econometric analysis of the impact of imports from emerging countries	Manufacturing industry
SESSI (De Gimel, 2005, p. 174)	1.3% of industry production in 1993; 2.4% in 1999; 2.7% in 2002	Ibid (Mathieu 1997)	Ibid (Mathieu 1997)
CAE (Fontagné and Lorenzi 2005: 60)	1% of indutrial employment (maximum), less of 0.5 percent of total employment from 1999 to 2002	Balance of employment	Ibid (Mathieu, 1997)
INSEE (Aubert and Sillard 2005)	0.35% of industrial employment in average by year between 1995 and 2001, meaning 13500 jobs by year (between 9000 and 20,000 jobs). 0.25% of industrial employment by year in average when some indirect effects of offshoring are taken into account (positive effects, reassignments), meaning around 10,000 jobs by year	Statiscal simultaneity of two conditions on a given period: (i) reduction of employment at least of 25% or closure of establishment; (ii) increase of imports from a given country, for the same type of good (+100% or less depending on whether labor costs of the foreign country are comparables or inferiors to French ones)	Manufacturing industry except energy sector, all firms
Sénat (Arthuis 2005)	0.1 percent to 2.6% of employment according sectors, meaning sum-total 8000 job threaten by offshoring in 2006 in the commercial service sector and 42,000 on the period 2006–2010	Estimations based on 100 individuals interviews of managers in January-March 2005 extrapolated with the evolution of sectoral imports	Commercial service sector
European Monitoring Center on Change (EMCC 2006)	34 cases of registered offshoring for France (for 443 cases of restructurations) between 2002 and 2005	Inventory from an expert informants network (for France: IRES)	Cases of restructurations which: lead to a decrease of at least 100 jobs; or are related to production sites with at least 250 workers and at least 10% of workers; or lead to the creation of at least 100 jobs

(*Continued*)

Table 6.1 (Continued)

Reference	Results	Methodology	Sectors
INSEE (Barlet et al. 2007)	On the period 1995–1999, 12,952 industrial jobs have been offshored each year, including 4858 toward low-wages countries. On the period 2000–2003, 14,975 industrial jobs have been offshored each year, including 8850 toward low-wages countries	Ibid (Aubert and Sillard 2005)	Ibid (Aubert and Sillard 2005)
Chanteau (2008)	0.15% of the establishments by year in average in 1993, 1997 and 2003	Inventory of confirmed cases by cross-checking of firms statements, experts investigations and professional and administrative resources	All sectors (except agricultural sector and non-profit service sector), firms with at least 20 workers in Rhône-Alpes
Kramarz (2008)	The relation between unions bargaining power, firms' response by outsourcing and the impact on workers' wage and employment is estimated. On the period 1986–1992, the firms that faced strong unions increased offshoring and decreased employment when the rest of the firms saw their relative employment increase and appeared to have used outsourcing much less intensively	Econometric analysis based on firm-level data (imports and wages) and data on unions activity and bargaining agreements	Most firms, subject to the fiscal report called the "Bénéfices industriels et commerciaux." All sectors, except the public sector, are covered
Jabbour (2010)	The impact of offshoring on firms' performance (productivity and profitablility, and not on employment) is estimated. Offshoring corresponds to a profit-maximising strategy and does not necessarily answer to the objective of enhancing productivity. It has a positive effect on productivity but a more substantial impact on profitability	Econometric analysis based on the "International Intra-Group Exchanges" survey, which provides information on offshoring activity by French manufacturing firms for the year 1999, and on the annual firm survey *Enquête Annuelle d'Entreprises* (EAE), produced by the French Ministry of Industry (SESSI)	Industrial sector. Firms affiliated to an industrial and international group, with more than one million euros of trade flows, or more than 500,000 euros of trade flows towards emerging countries

Note: Based on Chanteau (2008).

Offshoring to low-wage countries is concentrated in low-value-added activities. At best, it explains 14 percent of the decrease in employment in these sectors (textiles and home equipment). On the other hand, offshoring to developed countries in pharmaceuticals, aeronautics, and the automotive industry explains more than 20 percent of job decreases. Offshoring to developed countries is not limited to manufacturing industries: innovative services activities are also more and more offshored (for example the research and development activities in the computers, electronics, and pharmaceuticals sectors). These offshoring strategies generally emerge between key regions of industrialized countries with the objective of reinforcing the technological capabilities of the firm. The interest is to reinforce the technological advantage of the firm in its country of origin, with a focus on excellence rather than low labor costs. Regional systems of innovation are more and more open to globalization but still in patterns involving developed countries even if the weight of Asian developing economies is becoming more important (Bardhan and Jaffee 2005; Ernst 2006). Moreover, in the case of North-North offshoring, the localization of multinational firms can also be driven by horizontal strategies that aim at accessing new markets through foreign direct investment (Mouhoud 2006). Brainard (1993) built a theoretical model to explain why FDI involves mostly developed countries and why there is a trade-off between concentration and proximity that can explain firms' investment decisions. This model, together with others (Markusen 2002; Cogneau et al. 2000), points out that when transport costs between countries are high, it is less costly for a firm to create a subsidiary in the targeted market. The firm loses the benefits of the production in a single place (the scale economies) but does not have to bear the high trade costs. Empirically, a study on the localization of 3,902 foreign firms in France over the period 1985–1995 highlights the relevance of cluster dynamics in the strategies of localization and differences in the behavior of firms according to their country of origin (Crozet et al. 2004).

However, it should be stressed that the study of Aubert and Sillard (2005) finds no direct relationship between job losses in a specific industry and the volume of offshoring. Kramarz (2011) analyzes a panel of manufacturing firms over the period 1995–2004 and also finds no obvious pattern in the sign of the relationship between changes in imports and job creation or destruction.[3]

Departing from the common focus on the labor market, Jabbour (2010) assesses the impact of offshoring on firms' productivity and profitability and controls for variables influencing offshoring strategies. She shows that firms' economic performance depends strongly on governance, organizational forms (outsourcing appears generally to be more efficient than vertical integration), and the importance of imported inputs. This study follows previous empirical work (Jabbour 2008) in showing that the choice of offshoring by French firms depends on the kind of inputs and on market thickness.

Furthermore, another study (Chanteau 2008) assesses the determinants of foreign relocations using a new dataset of 15,000 establishments owned by firms with more than twenty employees. Comparing the data for three years (1993, 1997, and 2003), the study shows that foreign relocations are again quite marginal, with no more than 0.15 percent of firms involved yearly. The study then analyzes the determinants of offshoring decisions by French firms and highlights three strategies that are motivated not solely by differences in labor costs: offensive, defensive, and structural foreign relocations. While at the macroeconomic level no difference can be found in the impact of inward and outward offshoring, foreign relocations are not without consequences for the dynamic of firm strategies. Past offshoring may accelerate the international expansion of firms and lead to increased production abroad. For the author, foreign relocations can be considered as an adjustment variable for firms facing the challenges of globalization.

Finally, from a theoretical point of view, Kramarz (2008) constructs a bargaining model to show that offshoring can have a direct impact on wages by altering firms' threat point and thus changing the share of the rent between firms and workers. Offshoring appears to be a strategy for firms (especially for the ones facing strong unions) to decrease the size of the quasi-rent to discipline workers. Using French firm-level data, Kramarz shows that firms facing stronger unions increased offshoring and decreased employment, rents and wages.

In summary, as illustrated in Table 6.1, the literature suggests that in France offshoring is a limited phenomenon, which has a significant—but minor—direct negative impact on employment and which affects heterogeneously sectors and workers depending on their qualifications. Moreover, this phenomenon is not limited to developing countries, as developed countries are an important destination of offshored jobs. Finally, offshoring appears to be one of the factors that favor firms' productivity and profitability.

3 Methodology: how to measure offshoring in France

Offshoring refers to the geographical separation of production activities across countries. Firms relocate production abroad to seize the opportunity of differences in factor costs, resources, and in socioeconomic systems. The previous section has mentioned surveys where information on sourcing strategies is collected directly from firms. Our approach in this chapter is to work at a more macroeconomic level and to rely on national accounts and trade statistics to calculate offshoring indexes. This section first presents the data that we have collected and then explains the different offshoring measures that we have calculated to cover thirty-eight French industries over the period 1990–2009.

3.1 Data sources for France

As France collects industry-level data according to a national classification ("nomenclature d'activité française," NAF) that is slightly different from the European "nomenclature of activities" (NACE) and the International Standard Industrial Classification (ISIC), our analysis relies on the data provided by INSEE. The French office of statistics has recently released a consistent set of national supply-use tables for the period 1990–2009, based on benchmark year 2005. In this database, we can find time-series for output, value-added, domestic consumption, labor compensation, imports, and exports. The data are disaggregated for thirty-eight industries covering both the manufacturing and services sectors. Services are especially well covered, with nineteen industries (this is where the French classification departs from European and international classifications). The other advantage of using supply-use tables is that we have matrices on the use of inputs by French industries on the basis of which we can calculate offshoring measures (in particular the Feenstra–Jensen offshoring index, see section 3.2).

National accounts data are complemented with trade statistics from the Organisation of Economic Co-operation and Development (OECD). Bilateral trade data on goods come from the International Trade by Commodity Statistics (ICTS) database and services data from the Trade in Services by Partner country (TISP) database. In addition, we use estimates of bilateral trade in intermediate goods and services from the OECD dataset compiled by Miroudot et al. (2009). We have developed a correspondence between the product classifications used in the trade data (HS and EBOPS codes) and the thirty-eight industries of the supply-use tables. It should be noted that supply-use tables, unlike input–output tables, are tables constructed by product and by industry (and not industry by industry tables). Therefore, we do not face the issue of matching products with industries.

The only variable that we do not have in the national accounts is the number of employees, but these data are also available from INSEE for the same industries.[4] While the supply-use tables include information on the gross fixed capital formation, the data are partly confidential for France and hence provided at a more aggregated level. We have reconstructed detailed investment time-series on the basis of the available data and more disaggregated data from the OECD STAN database. We have expanded the coverage of investment data to 1982 in order to calculate capital stocks for each industry using the perpetual inventory method (PIM). We have also estimated a price index for inputs (a variable needed for the econometric analysis) on the basis of the supply-use tables.

While all our data are available for thirty-eight industries, the rest of the analysis focuses on twenty-five industries where offshoring matters. We have excluded all industries where the share of imports in output was less than 2 percent. Many service industries (such as real estate, construction, hotels and restaurants, health, education, and public administrations) import a negligible value of inputs, and offshoring measures cannot be properly calculated or meaningfully interpreted. We have also excluded commodities (agriculture, extractive industries, coke, and refined petroleum products), where imports cannot be interpreted as the offshoring of activities. The list of industries kept in the analysis can be found in Table 6.2.

3.2 Offshoring indexes

There is no single measure of offshoring. Authors have used a variety of indicators and indexes to indicate to what extent firms turn to foreign rather domestic producers for the provision of inputs.[5] Following Feenstra and Hanson (1999), a proxy for offshoring is the share of imported intermediate inputs in the total purchase of nonenergy inputs.

Winkler and Milberg (2009) show that a limitation in the way this proxy is calculated is the assumption that an industry's import of each input, relative to its total demand, is the same as the economy-wide imports relative to total demand ("proportionality assumption"). To provide a more accurate indicator, Feenstra and Jensen (2009) use a direct measure of imported intermediate inputs. We have calculated a similar index for French industries over the period 1990–2009 (offshoring index 1).[6] For any industry *i* using intermediate inputs *j* from industry *k*, the offshoring index is:

$$Offshore_i = \frac{\Sigma_{k=1}^{k}\ industry\, i\ purchases\, of\ inputs\ j\left(\dfrac{imports\, of\ inputs\ j}{total\, domestic\, consumption\, of\ j}\right)}{\Sigma_{k=1}^{k}\ industry\, i\ purchases\, of\ inputs\ j}$$

In the above calculation, we take into account inputs from all industries. A "narrow" measure of offshoring is sometimes used in the literature, where only inputs from the same industry ($i = k$) are included. In the case of France, we do not find the distinction between interindustry offshoring and intraindustry offshoring (i.e., narrow offshoring) very useful. In addition, when comparing industries, the two measures are influenced by the detail in the industry classification. For some sectors (e.g., wood, paper, and printing), most inputs are within the same industry code while for others inputs are in different industries (e.g., transport equipment, using inputs from "basic and fabricated metal products" and "rubber, plastic and other non-metallic mineral products" industries).

Moreover, because the Feenstra–Jensen index overlooks the offshoring of assembly activities, we use as a second measure (offshoring index 2) the share of imports from developing economies in total imports (following Milberg and Winckler 2010a). We cannot assume that all imports from developing economies correspond to the offshoring of assembly activities but this measure is useful to account for the fact that some offshoring is captured through final goods trade rather than trade in intermediate inputs. We have defined developing economies as low-income and middle-income countries in the World Bank classification. Most of the developing economies where offshoring happens are in the lower-middle-income (e.g., India and the Philippines) or upper-middle-income group (e.g., China, Tunisia, and Turkey). This is why we do not distinguish between middle-income and low-income countries, as the latter include mostly sub-Saharan African economies that are very marginal in world trade (especially for noncommodity trade).

4 An Acceleration of Globalization up to the Crisis

Some recent discussions have pointed to the consolidation of some global value chains, suggesting that at least in some sectors globalization is beginning to lose momentum (Cattaneo et al. 2010). In the case of France, however, the general picture

Table 6.2 Main aggregates, by industry

	Evolution of imports share	Imports share	Evolution of offshoring		Evolution of employment	Employment	Evolution of labor compensation share	Labor compensation share	Evolution of investment rate	Gross output
	Percentage points 1990–94/2005–09	imports as percentage of gross output 2005–09	Index 1 change 1990–94/2005–09	Index 2 change 1990–94/2005–09 (1999/2009 for services)	Thousands 1990–94/2005–09	Thousands 2005–2009	Percentage points 1990–94/2005–09	percentage of VA 2005–09	Percentage points 1990–94/2005–09	Current Mio euros 2005–09
Food products, beverages and tobacco	5.47	1864.6	9.27	−1.49	7	566	8.71	58	−0.96	140,015
Textiles, textile products, leather and footwear	81.12	12842.1	7.79	20.16	−232	149	4.79	73	1.52	21,136
Wood, paper, paper products and printing	6.89	3054.5	8.30	3.46	−90	246	1.75	71	−2.01	40,987
Chemicals and chemical products	13.88	6216.1	57.80	1.87	−61	165	11.91	64	3.66	59,966
Pharmaceuticals	43.31	6822.0	3.77	0.26	1	89	−2.15	46	−0.03	26,634
Rubber, plastic and other non-metallic mineral products	9.42	3341.6	34.87	7.03	−42	330	−2.51	66	6.77	58,067
Basic metals and fabricated metal products	10.39	3877.0	43.06	1.42	−87	440	1.78	71	1.46	92,574
Computing products and electrical and optical equipment	76.46	15150.6	4.96	20.06	−37	160	16.31	79	18.04	27,068
Electrical machinery and apparatus	27.96	6711.4	10.17	16.91	−36	133	16.70	75	1.44	26,350
Machinery and equipment, n.e.c.	24.98	8790.3	8.17	9.04	−50	229	−0.33	69	1.79	40,080
Transport equipment	12.38	5261.9	5.93	2.60	−44	393	4.37	80	−3.66	122,048
Other manufacturing	12.08	3285.5	8.44	15.23	−91	317	−10.12	74	−0.66	52,612
Collection, purification and distribution of water	0.87	441.0	3.09		85	174	−9.90	46	−6.99	31,731
Transport and storage	−0.21	1435.5	0.17		174	1341	−2.73	69	2.02	166,603

(Continued)

Table 6.2 (Continued)

	Evolution of imports share	Imports share	Evolution of offshoring		Evolution of employment	Employment	Evolution of labor compensation share	Labor compensation share	Evolution of investment rate	Gross output
	Percentage points 1990–94/2005–09	imports as percentage of gross output 2005–09	Index 1 change 1990–94/2005–09	Index 2 change 1990–94/2005–09 (1999/2009 for services)	Thousands 1990–94/2005–09	Thousands 2005–2009	Percentage points 1990–94/2005–09	percentage of VA 2005–09	Percentage points 1990–94/2005–09	Current Mio euros 2005–09
Publishing, audiovisual and broadcasting	−4.85	994.7	−2.15	4.80	39	206	1.25	62	8.28	47,885
Telecommunications	1.76	263.9	2.17	−10.61	−5	170	−2.86	30	−11.21	58,285
Computer and related activities	1.14	257.3	−0.94	9.15	155	296	8.94	73	7.23	59,662
Financial intermediation	−0.79	279.0	−1.17	4.07	108	809	9.79	68	8.56	166,029
Legal, accounting, architectural and engineering activities	−2.92	553.0	−2.37	8.35	283	830	−15.36	69	1.36	161,822
Research and development	1.56	995.2	1.71	8.40	25	151	13.71	87	18.35	36,812
Advertising, market research and other technical activitie	0.49	579.2	0.46	12.96	47	245	4.93	62	5.09	29,697
Other businessservices n.e.c.	0.89	466.0	0.25	6.24	716	1594	5.45	64	7.62	168,798
Other service activities	1.37	246.3	−1.37		125	524	0.64	63	−0.26	40,178

Source: INSEE Supply-Use tables 1990–2009, benchmark year 2005, INSEE employment statistics. The offshoring measure is the Feenstra-Jensen index (see Section 2).

does not confirm such an evolution: the indicators that we use point to a sustained and continuous increase in goods and services offshoring and even an acceleration since 2002.

Between 1990 and 2009, the share of imports in gross output for all the manufacturing activities (excluding commodities) has increased, sometimes dramatically (see Table 6.2). The same is true for most services industries, with the exception of "Publishing, audiovisual and broadcasting," "Financial intermediation," and "Legal, accounting, architectural, and engineering activities." Regarding the measure of offshoring focusing on inputs (offshoring index 1), the only difference is that "Computer and related activities" and "Other service activities" also experienced a small decline.

This evolution is related to an increase in the import share from developing countries in the case of manufacturing industries, as seen on Figure 6.1. The two offshoring indexes (the first one calculated on the basis of the share of imported inputs in intermediate consumption and the second one based on the share of imports from developing countries in total imports) grow at a similar rate over the period 1990–2009. There is an acceleration in the second decade, showing that France does not follow the consolidation scenario previously mentioned. In the case of services, there is no significant trend in offshoring: the first index is a flat line at a low level. The index is however not as reliable as for goods because of the proportionality assumption in the use of inputs by services industries (in the absence of statistics on trade in intermediate services by using industry). Due to data limitations, we can calculate the second offshoring measure only from 1999 onward and the data show some volatility related to the poor quality of bilateral trade statistics on services. The result is, however, consistent with the first offshoring measure, as no particular increase or decrease can be seen between 1999 and 2009.

In terms of employment, the dynamics of manufacturing and services industries contrast sharply as well. There has been a decline in employment in all manufacturing industries, except "food, beverages and tobacco" (+7,000) and "pharmaceuticals" (+1,000), with a net loss of 762,000 jobs. On the other hand, there has been an increase in employment in all the services industries considered except "telecommunications" (−5000), with an overall net gain of 1,752,000 jobs. This huge shift in jobs allocation represents the major structural transformation of the French labor market, as jobs in manufacturing and services do not have necessarily the same characteristics. However, this phenomenon is partly due to the development of extra and intrafirm outsourcing and the reallocation of labor activities, with some services activities being separated from manufacturing firms. The same jobs that were previously performed in-house in manufacturing firms are now part of services industries. One should therefore not overestimate the scope of the job reallocation. But, as the rest of the chapter will highlight, there are also industries that have really disappeared or are in strong decline following the specialization of the French economy in services activities. Concerning the evolution of the labor compensation share, no general trend appears, with some significant increase and diminution in manufacturing and services activities that we will further analyze.

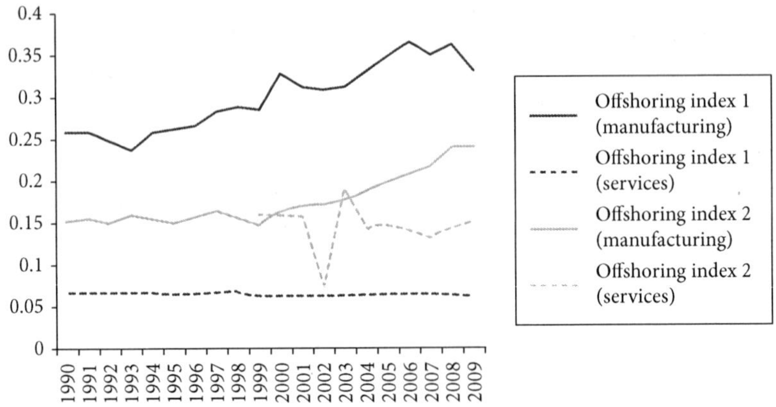

FIGURE 6.1 Offshoring indexes for France (1990–2009).

Comparing 1990–1999 and 2000–2008, a rapid look at the industry dynamics points out two elements (Tables 6.3 and 6.4). First, there is no sign of any significant slowdown in globalization. Between the two periods, the average compound annual growth rate (CAGR) of the import share has increased from 2.04 percent to 3.10 percent. An even clearer acceleration appears for the two indexes of offshoring, with a jump from −0.34 percent to 1.28 percent (offshoring index 1) and from 2.74 percent to 5.31 percent (offshoring index 2). It is worth noting that the phenomenon is especially important for goods but that the trend is much less uniform for services. For example, there has been a decline in "telecommunications" but a further internationalization of sourcing for "other business services" and "advertising, market research and other technical activities."

Second, in most of the sectors and on average, imports were more dynamic than exports in the second period. Consequently, there has been a deterioration of the trade balance (absolute or relative) for all manufacturing sectors, with the exception of "chemicals and chemical products," and for a majority of services activities (Table 6.5).

Finally, in 2009, the evolution of trade in France is consistent with the collapse of global trade (see Table 6.5). We observe a dramatic fall in imports and exports in all the sectors except "chemicals and chemical products," "telecommunications," and "financial intermediation." However, it is striking that in most sectors the decline of imports has been less severe than the decline of exports, resulting in further deterioration of the trade balance in most sectors (except four) and, contrary to the two previous periods, a negative overall trade balance. Concerning offshoring, there is a reduction of inputs offshoring (offshoring index 1) in all the industries except financial intermediation. However, the second offshoring index related to the share of imports from low- and middle-income economies progresses in most of the sectors and in some cases very significantly: in particular, the evolution of "computing products and electrical and optical equipment," "transport equipment," and "telecommunications," but also services such as "computers and related activities" and

Table 6.3 Industry dynamics of offshoring and international trade (1990–1999)

1990–1999	Offsshoring index 1	Offshoring index 2	Import share	Imports	Exports	Total trade balance	Relative total trade balance
	CAGR	CAGR	% of VA; CAGR	CAGR	CAGR	Constant Euros	%; calculated with constant euros
Food products, beverages and tobacco	0.59	−3.05	2.38	2.40	3.10	57,674	13.77
Textiles, textile products, leather and footwear	0.34	3.84	6.76	2.37	2.36	−52,867	−17.54
Wood, paper, paper products and printing	−0.36	−0.82	0.56	1.02	3.16	−25,324	−16.00
Chemicals and chemical products	−1.01	−1.18	2.17	2.51	5.41	30,111	6.41
Pharmaceuticals	0.67	−1.79	9.26	12.78	12.34	15,397	13.00
Rubber, plastic and other non-metallic mineral products	−0.80	6.99	2.57	2.88	3.79	5651	2.49
Basic metals and fabricated metal products	−1.08	−1.09	0.45	0.14	0.37	7555	1.93
Computing products and electrical and optical equipment	1.75	9.78	6.54	5.49	8.19	−48,052	−10.14
Electrical machinery and apparatus	1.25	10.15	4.63	5.63	7.33	8924	4.47
Machinery and equipment, n.e.c.	0.66	5.03	0.75	1.83	3.20	−7511	−1.78
Transport equipment	0.58	−0.39	2.67	4.83	5.84	123,779	16.04
Other manufacturing	0.67	5.43	2.19	2.62	4.16	−12,950	−7.97
Collection, purification and distribution of water	−1.18	n.a.	−2.24	−0.43	−0.24	2592	15.32
Transport and storage	−2.38	n.a.	−1.61	0.30	2.16	−12,231	−4.64
Publishing, audiovisual and broadcasting	−1.18	n.a.	−3.16	0.04	4.64	−24,319	−37.11
Telecommunications	0.03	n.a.	16.15	19.17	22.37	317	4.56
Computer and related activities	−1.06	n.a.	1.95	5.82	29.69	−1218	−15.63
Financial intermediation	−1.47	n.a.	−2.38	−2.07	−3.45	20,552	20.40
Legal, accounting, architectural and engineering activities	−1.48	n.a.	−0.69	2.87	1.87	25,446	17.61
Research and development	−0.40	n.a.	0.34	1.25	1.07	3403	7.43

(Continued)

Table 6.3 (Continued)

1990–1999

	Offsshoring index 1	Offshoring index 2	Import share	Imports	Exports	Total trade balance	Relative total trade balance
Advertising, market research and other technical activities	−0.85	n.a.	0.95	4.06	4.50	−3434	−18.82
	CAGR	CAGR	% of VA; CAGR	CAGR	CAGR	Constant Euros	%; calculated with constant euros
Other business services n.e.c.	−1.19	n.a.	−0.98	1.90	2.99	−789	−1.12
Other service activities	−0.29	n.a.	−0.40	3.84	0.85	1446	20.34
average/total	−0.34	2.74	2.04	3.24	5.44	137,529	4.02
				CAGR imports	> exports		

Note: Figures highlighted in gray are the ones illustrating the trend described in boxes at the bottom of the table. Relative total trade balance is calculated as (exports – imports) / (exports + imports).

Table 6.4 Industry dynamics of offshoring and international trade (2000–2008)

2000–2008	Offsshoring index CAGR	Offshoring index 2 % of total imports; CAGR	Import share % of VA CAGR	Imports CAGR	Exports CAGR	Total trade balance Constant Euros	Relative total trade balance %; calculated with constant euros
Food products, beverages and tobacco	5.54	1.56	3.60	2.86	1.00	51,757	11.30
Textiles, textile products, leather, and footwear	1.94	2.96	5.93	0.05	−0.95	−74,107	−21.39
Wood, paper, paper products, and printing	2.93	3.01	2.13	−1.06	−1.51	−28,866	−16.62
Chemicals and chemical products	7.46	5.47	4.12	1.94	1.36	57,151	9.23
Pharmaceuticals	−0.49	5.18	7.06	5.38	4.91	29,642	10.78
Rubber, plastic, and other nonmetallic mineral products	6.31	4.79	3.93	2.26	0.23	−11,992	−4.34
Basic metals and fabricated metal products	7.12	0.26	4.71	3.46	2.75	−22,052	−4.49
Computing products and electrical and optical equipment	−1.98	8.06	2.60	−3.64	−6.11	−78,359	−12.92
Electrical machinery and apparatus	0.32	5.91	4.95	0.37	0.44	3847	1.41
Machinery and equipment, n.e.c.	1.17	16.01	2.33	1.48	2.05	−16,504	−3.15
Transport equipment	1.01	8.17	5.64	2.16	0.10	179,629	15.86
Other manufacturing	1.64	3.57	3.78	2.49	1.01	−35,177	−16.18
Collection, purification, and distribution of water	1.63	n.a.	4.11	7.99	9.94	10,904	31.81
Transport and storage	0.82	n.a.	1.33	3.82	1.86	−17,081	−5.41
Publishing, audiovisual and broadcasting	−0.69	n.a.	−2.22	−2.23	−3.45	−12,030	−16.93
Telecommunications	−0.95	−5.11	1.71	4.80	6.03	6010	21.81
Computer and related activities	−1.43	n.a.	3.99	6.03	2.17	−281	−1.34
Financial intermediation	−0.92	9.16	−0.61	−1.64	−3.81	3117	3.95
Legal, accounting, architectural, and engineering activities	−0.77	n. a.	−3.81	1.51	−2.52	8641	5.69
Research and development	0.52	n.a.	3.83	3.92	0.43	−1809	−3.73

(Continued)

Table 6.4 (Continued)

2000–2008

	Offsshoring index CAGR	Offshoring index 2 % of total imports; CAGR	Import share % of VA CAGR	Imports CAGR	Exports CAGR	Total trade balance Constant Euros	Relative total trade balance %; calculated with constant euros
Advertising, market research, and other technical activities	0.59	n.a.	1.97	3.61	−3.82	−4968	−23.49
Other business services n.e.c.	0.76	n.a.	5.09	6.89	6.69	9495	8.61
Other service activities	−1.91	n.a.	8.15	9.11	1.99	−964	9.18
Average/total	1.28	5.31	3.10	3.05	0.86	77,509	2.26
	Acceleration: CAGR 2000–08 > 1990–99>0			CAGR imports > exports			Degradation: balance 2000–08 < 1990–99

Note: Figures highlighted in gray are the ones illustrating the trend described in boxes at the bottom of the table. Relative total trade balance is calculated as (exports − imports) / (exports + imports).

Table 6.5 Industry dynamics of offshoring and international trade (2009)

2009

	Offsshoring index 1 Annual % change	Offshoring index 2 Annual % change	Import share % of VA; CAGR	Imports Annual % change	Exports Annual % change	Total trade balance Current euros	Relative total trade balance %; calculated with current euros
Food products, beverages, and tobacco	−13.46	−8.33	2.05	−5.02	−9.18	3379	5.39
Textiles, textile products, leather, and footwear	−3.51	4.07	21.45	−6.72	−10.07	−10,384	−25.12
Wood, paper, paper products, and printing	−9.75	−5.07	−3.24	−13.51	−15.15	−3899	−20.32
Chemicals and chemical products	−14.96	−13.11	0.79	−20.21	−16.67	7497	10.10
Pharmaceuticals	−2.03	17.41	18.36	12.85	7.77	3914	8.23
Rubber, plastic, and other nonmetallic mineral products	−17.48	1.88	−11.42	−13.13	−18.11	−3942	−11.92
Basic metals and fabricated metal products	−19.48	−3.32	−18.67	−31.44	−30.23	−2673	−4.96
Computing products and electrical and optical equipment	−4.38	8.96	4.00	−11.94	−15.95	−13,401	−22.70
Electrical machinery and apparatus	−1.27	2.37	−5.06	−14.34	−17.78	−197	−0.60
Machinery and equipment, n.e.c.	−1.10	11.71	−11.96	−24.37	−23.36	−1692	−2.86
Transport equipment	−2.99	21.18	−8.22	−13.71	−16.45	10,483	8.06
Other manufacturing	−3.35	2.38	−4.76	−3.89	−0.88	−5033	−16.37
Collection, purification, and distribution of water	−14.57	n.a.	−39.97	−47.88	−39.35	1589	40.55
Transport and storage	−3.11	n.a.	−16.04	−17.31	−18.27	−3743	−9.36
Publishing, audiovisual, and broadcasting	−5.33	29.23	−6.74	−5.79	−5.64	−1718	−22.01
Telecommunications	−0.15	36.43	28.35	25.41	7.57	637	13.58
Computer and related activities	−3.05	99.39	−1.66	−3.79	−8.63	−325	−12.35
Financial intermediation	0.42	−17.06	−11.47	6.84	3.03	527	5.59
Legal, accounting, architectural, and engineering activities	−3.40	−2.29	−1.00	−3.89	−0.63	−92	−0.49
Research and development	−4.21	−1.90	−6.63	−0.68	−5.51	−791	−11.72
Advertising, market research, and other technical activities	−2.25	0.14	−5.15	−13.95	−20.55	−1152	−47.33
Other business services n.e.c.	−3.12	−4.17	8.44	0.79	−11.09	317	1.67

(Continued)

Table 6.5 (Continued)

2009	Offsshoring index 1 Annual % change	Offshoring index 2 Annual % change	Import share % of VA; CAGR	Imports Annual % change	Exports Annual % change	Total trade balance Current euros	Relative total trade balance %; calculated with current euros
Other service activities	−7.33	n.a.	−1.45	1.10	−11.28	−459	−26.39
Average/total	−5.83	9.00	−2.92	−7.11	−13.69	−20,487	−4.86
	Acceleration: growth2009>CAGR 2000–08>0			CAGR imports > exports			Degradation: relative balance 2009<2000–08

Note: Figures highlighted in gray are the ones illustrating the trend described in boxes at the bottom of the table. Relative total trade balance is calculated as (exports – imports) / (exports + imports).

"publishing, audiovisual and broadcasting" (for which data are not available in the previous period), suggests that imports from developing economies have been more resilient than overall trade.

To put it in a nutshell, between the nineties and the first decade of the century, there has been overall an acceleration of globalization. This evolution is very clear for all manufacturing activities but more nuanced in the case of services. The second important trend is the shift of employment from manufacturing activities towards services. Moreover, for most industries, but also at the aggregate level, exports have not increased in line with imports, resulting in a deterioration of the trade balance which even worsens with the crisis. In the context of the collapse of global trade during the 2008–2009 crisis, there has been a better resilience of imports from low- and middle-income economies which highlights the depth trade and industrial relationships established during the past decade with developing and emerging economies.

5 Econometric analysis: Does offshoring in France lead to lower employment and more profits?

Before analyzing the variety of sectoral regimes and identifying differences among industries, we propose in this section an econometric analysis of the data (with all sectors pooled together) in order to test some of the relationships previously discussed between offshoring, employment, and labor compensation.

The first variable that we test is the level of employment in French industries. Following Hijzen and Swaim (2007, 2010) and in line with the analysis of Milberg and Winkler (2010a) previously mentioned, we assume that the impact of offshoring on employment is twofold. First, there is a substitution effect: for a given level of output, firms faced with an increase in labor price turn to outsourcing and demand less domestic labor. This substitution effect can also be interpreted as a technology or productivity effect; a more efficient production process requires less labor. What is important is that for a given output, labor demand falls. Then there is a scale effect: having decreased their costs through offshoring, firms are expected to sell at a lower price and to expand their output, thus increasing employment (keeping constant this time the labor intensity). The scale effect can become a mark-up effect if, in the absence of a competitive market, the reduction in costs is not translated into a reduction of prices and the extra profit is used to invest and increase output with again a positive impact on employment for a given labor intensity. Of course, firms can also use the reduction in costs to increase their profits with no impact on employment (this is why we are also interested in the evolution of the labor compensation and investment). The impact of the scale/mark-up effect and the total impact of offshoring on employment are empirical questions.

As proposed by Hijzen and Swaim (2007), the following labor demand functions can be tested. The first one is the "conditional" labor demand testing the impact of offshoring for a given output, i.e. the substitution/productivity effect:

$$\ln L_{it} = \alpha_0 + \beta_1 \ln Y_{it} + \beta_2 \ln W_{it} + \beta_3 \ln K_{it} + \Sigma_{i=l}^{L} \gamma_l Z_{ilt} \quad (1)$$

where L is the level of employment (in industry *i* for year *t*), Y is gross output, W is the nominal price of variable factors (wage and the price of materials), K the capital stock. The model is augmented with demand shifters, *z*, that include the offshoring measures we have calculated and the share of imports in gross output. An assumption in this model is that capital is quasi-fixed to focus on the shift in labor demand. The capital stock rather than the cost of capital is thus the control variable. Firms determine the profit-maximizing level of labor demand by minimizing the costs of production conditional on output (and the capital constraint).

The second model is the "unconditional" labor demand, testing this time the total impact of offshoring. The assumption is that firms maximize profits for given input and output prices. They choose their optimal mix of inputs and the level of output. The model becomes:

$$\ln L_{it} = \alpha_0 + \beta_1 \ln p_{it} + \beta_2 \ln w_{it} + \beta_3 \ln K_{it} + \Sigma_{i=l}^{L} \gamma_l Z_{ilt} \quad (2)$$

where instead of gross output, p is the price of output.

The results of the estimation of the conditional and unconditional models over the period 1990–2009 can be found in Table 6.6. All the regressions are OLS estimations with year fixed effects and robust standard errors; the variables are in logs. In columns (1) and (5), the Feenstra–Jensen index and the share of imports in gross output are tested as labor demand shifters. We then have two other columns (2 and 6) where the second measure of offshoring (the share of imports from developing countries in total trade) is used. As this measure is collinear with the import share, we run separate regressions.[7] Both the conditional and unconditional models work very well for France. We have a very high R-squared (almost 90 percent). All the variables are significant at the 1 percent level. Controlling for output, nominal prices of factors, and capital stocks, we find a significant and negative relationship between employment and offshoring in the conditional model. As this specification should capture the substitution/productivity effect, this is the expected result. However, there is still a negative (and significant) relationship in the unconditional model capturing the total impact of offshoring on employment. Comparing the two coefficients for the offshoring index 1, one can see that the scale effect is small for French industries and that the substitution effect (loss of jobs) dominates. This result is not surprising as offshoring is particularly strong in manufacturing industries where France has lost a lot of jobs. All job creation, as seen in Table 6.2, is in services industries that have less offshoring.

To confirm this result, we also run the regressions in five-year differences (columns 3, 4, 7, and 8). First, the estimation in differences captures a dynamic view, the impact

Table 6.6 **Regression results: Labor demand functions (1990–2009).**

	Conditional				Unconditional			
	Level of employment		Five year difference		Level of employment		Five year difference	
Dependent variable: employment	(1)	(2)	(3)	(4)	(5)	(6)	(7)	(8)
Output	0.676***	0.461***	0.147***	−0.023				
	(0.065)	(0.071)	(0.052)	(0.042)				
Price of output/price of materials					0.656***	0.454***	0.077*	−0.023
					(0.064)	(0.070)	(0.044)	(0.039)
Wage/Price of materials	0.526***	0.634***	0.500***	0.886***	0.534***	0.636***	0.555***	0.889***
	(0.052)	(0.067)	(0.080)	(0.058)	(0.051)	(0.066)	(0.079)	(0.060)
Capital stock	−0.265***	−0.152***	0.317***	0.129***	−0.256***	−0.145***	0.319***	0.127***
	(0.023)	(0.028)	(0.034)	(0.041)	(0.023)	(0.028)	(0.036)	(0.042)
Offshoring index	−0.230***	−0.211***	−0.028**	−0.027***	−0.228***	−0.212***	−0.023**	−0.027***
	(0.026)	(0.031)	(0.011)	(0.008)	(0.025)	(0.031)	(0.011)	(0.008)
Import share	0.046***		−0.053***		0.048***		−0.050***	
	(0.014)		(0.012)		(0.014)		(0.012)	
2nd offshoring measure (imports from developing countries)		0.509***		0.03		0.532***		0.03
		(0.095)		(0.100)		(0.096)		(0.100)
Number of obs.	640	412	475	273	640	412	475	273
R-squared	0.898	0.933	0.702	0.779	0.896	0.933	0.697	0.779

Note: All variables are in logs. OLS regressions with year fixed-effects and robust standard errors. * significant at 10% ** at 5% *** at 1%.

of the change in offshoring on the change in employment. Long-difference estimations are recommended when working with labor data because of the time it takes for labor markets to adjust (see Hijzen and Swaim 2007). In addition, the advantage of the specification is that any time-invariant unobserved variable does not affect the results. We thus test the robustness of the previous relationship. The R-squared is slightly lower, with the estimation in difference and the offshoring index slightly less significant (at the 5 percent level in the unconditional estimation), but still we confirm the negative relationship between offshoring and employment (this time between the change in offshoring and the change in employment).

Another robust result from the two sets of estimations is that the share of imports in output is positively associated with the level of employment but negatively with the change in employment. The higher the competition in final products (or the offshoring of final assembly), the higher is employment in France in the same sector. But over the period of interest (1990–2009), an increase in the import share is associated with a decrease in employment, suggesting that an intensification of competition in a given sector leads to job destruction. A complementary result is that the share of imports from developing countries (our second offshoring measure) is positively associated with employment in the estimation in levels. It suggests that offshoring to other developed economies is what explains lower employment. The second offshoring measure is however not significant in the estimation in difference (columns 4 and 8), indicating that the positive relationship found between employment and trade with developing economies is static and does not last.

Changing slightly the model, we can also run regressions on the share of labor compensation in value-added, controlling for output, capital stock, and the nominal price of factors. Table 6.7 summarizes the results.

The specification is less robust than the labor demand functions, with a lower R-squared. But the control variables are very significant and the model explains a fair amount of inter-industry variations. The offshoring index is significant and positively correlated with the share of value-added going to labor in the estimation in levels. But the variable loses its significance when estimating the model in difference. While offshoring seems to decrease employment in the labor demand functions, the increase in the share of value-added to labor appears as a paradox. It could be explained, however, by a shift in skills (and thus higher wages paid). But again we cannot overinterpret this result as the coefficient is not robust in the estimation in difference. We have an indication that the import share might be negatively correlated with the share of labor and there the significance in the estimation in difference would appear as the sign of a more robust relationship than for the offshoring index. Regarding the second offshoring measure, the results suggest that the higher the imports from developing economies the lower the share of labor in value-added. But this relationship is not confirmed in the estimation in difference.

Overall, what the econometric analysis suggests can be summarized in three points:

- Because employment increases in services sectors in France where less offshoring occurs, we find a robust negative relationship between offshoring and the level of

Table 6.7 Regression results: Impact of offshoring on labor compensation (1990–2009)

	Dependent variable: share of labor compensation in VA			
	Level		Five year difference	
	(1)	(2)	(3)	(4)
Output	−0.409***	−0.165***	−0.633***	−0.586***
	(0.047)	(0.053)	(0.063)	(0.080)
Wage/price of materials	0.561***	0.362***	0.526***	0.563***
	(0.033)	(0.036)	(0.069)	(0.107)
Capital stock	−0.234***	−0.232***	−0.121**	−0.250**
	(0.028)	(0.029)	(0.052)	(0.097)
Offshoring index	0.150***	0.067***	0.024	0.009
	(0.026)	(0.020)	(0.043)	(0.042)
Import share	0.002		−0.027***	
	(0.017)		(0.009)	
2nd offshoring measure (imports from developing countries)		−0.333***		0.204
		(0.113)		(0.254)
Number of obs	680	432	510	288
R-squared	0.671	0.511	0.258	0.223

Note: All variables are in logs. OLS regressions with year fixed-effects and robust standard errors. * significant at 10% ** at 5% *** at 1%.

employment (both in a static and dynamic way; that is, more offshoring leads also to lower employment). The substitution effect (use of foreign rather than domestic labor) is stronger than the scale effect (higher market shares because production is more efficient with offshoring). In a panel of OECD countries Hijzen and Swaim (2007) find that on average the scale effect is stronger. France appears to be in the same situation as Japan, the United States, and a few other large economies where offshoring does not translate into more productivity.

- Overall, the negative relationship between offshoring and employment does not seem to result from higher competition from developing economies. If more competition in final products sourced from developing countries has an impact on labor, it is through a lower share of value-added going to wages in globalized industries (maybe because of a skill bias).
- Last, the extent to which industries face foreign competition in final goods has a complex relationship with employment. On the one hand, industries in which the import share is higher have a slightly higher level of employment, but an increase in the import share during the 1990–2009 period was associated with a relative decrease in employment. This suggests that French industries have specific difficulties in their integration in the world economy. Together with the lack of scale effect for offshoring, the productivity gains from trade seem elusive in the French context.

In the econometric analysis, we have pooled together all industries. It is time now to look more into the detail of sectoral dynamics. What is found on average to be correlated in the econometric analysis hides contrasted evolutions among industries.

6 Variety of Sectoral Regimes of Offshoring

In order to better understand the variety of dynamics associated with offshoring, we have built an analytical table using the various combinations of results we have for the offshoring measures, import share, labor share, level of employment, and investment rate (see Table 6.8).

On the basis of Table 6.8, we can distinguish three important driving forces related to offshoring. First, in some industries we observe at the same time an increase in the share of imports in output and a strong intensification of offshoring, which suggests that the main phenomenon is the fragmentation of production processes. In some other industries, we also observe an increase in the import share but no strong increase in offshoring; we regard this case as the intensification of competition on final products. The third case is the lack of globalization (at least on the import side), when both offshoring and the import share are decreasing (or growing very slowly). We have used different criteria to characterize the intensity of offshoring in manufacturing and services industries as by definition there are fewer material inputs in services industries and services are less tradable than goods. The contrast is really striking between, on the one hand, manufacturing industries where import shares are above 18 percent in all cases (18.6 percent is the minimum level of imports share for "food products, beverages, and tobacco," and the maximum one—151.5 percent—refers to "computing products and electrical and optical equipment") and, on the other hand, services activities where the highest share is 14.4 percent ("transport and storage") and others are generally below 10 percent. The same difference is observed with the offshoring indexes. It is worth noting that for all manufacturing industries considered in our study, none fits with the no-globalization scenario. This is consistent with our first stylized fact which is that during the period considered there has been a considerable deepening of globalization, although some services appear to have stay apart from such dynamic.

Our analytical table then allows us to distinguish four socioeconomic dynamics at the sectoral level, which can be linked to the three driving forces of offshoring, competition, and no-globalization.

The first socioeconomic dynamic is regressive. Despite a reduction in employment, the profit share and investment rate decrease (i.e., the labor share increases). This scenario corresponds to the decline of activities progressively eliminated by foreign competition ("transport equipment," "wood, paper, paper products, and printing") with net trade worsening.

Table 6.8 A mapping of French industries according to socioeconomic and offshoring dynamics.

SOCIO-ECONOMICS DYNAMICS	DECLINE	FINANCIAL PREDATION	TENTATIVE REBOUND	EXPANSION
DRIVING FORCES	Reduction in employment, increasing labor share and decline in investment rate	Decline in labor share and decline or weak growth in investment rate	Reduction in employment and rise in investment rate	Increase in employment and in labor share
Fragmentation of production process		**Predatory restructuring**	**Offensive restructuring**	**Expansionary insertion in global production networks**
Manufacturing: Increase in offshoring index 1 > 9 index points and increase in imports share > 5 percentage points Services: Increase in offshoring > 1 index point and > increase in import share		Basic metals and fabricated metal products	Rubber, plastic and other non-metallic mineral products	Food products, beverages and tobacco
		Collection, purification and distribution of water Telecom	Electrical machinery and apparatus	Research and Development
			Chemicals and chemical products	
Global competition	**Weakening**	**Financial-driven decline**	**Survival limited to some niches**	**Expansionary insertion in global competition**
Manufacturing: Increase in offshoring index 1 < 9 index points and increase in import share > 5 percentage points	Transport equipment	Pharmaceuticals	Machinery and equipment	
	Wood, paper, paper products and printing	Other manufacturing	Textiles, textile products, leather and footwear	

(Continued)

Table 6.5 (Continued)

SOCIO-ECONOMICS DYNAMICS	DECLINE	FINANCIAL PREDATION	TENTATIVE REBOUND	EXPANSION
Services: Increase in import share > 1 percentage point and > increase in offshoring			Computing products and electrical and optical equipment	Other service activities
				Computer and related activities
No apparent globalization		**Domestic predation**		**Domestic based expansionary path**
Manufacturing: Increase in offshoring index 1 < 5 index points and decrease in imports share Services: Increase in offshoring < 1 index point and increase in imports share < 1 percentage point		Legal, accounting, architectural and engineering activities		Publishing audiovisual and broadcasting
		Transport and storage		Other business services Financial intermediation Advertising, market research and other technical activities

The second dynamic is called "financial predation." In this category, a higher reliance on offshoring has allowed firms to compress the labor share. However, the resulting increase in the profit margin has not been used to reinvest in domestic sectors. On the contrary, investment rates have diminished or do not compensate for the decrease in the labor share. Such a dynamic is consistent with the literature that suggests that globalization and financialization should be analyzed as interrelated phenomena (for example, Milberg 2008). In this context, offshoring allows firms to diminish the cost of their inputs and to shrink the scope of their productive activities, which in turn reduces their productive investment and operating costs. Such a reorganization frees up financial resources to increase share buybacks and dividends as requested by impatient financial markets through the shareholder-value norm. Globalization thus participates in the general transformation of the relationship between financial markets and non-financial corporations, which is called "financialization." "Basic metals and fabricated metal products" appear to be the sole manufacturing sector of this kind and its trade balance deteriorates. Among services industries, "telecommunications" and "collection, purification and distribution of water" belong to this category. De facto protection from competition together with a recent deregulation may be the leading factors explaining the financial predation in these industries, which are nonetheless able to improve their trade balance. Such a phenomenon is probably also important in the retail sector, where global buyers have fueled their profits by cheaper inputs (Baud and Durand 2012), but this cannot be captured in our data (where only the commercial margin is affected to the distribution sector).

In the case of "pharmaceuticals" and "other manufacturing," financial predation occurs despite an increase in global competition and a relative deterioration of the trade balance, paving the way to a progressive decline of the sector while firms try to cope with shareholders requirements. Another important feature is the very existence of strong predatory dynamics in sectors that are relatively immune from global competition and that do not rely on the international fragmentation of production, such as "legal, accounting, architectural and engineering activities" and, to a lesser extent, "transport and storage." In such sectors, the lack of competition (because of trade restrictive measures and heavy regulations) seems to be the source of financial predation.

The third dynamic is that of tentative rebound. In the industries concerned, we observe a decline in employment but at the same time an increase in investment. In the case of "rubber, plastic, and other non-mineral products," there is a small decline in the labor share, which should be linked to a surge in offshoring, which has allowed efficiency gains and then has paved the way for new investments. In "chemicals and chemical products" and "electrical machinery and apparatus," the growth of offshoring is concomitant with an increase in the labor share, which may suggest a shift in intraindustry specialization towards high-skill activities. There is no common pattern for these sectors in terms of trade balance evolution.

Distinct from such an offensive restructuring configuration, we have some sectors where there is at the same time a decline in employment, an increase in investment, and an important increase in the share of imports, but no significant increase in offshoring.

In such sectors, we believe there is a general decline but an intraindustry specialization leading to survival in some niches. Such a dynamic fits very well with the case of "textiles, textile products, leather and footwear" and a similar trend is found for "computing products and electrical equipment" and "machinery and equipment." For all these sectors, the survival scenario is not able to compensate for the pressure of imports and as a consequence there is a decline in net trade.

Finally, we have a set of sectors following an expansionary path along three distinctive ways. First, "food products, beverage and tobacco" and "research and development" are the only sectors that expand both in terms of employment and increasing labor share, while relying more intensively on offshoring. This is the story of a successful globalization, although in the case of the food industry, the positive trade balance is declining.

Interestingly, "other service activities" and "computer and related activities" experience an expansion in the context of increasing competition from imports. Their domestic expansion occurs despite the fact that imports perform relatively better. In the case of "computer and related activities," the trade balance has even improved as compared to the 1990s.

Finally, other services industries expand strongly in terms of employment and labor share but without any significant increase in offshoring or pressure from imports. Relatively immune to the globalization of production, there is no common pattern in the trade balance for these four industries. The implementation of specific industrial policies in the case of "publishing, audiovisual and broadcasting" may be a factor explaining the significant reduction in the trade deficit. In the case of "financial intermediation," the improvement of the wage share is probably related to the surge in wages and bonuses for executives and top-ranked employees, which is a specific feature of this industry (Godechot 2008).

7 Conclusion

To conclude, the evolution of offshoring in France can be summed up in three stylized facts.

The first one is the acceleration of globalization in manufacturing activities. At a higher pace in the 2000s than in the 1990s, the share of imports in output has considerably increased and all manufacturing industries see a significant increase in their offshoring indexes. Beyond this general pattern of strong deindustrialization, we can distinguish three different types of dynamics. On the one hand, there are industries that are truly in decline in the sense that France has no comparative advantage and the open trade regime within the European Union and to some extent beyond it leads to interindustry specialization. Jobs are lost in such industries, as a consequence of interindustry labor reallocations. Then there are industries at the opposite end that are successfully expanding both domestically and internationally and that use offshoring as a source of productivity gains. In such industries, offshoring can be associated with an increase in employment. Most French industries, however, appear to be in between. In some cases, they fight to survive and use offshoring to improve productivity and find niche markets by differentiating products (intraindustry specialization). In some other cases, there are predatory strategies with no long-term prospects, just the postponment of an inevitable decline.

This diversity in outcomes in the French manufacturing sector has implications regarding industrial policy. To provide the right incentives, such a policy should help industries to move from predatory restructuring to tentative rebound. Industries shielded from foreign competition are often leaning towards the scenario of "financial predation" in our analysis, as exemplified by the fabricated metals (e.g., steel) or pharmaceuticals sectors. One can also see that no manufacturing industry is found in the "no apparent globalization" category. Therefore, the question for these industries is no longer whether offshoring should be encouraged or prevented; it has already happened, and the only successful manufacturing industry (in terms of labor outcomes) that we have identified is one with increasing offshoring intensity. Finally, as industrial policy at the sole national level is likely to be constrained, the issue could be better addressed through transnational industrial policy, for example—but not necessarily only—at the European level.

The second stylized fact is the major structural shift of employment from manufacturing to services. Between 1990 and 2009, 762,000 jobs have disappeared in the manufacturing sector, while 1,752,000 have been created in services industries. As previously mentioned, this is partly the result of outsourcing: the fact that the same job that was previously part of a manufacturing industry is now a service provided by an independent firm. But beyond this organizational restructuring of firms, the shift is also the result of the specialization of the French economy in services industries. A major implication of this shift is that France has now most of its jobs in sectors where offshoring is very marginal. This does not mean that globalization does not matter anymore in these industries, as services are essential inputs for manufacturing firms and our analysis has focused on the import and production sides. It should also be noted that it is generally through investment and foreign affiliates that services are "traded," something we do not capture in our data. But because offshoring and more generally cross-border imports are lower in services, we find not surprisingly a negative relationship between offshoring and employment in France. As productivity gains are generally lower in the services sector (Baumol et al. 1989), a challenge for the French economy will be how to face the socioeconomic consequences of this major shift towards services. There are in particular implications in terms of skill content and wage inequalities, but these issues were not covered by our analysis.

Lastly, the third stylized fact is that there is no one-way relationship between offshoring and the labor share. Despite interesting links between financialization and globalization, our data show that patterns are different at the industry level. In some sectors, offshoring is associated with a decrease in the labor share, in some others an increase. There are thus sectors where the fulfillment of the requirement of shareholder value norm and globalization are combined in such a way that the gains from offshoring are not mobilized for investment. But, for some services activities where the level of offshoring intensity is limited, we also observe a decrease in the wage share and a declining investment rate; that is, financialization with a slowdown of accumulation (Stockhammer 2004) but without strong globalization dynamics. Such sectors are often characterized by a lack of competition, allowing firms to not invest. Competition policy or adequate industry regulations appear necessary in such cases. However, part of the story about financialization is not well captured by our methodology as gains from global sourcing by retailers do not appear in the data we are using.

Notes

1. This threshold is chosen according a statistical criterion: a decrease of employment superior to 25 percent is more than a standard deviation below the average change of employment on the period.
2. Offshoring towards North African countries concerns manufacturing activities such as textile, electrical and electronics equipment but also services: call centers (for internet providers, mobile operators, etc.) for low value added activities, but also for high value added activities as computer maintenance or software development.
3. This study updates Biscourp and Kramarz (2007).
4. There are no data for agriculture which is not covered in our analysis. Data for public administrations are available only from 1999 onwards, but we have also excluded this sector from the scope of our analysis.
5. See Kirkegaard (2007) and Agnese and Ricart (2009) for a discussion of the empirical measurement of offshoring.
6. The advantage of using national accounts data is that services are covered as well as goods. But for services industries, the proportionality assumption has to be maintained due to data limitations.
7. The correlation coefficient between the second offshoring index and the import share is 0.45.

References

Agnese, P., and J. E. Ricart. 2009. "Offshoring: Facts and Numbers at the Country Level." Working Paper, IESE Business School, Universidad de Navarra.

Amiti, M., and S.-J. Wei. 2005, "Fear of Service Outsourcing: Is It Justified?" *Economic Policy* 20 (42): 308–347.

Arthuis, J. 2005. "Les délocalisations de métiers de services." In *La globalisation de l'économie et la délocalisation des activités et des emplois*. Commmission des finances, Rapport d'information au Sénat, no. 416, annexe 2, 95–142.

Aubert, P., and P. Sillard. 2005. "Délocalisations et réductions d'effectifs dans l'industrie française," Document de Travail de l'INSEE, n° 2005/03.

Bardhan, A. D., and D. M. Jaffee. 2005. "Innovation, R&D and Offshoring." University of California Berkeley: Fisher Center for Real Estate and Urban Economics.

Bardhan, A. D., and C. Kroll. 2003. "The New Wave of Outsourcing." University of California Berkeley: Fisher Center for Real Estate and Urban Economics.

Barlet, C., D. Blanchet, L. Crusson, P. Givord, C. Picart, R. Rathelot, and P. Sillard. 2007. "Les flux de main d'œuvre et les flux d'emplois dans un contexte d'internationalisation." In *L'économie française, Comptes et Dossiers*, INSEE, Paris.

Baumol, W. J., B. S. A. Blackman, and E. N. Wolff. 1989. *Productivity and American Leadership*. Cambridge: MIT Press.

Baud, C., and C. Durand. 2012. "Financialization, Globalization and the Making of Profits by Leading Retailers." *Socioeconomic Review* 10 (2): 217–240.

Besson, F., and C. Durand. 2006. "Délocalisations de services: quels enjeux pour les politiques publiques." Université Paris 1 Panthéon-Sorbonne: Post-Print and Working Papers, halshs-00135920_v1, HAL.

Biscourp, P., and F. Kramarz. 2007. "Employment, Skill Structure and International Trade: Film-Level Evidence for France." *Journal of International Economics* 72: 22–51.

Boulhol, H. 2004. "Quel impact du commerce extérieur international sur la désindustrialisation dans les pays de l'OCDE?" *Flash CDC Ixis*, 2004–06, 1 July.

Brainard, S. L. 1993. "A Simple Theory of Multinational Corporations and Trade with a Trade-Off between Proximity and Concentration," NBER Working Paper, no. 4269. Cambridge, MA: National Bureau of Economic Research..

Cattaneo, O., G. Gereffi, and C. Staritz (eds.). 2010. *Global Value Chains in a Postcrisis World: A Development Perspective*, Washington, DC: World Bank.

Chanteau, J. P. 2008. "Quantifications et analyse stratégique des délocalisations," *Revue d'Economie Industrielle* 124: 23–50.

Cogneau, D., J.-C. Dumont, and E. M. Mouhoud. 2000. "Regional Integration, Migration, Growth, and Direct Investment: A Reading of the Economic Literature." *Globalization, Migration, and Development*. Paris: OECD.

Cohen, D. 2006. "Les effets du commerce international sur l'emploi dans les pays riches." In *Délocalisation, normes de travail et politique de l'emploi: vers une mondialisation plus juste*, edited by P. Auer, G. Besse, and D. Meda, 29–53. Paris: La Découverte, coll. "Recherches."

Crinò, R. 2010. "Service Offshoring and White-Collar Employment." *Review of Economic Studies* 77 (2): 595–632.

Crozet, M., T. Mayer, and J. L. Mucchielli. 2004. "How Do Firms Agglomerate? A Study of FDI in France." *Regional Science and Urban Economics* 34: 27–54.

Daudin, G., and S. Levasseur. 2005. "Délocalisations et concurrence des pays émergents: mesurer l'effet sur l'emploi en France." *Revue de l'OFCE* 94: 131–160.

De Gimel, L. 2005. "Repères quantitatifs sur les délocalisations industrielles à partir des relations extérieures avec les pays émergents ou à bas salaires." In *Désindustrialisation, délocalisations*, Rapport du Conseil d'analyse économique, edited by L. Fontagné and J.-H. Lorenzi, 163–187. Paris: La Documentation française.

Demmou, L. 2010. "La désindustrialisation en France." *Document de Travail de la DGTPE*, 1, February.

EMCC (European Monitoring Centre on Change). 2006. *Restructuring and employment in the EU: Concepts, measurement and evidence*. European Foundation for the Improvement of Living and Working Conditions. Luxembourg: Office for Official Publications of the European Communities.

Ernst, D. 2006. "Innovation Offshoring: Asia's Emerging Role in Global Innovation Networks." East-West Center Special Report, 10; http://scholarspace.manoa.hawaii.edu/bitstream/handle/10125/12531/SR010.pdf?sequence=1sic.

Feenstra, R. C., and B. Jensen. 2009. "Evaluating estimates of Materials Offshoring from U.S. Manufacturing," In *Measurement Issues Arising from the Growth of Globalization*, edited by S. N. Houseman and K. F. Ryder, 359–378. Washington, DC: W. E. Upjohn Institute for Employment Research and National Academy of Public Administration.

Feenstra, R. C., and G. H. Hanson. 1999. "The Impact of Outsourcing and High-technology Capital on Wages: Estimates for the United States, 1979–1990." *Quarterly Journal of Economics*, 114 (3): 907–940.

Fontagné, L., and J.-H. Lorenzi. 2005. "Désindustrialisation, délocalisations." In *Désindustrialisation, délocalisations*, Rapport du Conseil d'analyse économique, edited by L. Fontagné and J.-H. Lorenzi, 9–131. Paris: La Documentation française.

Freeman, R. 2007. "The Expansion of the Global Labor Supply." In *Global Capitalism Unbound: Winners and Losers from Offshore Outsourcing*, edited by E. Paus. London: Palgrave Macmillan.

Geishecker, I. 2008. "The Impact of International Outsourcing on Individual Employment Security: A Micro-Level Analysis." *Labour Economics* 15 (3): 291–314.

Glyn, A. 2007. *Capitalism Unleashed*. Oxford: Oxford University Press.

Godechot, O. 2008. "'Hold-up' in Finance: The Conditions of Possibility for High Bonuses in the Financial Industry." *Revue Française de Sociologie* 49 (supplement annual English edition): 95–123.

Goos, M., A. Manning, and A. Salomons. 2009. "Job Polarization in Europe." *American Economic Review* 99 (2): 58–63.

Guscina, A. 2006. "Effects of Globalization on Labor's Share in National Income." IMF Working Paper, no. 06/294. Washington. DC: IMF.

Hijzen, A., and P. Swaim. 2007. "Does Offshoring Reduce Industry Employment?" Research Paper, no. 2007/24, Leverhulme Centre for Research on Globalisation and Economic Policy, University of Nottingham.

———. 2010. "Offshoring, Labour Market Institutions and the Elasticity of Labour Demand." *European Economic Review* 54 (8): 1016–1034.

IMF (International Monetary Fund). 2007. *World Economic Outlook*. Washington DC: IMF.

Jabbour, L. 2008. "Slicing the Value Chain Internationally: Empirical Evidence on the Offshoring Strategy by French Firms." GEP Working Papers 2, Leverhulme Centre for Research on Globalisation and Economic Policy, University of Nottingham.

———. 2010. "Offshoring and Firm Performance: Evidence from French Manufacturing Industry." *World Economy* 33 (3): 507–524.

Kirkegaard, J. F. 2007. "Offshoring, Outsourcing, and Production Relocation: Labor Market Effects in the OECD Countries and Developing Asia." Working Paper, no. 07–02. Washington, DC: Peterson Institute for International Economics.

Kramarz, F. 2008. "Offshoring, Wages, and Employment: Evidence from Data Matching Imports, Firms, and Workers," Paris: Crest Working Paper.

———. 2011. "Employment and Trade in France: A Firm-Level View (1995–2004)." Contribution to the International Collaborative Initiative on Trade and Employment (ICITE), Paris: OECD, TAD/TC/WP(2011)19.

Lazonick, W., and M. O'Sullivan. 2000. "Maximizing Shareholder Value: A New Ideology for Corporate Governance." *Economy and Society* 29 (1): 3–35.

Lipsey, R. E. 2006. "Measuring International Trade in Services." NBER Working Paper, no. 12271. Cambridge, MA: National Bureau of Economic Research.

Mankiw, G., and P. Swagel. 2006. "The Politics and Economics of Offshore Outsourcing." *Journal of Monetary Economics* 53 (5): 1027–1056.

Markusen, J. R. 2002. *Multinational Firms and the Theory of International Trade*. Cambridge, MA: MIT Press.

Mathieu, E. 1997. "La production industrielle française à l'étranger." *Le 4 pages des statistiques industrielles*, SESSI, 71 (January).

Milberg, W. 2008. "Shifting Sources and Uses of Profits: Sustaining US Financialization with Global Value Chains." *Economy and Society* 37 (3): 420–451.

Milberg, W., and D. Winkler. 2010a. "Financialisation and the Dynamics of Offshoring in the USA." *Cambridge Journal of Economics* 34 (2): 275–293.

———. 2010b. "Economic Insecurity in the New Wave of Globalization: Offshoring and the Labor Share under Varieties of Capitalism," *International Review of Applied Economics* 24 (3): 285–308.

Miroudot, S., R. Lanz and A. Ragoussis. 2009. "Trade in Intermediate Goods and Services." OECD Trade Policy Working Paper, no. 93. Paris: OECD.

Mouhoud, E. M. 2006. *Mondialisation et délocalisations des entreprises*. Paris: La Découverte, Collection Repères.

Orhangazi, O. 2008. "Financialization and Capital Accumulation in the Non-Financial Corporate Sector: A Theoretical and Empirical Investigation on the US Economy, 1973–2003." *Cambridge Journal of Economics* 32 (6): 863–886.

Peoples, J., and R. Sugden. 2000. "Divide and Rule by Transnational Corporations." In *The Nature of the Transnational Firm*, edited by C. Pitelis and R. Sugden, 174–191. London: Routledge.

Stockhammer, E. 2004. "Financialization and the Slowdown of Accumulation." *Cambridge Journal of Economics* 28 (5): 719–741.

Winkler, D. 2009. *Services Offshoring and its Impact on the Labor Market—Theoretical Insights, Empirical Evidence, and Economic Policy Recommendations for Germany* Heidelberg: Springer.

Winkler, D., and W. Milberg. 2009. "Errors from the "Proportionality Assumption" in the Measurement of Offshoring: Application to German Labor Demand." SCEPA Working Paper, no. 2009-12. New York: Schwartz Center for Economic Policy Analysis, New School. http://econpapers.repec.org/RePEc:epa:cepawp:2009-12.

SECTION IB

SMALL, DEVELOPED, AND OPEN ECONOMIES

CHAPTER 7

The Welfare State as an Investment Strategy

Denmark's Flexicurity Policies

ARTHUR DAEMMRICH AND THOMAS BREDGAARD

1 Introduction

Denmark has one of the most comprehensive and expensive welfare states in the world. Social expenditure as a percentage of GDP was 29.5 percent in 2012, compared to 22 percent averaged across the OECD.[1] Taxes are correspondingly high, peaking at a marginal rate of 63 percent for high earners and averaging 40 percent for all taxpayers.[2] The country's value added tax is 25 percent. Nonetheless, Denmark consistently ranks among the most competitive nations of the world. The workforce is well educated, and Danes switch jobs and start new businesses at rates far above those in other welfare states. The Danish version of "flexicurity" is often emphasized as key to understanding this unexpected complementarity between a generous welfare state, a competitive labor market, and entrepreneurial activity (Auer 2000; Daemmrich and Kramarz 2009; OECD 2004; Wilthagen and Tros 2004). Danish flexicurity can be described as a "golden triangle," combining a flexible labor market with low dismissal protection, a relatively generous social security system (notably in unemployment benefits and social assistance), and active labor-market and education policies (Madsen 1999; Bredgaard et al. 2005). Firms in Denmark gain global competitive advantages from a mobile labor force and government funding of public services and infrastructure, while workers benefit from domestic employment opportunities and continuing training.

This chapter examines how the welfare state can serve as a national strategy to invest in economic competitiveness and sustainable national prosperity and looks at the significant challenges associated with operating an open economy in a period of increased labor mobility. By calling the welfare state a national investment strategy we do not seek to argue that a set of leaders explicitly designed Denmark's institutions—welfare programs, citizen and worker associations, and private-sector organizations—and their interrelationships to respond effectively to challenges raised by globalization (Vietor 2007). As in most democracies, in Denmark different groups viewed the goals of economic growth and employment from different vantage points. Flexicurity is only identifiable as a national strategy in retrospective analysis. Yet the interaction of historical legacies, institutional-structural features, and reform-oriented leadership in Denmark combined to position the country and its populace to handle stresses from changing employment more effectively than in many other countries.

Much of the academic literature on labor-market policy is focused on policies for income insurance through unemployment programs and the relationship among welfare benefits, union representation, and ethnic homogeneity (Kahn 2012). This chapter explores Denmark's experiences related to its openness to globalization and shifts in national politics related to immigration and debates over multiculturalism. The sections that follow describe the origins of the Danish welfare state and its history of business–labor relations, the restructuring of welfare and labor policies that occurred in the 1990s, and present and near-term labor-market tensions related to immigration and the globalization of work. We also assess the policy responses in Denmark to the global financial crisis, and their effects on the balance between flexibility and security. Despite signs that the generosity of the welfare state is declining, thus far the basic complementarities between the welfare state and a competitive labor market remain intact. We conclude by assessing the possibilities and impediments for cross-national transfer of policy lessons from the Danish case.

2 Origins and Evolution of the Danish Welfare State

Modern Denmark reflects a long history of independence, but a notable decline in geographic size since the country's peak of military power in the fifteenth century. Perhaps uniquely among contemporary government descriptions of its nation's history, the official website of Denmark recently described the country in terms of lost wars and lost territory: "The present configuration of Denmark is the result of 400 years of forced relinquishments of land, surrenders, and lost battles."[3] Welfare programs, initially designed to moderate the impacts of industrialization on workers, were key to the largely tranquil transformation of the country from a large northern European superpower to a small and prosperous nation.

Although the origins of Danish welfare programs can be traced to "poor laws" enacted in 1708, formal institutions of the welfare state were established starting in the late nineteenth century to reduce tensions among an emerging urban industrial working class (Jonasen 1999; Madsen 2007). Welfare programs then shifted from the "deserving poor" to insure broader swaths of the population against the loss of livelihood due to old age (1891), sickness and chronic disease (1892), unemployment (1907), and disability (1921). The development of the welfare state continued through the interwar period, but accelerated after World War II with expanded social benefits and free education. Universal coverage of retirement (*folkepension*) was approved in 1956 for people over age 65, independent of former employment and income (Jørgensen 2008).

In 1973, a compulsory health insurance program funded through government tax revenue replaced "sickness funds" and other forms of health insurance. An extensive safety net became the norm; even conservative politicians and industry leaders rarely challenged the fundamental principles of redistributionist policies. By the late twentieth century, Denmark's comprehensive welfare state also sought to promote social cohesion and equality through maternity and paternity leave, childcare, and extensive cultural and educational programs. As a result, Denmark is among the world's most equal developed countries as measured by the Gini coefficient of income distribution (see also Table 7.1 for comparative indicators).[4]

Underpinning support for the welfare state, unions and employers' associations negotiate wages, working hours, working conditions, and other aspects of employment through a centralized collective bargaining process. A spirit of give and take has characterized negotiations since the historic "September compromise" of 1899. At the time, unions sometimes employed a tactic of sequential strikes in a particular region. However, when carpenters in several small towns initiated a small strike in April 1899, employers responded with a nationwide lockout. A month later, workers from eleven trades were blocked from employment. Lengthy negotiations ensued, culminating in an agreement that formalized labor negotiations and set the stage for collective bargaining to act as the primary mechanism for resolving disputes, rather than turning to the courts or government intervention (Jørgensen 2002). Trade unions accepted employers' "right to manage" and their authority to hire and fire the number and types of workers that they deemed necessary. Dismissal protection was modest under the agreement. In return, employers accepted the right of workers to join unions and to strike during negotiations on wages, benefits, and working conditions.

Since the September compromise, a scheduled and sequential negotiation process between employers and employees has been governed by cooperation agreements, which also are subject to periodic renegotiation. Cooperation agreements established a variety of rules, including when employees were allowed to strike. As a result, the government is only rarely drawn into the collective bargaining process. Similarly, regulation and implementation of dismissal protection is done through collective agreements negotiated by the social partners for each occupational group. This makes the system flexible and adaptable to the diversity in each occupational and sectoral group. Conflict resolution takes place in a specialized arbitration system administered by the social partners in consultation.

An important exception to this corporatist system is the 1938 law on salaried workers (*Funktionærloven*), which defines a salaried worker as someone who carries out office work, clinical work, or supervises the work of others. The majority of public employees and about half of the employees in the private sector are covered by the law. It stipulates, among other things, a set of dismissal rules, especially notice periods depending on the duration of employment.[5] There is no special protection for public employees, and notice periods and severance pay are comparatively low (Bredgaard 2012). In international comparison, Denmark's employment system is both highly coordinated among employers and unions and rather flexible.

Low job protection is integral to the Danish industrial structure, which is dominated by small and medium-sized enterprises. It is, furthermore, aligned with the long liberal tradition of the Danish welfare state, which relies on social partners—unions and employers—to regulate most of the terms and conditions of the labor market, in contrast to the state regulation found in other countries.

Comparing across developed economies (Table 7.1), Denmark combines an open and competitive economy, low taxes on employers, and high taxes on labor with a flexible labor market governed through collective regulation and bargaining. Whereas countries with high union density and collective wage bargaining typically also restrict

Table 7.1 Comparative indicators of welfare states and unionization

	Income equality (Gini coefficient)[a]	Days to start a business[b]	Corporate tax rate (%)	Income tax and social security (%)[c]	Union density (%)[d]	Collective bargaining coverage (%)	Trade as % GDP[e]	Enabling trade index (global rank)[f]
Denmark	.25	6	25	55	70	87	54	5.41 (3)
France	.33	7	33	41	8	95	28	5.02 (20)
Germany	.28	24	33	45	23	63	44	5.20 (13)
Japan	.25	31	41	50	20	24	17	4.80 (25)
Netherlands	.31	8	25	52	78	82	73	5.26 (10)
Sweden	.25	15	26	56	22	92	51	5.41 (4)
United Kingdom	.36	13	28	50	29	35	30	5.06 (17)
United States	.41	6	35	35	12	14	15	5.03 (19)

[a] World Bank, "World Development Indicators," http://www.worldbank.org, accessed December 2011.

[b] World Bank, "Doing Business," www.doingbusiness.org, accessed December 2011.

[c] The tax rate for a married couple with no children calculated as the total income tax and social security over gross income of $100,000 prior to any deductions. Source: KPMG, "Individual Income Tax and Social Security Rate Survey," www.kpmg.com, accessed December 2011.

[d] Union membership as a proportion of employed wage and salary earners. Source: Visser (2006: data from 2003).

[e] Share of trade in goods and services to the country's GDP. Source: OECD, "OECD Factbook 2010: Economic, Environmental, and Social Statistics," www.oecd-ilibrary.org, accessed December 2011.

[f] Index on scale of 0–6, measuring institutions, policies, and services that enable trade, with subindexes measuring market access, border administration, transport and communications infrastructure, and the business environment. Source: World Economic Forum, "The Global Enabling Trade Report 2009," www.weforum.org, accessed December 2011.

new-business formation and tax capital, Denmark, the Netherlands, and Sweden have followed a different economic strategy. The key to understanding complementarities among interests more typically in conflict with one another is flexicurity.

2.1 Danish flexicurity

The term "flexicurity" came into vogue among Danish policy makers in the early 2000s and soon captured the interest of European Union leaders and analysts worldwide. Attention to the Danish model coincided with an economic upturn (until 2008), declining unemployment, and stable macroeconomic performance. But a balance between labor-market flexibility and income security has characterized the Danish labor market for a century, including during an extended period of persistently high unemployment in the 1970s and 1980s (Bredgaard et al. 2008). We therefore caution that a low and stable unemployment rate is not automatically attributable to flexicurity (see Andersen and Svarer 2007).

In the Danish case, flexicurity should be understood as a historical byproduct of a specific combination of employment flexibility and income security (Wilthagen and Tros 2004). Neither the Social Democratic prime minister Poul Nyrup Rasmussen (1993–2001) nor his successor, the liberal Anders Fogh Rasmussen (2001–2009), invented flexicurity, though both have sought to take credit for it. But important policy changes did occur under both leaders that impacted the balance between flexibility and security.

Starting in the late 1980s, unemployment grew steadily in Denmark to a peak at 12.4 percent in 1993. A brief economic boom from 1985 to 1987 had been halted by a lack of skilled labor and rising inflation. This dilemma placed the concept of "structural unemployment" firmly on the political agenda and paved the way for significant changes of labor-market policies. In 1993, the newly elected Social Democratic coalition government introduced a labor-market reform package. The reforms aimed to motivate the unemployed to seek and take jobs on the ordinary labor market by reducing the length of unemployment benefits and by removing the right to extend unemployment benefits through participation in training and activation programs.[6]

At the same time, reforms sought to improve workplace skills among the unemployed by introducing new individual action plans and education and retraining programs. A key element in the reform package was an expansive fiscal policy to kick-start private consumption and the demand for labor. Finally, there were features in the package that served to reduce labor supply. First, persons participating in active labor-market programs were no longer registered as unemployed. Second, new entitlements for paid leave (parental, educational, and sabbatical) quickly became popular and reduced the labor supply in the short term. These leave schemes were gradually phased out as total unemployment started to fall in the late 1990s.

With these labor-market reforms, the third pillar in the "golden triangle" became more functional in relation to two separate aspects of active labor-market policy: motivating and qualifying the unemployed. The Danish version of flexicurity thus can be illustrated as a parallelogram (see Figure 7.1) in which workers do not simply cycle between employment and unemployment with benefits. Rather, they also may enter active labor-market programs and continuing education, even while still employed.

The *flexible labor market* is characterized by high rates of job turnover and job tenure comparable to liberal economies like the United Kingdom or the United States. High job-to-job mobility is generally found in countries with low dismissal protection.[7] Recent research on the effects of job protection has found that strict regulations can reduce workplace switching; negatively impact some groups of workers, notably youth; and encourage labor-market duality that hinders productivity and economic growth (Venn 2009: 5). Firms in Denmark, by contrast, can fire and hire with few restrictions, and entrepreneurs can start new companies with a minimal amount of bureaucratic delay.

The second element in Danish flexicurity is *generous income security*, especially unemployment benefits and social assistance for the unemployed. One of the main assumptions of flexicurity is that the availability of generous income replacements increases the risk-taking propensities of the labor force, thereby facilitating job mobility. For instance, seasonal unemployment in the construction industry is buffered by supplementary unemployment benefits. As a consequence, employers do not have to dismiss temporary workers. Compared to other OECD countries, Denmark has one of the longest entitlements periods for unemployment insurance (currently two years) and the highest maximum replacement rates for low-wage earners (up to 90 percent of former income). If unemployment benefits are exhausted, or the unemployed individual has not paid contributions into unemployment insurance funds, then means-tested social assistance is available as a last resort (between 60 and 80 percent of unemployment

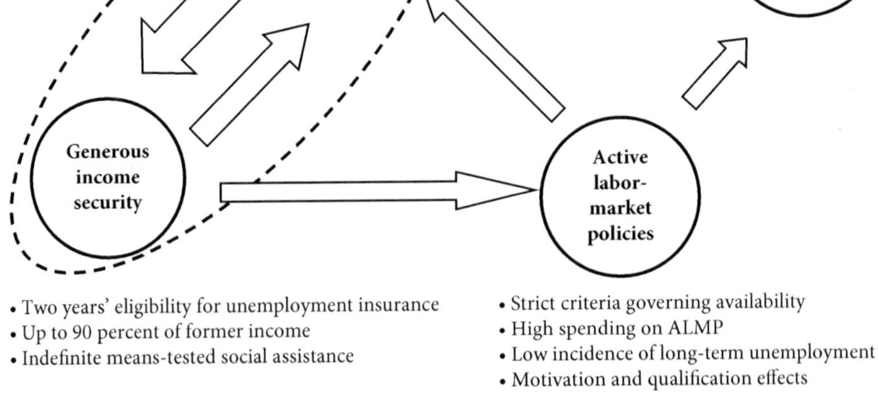

FIGURE 7.1 Danish flexicurity.

compensation, depending on care responsibilities). Unemployed individuals have to demonstrate "labor-market availability" by searching for jobs and participating in activation programs. In international comparison, the Danish rules for showing availability are relatively strict and have been tightened repeatedly during the last decade (Velfærdskommissionen 2005, 96).

The central dimension of complementarity in Danish flexicurity thus requires workers and trade unions to accept low job security offset by relatively generous income security. Companies and employers' associations, on the other hand, accept the costs of the relatively generous income security system because it creates a more flexible labor force.

The third element in Danish flexicurity is *active labor-market policies.* Among OECD countries, Denmark has one of the highest total expenditures on labor-market policies (3.48 percent of GDP in 2010) as well as the highest expenditure on active labor-market policies (nearly 2 percent of GDP in 2010) (OECD 2012). Active labor-market policies have two important and somewhat contradictory functions: first, to motivate the unemployed to find work without assistance, and second, to qualify those who cannot find employment on their own. As a metric of active labor-market policy effectiveness, long-term unemployment rates in Denmark have consistently remained among the lowest across the OECD.

Finally, *continuing vocational training*, or lifelong learning, plays an important role in Danish flexicurity. In international comparisons, Denmark's expenditures and share of training participants is among the highest in the world (Trepartsudvalget 2006). For instance, the Eurostat Labour Force Survey in 2009 found that Denmark had the highest rate of participation in adult vocational training in Europe. More than 30 percent of people aged between twenty-five and sixty-four years had participated in adult vocational training within the previous four weeks compared to a European Union (EU 27) average of 9 percent. Participation in continuing training underpins a flexible labor market by increasing the employability of Danes, improving both their numerical and functional flexibility (Bredgaard et al. 2009).

Although there is no clear-cut causality between flexicurity and unemployment, Denmark's unemployment rate began falling after the introduction of the 1993 labor-market reforms (Table 7.2). Job training and active labor-market policies likely contributed; a recent review of over 100 studies of labor-market intervention programs worldwide finds that job search assistance programs have short-term positive effects while classroom and vocational training reduce unemployment in the medium term (Card et al. 2010). The unemployment rate in Denmark continued falling until the 2008 global financial crisis. Unemployment more than doubled from 2008 to 2011, but remained among the lowest in the OECD.

Throughout the 1990s and the first decade of the 2000s, Denmark enjoyed steady national economic growth and a consistently positive balance of trade in goods and services (Table 7.3). While flexicurity cannot be singled out as the causal force behind this success story, the accommodative pattern of relations between business and labor made for a rather uniquely smooth transition from an economy dominated by manufactured goods and agricultural products to rising international

Table 7.2 Standardized unemployment rates, 1990–2011

	1990	1995	2000	2005	2008	2011
Denmark	7.2	6.8	4.3	4.8	3.4	7.6
France	8.4	11.4	9.0	9.3	7.8	9.7
Germany	4.8	8.0	7.5	10.6	7.3	5.9
Japan	2.1	3.2	4.7	4.4	4.0	4.6
Netherlands	5.9	6.6	2.8	4.7	2.8	4.4
Sweden	1.7	8.8	5.6	7.3	6.2	7.5
United Kingdom	6.9	8.5	5.4	4.8	5.6	8.0
United States	5.6	5.6	4.0	5.1	5.8	9.0

Source: OECD (2012): *Employment Outlook 2012*. Paris: OECD.

Table 7.3 Denmark's balance of payments

(US$ billion, current prices)	1990	1995	2000	2005	2010
Current account balance	1.4	1.9	2.3	11.1	17.1
Exports, goods	36.1	50.3	50.1	82.5	95.8
Exports, services	12.8	15.3	23.7	43.4	60.4
Imports, goods	31.2	43.8	43.4	75.2	87.1
Imports, services	10.2	14.0	21.1	37.0	51.9

Source: IMF, International Financial Statistics, http://elibrary-data.imf.org, accessed December 2011.

trade in services. Exported services including shipping, logistics, and consulting rose from one-third of goods exports in 1990 to two-thirds by 2010. Even a near doubling of imported goods between 2000 and 2010 could be paid for through rising exports of both goods and services. Unlike other small economies on the European periphery (e.g., Greece, Italy, and others) or even large economies like the United States, Danes did not respond to the combination of low borrowing costs and low-cost imported goods from manufacturing powerhouses in Asia by running up large trade deficits.

The complementarity we identify among the flexible labor market, generous income security, active labor-market policies, and education programs, however, are not the product of a deliberate national strategy designed and implemented in a single step. Danish and European Union politicians have become strong advocates for flexicurity in recent years and have sought to distill transferrable policy lessons. We find that the Danish version of flexicurity is the product of a gradual historical, political, and social evolution of welfare and labor-market institutions. While compromise among government, industry, and unions was key to flexicurity's emergence, Danish trade unions ultimately were key to securing the balance between flexibility and security by supporting vocational training and even the offshoring of certain kinds of work as economic transitions associated with globalization were underway.

2.2 Trade unions and globalization

In contrast to unions in many countries that have opposed free trade, open borders, and the offshoring of jobs to lower-wage countries, Danish unions adopted a strikingly different strategy in the 1990s. Opting not to confront industry or the government about workplace changes arising from globalization, they embraced flexicurity as a way to protect employment in Denmark through new job creation. While warning that "the focus must remain on flexibility *for* the employees not the flexibility *of* the employees," unions educated their members about the benefits of trade and which sectors were likely to undergo employment shifts (Danish Confederation of Trade Unions 2008: 6). In contrast to other European countries, the majority of workers remained members of unions even as employment changed from manufacturing to service jobs.

Furthermore, Danes retained union membership even while unemployed. Unionization rates declined significantly in the United Kingdom (from 53 percent in 1980 to below 30 percent by 2005), France (from 19 percent in 1980 to below 10 percent by 2005), and Germany (from 35 percent in 1980 to 20 percent by 2005). In Denmark, union density declined less rapidly and from a much higher level: 77 percent in 1995 to 70 percent in 2005 (Visser 2006). Traditionally, unemployment insurance funds were an additional recruitment channel for trade-union membership. Although there is no legal obligation to join both unemployment insurance funds and trade unions, many members are either not aware of the difference or decide to support the trade union movement when subscribing to unemployment insurance.[8]

Yet the movement of labor across national borders that accompanied globalization in the 1990s and early 2000s posed a challenge for union representation of workers. Officially, the unions walked a fine line between social integration and limits to immigration. The Danish Confederation of Trade Unions (LO), for example, issued a policy statement on globalization that argued: "Foreign labour should be welcome... provided that their employers observe the rules on pay and working conditions agreed between the social partners" (Danish Confederation of Trade Unions 2006: 39).

Rather than demanding employment for life and the retention of uncompetitive manufacturing sectors, Danish unions instead pushed for on-site skills enhancement, retraining of unemployed workers to make them attractive to new industries, and combined employer and government support for education. A 2007 LO report on employee-driven innovation thus emphasized: "It is widely agreed that a substantial part of Denmark's solution to globalization consists of a greater emphasis being placed on training, research, high technology and innovation. [...] If it hadn't been for globalization, Denmark would never have been able to maintain its position as one of the richest countries in the world at a time when competition grows increasingly fierce" (Danish Confederation of Trade Unions 2007: 6). Even on more controversial issues such as outsourcing, unions came to see workers' interests as aligned with the success of the country. If firms prospered, there would be more jobs even as some manufacturing moved to lower-cost locations.

When the liberal and conservative government of Anders Fogh Rasmussen sought to loosen regulations and lower taxes after 2001, it nevertheless continued to support flexicurity policies. Claus Hjort Frederiksen, the minister of employment, thus argued in 2007: "It is no secret that in Denmark we see flexicurity as an important response to the challenges presented by globalization. It means that enterprises can easily adapt to the changing needs and requirements resulting from globalization. Workers achieve a high degree of employment security and social security" (Frederiksen 2007).

Unions helped define a new concept of employment security as globalization changed the kinds of industries that prospered in Denmark. The outgoing head of LO argued in a speech at the annual party congress in 2007 that:

> When I was young, security meant having a good, solid job. This was not very exciting—but in a way, it was very safe. This security disappeared as globalization emerged. Security is no longer to hold on desperately to the same job throughout your life. Security is to stay cool when you hear rumours of outsourcing from the boardroom. Because deep down you know that you have solid skills and that you will quickly be able to find a new job if the old one is relocated. Security is not to be able to stay on. Security is to be able to move. It is precisely this new security through training and education that we have now embarked on creating for every worker.[9]

Echoing their union leaders and government officials, Danes felt secure that if they lost their jobs, they could find employment again quickly. Despite the low levels of formal job protection, there was—at least until the global financial crisis—a high feeling of job security among all subgroups of Danish workers (Auer 2007). In a Eurobarometer survey from 2005, more than 70 percent of Danes agreed it was "good for people to change jobs every few years," in contrast to fewer than 30 percent of Germans, Austrians, or Poles (European Foundation 2006). The positive attitude toward globalization in the Danish population meant that a similar Eurobarometer survey in mid-2008 found that 78 percent of respondents in Denmark agreed globalization was a good thing for domestic companies and would foster job growth, compared to a European average of 39 percent.[10]

Danes held a more positive view on globalization despite shifts in employment that workers in other countries found threatening and disruptive. Over the course of the past two decades, employment in traditional heavy industries, including agriculture, mining, manufacturing, and construction dropped by more than 25 percent (Table 7.4). Vocational training that was integral to flexicurity programs helped workers in traditional sectors to generate greater output despite lower total employment, and to produce niche products that sold globally. At the same time, investments in education made it possible for Danes to transition to new positions in service industries.

Few countries have resolved how to compensate the losers from globalization. Unrestricted welfare programs promote free riders and retraining programs assume

Table 7.4 Employment in Denmark

	1997	2000	2005	2010
Agriculture, forestry, fishing, and mining	120,590	107,877	92,228	79,056
Manufacturing, utility services, and construction	650,457	648,012	584,391	489,447
Trade, tourism, transportation, information, and communication	656,585	686,476	660,267	723,949
Financial, real estate, and insurance	296,343	344,225	382,021	388,748
Public administration, education, health, arts, and entertainment	931,801	962,198	979,560	989,353
Other	13,882	10,520	11,995	14,439
Total	2,669,658	2,759,308	2,710,462	2,684,992

Source: Adapted from Statistics Denmark (www.statbank.dk), accessed December 2011.

governments can predict which industries will succeed domestically in the future. Yet Denmark managed the transitions associated with our current era of globalization through negotiated compromises among unions, industry, and political parties. The country promoted skilled labor and high-value employment at globally competitive firms, even as it maintained the world's most generous welfare system. Consequently, Denmark over the first decade of the 2000s defied long-standing expectations that high taxes and extensive income redistribution inevitably lead to underinvestment by individuals to develop marketable skills and by firms to develop new products and services.

Denmark's labor-market reforms also countered the prediction that a decline in demand for unskilled work in developed countries, a product of the relocation of labor-intensive production to developing countries, would disproportionately hurt smaller rich countries. The economist Paul Krugman argued in the 1980s and early 1990s that shifts in the relative demand for skilled and unskilled labor was increasing unemployment in Europe (Krugman 1994). Yet when the political scientist Peter Katzenstein examined the economic disruptions confronting small states operating in world markets, he observed that they had historically adjusted policies in ways that sustained both openness to globalization and their unique welfare states (Katzenstein 1985, 2006). Denmark and other small countries had firms that nimbly filled niche markets; government monetary and fiscal policies were flexible, reactive, and incremental; and the political system had a tradition of pragmatic compromise among labor, industry, and parties. Katzenstein argued that "exposed to global markets that they cannot control, the small European states have accommodated themselves to a situation that Americans are now beginning to experience as a crisis" (1985: 38). Denmark's structural policies thus built on a historical foundation of responding to economic change thrust upon the country.

Even as Denmark reconfigured its welfare state, the country's prosperity, open borders, and liberal conception of citizenship also made it attractive to immigration. Significant tensions emerged concerning access to education, training, and welfare programs as well as the political and social values displayed by new immigrants, especially those from predominantly Muslim nations. As a result, just as Denmark was on the vanguard of reforming the classic welfare state in the 1990s, it has since been on the leading edge of calling into question aspects of immigration and labor mobility that are often ignored or downplayed in analyses of globalization.

3 Immigration and the Politics of Employment

Thanks to its northern location and small economy compared to Germany or France, Denmark was not a significant immigration destination until the last two decades of the twentieth century. Despite their ethnic homogeneity, Danes historically defined themselves primarily around shared values rather than ancestry, religion, or racial composition. Political, workplace, and many social activities are carried out through organized associations, with more than a million associations registered in Denmark. The country is noted for its equality, social responsibility, personal involvement in the good of the community, and high rates of participation by women in the workforce. For most Danes, the welfare state is an integral part of that self-conception, and democratic values are seen as part of the Danish identity. Danes consider democracy not just a form of government but also a way of life (Campbell et al. 2006).

In the initial post–World War II growth period, small numbers of immigrants were invited to Denmark from Turkey, Pakistan, Morocco, and Eastern Europe to work in manufacturing. During the first oil crisis of the early 1970s, a backlash in the form of restrictions on residency permits led to a slowing of immigration. A second wave of immigration began in the 1980s with refugees from Iran, Iraq, and Palestine, and continued in the 1990s with refugees from Somalia and Bosnia. Denmark's population by the early 1990s had grown to 5.1 million, with the vast majority identifying themselves as having Danish ethnic heritage. Alongside refugees, a new influx of immigrants working in blue-collar jobs and agriculture started in the 1980s and accelerated in the 1990s. With a domestic fertility rate of 1.7 (below the 2.1 needed to maintain a constant population), Denmark has come to rely on immigration for population growth and to fill undesirable jobs. As a consequence, the population composition changed significantly from 4 percent identified as of non-Danish origin in 1990. By 2010, immigrants and their offspring made up more than 10 percent of the country's 5.5 million inhabitants.[11]

Studies of welfare states have repeatedly suggested that homogeneity is critical to popular support for redistributionist policies (Alesina et al. 2001; Campbell and Hall 2009). In line with this finding, immigration also became politically contentious in Denmark, even though in both absolute and relative terms it was on par with other European countries, and even lower than some. Immigration became sufficiently contentious that the Danish People's Party (Dansk Folkeparti, or DPP) won thirteen seats (out of 179 seats in total) in the parliament starting in 1998. When a new coalition government led by Anders Fogh Rasmussen was forged in 2001 between Liberals and Conservatives, it came to rely on the DPP for votes to pass new legislation. The DPP, whose share of the popular vote grew from 7 percent in 1998 to nearly 14 percent in 2007, used strong nationalistic rhetoric during campaigns. The DPP introduced a distinctively anti-multicultural discourse into Danish politics with warnings that "Denmark is a paradise for fanatics who, with human rights in hand, will turn Denmark into a multi-ethnic society."[12]

While the Social Democrats and other left-of-center parties adopted pro immigration platforms, a series of controversies over free speech and democratic values put them on the defensive. Though reiterating the principle that "Solidarity... means automatic rejection of racism and animosity towards foreigners," Social Democrats grew concerned about the failure of recent immigrants to integrate into Danish society and adopt progressive values concerning, among others, the role of women in society (Danish Social Democrats 2005; Hedtoft 2003).

The issue came to a head in the wake of political cartoons depicting the prophet Mohammed and other icons of Islam that were published in the Danish paper *Jyllands-Posten* in 2005. Reprinted in early 2006, they set off protests throughout the Muslim world. At their most violent, crowds of protesters set fire to Danish embassies in Syria, Iran, and Lebanon. More than 70,000 Pakistanis took to the streets in protest in February 2006, and eight people were killed in 2008 when a powerful bomb ripped through Denmark's embassy in Islamabad. To many Danes, these protests suggested that Muslims—including immigrants to Denmark—held views on freedom of speech and press that were irreconcilable with Danish values. Even after the issue calmed through dialogue and the passage of time, the DPP took advantage of shifting demographics to repeatedly warn of risks to core Danish principles from immigration.

Migration and integration issues have calmed in recent years due to the more imminent political and policy attention to the financial crisis and rising budget deficits. In 2010, the DPP supported the liberal-conservative government's major retrenchment package, which included halving the period of eligibility for unemployment insurance (from four to two years), a freeze on municipal budgets until 2013, and proposals to reduce the length and generosity of early retirement benefits. In return, the DPP demanded increased border controls to fight organized crime by foreigners entering Danish soil, a measure which drew international media attention for its conflict with the Schengen agreement's principles of free movement of goods and people in the European internal market.

However, following the general election in October 2011 a new government, led by the Social Democratic prime minister Helle Thorning Schmidt repealed the border control legislation. Yet, a key party of the ruling coalition (Radikale Venstre) called for reform to early retirement policies as a precondition for its support. As a consequence, reforms to key welfare state policies are likely to move forward, with potential consequences for the core deal between labor and business that makes flexicurity work.[13]

4 Danish Flexicurity and the Global Financial Crisis

Broadly, the development of the Danish welfare state and employment system displays a hybrid character between the liberal welfare states characterized by high flexibility for employers and the generous Nordic welfare regimes characterized by high security for employees. To date, this hybrid model has managed to reconcile the dynamic forces of the free market economy with the social security of the universal welfare states. Some observers have been inclined to consider the balance unstable and bound eventually to become either fully liberal or a completely coordinated market economy (Hall and Soskice 2001). But it is evident that the Danish case of flexicurity is the result of a long evolutionary development and supported by relatively stable institutions and class compromises. Crucial in this institutional configuration is the legitimacy of strong and organised social partners capable of striking negotiated and flexible labor-policy agreements.

Nevertheless, Danish flexicurity is not a static policy program without tensions and challenges. The global financial crisis that started in 2008 and European debt crises of the past three years have brought four key conflicts to the fore that challenge the Danish flexicurity model's core principles.

First, Danish workers have begun to demand greater job protection. Since the beginning of the financial crisis in September 2008, registered unemployment has almost tripled, from 2.5 percent (2008, third quarter) to 6.1 percent (2012, second quarter). Around 175,000 jobs were lost between 2008 and 2010 (about 6 percent of total employment). It is, therefore, no surprise that the general feeling of job security has declined. Trade unions responded quickly. In 2009, they succeeded in achieving a new right to severance pay in the private sector. Dismissed employees became entitled to special severance pay, with double or treble the compensation upon six or eight years' seniority. The severance is calculated as the difference between the monthly unemployment benefit payment and the previous monthly wage, reduced by 15 percent. By itself, the new benefit will not sharply alter the flexibility of the labor market, but is has opened a path to raising the costs of firing employees that may be expanded in future collective bargaining.

Second, income security has declined in recent years. Demands by unions for greater job protection therefore are also a reaction to the decline in the generosity of unemployment benefits. While Denmark's net compensation rate is high for low-wage earners and the long-term unemployed by international comparison, it is surpassed by other countries for high-wage earners with short durations of unemployment. All types of welfare benefits, including unemployment benefits and social assistance, are regulated each year on the basis of average wages, minus a 0.3 percent deduction and excluding pension contributions. Since the mid-1980s, deductions and exclusions have led to a substantial decline in compensation. For the average blue collar worker, the net compensation rate has declined by 25 percent since 1982. In the current economic climate, the unemployment benefit period was reduced to two years. The relative decline in unemployment generosity has negatively affected both the support for the balance between employer flexibility and employee income security. Perversely, it also is reducing the likelihood that workers will voluntarily join the unemployment insurance system. As membership in unemployment insurance funds and trade unions declines, the legitimacy of the Danish model of voluntarist and flexible labor-market regulation declines as well, producing increased political pressure for state legislation.

Third, active labor market policies and adult vocational training policies have also been changed in the last decade. Since the liberal-conservative government took office in 2001, there has been a stronger focus on the motivation effects of employment policies, rather than improving worker qualifications. This is indicated by fewer opportunities for participation in education and training for the unemployed and instead a stronger focus on short-term job training and job search assistance accompanied by stronger sanctions for noncompliance. Changes have been characterized as a shift from "human capital" towards "work first" approaches (Larsen 2009). Reforms were implemented by a new and more local delivery structure consisting of municipal job centers, private employment service providers, and private unemployment insurance funds (Bredgaard 2011). Policy changes to the content and organization of employment policy coincided with a dramatic decline in registered unemployment. Consequently, until the beginning of the financial crisis changes to employment policies were largely invisible and untested at scale. However, during the crisis the "work first" approach quickly became unpopular and was shown to be ineffective as unemployment rose. The current social-democratic led government intends to shift the balance back towards "human capital" investments.

The adult vocational training system also underwent changes since 2001 that created challenges when unemployment spiked after 2008. At present, unskilled workers are less likely to participate in vocational training compared to other occupational groups. This is problematic in light of a skill bias in technological industries and the response to globalization by firms in Denmark of seeking creative and self-motivated workers. The financial crisis and the economic recovery plan of the government challenged the vocational system by reducing spending and cutting entitlements to training courses. However, the new Social Democratic coalition government has pledged to return to higher levels of spending on vocational training.

Fourth, mutual trust has declined. Dialogue and compromise between the social partners and the government are enabled by mutual trust and have been an important precondition of flexicurity in its pioneering countries, Denmark and the Netherlands (Wilthagen and Tros 2004). Trust between the trade unions and Anders Fogh Rasmussen's liberal-conservative government suffered a blow during the economic crisis, especially following the shortening of the unemployment benefit period and changes to the early retirement system. Similarly, the Social Democratic coalition government intended to strike a major tripartite labor market agreement with the social partners in early 2012, but failed.

Generally, mutual trust between the government and the social partners is an important precondition for the balance between external flexibility and security. The government must trust that the social partners are capable of regulating the labor market through collective agreements, necessitating an ability to compromise and implement policies that cover the entire labor market. In return, the social partners are granted institutionalised voice in the formulation and implementation of policy decisions on labor-market issues.

Similarly, the level of trust between the trade unions and the employers association and a climate of collaboration on workplace policy is vital for reaching balanced compromises and negotiated solutions. This is not to imply that conflicts do not exist or that the actors have inherently common interests, but rather that the viability of flexicurity requires a high level of social capital and trust to reach negotiated combinations of flexibility and security (Bredgaard et al. 2005).

5 Conclusions

The specific Danish combination of external numerical flexibility, income security, and employment security is the result of bargains struck over time as the country's employers and workers adjusted to economic change. While Denmark's social welfare institutions became a national strategy to invest in creating a well-trained and flexible workforce, it was not the product of a deliberate or recent policy plan. This makes Danish flexicurity impossible to export in a single step to other contexts where other institutional preconditions prevail. This is not to say that rapidly developing middle-income countries or other OECD members may not be inspired by the European welfare policy discourse in general, or by Danish flexicurity specifically.

More generally, Denmark offers an example of the tensions countries face when finding a balance between forces of globalization, in particular, greater trade in goods and services, free capital flows, and the offshoring of manufacturing jobs, and domestic social welfare policies. The Danish economy grew in the 1990s and 2000s through probusiness policies, labor-market reforms, and structural adjustments. Companies headquartered in Denmark learned to operate globally as niche players, while associations representing employers and workers together fostered public support for international trade and even the offshoring of jobs in many industries. The emergence of a new framing for employment security around education and mobility rather than holding the same job for a long period gave Danish companies a competitive edge and made Denmark an attractive European location to foreign firms.

In the 1980s and 1990s, some analysts held that small countries would find it impossible to maintain their social-welfare offerings in the face of impending growth in international trade and shifts in manufacturing to more populous and low-wage countries like India and China. As it turned out, Denmark and some other small northern European countries were able to reform their labor markets and offset the outsourcing of manufacturing with domestic growth of high-value jobs in services, design, and other areas. A new concept of employment security—based on skills and mobility—helped Danes adjust to changing economic conditions. Public consensus evolved to support international trade agreements and lower barriers to the flow of goods and services. The lack of large domestic markets helped companies in Denmark think globally at an early stage, leading to competitive advantages. At the same time, low corporate taxes and few restrictions on layoffs stimulated growth and provided incentives for foreign firms to invest in Denmark. Government revenues were used to provide public education, health care, and unemployment benefits that gave workers security even when jobs moved overseas. Rather than suffer as a small state in the global economy, Denmark prospered.

The welfare state proved more flexible than many analysts had expected and served to resolve dilemmas associated with growing international trade, manufacturing and services shifting to low-wage countries, and the consequent displacement of entire job categories. Unsurprisingly, Denmark's economic growth and generous welfare programs also made it attractive to immigrants. Importing specialists and technical experts is critical in a small country of five million people with a growing economy; furthermore, the process of upgrading domestic workers into better wage jobs left gaps in unskilled work filled by foreigners, and Danes' liberal values supported open borders for refugees.

As immigration increased in the 2000s, tensions emerged regarding the sustainability of welfare offerings in light of many immigrants' attitudes and preferences concerning women in the workforce and education of their children. Within Denmark, the Danish People's Party brought concerns about immigration to a head, forcing the prime minister to walk a fine line between continued integration with the EU and domestic concerns about multiculturalism. This raises a fascinating contradiction found in many countries: without domestic support, free trade agreements and open borders are not possible, but as economies grow at differential rates, those with significant in-migration find it difficult, if not impossible, to sustain the same political support for openness.

Academic studies of welfare states have found that redistributionist policies arise more frequently and are less politically contentious in more ethnically and racially homogenous nations. Following this line of argument, diverse countries like the United States have minimal social-welfare programs because its citizenry lacks solidarity with the notion that taxes will pay for benefits for people who do not look or act like them. There is no doubt that Denmark originated its welfare state in a period of cultural homogeneity. The interesting question now is whether a strong welfare state can build solidarity and help even quite diverse subgroups learn to view one another as sharing collective goals and values. Alternatively, Denmark may be at a tipping point of losing its historical collective support for the social-welfare state as it becomes more diverse. Growing trade in goods, services, and new dimensions of the "creative economy"—all key features to the current era of globalization—are linked to tensions concerning immigration. Greater diversity often promotes greater innovation. But even countries seeking to foster creativity and innovation cannot easily select who will immigrate. On a positive note, Denmark's experiences suggest that social welfare programs that are thought to inhibit innovation and economic growth can instead do the opposite, if properly designed and calibrated to changing economic conditions.

Contrary to a dominant view among free-market purists, the welfare state helps make globalization possible. Without broad domestic support, free-trade agreements (that benefit elites) are not possible, but without sharing benefits, broad support cannot be maintained. For Denmark, immigration is vital to the economy's future. But this is bringing to the fore tensions about ethnic and political identity. Denmark has a strong history of building solidarity and helping subgroups view one another as sharing collective goals and values. Who is a Dane does not have to be answered in terms of ethnicity or the number of generations one's family lived in Denmark; it can be answered through the development of values around work and participation in the public sphere.

Finally, many countries can take a modest but significant lesson from the Danish ability to find a common vision across industry, unions, and political parties. Globalization has made all countries relatively smaller and more exposed to the world, even the United States. Yet there is little to suggest that countries reform automatically in the face of outside pressure. Rather, it requires commitment and negotiated compromise to strike grand bargains that support continual retraining (and not just at moment of high unemployment in a business-cycle downturn) and provide a better social safety net for people whose jobs are most at risk from international competition.

Notes

1. Social expenditure includes public and private expenditures on pensions, survivor's benefits, incapacity-related benefits, health, family benefits, active labor-market programs, unemployment benefits, housing and other social policy areas (Adema et al. 2011).
2. Skatteministeriet, "Marginal Tax for all Taxpayers," www.skm.dk, accessed December 2011.
3. "About Denmark: History," www.denmark.dk/en/menu/About-Denmark/History, accessed February 2009.
4. World Bank, "World Development Indicators," www.worldbank.org, accessed July 2011.
5. The notice period for salaried workers is three months after one year's employment, four months after five years employment and six months after ten years employment. For construction workers the similar notice periods are three days, five days, and five days. For industrial workers they are twenty-one days, two months, and three months (Madsen 2007: 27).
6. Before the 1993 labor-market reform, the unemployment benefit period could in practice be indefinite because participation in active labor-market programs earned the participant a new period of unemployment benefits. When this link was removed, the maximum period became seven years (divided into three years of passive support, and four years with obligations to participate in active labor-market programs). In the later part of the 1990s, the maximum period was reduced to five years and then four years. In 2010, the maximum period was reduced to its current length of two years.
7. Since the early 1990s, the OECD has published measures on the strictness of employment protection as a composite index of protection for permanent workers against (individual)

dismissal, specific requirements for collective dismissal, and regulation of temporary forms of employment. From 1995, the Danish summary indicator has remained unchanged (1.5) and is consistently among the lowest in the OECD (Venn 2009).

8. There are indications that the close link between unemployment insurance funds and trade unions has eroded. This is seen in the increasing membership of "alternative/Christian" trade unions that oppose the right to strike and have few or no collective agreements (from 53,000 members in 1995 to 173,000 members in 2011). Another indication is the increase in the number of unorganized workers from 685,000 in 1995 to 879,000 in 2011. (Ibsen et al. 2011).
9. H. Jensen, "President's Statement" LO's 35th Ordinary Congress, October 28–31, 2007, www.lo.dk/englishversion/congress2007.aspx, accessed February 2009.
10. European Commission, Directorate-General Communication, "Eurobarometer 69: Public Opinion in the European Union," June 2008, 46, http://ec.europa.eu/public_opinion/archives/eb/eb69/eb_69_first_En.pdf, accessed November 2012.
11. Statistics Denmark, data series KRBEF3, www.dst.dk/homeuk.aspx, accessed January 2009.
12. P. Kjærsgaard, the leader of Dansk Folkeparti, interviewed in the newspaper *Jyllands-Posten* (January 20, 2002).
13. In January 2011, the former government proposed to gradually phase out early retirement benefits. Key elements of the reform will postpone retirement from age sixty to sixty-three and reduce the entitlement period from five to three years. Despite the change of government in October 2011, the new social-democratic led government could not build a majority to repeal the reform.

References

Adema, W. P., P. Fron, and M. Ladaique. 2011. "Is the European Welfare State Really More Expensive? Indicators on Social spending, 1980–2012; and a Manual to the OECD Social Expenditure Database (SOCX)." OECD Social, Employment and Migration Working Papers, no. 124. Paris: OECD.

Alesina, A., E. Glaeser, and B. Sacerdote. 2001. "Why Doesn't the U.S. Have a European-style Welfare State?" National Bureau of Economic Research, Boston, MA, Working Paper, no. 8524.

Andersen, T., and M. Svarer. 2007. "Flexicurity: Labour Market Performance in Denmark." *CESifo Economic Studies* 53 (3): 389–429.

Auer, P. 2000. *Employment Revival in Europe: Labour Market Success in Austria, Denmark, Ireland and the Netherlands*. Geneva: ILO.

———. 2007. "In Search of Optimal Labour Market Institutions." In *Flexicurity and Beyond*, edited by H. Jørgensen and P. K. Madsen, 67–99. Copenhagen: DJØF.

Bredgaard, T. 2011. "When the Government Governs: Closing Compliance Gaps in Danish Employment Policies." *International Journal of Public Administration* 34: 764–774.

———. 2012. "Flexibility and Security in Employment Regulation: What Can Be Learned from the Danish Case?" In *Employment Regulation after the Standard Employment Contract*, edited by H. Arthurs and K. Stone, 179–197. New York: Russell Sage.

Bredgaard, T., F. Larsen, and P. K. Madsen. 2005. "The Flexible Danish Labour Market: A Review." CARMA Research Paper 2005: 01. Aalborg: Centre for Labour Market Research.

———. 2008. "Flexicurity: In Pursuit of a Moving Target." *European Journal of Social Security* 10 (4): 305–325.

Bredgaard, T., F. Larsen, P. K.Madsen, and S. Rasmussen. 2009. "Flexicurity på Dansk." CARMA Research Paper 2009: 02. Aalborg: Centre for Labour Market Research.

Campbell, J. L., and J. A. Hall. 2009. "National Identity and the Political Economy of Small States." *Review of International Political Economy* 16 (4): 547–572.

Campbell, J. L., J. A. Hall, and O. K. Pedersen (eds.). 2006. *National Identity and the Varieties of Capitalism: The Danish Experience*. Montreal: McGill-Queens.

Card, D., J. Kluve, and A. Weber. 2010. "Active Labor Market Policy Evaluations: A Meta-analysis." *Economic Journal* 120: F452–F477.

Daemmrich, A., and B. Kramarz. 2009. "Denmark: Globalization and the Welfare State." Harvard Business School, case 709-015.

Danish Confederation of Trade Unions. 2006. *Denmark in a Globalised World*. Copenhagen: Landsorganisationen i Danmark.

———. 2007. *Employee-Driven Innovation*. Copenhagen: Landsorganisationen i Danmark.

———. 2008. *A Flexible Labour Market Needs Strong Social Partners*. Copenhagen: Landsorganisationen i Danmark.

Danish Social Democrats. 2005. "Policy and principles." October 20. http://socialdemokraterne.dk.

European Foundation for the Improvement of Living and Working Conditions. 2006. *Mobility in Europe: Analysis of the 2005 Eurobarometer Survey on Geographical and Labour Market Mobility*. Dublin: European Foundation for the Improvement of Living and Working Conditions.

Frederiksen, C. H. 2007. "Pathways Towards a Better Combination of Flexibility and Security." Paper to the European Commission conference "Pathways Towards a Better Combination of Flexibility and Security," 20 April.

Hall, P. A., and D. Soskice. 2001. *Varieties of Capitalism: The Institutional Foundations of Comparative Advantage*. Oxford: Oxford University Press.

Hedtoft, U. 2003. "Cultural Transformation: How Denmark Faces Immigration." www.OpenDemocracy.Net, accessed February 2009.

Ibsen, F., L. Høgedahl, and S. Scheuer. 2011. *Kollektiv Handling: Faglig Organisering og Skift af Fagforening*. Copenhagen: Nyt fra Samfundsvidenskaberne.

Jonasen, V. 1999. *The History of the Danish Welfare State in Denmark*. Aarhus: National Danish School of Social Work.

Jørgensen, H. 2002. *Consensus, Cooperation and Conflict: The Policy-making Process in Denmark*. Cheltenham: Edward Elgar.

———. 2008. "Flexible Labour Markets, Workers' Protection, and the 'Security of the Wings.'" CEPAL Serie Macroeconomía del Desarrollo, no. 76. Sandiago: United Nations.

Kahn, L. 2012. "Labour Market Policy: A Comparative View on the Costs and Benefits of Labor Market Flexibility." *Journal of Policy Analysis and Management* 31: 94–110.

Katzenstein, P. J. 1985. *Small States in World Markets: Industrial Policy in Europe*. Ithaca: Cornell University Press.

———. 2006. "Denmark and Small States." In *National Identity and the Varieties of Capitalism: The Danish Experience*, edited by J. L. Campbell, J. A. Hall, and O. K. Pedersen, 431–441. Montreal: McGill-Queens.

Kitromilides, Y. 2011. "Deficit Reduction, the Age of Austerity, and the Paradox of Insolvency." *Journal of Post-Keynesian Economics* 33: 517–536.

Krugman, P. 1994. "Past and Prospective Causes of High Unemployment." *Federal Reserve Bank of Kansas City Economic Review* 79: 23–43.

Larsen, F. 2009. *Kommunal Beskæftigelsespolitik: Kommunale Jobcenter Mellem Statslig Styring og Kommunal Autonomi*. Frederiksberg, Denmark: Frydenlund Academic.

Madsen, P. K. 1999. "Denmark: Flexibility, Security and Labour Market Success." Employment and Training Papers, no. 53. Geneva: International Labour Organization.

———. 2007. "Distribution of responsibility for social security and labour market policy country report: Denmark." Amsterdam Institute for Advanced Labour Studies, Working Paper, no. 07/51.

OECD (Organisation for Economic Co-operation and Development). 2004. *Employment Outlook*. Paris: OECD.

———. 2012. *Employment Outlook*. Paris: OECD.

Trepartsudvalget. 2006. *Livslang opkvalificering og uddannelse for alle på arbejdsmarkedet: Rapport fra trepartsudvalget*. Copenhagen: Finansministeriet.

Velfæ rdskommissionen. 2005. *Fremtidens velfærd: Sådan gør andre lande*. Copenhagen: Velfærdskommissionen.

Venn, D. 2009. "Legislation, Collective Bargaining and Enforcement: Updating the OECD Employment Protection Indicators." OECD Social, Employment and Migration working paper, no. 89. Paris: OECD.

Vietor, R. 2007. *How Countries Compete: Strategy, Structure, and Government in the Global Economy*. Cambridge, MA: Harvard Business School Press.

Visser, J. 2006. "Union Membership Statistics in 24 Countries." *Monthly Labor Review* 129: 38–49.

Wilthagen, T., and F. Tros. 2004. "The Concept of 'Flexicurity': A New Approach to Regulating Employment and Labour Markets." *Transfer: European Review of Labour and Research* 10 (2): 166–187.

CHAPTER 8

THE IMPACT OF OVERSEAS R&D ON DOMESTIC R&D EMPLOYMENT

MATTHIAS DESCHRYVERE*
AND JYRKI ALI-YRKKÖ**

1 INTRODUCTION

The offshoring practices of firms have been moving up the value chain, also affecting R&D activities. From a home-country perspective a major concern is that overseas R&D starts to replace domestic R&D and that this hollows out the National Innovation System (NIS) and threatens the human capital accumulation (UNCTAD 2005). Decreasing costs of communication and coordination encouraged multinationals to think about their organization as a matrix with different tasks feedings into their range of products and services (Bardhan 2006). This evolution led to a fragmentation of the value chain allowing all or parts of the matrix cells of the firm to move abroad in search of lower costs, other efficiency gains, and/or access to skilled labor and new market opportunities. The fact that global competition occurs now on a task level explains why offshoring or relocation practices move up the value chain, eventually affecting R&D activities (Baldwin 2006).

Figure 8.1 shows the recent evolution of R&D activities in the Finnish private sector (R&D personnel). Until 2006 there was a clear upward trend in R&D personnel but lately that development has come to a hold. This chapter focuses on the role of R&D relocation abroad in explaining changes in domestic R&D employment. According to Freeman (2005), the fact that MNEs are building R&D facilities in developing countries is one of the logical consequences of a declining comparative advantage of high-tech in the West. Relocation dynamics in R&D have been found to favor R&D employment in developed Asia, putting not only the United States but also Western Europe under pressure (Thursby and Thursby 2006; LTT 2007). R&D offshoring triggers direct

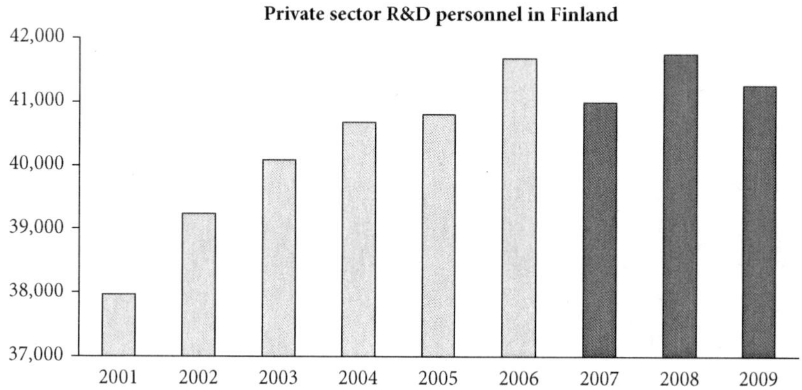

FIGURE 8.1 Recent evolution of R&D personnel in the Finnish private sector.
Source: Statistics Finland, Science and Technology Statistics.

job displacement and potentially redirects R&D job growth to lower-cost developing nations (Kenney and Dossani 2005). Although there seems to be enough evidence that R&D offshoring gained momentum (see also Hall 2011), empirical papers that look deeper into the effects of R&D offshoring on the home country are scarce (Ali-Yrkkö and Deschryvere 2008). Our empirical analysis makes an attempt to fill a part of that important research gap by focusing on the impact of R&D offshoring on the labor market of the home country. To us, this seems to be a necessary step towards a better understanding of the impact of R&D offshoring on the home country's NIS.

The contribution in this chapter is an empirical analysis of the consequences of international sourcing of R&D for domestic R&D employment. Our analysis builds on the literature of service offshoring but specifically looks at the offshoring of R&D services, an exceptional kind of service inputs. The process of R&D offshoring involves a relocation of R&D tasks to a foreign country and implies that (a part of) the output of the R&D tasks will now be produced abroad and will have to be imported as intermediate R&D inputs. The analysis is based on survey data on international sourcing from Statistics Finland and builds on earlier work that looked at the effect of R&D offshoring on expected R&D employment (Ali-Yrkkö and Deschryvere 2008). As Finland has an open economy that scores high in innovation rankings, the available data offer an interesting opportunity to analyze R&D offshoring. The final sample contains 464 medium-sized and large firms that all had R&D employees in Finland at the time of the survey.

We contribute to the literature in two respects. First, we address the statistical relationship between R&D offshoring and a subsequent change in R&D employment in the home country. In this respect, our results are twofold. Our basic statistical results indicate that the overall short-term relationship between R&D relocation and R&D employment in the home country is not statistically significant. However, R&D offshoring does have statistically significant impact when we separated different offshoring channels (captive offshoring and offshore outsourcing). We found evidence that relocating R&D to foreign affiliates has a negative relationship with domestic R&D employment, whereas relocating to foreign subcontractors has a positive relationship with domestic R&D employment. Second, we assessed the consistency of answers on R&D offshoring surveys. Comparing answers for a subsample of firms that answered both available surveys brought to light that answers on R&D offshoring can differ for a rather large share of firms. The available data also allowed for an ex post comparison of expected R&D employment changes with the actual R&D employment changes. Differences between both variables were surprisingly high. The results advocate being prudent with the construction and use of R&D surveys.

The chapter proceeds as follows. The section 2 covers a brief review of the literature on which we base the formulation of three hypotheses. Section 3 describes the survey data and lists the sample properties. Part 4 describes the methodology. Section 5 presents the econometric results and section 6 concludes.

2 Literature review

2.1 Effect of overseas relocation of R&D on domestic R&D employment

Originally influenced by the international trade literature, a group of studies focuses specifically on the effects of service offshoring on relative labor demand for skilled white collar workers (Crinò 2007). Traditional studies are based on trade theory, and state that service offshoring leads developed countries to specialize in high skill intensive service tasks, in line with the standard law of comparative advantage.

Studies following a new approach are based on the theory of firm organizations and hierarchies and state that it is not the skill intensity of the tasks that matters but the ease in the tradability of the services. The key point is that global competition occurs now also on a task-by-task basis and not only on a firm-by-firm and sector-by-sector basis (Baldwin 2006; Grossman and Rossi-Hansberg 2006a; Grossman and Rossi-Hansberg 2006b). In practice, the tasks that show tradability characteristics are mostly routinized and low-skill intensive. As such both approaches lead to the same conclusion: developed countries' service offshoring will shift relative labor demand in favor of high-skilled white-collar workers (Antràs et al. 2006). Based on the above conclusions and the fact that R&D activities are a special form of services it could be expected that firms would offshore the R&D tasks that are tradable. Whereas the expected effect of the offshoring of R&D would be that it would shift relative demand for domestic R&D employees to the most skilled—demanding or strategically important—R&D tasks.

A priori, the effect of service offshoring on net employment is not clear as it depends on several factors such as the time frame considered, the labor mobility, and the level of disaggregation (Amati and Wei 2005a; Jaffee 2004). In the short term a researcher who loses his job in a certain firm because of offshoring could be unemployed but after that he probably can get a research job in another firm. Due to the flexibility of service workers the net employment effect for the R&D sector is eventually zero but in the long term adverse effects could rise as the comparative advantage in R&D shifts, or offshoring of initially nontradable R&D increases. In a labor market with rigidities, the offshoring of tasks, in our case R&D tasks, can affect the labor demand through three channels (Amiti and Wei 2005b). First, a substitution effect operates through the price of R&D inputs. A fall in the price of imported R&D services would lead to a fall in labor demand if R&D labor and R&D services are substitutes. Second, if offshoring leads to an improvement of productivity the same R&D output can be produced with less R&D inputs. Baldwin and Okubo (2006) find that when countries are asymmetric, the small country firm is more likely to offshore its R&D activities into the large country than conversely. This firm migration accelerates productivity gains in the big nation while reducing productivity gains in the small nation. Third, offshoring can affect labor demand through a scale effect. An increase in R&D offshoring can make a firm more efficient and competitive, increasing demand for its output and hence labor. In sum, offshoring may have a positive or negative effect on employment depending on whether the scale effect outweighs the negative substitution and productivity effects. However, conditional on a given level of R&D output, offshoring is expected to reduce the demand for R&D labor. This leads us to formulate the **first hypothesis** (H1) we test in this analysis: **Relocated R&D replaces domestic R&D**.

In the literature the very few studies looking at the labor-market effects of R&D offshoring have been complemented with an important category of studies looking at the innovation-system effects and welfare effects of R&D offshoring. That is, R&D offshoring may lead to a decline of capacity for innovation. The scale of this effect depends on the nature and composition of the R&D (OECD 2007). In addition, effects of R&D offshoring depend on international spillover effects. There is some empirical and theoretical evidence that innovations and new findings developed abroad spill back domestically. Kiyota (2005) found that the positive effect of FDI-related (captive offshoring) R&D spillover effects last longer than import-related (offshore outsourcing) R&D spillover effects, though both accelerate productivity growth. This international diffusion of technology advocates that the effect of R&D offshoring should be analyzed on the technological potential of the country (OECD 2008). For the United States and other Western countries, developing new ways of benefiting from scientific and technological advances in other countries is one of the keys to easing the adjustment to a less dominant position in science and engineering (Freeman 2005). Gersbach and Smutzler (2006) took even a broader perspective when assessing the effects of R&D offshoring on the welfare of the home country. They found that based on a two-country model, the relocation of R&D activities increases domestic welfare since relocation only occurs if intrafirm communication is well developed and therefore knowledge generated and obtained abroad flows back to the domestic country.

2.2 The overseas relocation of R&D is gaining momentum

Global competition gradually eroded the comparative advantage of the West in high-skilled jobs in general and in science and engineering specifically (Freeman 2005), fueling the offshoring of high-skilled jobs and high-tech jobs. In the last ten years R&D offshoring has been steadily increasing but its relative weight and its strategic importance are said to be still limited (European Commission 2006).

Recent or planned facilities central to the firm's current R&D strategy on average only make up 15 percent of all technical employees worldwide (Thursby and Thursby 2006). However, looking at the offshorability of jobs by sector and occupations reveals that one could expect the relocation of R&D tasks to continue. In a paper of van Welsum and Vickery (2005), tasks that can potentially be offshored are defined on the basis of four criteria: (1) intensive use of ICT; (2) an output that can be traded/transmitted enabled by ICTs; (3) high "codifiable" knowledge content; and (4) no face-to-face contact requirements. Based on those criteria they found that in the EU15 roughly 40 percent of the R&D sector employment will potentially be affected by offshoring. Autor et al. (2003) look at the tradability of occupations by assessing their share of routine and nonroutine tasks. Applying a similar methodology on Sweden, Nilsson-Hakkala et al. (2008) found that occupations that could consist of R&D tasks, like science professionals, are typically characterized by a high share of nonroutine tasks (between 80 percent and 100 percent) and interactive tasks (between 48 percent and 66 percent). However, these figures do also imply that potentially still 20 percent to 34 percent of the tasks in the science professions are routine tasks and noninteractive tasks and could, it is argued, be more easily traded and offshored.

In addition to direct job displacement, R&D offshoring potentially redirects job growth to lower-cost developing nations (Kenny and Dossani 2005). Not only do big firms engage in offshoring, but also high technology start-ups may, early in their life, start to offshore so as to be more competitive.

2.3 Offshoring channel and industry matter

R&D can be relocated overseas via a range of channels. A firm can either relocate R&D overseas through captive offshoring (via FDI) or through offshore outsourcing (to subcontractors). In addition, the firm can engage in several types of partnerships and joint ventures with other firms, institutions, and universities.

Bardhan (2006) illustrates that firms with a cellular-form organization can offshore different R&D tasks to one or more competence clusters around the world. This leads to much heterogeneity in the R&D that has been offshored and to a dispersed location of technology development. The composition of offshored R&D depends on two main dimensions: the type of technology (familiar technology versus new technology) and the category of market (familiar markets versus new markets). Antràs (2005) states that the transfer of younger technology should be captive offshored so as to minimize incomplete contracts. LTT (2007) states that complex and less codifiable technologies are less frequently offshore outsourced and more frequently captive offshored. Most of the literature on the motivation to offshore R&D focuses on large multinational firms. According to the empirical firm-perspective literature, overseas R&D activities can either be motivated by *support-oriented R&D* or *knowledge-sourcing R&D*. The first and conventional type involves the adaptation of the home-made technology and products to the host country. The second type combines both local and worldwide R&D resources so as to generate new technological knowledge (Ito and Wakasugi 2007). The home-country effects of R&D offshoring depend on what kind of R&D is involved. The fact that firms may prefer different kinds of offshoring channels for different kinds of R&D is important to take into consideration when assessing home-country effects of R&D offshoring (Ali-Yrkkö and Deschryvere 2008). This leads us to formulate our **second hypothesis** (H2) to be tested: **The relation between R&D offshoring and employment varies by offshoring channel.**

The sources of knowledge for innovation between the service sector and the manufacturing sector differ (Leiponen 2008). R&D investments or permanent R&D teams are not very strongly statistically associated with the introduction of new services. Service firms tend to rely more than manufacturing firms on consulting companies as inputs for innovation. Intrafirm training may compensate for formal R&D activities in many service firms. Service innovators utilize formal intellectual property rights much less intensively than good innovators. Service firms tend to rely on confidentiality agreements, lead time, trademarks, and secrecy rather than patents. Based on the above findings it seems appropriate to study the R&D offshoring between the manufacturing and service sector separately. We formulate our **third hypothesis** (H3) as follows: **The relation between R&D offshoring and domestic R&D employment varies by industry**.

3 Data description and sample properties

3.1 Data description

The analysis presented in this chapter is based on new Finnish survey data on international sourcing. The data were collected by Statistics Finland within a project of the Statistical Office of the European Communities (EUROSTAT). The economy-wide ad hoc survey covers the nonfinancial business economy and focuses on larger enterprises (at least fifty employees), as the key players in international sourcing are considered to be multinational groups of enterprises. In the case of Finland a total of 1729 medium-sized firms (between 50 and 249 employees) and large firms (at least 250 employees) were contacted in the second and third quarter of 2007. As the survey was mandatory, most of the companies answered the questionnaire (81 percent), leaving us with an initial sample of 1407 firms. The report by Statistics Denmark (2008) describes the Statistics Finland's survey in more detail.

A comparison of the survey data of Statistics Finland with an earlier set of survey data revealed interesting differences. The earlier set of survey data was collected by ETLA (Research Institute of the Finnish Economy) for the prime minister's office in Finland. The ETLA dataset was used in a paper of Ali-Yrkkö and Deschryvere (2008) that analyses the relationship between R&D offshoring and expected R&D employment. For a general overview of both surveys we refer to the appendix (Table 8.A1). Both surveys had 320 firms in common and returned information on R&D offshoring for the same reference period. In Table 8.1 and Table 8.2 we compare striking differences in the answers to both surveys.

A first finding of the comparison is that a considerable share of firms answered both surveys differently when asked if they relocated R&D abroad in the 2001–6 period. Table 8.1 shows that respondents to the ETLA survey reported their firms to have offshored R&D more often than respondents in the Statistics Finland survey. Out of 14 percent of the total sample reporting R&D offshoring in the ETLA survey only 1 percent of the sample reported R&D offshoring in the Statistics Finland sample. One consequence of this finding relates to the definition of relocation we will use in the analysis. For the sample used in our econometric analysis, we will assume firms to have relocated R&D in the 2001–6 period if they reported this in at least one of the two surveys. Another consequence of the finding is that survey data on R&D offshoring should be treated with care, especially in bigger firms, as the answers to the use of R&D offshoring may depend on which person is contacted. Ideally the setup of a survey would require multiple answers per firm as this would allow us to test the consistency of the answers.

A second important finding of the comparison between both surveys is that expected R&D employment changes and actual R&D employment changes can differ to a great extent. The expected change of R&D employment captures valuable information about the innovative capacity of the firm in the future. Therefore it is a variable that has been collected in R&D surveys (Thursby and Thursby 2006; SEC 2006) and used in empirical analyses (Ali-Yrkkö and Deschryvere 2008). The latest available data from Statistics Finland on the actual evolution of R&D employment allowed for an ex post comparison between the expected R&D employment in the home country and the actual R&D employment

Table 8.1 Comparison of the R&D offshoring dummy between the two surveys

		Relocated R&D (ETLA survey)		
		NO (%)	YES (%)	%
Relocated R&D (Statistics Finland survey)	NO	84	13	97
	YES	2	1	3
		86	14	100

Source: Statistics Finland, ETLA.

Note: The comparison in the above table is based on 320 firms that had information on both variables.

Table 8.2 Expected versus actual R&D employment changes

		Planned to increase R&D employment (expected change)		
		NO (%)	YES (%)	%
Increased R&D employment (actual change)	NO	46	24	70
	YES	15	15	30
		61	39	100

Source: Statistics Finland, ETLA.

Note: The "Increased R&D employment" variable refers to the 2006–8 period and is based on the most recent available Statistics Finland data. The "Planned to increase R&D employment" variable refers to the 2006–9 period and was obtained from the ETLA survey. The comparison in the above table is based on 233 firms that had information on both variables.

evolution in the home country. Table 8.2 compares to what extent the firms' expectations (in 2006) to change their R&D employment in the following three years (2006–9) differ ex post facto from the actual changes of R&D employment (2006–8[1]). As time periods of expected and actual changes do not fully overlap the data in table 8.2 are illustrative and should be carefully interpreted. From the cells in Table 8.2 emerges that in fact only 61 percent of the firms actually changed R&D employment in the home country in the direction they originally reported. An additional finding of interest the table highlights is that the negative expectations (46/61) were borne out more than the positive (15/39).

Intuitively, the expected R&D employment and actual R&D employment can diverge for several reasons. A first reason is the change in macroeconomic context. Uncertainty about the economic outlook may have started to increase already in the second quarter of 2007. It was exactly in the period 2006–8 that the global financial crisis started to unwind and one would therefore expect the share of firms that did increase R&D employment to be lower than the share of firms that originally expected to increase R&D employment. Although 39 percent of the firms said they would increase R&D in the home country, only 15 percent of the sample did what they earlier reported. However, looking at aggregated annual figures of private R&D expenditure in Finland shows that the drop in R&D expenditure did not take place before 2009 (Research.fi 2011). A second reason for divergence can be related to the fact that the respondent does not want to reveal the intentions of the company. R&D survey results can attract a lot of attention from policy makers and respondents may therefore be inclined to bring a too positive or a too negative message. A third explanation of divergence lies in the fact that the management of firms is by nature too positive and always has high expectations. In addition firms act in a highly uncertain environment and often don't know which decisions to make. There is also a difference between long term strategy of the firm and the middle term strategy or tactics that can constantly change along the road. Divergence can further be explained by globalization, as it rapidly transformed the importance of the global organization of R&D activities. In sum, information on expected R&D employment has limited value and results based on that variable cannot be generalized.

As the focus of this analysis is on international sourcing of R&D functions, only firms that had R&D employees in Finland in 2006 were retained. The sample used in our econometric analysis contains 464 medium-sized and large firms. The focus on a sample with only firms with at least 50 employees in Finland—having also R&D employees—creates a selection bias that has to be taken into account when interpreting all results presented in this chapter. Unless otherwise mentioned, all results reported in the remaining chapter employ sampling weights. The next section will describe the descriptive statistics of the sample.

3.2 Sample properties

Table 8.3 shows the descriptive statistics of the data consisting of 464 businesses with 50 or more employees operating in Finland and having reported R&D employees in 2006.

In the first two numerical columns the mean and standard deviation refer to the whole sample. Since we are investigating the relationship between the relocation of R&D abroad and the subsequent change in R&D employment, it is useful to list the same information across the group of firms who did relocate R&D activities abroad and those who did not. The last three columns report the means of firms who did offshore R&D and those who did not, as well as the statistical significance of the difference between these means (a two-sided t-test without assuming equal variances across the two groups).

The first line of Table 8.3 lists our dependent variable, "Decreased firm's R&D employment in Finland" in the period 2006–8. On average about 56 percent of the firms did decrease their R&D employment in Finland during 2006–8. A lower share of firms (35 percent) increased their R&D employment in Finland. That share is higher (at a 20 percent significance level) for firms that did offshore R&D activities abroad. On average Finnish firms reduced their R&D employment with eleven employees during that two-year period. The high average is mainly driven by very large companies. The remainder of Table 8.3 refers to a set of indicator explanatory variables, as well as a couple of noncategorical explanatory variables.

The second section of Table 8.3 lists the shares of firms that relocated R&D abroad. The survey data allow a distinction between two relocation channels. Roughly 10 percent of the firms relocated R&D from Finland during the 2001–6 period. But still more firms (17 percent) outsourced R&D activities domestically. Zooming in on the relocation channels reveals that offshore outsourcing is slightly more common (6 percent) than captive offshoring (5 percent). The fact that some firms used both channels shows that they may be complementary and that they may be used for different kinds of R&D. It is also of interest to note that compared to R&D relocation (10 percent) more than

Table 8.3 Descriptive statistics

	Total			Offshored[b] R&D	Did not offshore[b] R&D	
	Obs.	Mean	S.D.	Mean	Mean	Signif.
Decreased firm's R&D employment in Finland[a]	464	0.56	0.027	0.54	0.56	
Increased firm's R&D employment in Finland[a]	464	0.35	0.026	0.46	0.33	'
Change in firm's R&D employment in Finland (absolute change)[a]	464	−11.35	10.6854	−103.74	−1.46	
Firm: Relocated R&D from Finland to abroad[b]	464	0.1	0.015			
Firm: Captive offshoring of R&D[b]	464	0.05	0.01			
Firm: Offshore outsourcing of R&D[b]	464	0.06	0.012			
Firm: Domestic outsourcing of R&D[b]	464	0.17	0.022			
Firm: Relocated production from Finland to abroad[b]	464	0.22	0.019	0.68	0.17	***
Firm: Captive offshoring of production[b]	464	0.16	0.016	0.52	0.12	***
Firm: Offshore outsourcing of production[b]	464	0.12	0.016	0.43	0.09	***
Firm: Domestic outsourcing of production[b]	464	0.25	0.024	0.53	0.22	***
Firm: Age (years)	461	21.55	1.0864	27.07	20.95	'
Firm: Age (log of years)	461	2.65	0.054	2.76	2.63	
Firm: Infant	464	0.31	0.025	0.31	0.31	
Firm: Old	464	0.33	0.028	0.42	0.33	
Firm: Size in 2006 (Finnish employment)	464	442.26	52.706	879.60	395.48	
Firm: Size in 2006 (log of Finnish employment)	464	5.22	0.0333	5.63	5.18	**
Firm: Small[c]	464	0.34	0.009	0.22	0.36	+
Firm: Mid size (reference)[c]	464	0.32	0.02	0.23	0.33	'
Firm: Large[c]	464	0.34	0.018	0.55	0.32	***
Firm: Multi establishment in 2006	464	0.62	0.026	0.8	0.6	***
Firm: Profitability in 2006 (ROI)	462	14.87	4.266	17.72	14.57	
Firm: R&D intensity	460	0.06	0.007	0.10	0.05	'
Firm: Export propensity in 2006	411	0.9	0.018	0.93	0.9	
Firm: High education employment share	460	0.11	0.006	0.16	0.11	**

(Continued)

Table 8.3 (Continued)

	Total			Offshored[b] R&D	Did not offshore[b] R&D	
	Obs.	Mean	S.D.	Mean	Mean	Signif.
Firm: Med education employment share	460	0.28	0.006	0.32	0.28	*
Firm: Other (low) education employment share	460	0.6	0.008	0.52	0.61	***
Firm: Foreign owner	461	0.26	0.022	0.31	0.25	
Region: Helsinki metropolitain area[d]	464	0.34	0.026	0.46	0.33	+
Region: South	464	0.15	0.018	0.1	0.16	
Region: West	464	0.36	0.026	0.27	0.37	
Region: East	464	0.09	0.016	0.05	0.09	
Region: North	464	0.06	0.017	0.12	0.05	
Industry: Foods, textiles, apparel	464	0.07	0.003	0.06	0.08	
Industry: Wood, pulp, paper	464	0.06	0.007	0.02	0.06	**
Industry: Chemicals	464	0.12	0.011	0.15	0.12	
Industry: Metals	464	0.09	0.003	0.14	0.08	
Industry: Machinery, equipment	464	0.19	0.004	0.1	0.2	**
Industry: Electronics, electronic equipment	464	0.11	0.007	0.18	0.11	
Industry: Other manufacturing (reference)	464	0.12	0.013	0.09	0.12	
Industry: Construction	464	0.04	0	0	0.05	***
Industry: Trade	464	0.03	0.004	0.04	0.03	
Industry: Transportation	464	0.01	0	0.02	0.01	
Industry: KIBS	464	0.15	0.005	0.2	0.14	
Industry: Other services	464	0.01	0.002	0	0.01	***
Industry: Manufacturing	464	0.81	0.006	0.74	0.81	

Notes: [a]Refers to the 2006–8 period; [b]All relocation/offshoring/outsourcing variables refer to the 2001–6 period and are based on combined information from the Statistics Finland and ETLA survey; [c]Small firms are defined as firms with fifty to ninety-nine employees; Mid-size firms are defined as firms with 100 to 249 employees; Large firms are firms with at least 250 employees. [d]Helsinki Metropolitan Area includes Helsinki, Espoo and Vantaa. Statistical significance: $^{***}p < 0.01$, $^{**}p < 0.05$, $^{*}p < 0.10$, $+p < 0.15$, $'p < 0.20$.

twice as many firms (22 percent) relocated (service- or product-) production tasks. For your information a comparison of the use of offshoring of eight categories of tasks is listed in Table 8.A2.

Additional firm-level related variables show that firms that relocated R&D abroad are on average older (twenty-seven versus twenty-one years) and bigger (the average number of employees in Finland: 879 versus 395). Firms with R&D abroad are, on average, more likely to have many establishments (80 percent versus 60 percent) and a higher share of highly educated employees. Almost all of the firms in both subsamples (roughly 90 percent) do have exports. The sizable difference in the means would seem to suggest that firms who relocated R&D abroad are more R&D intensive (10 percent) than firms who did not relocate R&D abroad (5 percent). The difference is statistically significant at a 0.2 level. Interestingly there is no statistically significant difference in terms of profitability. Foreign firms would be expected to offshore R&D more often than Finnish-owned firms. In our sample this turns out to be the case but the difference is not statistically significant. The firms that offshored R&D are significantly less represented in the wood, pulp and paper industry, the machinery and equipment industry, the construction sector and in the category other service sectors. The above results suggest that there may be variation across industries and firm size, therefore, Table 8.4 pays attention to these two dimensions.

Table 8.4 provides us with four main findings. First, compared to manufacturing firms, service firms increased their R&D employment in Finland less often and decreased it more often. This holds for large firms. Second, large firms have relocated R&D more often than medium-sized firms. Third, service firms use the offshore outsourcing

Table 8.4 R&D activities by sector and firm-size (shares of firms)

	All sectors[a]			Manufacturing[b]			Services[c]		
	Total	Large	Medium (%)	Total	Large	Medium (%)	Total	Large	Medium (%)
Increased firm's R&D employment in Finland[d]	35	37	34	35	39	33	33	28	36
Decreased firm's R&D employment in Finland[d]	56	58	54	55	55	55	61	70	56
Relocated R&D from Finland to abroad[e]	10	15	7	9	15	6	13	17	10
Captive offshoring of R&D[e]	5	7	4	4	7	3	5	5	5
Offshore outsourcing of R&D[e]	6	12	3	5	10	3	10	17	6
Domestic outsourcing of R&D[e]	17	28	11	17	28	11	19	32	12
R&D intensity	6	5	6	4	4	4	11	5	14

Notes: [a]Based on 464 observations; [b]Based on a subsample of 376 firms of the manufacturing sector; [c]Based on a subsample of eighty-eight firms of the service sector; [d]Refers to the 2006–8 period; [e]All relocation/offshoring/outsourcing variables refer to the 2001–6 period and are based on combined information from the Statistics Finland and ETLA surveys.

channel more often than manufacturing firms. Fourth, R&D intensity[2] is higher in the service sector, especially for medium-sized firms.

The survey data of statistics Finland also returned information on the drivers of offshoring (see Table 8.A3). For firms that also offshored R&D the main drivers were labor costs (for 83 percent of the firms), pressure from clients and competitors (75 percent) and other costs (72 percent). But it is important to note that drivers can vary by offshoring channel. Captive offshoring is mainly driven by costs savings, entry to market, or improved consideration of customer needs and increasing flexibility, while offshore outsourcing is mainly driven by acquiring technology, knowhow, and capacity and by cost savings (Ali-Yrkkö and Deschryvere 2008).

In addition the data returned information on the impact of offshoring (see Table 8.A4). A positive impact mainly occurred on the level of the competitiveness of the firm and the reduction of labor and other costs. A negative impact may occur on the level of internal knowhow of the firm. This section had a simple look at the data without controlling for the potential impact of any other variable. This will be tackled in the next two sections.

4 Methodology

In modeling the short-term impact of R&D internationalization on R&D employment we consider a firm-level R&D employment equation. Estimating a *logit model* by taking into account the data availability[3] leaves us with the following specification:

$$Employment_{R\&D\ i\ 2006-2008} = \begin{cases} 1\ if\,(Employment_{R\&D\ i\ 2008} - Employment_{R\&D\ i\ 2006}) < 0 \\ 0\ if\,(Employment_{R\&D\ i\ 2008} - Employment_{R\&D\ i\ 2006}) \geq 0 \end{cases} \quad (1)$$

With the measure of domestic R&D employment, $Employment_{R\&D\ i\ 2006-2008}$, equaling 1 if the firm *i* decreased domestic R&D employment in the period 2006 to 2008 or 0 if this is not the case.

The empirical latent model with latent metric $Employment^*_{R\&D\ i\ 2006-2008}$ (the probability that a firm decreased domestic R&D employment in the period 2006 to 2008) becomes:

$$Employment^*_{R\&D\ i\ (2006-2008)} = \beta_1 \left(R\&D\,relocation\ abroad\right)_{i\ (2001-2006)} + \beta_2 X_{i2006} + \varepsilon_{i2006} \quad (2)$$

We stress the fact that the specification in the above equation is not based on any particular theoretical framework. It is thus purely ad hoc and meant to give some indication of the relationship between R&D relocation abroad and a subsequent change in domestic R&D employment. We do not wish to give our regressions a causal interpretation, even if that might in some cases be appropriate, but rather simply uncover the partial correlations. The above specification will return biased estimates if there is a causality or endogeneity problem. This is likely as a firm is expected to make at the same time a decision about its domestic R&D employment and about the use of R&D relocation abroad. However, the time difference between the left hand side and right hand side of equation (2) may reduce these endogeneity problems.

The employment variable on the left hand side of equation (2) represents the probability that a firm decreased domestic R&D employment in the period 2006 to 2008.[4] In choosing the dependent variable to be based on actual employment this analysis follows standard practice of econometric analysis studying the labor-market effects of offshoring. The most frequently used dependent variables have been aggregate employment (on industry or regional level), plant-level employment, or the individual job hazard rate (probability of becoming unemployed). In using freshly available data on actual R&D employment our current analysis adds value to an earlier paper of ours that looked at the effect of R&D offshoring on anticipated R&D employment (Ali-Yrkkö and Deschryvere 2008). Earlier studies that did use the anticipated R&D employment to screen the employment effects of offshoring are mainly descriptive (Thursby and Thursby 2006; Statistics Denmark 2008). Comparing anticipated R&D employment with actual R&D employment for a sample of Finnish firms in section 3.1 revealed that both variables can vary considerably. This certainly puts the value of anticipated R&D employment obtained via surveys into perspective.

The right-hand side of the equation contains variables that capture whether the firm relocated R&D abroad in the period 2001–6 (light-colored bars in Figure 8.1). The international trade literature quantifies offshoring mostly based on the sum of imported intermediate inputs. When taking into account the lack of precise data this seems to be the optimal way to proceed but it also has several drawbacks. A first drawback is that imported intermediate inputs are expressed in money terms and therefore cheaper imports may underestimate the value of offshoring (Amiti and Wei 2005). A second downward bias may originate from the fact that offshoring of the final stages of production will not show up in the figures of imported intermediate imports. In the Finnish case this bias may be considerable as the Finnish market for final goods is rather small (see Ekholm and Hakkala 2006). A third drawback is that it doesn't allow us to make a distinction between captive offshoring and offshore outsourcing. A final drawback of the above measure we mention is that the data on imported intermediate inputs related to R&D and other service-type of tasks are not available in the international trade statistics.

Due to the above-mentioned drawbacks, our analysis will be based on firm-level survey data. The relocation variables on the right-hand side of equation (2) are all dummy variables. The first dummy variable that is used in the analysis tells if the firm relocated R&D activities during 2001–6. The available data also allow us to take into account the way R&D offshoring activities are organized, whether they involve a shift to an independent foreign supplier or a shift to a foreign affiliate belonging to the same group.[5] From the literature we know that the distinction is important, as different channels may have different domestic employment effects because they may be used for different kinds of R&D and may have different spillover effects.

The vector *X* contains a number of (available) control variables that have been identified in the literature as potentially affecting employment. All variables refer to 2006, the year before the survey was sent out. As a proxy for firm size, two dummies are used that tell if the firm is either large or small and where the reference category is the mid-sized firm. To capture information from the plant level, a dummy is used that tells if a firm has more than one establishment or not. Based on previous literature it can also be expected that R&D offshoring influences the R&D employment variable both directly and indirectly (via profitability and R&D intensity). For manufacturing firms R&D intensity was found to positively affect the internationalization intensity of R&D and the offshoring mode of R&D (European Commission 2006). Görg and Hanley (2009) found that offshoring can have a direct impact on R&D intensity and an indirect (lagged) impact on R&D intensity via profitability. Entering these three variables in our specification may possibly lead to multicollinearity and asks for a careful interpretation of those explanatory variables. Profitability is defined as return on investment and is supposed to have a positive impact on R&D employment. R&D intensity is defined as R&D expenses as percentage of turnover and its impact is ambiguous. Also the shares of total firm employment per educational level (high education and low education) are taken into account with the mid-education level being the reference category. A final group of variables that is included in all econometric specifications is a dummy for the Helsinki metropolitan area and industry dummies, which aims to control for any regional and sector-specific effects.

Domestic outsourcing propensities of R&D can give information on the differences in effects between domestic and international outsourcing on the domestic R&D employment (Görg and Hanley 2009). A priori, it is unclear to what extent the effects will be different. To evaluate this, domestic R&D outsourcing propensities will be introduced to test robustness of the effects of the R&D offshoring propensities.

Offshoring in the period 2001–6 may also affect employment sooner or later than 2006–8. Ideally one would allow for more detailed lags but this is not possible as it would require panel data; another reason why panel data would improve our results is the possibility of isolating other firm-specific effects. The R&D employment equation (2) will be run for the manufacturing and service sector separately, because the industries are expected to behave differently. Section 5 tabulates and discusses the results of our multivariate analysis described above.

5 Multivariate analysis

Based on our representative recent cross-section of firms, some clear results can be deduced. However, it is important to stress that results should be interpreted with care.

The first reason that asks for a careful interpretation is the relative small absolute number of firms that relocated R&D abroad. From the descriptive statistics it follows that the analysed sample of 464 firms with R&D returned merely 10 percent of firms that relocated R&D abroad between 2001 and 2006. The second reason for a cautious interpretation of the results relates to problems of endogeneity. The decision on R&D location at home and abroad may be simultaneous implying a dual causality. The final reason advocating a cautious interpretation relates to the multicollinearity between certain variables. For the above reasons we do not wish to give the regressions presented in this chapter a causal interpretation, even if that might in some cases be appropriate, but rather simply uncover the partial correlations. In what follow we present the main test results of our three hypotheses that we deducted from the literature and described in section 2.

The tables in this section list the partial correlations between R&D relocation variables and a subsequent decrease of R&D employment in the home country. As a robustness test the analysis also looked at the relationship between relocation variables and a subsequent increase of R&D employment[6]. All tabulated results of our LOGIT models list the coefficients. As described in the methodology section, all specifications control for variables that turned out to be important for the level of R&D employment. The results of the base-line regression are tabulated in column (a) in Table 8.5.

Our first hypothesis (H1) to be tested stated that "Overseas R&D replaces domestic R&D." In our sample, having relocated R&D abroad (dummy variable) has a positive impact on R&D employment in the home country, but the effect is statistically insignificant. Further results show a positive partial correlation between having relocated R&D abroad and a subsequent increase in R&D employment in the home country, the effect again being nonsignificant. This implies that at first sight there is no firm-level evidence that having relocated R&D abroad is combined with a decrease or an increase in domestic R&D employment. Hence, these results do not support the substitution hypothesis (H1) between foreign and domestic R&D. Looking at the correlation matrix in Table 8.A5 shows that the sign of the correlation between the dependent variable and the main explanatory variables depends on the relocation channel. This finding raises the question if the relocation channel does matter for the employment effect. In columns (b–f) we have studied separately the relationship between those channels and domestic R&D employment.

Our second hypothesis (H2) tests whether the relation between R&D relocation and R&D employment varies by relocation channel. When looking at the mode of relocating R&D activities abroad two major categories of modes can be distinguished, namely captive offshoring and offshore outsourcing.

Column (b) shows that firms that undertook captive offshoring are more likely to decrease their domestic R&D employment, an effect significant at a 0.15 level. This is weak evidence that within firm groups R&D in Finland and R&D at their foreign subsidiaries are substitutes.

Another picture arises—in column (c)—when the internationalization of R&D via offshore outsourcing is concerned. Firms undertaking offshore outsourcing are less likely to decrease their R&D employment and more likely to raise their domestic R&D employment. The latter effect is significant at a 0.05 level indicating that offshore outsourcing of

Table 8.5 Estimation results for the full sample

Dependent variable in LOGIT model: DECREASE in R&D employment in Finland in 2006–08

Full sample; table lists coefficients

	(a)	(b)	(c)	(d)	(e)	(f)
Relocated R&D from Finland (d)	−0.035					
	(−0.10)					
Captive offshoring of R&D (d)		0.824 +		0.998 *		0.963 *
		(1.50)		(1.82)		(1.78)
Offshore outsourcing of R&D (d)			−0.675 *	−0.835 **		−1.306 **
			(−1.67)	(−1.97)		(−2.64)
Domestic outsourcing of R&D (d)					0.284	0.637 *
					(0.93)	(1.72)
Small (d)	−0.169	−0.146	−0.169	−0.145	−0.185	−0.182
	(−0.55)	(−0.48)	(−0.55)	(−0.48)	(−0.60)	(−0.59)
Large (d)	0.051	0.047	0.105	0.112	−0.010	0.023
	(0.21)	(0.19)	(0.43)	(0.46)	(−0.04)	(0.09)
Multi-establishment (d)	−0.274	−0.306	−0.258	−0.291	−0.281	−0.284
	(−1.05)	(−1.17)	(−1.00)	(−1.11)	(−1.07)	(−1.07)
Profitability (ROI)	0.001	0.001	0.001	0.001	0.002	0.002
	(0.76)	(0.76)	(0.81)	(0.82)	(0.85)	(1.05)
R&D intensity	1.066	0.942	1.295	1.211	0.972	1.216
	(0.74)	(0.66)	(0.86)	(0.80)	(0.68)	(0.81)
High educ. empl. share	−2.774 +	−2.729 +	−2.721 '	−2.670 '	−2.681 '	−2.437
	(−1.47)	(−1.46)	(−1.42)	(−1.40)	(−1.42)	(−1.27)
Low educ. empl. share	−0.234	−0.117	−0.259	−0.143	−0.118	0.06
	(−0.23)	(−0.12)	(−0.26)	(−0.14)	(−0.12)	(0.06)
Helsinki metropolitan area (d)	0.507 *	0.511 *	0.524 *	0.532 *	0.504 *	0.536 *
	(1.77)	(1.80)	(1.82)	(1.85)	(1.79)	(1.90)
Industry: Metals	−0.789 *	−0.767 *	−0.709 *	−0.662 +	−0.819 *	−0.655 +
	(−1.87)	(−1.81)	(−1.70)	(−1.58)	(−1.90)	(−1.55)
Industry: Machinery, equipment	−0.418 +	−0.404	−0.426 +	−0.414 '	−0.428 +	−0.448 +
	(−1.46)	(−1.41)	(−1.48)	(−1.44)	(−1.49)	(−1.53)
Industry: Trade	0.378	0.408	0.362	0.395	0.395	0.423
	(0.58)	(0.63)	(0.55)	(0.60)	(0.62)	(0.64)
Industry: KIBS	−0.061	−0.026	−0.060	−0.023	−0.034	0.024
	(−0.14)	(−0.06)	(−0.13)	(−0.05)	(−0.08)	(0.05)
Constant	0.813	0.708	0.81	0.699	0.715	0.506
	(0.93)	(0.82)	(0.93)	(0.81)	(0.82)	(0.58)
Observations	458	458	458	458	458	458
Adjusted Wald test (Model)	1.02	1.175	1.225	1.379 '	1.167	1.6 *
Goodness-of-fit test[a]	0.94	0.53	0.36	0.59	0.51	0.97

Notes: The table lists coefficients. Between brackets are the t-values. Statistical significance: ***p < 0.01, **p < 0.05, *p < 0.10, +p < 0.15, 'p < 0.20. Mid-size is the reference category of size; Mid-education is the reference level of education; Greater Helsinki Metropolitan area includes Helsinki, Espoo, and Vantaa.
[a]The table lists the test results of the F-adjusted mean residual test according to Archer and Lemeshow (2006). Test results were obtained by running the -estat gof- command after -svy: logit- in Stata 11.1. The goodness-of-fit test indicates a good fit for all six specifications in the above table.

R&D abroad and domestic R&D are complementary. The above findings offer evidence in favor of H2. In column (d), both captive offshoring and offshore outsourcing variables were included. The result of this regression is in line with columns (b) and (c).

From the literature (Görg and Hanley 2009) it became clear that a specification that does not include domestic outsourcing may suffer from an omitted variable bias. Domestic outsourcing of R&D can affect the evolution of domestic R&D employment and it correlates with offshoring variables of R&D. Table 8.A5 shows this correlation to be 0.49.

In column (f) we have controlled for this concern by adding the domestic outsourcing of R&D variable in the regression. This addition does not change our results reported in columns (a–d).

In sum, these findings indicate that different modes of R&D internationalization have different impacts on the domestic R&D employment. The obtained results also have implications for the National Innovation System. The literature section paid attention to the heterogeneity of R&D tasks and one should analyze in more detail what tasks are more prone to captive offshoring than others. The results presented in this section are partially in line with Ali-Yrkkö and Deschryvere (2008). The main reasons for the differences are that: (1) companies with less than fifty employees are not included, reducing the share of service-sector firms in the total sample to less than 20 percent (compared to 50 percent); and (2) instead of expected R&D employment changes in the home country the analysis in the current chapter is based on actual R&D employment changes in Finland.

Answering our third hypothesis (H3) requires checking whether the relation between R&D offshoring and domestic employment varies by industry. Findings from the literature (Leiponen 2008) and the fact that the manufacturing and service sector displayed on average different shares of R&D internationalization (Table 8.4) suggest that it is useful to analyze the two industries apart. Table 8.3 shows that the total sample consists of 81 percent of manufacturing firms. The small absolute number of service firms implies that the service-sector results tend not to be significant.

We proceed by analyzing manufacturing and service firms separately using the same specification as in Table 8.5. First we report the results concerning the manufacturing sector (Table 8.6).

In the manufacturing sector, the coefficient of "*relocated R&D abroad*" does not differ statistically significantly from zero. But looking at the relocation channels separately (columns b–d) shows that both channels have significant but opposite effects. If the firm relocated R&D abroad to its subsidiaries (captive offshoring) the effect on domestic R&D employment tends to be negative. Within a company group relocated R&D and home-country R&D tend to be substitutes. This result is in line with the findings in our earlier paper (Ali-Yrkkö and Deschryvere 2008). On the contrary, firms that relocated R&D abroad by externalizing it (offshore outsourcing) subsequently tend to increase R&D employment in the home country. This is an indication that offshore outsourced R&D and domestic R&D are complementary.

Columns (e) and (f) show that domestic outsourcing of R&D does have a negative effect on domestic employment although the effect tends only to be significant in specification (f).

Next, we report the same analysis for the service sector (Table 8.7).

Table 8.6 Estimation results for the manufacturing sector

Dependent variable in LOGIT model: DECREASE in R&D employment in Finland in 2006–2008

Manufacturing sector sample; table lists coefficients

	(a)	(b)	(c)	(d)	(e)	(f)
Relocated R&D from Finland (d)	−0.052					
	(−0.13)					
Captive offshoring of R&D (d)		0.984 +		1.118 ·		1.068 +
		(1.50)		(1.67)		(1.62)
Offshore outsourcing of R&D (d)			−0.776 +	−0.925 ·		−1.312 ··
			(−1.58)	(−1.78)		(−2.26)
Domestic outsourcing of R&D (d)					0.207	0.513 '
					(0.63)	(1.33)
Small (d)	−0.049	−0.044	−0.045	−0.039	−0.059	−0.057
	(−0.15)	(−0.13)	(−0.13)	(−0.12)	(−0.17)	(−0.17)
Large (d)	0.011	−0.010	0.063	0.051	−0.033	−0.015
	(0.04)	(−0.04)	(0.23)	(0.18)	(−0.12)	(−0.05)
Multi-establishment (d)	−0.207	−0.234	−0.204	−0.234	−0.204	−0.217
	(−0.72)	(−0.81)	(−0.71)	(−0.81)	(−0.71)	(−0.75)
Profitability (ROI)	0.003	0.003	0.003	0.003	0.003	0.003 '
	(1.18)	(1.17)	(1.20)	(1.20)	(1.22)	(1.32)
R&D intensity	2.066	2.045	2.149	2.102	2.055	2.116
	(1.01)	(1.00)	(1.01)	(1.02)	(1.00)	(1.01)
High educ. empl. share	−4.059 *	−3.975 +	−3.930 +	−3.802 +	−3.960 +	−3.504 '
	(−1.66)	(−1.64)	(−1.59)	(−1.56)	(−1.61)	(−1.41)
Low educ. empl. share	−0.035	0.145	−0.052	0.128	0.072	0.32
	(−0.03)	(0.11)	(−0.04)	(0.10)	(0.06)	(0.25)
Helsinki metropolitan area (d)	0.739 **	0.732 ··	0.768 ··	0.767 ··	0.721 ··	0.741 ··
	(2.32)	(2.31)	(2.40)	(2.39)	(2.31)	(2.36)
Industry: Metals	−0.775 *	−0.747 ·	−0.687 +	−0.636 +	−0.8 ·	−0.632 +
	(−1.78)	(−1.71)	(−1.59)	(−1.46)	(−1.81)	(−1.45)
Industry: Machinery, equipment	−0.366	−0.349	−0.372	−0.356	−0.375	−0.387
	(−1.23)	(−1.17)	(−1.24)	(−1.19)	(−1.26)	(−1.28)
Constant	0.577	0.423	0.573	0.417	0.482	0.229
	(0.52)	(0.39)	(0.51)	(0.38)	(0.43)	(0.21)
Observations	370	370	370	370	370	370
Adjusted Wald test (Model)	1.453 +	1.67	1.675 ·	1.766 ·	1.492 +	1.817 ··
Goodness-of-fit test[a]	0.34	0.53	0.77	0.82	0.23	1.07

Notes: The table lists coefficients. Between brackets are the t-values. Statistical significance: ***p < 0.01, **p < 0.05, *p < 0.10, +p < 0.15, 'p < 0.20. Mid-size is the reference category of size; Mid-education is the reference level of education; Greater Helsinki Metropolitan area includes Helsinki, Espoo, and Vantaa. [a]The table lists the test results of the F-adjusted mean residual test according to Archer and Lemeshow (2006). Test results were obtained by running the -estat gof- command after -svy: logit- in Stata 11.1. The goodness-of-fit test indicates a good fit for all six specifications in the above table.

Table 8.7 Estimation results for the service sector

Dependent variable in LOGIT model: DECREASE in R&D employment in Finland in 2006–08

Service sector sample; table lists coefficients

	(a)	(b)	(c)	(d)	(e)	(f)
Relocated R&D from Finland (d)	−0.093					
	(−0.11)					
Captive offshoring of R&D (d)		0.283		0.607		0.608
		(0.23)		(0.53)		(0.52)
Offshore outsourcing of R&D (d)			−0.731	−0.874		−1.46
			(−0.79)	(−0.90)		(−1.05)
Domestic outsourcing of R&D (d)					0.226	0.847
					(0.23)	(0.60)
Small (d)	−0.431	−0.382	−0.439	−0.365	−0.454	−0.499
	(−0.45)	(−0.39)	(−0.46)	(−0.38)	(−0.48)	(−0.52)
Large (d)	0.548	0.555	0.662	0.709	0.481	0.571
	(0.74)	(0.74)	(0.86)	(0.91)	(0.60)	(0.70)
Multi-establishment (d)	−0.674	−0.698	−0.631	−0.653	−0.718	−0.737
	(−0.72)	(−0.74)	(−0.69)	(−0.71)	(−0.80)	(−0.82)
Profitability (ROI)	0.001	0.001	0.001	0.001	0.001	0.002
	(0.26)	(0.24)	(0.32)	(0.32)	(0.27)	(0.47)
R&D intensity	0.423	0.291	0.816	0.783	0.292	0.899
	(0.18)	(0.13)	(0.35)	(0.33)	(0.13)	(0.39)
High educ. empl. share	−0.334	−0.345	−0.205	−0.195	−0.411	−0.307
	(−0.09)	(−0.10)	(−0.06)	(−0.06)	(−0.12)	(−0.09)
Low educ. empl. share	−1.796	−1.748	−1.876	−1.843	−1.689	−1.605
	(−0.88)	(−0.86)	(−0.92)	(−0.91)	(−0.82)	(−0.77)
Helsinki metropolitan area (d)	−0.427	−0.406	−0.459	−0.440	−0.376	−0.315
	(−0.49)	(−0.47)	(−0.53)	(−0.51)	(−0.43)	(−0.35)
Industry: Trade	−1.403	−1.420	−1.417	−1.454	−1.379	−1.352
	(−0.79)	(−0.80)	(−0.79)	(−0.80)	(−0.80)	(−0.76)
Industry: KIBS	−2.335	−2.34	−2.381	−2.42	−2.27	−2.258
	(−1.27)	(−1.27)	(−1.28)	(−1.29)	(−1.27)	(−1.22)
Constant	3.879 '	3.879 '	3.893 '	3.862 '	3.796 '	3.632 '
	(1.37)	(1.36)	(1.38)	(1.38)	(1.34)	(1.30)
Observations	88	88	88	88	88	88
Adjusted Wald test (Model)	0.28	0.279	0.333	0.321	0.271	0.283
Goodness-of-fit test[a]	0.5	0.93	1.68	1.68	2977.11	2.35

Notes: The table lists coefficients. Between brackets are the t-values. Statistical significance: ***p<0.01, **p < 0.05, *p < 0.10, +p < 0.15, 'p < 0.20. Mid-size is the reference category of size; Mid-education is the reference level of education; Greater Helsinki Metropolitan area includes Helsinki, Espoo, and Vantaa. [a]The table lists the test results of the F-adjusted mean residual test according to Archer and Lemeshow (2006). Test results were obtained by running the -estat gof- command after -svy: logit- in Stata 11.1. The goodness-of-fit test indicates a good fit for specifications (a) to (d) in the above table.

Table 8.7 shows that, based on a small sample of eighty-eight service firms, the link between R&D relocation and a subsequent decrease in domestic R&D employment is not significant. The analysis further revealed scant evidence that offshore outsourcing tends to have a positive effect on a subsequent increase of R&D employment in the home country. Although the descriptive statistics in Table 8.4 show differences in R&D relocation between the service and the manufacturing sector, the multivariate analysis did not deliver strong evidence that both sectors differ. However, according to the literature the sectors are different when it comes to the kind of R&D they have (Leiponen 2008). Ali-Yrkkö and Deschryvere (2008) found evidence that the R&D employment effects of R&D offshoring do vary between both sectors. The fact that our sample does not include small firms (firms with between ten and forty-nine employees) excludes many service firms, leading to a restricted service-sector sample. To fill an important research gap future research should in the first place pay attention to R&D relocation in the service sector.

6 Conclusions

The focus of this chapter was on global sourcing for R&D and its impact on the home country. The empirical analysis presented is based on detailed survey data on international sourcing from Finland, a small open economy that scores high on innovation rankings. Notwithstanding our data covers only a single country, we do not see reasons why our results would be specific to one country.

Using a unique data set on international sourcing allowed for making a distinction between two channels a firm can use to offshore R&D: an internal channel (via FDI) or an external channel (via subcontractors). In our data, roughly 5 percent of firms internationalized R&D through captive offshoring in the 2001–6 period while almost 6 percent engaged in offshore outsourcing. In sum roughly 10 percent of the firms relocated R&D activities to abroad but almost two times more firms (17 percent) outsourced R&D activities domestically.

The analysis contributes to the literature with four main findings. A first finding is that overseas R&D replaces domestic R&D if relocation happens within the firm. Thus, firms that offshored R&D to their overseas affiliates are more likely to subsequently decrease domestic R&D employment. A second finding is that overseas R&D does have a positive effect on domestic R&D when relocation is done to external subcontractors. Firms that did offshore outsource R&D are more likely to increase R&D employment. A third finding is that industry matters. Hence, manufacturing sector and service sector present different effects. Our fourth finding is that firm-level survey data on R&D activities should be treated with care. A comparison of a sample of firms between two surveys revealed that for a considerable share of companies their answers between both surveys diverge. This implicates that constructing surveys on R&D activities requires a clear strategy on how many and which people to contact in firms as to test and maximize the correctness of the answers. Our findings also imply that questions on expected changes in R&D employment have limited value.

We conclude this chapter by underlining the need to broaden the perspective when assessing the home-country impact of relocation of R&D abroad. Such a broad assessment should both include a long-term view and an impact study on the national innovation system as a whole. In addition, more attention should be paid to the heterogeneity of R&D. It is important to get more detailed information on exactly which categories of R&D stay and go and which kinds of R&D innovation policy should focus on. Future research should concentrate on a better understanding of service-sector R&D and its relocation abroad.

Acknowledgment

The analysis in chapter 8 is part of Etlatieto's (subsidiary of ETLA) research project "Finland and Finnish companies in global value chains". Matthias Deschryvere contributed to the finalisation of the paper while employed by VTT Technical Research Centre of Finland. Financial support from the Finnish Funding Agency for Technology and Innovation (TEKES) is gratefully acknowledged. In addition the authors want to thank Statistics Finland for the access to the data.

Notes

* VTT Technical Research Centre of Finland.

** ETLA, The Research Institute of the Finnish Economy.

1. At time of analysis the last available firm-level data on R&D employment at Statistics Finland is 2008.
2. R&D intensity is defined as the ratio between total R&D expenses and sales.
3. A common way to analyze the effect of offshoring on domestic labor demand is the trans-log cost function approach. Cost minimization leads to an optimal demand for inputs for a given level of output. The conditional short-run labor demand equations are than estimated in first differences as log-log specifications and as a function of wages, rental, input prices of material and services, capital stock and output. In many applications of the trans-log cost function approach that rely on cross-industry variation to identify parameters, input prices are excluded from the estimations. Excluding input prices implies that we introduce potential omitted variable bias.
4. Latest available year for Finnish firm-level R&D employment data is 2008 whereas aggregate data on R&D employment in the Finnish private sector are available till 2009.
5. The original question we used to construct the three R&D offshoring dummies from the Statistics Finland survey is: To what kind of business partners has your enterprise sourced R&D functions internationally during 2001–2006? Possible answers were: (1) to foreign enterprise of the same group and (2) to other foreign enterprises (no ownership or 50 percent or less).
6. Results are described in the text but not tabulated in this chapter. Tables with these specific results available on request.

References

Ali-Yrkkö, J. and Deschryvere, M. (2008). "Domestic R&D employment effects of offshoring R&D tasks: some empirical evidence from Finland." *ETLA Discussion Paper Series*, 1163. Helsinki: Research Institute of the Finnish Economy.

Amiti, M., and S.-J. Wei. 2005a. "Fear of Service Outsourcing: Is It Justified?" *Economic Policy* 20 (42): 308–347.

———. 2005b. "Service Offshoring, Productivity, and Employment: Evidence from the United States." IMF working paper 05/238, Washington, DC.

Antràs, P. 2005. "Incomplete Contracts and the Product Cycle." *American Economic Review* 95 (4): 1054–1073.

Antràs, P., L. Garicano, and E. Rossi-Hansberg. 2006. "Offshoring in a Knowledge Economy." *Quarterly Journal of Economics* 121 (1): 31–77.

Archer, K. J., and S. Lemeshow. 2006. "Goodness-of-fit Test for a Logistic Regression Model Fitted Using Survey Sample Data." *Stata Journal* 6: 97–105.

Autor, D., F. Levy, and R. Murname. 2003. "The Skill Content of Recent Technological Change: An Empirical Exploration." *Quarterly Journal of Economics* 118 (4): 1279–1333.

Baldwin, R. 2006. "Globalisation: The Great Unbundling(s)." In *Globalisation challenges for Europe*, Report by the Secretariat of the Economic Council, 11–54. Helsinki: Prime Minister's Office Publications.

Baldwin, R. and Okubo, T. 2006. "Agglomeration, Offshoring and Heterogenous Firms." CEPR Discussion Paper Series, no. 5663. Washington, DC: Center for Economic Policy Research.

Bardhan, A. D. 2006. "Managing Globalization of R&D: Organizing for Offshoring Innovation." *Human Systems Management* 25: 103–114.

Bardhan, A. D., and D. Jaffee. 2005. "Innovation, R&D, and Offshoring." Research Report of the Fisher Center for Real Estate and Urban Economics, Paper 1005, 1–20. Berkeley: University of California.

Cochran, W. G. 1977. *Sampling Techniques*. 3rd ed. New York: John Wiley & Sons.

Crinò, R. 2009. "Offshoring, Multinationals and Labor Market: A Review of the Empirical Literature." *Journal of Economic Surveys* 23 (2), 197–249.

Ekholm, K., and K. Hakkala. 2006. "The Effect of Offshoring on Labour Demand: Evidence from Sweden." CEPR Discussion Paper Series, no. 5648. Washington, DC: Center for Economic Policy Research.

European Commission. 2006. *The 2006 EU Survey on R&D Investment Business Trends*. Joint Research Centre, Directorate General Research, Luxembourg.

Freeman, R. B. 2005. "Does Globalization of the Scientific/Engineering Workforce Threaten US Economic Leadership?" Paper for conference, "Innovation Policy and the Economy," Washington, DC, April 19.

Gersbach, H., and A. Schmutzler. 2006. "Foreign Direct Investment and R&D offshoring." CEPR Discussion Paper Series, no. 5766. Washington, DC: Center for Economic Policy Research.

Grossman, G. M., and E. Rossi-Hansberg. 2006a. "Trading Tasks: A Simple Theory of Offshoring." NBER Working Paper, no. 12721. Cambridge, MA: National Bureau of Economic Research.

———. 2006b. "The Rise of Offshoring: It's Not Wine for Cloth Anymore." In *The New Economic Geography: Effects and Policy Implications*. Federal Reserve Bank of Kansas City Proceedings, 59–102.

Görg, H., and A. Hanley. 2009. "Services Outsourcing and Innovation: An Empirical Investigation." CEPR Discussion Paper Series, no. 7390. Washington, DC: Center for Economic Policy Research.

Görg, H., and E. Strobl. 2003. "'Footloose' Multinationals?" *Manchester School* 71 (1): 1–19.

Hall, B. H. 2011. "The Internationalization of R&D." UNU-MERIT Working Paper Series, no. 2011, 49.

Ito, B., E. Tomiura, and R. Wakasugi. 2007. "Dissecting Offshore Outsourcing and R&D: A Survey of Japanese Manufacturing Firms." RIETI Discussion Paper Series, no. 60. Research Institute of Economy, Trade and Industry, Japan.

Ito, B., and R. Wakasugi. 2007. "What Factors Determine the Mode of Overseas R&D by Multinationals? Empirical evidence". *Research Policy* 36: 1275–1287.

Jaffee, D. 2004. "Globalization, Offshoring, and Economic Convergence: A Synthesis." Paper presented at the conference "Understanding Global Outsourcing," Stern School of Business, New York University, December 10, 2004.

Kenney, M., and R. Dossani. 2005. "Offshoring and the Future of U.S. Engineering: An Overview." *The Bridge* 35 (3): 5–12.

Kiyota, K. 2005. "Reconsidering the Effects of Intra-national and International R&D Spillovers: Firm Level Evidence from Japan." Manufacturing Management Research Center, University of Tokyo.

Leiponen, A. 2008. "Is Service Innovation Different"? ETLA Discussion Paper Series, no. 1151. Helsinki: Research Institute of the Finnish Economy.

LTT. 2007. "The Implications of R&D Offshoring on the Innovation Capacity of EU Firms." Helsinki School of Economics. http://www.proinno-europe.eu/sites/default/files/page/10/07/off_shoring_study.pdf.

Nilsson-Hakkala, K., F. Heyman, and F. Sjöholm. 2008. "Multinational Firms and Job Tasks." Research Institute of Industrial Economics [Stockholm], Working Paper Series, no. 781.

OECD (Organisation of Ecomonic Co-operation and Development). 1998. "Internationalisation of Industrial R&D, Patterns and Trends." Paris: OECD.

———. 2007. *Offshoring and Employment, Trends and Impacts*. Paris: OECD.

———. 2008. "The Internationalisation of Business R&D: Evidence, Impacts and Implications." Paris: OECD.

Research.fi. 2011. Finnish Science and Technology Information Service. http://www.research.fi/en/resources.

SEC (Secretariat of the Economic Council). 2006. "Finland's Response to the Challenge of Globalisation: Report by the Secretariat of the Economic Council. Part II." Prime Minister's Office Publications, 19, Helsinki.

Spencer, B. 2005. "International Outsourcing and Incomplete Contracts." *Canadian Journal of Economics* 38 (4): 1107–1135.

Statistics Denmark. 2008. "International Sourcing, Moving Business Functions Abroad," June 2008. http://www.dst.dk/HomeUK/Statistics/ofs/globalisation/InterSourcingPubl.aspx.

Thursby, J., and M. Thursby. 2006. *Here or There, a survey of factors in multinational R&D location*. Washington, DC: Ewing Marion Kauffman Foundation.

UNCTAD (United Nations Conference on Trade and Development). 2005. "World Investment Report: Transnational Corporations and the Internationalization of R&D." New York and Geneva: UNCTAD.

van Welsum, D., and X. Reif. 2005. "Potential Offshoring: Evidence from Selected OECD Countries." Paris: OECD, Directorate for Science, Technology and Industry.

van Welsum, D., and G. Vickery. 2005. "Potential Offshoring of ICT-intensive Using Occupations," DSTI, Information Economy Working Paper, DSTI/ICCP/IE(2004)19/FINAL. Paris: OECD.

APPENDIX

In the Statistics Finland survey, the original question concerning relocation was:

What types of functions has your enterprise sourced in the period 2001–06? (tick all that apply)

	Domestic	Internationally	No functions sourced
Core business functions			
Production of goods and services for the market	□	□	□
Support business functions			
Distribution and logistics	□	□	□
Marketing, sales and after sales services, including help desks and call centers	□	□	□
ICT services	□	□	□
Administratice and management functions	□	□	□
Engineering and related technical services	□	□	□
R&D	□	□	□
Other types of functions, pls. specify	□	□	□

The target population of the ETLA survey consisted of firms with at least 10 employees in manufacturing and private services. The stratified random sample and associated weights were determined in association with the Statistics Finland Register of Enterprises and Establishments. The survey was sent to 1827 firms in summer 2006 and yielded 653 usable observations; the response rate was 40%. A description of these survey data has been published by the Secretariat of the Economic Council (2006). In the ETLA survey, the original questions concerning R&D relocation were "During 2000's, did your firm offshored R&D to your overseas affiliates?" and "To what countries has your company outsourced R&D (only to Finland, only to overseas, both)?" For a detailed description of the ETLA survey see Ali-Yrkkö and Deschryvere (2008).

Table 8.A1 Number of firms in the two Finnish surveys on international sourcing

	Statistics Finland survey	ETLA survey
Small firms (10–49 employees)		
Population		9985
Sample		500
Response		125
Response rate		25%[a]
Medium and large firms (50+ employees)		
Population	2539	2487
Sample	1729	1327
Response	1407	528
Response rate	81%	40%[a]

Note: The Statistics Finland survey and the ETLA survey had 320 firms in common. [a]Response rates of the ETLA survey: using as a denominator the number of contacts reached (instead of the random sample) returns a response rate of 27 percent for the small firms and 45 percent for the medium and large firms.

Table 8.A2 The use of offshoring in Finland for different categories of tasks in the 2001–6 period

	Obs.	Total Mean	S.D.	Offshored R&D Mean	Did not offshore R&D Mean	
Relocated R&D from Finland to abroad	464	0.05	0.011			
Relocated production from Finland to abroad	464	0.18	0.018	0.64	0.16	***
Relocated distribution and logistics from Finland to abroad	464	0.05	0.011	0.22	0.05	*
Relocated marketing sales and after sales services from Finland to abroad	464	0.08	0.014	0.41	0.06	***
Relocated ICT from Finland to abroad	464	0.07	0.014	0.38	0.05	**
Relocated administration and management from Finland to abroad	464	0.06	0.012	0.37	0.04	***
Relocated engineering and technical services from Finland to abroad	464	0.04	0.011	0.41	0.02	***
Relocated other tasks from Finland to abroad	464	0.01	0.006	0.17	0.01	+

Note: Based on Statistics Finland survey data. Information from ETLA survey data not included.
***p < 0.01, **p < 0.05, *p < 0.10, +p < 0.15, 'p < 0.20.

Table 8.A3 The drivers of offshoring (of a sample of firms that did offshore R&D too)

		(a)	(b)	(c)
Ranking	Drivers of offshoring[a]	Captive offshoring of R&D	Offshore outsourcing of R&D	Relocation of R&D abroad[b]
1	Labor costs	75%	100%	83%
2	Pressure from clients and competitors	64%	100%	75%
3	Other costs	64%	81%	72%
4	Access to new markets	48%	100%	64%
5	Strategic decisions made in parent company	62%	56%	60%
6	Poor labor availability in Finland	32%	90%	53%
7	Concentration on core business	27%	90%	49%
8	Access to expertise and technology	43%	56%	48%
9	Improvement of quality of existing products and launching of new products	27%	81%	45%
10	Taxes	21%	71%	38%
11	Other reasons	5%	1%	4%

[a]The above table summarizes which factors were the drivers to offshore (R&D or other activities) and shows percentages of all firms that did offshore R&D. All shares are based on the available answers from the Statistics Finland survey. [b]Column (c) presents results for all firms that used at least one R&D offshoring channel (captive offshoring (a) or offshore outsourcing (b)).

Table 8.A4 The impact of offshoring on the firm (of a sample of firms that did offshore R&D too)

	The impact of offshoring[a]	
	Positive impact (%)	Negative impact (%)
Competitiveness of the firm	78	4
Labor costs	64	4
Other costs	61	8
Access to expertise and technology	59	4
Internal know how of the firm	55	15
Access to new markets	47	0
Improvement of quality of existing products and launching of new products	31	7
Logistics	26	8

[a]The above table includes only the firms that did offshore R&D. Those firms were asked what was the impact of offshoring (R&D OR other activities).

Table 8.A5 Nonweighted correlations between the outsourcing and offshoring variables (dummies) of R&D

	Increased firm's R&D employment in Finland	Decreased firm's R&D employment in Finland	Relocated R&D from Finland to abroad	Offshore in-house sourcing of R&D	Offshore outsourcing of R&D	Domestic outsourcing of R&D
Increased firm's R&D employment in Finland	1					
Decrease firm's R&D employment in Finland	−0.842	1				
Relocated R&D from Finland to abroad	0.054	0.0047	1			
Offshore in-house sourcing of R&D	−0.0302	0.0677	0.6797	1		
Offshore outsourcing of R&D	0.1012	−0.0526	0.7921	0.2053	1	
Domestic outsourcing of R&D	−0.004	0.0355	0.4434	0.1449	0.4943	1

Source: Statistics Finland, ETLA.

CHAPTER 9

THE IMPACT OF OFFSHORING BY SERVICE FIRMS ON A COUNTRY'S COMPARATIVE ADVANTAGE

DÉSIRÉE VAN GORP AND DESIRÉE VAN WELSUM

THIS chapter discusses the impact of offshoring by service firms on a country's comparative advantage, with a focus on the labor market in the country of origin. The reason for focusing on the labor market is that research results in our studies imply that the competitiveness of countries is largely determined by the labor market, in terms of both the size and skills of the labor pool. Research also indicates that offshoring by firms in OECD countries has created substantial value addition for firms by enhancing quality of products and processes and by reducing costs. In addition, domestic firms that sourced their products or services globally experience lower exit probabilities and are more likely to be competitive internationally. Many developed countries were found to be net receivers of relocated activities; that is, contrary to what is often thought, the rest of the world relocates more to them than they offshore, including for example in business services and computer and information services. We argue, therefore, that governments should focus on the positive effects of offshoring such as job creation and increased productivity. In doing so we acknowledge that offshoring may result in challenges which may require adjustment policies; it is important not to just cave in to pressure coming from those who view offshoring as a threat resulting in negative labor market outcomes such as higher unemployment.

1 THE SOURCING TRINITY

Global sourcing is a common strategy used by both service and manufacturing firms, allowing them to coordinate activities and exploit competitive (firm-specific) advantages as well as comparative (location-specific) advantages on a global scale (Kotabe and Murray 2004). Global sourcing or international sourcing refers to a strategy whereby firms determine which part of the value chain will serve which particular market and how components, finished goods, or services will be produced (Cheng and Zang 2006; Murray and Kotabe 1999). Offshoring and outsourcing, although they are related, are two distinct phenomena (Jahns et al. 2006). Offshoring always involves a foreign location and in the case of captive offshoring, direct or shared control. This is not the case for outsourcing, which can be executed on the domestic market and always involves a third party. Consequently, captive offshoring and offshore outsourcing refer to different foreign market-entry modes (Kedia and Mukherjee 2009):

- Offshore outsourcing: externally, by outsourcing services to a third party.
- Captive offshoring: internally, through the establishment of foreign affiliates.

In the absence of data on various types of offshoring, proxies have to be used under certain assumptions. Thus, captive offshoring is considered to be part of foreign direct investment (FDI) outflows, and offshore outsourcing gives rise to cross-border trade in services (UNCTAD 2004).

2 Offshoring and Policy Implications

Although the phenomenon of offshoring at firm level is now relatively well understood, less is known about the policy implications (GAO 2006; Geishecker et al. 2008). One of the reasons for the knowledge gap regarding the policy implications is that even today there is a lack of quantitative information. This is due to the fact that the consequences of offshoring are difficult to measure (OECD 2010).

Despite the lack of precise data, many studies have attempted to measure the impact of offshoring on the labor market in the country of origin. Some studies focus on the negative effects of offshoring, arguing that the integration of lower-income economies into the worldwide division of labor tends undermine the protection of domestic workers through labor market regulations and traditional institutions (Neureiter and Nunnenkamp 2010; Dreher and Gaston 2007). Other research studies focus on the benefits of offshoring. The perceived benefits for firms include: cost savings, higher profits, higher consumer incomes because of the low prices of imported offshored goods, better quality of products and services, increasing productivity and efficiency gains, investments in new activities, better control over inflation thanks to the impact of low import prices, enhancement export capacity and increased competitiveness of the local business community allowing service firms to expand their market shares, profits and capital spending, and the creation of jobs in their home countries (EMCC 2004; Werner 2009; OECD 2010).

Although it is often perceived that developing countries are benefiting more from offshoring than developed countries, research shows that most developed countries are not more offshoring-intensive (when adjusted for economic size) than many developing countries (Amiti and Wei 2005). In fact, many developed countries are found to be net receivers of offshored activities, that is, the rest of the world relocates more activities to them than the reverse, including for example in business services and computer and information services. In addition, with the income elasticity of demand of internationally traded services greater than one (e.g. Pain and van Welsum 2004; van Welsum 2004; Mann 2004), rapid growth in countries such as India and China should also lead to reinforced exports from OECD countries.

Currently the offshoring of goods by the manufacturing sector is still the most prevalent type of relocating activities abroad (OECD 2010). However, the offshoring of both goods and services by the service sector is growing more rapidly, as so eloquently elaborated on by Pascal Lamy:. "I believe a further important area where we are only scratching the surface is trade in services. There is a growing realization of the fundamental importance of service industries in almost all activity in modern economies, yet we remain far behind in our ability to solidify international cooperation in this field." (Pascal Lamy, director-general, World Trade Organization; World Trade Report, 2007: v, vi).

Technological advances in ICT and trade and investment liberalisation have enabled the emergence of offshoring of especially IT-enabled services and a global labor market for (white-collar) skilled workers (van Welsum and Vickery 2005a, 2005b). The growing importance of offshoring in the service sector justifies extra attention from policy makers in analyzing the impact of this development on countries' competitive advantages.

3 Economic Impact and Employment Effects of Offshoring

The majority of studies measuring the impact of offshoring have concluded that for the time being offshoring has little impact on job losses in the country of origin (e.g., van Welsum and Vickery 2005a; van Welsum and Reif 2006; OECD 2010). As a rule, the short-term employment effects of offshoring are more important for manufacturing than for services. For example, for a 1 percent increase in the proportion of imported intermediate manufactured goods, sectoral employment in the country of origin contracts by 0.15 percent, as opposed to roughly 0.08 percent in the case of services (OECD 2010). However, there is no systematic evidence that offshoring of services is associated with a significant decline of aggregate job losses (van Welsum and Vickery 2005a). According to the European Monitoring Centre on Change (EMCC 2004), offshoring by European firms is responsible for a relative low percentage (i.e., less than 5 percent) of total job losses in Europe. Other reasons such as bankruptcies, shut-downs, and restructuring have far more impact on the labor market.

Furthermore, the perception that companies relocate activities mostly to low-wage regions is not supported by any evidence. On the contrary, firms locate offshoring facilities to destinations where wages are closer to those in the home country (Konings and Murphy 2006; van Gorp 2008, 2010). For example, the relocation of activities of multinational companies to their affiliates shows that the employment effect takes mainly place between parent companies (often based in the north of the European Union, EU) and their affiliates located also in the North EU, rather than their affiliates located in the South EU and Central and Eastern Europe.

This does not mean that there are no effects at all on the labor market as the composition of the labor market changes. Offshoring and technology may have a different effect on workers with different types of skills (e.g., van Welsum and Reif 2006; Liu et al. 2010; Head and Ries 2002). In general it is the case that labor markets across industrialized countries suffer from a decline of low-skilled workers in total employment and this process has been taking place within most manufacturing industries (Geishecker et al. 2008). There is evidence that the number of jobs involved in offshoring is larger when relatively low skilled tasks were offshored than in the case of higher-skilled functions (Huws 2003). Certain types of occupations will probably experience slower growth than they otherwise might have done (van Welsum and Reif 2006).

Moreover, for offshoring in the service sector new job creation offsets job destruction. Indeed, the offshoring phenomenon itself also creates new jobs in the domestic economy as existing services sectors have expanded and new services have emerged. This effect can be expected to become more important over time as with ongoing technological developments and services trade liberalization, more are likely to be created and at unprecedented pace.

4 Creating Comparative Advantages by Offshoring Policies

Although differences in comparative locational advantages have always played a role in the internationalization of firms, today's developments in the service sector happen at a much more rapid pace than was the case in the manufacturing industry (OECD 2010). An important reason for this development is the ICT-enabled aspect of services tradability—which means activities can be offshored more easily. Furthermore, these technological developments in ICT are taking place at unprecedented pace.

Although wage differentiation is one of the reasons behind offshoring, it also reflects underlying differences in productivity. Moreover, locational advantages based on cost advantages, especially if they are built solely on low wages, are often short lived. Indeed, they are relatively quickly subject to change as countries offering even lower costs develop pace rapidly. In addition, a country is more likely to be a destination of services offshoring as the average wage of a country is increasing (Konings and Murphy 2006; van Gorp 2008, 2010). High educational levels and cultural similarity, not to be confused with geographical proximity, are more important comparative advantages than cost advantages (Bunyaratavej et al. 2007; van Gorp 2008, 2010). Issues regarding the protection of intellectual property, for example, are also important locational factors for service firms when relocating their activities to offshore locations and in deciding on whether to resort to FDI or relocate activities via a third party to a specific country.

To respond to any perceived negative effects of offshoring, and to exploit the opportunities that may result from service offshoring, countries must create sustainable comparative locational advantages for the longer term. As research results in our studies indicate, offshoring is not just about costs and low-skilled labor but increasingly about the availability of highly skilled employees and management, implying that the competitiveness of countries takes place on the labor market to a considerable extent in terms of both numbers and skills. Effects of service offshoring will not be the same for all OECD countries. The flexibility of the labor market will be a differentiating factor for responding to challenges posed by services offshoring (Werner 2009).

Developed economies are largely dependent on the service sector, and their labor force, legal and regulatory framework, and productivity are under pressure with the emergence of competing locations for the offshoring of services activities. In addition to careful monitoring, these developments require special attention to be paid to developing an adequately skilled and trained labor force. Whereas many developing countries were competing on cost and especially low wages, more recently they compete on highly skilled labor and innovation framework conditions. This has triggered several countries to initiate protective measures. However, rather than fearing a powerful economic force and requesting protective measures, it may be more advantageous to join forces and jointly explore opportunities to create comparative advantages between countries.

5 The Netherlands as a Case Study

This section examines the Netherlands as a case study to illustrate the importance for countries to use their offshoring policy to create comparative advantages. The Netherlands is considered to be representative of the following European countries:[1] Austria, Belgium, Denmark, Finland, France, Germany, Greece, Luxembourg, Norway, Portugal, Sweden, Spain, and Switzerland. We have not taken the new member states in Eastern Europe into account, because wage differentials between old and new member states put them in different positions as regards the impact of services offshoring on their national economies (Werner 2009). They are more often than not net receivers of offshored activities. The United Kingdom and Ireland are also excluded from the analysis because they showed early on relatively high levels of offshoring activities compared to the other Western European countries (Werner 2009). They are also—together with the United States—the frontrunners due to the English language facilitating the offshoring process at an early stage to countries such as India. The European Union—except for the United Kingdom—is lagging substantially behind the United States in international services offshoring. An explanation for these differences may be the fact that

EU firms tend to externalize services to a much lesser extent than US firms do; their internationalization is lower than their US counterparts; there is a language barrier in non–English-speaking EU countries; and there is market fragmentation due to other natural or artificial barriers, such as regulations and lack of an internal market (Stare and Rubalcaba 2009). Although in the United Kingdom and the United States offshoring activities have been reduced during the period 1995–2002 (OECD 2010), according to the latest survey of Eurostat (2010) the United Kingdom and Ireland are still front-runners with regard to offshoring of products and services. However, fewer firms located in these countries indicated plans to source internationally during 2007–9.

5.1 A brief overview of the economic structure of the Netherlands

The Netherlands is an advanced service-based small open economy with strong dependence on the service sector.

Since 1999, the service sector in the Netherlands accounted for more than 70 percent of GDP. In 2008, services such as transportation, distribution, logistics, and financial services (banking, insurance, and pensions) accounted for nearly three-quarters of the national income, while industrial activities such as metalworking, oil refining, chemical and food processing generated a quarter of national income.[2] Agricultural activities contribute about 2 percent of GDP. The nation is heavily dependent on foreign trade, which accounts for more than 60 percent of its GDP (Economic Intelligence Unit 2008).

The economic structure of the Netherlands shows similarity with the other European economies (Figure 9.1).

The World Economic Forum's Global Competitiveness Report (GCR 2010–11)[3] classifies countries and economies in three stages, based on their current level of development. The first stage is referred to as the "factor-driven stage," where countries compete based on their factor endowments such as unskilled labor and natural resources. In this stage, the countries perform basic economic activities such as primitive farming and mining natural resources. Therefore, export of raw materials contributes in a major way to GDP. As countries evolve, they move up the value chain by acquiring skills to process the raw materials. This stage is referred to as "efficiency-driven stage," in which countries strive to enhance efficiency and product quality. In order to achieve this objective, nations will invest in development of industrial sector, which will lead the economic growth of the country. The growth of industrial sector contributes to increased wages, which in turn will stimulate domestic demand for products and services. Therefore, export of finished products, import of industrial equipment, and domestic consumption of finished products contributes to GDP. Lastly, countries evolve to compete with new and unique products and services using most sophisticated production processes and innovation. This stage is referred to as the "innovation-driven stage," where innovation is the key driver of the economy.

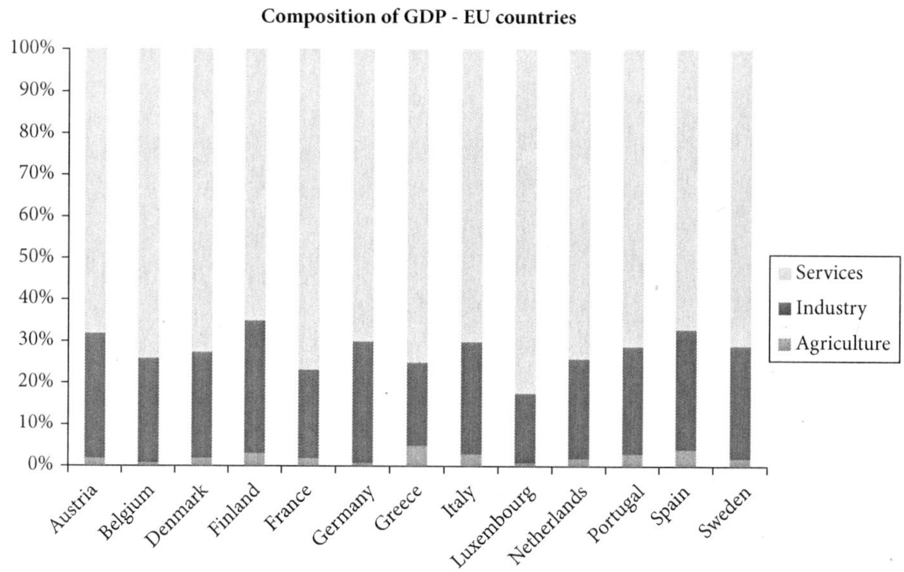

FIGURE 9.1 Economic structure of fifteen western European countries (Agriculture value-added, industry value-added, and services value-added as % of GDP) in 2008.

Source: World Bank, Key Development Indicators, 2010.

According to the GCR 2010–11, all European countries included in our analysis in this chapter are classified as innovation-driven economies that have higher GDP per capita income. The Netherlands has a services-dominated economic structure similar to the other countries (Figure 9.2). Moreover, firms in the Netherlands are comparable in terms of their offshoring activities with firms in those countries.

5.2 Developments in the labor force and demographics

A popular belief is that globalization including offshoring is a threat to jobs especially at the bottom end of the labor market in advanced countries putting pressure on wage equality (CPB 2007). This fear of job losses resulting from offshoring is often based on the assumption that the number of jobs is exogenously given and that a rise in employment in one country (offshore location) unavoidably leads to a reduction in another country (in this case the Netherlands). In the longer term, however, the number of jobs in a country is determined by interactions between the demand and supply of labor and the factors influencing them (such as growth and GDP, domestic and foreign demand for its goods and services, the tax burden, the educational system, and labor market institutions). At the same time, the efficiency and productivity gains enabled by offshoring should lead to further growth opportunities with potential new job creation.

Over the past decades both the skill premium and the supply of and demand for skilled workers have risen simultaneously in advanced countries (Nahuis and De Groot 2003).

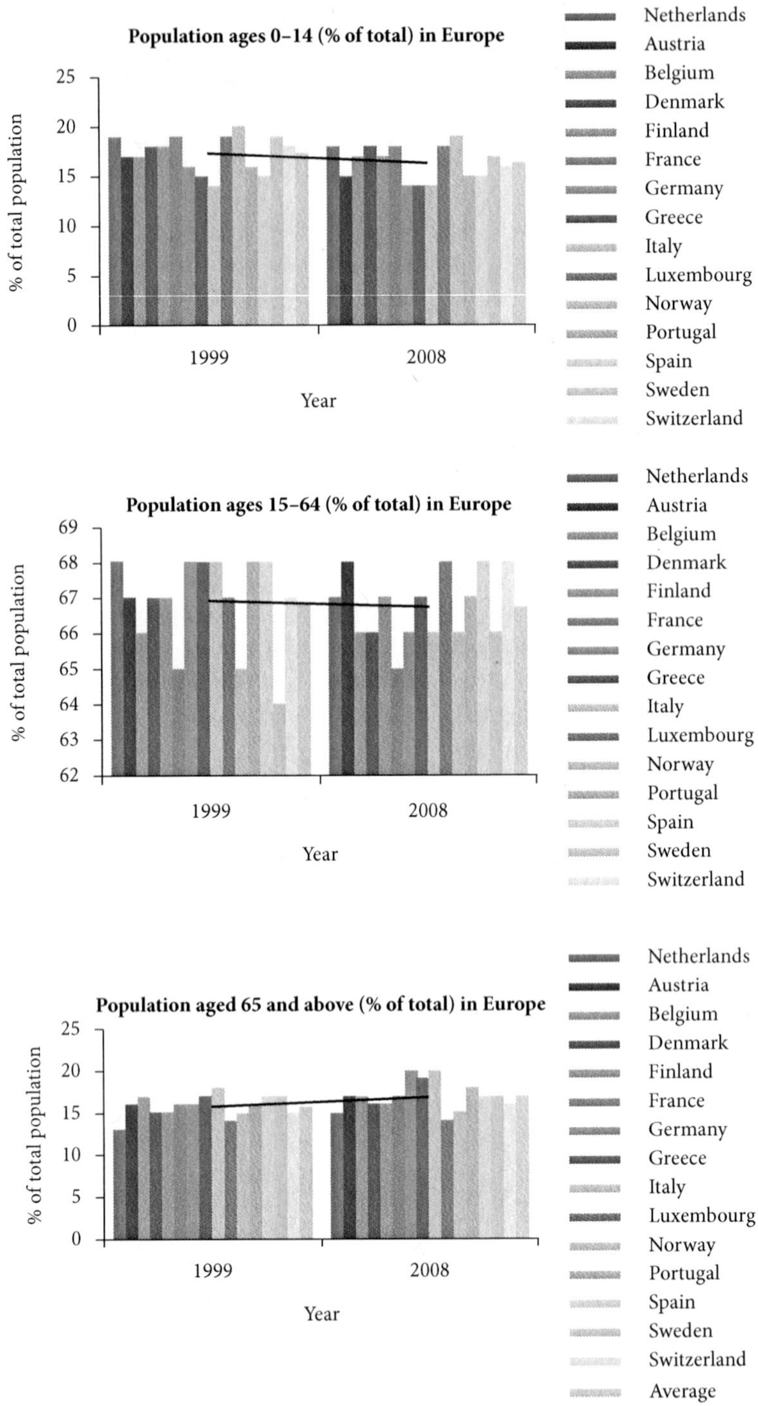

FIGURE 9.2 Demographic developments in Europe during the period 1999–2008.

Source: World Bank Key development indicators for population in Europe: http://data.worldbank.org/topic/health.

The fact that globalization overall benefits the average citizen does not mean that the gains are shared equally in society. Furthermore, technological progress also has an impact on wage inequality and the employment structure of advanced economies. Technological progress would eventually result in a lower price for low-skilled labor competing with new technologies and a higher price for high-skilled labor gaining in productivity. The skill-biased higher wages for skilled workers leads again to wage inequality, which has been the case in the past two decades in most OECD countries (OECD 2007a).

The Netherlands appears to be one of the few exceptions to the general trend, due to a relatively strong increase in the supply of skilled labor, which has largely neutralized the effects mentioned before and which did not result in wage inequality during the past decades (CPB 2007). There is some variety in studies that rank countries based on wage inequality, but the Netherlands is generally viewed as a country with a relatively egalitarian distribution and only a slight increase of inequality (Förster and Mira d'Ercole 2005; Burniaux et al. 2006). This points to a potential role of changing working habits, in particular increased part-time work, in explaining developments in wage inequality. This is in line with previous studies on wage inequality in the Netherlands suggesting that inequality has been rather stable (Van den Brakel-Hofmans 2007). More recently this picture has changed due to a reduced supply of skilled labor, which is likely to raise the skill premium and inequality again. In terms of demographics, European countries have a growing older population (≥65 years), whereas the population in the age categories 0–14 years and 16–64 years is declining (Figure 9.2).

This development, combined with the reduced supply of skilled labor and an increasing demand for highly skilled employees, will make offshoring almost a prerequisite for companies to compete for talent on a globalizing market place.

5.3 Offshoring by firms based in the Netherlands and in other European countries

Firms engage in offshoring for a variety of reasons, such as: retaining or enhancing competitive position, lowering overall costs, lowering labor costs, access to new markets, access to skilled labor (van Gorp 2008). A survey on offshoring conducted in the EU survey identified seven broad groups of business functions that are impacted by offshoring (EMC 2004): software development; data processing, including data capture; sales; customer services; creative and content-generating functions including research, development, and design; financial functions; and management, HR, and training functions. The latest large offshoring study in the Netherlands shows that firms in a wide variety of industries, in both manufacturing and services, are involved in offshoring. These firms show a preference for captive offshoring (77 percent), while less than a third are involved in offshore outsourcing (van Gorp 2010). The reason for this particular form of offshoring is likely to be related to the finding that the majority of activities being relocated are services (61 percent), whereby captive offshoring is in general the preferred form of offshoring, especially when the services are less standardized and more knowledge driven. India is the most popular offshore location for firms relocating activities from the Netherlands, followed by China, the United States, and Germany.

Interestingly, as shown in Figure 9.4, firms in the Netherlands just like in other parts of Europe are relocating not only their support activities but also their core business functions including various knowledge-intensive service activities to foreign locations (OECD 2007b; van Gorp 2008). On average about 11 percent of European companies (UK and Ireland excluded) sourced core business function from global locations, against 10 percent that sourced support business functions (Eurostat 2010). The Eurostat (2010) survey was conducted in twelve EU member states[4] to estimate the level of offshoring in Europe during the period 2001–6 and plans for offshoring during the period 2007–9 (Figure 9.3). On average, about 16 percent of the firms offshored activities during 2001–6.

In comparison, offshoring by firms in OECD countries increased significantly over the past decade, creating substantial value-added for firms by enhancing quality of products and processes and by reducing costs (OECD 2010). On the contrary, nonadoption of offshoring may eventually lead firms to either exit or downsize their operations. The Coucke and Sleuwaegen (2008) study of Belgian manufacturing firms indicated that domestic firms that sourced their products or services globally have lower probability of exit and stand a good chance to compete with other firms. Marin (2006) studied the offshoring pattern of German and Austrian firms to Eastern European countries. The study results showed that while relative labor costs and transportation costs are the main drivers for German and Austrian firms to offshore their labor intensive activities, they relocate their R&D activities because of skilled human capital shortages. Servais et al. (2006) found that international sourcing is the core of the internationalization of SMEs located in Italy. Further, offshoring, in the form of captive offshoring by firms located in Spain has increased since 1999–2000 (Guarasa 2007).

Overall, European companies relocated more core business than support functions. Though compared to the manufacturing companies, service companies relocated relatively

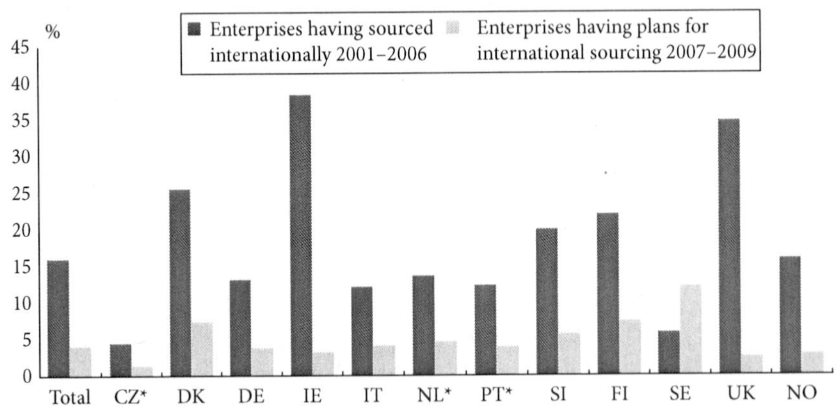

FIGURE 9.3 Level of offshoring in Europe during the period 2001–06.

Source: Eurostat 2010.

* CZ, PT: provisional date: NL unreliable data for enterprises having international sourcing plans 2007–2009.

Note: Enterprises with plans for 2007–2009 only include enterprises not having sourced internationally in the previous period 2001–2006.

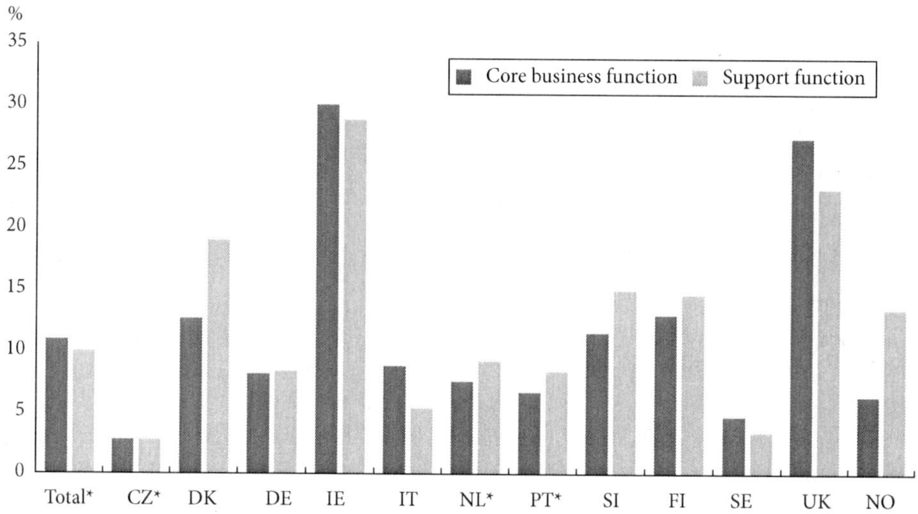

FIGURE 9.4 Offshoring core versus support business functions in Europe during the period 2001–2006.

Source: Eurostat 2010.

* CZ, PT: provisional date: Total, NL: unreliable data.

more support functions than core business functions. Different studies show an increase in offshoring of especially service activities in the countries included in our analysis. Cost savings remain a driver of European countries for offshoring. However, other drivers such as a search for talent and entering new markets become increasingly important.

5.4 Measuring offshoring

Given the complex nature of measuring offshoring, the relocation of jobs often is considered to measure the extent to which activities are relocated to foreign locations (Werner 2009). According to the OECD (2010) there are three parameters that measure offshoring or outsourcing:

1. The degree of outsourcing refers to the ratio of value-added to the total turnover in an economy. It is observed that the more a sector outsources its activities, the more the likely the ratio of value-added to turnover is to be low. Therefore lower values of the ratio indicate higher outsourcing in an economy and the higher the values the less the outsourcing in the economy.
2. The index of outsourcing abroad indicates the level of intermediate imports (of goods and services) used to produce final goods and services. It includes four overall possibilities: manufacturing sector imports intermediate goods; manufacturing sector imports intermediate services; service sector imports intermediate goods; and services sector imports intermediate services.
3. The employment trends measured as job gain or job loss in a sector.

Based on these parameters, the following general observations can be made. Between 1995 and 2002 offshoring took place sequentially: (1) offshoring goods by manufacturing sector; (2) Offshoring of goods by service sector; (3) offshoring of services by service sector; and (4) offshoring of services by manufacturing sector. The strongest growth between 1990 and 2000 was in offshoring of goods and services by the service sector. In addition, all countries except Spain offshore slightly more in services than in manufacturing industries. The top three countries that offshore most are Hungary, Japan, and the Netherlands. The top four countries whose manufacturing sectors offshore most goods are Belgium, the Netherlands, Austria, and Denmark. In general, smaller countries tend to offshore relatively more than larger countries. It also interesting to know that subsidiaries under foreign control offshore more than firms under the control of residents or that are nationally owned.

Looking at employment trends, it appears that job losses due to offshoring exclusively occurred in the manufacturing industry. However, all countries (expect for Japan, Slovakia, and the Czech Republic) compensated for losses recorded in the manufacturing sector by jobs created in the service sector and they all benefited from net job creation in that sector (OECD 2010).

6 Main findings from previous offshoring studies in the Netherlands

This section provides the main findings of the offshoring studies regarding the offshoring behavior of service firms operating from the Netherlands (van Gorp 2008, 2010). Apart from providing insights in the offshoring behavior of firms, the findings of these studies contribute to improving the understanding of the strategic logic for the choice between captive offshoring and offshore outsourcing. The findings present a decision-making model that shows how different determinants in the offshoring behavior of service firms interrelate and determine the foreign entry mode choice for relocating activities.

6.1 Exploiting competitive advantages at the firm level

Findings in the research were in line with the trend that service firms split up various business processes and tasks to locate them around the world, allowing the firms to exploit both their competitive advantages and the comparative advantages of various countries. This implies that the firms should increasingly move from efficiently attending single offshoring activities to reconfiguring whole processes and value chains in order to realize more value across the whole organization. In doing so, they needed to learn to source, locate, and manage human capital and activities on a structural basis anywhere in the world, which is perceived by many firms as a challenging managerial practice

(Lewin and Peeters 2006; Jagersma and van Gorp 2002). Offshoring brings competitive advantages much more than cost savings. For example, it can provide higher-quality resources as most of the employees of third-party offshoring are generally more highly qualified their US or European counterparts (Kedia and Lahiri 2007).

These developments are in contrast with some of the early offshoring literature, in which offshoring was perceived as a cost-cutting procurement tool for relocating non-core activities via third parties to so-called low-wage countries; that is, a method of procurement in search of lowest costs around the globe. The difference with purchasing decisions which simply involve procurement is that offshoring may affect the entire organization, not just the procurement department, and it often requires a strategic decision (Grossman and Helpman 2005; Gilley and Rashid 2000).

The findings in the underlying offshoring studies imply that service firms are required to take a long-term perspective regardless of which type of offshoring they choose for relocating activities to foreign locations. The reason is that service firms often engage in offshoring in long-term commitments for making investments and long-term agreements with third-party offshore providers. Furthermore, a long-term perspective is required for seamless alignment with activities in the domestic market. These studies also imply that service firms consider the lessons learned from those with prior offshoring experience and especially the level to which they have achieved their objectives, because this is one of the determinants regarding their choice for a foreign entry mode.

6.2 Exploiting comparative advantages and national offshoring policies

Although differences in comparative locational advantages have always played a role in the internationalization of firms, today's developments in the service sector happen at a much more rapid pace than was the case in the manufacturing industry. Comparative locational advantages based on cost advantages are often short lived in this context, especially if they are built solely on low wages, which is relatively quickly subject to change as countries offering even lower costs develop at a relatively rapid pace. In addition, research shows that a country is more likely to be a destination of services offshoring as its average wage is increasing; that is, firms locate offshoring facilities to destinations where wages are closer to those in the home country (Clark 2010). Non-core activities are more often associated with low-income-level offshore locations and offshore outsourcing, whereas core activities tend to be associated with high-income-level offshore locations and captive offshoring (van Gorp 2008). This is in line with our research findings indicating that high educational levels and cultural similarity, not to be confused with geographical closeness, are more important drivers of comparative advantages for the relocation of some activities than cost advantages are (Kedia and Mukherjee 2009).

To further illustrate the importance of comparative advantages for offshoring we take offshoring from the Netherlands (a small and advanced country) to India (a large and emerging country) as an example. In general, a smaller economy like the Netherlands would have more need for offshoring due to the fact it would tend to lack balanced resource endowments and a large home market that allows for economies of scale. At the same time, comparative advantages are expected to change more quickly in emerging economies like India than in advanced economies like the Netherlands. Hence there is a need for India to have a specialized economy notwithstanding the fact that large economies normally have less need for specialization. Over 60 percent of Dutch exports in 2005 were technology intensive or human capital intensive, whereas unskilled-labor intensive and natural-resource intensive products are negligible. For India the two categories of technology and human capital are important and account for approximately 35 percent of the exports that same year. This implies a shift compared to 2005 when the main categories for India were primary products (27 percent) and unskilled-labor-intensive products (20 percent). This partly reflects the characteristic pattern of economic development in which export patterns evolve from initially primary-sector oriented towards becoming more high-tech and skilled-intensive oriented. Another cluster of product groups that can be clearly identified consists of unskilled-labor-intensive products such as textile yarn, fabrics, made-up articles and related products, travel goods, handbags and similar articles of apparel, and clothing accessories and footwear. India is strong and the Netherlands is weak in these sectors (CPB 2007). When companies look at why they are interested in locating activities in the Netherlands, they refer to high labor productivity, organizational cultures, the availability of highly qualified employees, and the innovative capabilities present in the country (van Gorp 2010).

In contrast to the media attention for job losses from the West to the East, European countries are still major beneficiaries from offshoring, and there is no evidence that the perceived job losses due to offshoring can be explained by the dichotomy between low- and high-wage locations (Neureiter and Nunnenkamp 2010). Generally, investors' location decisions are not driven by low wages. Furthermore, their wage sensitivity declines as the skill intensity of the industry increases (Liu et al. 2010). Issues regarding the protection of intellectual property are also important indicators for service firms when relocating their activities to offshore locations and deciding on whether to engage in FDI in the country or to relocate activities via a third party to a specific country. Thus, in order to respond to any negative effects of offshoring, such as potential initial redundancies, and to exploit the possibilities regarding service offshoring, countries must create sustainable comparative locational advantages for the longer term.

7 Conclusions

The finding that the increase in service firms relocating core activities to foreign locations based more on long-term competitive advantages and less on creating short-lived cost advantages is sometimes met with surprise. The phenomenon of offshoring was previously perceived as a tool of cutting costs by relocating non-core activities via third parties to so-called low-wage countries, especially in the manufacturing sector. Academics, policy makers, and the media have taken this view as a point of departure for their thinking and writing about offshoring. However, with offshoring of service activities increasing, it is important to face a new reality: although offshoring may often be the result of pressure on cost reductions, service firms are increasingly also relocating their activities to explore strategic opportunities, such as following customers and suppliers, entering new markets, and realizing scalability due to the availability of large numbers of qualified workers. This is important as different objectives or motivations for offshoring may result in different employment effects and these effects may be shaped by labor market rigidities in various continental European home countries (Neureiter and Nunnenkamp 2010). This implies that economies with a more flexible job market and integrated economy are in a better position to benefit from offshoring than countries with a rigid labor market, weak regional and sectoral mobility of workers, low mobility between professions, and limited opportunities for reemployment, as is the case in the European Union (Stare and Rubalcaba 2009). A flexible labor market is crucial to increase the benefits from offshoring for European countries.

The increasing demand for high-skilled jobs and the lack of labor supply largely due to developments in the demographics—that is, a growing population of older people in the Netherlands and Europe at large—will enlarge the gap between demand and supply in the labor market. So far, the European economy has profited from the offshoring of companies as job creation has outweighed any job losses. This may be the case in general, though the demand for unskilled jobs has decreased while demand for high-skilled jobs has increased throughout Europe. Therefore, the impact of offshoring may be different at the level of the individual worker than for the economy as a whole, with negative effects especially for low-skilled employees losing their jobs and not easily finding new ones. The comparative advantages are expected to change more quickly in emerging economies than in Europe, where the majority of countries have advanced economies. Emerging economies are moving up the value chain and specialize in more knowledge- and human capital-intensive products and services. This brings them in direct competition with the advanced economies.

Whereas many developing countries were competing on cost and especially low wages, more recently they have started to also compete on highly skilled labor and innovation. Investors in the least skill-intensive industries exhibit the largest wage sensitivity in choosing a host, which is in contrast with those who are in search of a high-skilled labor force. Unfortunately, some are still of the belief that developed countries have "a monopoly on innovation," carrying out high-skilled and high value-added activities while other countries specialize in the lower-skill, lower-cost, and lower value-added labor-intensive activities. However, countries such as India have led the way in creating comparative advantages, such as through their educational system (and even though many in India still do not receive adequate education, the numbers are so large that even a relatively small percentage of educated people still represents a huge pool of talent), large numbers of highly qualified employees, and by creating innovative approaches to service delivery. Offshoring and innovation can go hand in hand and may go in both directions. For example, today "the thinking" may be accomplished in India while "the delivery" is accomplished in the Netherlands. "Made in China" may soon change to "Made by China."

Wage pressures on host countries change as the development in offshoring matures. The trend that offshoring is not just about reducing costs and finding low-skilled labor but increasingly about the availability of highly skilled employees and management implies that the competitiveness of countries takes place on the labor market to a considerable extent in terms of both numbers and skills. The Dutch economy, like the other European economies included in our analysis, is largely dependent on the skill-intensive service sector. The labor force, legal and regulatory framework, and productivity in these countries are under pressure as a result of the offshoring of service activities. These developments require special attention for an adequately skilled and trained labor force. The lower the supply of skilled and experienced workers, the higher the probability of offshoring activities higher up the value chain such as R&D, engineering services, and product design. This has triggered several countries to initiate protective measures. However, rather than fearing a powerful economic force and requesting for protective measures, it may be more advantageous to join forces and jointly explore opportunities to create comparative advantages between countries.

As discussed in this chapter, European countries are still net beneficiaries of offshoring as host countries. In Europe, just like in the United States, layoffs attributable to relocation abroad represent just a small fraction of the total number of workers laid off. Those activities and jobs involved that are being relocated from Europe to foreign destinations are generally compensated for by job creation. However, this does not mean that there may not be severe consequences for individual employees employed in lower skilled jobs due to a shift from low- to higher-skilled jobs. Offshoring has an impact on domestic skill intensity; that is, offshoring to low-income countries increases the domestic skill level in relative terms, whereas offshoring to high-income countries may result in skill downgrading.

In order to increase the benefits from offshoring, offshoring policies should focus on creating an adequately skilled labor force and increasing the flexibility of the labor market. At the same time, it is important to monitor closely the offshore behavior of firms both in the manufacturing and service sectors in order to create and exploit comparative advantages, attract FDI, and increase trade in services.

NOTES

1. http://unstats.un.org/unsd/methods/m49/m49regin.htm#europe.
2. Background notes on countries of the world: Netherlands, 2008.
3. http://www3.weforum.org/docs/WEF_GlobalCompetitivenessReport_2010–11.pdf
4. Czech Republic, Denmark, Germany, Ireland, Italy, Netherlands, Portugal, Slovenia, Finland, Sweden, United Kingdom, and Norway.

References

Amiti, M., and S.-J. Wei. 2005. "Fear of Service Outsourcing: Is It Justified?" *Economic Policy* 20 (42): 308–347.

Bunyaratavej, K., J. Doh, E. Hahn, A. Lewin, and S. Massini. 2011. "Conceptual Issues in Services Offshoring Research: A Multidisciplinary Review." *Group & Organization Management* 36 (1): 70–102.

Burniaux, J., F. Padrini, and N. Brandt. 2006. "Labour Market Performance, Income Inequality and Poverty in OECD Countries." OECD Economics Department Working Paper 500.

Cheng, W., and D. Zhang. 2006. "Domestic and global sourcing." *Division of Labor & Transaction Costs* 2 (1): 37–53.

Clark, D. 2010. "Vertical Specialization with Developed and Developing Countries." *Journal of Developing Areas* 43 (2): 327–339.

Coucke, K., and L. Sleuwaegen. 2008. "Offshoring as a Survival Strategy: Evidence from Manufacturing Firms in Belgium." *Journal of International Business Studies* 39 (8): 1261–1277.

CPB (Netherlands Bureau for Economic Policy Analysis). 2007. "India and the Dutch Economy: Stylised Facts and Prospects." CPB Document, Netherlands, no. 155. http://www.cpb.nl/publicatie/india-and-dutch-economy-stylised-facts-and-prospects.

EMCC (European Monitoring Centre on Change). 2004. "Employment in Europe Report 2004: Recent Trends and Prospects." European Communities, Belgium. http://ec.europa.eu/social/keyDocuments.jsp?policyArea=&type=0&country=0&year=2004&advSearchKey=empleuropereport&mode=advancedSubmit&langId=en.

Economic Intelligence Unit. 2008. "The Netherlands, Country Profile." London.

Eurostat. 2010. "International Sourcing in Europe. Statistics in focus." Eurostat http://epp.eurostat.ec.europa.eu/cache/ITY_OFFPUB/KS-SF-09-004/EN/KS-SF-09-004-EN.PDF.

Förster, M., and M. Mira d' Ercole. 2005. "Income Distribution and Poverty in OECD Countries in the Second Half of the 1990s." OECD Social, Employment and Migration Papers, no. 22. Paris: OECD.

Geishecker, I., H. Görg, and S. Maioli. 2008. "The Labour Market Impact of International Sourcing." In *Globalisation and labour market adjustment,* edited by D. Greenaway, R. Upward, and P. Wright, 152–173. New York: Palgrave Macmillan.

Gilley, K. M., and A. Rasheed. 2000. "Making More by Doing Less: An Analysis of Outsourcing and its Effects on Firm Performance." *Journal of Management* 26 (4): 763–790.

Grossman, G. M., and E. Helpman. 2005. "Outsourcing in a Global Economy." *Review of Economic Studies* 72 (1): 135–159.

Guarasa, M. 2007. "Are Foreign Firms Delocalizing Services from Spain?" *Services Industry Journal* 27 (3): 305–320.

Haveman, J., and J. Shatz. 2004. *Services Offshoring: Background and Implications for California.* San Francisco: Public Policy Institute of California.

Head, K., and J. Ries. 2002. "Offshore production and Skill Upgrading by Japanese Manufacturing Firms." *Journal of International Economics* 58 (1): 81–105.

Hejazi, W. 2009. Does China Receive More Regional FDI than Gravity Would Suggest?" *European Management Journal* 27: 327–335.

Jagersma, P. K., and D. M. van Gorp. 2002. "International HRM: The Dutch Experience." *Journal of General Management* 28 (2): 75–87.

Jahns, C., E. Hartmann, and L. Bals. 2006. Offshoring: Dimensions and Diffusion on a New Business Concept." *Journal of Purchasing & Supply Management* 12 (4): 218–231.

Kedia, B., and S. Lahiri. 2007. "International Outsourcing of Services: A Partnership Model." *Journal of International Management* 13: 22–37.

Kedia, B., and D. Mukherjee. 2009. "Understanding Offshoring: A Research Framework Based on Disintegration, Location and Externalization Advantages." *Journal of World Business* 44: 250–261.

Konings, J., and P. Murphy. 2006. "Do Multinational Enterprises Relocate Employment to Low-wage Regions? Evidence from European Multinationals." *Review of World Economics* 142 (2): 267–286.

Kotabe, M., and J. Y. Murray. 2004. "Global Sourcing Strategy and Sustainable Competitive Advantage." *Industrial Marketing Management* 33 (1): 7–14.

Lewin, A. Y., and C. Peeters. 2006. "Offshoring Work: Business Hype or the Onset of Fundamental Transformation." *Long Range Planning* 39 (3): 221–239.

Liu, X., M. Lovely, and J. Ondrich. 2010. "The Location Decisions of Foreign Investors in China: Untangling the Effect of Wages Using a Control Function Approach." *Review of Economic and Statistics* 92 (1): 160–166.

Mann, C. L. 2004. "The US Current Account, New Economy Services and Implications for Sustainability." *Review of International Economics* 12 (2): 262–276.

Marin, D. 2006. "A New International Division of Labor in Europe: Outsourcing and Offshoring to Eastern Europe." *Journal of European Economic Association* 4 (2–3): 612–622.

Murray, J. Y., and M. Kotabe. 1999. "Sourcing Strategies of U.S. Service Firms: A Modified Transaction-cost Analysis." *Strategic Management Journal* 20 (9): 791–809.

Nahuis, R., and H. De Groot. 2003. "Rising Skill Premia: You Ain't Seen Nothing Yet." CPB Discussion Paper 20. The Hague.

Neureiter, M., and P. Nunnenkamp. 2010. "Outsourcing Motives, Location Choice and Labour Market Implications: An Empirical Analysis for European Countries." *KYKLOS* 63 (2): 206–230.

OECD (Organisation for Economic Co-operation and Development). 2010. *The Impact of Offshoring on Employment: Measurement Issues and Implications*. Paris: OECD.

———. 2007a. "OECD workers in the global economy: increasingly vulnerable?" *Employment Outlook*. Paris: OECD.

———. 2007b. *Moving Up the Value Chain: Staying Competitive in the Global Economy*. Paris: OECD.

Pain, N., and D. van Welsum. 2004. "International Production Relocation and Exports of Services." *OECD Economic Studies* 38 (1): 67–94.

Servais, P., A. Zucchella, and G. Palamara. 2006. "International Entrepreneurship and Sourcing: International Value Chain of Small Firms." *Journal of Euromarketing* 16 (1/2): 105–117.

Stare, M., and L. Rubalcaba. 2009. "International Outsourcing of Services: What Role for Central and East European Countries?" *Emerging Markets Finance & Trade* 45 (5): 31–46.

UNCTAD (United Nations Conference on Trade and Development). 2004. *The Shift towards Services*. World investment report. Geneva: UNCTAD.

van den Brakel-Hofmans, M. 2007. "De ongelijkheid van inkomens in Nederland." CBS Sociaaleconomische Trends. 3rd quarter: 7–11.

van Gorp, D. 2008. "Offshoring in the Service Ssector: An Empirical Investigation on the Offshoring Behavior of Service Firms and its Influence on their Foreign Entry Mode Choice." PhD diss., Nyenrode Business Universiteit, The Netherlands.

———. 2010. "Offshoring by Manufacturing and Service Firms in the Netherlands: Offshoring Behavior in Times of a Financial Crisis." Ministry of Economic Affairs in the Netherlands. http://www.nyenrode.nl/bio/Documents/NyenrodeOffshoringReport_May2010.pdfvan.

Welsum, D. 2004. "In Search of "Offshoring": Evidence from U.S. Imports of Services," Birkbeck College, London, Economics Working Paper 2004 No. 2.

van Welsum, D., and X. Reif. (2006). "We Can Work it out: The Globalization of ICT-enabled Services." NBER Working Paper, no. 12799. Cambridge, MA: National Bureau of Economic Research.

van Welsum, D., and G. Vickery. 2005a. "The Share of Employment Potentially Affected by Offshoring: An Empirical Investigation." DSTI Information Economy Working Paper, DSTI/ICCP/IE(2005)8/FINAL. Paris: OECD.

———. 2005b. "Potential Offshoring of ICT-intensive Using Occupations." DSTI Information Economy Working Paper, DSTI/ICCP/IE(2004)19/FINAL. Paris: OECD.

Werner, W. 2009. "Service Offshoring: Is Europe Different?" *Intereconomics* 44 (2): 96–104.

World Trade Organization. 2007. "Six Decades of Multilateral Trade Cooperation: What Have We Learnt?" World Trade Report 2007: v, vi.

SECTION II

OTHER DEVELOPED COUNTRIES

CHAPTER 10

OFFSHORING AND JAPANESE FIRMS

EIICHI TOMIURA*, BANRI ITO,**
AND RYUHEI WAKASUGI***

1 INTRODUCTION

Firms are offshoring a wide range of tasks, partly facilitated by trade liberalization and the development of information technologies. Sourcing high-quality inputs from low-cost suppliers across national borders is a vital concern for many firms competing in the global market. In the United States, the offshoring of software programming to India attracts political reactions. German firms are actively offshoring their production activities to Eastern Europe. In East Asia, Japanese firms have established dense trade-production networks through exports of intermediates and accumulation of foreign direct investment (FDI). This chapter reports the current status of offshoring by Japanese firms based on our unique firm-level data and summarizes how offshoring firms differ from nonoffshoring firms in Japan to derive implications of offshoring for national economies.[1]

In international economics, the theory of offshore sourcing decisions by heterogeneous firms has become one of the hottest research topics, pioneered for example by Antràs and Helpman (2004), but empirical investigations of this "New New Trade Theory" have been seriously constrained by the limited availability of microdata. To fill this gap, we conducted a survey on large and medium-sized firms across all manufacturing industries in Japan. The survey has direct information on offshore sourcing, explicitly distinguished from domestic sourcing, and covers not only production offshoring but also service offshoring, such as R&D, information services, customer supports, and professional services. The survey also distinguishes the type of suppliers: own offshore subsidiaries, subsidiaries owned by other Japanese firms, and foreign-owned suppliers. As these data have been largely unavailable in previous datasets used for similar purposes, this chapter will contribute to our understanding of offshoring by Japanese firms in particular, but also offshoring in general.

The rest of this chapter is organized as follows. Section 2 overviews aggregate statistics related with Japanese offshoring. Section 3 explains our survey and reports the current state of offshoring by Japanese manufacturing firms. Section 4 reviews how offshoring firms differ from nonoffshoring firms in terms of productivity, employment, and innovation based on previous empirical studies of Japanese firm-level data. Section 5 adds concluding comments.

2 Overview of Japanese offshoring at aggregate levels

Before reporting our results from firm-level data in detail, this section briefly overviews the aggregate trends of offshoring in Japan. To discuss offshoring, the summary statistics on imports, FDI, production, and employment are informative.

The upward trend in Japan's dependence on imported intermediates is summarized in Figure 10.1. The share of imports of final goods and that of intermediates are shown relative to industrial value added. While the share of final imports remains stagnant, the share of intermediate imports has remarkably increased from 1 percent to 5 percent in the recent decade. This rapid growth of input imports reflects the changing composition

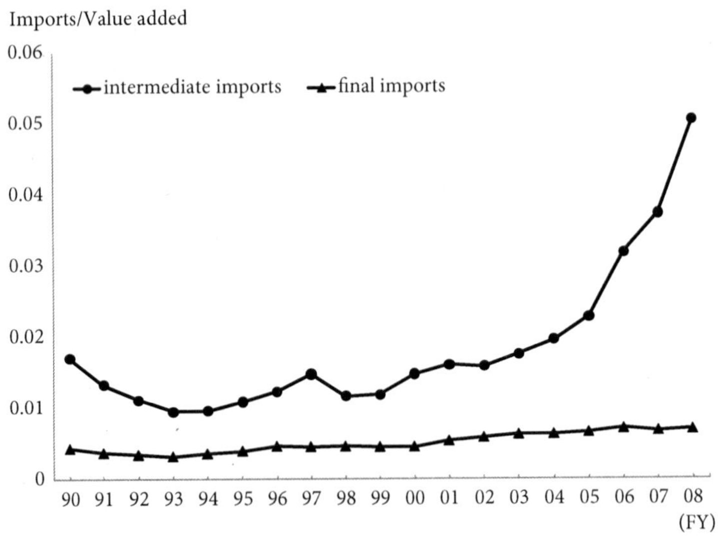

FIGURE 10.1 Japan's import shares.

Note: The denominator is industrial value-added retrieved from World Development Indicators.

Source: Authors' calculation based on RIETI-TID database.

of Japan's imports and implies active offshoring. While expanding imports should generally be welcomed for the national welfare (final goods for consumers and intermediates for producers), Wakasugi et al. (2008) report that both expanding offshoring and declining value-added are observed in Japan, and argue that some of the high-value-added portions of production processes might be relocated to offshore sites. The contrast between final versus intermediate imports in Figure 10.1 is consistent with this interpretation.

Japanese firms have expanded FDI and shifted their production to offshore locations over the recent decades since the historic yen appreciation in the middle of the 1980s. Figure 10.2 confirms the accelerating trend of FDI from Japan based on cross-border capital flow data derived from the balance of payment statistics. Following this FDI trend, Japanese firms have substantially expanded their offshore production. Figure 10.3 displays the offshore production ratio of Japanese manufacturing firms based on the official statistics.[2] Among the firms operating offshore subsidiaries, nearly one-third of their outputs are now produced abroad. A persistent rising trend is evident. Even for the entire Japanese manufacturing (including the overwhelming majority of domestic firms without FDI), the share of offshore production in total production has more than doubled since the middle of the 1990s. As this rise of offshore production is likely to result in fragmentation of production processes, these pieces of evidence indicate active cross-border sourcing of intermediates and various other tasks.

While accelerating FDI indicates active offshoring, not all transactions associated with offshoring are accomplished within the boundary of multinational firms. Figure 10.4 displays the ratio of intrafirm imports in total imports. Although the level is generally

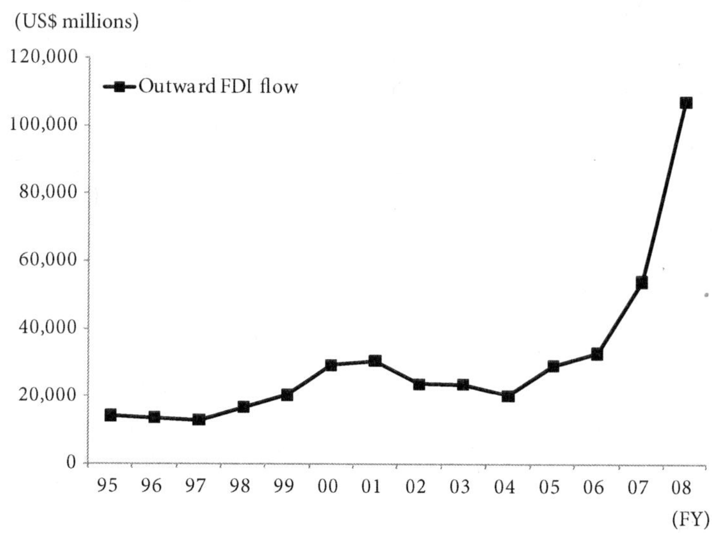

FIGURE 10.2 Japan's outward FDI.

Note: Net capital flow data are from the balance of payments statistics.

Source: JETRO database.

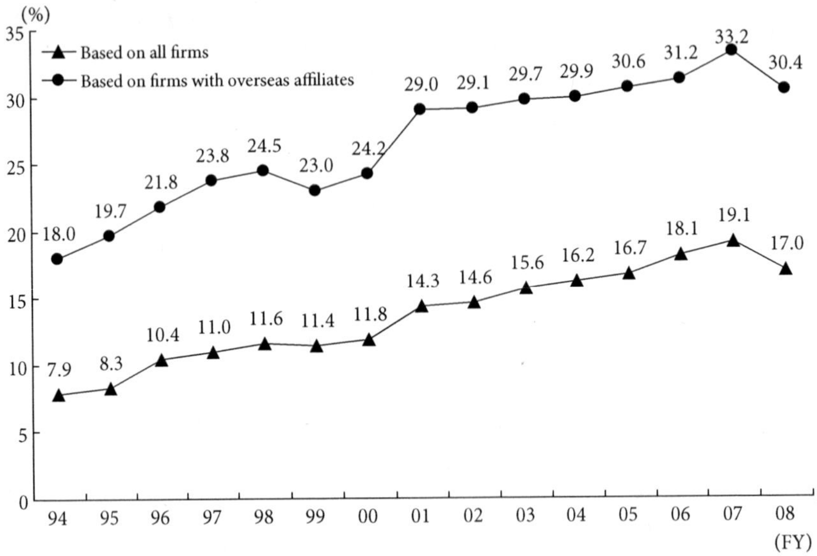

FIGURE 10.3 Offshore production ratios of Japanese manufacturing firms.

Note: Ratio based on all firms = Sales of overseas affiliates/(Sales of overseas affiliates + Sales of all domestic firms) × 100.

Ratio based on firms with overseas affiliates = Sales of overseas affiliates/(Sales of overseas affiliates + Sales of parent firms) × 100.

Source: Survey of Overseas Business Activities by METI.

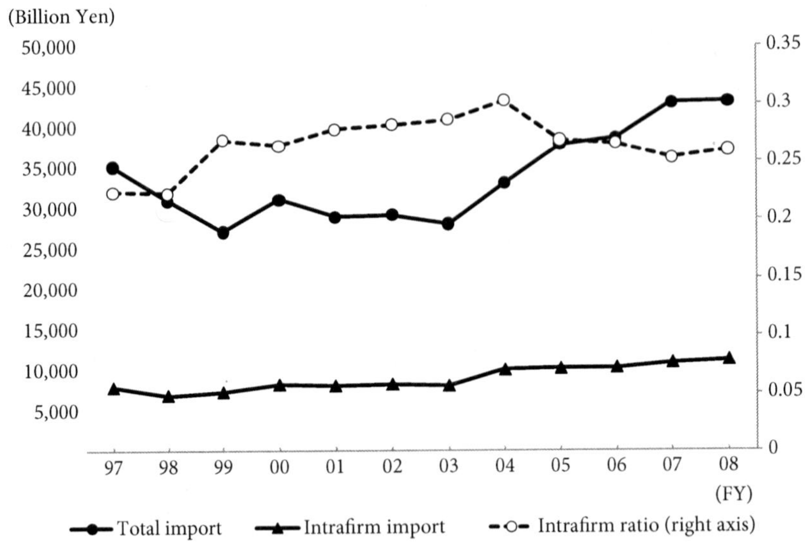

FIGURE 10.4 Japan's intrafirm trade.

Note: Intrafirm trade share is measured on the right scale.

Source: Basic Survey of Japanese Business Structure and Activities.

high, no increasing trend is observed in this graph. Combined with the accelerating FDI and rising share of offshore production explained in the previous paragraph, this relatively stable share of intrafirm trade suggests active offshoring across firm boundaries, that is, expanding offshore outsourcing (sourcing from independent foreign suppliers without ownership relations). Offshoring is not necessarily contained within multinational corporations, but also includes arm's-length contract-based sourcing activities crossing firm boundaries as well as national borders. We will later compare outsourcing with intrafirm sourcing based on our disaggregated offshoring data.

Following the trend in production explained above, Japanese manufacturing firms have substantially shifted their employment to offshore locations. Figure 10.5 reports the manufacturing employment in Japan and the offshore employment by Japanese subsidiaries. Domestic manufacturing employment has continued to shrink since the early 1990s, while the number of workers employed by Japanese subsidiaries abroad has almost doubled in the last decade. The size of offshore employment by Japanese FDI subsidiaries has already surpassed one-third of that of manufacturing employment in the home country. Given the apparent comparative advantage of Japanese manufacturing, this share of offshore employment should be noted. Although this does not necessarily mean the direct substitution by FDI, this trend should have serious impacts on immobile production factors in Japan, especially on employees working in manufacturing plants and potentially all those people in Japan with skills for production activities. This chapter reports the current state of offshoring by Japanese manufacturing firms and summarizes the differences between offshoring firms versus nonoffshoring firms to derive implications for Japanese manufacturing firms and industries.

Before concluding this section, we must note, however, that the share of manufacturing keeps declining in Japanese employment and outputs. As the major portion of the

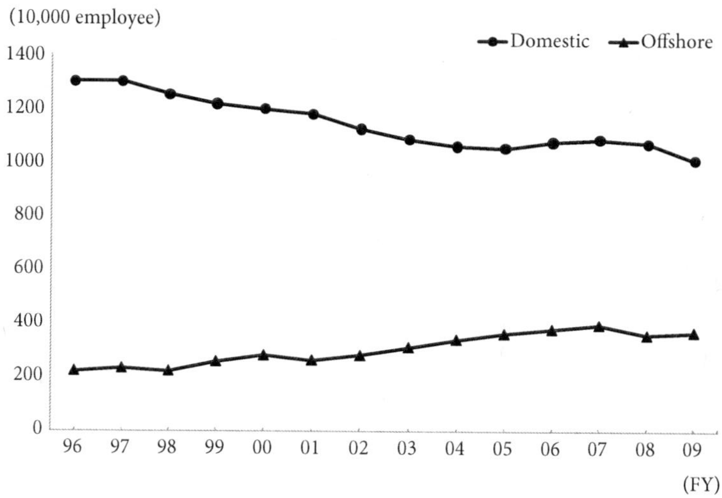

FIGURE 10.5 Japan's domestic and offshore manufacturing employment.
Source: Labor Force Survey and *Survey of Trends in Business Activities of Foreign Affiliates.*

Japanese economy is shifting toward service activities, the overemphasis on manufacturing might be misleading as a description of the entire Japanese economy. Intermediate import data derived from custom-clearance statistics and employment data based on manufacturing census are reliable indicators for production offshoring, but are not suitable for investigating offshore sourcing of nonproduction corporate activities. This chapter will fill a part of this gap by reporting our offshoring survey, which disaggregates offshoring by tasks including services.

3 Dissecting Japanese offshoring based on firm-level data

This section describes offshoring by Japanese manufacturing firms based on microdata derived from our unique survey. The survey was conducted for our research project by the Research Institute of Economy, Trade and Industry (RIETI), which is affiliated with Japan's Ministry of Economy, Trade and Industry.[3] By making use of the strength of microdata, we report how many firms are actually engaged in offshoring. The overall Japanese offshoring is disaggregated in terms of destinations (e.g., China, ASEAN, other Asia, United States/Europe), as well as of task categories (e.g., intermediate production, final assembly, R&D, information services, professional services, customer supports). Our data show that Japanese offshoring is overwhelmingly toward neighboring low-wage Asian developing countries and remains mostly through offshoring of production tasks. These disaggregated descriptive data are straightforward and useful as a guide for the precise understanding of Japanese offshoring.

3.1 Design of the survey

The survey asked whether or not the firm was sourcing across borders. In this survey, the "offshoring" (or offshore sourcing) is defined as "contracting-out" (*gaichu* or *itaku*, in Japanese) to other independent legal entities located overseas[4] based on explicit contracts detailing specifications or other dimensions of the outsourced tasks. This restrictive definition is appropriate for investigating the empirical implications of make-or-buy decision models in contract theory or the theory of the firm.

The survey also asked each firm about its experience of offshoring five years before as a retrospective question to alleviate the limitation of a one-shot survey. As we distributed the questionnaire at the end of the 2006 fiscal year (January to March 2007), the offshoring status at 2005 is surveyed. As a result, "five years ago" in the survey means the year 2000.

Although no quantitative data are available on how much each firm is offshoring, the survey had detailed questions on what kind of tasks are offshored to which type of suppliers in which regions. On the disaggregation on offshored tasks, the survey distinguishes the following eight categories:

(1) Production of jigs or dies,
(2) Production of parts, components, or other intermediates,
(3) Final assembly or processing of final products,
(4) R&D,
(5) Information services (e.g., software programming),
(6) Customer supports (e.g., operations of call centers),
(7) Professional (legal, accounting, or financial) services, and
(8) Other tasks.

As not only production but also services are covered as tasks offshored, this survey has a wider coverage of offshoring than previous surveys. The most popular offshoring measure based on sector-level intermediate import data derived from input-output tables, which has been widely used since Feenstra and Hanson (1996), focuses on (2) but certainly fails to cover (3) as well as some parts of other categories. Even for the category (2), intermediate import data are inevitably contaminated by the inclusion of standardized inputs purchased at the marketplace.[5] At least for Japan, this is the first survey squarely capturing service offshoring at the firm level.[6] Even in other countries, service offshoring can be captured mostly through sector-level input-output tables.[7]

On the offshoring destinations, the survey identifies the following five regions:

(1) China (including Taiwan and Hong Kong),
(2) ASEAN countries,
(3) Other Asian countries,
(4) United States and European countries, and
(5) Rest of the world (ROW).[8]

The disaggregation by geographical destinations will enable us to discuss the impacts of market institutions or the level of development on offshoring decisions.

On the offshoring partners, the survey distinguishes the following three types of firms:

(1) Own offshore subsidiaries,
(2) Subsidiaries owned by other Japanese multinationals, and
(3) Foreign-owned firms.

"Subsidiaries" (*kogaisha*, in Japanese) are defined by the majority ownership. Although a 10 percent threshold is often used in FDI studies, the majority ownership is critical for identifying the relationship between the supplier and the offshoring firm. The firms in the last category are either local firms or subsidiaries of multinationals from third countries.[9] The comparison of these three categories will reveal how offshoring decision is affected by the boundary or the nationality of the firms. Furthermore, since the offshoring defined by contracts includes transactions between the parent firm and offshore subsidiaries as long as they are independent legal entities, it will be informative to identify how much of the offshoring transactions are within the boundary of multinational firms (intrafirm offshoring).

The questionnaire was sent to 14,062 manufacturing firms in Japan.[10] As the population of firms chosen for this survey was the same as those used for the previous wave of the annual national legal mandatory survey (*The Basic Survey of Business Structure and Activities*, Ministry of Economy, Trade and Industry [METI]), these 14,062 firms comprise virtually all firms with fifty or more employees in all manufacturing industries.[11] We obtained responses from nearly 40 percent of these 14,062 firms.[12] This response rate, which is high for an academic survey, implies that our sample should be regarded as reasonably reliable in deriving implications to the whole manufacturing. Since other previously available firm-level data sets on offshoring include only a limited number of firms and are not designed to cover the entire manufacturing, this survey has a clear advantage in its coverage.[13]

While different official statistics (*The Basic Survey of Commercial and Manufacturing Structure and Activity*, or *Sho-kogyo Jittai Kihon Chosa* in Japanese) covered production offshoring by 118,300 Japanese manufacturing firms without any firm-size threshold in 1998, previous investigations of that survey by Tomiura (2005, 2007) have confirmed that offshoring is actually quite rare among small-sized firms.[14] Consequently, in spite of the firm-size threshold, this survey should capture the predominant portion of offshoring activities by Japanese firms.

3.2 Survey results on offshoring

3.2.1 *Share of offshoring firms*

As the first notable finding from the survey, offshoring has spread to more firms over recent years. Of the 5,528 firms that responded to the survey, 21 percent are currently involved in offshoring. As only 15 percent were offshoring five years ago, the number of offshoring firms has increased by more than 35 percent (from 840 to 1,136 firms) over this five-year period.[15] This growth should be regarded as high, considering the recent trend that many firms are trying to replace specialized parts and components by those available at reduced cost at the marketplace. This spread of offshoring is even more remarkable when we consider that the number of domestic sourcing firms increased merely by 4 percent (from 3,252 to 3,391 firms) during the same period. As expected, the growth of offshoring clearly outpaced that of domestic sourcing.

However, as far as we count the number of firms, the share of firms active in offshoring remains lower than those active in domestic sourcing. Of the surveyed firms, 61 percent are sourcing within the national border. This gap in participation indicates that entry costs are likely to differ depending on sourcing locations. Differences in languages, legal systems, or business practices are likely to result in this gap in offshore versus domestic sourcing participation.

Table 10.1 Cross-tabulations on offshore sourcing

		Offshore sourcing		
		Yes	No	Total
Domestic sourcing	Yes	19.78	42.38	62.16
	No	1.20	36.64	37.84
	Total	20.99	79.10	100.00
Offshore sourcing		2000		
		Yes	No	Total
	Yes	14.74	6.04	20.78
2005	No	0.83	78.39	79.22
	Total	15.57	84.43	100.00

Notes: Shown are the percentages of the firms.

By combining questions from the survey, Table 10.1 displays useful cross-tabulations. Several findings are noteworthy. First, as expected from the explanation above, the firms engaged in offshoring without sourcing from domestic suppliers, or jumping to offshore sourcing by bypassing domestic sourcing, are quite exceptional, possibly reflecting different levels of contractibility and/or entry costs. Second, 1 percent exited but another 6 percent of the firms newly entered into offshoring during the five-year period. Though more firms (in net terms) are offshoring than in the past, not all firms active in offshoring five years ago continue offshoring now. The answers to other questions in the survey indicate that these exits from offshoring are relatively often induced by concerns of input quality or unexpected coordination costs with offshore suppliers.[16] As the decomposition of net employment changes into gross job creation and destruction has become popular in labor economics, this entry/exit decomposition is informative for our understanding of the dynamics of offshoring.

3.2.2 *Disaggregation by tasks*

The survey contains disaggregated information on the types of offshored tasks. Before discussing offshore sourcing, Table 10.2 summarizes the task distribution among domestic sourcing as a comparison. Percentages shown in the table are task counts, where we count multiple tasks sourced by the same firm separately. The three production-related tasks (production of intermediates, final assembly, and production of jigs/dies) occupy more than 70 percent of the domestic sourcing cases. The service-related tasks are far less frequently sourced in Japan.

Table 10.3 presents the task allocations in offshoring disaggregated across geographical destinations.[17] When a firm is offshoring multiple categories of tasks, we treat them as separate offshoring cases, as in Table 10.2, even if the firm is sourcing from the single type of suppliers (its own subsidiaries for example) in the single country.[18] As shown in the table, the two types of tasks most frequently offshored are the production of intermediates and final assembly, each of which occupies 35 percent. In third place is the

Table 10.2 Distribution of tasks in domestic sourcing

Production of jigs or dies	16.87
Production of intermediates	30.68
Final assembly	25.10
R&D	3.24
Information services	6.72
Customer supports	1.66
Professional services	5.92
Other tasks	9.80

Notes: Shown are the percentages of the firms sourcing each task. As a firm can source multiple tasks, the percentage is relative to the total number of choices.

production of jigs/dies (13 percent).[19] These top three tasks most frequently offshored are all directly related with production activities. Consequently, Japanese manufacturing firms are actively sourcing production-related tasks from suppliers located both within the home country and overseas.

On the other hand, the offshoring of service-related tasks remains severely limited, as in domestic sourcing reported in Table 10.2. Japanese firms are offshoring less than 5 percent in customer support (4.51 percent), R&D (3.58 percent), information services (3.01 percent), and professional services (2.13 percent).[20] Since the share of tasks currently offshored and that offshored five years ago do not differ much (omitted from the table), the central role of production-related tasks among offshore sourcing remains untouched for Japanese firms over the recent years. While the serious concerns are expressed in the United States over offshoring of software programming to India, the offshoring of services is still limited to a small segment of firms in the case of Japanese manufacturing industries, in spite of the general rise of offshoring to China.[21]

Table 10.3 Offshoring disaggregated by tasks and geographical destinations

Region task	China	ASEAN	Other Asia	USA and Europe	ROW	World Total
Jigs/dies	7.35	2.64	1.93	0.51	0.09	12.52
Intermediates	19.19	7.61	4.37	3.32	0.85	35.34
Final assembly	19.56	8.57	3.52	2.92	0.68	35.25
R & D	1.22	0.45	0.40	1.39	0.11	3.58
Information services	1.28	0.65	0.20	0.79	0.09	3.01
Customer supports	1.79	0.91	0.51	1.16	0.14	4.51
Professional services	0.71	0.37	0.31	0.65	0.09	2.13
Other tasks	1.70	0.71	0.34	0.71	0.20	3.66
Total	52.80	21.91	11.58	11.47	2.24	100.00

Notes: Shown are the percentages in the total number of offshoring cases.

While the task distributions are largely similar in offshore and domestic sourcing, several differences should be noted. First, among the production-related tasks, jigs and dies are more often sourced from suppliers within Japan, while intermediates are more often offshored. This contrast may be at least partly because the production of jigs and dies is supposed to be deeply integrated into the firm's technology choice and R&D strategy and supposed to require frequent face-to-face interactions for engineering adjustments. On the other hand, the production location of parts and components is supposed to be strongly affected by intercountry cost differentials. Second, among service-related tasks, the customer support and R&D are sourced more often across borders, but the offshoring of information processing and professional services are noticeably more often within the home country. This gap may be partly due to language barriers for Japanese firms.

3.2.3 *Disaggregation by geographical destinations*

Following the description of task allocations in offshoring, this section reports the regional disaggregation of sourcing destination based on Table 10.3.

First, China (including Taiwan and Hong Kong) occupies more than half of the offshoring cases, followed by ASEAN (22 percent). Nearly three-quarters of offshoring cases are within East Asia (China and/or ASEAN).[22] Furthermore, nearly three-quarters of the increases during 2000–2005 are due to the expansion of offshoring to China, though these are not shown in the table. Thus, the large and expanding share of offshoring to China strongly characterizes Japanese offshoring, as expected from the geographical proximity and large wage gap between Japan and China. As wage levels in China have recently risen, the future prospect of Japanese offshoring to China should be viewed with caution.

Other regions are relatively minor as offshoring destinations (other Asia, 11.58 percent; United States and Europe, 11.47 percent; the rest of the world, 2.24 percent). While the offshoring to India by American firms attracts political attentions in the United States, the offshoring from Japan to India (included in "other Asia") remains limited, possibly due to language barriers. The share of Korea, which is also included in "other Asia," was low, possibly due to the narrow wage gap and intense business competition between Korea and Japan. Though not shown in the table, during the five-year period, the share of "other Asia" has nonetheless surpassed that of the United States and Europe.

Second, the composition of tasks offshored to these two major destinations is not drastically different from that sourced within Japan, while the share of intermediate production and final assembly is slightly higher and the share of jigs and dies production is lower. More than half of the three production-related tasks are offshored to China. Combined with the previously reported figures on offshored tasks, the offshoring by Japanese manufacturing firms can be mainly characterized by the offshoring of production tasks to East Asian developing countries.

In terms of task composition in offshoring to other advanced countries (United States and Europe), the share of services is relatively high. Notwithstanding, even in the offshoring of information services, professional services, and customer supports, China surpasses these high-cost developed countries. On R&D, however, the United States and

Europe are the most popular offshoring destinations (39 percent: 1.39 of 3.58). By task composition, the share of R&D and of customer supports is higher than that for domestic sourcing. This may be partly due to the high level of R&D and large market size in the United States and Europe. While the share of production of jigs and dies is lower than that from domestic sourcing, the share of information services and of professional services is as high as from domestic sourcing, possibly suggesting the high competitiveness of these sectors in the United States and Europe.

3.2.4 *Disaggregation by suppliers*

This section identifies the types of partner firms in offshoring. Table 10.4 compares the task decomposition across three distinct types of supplier. Several differences must be noted.

First, R&D, customer supports, and final assembly tend to be relatively often offshored to own subsidiaries within multinationals. This appears consistent with the interpretation that R&D and customer supports are deeply linked with firm-specific inside knowledge. Firms may prefer their own subsidiaries in offshoring of final assembly at least partly due to brand-name concerns. These three tasks are offshored within the boundary of multinationals in around half of the cases (1.96/3.58; 2.36/4.51: 15.55/35.25 respectively; see Table 10.4). Even if all types of tasks are combined, 39 percent of offshore sourcing cases are to subsidiaries abroad owned by the offshoring firms. In other words, more than one-third of the offshoring cases are intrafirm transactions within multinationals, even if they are regarded as offshoring between legally independent entities. While we cannot estimate the magnitude of these intrafirm transactions from our survey, we must be cautious in claiming the spread of offshoring among independent firms.[23]

Second, subsidiaries owned by other Japanese firms play a larger role in offshoring of intermediate production, while their share in R&D is substantially lower. Japanese firms have an established reputation for their advantages in manufacturing parts and components. On the other hand, firms may find less incentive in offshoring R&D to other Japanese firms, who are often competing in the same industries based on similar advantages.

Table 10.4 Offshoring disaggregated by types of suppliers

Supplier task	Own subsidiaries	Other Japanese subsidiaries	Foreign-owned suppliers	Total
Jigs/dies	4.06	2.19	6.27	12.52
Intermediates	11.92	6.24	17.17	35.34
Final assembly	15.55	4.74	14.96	35.25
R & D	1.96	0.28	1.33	3.58
Information services	1.11	0.60	1.31	3.01
Customer supports	2.36	0.62	1.53	4.51
Professional services	0.45	0.31	1.36	2.13
Other tasks	1.73	0.43	1.50	3.66
Total	39.14	15.41	45.44	100.00

Notes: See notes to Table 10.3.

Third, foreign suppliers other than those owned by Japanese multinationals occupy high shares in offshore sourcing of any tasks: 42–50 percent in production-related tasks and 64 percent in professional services. Even when all tasks are summed, 45 percent of offshoring cases are to foreign suppliers without Japanese ownership, while the share of offshoring to subsidiaries owned by other Japanese firms is as low as 15 percent. Consequently, the perception that Japanese firms are sourcing from each other within a closed interlocked network no longer captures the reality of Japanese offshoring today.[24]

The survey contains additional information on the types of partner firms by disaggregating the geographical destination of offshoring, though this has been omitted from the tables for the sake of brevity. While the aggregate characteristics summarized in Table 10.4 are strongly affected by those of offshoring to China, the offshoring to ASEAN is characterized by the high share of sourcing from own subsidiaries, especially offshoring of final assembly and R&D within multinationals. This observation is consistent with Japanese accumulated FDI in ASEAN. On the other hand, in the offshoring to other advanced countries, more than half of the cases are sourcing from local suppliers (without Japanese majority ownership), especially in offshoring of service tasks, possibly reflecting the competitiveness of American and European firms in service sectors.

As a related early finding, Head and Ries (2002) find that production offshoring (measured in terms of purchases of finished goods from other firms relative to total variable costs) increases with the firm's FDI in low-income countries, based on a different Japanese firm-level data set (publicly traded companies captured in a commercial data base). Their result is consistent with our evidence on active production offshoring to East Asian low-wage countries, especially ASEAN with Japanese accumulated FDI.

The description of Japanese offshoring in this section, based on firm-level data, has revealed that more but a substantially limited fraction of Japanese firms (mostly large-sized firms) are active in offshoring, mainly of production tasks, predominantly to East Asian neighbors, overwhelmingly to China. The impact of the recent surge in local wage levels in China on Japanese offshoring, however, remains to be seen. On the other hand, offshoring of service tasks and by small firms remain inactive, possibly due to language barriers and/or management capability constraints. Whether or not the further development of information and communication technologies will trigger the spread of service offshoring should certainly be an important future research topic.

4 Whether and how offshoring firms are different in Japan

This section surveys previous studies on Japanese offshoring and discusses whether and how offshoring firms are different from nonoffshoring firms in Japan. The key variables on which we focus are productivity, employment, and R&D. Summarizing the established results on this contrast will be useful for discussing the potential impacts of offshoring on the domestic economy.

4.1 Productivity

The main prediction from the recently developed "New New Trade Theory." is that the firms engaged in offshoring are more productive than domestic firms but less productive than the firms engaged in FDI. In most of the theoretical models, the difference in cut-off productivity levels is derived from different entry costs. This theoretical productivity ordering has been clearly confirmed by Tomiura (2007). His finding provides evidence on Japanese firms but also contributes to the direct firm-level confirmation of the theoretical prediction itself. The principal finding remains robust irrespective of productivity measures (labor productivity, approximate total factor productivity, or domestic sales) or even after controlling for firm size or capital-intensity classes as well as industry. The productivity gap between the firms with different globalization modes is found really sizable. While the productivity ranking among FDI firms, exporters, and domestic firms has been confirmed in many other countries, the investigation of offshoring firms has so far been quite rare due to the data constraint even outside of Japan.[25] Based on a rare firm-level data set, Tomiura (2007) demonstrates that offshoring firms tend to be more productive than domestic firms but less productive than FDI firms. Although the identification of exact causes behind this productivity ordering is beyond the scope of his research, this productivity differential suggests higher entry barriers due to management overloads associated with offshore subsidiaries.

While the research results explained above have established the productivity ordering exactly predicted by "New New Trade Theory," the direction of causality is not investigated within the limit of cross-section data set. By using the firm-level panel data derived from the RIETI survey, Ito et al. (2012) examine this issue. On this point, Figure 10.6 confirms that intrafirm offshoring firms are on average more productive than outsourcing firms but it also shows that the productivity gap between them expands over time.[26] This dynamic pattern is more in line with the learning effect (becoming more productive after offshoring) rather than self selection (more productive firms entering into offshoring). Ito et al. (2012) confirm this impression by econometric propensity-score matching technique.[27] Their finding of the gap between intrafirm offshoring versus offshore outsourcing is consistent with nonnegligible costs for monitoring suppliers abroad without ownership. Even in the more researched topic on export versus FDI in other economies, it remains undecided which of these two mechanisms (learning or selection) works in the real world. More evidence will certainly be required for offshoring research.

While the analyses cited above investigate the contrast between intrafirm offshoring and offshore outsourcing, the impact of offshoring on productivity should also vary depending on the offshored task content or on the offshoring destinations. One of the research results from the RIETI survey by Ito et al. (2011) shows that the positive relation with productivity is significant for firms offshoring both manufacturing and service tasks and for firms offshoring to various destinations. This finding indicates some forms of economies of scope in offshoring, though the task content appears different depending on sourcing destinations or sourcing modes (see the descriptive evidence from the

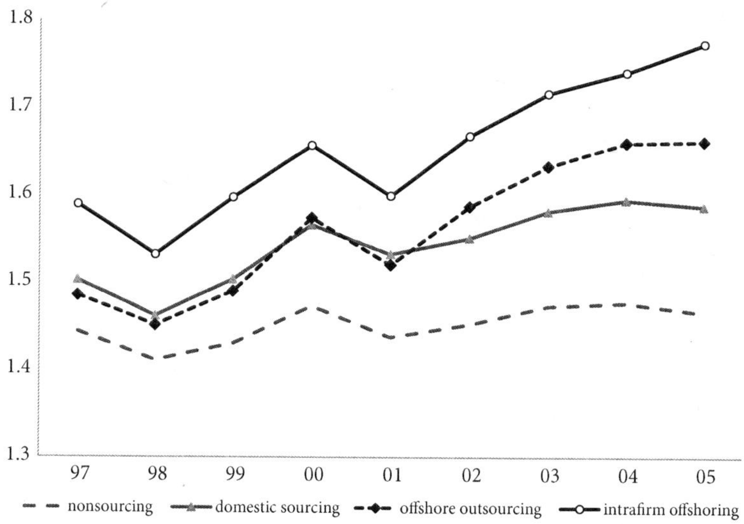

FIGURE 10.6 Offshoring and productivity differences.

Note: Firms are grouped by their offshoring status at 2000. Measured on the vertical axis is total factor productivity in logarithms.

same survey cited as Tables 10.3 and 10.4 in this chapter). While theoretical and empirical studies have been accumulated, the exact understanding of the productivity impact of offshoring requires detailed and wider-ranging data than that normally collected in standard statistics.

4.2 Employment

The impact of offshoring on domestic employment is a serious social concern in many developed countries. Manufacturing employment in developed economies has long been threatened by imports from developing countries, but furthermore, employment in service sectors, most of which have been sheltered from international competition as nontradable sectors, is increasingly exposed to risks of employment shifts to offshore competitors. The detection of exact impacts, however, is practically difficult due to the limited availability of offshoring data. This subsection instead summarizes findings on the relation between offshoring and the employment of offshoring firms compared with nonoffshoring firms based on Japanese firm-level data.

The size (in terms of employment) of offshoring firms is found to be larger than that of nonoffshoring firms. Tomiura (2007) reports that offshoring firms tend to be noticeably larger than domestic firms within a sample of 118,300 manufacturing firms in Japan without any firm-size threshold. The size premium remains significant even within the same industry. Furthermore, even within the sample excluding small firms, Ito et al. (2011) confirm a notable size premium associated with offshoring in Japanese manufacturing firms. While our firm-level offshoring data contain information not on the magnitude of offshoring but only on the number count of firms, the above findings of active offshoring by large firms suggest that the impact of offshoring on domestic employment might be nonnegligible because of the dominant shares occupied by large firms.

The difference between offshoring firms and nonoffshoring firms is summarized in Table 10.5. Shown in this table is the estimated coefficient on the offshoring dummy in the cross-section firm-level regression of each firm attribute. All the differences are statistically significant. These estimation results show that offshoring firms tend to be large, productive, and skill intensive.[28] The size premium (both in sales and employment) remains significant in both years, though it becomes slightly slim in 2005. The detailed employment composition is not identified in our firm-level data, but the average wage level (total wage payment divided by the number of employees) at offshoring firms is higher than that at nonoffshoring firms. As evidenced from a different data source related to wage differentials, the average wage level of Japanese workers engaged in production tasks, which occupy a major portion in Japanese offshoring, is lower than that in nonproduction tasks.[29] The higher average wage of offshoring firms may result from more profitable operations due to cost reduction by offshoring, though workers at offshoring firms are likely to be richer in human skills. This observation is in line with the established finding of the high wage of exporters and of multinationals.

By disaggregating nonproduction employment, Tomiura et al. (2012) further find that the employment share of skilled nonproduction workers, not of unskilled nonproduction workers, tends to be higher in offshoring firms than in nonoffshoring firms.[30] Although the share of nonproduction workers relative to production workers has been often used as a measure of skill intensity, the detailed analysis within nonproduction workers becomes more critical as the scope of offshoring expands from production to nonproduction corporate activities.

As consistent with the firm size premium, Tomiura (2007) confirms that offshoring is actually very rare among small firms, based on the firm-level data without any size threshold. In other words, offshoring activities are in only a limited fraction of large

Table 10.5 Offshoring premium

	2000	2005
Sales	0.949	0.904
Employment	0.700	0.631
Wage	0.074	0.110
Capital-labor ratio	0.245	0.313
Skill intensity	0.020	0.028
R&D intensity	0.034	0.027
Labor productivity	0.110	0.182
Total factor productivity	0.055	0.119

Notes: Shown is the estimated coefficient on the offshoring dummy in the regression of each firm attribute, adapted from Ito et al. (2011: table 2).

firms. This implies that offshoring should require highly skilled workers and/or strong corporate headquarters to handle contracting under different legal systems in remote locations, even in our Internet era.

As a related issue, the capital-labor ratio of intrafirm offshoring firms compared with offshore outsourcing firms is also an important variable. Antràs (2003) shows that FDI firms are more capital intensive than outsourcing firms. This theoretical prediction is based on the presumption that cost-sharing of investment in capital tends to be easier than that in labor. He also finds supportive evidence from aggregate industry- and country-level data. Tomiura et al. (2011) confirm, directly at the firm level, that firms engaged in offshore intrafirm sourcing tend to be significantly more capital intensive than firms engaged in offshore outsourcing, even after offshoring destinations and firm characteristics are controlled for, based on the firm-level data derived from the RIETI survey. This finding demonstrates that, while globalized firms are more capital intensive than domestic firms, offshore outsourcing firms are less capital intensive compared with FDI firms active in intrafirm sourcing. We must also note, however, that the research cited above has examined the static relation between capital intensity and offshore make-or-buy decision, as indicated by the self selection of capital-intensive firms into intrafirm sourcing within offshoring. Future studies will be required to investigate dynamic effects of offshoring on capital intensity, as relatively labor-intensive production processes are generally supposed to be easily offshored to low-wage countries.

4.3 Innovation

Innovation is certainly one of the vital concerns for firms competing in the modern global marketplace. As confirmed by the R&D-sales ratios reported in Table 10.5, offshoring firms are on average more innovative than nonoffshoring firms. This observation is consistent with the interpretation that only sufficiently innovative firms can enter into offshoring transactions. Previous empirical studies on the relation with innovation, as summarized below, have focused on the comparison of offshoring with other sourcing modes: intrafirm offshore sourcing via FDI and domestic sourcing.

The link between offshoring and innovation is examined theoretically by Antràs (2005) in comparisons with other globalization modes (FDI and exporting). The product-cycle theory originally proposed by Vernon (1966) has been extended in that paper to include offshore outsourcing. Antràs's model shows that the production is shifted to offshore locations first by FDI and then by offshore outsourcing, as the product becomes more matured (standardized). Motivated by this theoretical prediction, Tomiura (2008) empirically investigates the firm-level data set of 118,300 Japanese manufacturing firms. His comparison of the average R&D-sales ratio shows that exporters (combined with firms with FDI out of Asia) are the most R&D intensive, followed by firms with FDI in Asia. Firms engaged in production offshoring are on average less R&D intensive than these other globalized firms. This ordering in R&D intensity is exactly consistent with the theoretical hypothesis.

The different impact of innovation on domestic and offshore sourcing is empirically investigated by Tomiura (2009) based on the same 118,300 Japanese firms. His estimation results from multinomial logit model show that firms with higher R&D intensity tend to choose domestic sourcing rather than offshore sourcing. This finding implies that innovative firms prefer sourcing from suppliers within the home country possibly due to the importance of face-to-face contacts in technologically complex production.

These two empirical studies of Japanese firm-level data demonstrate how critically offshoring is related with innovation. However, neither of these research results established any direction of causality. The higher average R&D-sales ratio of offshoring firms, as shown in Table 10.5, could be a result merely from hollowing out (cross-border relocations of labor-intensive production processes through offshoring). If this is the case, apparent high R&D intensity of offshoring firms and eroded production base at home are the other side of the same coin. On the other hand, if the selection mechanism (innovative firms self-selected into offshoring) works, expansion of offshoring implies that innovative firms efficiently allocate corporate activities around the globe. The identification of the causality direction (innovation to offshoring or vice versa) will be required in the future.

5 Concluding remarks

In recent years, more and more firms are actively offshoring broader ranges of tasks. The main body of this chapter has described Japanese offshoring based on our unique survey. In spite of ample anecdotal episodes, statistical information on the precise state of offshoring is severely limited not only for Japan but also for many other countries. Consequently, the firm-level data reviewed in this chapter certainly contributes to our understanding of offshoring by Japanese firms and of offshoring in general. This chapter summarized the main descriptive results from the survey and discussed their implications. We have also reviewed established results from previous empirical research on Japanese offshoring.

The principal findings from our survey on Japanese offshore sourcing are as follows. Noticeably more firms are sourcing across national borders compared with five years ago, but still only around one-fifth of the medium-sized or large firms are actively offshoring. Offshoring firms tend to be substantially more productive than domestic firms. Production-related tasks offshored within East Asia occupy the major share in Japanese offshoring, while service offshoring remains limited. In more than one-third of offshoring cases, tasks are sourced from own offshore affiliates within the boundary of multinational firm. These intrafirm offshoring firms tend to be more capital intensive and R&D intensive than outsourcing firms. These may indicate still serious obstacles for active offshoring, especially of service tasks, across firm boundaries and beyond the neighboring countries, or unsolicited ample opportunities of global sourcing ahead of many firms in Japan.

Although firm-level data from our survey are informative, many important issues remain unresolved. For example, the magnitude of offshoring is not measured by our binary "yes or no" questions but they are certainly critical in evaluating the impact of offshoring on the Japanese economy. While our survey shows that only a limited fraction of Japanese firms are engaged in offshoring, the magnitude should not be underestimated as these offshoring firms are on average substantially large-sized. Figure 10.7 confirms the substantial variations in offshoring frequency across firm sizes.

Another topic left for future studies is the identification of causality direction. The simultaneous expansion of offshoring and decline in manufacturing employment are observed in many mature economies, including Japan. However, we should be cautious in concluding that offshoring causes domestic employment shrinkage. The size of manufacturing employment in a country is determined by various factors, ranging from macroeconomic business cycles, international competitiveness, population dynamics, and labor market institutions to technological changes. Offshoring is merely one of them, and these factors are often intertwined. Especially, technological innovations, such as more advanced communication technologies, will expand the scope of offshoring, while offshoring is likely to affect firms' choices of technology. Comprehensive data-collecting efforts will become increasingly important for our understanding of offshoring, not only in Japan and many other developed countries from which their firms are offshoring but also in developing countries to which globalized firms are offshoring.

While our firm-level data themselves have revealed no background explanations, the development in Japanese offshoring should be a part of corporate strategies to exploit the benefits of information technologies. Furthermore, as Japan has gone through a severe adjustment process after the burst of the bubble, the pressures for cost reduction

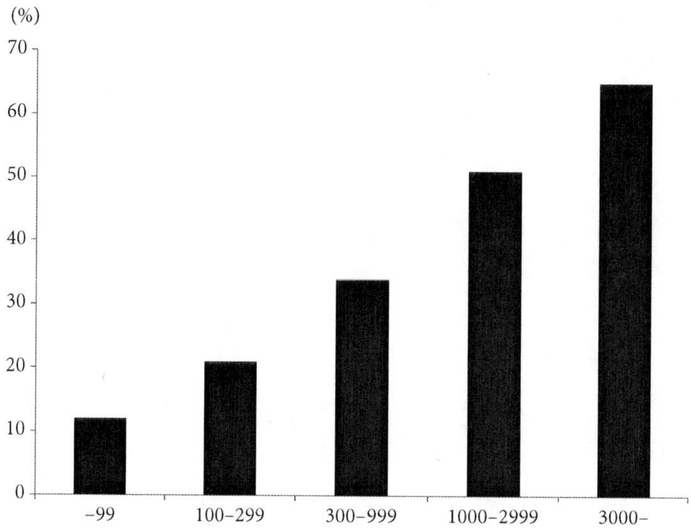

FIGURE 10.7 Offshoring by firm sizes.

Note: The horizontal axis presents firm-size classes in the number of employees. Measured on the vertical axis is the percentage of offshoring firms in each firm-size class. Firm-level data at 2005 are derived from RIETI survey.

should have been particularly serious for Japanese firms. Although the great earthquake in March 2011 uncovered the vulnerability of cross-border supply chain networks, the survival of Japanese firms will continue to critically hinge on offshoring in the era of global competition intensified by developments of emerging economies.

Acknowledgment

The authors appreciate the financial and administrative supports of Japan's Research Institute of Economy, Trade and Industry (RIETI). Section 3 of this chapter is based on a sunstantially revised version of our discussion paper (Ito et al. 2007).

Notes

*. Department of Economics, Yokohama National University, 79–4 Tokiwa-dai, Hodogaya-ku, Yokohama City, 240–8501, Japan. E-mail: tomiura@ynu.ac.jp.

**. School of Economics, Senshu University, 2–1-1 Higashimita, Tama-ku, Kawasaki-shi Kanagawa, 214–8580, Japan. E-mail: ito-banri@isc.senshu-u.ac.jp.

***. Center for Economic Growth Strategy, Yokohama National University, and Institute of Economic Research, Kyoto University, Yoshida-honmachi, Sakyo-ku, Kyoto, 606–8501, Japan. E-mail: wakasugi@ynu.ac.jp.

1. For Japanese offshoring, see also chapter 11 by Yasuyuki Todo in this volume.
2. The sample coverage of this statistics is relatively limited as the response is not legally mandatory. However, this is the only official data source for Japanese offshore production and can be traced for a long period.
3. This section is based on the first part of Ito et al. (2007) with adaptations to the context of this volume.
4. The distinction between offshore versus domestic sourcing is based on the location, not the ownership of suppliers.
5. Another offshoring measure includes inward/outward processing trade, which is unavailable for countries without such a special duty treatment scheme. As still another measure, Yeats (2001) uses exports of parts and components in trade statistics, readily available but with limited scope.
6. To the best knowledge of the authors, all the offshoring data of Japanese firms (*The Basic Survey of Business Structure and Activity* and *The Basic Survey of Commercial and Manufacturing Structure and Activity*) capture only production offshoring. The latter survey has not been conducted since 1998. The former survey resumes collecting data on production offshoring, of which Hijzen et al. (2010) analyzed earlier years, and additionally introduces questions on service offshoring in the most recent survey at the time of this writing.
7. Görg and Hanley (2005) distinguish expenditures on imported services from those on imported materials at the plant level, while Cusmano et al. (2010) disaggregates offshoring into three categories (production-assembling, R&D-design, and services). However, our disaggregation is more detailed than these.

8. Korea, India and Middle East are included in "other Asian countries." Eastern Europe is included in "United States and Europe." Latin America and Australia are included in ROW. These definitions are explicitly given in the survey question.
9. Since category (1) concentrates on the majority-owned subsidiaries, the categories (2) and (3) could include minority-owned affiliates of the offshoring firm.
10. See Ito et al. (2007) for the details of the survey.
11. We cannot cover firms those entered after 2005, while some firms previously included in the list are no longer accessible (e.g., exits, address changes). While all the firms should have been above the threshold size (fifty employees) at the time of the mandatory survey, 10.6 percent of surveyed firms are below the threshold this time. In addition to this employment size threshold, the original statistics on which our survey is based impose a threshold on capital at 30 million yen.
12. As firms did not necessarily answer all questions, the response rates for individual questions are inevitably lower.
13. The sample size in previous micro-data studies is generally limited: 652 plants within Irish electronics industries by Görg and Hanley (2005), and 1,148 manufacturing firms within Lombardy region by Cusmano et al. (2010), for example. Kurz (2006) documents 34,649 US manufacturing plants, but he uses foreign content cost of materials, which could include imports of standard raw materials and fails to include many other forms of offshoring.
14. Tomiura (2007) reports that only around 3 percent of the firms are offshoring production at 1998 among 118,300 surveyed firms, of which nearly 80 percent are with less than 50 employees. Cusmano et al. (2010) similarly find that merely 7.84 percent of the firms are offshoring among 1,148 firms, about half of which belong to 10–49 employee class.
15. As entry/exit is rare among Japanese large/mid-sized firms in our sample period, this observation is qualitatively unchanged even within the balanced panel of continuing firms.
16. This survey asks each firm on the reasons for entry/exit by multiple-choice questions. See Ito et al. (2007).
17. Among 1,136 firms answering affirmatively to the binary offshoring-or-not question, seventeen firms did not report any breakdown data and thus are excluded from the disaggregated tables.
18. On the other hand, when a firm is sourcing the single category of task from the single type of suppliers in the single country, we count it as one case even if many suppliers are involved.
19. This observation remains unchanged even if we count the numbers of firms for each task (without distinguishing destinations and suppliers). 63, 62, and 24 percent respectively of the offshoring firms are offshoring final assembly, production of intermediates, and production of jigs and dies respectively.
20. When we do not distinguish destinations or tasks, 7.5, 7.0, 5.0, and 3.1 percent respectively of the offshoring firms are offshoring customer supports, R&D, information services, and professional services, respectively. This confirms the same ordering as in the task-destination-supplier count.
21. We must note that the survey does not cover service or commercial industries.
22. When we do not distinguish task or suppliers, 77 percent of the offshoring firms are offshoring to China. 33% are offshoring to ASEAN. As some firms are offshoring to multiple destinations, the sum of percentages thus defined (different from those in the tables) over all regions exceeds 100.

23. Tomiura et al. (2011) find that firms engaged in intrafirm offshoring tend to be more capital-intensive than offshore outsourcing firms, even after industry and relevant firm characteristics are controlled for. Ito et al. (2012) report that intrafirm offshoring firms tend to be more productive and to exhibit higher productivity growth compared with outsourcing firms. Both are based on the same RIETI firm-level data.
24. When we look at the growth from five years ago, the share of subsidiaries owned by other Japanese firms is still high. Hence, we must be cautious in concluding that Japanese offshoring will shift further from Japanese subsidiaries to foreign suppliers.
25. As a rare exception, Defever and Toubal (2007) analyze French firm-level offshoring data for a similar purpose.
26. Productivity in logarithm is measured in terms of Total Factor Productivity (TFP), which we estimate by applying the Levinsohn–Petrin method for handing endogeneity in the estimation of Cobb–Douglas production function. Firms engaged in multiple sourcing modes are classified in the mode with the highest entry costs, assuming that entry costs are the highest in intrafirm offshoring, followed by offshore outsourcing, which are in turn followed by domestic sourcing and entry costs are the lowest in firms not involved in any sourcing. For example, firms active both in intrafirm offshoring and domestic sourcing are included in the graph as intrafirm offshoring firms.
27. Based on Japanese different firm-level data, Hijzen et al. (2010) also discover that the impact on productivity is significantly positive not in offshore outsourcing but in intrafirm offshoring, though their data cover only production offshoring during an earlier period (1994–99).
28. Labor productivity is defined by per-employee value-added. TFP is estimated by the Levinsohn–Petrin method as explained earlier. The skill intensity is measured by the employment share of nonproduction workers (employees at corporate headquarters sections), as no employment data disaggregated by skills, occupations, or educational attainments are available in Japanese corporate statistics.
29. According to the most recent Japan's Wage Census in 2010, the scheduled monthly wage (before tax, excluding overtime pay) of workers averaged over all production occupations is 236 thousand yen, while that of science researchers, system engineers, computer programmers, lawyers, and accountants is 400, 332, 265, 955, and 580 respectively.
30. Skilled nonproduction workers are defined as employees in corporate headquarters for corporate planning, R&D, and information processing, while unskilled non-production workers are those for other miscellaneous functions, such as clerical works. Workers managing overseas business at corporate headquarters increase in offshoring firms.

References

Antràs, P. 2003. "Firms, Contracts, and Trade Structure." *Quarterly Journal of Economics* 118: 1375–1418.

———. 2005. "Incomplete Contracts and the Product Cycle." *American Economic Review* 95 (4): 1054–1073.

Antràs, P., and E. Helpman, E. 2004. "Global Sourcing." *Journal of Political Economy* 112: 552–580.

Cusmano, L., M. Mancusi, and A. Morrison. 2010. "Globalisation of Production and Innovation: How Outsourcing is Reshaping an Advanced Manufacturing Area." *Regional Studies* 44, 235–252.

Defever, F., and F. Toubal. 2007. "Productivity and the sourcing modes of multinational firms: Evidence from French firm-level data." CEP Discussion Paper, no. 0842, London.

Feenstra, R. C., and G. H. Hanson. 1996. "Globalization, Outsourcing, and Wage Inequality." *American Economic Review* 86 (2): 240–245.

Görg, H., and A. Hanley. 2005. "International Outsourcing and Productivity: Evidence from the Irish Electronics Industry." *North American Journal of Economics and Finance* 16: 255–269.

Head, K., and J. Ries. 2002. "Offshore Production and Skill Upgrading by Japanese Manufacturing Firms." *Journal of International Economics* 58 (1): 81–105.

Hijzen, A., T. Inui, and Y. Todo. 2010. "Does Offshoring Pay? Firm-level Evidence from Japan." *Economic Inquiry* 48: 880–895.

Ito, B., E. Tomiura, and R. Wakasugi. 2007. "Dissecting Offshore Outsourcing and R&D: A Survey of Japanese Manufacturing Firms." Discussion Paper, no. 07-E-060, Research Institute of Economy, Trade, and Industry, Tokyo.

———. 2011. "Offshore Outsourcing and Productivity: Evidence from Japanese Firm-level Data Disaggregated by Tasks." *Review of International Economics* 19: 555–567.

———. 2012. "Does Firm Boundary Matter? The Effect of Offshoring on Productivity of Japanese Firms." In *Quantitative Analysis of Newly Evolving Patterns of International Trade*, edited by R. M. Stern, 100–138. New Jersey: World Scientific.

Kurz, C. 2006. "Outstanding outsourcers: A Firm and Plant-level Analysis of Production Sharing." FEDs Working Paper, no. 2006–04, Washington, DC.

Tomiura, E. 2005. "Foreign Outsourcing and Firm-level Characteristics: Evidence from Japanese Manufacturers." *Journal of the Japanese and International Economies* 19: 255–271.

———. 2007. "Foreign Outsourcing, Exporting, and FDI: A Productivity Comparison at the Firm Level." *Journal of International Economics* 72: 113–127.

———. 2008. "Foreign Outsourcing and the Product Cycle: Evidence from Micro Data." *Applied Economics Letters* 15: 1019–1022.

———. 2009. "Foreign Versus Domestic Outsourcing: Firm-level Evidence on the Bole of Technology." *International Review of Economics and Finance* 18: 219–226.

Tomiura, E., B. Ito, and R. Wakasugi. 2011. "Offshore Outsourcing Decision and Capital Intensity: Firm-level Relationships." *Economic Inquiry* 49: 364–378.

———. 2012. "Offshore Outsourcing and Non-production Workers: Firm-level Relationships Disaggregated by Skills and Suppliers." *The World Economy*, doi: 10.1111/j.1467-9701.2012.01477.x.

Vernon, R. (1966) "International investment and international trade in the product cycle." *Quarterly Journal of Economics* 80: 190–207

Wakasugi, R., B. Ito, and E. Tomiura. 2008. "Offshoring and Trade in East Asia: A Statistical Analysis." *Asian Economic Papers* 7: 101–124.

Yeats, A. 2001. "Just How Big is Global Production Sharing?" In *Fragmentation: New Production Patterns in the World Economy*, edited by S. Arndt and H. Kierzkowski, 108–143. Oxford: Oxford University Press.

CHAPTER 11

Offshoring of Japanese Small and Medium Enterprises*

YASUYUKI TODO†

There is already an abundant literature on offshoring using firm-level data for Japan. However, such firm-level studies are mostly based on data for medium and large firms. For example, Wakasugi et al. (2008), Hijzen et al. (2010), Yamashita and Fukao (2010), and Jinji et al. (2011), as explained in detail later, draw on data for firms with fifty employees or more and paid-up capital of at least 30 million yen.

Not only large firms but also small and medium enterprises (SMEs) may engage in offshoring. However, although the characteristics, determinants, and impact of SME offshoring differ from those of larger firms, few studies have yet quantitatively examined this using firm-level data in any country. The exception is Tomiura (2007), who employed census data for all firms, including SMEs. This chapter particularly focuses on the offshoring of Japanese SMEs, using a unique data set that contains detailed information on offshoring.

The chapter is structured as follows. Section 1 describes the data. Section 2 summarizes the offshoring characteristics of Japanese SMEs. Section 3 examines the determinants of offshoring, focusing on the choice between intrafirm and arm's-length offshoring. Sections 4, 5, and 6 investigate the impact of offshoring on employment, skill upgrading, and productivity respectively. Section 7 summarizes the results and concludes. Throughout the chapter, the results for Japanese SMEs are compared with the results for larger firms as evidenced in past studies.

1 Description of the Data

We construct the data set for Japanese SMEs from two sources. The first is a confidential survey of Internationalization and Enterprise Activities by SMEs (*Kokusaika to*

Kigyo Katsudo ni Kansuru Anketo Chosa), hereafter the SME Survey. This survey was conducted in December 2009 by Mitsubishi UFJ Research and Consulting in cooperation with the Small and Medium Enterprise Agency under the Ministry of Economy, Trade and Industry (METI) of Japan. In accordance with the definition of the Small and Medium Enterprise Agency, the survey defines SMEs as firms with fewer than 300 employees or less than 300 million yen of paid-up capital. The survey targets about 8,000 SMEs identified as engaging in export or foreign direct investment (FDI) according to existing census surveys by METI, along with about 10,000 SMEs randomly selected from those not previously recorded as engaging in FDI or export. Of the 18,407 SMEs sent the survey, 3,512 SMEs (19.1 percent) responded.

The second source of data is METI's Current Survey of Production (*Kogyo Tokei Chosa*), hereafter CSP.[1] Conducted annually, the CSP includes all enterprises producing manufactured goods or mineral products at the establishment level. Responding to the CSP is compulsory, and more than 100,000 establishments respond every year. The CSP data for 2006, the most recent year available at the time of the data collection, were converted to firm-level data and merged with the data from the SME Survey. After merging and cleaning the data, the sample comprises 1,511 manufacturing firms.

Besides its focus on SMEs, this data set is unique in that it contains detailed information on international transactions of the SMEs, including FDI and international contracting-out. This information enables us to identify offshoring SMEs. Offshoring is often defined as "the transfer, through foreign direct investment or sub-contracting, of all or part of the production of goods and services to another country with the intention to re-import them to the home country" (Yeaple 2006). Offshoring is then often further classified into two types, intrafirm offshoring, sometimes referred to as offshore insourcing, that is, offshoring to the firm's own foreign subsidiaries, and arm's-length offshoring, or offshore outsourcing, that is, offshoring to unaffiliated firms. It is possible to distinguish between the two types of offshoring in this data set because firms report both the destination and the buyer of goods produced in foreign countries for each international transaction. In the benchmark estimations, we define intrafirm offshoring as FDI in which products are exported to Japan and arm's-length offshoring as international contracting-out to unaffiliated foreign firms where the products are exported to Japan.

However, offshoring is occasionally defined more broadly as the relocation of business activities to any foreign country, regardless of whether the firms involved reexport products to the home country (Wagner 2009). Therefore, in an alternative specification, we define intrafirm offshoring as FDI of any kind and arm's-length offshoring as international contracting-out of any kind. To avoid notational confusion, we refer to FDI and international contracting-out as broadly defined offshoring.

In addition, this data set contains information on the characteristics of the chief executive officer (CEO) of each SME, including information on each CEO's international experience and risk and time preferences. We consider a CEO to have international experience prior to the decision on offshoring if he or she has worked, lived, or studied abroad.

The CEO's risk preference can be measured from the response to the following question in the survey: "If there were an investment opportunity that presents a 50 percent probability of earning 1 million yen and otherwise earning nothing, what is the most you would pay for this investment?" The ten responses available range from 100,000 to 1 million yen plus the option, "I would not even pay less than 100,000 yen." Using this information, we construct a risk preference variable that takes a value of 1 if the CEO chooses not to invest, 2 if 100,000 yen, 3 if 200,000, 4 if 300,000, 5 if 400,000, and 6 if 500,000 or more. Accordingly, larger values imply the CEO is more risk tolerant.

We infer the time preference of CEOs from their response to the following question: "What is the minimum amount you would prefer receiving one year and one month from now to receiving 100,000 yen one month from now?" Using this information, we construct a binary variable that takes a value of 0 if the CEO responds, "I would prefer receiving 100,000 yen one month from now, regardless of the amount of money I would get one year and one month from now," and 1 otherwise. We assume this variable approximates whether the CEO is forward-looking (1) or myopic (0). Estimating risk and time preferences from similar hypothetical questions is featured in work by Cramer et al. (2002), Frederick et al. (2002), and Tanaka et al. (2010), although not in the context of the internationalization of firms.

2 Characteristics of Japanese Firms' Offshoring

2.1 Evidence from existing studies

Before looking at the characteristics of the offshoring of Japanese SMEs, let us summarize what we know from existing work on the offshoring of Japanese firms more generally. According to the definition of offshoring in Yeaple (2006), a natural measure of the extent of offshoring at the industry level is the share of imports of intermediate inputs in the total inputs purchased by the industry. However, as data on the imports of intermediate inputs for a particular industry are often unavailable, Feenstra and Hanson (1999) propose a measure of offshoring for industry *i* given by:

$$\sum_j (\text{share of good } j \text{ in total purchases by industry } i)$$
$$\times (\text{Share of imports in total consumption of good } j)$$
$$= \sum_j \left[\frac{\text{Input purchases of good } j \text{ by industry } i}{\text{Total input purchases by industry } i}\right] \times \left[\frac{\text{Improts of good } j}{\text{Domestic consumption of good } j}\right]$$

In other words, Feenstra and Hanson assume that the share of imports of a particular good purchased by any industry is equal to the share of imports of the good in the whole country. Correspondingly, Feenstra and Hanson define a "narrow" measure of offshoring for a particular industry as the share of imports in intermediate inputs purchased from the same industry. These measures are widely used in other offshoring studies, such as Amiti and Wei (2006).

To construct these offshoring measures at the industry level for Japan, existing studies often rely on the Japan Industry Productivity (JIP) Database, constructed and annually updated by Kyoji Fukao at Hitotsubashi University, Tsutomu Miyagawa at Gakushuin University, and their collaborators. The JIP Database includes detailed information on inputs, outputs, trade, and FDI at the industry level and is freely available on the website of the Research Institute of Economy, Trade and Industry (RIETI). See http://www.rieti.go.jp/en/.

Using the JIP Database, Agnese (2009a, 2009b) follows Feenstra and Hanson (1999) and constructs both narrow and broad measures of offshoring. Moreover, Agnese (2009a, 2009b) follows Amiti and Wei (2006) and distinguishes between material and service offshoring, defining the measure of service offshoring as the share of estimated imported purchases from service sectors by each industry in the total purchases from service sectors by the industry. Agnese (2009a, 2009b) documents a remarkable increase in the material offshoring intensity from 3 percent in 1980 to 10 percent in 2005, while the service offshoring intensity remained relatively low at about 2 percent during the same period.

Although increasing, the intensity of offshoring in Japan is relatively small compared with that found in other developed countries. For example, Campa and Goldberg (1997) concluded that the imported input share in the manufacturing sector for Japan was about 4.1 percent in 1993, while the corresponding share for the other three countries considered in the study (the United States, the United Kingdom, and Canada) was substantially higher (about 8 percent in the US and 20 percent in the UK and Canada in the mid-1990s). More recently, using the OECD input–output database to construct Feenstra–Hanson offshoring measures, Agnese and Ricart (2009) find that the offshoring intensity for Japan in 2005 was the second lowest among 26 countries.

One drawback of the measures developed by Feenstra and Hanson (1999) is that the share of imports in domestic consumption of good *j* may differ from the share of imports in domestic consumption of good *j* by industry *i*, such that the estimated imports of intermediate inputs for each industry are biased.

To correct for this possible bias, Ito and Tanaka (2010) combine the JIP Database and detailed input–output tables constructed by the Ministry of Internal Affairs and Communications for 1990, 1995, and 2000 (available at http://www.stat.go.jp/english/data/io/index.htm) and construct a more direct measure of material and service offshoring, defined as the ratio of the imports of intermediate goods/services to the total inputs of intermediate goods/services in each industry. Their estimates are similar to those of Agnese (2009a, 2009b), showing that material offshoring intensity in Japan increased from 6.0 percent in 1990 to 8.9 percent in 2004, while service offshoring intensity remained low at 0.21 percent in 1990 and 0.19 percent in 2004 (see Figure 11.1). Ito and Tanaka (2010) further disaggregate offshoring intensity based on the host country using the regional distribution of imports in 1996. In 2004, about half of material offshoring was to Asia, increasing from a quarter in 1990, while offshoring to North America and the European Union accounted for some three-quarters of service offshoring. These

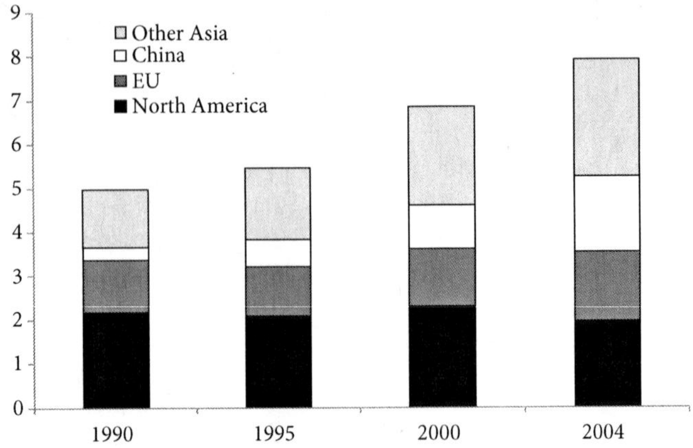

FIGURE 11.1 Material offshoring intensity by destination.

Note: Material offshoring intensity is defined as the ratio of imports of intermediate goods to total inputs.

Source: Ito and Tanaka (2010: table 1).

findings, as summarized in Figure 11.1, clearly indicate that material offshoring to Asia, most notably China, expanded rapidly from 1990 to 2004.

Another source of information on offshoring in Japan is a survey conducted by the RIETI at the firm level in 2006, *Kigyo Kaigai Katsudo Chosa* (Survey of Corporate Offshore Activities), hereafter referred to as the RIETI Survey. This survey targeted 14,062 medium and large firms in Japan and received 5,528 responses. See chapter 10 for further details of the survey. The data from the RIETI Survey are unique in several ways. First, the data classify the work offshored into several types, including the production of jigs or dies, the production of parts and components, final assembly, R&D, information services (such as programming and customer services), and professional services (such as legal, accounting, and financial services). Second, the data include the geographic destination of offshoring using the categories of China, Association of Southeast Asian Nations (ASEAN), other Asian countries, the United States, Europe, and rest of the world. Finally, the data reveal the type of firm to which the tasks are sourced, namely, own subsidiaries, subsidiaries owned by other Japanese firms, and others.

Wakasugi et al. (2008) provide a summary of the RIETI Survey in relation to offshoring. Of the 5,528 respondent firms, 42 percent practiced domestic sourcing, that is, sourcing some tasks to firms in Japan, while 21 percent practiced offshoring, that is, sourcing some tasks to firms abroad, and 20 percent practiced both domestic sourcing and offshoring. This work also indicated that offshoring is more prominent in industries such as the apparel, machinery, electric machinery, information and telecommunications, and electronics and devices industries, as these are often characterized by the modularization of parts and components.

Wakasugi et al. (2008) also report that of all offshored tasks, 53 percent are sourced to China, 22 percent to ASEAN, and 12 percent to other Asian countries (see chart A in Figure 11.2). Clearly, the role of China and ASEAN is substantially greater than that estimated

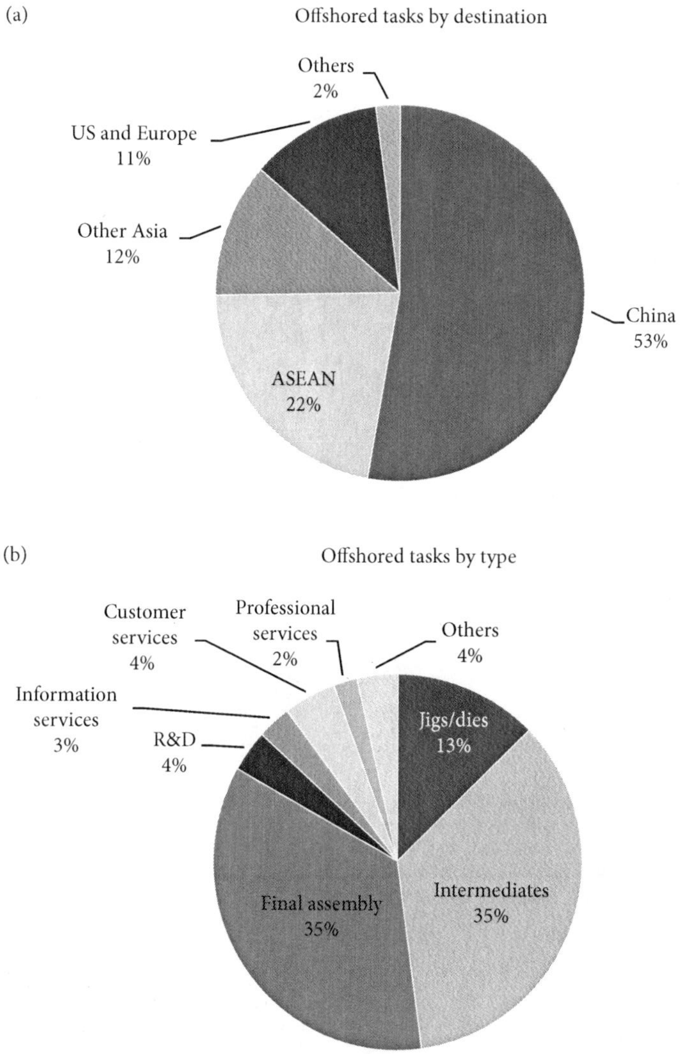

FIGURE 11.2 Destinations and types of offshored tasks in 2005.

A. Offshored tasks by destination.

B. Offshored tasks by type.

Source: Wakasugi et al. (2008: fig. 3 and table 4).

for 2004 by Ito and Tanaka (2010). One possible reason for this difference is that Ito and Tanaka (2010) use the regional distribution of imports in 1996, when imports from China were substantially smaller than in 2004, to estimate the imports of intermediate goods from China. Another possible reason is that Wakasugi et al. (2008) do not take the value of offshored tasks into account; rather, they consider only the *number* of offshored tasks.

In addition, Wakasugi et al. (2008) find that 35 percent of offshored tasks involve the production of intermediate goods and that another 35 percent include final assembly. A further 13 percent involve the production of jigs or dies and 3.6 percent involve R&D

activity. Service offshoring accounts for 10 percent of tasks, including the offshoring of information services, customer support, and professional services (see chart B in Figure 11.2). This is consistent with the findings in Agnese (2009a, 2009b) and Ito and Tanaka (2010) that service offshoring in Japan is relatively minor. Finally, Wakasugi et al. (2008) report that 39 percent of tasks are offshored to the firm's own foreign subsidiaries, 15 percent to the foreign subsidiaries of other Japanese firms, and 45 percent to other firms. This highlights that intrafirm offshoring is just as important as arm's-length offshoring.

2.2 Evidence on SMEs

Of the 1,511 SMEs in the sample described in section 1, 288 firms engaged in either FDI or international contracting-out, or broadly defined offshoring, and 92 firms engaged in (narrowly defined) offshoring, specifying both the buyer and the destination (the first row of Table 11.1).[2] Of the 288 broadly defined offshoring firms, 155 and 177 firms reported their engagement in FDI and international contracting-out respectively. The sum of 155 and 177 exceeds the total number, 288, since some firms engage in both. Of the 92 narrowly defined offshoring firms, 61 and 45 firms respectively engage in intrafirm and arm's-length offshoring, defined as FDI or international contracting-out in which the products are reexported to Japan. Further, offshoring to China accounts for about 60–70 percent of total offshoring, an even larger share than that of the larger firms documented in previous studies and summarized in section 1. We should emphasize,

Table 11.1 Offshoring of Japanese SMEs. Total number of firms: 1,511

	Number of firms		Number of firms
FDI or international contracting-out (broadly defined offshoring)	288	Offshoring (narrowly defined offshoring in which products are exported to Japan)	92
Of which		Of which	
FDI (broadly defined intrafirm offshoring)	155	Intrafirm offshoring	61
Destination		Destination	
China	85	China	38
ASEAN	57	ASEAN	22
Other Asia	19	Other Asia	4
Others	27	Others	0
International contracting-out (broadly defined arm's-length offshoring)	177	Arm's-length offshoring	45
Destination		Destination	
China	108	China	32
ASEAN	68	ASEAN	7
Other Asia	50	Other Asia	7
Others	95	Others	7

Note: The total number of firms by destination of intrafirm or arm's-length offshoring exceeds the total number of offshoring firms as firms may engage in offshoring in more than one country.

Table 11.2 Summary statistics

	Number of observations	Mean	Standard deviation	Median	Minimum	Maximum
No. of workers in 2009	1511	61.3	68.8	38	1	590
(in logs)	1511	3.66	0.983	3.64	0	6.38
No. of workers in 2006	1511	62.2	66.6	39	4	708
(in logs)	1511	3.72	0.900	3.66	1.39	6.56
Sales in 2009 (million yen)	1408	1774	4636	678.5	6	122473
(in logs)	1408	6.57	1.34	6.52	1.79	11.7
Sales in 2006 (million yen)	1511	1635	2992	705	9	59031
(in logs)	1511	6.63	1.25	6.56	2.20	11.0
Share of exports in sales in 2006	1511	5.74	14.6	0	0	100
Firm age in 2009	1511	52.0	33.8	47	2	505
Index of risk preference of the CEO (1–6, where 6 = risk taking)	1495	3.20	2.24	2	1	6
Index of time preference of the CEO (0, 1, where 0 = myopic)	1511	0.497	0.500	0	0	1
International experience of the CEO (0, 1)	1511	0.267	0.442	0	0	1

however, that as about half of the sample was from internationalized firms and the other half from other firms, the share of offshoring firms in the sample (about 6 percent if narrowly defined and 20 percent if broadly defined) significantly overestimates the actual share in the population of SMEs. Thus, the actual share of offshoring SMEs should be quite small, and probably much smaller than the share of larger firms of 21 percent found in Wakasugi et al. (2008) (as shown in section 2.1).

Table 11.2 provides summary statistics of the variables subsequently used in the analysis. The median numbers of firm workers and sales in 2009 were 38 and 647 million yen respectively, both indicating that the firms included in the data set are relatively small.[3] The average share of exports in sales in 2006 was 5.7 percent, and 60 percent of all firms in the sample did not export. We ascertain that about half of the CEOs in the SMEs are myopic (the rest are forward-looking) and 26.7 percent of CEOs have international experience as defined.

3 The choice between intrafirm and arm's-length offshoring

3.1 Evidence from existing studies

As explained in section 1, there are two types of offshoring, intrafirm offshoring and arm's-length offshoring. Trade theory has examined how firms make the choice between the two types of offshoring available, providing three key predictions. First, Antràs (2003) incorporates the theory of the firm with incomplete contracts developed by Grossman and Hart (1986) into the new trade theory of Helpman and Krugman (1985), predicting that firms are more likely to engage in intrafirm offshoring in more capital-intensive (less labor-intensive) industries. The reason is that sharing the costs of investment in physical capital between final-good firms and their intermediate suppliers is easier than sharing the costs of investment in labor. Antràs (2003) finds a positive relation between the capital–labor ratio and the share of intrafirm imports in total imports at the industry level for the United States, thereby supporting this theoretical prediction.

Second, Antràs and Helpman (2004) extend Antràs (2003) to incorporate firm heterogeneity into the model. Their main conclusion is that productivity determines the organizational form of the relation between final-good firms and their suppliers. In sectors where headquarter services are used more intensively than intermediate goods, the most productive firms engage in intrafirm offshoring, while less productive firms engage in arm's-length offshoring. This is because intrafirm offshoring requires larger initial fixed costs, but also leads to larger profits for more productive firms.

Finally, Chen et al. (2008) incorporate into their model knowledge capital that can be easily learned and used by intermediate-good suppliers and they find that knowledge-capital-intensive firms are more likely to engage in intrafirm offshoring to prevent the dissemination of knowledge. They further argue that, as knowledge-based assets should be reflected by the market value of firms, Tobin's q, or the ratio of a firm's market value to the replacement value of physical assets, is positively correlated with the likelihood of intrafirm offshoring.

Several studies test these theoretical predictions using Japanese data. Because of the richness of the data on offshoring for Japan compared with other countries, the following three studies are the first to test these theoretical predictions using firm-level data. First, Tomiura (2007) employs census data for Japanese firms from *Sho-Kogyo Jittai Kihon Chosa* (the Basic Survey of Commercial and Manufacturing Structure and Activities)[4] conducted by METI in 1998 and examines how firms' productivity affects their globalization decisions. One advantage of this particular data set is that there is no firm size threshold, so that it covers 118,300 firms across all manufacturing industries. Another unique feature of this data set is that the survey directly asks sample firms whether they "contract out manufacturing or processing tasks to other firms overseas" so that arm's-length offshoring firms can be clearly identified. However, because this question is limited to manufacturing offshoring, the data set excludes service offshoring. In addition, information on the ownership of foreign affiliates is included in the data, and Tomiura (2007) defines FDI firms as firms that own one or more foreign affiliates with an ownership share of 20 percent or more. Although Tomiura (2007) does not perform any statistical tests, he draws conclusions on the basis of the distribution of productivity by firm type, finding evidence consistent with the predictions in Antràs and Helpman (2004). In particular, firms engaging in FDI have the highest average productivity, followed by arm's-length offshoring firms. Firms without any globalized activity display the lowest level of average productivity.

Second, Tomiura et al. (2011) test the hypothesis derived by Antràs (2003) using a unique data set on offshoring by Japanese firms derived from the *Kigyo Kaigai Katsudo Chosa* (Survey of Corporate Offshore Activities, or the RIETI Survey) previously used in Wakasugi et al. (2008). As mentioned in section[2], this data set includes information on offshoring activities directly reported by each firm, including both material and service offshoring. Using a multinomial logit model, Tomiura et al. (2011) examine how the choice between intrafirm, arm's-length, and no offshoring is determined and confirm the finding in Antràs (2003) that capital-intensive firms, or firms with a higher capital–labor ratio, are more likely to engage in intrafirm offshoring than in arm's-length offshoring. In addition, they find that firm size (as measured by the number of employees) has a larger positive effect on the likelihood of intrafirm than of arm's-length offshoring. Given that firm size is often positively correlated with the level of productivity, this finding is also consistent with the theoretical predictions in Antràs and Helpman (2004).

Finally, Jinji et al. (2011) test the hypothesis in Chen et al. (2008) by merging three data sets for Japanese firms: *Kigyo Katsudo Kihon Chosa* (Basic Survey of Japanese Business Structure and Activities, hereafter *KKKC*), *Kaigai Jigyo Katsudo Kihon Chosa* (Basic Survey of Overseas Business Activities, *KJKKC*),[5] and the Company Financial Reports of Nikkei NEEDS (NEEDS). The first two surveys are conducted annually by METI. The *KKKC* data, particularly from 1994 to 1999, contain information on domestic and arm's-length offshoring, including how much each firm is paid for contracting out manufacturing or processing tasks. Therefore, Jinji et al. (2011) focus on the data gathered during this period. However, as the NEEDS data cover only about 4,000 listed firms, and given the difficulty in merging the firm-level data in the *KKKC* and *KJKKC* with those in NEEDS, the sample in Jinji et al. (2011) comprises only 1,100 parent firms. Their chosen measure of FDI is the ratio of the sales of foreign affiliates to domestic sales, whereas the measure of arm's-length offshoring is the ratio of total expenditure on arm's-length offshoring to domestic sales.

The estimation in Jinji et al. (2011) employs quantile regression of either the measure of FDI, the measure of arm's-length offshoring, or their ratio. They find that labor productivity has a positive impact on the measure of FDI, but no significant effect on the measure of arm's-length offshoring or the ratio of FDI and arm's-length offshoring. In addition, Tobin's q has a positive effect on FDI, arm's-length offshoring, and FDI relative to arm's-length offshoring. These findings support the hypothesis in Chen et al. (2008) that knowledge-capital intensive firms, or firms with a high Tobin's q, are more likely to engage in intrafirm offshoring because of the importance of knowledge assets in these firms. By comparing the results for productivity and Tobin's q, Jinji et al. (2011) further argue that productivity is less important than Tobin's q in this regard.

3.2 Evidence on SMEs

To examine how SMEs make choices between no offshoring, arm's-length offshoring, and intrafirm offshoring, we employ a multinomial logit model as in Tomiura et al. (2011). To simplify the model, we categorize firms engaging in both intrafirm and arm's-length offshoring as firms engaging in intrafirm offshoring. In other words, "firms engaging in intrafirm offshoring" consist of firms engaging in intrafirm offshoring but not in arm's-length offshoring and firms engaging in both intrafirm and arm's-length offshoring.[6] To alleviate possible biases associated with endogeneity, we specify past values of the independent variables when necessary. For example, productivity is measured by the log of value-added per worker three years before the offshoring decision.[7] Similarly, the share of exports in total sales, the log of employment, and the capital–labor ratio three years before are used as potential determinants of offshoring. We assume that the international experience and time preference of CEOs are determined before their offshoring decision and hence are exogenous.[8] To control for unobserved industry and regional characteristics, we also incorporate twenty-four industry and ten region dummies.

The results from the narrow definition of offshoring are presented in column (1) of Table 11.3, while the results from the broad definition are in column (2). The results indicate that the time preferences and international experiences of CEOs affect the offshoring decision; that is, firms are more likely to engage in offshoring when CEOs are more forward looking and have international experience. The effect of international

Table 11.3 Determinants of offshoring

	(1)		(2)	
	Arm's-length offshoring	Intrafirm offshoring	International contracting-out	FDI
Time preference of the CEO	0.416	0.901***	0.300**	0.381*
	(0.501)	(0.244)	(0.145)	(0.215)
International experience of the CEO	0.882**	1.474***	0.868***	1.318***
	(0.425)	(0.260)	(0.197)	(0.214)
Firm age	−0.000354	0.00463*	0.00519*	0.00625***
	(0.00479)	(0.00242)	(0.00272)	(0.00182)
Share of exports three years before	0.00167	0.0109	0.0219***	0.0239***
	(0.0131)	(0.0110)	(0.00555)	(0.00672)
Log of value-added per worker three years before	0.199	0.378	0.265	0.258*
	(0.359)	(0.306)	(0.197)	(0.138)
Log of employment three years before	0.433*	0.642***	0.224***	0.566***
	(0.241)	(0.182)	(0.0758)	(0.144)
Capital–labor ratio three years before	−0.111	−0.110**	0.000970	−0.0217
	(0.0767)	(0.0458)	(0.0129)	(0.0162)
Number of observations	1511		1511	
Log likelihood	−330.0		−774.4	

Notes: Coefficients from multinomial logit estimations reported. The base case is no offshoring. Standard errors in parentheses. *, **, and *** denote statistical significance at the 10, 5, and 1 percent level respectively. Industry and region dummies are included, but for brevity the results are not reported.

experience is also larger on intrafirm offshoring than on arm's-length offshoring. These results provide new evidence for the literature that at least some CEO characteristics affect the offshoring decision of SMEs.

As shown in column (1) of Table 11.3, productivity (as measured by the log of value-added per worker) has no significant effect on decisions on intrafirm or arm's-length offshoring, although it does have a positive and significant effect on FDI (or broadly defined intrafirm offshoring), as shown in column (2). Firm size (as measured by the log of employment) has a positive and significant effect on both types of offshoring, regardless of definition, although its effect on intrafirm offshoring is larger than that for arm's-length offshoring. These findings concerning productivity are only partly consistent with the hypothesis in Antràs and Helpman (2004) and the empirical findings in Tomiura (2007), whereas the results concerning firm size are consistent with the empirical findings in Tomiura et al. (2011). Moreover, the capital–labor ratio has a negative and significant effect on intrafirm offshoring but no significant effect on any of the other offshoring measures. The negative effect of capital intensity is inconsistent with both the theoretical predictions in Antràs (2003) and the empirical findings in Tomiura et al. (2011). One possible reason for this is that the amount of capital stock, which is the book value of the firm from the CSP data, is not reliable. In evidence, 691 of the 1,511 firms in the sample reported that their book value was zero.

4 Impact of Offshoring on Employment

4.1 Evidence from existing studies

Whether offshoring worsens the level of domestic employment remains a major subject of debate in both academic circles and the political arena. Certainly, offshoring may potentially affect employment in the home country, but the direction of change could go either way. For example, for a given level of output, offshoring, or the relocation of part of the business activities overseas, lowers labor demand at the headquarters in the home country. Domestic employment will fall. However, if firms become more productive and competitive through offshoring, as is often suggested in the literature (see section 6 below), it is also likely that firms increase their output and correspondingly their demand for labor (Amiti and Wei 2006). Domestic employment will then rise. Therefore, whether offshoring increases or decreases domestic employment is an empirical question.

Using the industry-level JIP Database, Agnese (2009a, 2009b) provides a response to this question for Japan, using the method in Feenstra and Hanson (1999) to measure the extent of offshoring and distinguishing between material and service offshoring. Applying the dynamic generalized method of moments (GMM) estimation from Arellano and Bover (1995), Agnese (2009b) finds that service offshoring has a large positive effect on domestic employment. An increase in the measure of service offshoring as in Feenstra and Hanson (1999), or the share of estimated imported intermediate services in total purchases of intermediate goods and services at the industry level, by one percentage point leads to an increase in employment by 2 percent (Agnese, 2009b: table 11.A1, third column). In contrast, material offshoring has a small negative effect on employment; that is, an increase in the measure of material offshoring by one percentage point leads to a decrease in domestic employment of 0.24 percent. Thus, increasing material and service offshoring by 1 percent at the same time increases domestic employment by 1.76 percent (= 2 – 0.24). Agnese (2009a) examines the same issue for each of eighty-three industries, finding that material and service offshoring have, respectively, positive and significant effects in fourteen and twenty-nine industries and negative significant effects in thirty-two and thirteen industries.

There is no known econometric analysis using firm-level data for Japan on the impact of offshoring on domestic employment. Using the *KKKC* and *KJKKC* data, Yamashita and Fukao (2010) estimate the effects of FDI on employment after disaggregating FDI by destination. Yamashita and Fukao (2010) find no significant negative effect of FDI on employment, although they do find a significant positive effect in some specifications. Given that intrafirm offshoring is more likely associated with FDI to Asia, the insignificant effect of FDI to East Asia may indirectly reflect the absence of the effect of intrafirm offshoring to the region on employment.

4.2 Evidence on SMEs

To examine the impact of offshoring on employment in SMEs in particular, we follow a standard dynamic model of employment used in, for example, Yamashita and Fukao (2010), and regress the log of the number of workers on its lagged value three years before and the log of sales, along with dummies for industries, regions, and engagement in offshoring. To alleviate any endogeneity arising from the apparent reverse causality from employment to sales, we specify the log of sales three years before, rather than at its current value. However, the data set used does not include information on current wage expenditure, and so we cannot incorporate the variation in wages at the firm level into the estimation. Nevertheless, the industry and region dummies enable us to capture some of the variation in wages at the industry and region level.

A more important econometric issue arises given that in section 4.1 we found that firms are more likely to engage in offshoring when the level of employment three years before was high. Correcting for the endogeneity of offshoring from this source of reverse causality is of course necessary, but it is often difficult to find good instruments. An advantage of this data set for SMEs is that it includes variables on the characteristics of CEOs, such as their time preference and level of international experience, that were found in section 3.2 to influence the offshoring decision. As these CEO characteristics do not appear to affect the employment level directly, they can be used as instruments in the estimation of employment. Thus, one way to correct for the endogeneity is to employ two-stage least squares (2SLS) by specifying CEO characteristics as instruments.

However, as there are three offshoring choices, simply employing them as instruments may not be appropriate. Consider, for example, the first-stage regression of the dummy variable for arm's-length offshoring on the instruments and exogenous variables. The dummy for arm's-length offshoring is zero either when firms do not engage in offshoring or when they engage in intrafirm offshoring. As the two firm states should be systematically different, the regression of the arm's-length offshoring dummy may be biased such that the second-stage regression may also be biased. Therefore, instead of the CEO characteristics, we use the predicted probabilities of engaging in intrafirm and arm's-length offshoring from the multinomial logit estimation in section 3.2 as instruments. In other words, the instruments are nonlinear combinations of the characteristics of CEOs and the other determinants of offshoring.

Table 11.4 presents the estimation results from both ordinary least squares (OLS) as a point of reference and 2SLS using the benchmark definition of offshoring. Columns (1) and (2) show the results on the effect of offshoring from OLS and 2SLS, respectively, ignoring the difference between intrafirm and arm's-length offshoring. Columns (3)–(8) provide the results on the effect of intrafirm and arm's-length offshoring separately, after changing the specifications slightly. Although the overall offshoring dummy and the arm's-length offshoring dummy have a positive and significant effect on employment in the OLS estimations, no offshoring dummy has a significant effect in the 2SLS estimations. The difference between the OLS and the 2SLS results reveals that while larger

Table 11.4 Impact of offshoring on employment. Dependent variable: log of employment

	(1)	(2)	(3)	(4)	(5)	(6)	(7)	(8)
Estimation method	OLS	2SLS	OLS	2SLS	OLS	2SLS	OLS	2SLS
Offshoring	0.0821**	0.319						
	(0.0307)	(0.208)						
Intrafirm offshoring			0.0209	0.200	0.0462	0.166		
			(0.0599)	(0.173)	(0.0543)	(0.203)		
Arm's-length offshoring			0.124**	-0.0742			0.129**	0.106
			(0.0521)	(0.390)			(0.0466)	(0.373)
Log of sales three years before	0.132***	0.130***	0.132***	0.131***	0.132***	0.131***	0.132***	0.133***
	(0.0141)	(0.0137)	(0.0143)	(0.0134)	(0.0142)	(0.0135)	(0.0140)	(0.0136)
Log of employment three years before	0.852***	0.845***	0.852***	0.852***	0.853***	0.852***	0.852***	0.853***
	(0.0200)	(0.0199)	(0.0203)	(0.0198)	(0.0199)	(0.0200)	(0.0206)	(0.0205)
Number of observations	1511	1511	1511	1511	1511	1511	1511	1511
R-squared	0.851	0.851	0.851	0.849	0.851	0.850	0.851	0.851

Notes: Standard errors in parentheses. *, **, and *** denote statistical significance at the 10, 5, and 1 percent level respectively. Industry and region dummies are included, but for brevity results are not reported.

Table 11.5 Impact of broadly defined offshoring on employment. Dependent variable: log of employment

	(1)	(2)	(3)	(4)
Estimation method	2SLS	2SLS	2SLS	2SLS
FDI/international contracting-out	0.0358 (0.115)			
FDI		0.262* (0.157)	0.0739 (0.137)	
International contracting-out		−0.307 (0.256)		−0.159 (0.208)
Number of observations	1511	1511	1511	1511
R-squared	0.851	0.838	0.851	0.847

Notes: Standard errors in parentheses. *, **, and *** denote statistical significance at the 10, 5, and 1 percent level respectively. The log of sales three years before, the log of employment three years before, and industry and region dummies are included, but for brevity the results are not reported.

firms are more likely to engage in offshoring, offshoring neither increases nor decreases employment at the firm level. As expected, the effects of sales and lagged employment have a positive and significant effect in all specifications.

In Table 11.5, we estimate the effect of overall FDI and international contracting-out, broadly defined as the combination of intrafirm and arm's-length offshoring. The 2SLS results show that in most specifications the effect of FDI or international contracting-out has no significant impact on employment. In contrast, as shown in column (2), the effect of overall FDI is positive and significant, but its positive effect is not robust, because the same effect is negative and insignificant in column (3). Note also that offshoring, FDI, and international contracting-out as defined here all include transactions of both manufacturing goods and services. Thus, the conclusion from this firm-level analysis that material and service offshoring together do not affect domestic employment is consistent with the industry-level findings in Agnese (2009a, 2009b).

5 Impacts of offshoring on skill upgrading

5.1 Evidence from existing studies

As discussed in the previous section, offshoring in Japan has little effect on total labor demand. However, offshoring may affect employment through higher demand for skilled than unskilled labor, as offshoring firms often relocate less skill-intensive business activities overseas. An early attempt to address this issue is available in Head and Ries (2002), who employ firm- and industry-level data from Japanese Overseas Investment,

1992–1993, compiled by Toyo Keizai, Inc. Head and Ries find that the share of a firm's total workforce located offshore out of its total worldwide employment has a positive effect on the share of nonproduction workers in the total wage bill of the parent firm. This finding indeed suggests that offshoring leads to the upgrading of worker skills.

Ahn et al. (2008) and Yamashita (2008) subsequently revisit this issue using a more comprehensive industry-level data set, the JIP Database. Both of these studies construct a measure of offshoring defined as the share of imports in total purchases of intermediate goods for each industry. To obtain precise measures of the purchases of imported goods, Ahn et al. (2008) draw on detailed input–output tables constructed by the Ministry of Internal Affairs and Communications for 1990, 1995, and 2000, and Yamashita (2008) employs the UN Comtrade Database. Note that when using only the JIP Database, it is possible to construct the offshoring measure in Feenstra and Hanson (1999), as does Agnese (2009a, 2009b), but not the share of imports in the total purchases of intermediate goods.

Ahn et al. (2008) find that manufacturing offshoring increases the demand for workers with lower-secondary education (nine years of education) and those with tertiary education (sixteen years) but decreases the demand for workers with upper-secondary education (twelve years). According to their estimates, the increase in offshoring in Japan during the period 1995–2000 contributed to an increase in labor demand for workers with lower-secondary education by 44,000, for workers with tertiary education by 14,000, and a decrease in the demand for workers with upper-secondary education by 59,000. Thus, the effect of offshoring on total employment is negligible, although it varies substantially depending on the level of worker education. In particular, when Ahn et al. (2008) consider the effect of offshoring to East Asia, they find a larger positive effect on the demand for workers with tertiary education. Using a somewhat different estimation framework, Yamashita (2008) finds a positive and significant effect of offshoring to East Asia, as measured by the share of imports from East Asia in total inputs, on the share of nonproduction workers at the industry level. Although the total effect of offshoring in this study is insignificant, the findings in Yamashita (2008) and Ahn et al. (2008) are generally consistent.

5.2 Evidence on SMEs

We examine whether offshoring leads to skill upgrading, particularly for Japanese SMEs, using the framework in Yamashita (2008). We specify a 2SLS model in which the dependent variable is the share of university graduates in total employment at the firm level and the independent variables are the offshoring dummies, the log of sales three years before, firm age, and the industry and region dummies. The offshoring dummies are instrumented using the log of employment, the share of exports three years before, and the time preference and international experience of the CEO to correct for possible endogeneity.

The 2SLS results in Table 11.6 for several different specifications indicate that offshoring has a positive and significant effect on the share of university graduates in Japanese

Table 11.6 Impact of offshoring on skill upgrading. Dependent variable: share of workers with tertiary education

	(1)	(2)	(3)	(4)
Estimation method	2SLS	2SLS	2SLS	2SLS
Offshoring	22.59***			
	(6.625)			
Intrafirm offshoring		19.33	28.43***	
		(25.33)	(10.12)	
Arm's-length offshoring		17.12		34.05**
		(38.04)		(17.30)
Log of sales 3 years before	1.768***	1.779***	1.723***	2.028***
	(0.517)	(0.562)	(0.530)	(0.510)
Firm age	0.0185	0.0194	0.0170	0.0234
	(0.0158)	(0.0159)	(0.0156)	(0.0150)
Number of observations	1351	1351	1351	1351

Notes: Standard errors are in parentheses. *, **, and *** denote statistical significance at the 10, 5, and 1 percent level respectively. Industry and region dummies are included, but for brevity the results are not reported.

SMEs. Although both intrafirm and arm's-length offshoring have an insignificant effect when together in the same estimation, as shown in column (2), this somewhat puzzling result probably arises because of the correlation between intrafirm and arm's-length offshoring. We find similar results using the broader measures of offshoring in the form of overall FDI and international contracting-out.[9] Even when both measures are specified in the same estimation, international contracting-out has a positive and significant effect on skill upgrading, in contrast with the situation shown in column (2) of Table 11.6. Note that the effect of offshoring on skill upgrading is quite large, with offshoring, whether intrafirm or arm's length, increasing the share of university graduates in total employment by 20–30 percent.

6 Impact of offshoring on productivity

6.1 Evidence from existing studies

Amiti and Wei (2006, 2009) argue that there are at least four possible channels through which offshoring can affect productivity. First, when firms engage in offshoring, they relocate less efficient production stages so that average productivity increases. Second, domestic production may become more efficient through restructuring. For example, offshoring labor-intensive or less skill-intensive production stages to less developed countries allows firms to make more efficient use of the remaining production factors in more skill-intensive stages. Third, firms may learn from imported materials and services. Finally, productivity could increase because of the use of new material or service input varieties.

Several studies investigate the impact of offshoring on productivity using either firm- or industry-level data. For example, Ito et al. (2008), using unique data on offshoring from Wakasugi et al. (2008), estimated the effect of engaging in offshoring on total factor productivity (TFP), finding that engaging in offshoring increases TFP by 2.7 percent. Ito et al. (2008) further disaggregate offshoring depending on the types of task and find a positive and significant effect of offshoring of the production of jigs and dies, the production of intermediate goods, the assembly of final goods, R&D activity, and information services, but an insignificant effect on customer and professional services. The marginal effect of offshoring is particularly large for R&D (11 percent) and information services (8 percent).

In other work, Ito and Tanaka (2010) employ the JIP Database to estimate the productivity effects of offshoring at the industry level. Ito and Tanaka (2010) also distinguish between material and service offshoring, by measuring the offshoring of materials and services by the share of imported materials and services in the total purchases of intermediate inputs. Using a first-differenced estimation model, Ito and Tanaka (2010) find that the effect of material offshoring on TFP and labor productivity is positive and significant in many of their specifications, while the effect of service offshoring is always insignificant. The positive effect of material offshoring is also robust when they focus on offshoring to Asia. Note that the positive effect of material offshoring and no significant effect of service offshoring are opposite from Amiti and Wei's (2006, 2009) finding that service offshoring in the United States has a larger productivity effect than material offshoring.

Similarly, Hijzen et al. (2010) distinguish between domestic sourcing, arm's-length offshoring, and intrafirm offshoring using data from the *KKKC* and *KJKKC* for the period 1994–99 for which data on the contracting-out of production activities are available (see the description of the data used in Jinji et al. 2011 in section 3.1). Hijzen et al. (2010) measure the extent of domestic sourcing and overall (including intrafirm and arm's-length) offshoring by the respective ratios of purchases of products, parts, and components from domestic and foreign providers to domestic value-added. In addition, they measure the extent of intrafirm offshoring by the ratio of purchases of any kind from the firm's own affiliates to domestic value-added. Using the measures of overall and intrafirm offshoring together as independent variables in the same regression, they thus distinguish between the effect of intrafirm and arm's-length offshoring on productivity. Using the system GMM developed by Blundell and Bond (1998), Hijzen et al. (2010) conclude that intrafirm offshoring has a positive effect on TFP, while arm's-length offshoring or domestic sourcing has no significant effect. The difference between the two types of offshoring suggests that sourcing intermediate inputs to affiliated foreign firms is more effective than to unaffiliated foreign firms. This finding is consistent with the findings by Görg et al. (2008), both using Irish plant-level data, that offshoring improves productivity only for firms with experience in international markets.

6.2 Evidence on SMEs

To examine impacts of offshoring on productivity in the case of SMEs, we face some challenges due to data limitation. First, the data set for SMEs does contain sufficient information on sales, profits, and employment in 2009, but not information on intermediate inputs, assets, or capital stocks in 2009. Thus, the best measure of productivity available from the data set is sales per worker. However, we should emphasize that in using sales per worker as the productivity measure, we effectively ignore intermediate inputs, which are the most important aspect of offshoring. In other words, offshoring can increase sales per worker simply because firms purchase intermediate inputs from foreign countries and domestic workers can then be devoted to final-good production. However, the increase in sales does not necessarily mean an increase in value-added (which equals sales less the purchases of intermediate goods). Therefore, the effect of offshoring on productivity is most likely to be overvalued when productivity is measured by sales per worker.

Second, since data on sales in 2009 are from the SME Survey, a noncompulsory survey, the data may not be as accurate as those for 2006 from the CSP, a compulsory survey conducted by the government. Table 11.2 shows that the standard deviation of sales in 2009, 4636, is much larger than that of sales in 2006, 2992. For reference, the standard deviation of the number of workers in 2009 from the SME Survey, 68.8, is similar to that

Table 11.7 Impact of offshoring on productivity. Dependent variable: log of sales per worker

	(2)	(4)	(6)	(8)
Estimation method	2SLS	2SLS	2SLS	2SLS
Offshoring	0.131			
	(0.270)			
Intrafirm offshoring		−0.789	0.0178	
		(0.727)	(0.280)	
Arm's-length offshoring		1.730*		1.068*
		(0.905)		(0.623)
Log of sales per worker 3 years before	0.783***	0.785***	0.785***	0.776***
	(0.0193)	(0.0259)	(0.0190)	(0.0231)
Log of employment 3 years before	-0.00162	−0.00122	0.00247	-0.0120
	(0.0183)	(0.0180)	(0.0174)	(0.0193)
Capital–labor ratio 3 years before	0.00588**	0.00569*	0.00553**	0.00669**
	(0.00268)	(0.00315)	(0.00257)	(0.00299)
Number of observations	1,408	1,408	1,408	1,408
R-squared	0.593	0.459	0.595	0.550

Notes: Standard errors in parentheses. *, **, and *** denote statistical significance at the 10, 5, and 1 percent level respectively. Industry and region dummies are included, but for brevity results are not reported.

in 2006 from the CSP, 66.6. Therefore, we may conclude that data on sales in 2009 are less reliable than data on sales in 2006 or the number of workers in 2009.

As in the estimation of the impact on employment, we employ a dynamic equation in which the dependent variable is the log of sales per worker and the independent variables are the log of lagged sales per worker, lagged employment, the lagged capital–labor ratio, and the offshoring, industry, and region dummies. To correct for the endogeneity of the offshoring dummies, we utilize the same estimation strategy as before (using the predicted probability of offshoring as instruments in 2SLS estimations).

The estimation results in Table 11.7 indicate that arm's-length offshoring has a positive and significant effect on productivity, while intrafirm offshoring has no significant effect. The size of the effect is very large, since arm's-length offshoring apparently improves productivity by more than 100 percent. The large impact of arm's-length offshoring may be due to the limitation in the use of sales per worker as a measure of productivity, as mentioned above. In addition, our finding that arm's-length offshoring has a positive productivity effect while intrafirm offshoring does not is contradictory to the previous findings by Hijzen et al. (2010). This may also reflect the data limitation. Therefore, although we find some evidence of positive effects of offshoring on productivity, the results should be treated with caution.

7 Summary and Discussion

This section summarizes the results on offshoring of Japanese firms, including larger firms and SMEs, and discusses the key results. First, although the material offshoring of Japanese firms has been expanding, service offshoring remains stagnant at a substantially lower level than that of other developed countries. Offshoring to Asia, particularly China, is the driving force of the expansion in material offshoring. Although some SMEs engage in offshoring, the share of offshoring SMEs is smaller than the corresponding share for larger firms.

Second, three existing studies and section 3 of this chapter examine how the choice between no offshoring, arm's-length, and intrafirm offshoring is determined, leading to mixed results. To start with, Tomiura (2007) and Tomiura et al. (2011) find that productivity determines the offshoring decision, as theoretically predicted by Antràs and Helpman (2004). That is, firms engaging in intrafirm offshoring are the most productive, followed by those engaging in arm's-length offshoring, and finally, nonoffshoring firms. In addition, Tomiura et al. (2011) find that capital-intensive firms are more likely to engage in intrafirm offshoring, as theoretically predicted and empirically evidenced at the industry level by Antràs (2003). However, Jinji et al. (2011) conclude that the impact of productivity is limited, while Tobin's q has a large impact, as reasoned by Chen et al. (2008). This evidence implies that knowledge-intensive firms are more likely to engage in intrafirm than arm's-length offshoring in order to prevent the dissemination of firm-specific knowledge. Section 3 in this chapter also finds that in the case of

SMEs, the effect of productivity is mostly insignificant, whereas CEO characteristics, such as international experience and time preference, largely affect the offshoring decision itself. Of course, given that the four studies employ distinct data sets and estimation methodologies, the differences in how the offshoring decision is determined may stem from these differences in data or methodology. Further investigation of these important matters for Japan and other countries is then necessary.

Third, material offshoring, particularly to Asia, has a large positive impact on productivity. The evidence suggests that Japanese firms improve productivity by relocating labor-intensive production stages to Asia so as to allocate any remaining production factors to more skill-intensive stages. In contrast, service offshoring, with the exception of the offshoring of information services, does not appear to have a significant impact on productivity. Given that service offshoring has often been found to have a large positive effect on productivity in other countries, such as the United States (Amiti and Wei 2006, 2009), Ireland (Görg et al. 2008), and the United Kingdom (Criscuolo and Leaver 2005), the absence of a productivity effect in service offshoring for Japan is unique. This uniqueness may relate to the fact that service offshoring has continued at a very low level in Japan. Because of Japan's unique linguistic, cultural, and institutional features, it is difficult for Japanese firms, unlike their European or US counterparts, to find good partners for the effective offshoring of services. These difficulties may result in the apparently minor and ineffective use of service offshoring by Japanese firms.

Fourth, offshoring of Japanese firms, including that of SMEs, does not appear to reduce domestic employment. This is probably because the short-run negative effect of offshoring through the relocation of business activities to foreign countries can be offset by the long-run positive effect of offshoring through productivity growth and business expansion. Given the insignificant effect of offshoring on employment at the industry level, the offshoring of a particular firm also does not appear to reduce industry employment when nonoffshoring firms with low levels of productivity are eliminated.

In an industry-level study by Agnese (2009a, 2009b), material offshoring is found to have a small negative effect on employment, while service offshoring has a positive effect. As we find a positive effect of material offshoring on productivity and no significant effect of service offshoring, our finding is not consistent with Agnese (2009a, 2009b). The difference probably arises because the effects of offshoring on productivity and employment vary depending on the characteristics of both the offshoring and the firm. Further investigation of types of offshoring and conditions that affect impacts of offshoring is required to solve this puzzle.

Finally, offshoring does affect the domestic labor market as it leads to the upgrading of skills in domestic business activities and hence to an increase in the demand for skilled (or more educated) labor. Offshoring by SMEs in particular has a large effect on skill upgrading. An important policy implication of these findings is that although offshoring should not necessarily be discouraged to protect domestic employment, policymakers should provide better education and business training to deal with the increase in demand for skilled labor.

NOTES

*. This research was conducted as part of a project entitled "International Trade and Firms" undertaken at the Research Institute of Economy, Trade and Industry (RIETI). The author would like to thank RIETI and the Japan Society for the Promotion of Science for financial support and the Ministry of Economy, Trade and Industry (METI) for providing the firm-level data used in the analysis. The author is also grateful to Toshiyuki Matsuura for his assistance in constructing the data set. The opinions expressed and arguments employed in this paper are the responsibility of the author and do not necessarily reflect those of RIETI, METI, or any institution with which the author is affiliated.

†. Department of International Studies, the University of Tokyo (5–1-5 Kashiwanoha, Kashiwa, Chiba 277–8563 Japan), and the Research Institute of Economy, Trade and Industry (e-mail: yastodo@k.u-tokyo.ac.jp; URL: http://park.itc.u-tokyo.ac.jp/yastodo/)

1. Official information on the CSP is available at http://www.meti.go.jp/english/statistics/tyo/seidou/index.html.
2. Forty-five and fifty-four firms reported their engagement in FDI and international contracting-out respectively, but they did not specify the buyer or the destination.
3. When firms reported sales in 2009 to the SME Survey, some apparently misunderstood the unit of sales (million yen). These misunderstandings were identified by comparing sales in 2006 and 2009 and corrected. In addition, sales in 2009 were replaced with a missing value if sales per worker in 2009 are more than 10 times greater than or less than 0.1 times smaller than sales per worker in 2006, even after the correction.
4. Official information on this survey is available at http://www.meti.go.jp/english/statistics/tyo/syokozi/index.html.
5. Official information on the KKKC and KJKKC is available at http://www.meti.go.jp/english/statistics/tyo/kikatu/index.html and http://www.meti.go.jp/english/statistics/tyo/kaigaizi/index.html respectively.
6. The main results do not change if we instead consider four categories: no offshoring, only arm's-length offshoring, only intrafirm offshoring, and both arm's-length and intrafirm offshoring.
7. The SME data were collected in 2009. The most recent year available for the CSP data at the time of the data collection in this study is 2006.
8. The risk preferences of CEOs, information for which is available in the data set, are another potential determinant of offshoring. For instance, Todo and Sato (2011) find a positive and significant effect of risk preferences of CEOs on the broadly defined internationalization of firms, including export, FDI, and international contracting-out, using the same data set as in this chapter. However, as we find that the index for risk preferences has no significant effect on offshoring, we remove it from further analysis.
9. The results (not shown for brevity) are available upon request.

REFERENCES

Agnese, P., 2009a. "Employment Effects of Offshoring: An Application to Japanese Industries, 1980–2005." MPRA Paper, no. 16506. Munich Personal RePEc Archive.

——. 2009b. "Japan and Her Dealings with Offshoring: An Empirical Analysis with Aggregate Data." IESE Business School Working Paper, no. 793. IESE Business School of the University of Navarra.

Agnese, P., and J. E. Ricart. 2009. "Offshoring: Facts and Numbers at the Country Level. MPRA Paper, no. 16503. Munich Personal RePEc Archive.

Ahn, S., K. Fukao, and K. Ito. 2008. "The Impact of Outsourcing on the Japanese and South Korean Labor Markets: International Outsourcing of Intermediate Inputs and Assembly in East Asia." Global COE Hi-Stat Discussion Paper, no. 1, Tokyo: Institute of Economic Research, Hitotsubashi University.

Amiti, M., and S.-J. Wei. 2006. Service Offshoring, Productivity and Employment: Evidence from the US. CEPR Discussion Paper Series, no. 5475. Washington, DC: Center for Economic Policy Research.

———. 2009. "Service Offshoring and Productivity: Evidence from the US." *World Economy* 32 (2): 203–220.

Antràs, P. 2003. "Firms, Contracts, and Trade Structure." *Quarterly Journal of Economics* 118: 1375–1418.

Antràs, P., and E. Helpman. 2004. "Global Sourcing." *Journal of Political Economy* 112: 552–580.

Arellano, M., and O. Bover. 1995. "Another Look at the Instrumental Variable Estimation of Error-components Models." *Journal of Econometrics* 68: 29–51.

Blundell, R., and S. Bond. 1998. "Initial Conditions and Moment Restrictions in Dynamic Panel Data Models." *Journal of Econometrics* 87: 115–143.

Campa, J., Goldberg L.S., 1997. The Evolving External Orientation of Manufacturing: A Profile of Four Countries. *Economic Policy Review* 3: 53–81.

Chen, Y., I. J. Horstmann, and J. R. Markusen. 2008.*Physical Capital, Knowledge Capital and the Choice between FDI and Outsourcing*. Cambridge, MA: National Bureau of Economic Research.

Cramer, J. S., J. Hartog, N. Jonker, and C. M. Van Praag. 2002. "Low Risk Aversion Encourages the Choice for Entrepreneurship: An Empirical Test of a Truism." *Journal of Economic Behavior and Organization* 48: 29–36.

Criscuolo, C., and M. Leaver. 2005. "Offshore Outsourcing and Productivity." http://www.oecd.org/dataoecd/55/23/35637436.pdf.

Feenstra, R. C., and G. H. Hanson. 1999. "The Impact of Outsourcing and High-technology Capital on Wages: Estimates for the United States, 1979–1990." *Quarterly Journal of Economics* 114 (3): 907–940.

Frederick, S., G. Loewenstein, and T. O'Donoghue. 2002. "Time Discounting and Time Preference: A Critical Review." *Journal of Economic Literature* 40: 351–401.

Görg, H., A. Hanley, and E. Strobl. 2008. "Productivity Effects of International Outsourcing: Evidence from Plant-level Data." *Canadian Journal of Economics* 41: 670–688.

Grossman, S. J., and O. D. Hart. 1986. The Costs and Benefits of Ownership: A Theory of Vertical and Lateral Integration." *Journal of Political Economy* 94: 691–719.

Head, K., and J. Ries. 2002. "Offshore Production and Skill Upgrading by Japanese Manufacturing Firms." *Journal of International Economics* 58 (1): 81–105.

Helpman, E., and P. Krugman. 1985. *Market Structure and Foreign Trade: Increasing Returns, Imperfect Competition, and the International Economy*. Cambridge, MA: MIT Press.

Hijzen, A., T. Inui, and Y. Todo. 2010. "Does Offshoring Pay? Firm-level Evidence from Japan." *Economic Inquiry* 48: 880–895.

Ito, K., and K. Tanaka. 2010. "Does Material and Service Offshoring Improve Domestic Productivity? Evidence from Japanese Manufacturing Industries." RIETI Discussion Paper Series, no. 10-E-010. Tokyo: Research Institute of Economy, Trade and Industry.

Ito, B., R. Wakasugi, and E. Tomiura. 2008. "*Offshoring and Productivity: Evidence from Japanese Firm-level Data*." RIETI Discussion Paper Series, no. 08-E-028. Tokyo: Research Institute of Economy, Trade and Industry.

Jinji, N., X. Zhang, and S. Haruna. 2011. "Does Tobin's q Matter for the Choice of Globalization Mode?" RIETI Discussion Paper, no. 11-E-061. Tokyo: Research Institute of Economy, Trade and Industry.

Tanaka, T., C. F. Camerer, and Q. Nguyen. 2010. "Risk and Time Preferences: Linking Experimental and Household Survey Data from Vietnam." *American Economic Review* 100: 557–571.

Todo, Y., and H. Sato. 2011. "Effects of CEOs' Characteristics on Internationalization of Small and Medium Enterprises in Japan." RIETI Discussion Paper, no. 11-E-026. Tokyo: Research Institute of Economy, Trade and Industry.

Tomiura, E. 2007. "Foreign Outsourcing, Exporting, and FDI: A Productivity Comparison at the Firm Level." *Journal of International Economics* 72: 113–127.

Tomiura, E., B. Ito, and R. Wakasugi. 2011. "Offshore Outsourcing Decision and Capital Intensity: Firm-level Relationships." *Economic Inquiry* 49: 364–378.

Trade Union Advisory Committee to the OECD. 2004. "Trade, Offshoring of Jobs and Structural Adjustment: The Need for a Policy Reponse." TUAC Discussion Paper. Paris: Trade Union Advisory Committee to the OECD.

Wagner, J. 2009. "Offshoring and Firm Performance: Self-selection, Effects on Performance, or Both?" *Review of World Economics* 147: 1–31.

Wakasugi, R., B. Ito, and E. Tomiura. 2008. "Offshoring and Trade in East Asia: A Statistical Analysis." *Asian Economic Papers* 7: 101–124.

Yamashita, N. 2008. "The Impact of Production Fragmentation on Skill Upgrading: New Evidence from Japanese Manufacturing." *Journal of the Japanese and International Economies* 22: 545–565.

Yamashita, N., and K. Fukao. 2010. "Expansion Abroad and Jobs at Home: Evidence from Japanese Multinational Enterprises." *Japan and the World Economy* 22: 88–97.

Yeaple, S. R. 2006. "Offshoring, Foreign Direct Investment, and the Structure of US Trade." *Journal of the European Economic Association* 4: 602–611.

CHAPTER 12

TRADE IN MIDDLE PRODUCTS BETWEEN SOUTH KOREA AND CHINA

A Survey on the Extent of Offshore Production Sharing

GOURANGA DAS[1] AND HONGYUL HAN

"We live in an age of outsourcing."

Grossman and Helpman (2002: 1).

"Some claims about the borderless world may be exaggerated, but there is no doubt that firms increasingly disperse production to wherever it can be done most efficiently. If China is the world's most efficient workshop, perhaps it does not also need to be the world's most cutting-edge laboratory." *Economist*, May 7, 2011, 64.

1 PRELUDE

The quotations that open this chapter signify the pervasive impact of globalization, its multifaceted manifestations such as the shifting of global wealth to emerging giants like India and China, among other "Southern Engines." The trade pattern that has evolved in the wake of globalization has experienced a dramatic shift, underscoring growing structural interdependence between nations. The aspect of cross-border component sharing (delocalization) is a crucial feature of it, thanks to global integration, falling trade barriers, and the rise of global production networks (GPNs) or global value chains (GVC).[2] The growth in world trade in manufactured goods has overtaken the growth in world trade and GDP. Not only that, world trade in intermediates and parts and components (P&C) has swelled significantly, from US$400 billion in 1992 to US$1.25 trillion in 2005

(Li et al. 2010). Global production sharing, by "slicing the value chain," has occurred because of fragmented production technology in globally dispersed production networks. This type of intraproduct specialization is called "vertical specialization" (VS) and has led to international division of labor across a continuum of stages via subcontracting noncore activities in different locations. This involved the relocation of manufacturing and services, and encompasses R&D and innovation, happening via modes such as subcontracting of subfunctions, intrafirm sourcing (i.e., captive offshoring), via foreign direct investment (FDI) undertaken by multinational corporations (MNCs) (Bardhan and Jaffe 2005).[3]

Also, with rapid technical progress, trade, and investment liberalization, the industrialization pathways have experienced a major shift in countries like India, China, Russia, and other emerging economies with backward and forward linkages (Szirmai 2009). With the emergence of the Southern Engines of growth and declining speed of innovations in the North, the shift in the economic centre of gravity has led to intense North-South outsourcing of innovative activities (*Economist*, March 5, 2011, 80). According to Athukorala and Menon (2010), trade in P&C grew from 18.9 percent of global trade to 23 percent, with the rise in East Asia's share in such exports from 27 percent to 39 percent, dominated by China. Such trade, defined broadly, covers VS in goods-in-process, intermediate goods (IG), and P&C (Athukorala 2005; Athukorala and Menon 2010; Athukorala and Yamashita 2006; Feenstra and Wei 2011).

As evidenced in the literature (Lall et al. 2004), the pattern differs across regions. This chapter traces the level and growth of offshoring between South Korea (SK) and China in the overall context of East Asia. Given the vicinity and rising imports from SK, our contribution is an analysis of commonalities and differences in the bilateral processing trade relationship of China with Japan vis-à-vis SK. In fact, a recent study by Samsung Economics Research Institute (SERI) (June 2011) analyzes the prospects for Korea-China free trade agreement (FTA) with Korea having revealed a comparative advantage in manufacturing while China's is in agricultural products.

As production relocation involves trade in tasks, it has ramifications in labor markets and hence the employment effects and wage differences are pertinent to study. In particular, through the lens of recent theoretical work we ask questions such as: What form of organization of production (fragmentation or internalization by MNEs via foreign investment) is prevalent for such trade? What sectors are subject to such value-chains? What are the prospects (and problems) of such trade between Korea and China? Finally, what are the repercussions in the labor market?

Section 2 reviews definitions and measurements. Apart from anecdotes based on management consulting firms, not much systematic evidence quantifying vertical trading exists. Thus, based on the foregoing presumptions, sections 3 and 4 synthesize evidence of outsourcing in China, provide a comparative perspective for SK with China vis-à-vis other countries. Section 5 explores underlying factors and the labor market effects. Section 6 offers a summary.

2 Definitions and Measurements: A Brief Review

Trade in goods-in-process is due to vertical integration of production, where sequentially different stages of production are vertically stretched across separate locations. It involves increasing interconnectedness and vertical specialization (VS).[4] Outsourcing—*either inside* the national border or *offshore*, across national borders—is based on such production sharing with *local* or *global* value chains. In broader terms, it refers to the splitting or fragmentation of an integrated production process *and* to the procurement of the production segments or blocks involving middle products (services and goods) from outside the firm (i.e., *domestic inshore* via arm's length transactions) or, within the firm (insourcing) or internationally (offshore), via arm's length purchase or intra-firm trade (foreign investment enterprises).[5] Offshoring is international in scope as it is procured from abroad (intraindustry trade IIT, within the enterprise) by multinational firms' transfer of tasks either through their existing *own affiliates*, by or creating *new foreign ones*, or by subcontracting to independent third-party *non-affiliated* foreign enterprise, (OECD 2007a).[6] Externalization tasks involve MNEs as well as small and medium enterprises (SMEs).

Although previous studies recognize this (Balassa 1967), there have been few systematic studies concerning its growth and impacts, with the exception of Krugman (1995), Feenstra and Hanson (1996, 2003), Jones and Kierzkowski (2001, 2005), Athukorala and Menon (2010), among others. Alternative terms have proliferated. For example, "multistage production" (Dixit and Grossman 1982), "trade in middle products" (Sanyal and Jones 1982), "slicing the value chain" (Krugman 1995), "intra-product or super-specialization" (Arndt and Kierzkowski 2001), "disintegration of production" (Feenstra 1996), "vertical fragmentation" (Jones and Kierzkowski 2001), "trade in tasks" (Grossman and Rossi-Hansberg 2006), "international production sharing" (Ng and Yeats 2001/2003), "vertical specialization" (Hummels et al. 1998; Yi 2003). Overall, globalization of value chains caused a fall in share of value-added in production in national territories as imported intermediates increased share in supply chains across nations. In the context of the German economy, Sinn (2003) has called this the "bazaar economy effect"—causing high unemployment in Western Europe after the relocation of production to transition economies of East Europe and South-East Asia. Terminological differences aside, these studies converge on the phenomenon of global production sharing carried out in vertically sequenced stages according to comparative advantage and relative cost differences. Typically, final goods production involves broadly two stages: Stage 1 for *intermediate goods procurement* (either by own production or subcontracting via arms' length trade and/or intrafirm trade), and stage 2 for final goods *processing* (in a low-cost location).[7] As outsourcing has expanded beyond the traditional confines of manufacturing or materials, it has encompassed services and, more recently, innovations thanks especially to IT-enabled services. Given the definitional differences, the extent of such a phenomenon and its effects are empirical questions and so results depend on the level of industry aggregation (i.e., identifying appropriate intermediate stages) and the outsourcing or offshoring indices. Being firmly embedded in empirical domain, the applied trade literature has some lacunae because of the lack of appropriate data categorizing the products, despite a proliferation of theoretical papers (Baldwin and Robert-Nicoud 2007; Jones and Kierzkowski 2001, 2005; Cheng and Kierzkowski 2001).

2.1 Calculus of fragmentation: a taxonomy of nomenclature

OECD (2007/2008) is a comprehensive survey of outsourcing for the OECD countries. However, we are not reinventing the wheel. It is important to note that although intrafirm trade is one factor for trade in fragments, using the typical Grubel-Lloyd index (1975) is misleading as it fails to capture the essential nature of such trade. As Jones and Kierzkowski (2005) have pointed out, trade in fragments and middle products is distinct from IIT as the former opens up scope for developing economies to participate in international exchange of production segments with the developed ones, unlike IIT, occurring mainly between industrialized nations. The increasing participation of China in East Asia's production network is exemplary in this line.

Often, as intrafirm level microdata are hard to get, most of these measures are at aggregate industry level. Feenstra and Hanson (1996) defined vertical specialization as the "share of imported intermediate inputs in total purchase of non-energy materials" (241). It is one of the important systematic measures of the relation between offshoring and wage inequality. Using input-output data for OECD nations, Hummels et al. (1998) and Yi (2003) defined two measures of VS as the share of imported inputs in the final product, provided after the value-addition the final output is exported. Yeats (1998), Ng and Yeats (2003) studied the East Asian context using imported inputs in total imports as proxy measure. Ahn et al. (2008) offer a comprehensive analysis of outsourcing and labor market effects for Korea and Japan vis-à-vis China.

Here, we are adopting Amiti and Wei's (2004) broader definition, as the ratio of imported inputs to total inputs or "outsourcing intensity of intermediate inputs" (1). Thanks to advances in ICT, falling transmission costs, internet, and e-mail, as they are spreading to the service sectors (R&D, business process outsourcing, call centers, data entry and research and consultancy services, medical transcriptionist, etc.), we can reformulate it: for a given final goods sector j in a region r, we define OS_SM (j, r) as the measure of *service and material* outsourcing intensity, based on Feenstra and Hanson (1996). Our specification has a regional dimension, so that we compute it across selected regions of the Global Trade Analysis Project (GTAP).[8] Thus, for region r, we calculate the extent of outsourced material or services for industry j, OS_SM (j, r), as:

$$OS\_SM_{jr} = \sum_i \left[\frac{a_{ijr}}{a_{jr}}\right] \times \left[\frac{G_{ir} + P_{ir} + a_{ir}}{Y_{ir} + M_{ir} - X_{ir}}\right]$$

Which represents the following:

a_{ijr}: the use of intermediate i in final user sector j;
a_{jr}: total of *all intermediate inputs* (summed across i) used for production in j;
G_{ir}: government consumption of import of commodity i;
P_{ir}: private household consumption of import i;
a_{ir}: for each ith intermediate input, the total intermediate use of i by all user j (summed across j);
Y_{ir}: production/output of i,
M_{ir}: imports of i;
X_{ir}: exports of i from r.

The first bracketed term is the share of the ith intermediate in overall intermediate input usage for industry j, giving an intermediate input intensity for industry's of use j. The second term calculates the import share by usage, which is applied to each i. These two together give outsourcing intensity of material/services i for a typical industry j in region r. By aggregating over all the intermediate (i.e., summing across all i) used in a particular final goods sector j, we derive the average outsourcing intensity ratio for each j.

Table 12.1 shows that developing regions experience higher outsourcing intensity (ratio) compared to developed regions, thus confirming their emergence as the kingpin of production sharing. Clearly, East Asia is major hub of such networks. In fact, Feenstra and Wei (2011) have documented the growing importance of China as manufacturing base for firms worldwide via their engagement in "contract manufacturing" with mostly foreign invested enterprises (FIEs).

Table 12.1 Outsourcing of materials and services for selected sectors across regions (%)

	Developed Regions				Developing Regions				
Sectors	USA	Canada	Japan	EU	India	China	South-East Asia	Mercosur	South America
Light Manufactures	10.9	20.8	9.9	21.9	9.9	12.6	28.4	6 9	18.6
Heavy Manufactures	14.9	34.6	8.9	28.3	14.2	12.7	36.3	10.3	23.9
Hi-Technology Products	17.1	50.1	8.1	29.9	14.6	18.2	55.8	14.02	35.7
Services	5.8	15.6	5.2	13.1	8.8	11.8	27.7	6.2	17.4
Capital Goods	11.5	22.3	4.9	21.5	11.6	9.6	34.9	9.2	24 2

Source: Das (2007).

2.2 A brief sketch of the literature

A rich array of neoclassical production models in the trade literature consider different theoretical structures (Sanyal and Jones 1982; Marjit and Acharyya 2003; Deardorff 2005). However, Sanyal and Jones (1982) is one of the pioneering works for initiating "fragmentation" theory by incorporating trade in intermediates in Ricardian and Heckscher-Ohlin structures and their variants. The production-sharing phenomenon was not mentioned explicitly, but subsequently stronger evidence of such production organization led to works addressing intraproduct specialization. Grossman and Helpman (2002) is one such work. Labor outsourcing is driven by the objective of cost cutting via contracting services to firms offering fewer wages. Employment depends on workers' skill and quality. However, by creating demand for a specific type of labor with relatively more skill and technological expertise the technology spillover from hub to spokes affects the factor market via earning differential. Jones, Kierzkowski, and Chen (2005) developed an analytical framework after presenting evidence from East Asia and emphasized the role of globalization, the spread of telecommunications technology, service links, decline in entry barriers. Macroeconomic factors, among others, worked better for East Asia and hence there was a shift of destination from Latin America during the last several years.

According to Grossman and Helpman (2002: 2), "[because] outsourcing involves more than just the purchase of a particular type of good or service, it has been difficult to measure the growth in international outsourcing. While these are all imperfect measures of outsourcing as we would define it, the authors do show that there has been rapid expansion in international specialization for a varied group of industries that includes textiles, apparel, footwear, industrial machinery, electrical equipment, transportation equipment, chemicals and allied products." The sectors experiencing splitting of subfunctions are predominantly manufacturing (for example, export-platform FDI) and, with increasing trade, service and now R&D innovation activities. Structural change and the composition of GDP raise a concern about the relative decline of the manufacturing share in GDP and the rise in services, and there have been calls for investment in innovation to boost the manufacturing sector to counter the loss of employment caused by shifting toward the lower end of the value-added chain in low-cost countries like India and China.

China's formation of FTAs or PTAs with regional neighbors in East Asia, especially Korea, calls attention to whether SK could establish itself as a technological hub of outsourced production to a "spoke" country like China. Establishing themselves as dynamic economies, they have emerged as subhubs in their geographical regions and thus they could become outsourcers to closely neighboring regions and engage in technology flows. A regional production network emerged in East Asia with substantial East Asian trade in P&C. Sectors are predominantly: P&C of office and adding machinery, telecom equipment, motor vehicles and accessories, and services (which make positive use of the fact that neighboring countries do not have time zone differences). Japan is the main driver of exports and imports of P&C—more as an exporter of P&C, as other East Asian regions assemble Japanese products. Taking Korea as source and China as destination or preferred location for outsourcing, production sharing between them could promote growth in the destination, China. Korea's technological superiority and sophistication have caused a switch in its production-sharing pattern.

3 Bird's eye (re)view of East Asian production sharing: emergence of a dominant triangle?

> "China is ideally placed to be the world's middleman: close enough to the frontier of innovation to keep up with the latest developments, and skilled at adapting new ideas for the mass market." *Economist*, May 7, 2011, 64.

China is one of the world's top exporters (with 68 percent trade dependency ratio, UNCTAD 2006), with her exports in the share of world exports growing at an annualized rate of 19 percent. China's emergence as the dominant trade partners of major OECD countries has made it a leader in global value chains. Harrigan and Deng (2011) find that Korea ranks fourth among the export markets for China, while Taiwan, Korea, and Japan lost market share to her in major markets (Chen and Chang 2006). The rise of China's share in total world exports and manufacturing value-added is dominated by processed exports—both component production and assembly into intermediates, subsequently processing and exporting final goods—in regional as well as global production networks. This hinges on three factors: low labor cost (a natural comparative advantage), geographic vicinity to the dynamic East Asian region with its large market size, and a processing *trade regime* which allows export promotion (Ma et al. 2009). It is also due to establishment of a regime facilitating the domestic processing trade by allowing duty exemptions of imported inputs, giving rise to the unbundling of production stages by the MNEs' intrafirm trade. However, apart from low labor cost and its contribution in value-added, the share of imported intermediates/parts sourced from Japan and South Korea is 80 percent, in contrast to its 20 percent share of domestic value-added via low labor-cost and domestic intermediates (Ma et al. 2009). One of the important aspects of China's dominance in processing exports is its heavy dependence on Japan and Korea for imported inputs and materials—almost 80 percent of the value of processed exports comes from imported inputs (Dean et al. 2009, Kimura et al. 2007). Not only that, Ma et al. (2009) have shown that location plays an important role for China. In particular, compared to non-Asian countries, processing exports to East Asian countries are more sensitive to the average distance traveled by imported inputs and final goods exports (i.e., import distance and export distance) and are negatively affected by them. Procurement of P&C and hence production sharing in East Asia led to a regional production network

(RPN) paving the way for a GPN.[9] Heavy reliance on East Asian neighbors for sophisticated imported inputs (for P&C) and technology-intensive sectors (like SITC 7 and 8) has made China a net importer of such P&C and turned it into a powerhouse of global processing exports (55 percent share of total Chinese exports) via export-platform FDI. According to Ma et al. (2009), "geographic location explains this pattern via negative impact of import distance on processing export distance in trading border regions."

China is pursuing the path of developing capacity for independent innovation—processes or products—as part of a broader national development strategy. Thus, the bigger dividends accrue via innovation, enabling it to garner existing technologies, become involved in routine assembly, and engage in adapting new ideas for catering to world market. Hence, getting involved in the business of trade in intermediates pursued by inventive and technologically sophisticated firms (MNEs) from Japan and Korea via unbundling products opens China's door for regional mass production. According to Li et al. (2010), the growing importance of China in trade in P&C has shown dynamic patterns in sectors classified in UNCTAD data (UN Commtrade dataset) under SITC 7 (machinery and transport equipment) and 8 (miscellaneous manufacturing commodities) sectors (Revision 3), as well as with twenty-five trading partners across the globe. Considering 219 kinds of P&C with 2,800 commodities, the study finds that in 2005 the shares of imports and exports of parts and components for SITC 75 (office machinery and equipment), SITC 76 (telecommunications and recording equipment), and SITC 77 (electrical machinery and parts) accounted for 97 percent and 94 percent respectively of total imports and exports of parts and components. Thus, component trade's share in total manufacturing imports increased to 35 percent in 2005, while the share of such imports in total manufacturing imports exceeds the exports shares (16.9 percent). In total manufacturing imports, the share of P&C is 34.3 percent, dominated by parts and components for SITC 7 (Table 12.2). However, since 2000 China has turned into a net importer of P&C in SITC 7 category and net exporter of P&C for relatively labor-intensive other manufacturing products (SITC 8). Also, of all its trading partners, among the regional neighbors in East Asia, Japan, SK, and the ASEAN 6 (Indonesia, Malaysia, Philippines, Singapore, Thailand, Vietnam) play a major role (more than 50 percent of total imports of P&C) with visible interregional and intraregional shifts in sourcing imports of P&C.

Table 12.3 shows that over time, trade in P&C from Japan and South Korea in China increased while that of North America and Europe experienced relative decline. Although this does not mean decoupling necessarily from the global chain, Japan's share shrank while that of South Korea and ASEAN 5 has increased. Korea and the large ASEAN countries are replacing Japan and Hong Kong as subsuppliers of parts and components in China.[10] The emergence of Korea as a technologically dynamic nation established it as a supplier of sophisticated technology- and capital-intensive components and intensified offshoring to China (Kimura and Ando 2005).

All of this suggests that China is predominantly an exporter of final goods (more than 60 percent of her total trade), while for intermediate goods (including P&C), it imports, processes, assembles, and exports them to the rest of the world. Low labor costs and the

Table 12.2 Regional shares of source-wise component imports and exports with China

Component imports trade in China (%)

Region/Country	1992	1993	1996	1997	2000	2001	2004	2005
US	9.6	10.3	9.8	10.9	8.5	9.4	5.8	5.5
Canada	0.6	0.4	0.9	0.9	1.6	1.2	0.5	0.4
EU4	13.9	13.7	10.2	10.8	10.9	11.2	7.6	6.1
North-east Asia	61.5	54.5	58.8	57.6	52.7	51.1	52.9	53.4
Hong Kong	38.7	16.2	9.5	7.6	5.4	5.1	2.6	2.1
Japan	20.2	32.1	35.1	32.3	25.9	24.2	20.8	17.9
Korea	1.8	3.9	7.5	8.4	9.3	8.4	12.6	15.3
ASEAN 5	0.8	2.2	6.7	9.3	12.1	13.4	16.8	18

Component exports trade from China (%)

	1992	1993	1996	1997	2000	2001	2004	2005
US	6.8	16.1	15.2	15	14.4	14.9	15.5	15.4
Canada	0.3	0.9	0.7	0.7	1	0.7	0.6	0.7
EU4	2.2	9.1	5.8	6.2	7.4	6.6	7.1	7.1
North-east Asia	77.1	56.7	63.6	62.5	59.5	59.6	57.4	55.7
Hong Kong	62.3	30.1	26.7	26.4	26.6	27	28	28.4
Japan	9.1	17.4	20.5	19.6	15.4	15	11.7	10.5
Korea	1.2	2.4	5.5	4.9	4.8	4.6	5.3	4.9
ASEAN 5	4.1	6.4	10.7	11.2	12.4	12.7	12.3	11.8

Source: Adapted from Li et al. (2010), chapter 12.

size of the market attract larger volumes of imports of such components for assembly. Therefore, China typically gains from specialization in relatively labor-intensive production block of vertically separated stages by assembling the P&C (and sophisticated intermediate goods) and reexporting them. Given the proximity of China's location there is immense scope for "trade in middle products" between China, Korea, and Japan (CJK). In this case, a *dominant triangular mode* of trade network can be seen. For example, suppose heterogeneous firms from OECD countries like Japan (highly advanced) and Korea (advanced) trade products. To serve the foreign markets, they can directly export from their home base and/or assemble P&C into intermediate goods, or intermediates into final goods, in a third export-platform country, in this case China (primarily because of its low labor cost and regional proximity), then indirectly export to each other's markets. As generally speaking delocalization, or the unbundling of production blocks/stages into "tasks" dispersed to a different location, depends on the trade costs related to the geographical proximity of the processing platform, China's vicinity to the large markets of East Asia (and ASEAN), especially to Korea and Japan, gives it a comparative geographical advantage compared to the Latin American nations (say, Mexico) neighboring North America, or those of Eastern Europe (say, Poland) bordering Western Europe.

Table 12.3 International outsourcing in 1990, 1995, 2000: Imported inputs as a percentage share of output and inputs

Measure			1990		1995		2000	Change 1990–2000 (% points)			
		(%)		(%)		(%)				(%)	
(a) Japan											
Share in output											
All industries	Narrow		0.73		0.78		0.85		0.12		15.97
	Broad		2.5		2.26		2.54		0.04		1.43
	Narrow									32.62	
Manufacturing	Broad	1.39	4.25	1.61	4.26	1.84	5.17	0.45	0.92	21.66	
Services	Narrow		0.32		0.37		0.39		0.07		22.31
	Broad		1.41		1.27		1.32		−0.1		−6.8
Services within mfg.			0.18		0.17		0.19		0.02		8.97
Share in inputs											
All industries	Narrow		10.1		12.71		14.11		4.01		39.69
	Broad		5.1		4.84		5.51		0.4		7.91
	Narrow									46.68	
Manufacturing	Broad	8.96	6.49	11.20	6.64	13.15	8.05	4.18	1.56	24.09	
Services	Narrow		17.23		19.01		17.38		0.15		0.86
	Broad		3.72		3.37		3.53		−0.19		−5.05
(b) Korea											
Share in output											
All industries	Narrow		3.67		3.79		5.12		1.45		39.56
	Broad		8.87		8.7		10.63		1.76		19.81
	Narrow									26.68	
Manufacturing	Broad	6.99	15.90	7.38	15.85	8.85	17.74	1.86	1.83	11.52	
Services	Narrow		0.65		0.74		1.75		1.1		169.31
	Broad		2.51		2.66		4.18		1.68		66.82
Services within mfg.			0.11		0.15		0.65		0.55		500.04
Share in inputs											
All industries	Narrow		29.65		29.52		33.5		3.86		13
	Broad		15.29		15.39		18.08		2.79		18.25
	Narrow	30.27		31.02		34.12				12.72	
Manufacturing	Broad	20.99		21.43		23.72		3.85	2.72	12.98	
Services	Narrow		27.87		20.97		31.18		3.31		11.87
	Broad		5.89		6.29		9.4		3.52		59.79

Source: Adapted from Table 3.2, Ahn et al. (2008), OECD Trade Policy Working paper 65.

Despite the negative impact of import and export distances on such trade in fragments with neighbors in East Asia, compared to non-Asian countries, proximity facilitates the scope of triangular trade between CJK. As Korea and Japan are advanced industrialized nations, sourcing processing imports from them is quite straightforward. This opens up the scope of a potential regional *trilateral trade*, with China standing as the low-cost haven.[11] This triangular mode of organizing offshore outsourcing for CJK is shown in Figures 12.1 and 12.2, a conceptual framework of offshoring tasks, including direct exports and indirect exports. Considering their tripartite cooperation, we could think about the following scenarios in which either Japan or Korea engage in outsourcing to China before exporting to each other's market. Given the colonial legacy of Korea and historical precedence, apart from domestic firms (coordinating both stages domestically and selling locally), some foreign firms produce final goods and their components in Korea and export them back to Japan and others. In another arrangement, some foreign firms produce their components in Korea (stage 1) and process the final goods in China (stage 2), subsequently exporting them to Japan. This chapter focuses on this last arrangement. In Figure 12.1, stage 1 is split in two countries, the home country and its advanced neighbor, with a high level of technological sophistication. Subsequently, in stage 2, unbundling occurs, to take advantage of the low wage rate (skilled and especially unskilled) in the processing platform, China.

Figure 12.1 presents a general scheme of such production sharing *involving three countries* where the third country is the export destination. One example of such trade involving Japan and Korea is "microcontrollers," which Korea imports from Japan. In

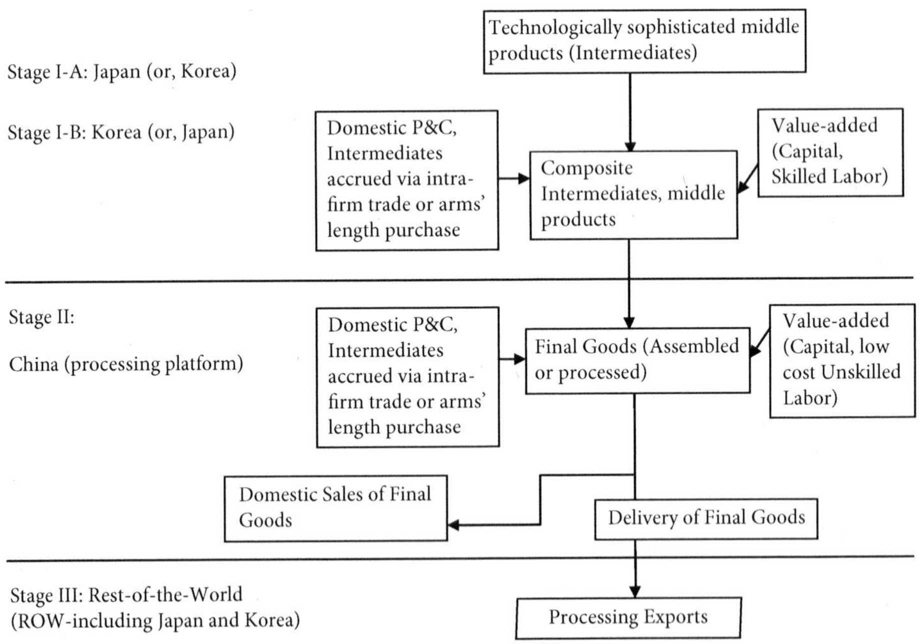

FIGURE 12.1 Principal pathways of triangular mode of offshore fragmentation.

fact, in 2010–11 Korea had a huge trade deficit of US$36.2 billion, of which $24.3 billion (two-thirds) are attributed to deficits in P&C.[12] These are assembled either locally or sometimes via offshore assembly, taking advantage of labor arbitrage, especially in neighboring countries like China (Figure 12.2).

In the current context j = Korea, Japan, or any country taking outsourcing offshore to i for delivering finally to l, where l = the rest of the world (or another country including the outsourcing country) and i = intermediate processing platform (say India or China). Thus, the emergence of a new regional division of labor and regional production network (RPN) needs to be discussed in the context of these structural changes in trade and industrial development of the nations. From the conceptual diagram, it can be inferred that China's ascent as a global workshop has opened up scope of *shifts* in the organization of production. In the next section, based on these flow charts of structural interdependence (bilateral Sino-Korean or triangular, involving CJK), we reveal the extent of such fragmentation via either trade with unaffiliated foreign subcontractor or procuring through intrafirm mode of organizing processing via MNEs' affiliates. In particular, we focus on South Korea's emergence as supplier of hi-tech products, namely electronics, machinery, chemicals, and its delocalization of production segments in China.

However, production data capturing the contribution of components of value-added assessment of China's upgrading and catching up in the electronics sector and its subcategories showed that electronics production activities are not as sophisticated as they are normally expected to be (Assche and Gangnes 2009).[13] Due to offshoring of assembly

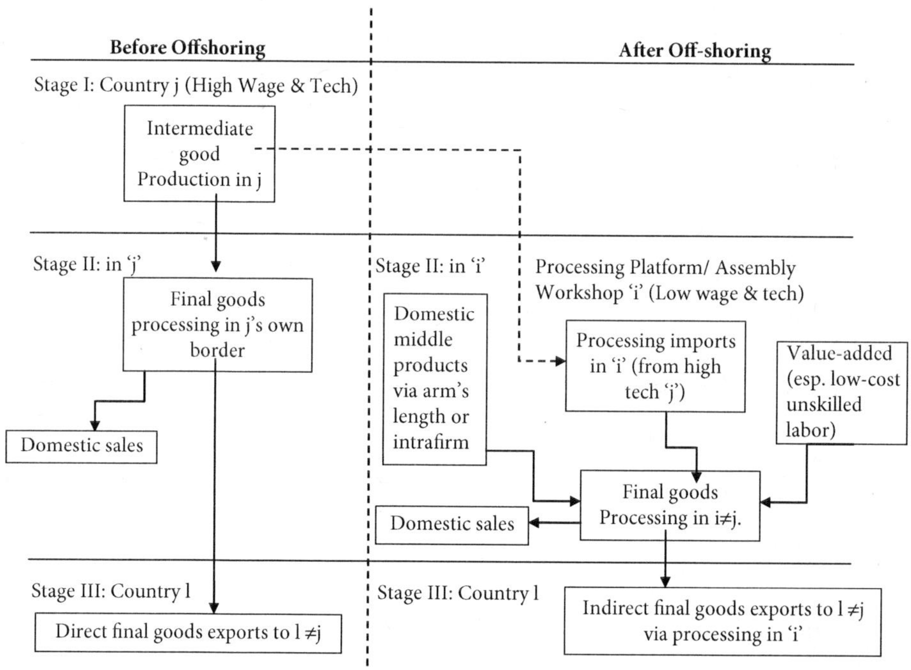

FIGURE 12.2 Principal pathways of a conceptual tripartite cooperation between CJK.

plants, such indexes in less sophisticated categories such as electronic data processing, audio-video equipment, office and industrial equipment increased between 1995 and 2005 for China (including ASEAN 4 countries, Mexico and some Eastern European nations). In terms of country technology index, the study finds little support for China's climbing up the technological ladder; its ranking marginally improved from 42nd in 1994 to 39th in 2005. By contrast, the findings confirm that Korea has improved her ranking from 43rd in 1994 to 29th in 2005, whereas Japan went down from 29th in 1994 to 31st in 2005. The compound annual growth rate of electronics production in Korea (11.5%) exceeds that in Japan and the share of electronics production in GDP of Korea is 13.5 percent compared to 4.2 percent in Japan and 11.7 percent in China. Therefore, although machinery and electronics occupy the biggest category (63 percent) in China's processing exports, it is due more to "imported sophistication" based on FIEs and their spillovers than to state-owned enterprises. Export promotion policies, large market and processed import supply from East Asian neighbors paved the way for China's export-led growth.

4 Evidence of Korea-China bilateral trade and outsourcing

Sometimes Korea's stellar progress from one of the poorest country to an industrialized high-income country, strongly based on heavy industry, chemicals, and IT, might seem mysterious. The Korean case in the last half of the twentieth century is so exceptional that exploring her path of development offers valuable insights even now. The dramatic turnaround of the world economy in 1986 particularly helped Korea's miracle, thanks to the so-called "three lows"—a weak dollar and the Korean won (which was pegged to the dollar), low interest rates, and low oil price—which together boosted the world demand as well as providing Korean exports with favorable price competitiveness. Thus, a favorable international economic environment made it possible for the Korean economy, suffering from over-capacity for a long time, to breathe again and establish a strong industrial base.

However, sometimes it is easy to forget that at the same time Korea was struggling with rising labor costs in the late 1980s, caused by democratic reform triggered by the civil movement against the dictatorship. While firms were enjoying an export boom, they also suffered from unprecedented wage increases. In the context of the subject of this chapter, it is worthwhile noting that the fast increase in labor costs in the late 1980s led the Korean industries to the path of globalization. First of all, the high labor cost drove many FIEs *out* of Korea. Particularly, Japanese firms investing in the free export zones moved their production facilities to the Southeast Asian region. Also, many Korean firms, particularly small and medium firms which were highly vulnerable to the weakened price competitiveness against exports from Southeast Asia, started to look for ways to overcome the situation. Then China arrived on the scene. The opening of the Chinese economy not only provided strong demand for Korean exports but also new ground for damaged Korean firms to fill the cost gap. Although it is hard to judge whether the success story of Korea's economic development could partly, at least, be attributed to "luck" (the dramatic turnaround of the world economy and timely opening up of China), however, it is evident that the political reform both in Korea and China triggered the structural change. A recent SERI report (June 2011) highlights the areas of revealed comparative advantage of both nations and identifies areas of cooperation in the case of unfolding of Korea-China FTA.

4.1 Korea-China trade: any room for production sharing?

Superseding the United States, China became the biggest destination of Korea's exports for the first time in 2002. Also, according to Kang et al. (2011: 106), "the growth rate of China-bound shipments was 1.3 times greater than overall export growth." Heavy export dependence on the United States and the European Union had been regarded one of the most chronic problems and hence the major attention of trade policy was constantly turned toward export diversification. China's weight in Korea's trade has registered substantial increase, replacing the United States. According to SERI (June 2011), China's share in Korea's aggregate exports and imports are 25 percent and 27 percent respectively, as opposed to 10.7 percent and 9.5 percent in the case of the United States. Bilateral trade between Korea and China is expected to increase from US$58 billion in 2003 to US$200 billion in 2011. Keeping that in mind an FTA is in the making, since the joint study was launched in September 2004 and completed in September 2010. That, and its growth miracle, has established Korea as a net FDI outflow country with a favorable external economic environment. As per SERI (June 2011), Korea's largest investment destination (US$30.8 billion) is China, as its geographical vicinity and symmetries encouraged Korean companies (154 out of 204 making foreign investment) to relocate via MNEs or SMEs. The report also identified rapid expansion of *intraindustry trade*, especially in the sectors of electrical goods, electronics, and machinery, using Korea's technological superiority in sophisticated skill-intensive products such as liquid crystal displays and wireless components. During the 1980s and 1990s, Korea recorded a trade surplus with China in all categories except agricultural trade. Starting in the early 2000s, Korea started to record a deficit in light industry primarily in textile and leather products.

Table 12.4 reveals that the structure of Korea-China trade by sector has not only changed but also deepened, especially its heavy reliance on the exports of electrical machines and electronics. The share of this sector is expected to rise to 50 percent of total trade with China by 2012 from 33.1 percent in 2002. In contrast with this sector, shares of trades in primary products and textiles have shrunk significantly. It is worthwhile to note that automobile parts have increased in share by fourfold during the same period. The rapid increase of auto parts symbolizes the changing nature of Korea-China trade. This is attributable to the establishment of Hyundai Beijing in 2001, a joint venture of

Table 12.4 Major export destinations of Korea, Japan, and China (%)

Rank by Destination	Korea	Japan	China
1	China (21.3)	US (22.8)	US (21.0)
2	EU (14.9)	EU (14.5)	EU (18.8)
3	US (13.3)	China (14.3)	Hong Kong (16.0)
4	Japan (8.2)	Korea (7.8)	Japan (9.5)
5	Hong Kong (5.8)	Taiwan (6.8)	Korea (4.8)
Total	63.5	66.2	70.1

Source: Compiled from WTO, Trade Profiles 2008.

Hyundai Motors and Beijing Motors. Considering the fact that more than 4,000 companies, big and small, are present in China and Korea is the world's leading investor in China, the nature of China-Korea trade is switching more and more towards intraindustry and intrafirm trade.

Table 12.5 shows trade in SITC categories 7 and 8 and offers a glimpse into the scope of Sino-Korean outsourcing (Korea International Trade Association [KITA] Report).

Table 12.5 Korea's trade with China by major category

	Total trade (Exports +Imports)			Annual growth (%)		Share (%)		
Category	2002	2007	2012	03–07	08–12	2002	2007	2012
Total	411.5	1240.0	2350.0	24.7	13.6	100.0	100.0	100.0
Primary products	57.1	94.4	133.9	10.6	7.2	13.9	7.6	5.7
Textile	53.2	108.7	185.7	15.4	11.3	12.9	8.8	7.9
Steel	36.9	97.1	183.0	21.4	13.5	9.0	7.8	7.8
Machinery	31.9	93.4	170.0	24.0	12.7	7.8	7.5	7.2
Electric and electronics	136.4	564.3	1202.0	32.8	16.3	33.1	45.5	51.1
industrial use	61.2	265.3	557.4	34.1	16.0	14.9	21.4	23.7
* computer	28.5	122.0	270.3	33.8	17.3	6.9	9.8	11.5
*communication	29.1	136.1	236.0	36.2	11.6	7.1	11.0	10.0
electronics parts	41.8	185.1	431.5	34.6	18.4	10.2	14.9	18.4
* semiconductors	19.5	83.4	184.4	33.8	17.2	4.7	6.7	7.8
Petrochemicals	40.8	68.1	92.8	10.8	6.4	9.9	5.5	4.0
Automobile and parts	4.2	27.4	71.0	45.4	21.0	1.0	2.2	3.0
Automobiles	2.3	10.0	20.3	34.8	15.1	0.5	0.8	0.9
parts	2.0	17.3	50.7	54.7	24.0	0.5	1.4	2.2

Source: IIT (2008). Note, figures for 2012 are estimates by KTI.

Table 12.6 Product with high export reliance on China

Product	Export Reliance to China %	Product	Export Reliance to China %	Product	Export Reliance to China %
Synthetic textile materials	83.1	Dry cell and storage battery	58.3	Illumination equipment	42.8
Intermediate petrochemical materials	72.9	Flat display panels	55	Copper products	42.4
Leather goods	66.7	Fur products	50.0	Machine tools	42.4
Other heavy electrical equipment	63.2	LPG	49.5	Semiconductor manufacturing equipment	40.8
Display manufacturing equipment	61.9	Office supplies	44.4	Synthetic resin	40.3
Woolen products	60.0	Basic petrochemical elements	44.4	Footwear	40.1
Optical equipment	59.8	Paint and ink	43.5	Audio equipment	40.0

Source: KITA, reproduced from *Korea Focus*, 19 (1), spring 2011, table 4.

For economic reliance on each other's market, *major export industries* are: electronic parts (56 percent), petrochemicals (44 percent), synthetic textile materials (83 percent), and intermediate petrochemicals (73 percent). Also, after the financial crisis, Korea's export boom involved predominantly parts and materials and consumer durables. In fact, Korea's *post-crisis* export growth rate to China is 19.2 percent—the highest among others including the OECD nations, with 31 percent of Korea's total exports bound for China in 2010.

Also, the *share of imports* from China to Korea is large, exceeding that of Japan and the United States. The report identifies the major industries showing such resilience for Sino-Korean exports (more than 50 percent of ten Korean export products) and imports, mostly electronic parts (56 percent Korean exports), with the remaining 44 percent as petrochemicals, precision machinery, non-ferrous metal products. These are mostly intermediate and capital goods assembled and reexported. Imports from China are primarily "reimports" of domestically manufactured products from China. They are: assembled metal and textile industries (50 percent), audio-visual and communication equipment, electric equipment and computer industries (40 percent approximately). Considering the trade balance (Table 12.7), it is evident that the technological superiority of Korea over China enables her to amass a trade balance growing over the years in exporting sophisticated products. Although China's catching up process is altering the situation, it is not causing a total reversal. In fact, Table 12.8 shows that Korea's exports to China mostly consist of intermediate and capital goods, and the export shares of primary products and consumer goods are extremely small. Intermediate goods and capital goods take more than 90 percent of total exports. During the 1990s, more than 70 percent of total exports were processed goods. Entering 2000, exports of parts and capital

Table 12.7 Korea's trade balance with China: Electric & Electronic Products and Machinery (Unit: US$100 million, %)

Classification		1995	2000	2003	2005	2007	2009	Growth (1995–2005)
Total	Export	91.4	184.6	351.1	619.2	819.9	867.0	17.4
	Import	74.0	128.0	219.1	386.5	630.3	542.5	15.3
	Balance	17.4	56.6	132.0	232.7	189.6	324.6	23.2
Electric, electronic, machinery (SITC 7 & 8)	Export	24.8	63.5	188.1	364.7	490.0	537.8	24.6
	Import	15.9	56.5	116.1	202.7	335.7	328.8	24.2
	Balance	8.9	7.0	72.0	162.0	154.3	208.9	25.3
Electric, electronic, machinery parts	Export	5.1	21.3	95.3	182.7	263.7	324.9	34.6
	Import	3.6	15.5	31.7	58.1	97.6	91.7	26.1
	Balance	1.5	5.8	63.6	124.5	166.1	233.2	43.5

Source: Based on US Comtrade. SERI, *Monthly Focus*, no. 6, June 2011, table 4.

goods significantly replaced processed goods. Of course, the fast increase of Korea's FDI to China in the area of electronics, automobiles, and so on induced the change. In particular, the share of parts exports increased from 10.3 percent in 1996 to 35.9 percent in 2006, mostly due to expansion of FDI in the cellular phone and automobile industries. Secondly, exports by trade business take more than half of total exports. For instance, firms that have export-import licenses import primary materials from China and reexport final goods or semiprocessed products to China. This type of export took 38.2

Table 12.8 Korea's trade structure by processing category

		1997	2000	2006
A. Exports to China				
primary product		0.3%	0.4%	0.1%
Intermediate goods	semiprocessed	72.3%	62.2%	44.0%
	parts	10.3%	19.7%	35.9%
Final goods	capital goods	11.2%	9.9%	16.7%
	consumer goods	5.9%	4.8%	3.3%
B. Imports from China				
primary product		20.6%	16.1%	5.9%
Intermediate goods	semiprocessed	44.4%	34.4%	36.9%
	parts	8.9%	16.0%	20.9%
Final goods	capital goods	6.6%	13.7%	18.7%
	consumer goods	19.5%	19.8%	17.5%

Source: Yang (2007).

percent of total exports in 2006. Finally, a major portion of total exports to China is destined to foreign-invested firms in China, the share increasing from 59.1 percent in 2000 to 75.3 percent in 2006.

As far as imports from China are concerned, consumer goods still take relatively high shares. However, imports of intermediate goods from China have increased significantly during the same period implying an expansion of horizontal integration between the two countries.

With Korea's soaring FDI since 1990s, trade between Korean firms and their affiliates in China increased significantly. According to Lee and Lim (2007), overall intrafirm exports of Korea's listed firms have increased 45.6 percent annually during 1999–2005. This is in sharp contrast with Japan (Table 12.9). During 2000–2008, Korea's exports of parts and capital goods *increased their share* significantly while there was a drop in the share of consumer goods by a third. The Japanese export structure shows only an opposite trend: while the total share of intermediate goods and capital decreased, primary and consumer goods increased their share during the past decade. Both Korea and Japan lost export shares of intermediate goods between 2000 and 2008. Korea's export composition of intermediate and capital goods looks much similar with that of Japan as parts export rapidly replaced semiprocessed products. Korea's export share of semiprocessed goods decreased from 63.6 percent in 2000 to 39.8 percent in 2008. This change in trade pattern implies that the processing trade among Korea, Japan, and China is weakening, even though it is still the dominant nature among the triad. The driving factor of the change is the fast development of Chinese industry transforming China's export structure to become more capital and technology intensive. The preceding discussion shows that China's trade structure exhibits clear dominance of larger import share of middle products—P&C and semifinished goods (intermediates) and a growing share of finished (final) goods exports, thus establishing it as a platform for processing and as an assembly for finished products bound for the world market. Export diversification from consumption to capital goods suggests China's upward movement in the value chain.

The growing volume of intraregional trade in P&C in East Asia (and its manifestation in the formation of various FTAs and regional cooperation agreements) through fragmented production has been taking place owing to foreign investment in host countries like China, as well as via bilateral or trilateral arm's length transactions. MNEs from

Table 12.9 Comparison of export structure between Korea and Japan to China (%)

		Primary products	Semiprocessed	Parts	Capital goods	Consumer goods
Korea	2000	0.4	63.6	19.7	11.0	5.3
	2008	1.0	39.8	30.2	25.5	5.3
Japan	2000	1.3	41.9	29.6	23.2	4.0
	2008	3.5	36.6	30.3	23.4	6.2

Source: Oh et al. (2010).

Japan and Korea have been instrumental in the prevalence of such trade, taking advantage of endowment dissimilarities between relatively capital-abundant Korea (and Japan) and relatively labor-abundant China. As China is Korea's largest FDI destination, with about 25 percent share of overseas Korean investment, it is worthwhile to analyze the evidence of such MNE activities. Prevalence of intrafirm trade is symptomatic of such FIE-based regional production networks within East Asia. Taking the schemes from Tables 12.1 and 12.2 into consideration, we could also envisage a practical scenario where the trade-creating effect of FDI-induced international production network between, say, Japan (source/host) and Korea (host/source), is changed as both of these nations' foreign affiliates source intermediate goods from China (a third country).[14] Alike the case of Japan, FDI outflows by MNCs from Korea facilitates production-sharing in segments. Initiation of processing trade regime in China in the 1980s (i.e., duty exemption for intermediates and raw materials conditioned on its usage in promoting exports), economic reforms leading to open door policy, gradual economic transition from bureaucratic socialism to scientific socialism, and rural to urban transformation all created a conducive environment for Korea's participation, herself undergoing transition from dictatorship to democracy and embracing export-oriented trade policy.

4.2 Korea's FDI in China

In this section, we analyze the impact of inward FDI on trade flows: intermediate goods, P&C, and finished goods; that is, capital goods and consumption goods. After the financial crisis in 1997, East Asia has been a large recipient of FDI inflows (US$151.3 billion; i.e., over 20 percent of global FDI inflows in 2005), owing to its miraculous growth performance, favorable FDI policy environment, mergers and acquisitions. Extensive policy reforms favoring FDI caused a surge in flows into Korea after the 1997 crisis. But over the years, Korea's FDI to China has highlighted Korea's trade structure with China. Ever since 1990, Korea's FDI has rapidly increased except for the period of the global economic crises in 1998 and 2008. Considering the fact that world FDI is mostly directed to advanced economies, Korea's concentration on China stands apart. The primary reason behind the difference is that Korea's investment in China has been driven by the motivation of saving cost (Ha and Lee 2011). According to a Korea Trade-Investment Promotion Agency (KOTRA) survey (2009), in the 1990s, primary motivations of FDI were to take advantage of China's cheap labor and domestic market access.[15] However, recent studies show a changing pattern of FDI in terms of FDI motivation, the form of investment, and industrial composition. In 2008, out of 1,343 FDIs, the primary motivation of 775 firms was access to local markets whereas 228 firms considered low labor cost. This conforms to the KIEP (2010) report. In order, such motivations are: domestic market (34.0 percent), low labor cost (20.9 percent), worsening business environment in Korea, (10.6 percent), and so on.

As of 2009, unlike the case with Japan, where it is most active in the area of financial service and insurance, almost 80 percent of Korea's FDI inflows to China are in the

Table 12.10 Korea's total exports and intrafirm exports (US$ billion, %)

	Total exports	Intrafirm exports	Excluding intrafirm exports	Share of intrafirm exports (%)
1999	144	13	131	9
2002	162	34	128	21
2005	284	91	193	32
Annual growth	12.9%	45.6%	7.2%	

Source: Lee and Lim (2007).

manufacturing sector, mostly concentrated in the areas of electronics and telecommunication equipment manufacturing. Out of thirty-three Korean companies ranked in the top 500 foreign-invested firms in China, twenty-three firms are investing in the area of electrical machine and electronics manufacturing (KIEP 2010). However, the areas of wholesale and retail distribution, publishing, media, and information services have increased their shares in recent years.

Regarding the organizational mode of such Sino-Korean intrafirm networks, most of Korea's FDI in China is in the form of new incorporation. In terms of total FDI stock, new incorporation takes 96 percent of total numbers and 85 percent of total amount. So FDI in the form of M&A investment is rare. However, KIEP (2010) reports that M&A investment is gaining importance, although before 2000 there had been practically no M&A investment in China by Korean companies. Even in terms of the number of investments, investment by acquisition reached 6.7 percent. Also, the foreign investing firm contributes to the overall trade surplus. According to Ha and Lee (2011), trade surplus from intrafirm trade is four times bigger than the overall trade surplus. The Korean firms investing in China usually conduct the later stage of production processes with imported intermediated and capital goods from Korea, with sales to local or third countries' markets (Tables 12.10 and 12.11). Lee (2008) reports that only 16.4 percent of the processed products are exported to the Korean market.

Table 12.12 provides the current state of division of labor between Korea and China. Overall, while the share of interindustry trade is slightly higher than IIT, the latter has increased significantly during 1996–2007. Particularly the share of IIT for capital goods and intermediate goods has increased from 39.7 percent in 1996 to 60.6 percent in 2006. Vertical integration between Korea and China reflects the fact that Korea is still

Table 12.11 Annual growth of intrafirm exports of Korea by country

	China	Germany	Singapore	Italy	Japan	France	Hongkong	U.S
Intrafirm exports	398%	290%	243%	100%	98%	81%	55%	49%
Total exports	48%	19%	5%	20%	5%	11%	8%	4%

Source: Lee and Lim (2007).

Table 12.12 Korea-China division of labor by production process (%)

		All Industries excl. agriculture goods	
		1996	2006
Capital goods	Interindustry	60.3	39.4
	Korea to China	52.6	24.4
	China to Korea	8.7	15.0
	Intraindustry	39.7	60.6
	Horizontal	2.9	3.6
	Vertical	36.8	57.0
Intermediate goods	Interindustry	65.8	51.6
	Korea to China	44.2	19.5
	China to Korea	21.6	32.1
	Intraindustry	34.2	48.4
	Horizontal	4.7	9.8
	Vertical	29.5	38.6
Consumer goods	Interindustry	63.5	60.4
	Korea to China	23.0	7.9
	China to Korea	40.5	52.5
	Intraindustry	36.4	39.6
	Horizontal	3.2	4.4
	Vertical	33.2	35.2

Source: KIEP, Ahn and Bang (2007).

maintaining its technological distance from China and its technological advantage over China in every area of capital, intermediate, and consumer goods. Kim and Ju (2007) confirm faster vertical integration than horizontal integration between Korea and East Asian countries and shows that IIT in higher-value-added product is growing compared to lower-quality product, even though Korea's trade with Japan is still characterized by IIT in relatively lower-value-added product. However, China is believed to be catching up with Korea in some intermediated goods because of the expansion of horizontal IIT in intermediate goods. In the case of Korea-Japan trade, Korea seems to have reduced the technological gap for capital goods although the distance between the countries has widened for intermediate goods. According to Ok et al. (2007), both horizontal and vertical IIT increased by 15 percent and 35 percent respectively. The ratio of VIIT (Korea-China) to domestic production increased, which results in a widening wage gap in the Korean labor market. However, as Korea catches up with the United States and Japan, the ratios of VIIT to total domestic production with these countries decreased in each industry. Overall increase in VIIT with China overwhelms decreases in VIITs with the United States and Japan. The fastest increases in VIIT with China are observed in: audio-video, communication equipment, automobile, refinery, basic metal, other transportation equipment. VIIT decreases in: textile products, food and beverages, minerals, leather products, footwear, clothing and fur products.

4.3 How "big" is Sino-Korean offshore outsourcing?

In order to demystify the dynamics of production networks between Korea and China, we need to consider the underlying motivation driving Korea to outsource to China.[16] This will enable us to sift through the panoply of factors. We observed that growth of imports of intermediates for assembly and transformation in China from Korea increased relatively more than import growth from the US and Japan. In fact, the calculation by Dean et al. (2009) of the export similarity index shows that China has its highest, over 50 percent, with Asian tigers, as compared to the United States and European Union (42 percent). Hyun et al. (2008) report survey results from Korean firms on offshoring: the dominant motivation of Korean companies' offshoring strategies is to save production costs (Table 12.13). Also, according to this study, 84 percent of surveyed companies responded that offshoring has improved their performance in terms of sales, profit, and overall competitiveness.

According to Lee et al. (2010), based on a survey of business activities by the Bureau of Statistics, less than 8 percent of Korean companies are involved in offshoring activities. From Das (2007) we learn that China receives almost half of the total offshoring of Korean firms as of 2006. Lee et al. (2010) report that China's share of Korea's aggregate offshoring increased from 41 percent to 49 percent between 2001 and 2004 and

Table 12.13 Motivations for offshoring (survey data). Number of firms

Motivations	Cost saving	Business flexibility	Technology transfer	Access to foreign skilled manpower	Access to foreign market	others
1st	125	23	7	1	10	1
2nd	20	79	8	5	44	2

Source: Hyun (2008).

Table 12.14 Regions of offshoring

	2001		2006	
Area	No. of firms	%	No. of firms	%
China	75	41.44	136	49.10
Japan	23	12.71	32	11.55
ASEAN	20	11.05	29	10.47
North America	25	13.81	30	10.83
EU/EFTA	25	13.81	29	10.47
Others	13	7.18	21	7.58
Total	181	100.00	277	100.00

Source: Hyun (2008).

Table 12.15 Areas of mutual competitiveness between China and Korea

Classification	Korea	China	Remarks
Automobiles	Competitive edge in finished cars and parts	Maintains competitive edge in certain car parts	
Electronics	Comparative advantage in home appliances (Telecom equipment, semiconductors and LCDs)	Upgrading competitiveness (Automatic data processors and fixed-line telephones)	More mutually complementary (Electronic tubes, semiconductors, telecommunication Equipments) Decrease in technological gap
Petrochemicals	Competitive in organic chemistry and plastic goods (Accounts for 20% of China's petrochemical imports)	Competitive in fertilizers and others	Korea's overall competitiveness over China
Textiles and clothing	Competitive in high-quality and functional textile products and clothes	Secures competitiveness in the low-priced textile products and clothing	Mutual competition in the world market

Source: Adapted from Samsung Economic Research Institute (*Monthly Focus*, no. 6, June 2011), table 8.

this takes the form of "intrafirm offshoring," that is, procurement from affiliates (already exisiting or green field) or subsidiaries in foreign countries. Japan and North America are the second and third largest areas for offshore outsourcing.

The composition of offshoring firms by industry shows manufacturing and construction are the most active sectors (Lee et al. 2010). Table 12.15 highlights areas of Korea's and China's mutual competitiveness (SERI 2011).

5 Learning from the Facts: A Qualitative Exploration[17]

5.1 Labor market effects

In terms of employment effects and labor market ramifications, the change in mix of jobs (i.e., skilled and unskilled labor-intensive jobs) and wage dispersion is worthy of consideration. The typical negative employment impact of offshoring could be attributed to imports of raw materials and services replacing domestic workers. That triggers policy debates. Also, offshoring is expected to enhance productivity via resource reallocations to foreign production facilities with better productivity. Mixed reactions exist: offshoring activities in the more strategic and core areas such as designing, R&D, could have negative impacts on overall performance and competitiveness of domestic industries, whereas efficiency effects of offshoring can contribute to strengthened labor demand in the longer run by enhancing business performance.

As skilled and unskilled wage rates in China are relatively lower than Japan and Korea, the relocation of production fragments will have wage effects. As Korean firms specialize more in technology-intensive products, trade expansion with China is expected to increase the wages of skilled labor in these industries with skill bias. Often, the educational attainment of workers is taken as indicator of the skill content of the labor force and hence, depending on the nature of production blocks being relocated, the wage dynamics change (Jones 2000; Das 2009).

According to the report by the Ministry of Strategy and Finance (MOSF), Korea's overseas investment has increased almost 30 percent in 2011 to US$44.4 billion from US$34.3 billion in 2010. This is a second consecutive double-digit increase since 2009, after a slight decline in 2008, due to the international financial crisis. The increase in overseas investment reflects more offshoring activities by Korean firms. There has been growing concern over the expansion of overseas investment that it could accelerate the hollowing out of Korea's manufacturing industries and aggravate the sluggish employment market. As the recent overseas investment is mostly made by bigger firms and their global production networks help increase global demand for Korean products leading to higher investment domestically, it could help employment by inducing domestic investment. However, the recent characteristics of Korea's overseas investment show a high concentration in the area of resource development and distribution service sectors compared to the investment in manufacturing sectors. In 2011, overseas investments in those areas recorded 100 percent and 45 percent increases while the latter recorded only 9 percent, even though the manufacturing sector still takes the largest share of overseas investment. According to Park et al. (2011), in the wake of Korea-China competition the pressure on restructuring of various sectors, especially the Korean SMEs, could cause "biplolarization" because of vulnerability to trade shocks. Employment increased in electronics, IT-related industry and transport equipment during 1993–2005, while deindustrialization in light industry (leather and footwear) led to a fall in employment by 8.6 percent. Thus, a negative feeling could grip the offshore outsourcing prospect even with an FTA in the making.

Ahn et al. (2008) explored the impact of production sharing with China on the Japanese and Korean labor market in a comparative perspective. According to them, total outsourcing to Asia had a negligible effect—unlike the case with Japan—on labor demand; however, Japanese outsourcing to China had a significant adverse impact on the demand for workers with lower secondary education, though a favorable positive effect on the demand for labors with tertiary level of education. In case of outsourcing to Japan, the converse is true: that is, inflating the demand for workers with lower secondary education. In other words, in a triangular mode of organizing production sharing in East Asia (Figure 12.1), the wage impact has different inherent dynamics, namely that the Korea-Japan mode shifts demand away from workers with tertiary-level skill to the workers with lower-secondary education, whereas the Korea-China mode switched demand away from workers with upper- or lower-secondary education to those with tertiary education. On the whole, it is envisaged that the positive impact on the demand for skilled workers is significant and could be attributed to the outsourcing in the electrical machinery sector alone.

With already existing higher wage share of workers with tertiary and upper secondary level in both manufacturing and services (and in total economy), net export of sophisticated intermediates in electrical and general machinery from Korea to China (and other Asia) led to diverging wage gap between employees with different educational attainment. Imported inputs *from* Korea has embodied skilled labor content with higher education and substitutes skill-intensive activities in China (causing wage of skilled Chinese workers to fall and relative rise in wage of unskilled workers there needed to assemble the sophisticated Korean intermediates); on the other hand, imported intermediates (processed) and final goods from China *into* Korea embodies unskilled labor with low secondary education and hence, substitutes unskilled-intensive blocks in Korea, causing wage of unskilled to relative decline, but Korean skilled labor's wage increase as more intermediates are exported to China. However, according to Ahn et al. (2008: 58), "the overall effects of total outsourcing in terms of increasing (decreasing) the relative demand for workers with higher (lower) education have been insignificant in Korea partly because a substantial part of Korean outsourcing remained directed towards Japan, shifting labor demand away from workers with tertiary education towards workers with lower education. For Korea, [results] imply that labor demand would shift away from less-skilled workers towards more skilled workers if outsourcing to China increased and outsourcing to Japan decreased in the future."

Empirical studies by Ok et al. (2007), Suh et al. (2008), and Park (2009) show that offshoring has very negligible negative impacts on employment. Lee et al. (2008) show that a 1 percent increase of the ratio of firms' offshoring activities to total sales reduces employment by 0.08 percent. This effect is dominant in service industries than in manufacturing and, particularly, forceful against higher skilled workers. Furthermore, it reports that increase in the overseas investment induces domestic investment via strengthened global production network. Using the "Survey of Business Activities" (a firm-level panel data set surveyed by the Statistics Korea between 2006 and 2008), and using Panel Logit and Fixed Effect Panel models, Lee et al. (2010) identify that firm size, export ratio, and R&D intensity are positively related to offshoring. Secondly, on the labor productivity aspect, it has an adverse negative effect (in the service industry) and statistically insignificant effect (in the manufacturing industry) while it negatively affects total employment. The findings of this study imply that offshoring by Korean domestic firms is in a primitive stage and therefore reduces employment *without* increasing productivity. This suggests the importance of long-term strategies and policies to support improvements in the quality of offshoring and the adjustment of the industry structure for strengthening the competitiveness of Korean firms. Similarly, using data for forty-nine manufacturing sectors between 1999 and 2000, Kim (2006) showed that Korean firms' offshoring activities for raw materials and services have negative employment effects.

The general negative employment effect is confirmed by Nahm (2010), in an empirical analysis of the effect of global outsourcing on the wage inequality in manufacturing during 1999–2006, with data obtained from the Mining and Manufacturing Surveys, Input-Output Tables, and Trade Statistics. It shows a significant widening of the wage gap between skilled and low-skilled labor in Korea's manufacturing sectors for 1999–2006. Depending on the definition of the scopes of offshoring (narrow and wide), the wage gaps had increased as much as 7.1 percent and 12.6 percent respectively, with narrow outsourcing having a significant impact on the wage inequality while the effect of wide outsourcing was insignificant. Although generally offshoring has negative impacts on employment and wages, this is contrary to the empirical results for other developed countries with positive productivity and employment long-run effects. It is hard to conclude that this is embedded characteristic of Korea and needs further exploration in future. It was not until 2000s that Korea's large firm actively started to establish global production network. As large high technology firms are leading offshoring activities, one can expect that the employment effects in these sectors would be greater in the longer term.

5.2 A view through the theoretical lens

Drawing upon the discussions, we can look through the lens of theoretical literature. However, typical neoclassical models concentrating on the final goods trade is inadequate in handling such production organization. We will probe beyond theoretical complexities for unearthing the commonalities and differences in trade flows between CJK. Possible candidates for explaining such trade can be lined up in two sets: core (*sui generis*) specific factors pertinent to China and Korea and some general factors. These are mostly due to *onshore factors* in China as well as *near-shore* or offshore factors as documented below:

(1) The countries are tied by cultural similarity, especially Confucian culture, the affinity of language, and their common land border. This cultural coherence is conducive to organizing production, improving competencies and service quality by dint of commonalities (Liang 2010). About one-third of China's outsourcing revenues are attributed to Korea and Japan (Tholons 2010). According to this report, it is due to *Guanxi* effect: relationships signifying business connections, its power in making cooperation possible for doing business (7). Samsung moved its outsourcing segments from Hong Kong to China in 2006 by leveraging on cost-arbitrage and business efficiency enhancement. Then it started running offices in Tianjin and Shenzhen. This was because of the cultural affinity, which made negotiations easier between clients, encompassing various facets including technological capabilities.[18]

(2) Political relations between Japan and China, Japan and Korea, and Korea and China are also instrumental in terms of increasing Sino-Korean interactions. Rooted in their colonial past, China, Japan, and Korea often have a conflicting relationship. This is more so in the context of Japan and Korea. As both of these countries are still involved in imbroglios over territorial claims, Korea's tilt over China could be a "substitution effect." The geopolitical factor could lead to more intraregional Sino-Korean trade replacing Japan's predominance. In this context, a possible Korea-China FTA is a step forward to this direction for intensifying further production sharing. As SERI (June 2011) reports, this FTA could have *threefold* benefits: (1) reinforcing competitiveness of Korean products in China's markets; (2) Korea's establishment of FTAS with Japan, the United States, and China, becoming a center of economic dynamism; (3) exploiting mutual comparative advantage as Korea is gaining competitive advantage over Japan in P&C, electronics, P&C. Proximity to clients leads to RPN.

(3) According to Li et al. (2010: 245), the "composition of China's exports has been moving quickly towards capital and technology-intensive products in recent years," especially in office machinery and equipment (SITC 75), telecommunications and recording equipment (SITC 76), and electrical machinery and parts (SITC 77). As China diversifies export and sophisticated products, Korea could reap advantage from sourcing such processing imports. The learning effect, by participating in trade in middle products with the United States, Japan, and Korea, is instrumental behind the proliferation of such trade.

(4) China's *economic reforms* favoring processing trade regime pave the way for its role as an assembly base in East Asia. China's political leadership support

outsourcing sector's growth and there are twenty-four designated outsourcing cities with many vendors. Not only had that, policy-related variables such as tariff barriers (import duty and corporate tax rates) became favorable, especially after its accession to the WTO. It would be interesting to study whether an FTA among Korea, United States, and China (in the process of negotiations) would bring more economic benefits for China and Korea at the detriment of others. But an FTA involving CJK has a good prospect of delivering large benefits via triangular mode of fragmentation.

(5) As emphasized by Jones and Kierzkowski (1990, 2005), production blocks need to be connected via *service links* or bundle of activities such as transport and communication, insurance, telecommunications, quality assurance, coordination of tasks, and so on. ICT-induced technological changes transforming and increasing tradability of modern services are important for such trade to happen. China's improvement in telecommunications facilitated quality infrastructure so as to improve logistics, coordination of shipments, sale of final goods, and so forth. According to Li et al. (2010), the number of civil aviation routes increased by 3.4 times between 1986 and 2005, the number of fixed telephone lines per 1,000 went up by 25 times between 1992 and 2004, and China has the largest mobile phone market in the world.

(6) Geographical proximity and similar time zones are important factors behind cost arbitrage. In fact, flights connecting major cities with Seoul take two hours.[19] But considering Japan and Korea vis-à-vis China, this does not offer additional insight apart from the fact of reduction of transport cost and information cost. Most importantly, Chinese provinces source intermediate inputs from dynamic Korea, Japan and Taiwan for exporting to the Western world and being in near-vicinity of Korea, the prospect of such trade looms large in the horizon (Ma et al. 2009). In particular, access to a steady supply of talent pools of skilled workers from Korea with relatively better English skills is important for Korea-China case. Not only that, aging population problem in Korea (and also in Japan) is a factor driving Korean companies to seek for young pool of workers at cheaper price and hence the demographic factors changing the composition of labor force in Korea against working-age population are causing her to tap nearby China with diverse language skill with proficient analytical skills apart from acumen for hard work.[20]

(7) Onshore domestic demand for outsourced services driven by expansion of Chinese economy acts as a catalyst. Unlike India where mostly outsourcing industry flourishes due to offshore-demand pull, in the case of China, local demand for outsourcing services such as telecommunications, automotive, and so on, are also instrumental for Korean firms' recent success. Apart from the world market destination for processed exports, the fueling of domestic consumption demand—because of the rural to urban transition and the annual average economic growth above 9 percent—has also led to demand for outsourced services. Thus, the government's support for domestic companies to

outsource for catering domestic market works fine for near-shore Korean (and Japanese) companies. As the scenario changed in the post-crisis period, China's major source of outsourcing segments shifted from offshore United States and the European Union to near-shore industrial bases like Korea and onshore local demand by state-owned enterprises.[21]

6 Concluding remarks

The growing volume of intraregional trade in East and South-East Asia can in no way be overlooked at this juncture. In fact, the post-crisis world economy has experienced a rise of Southern Engines of growth, especially India and China (Santos-Paulino and Wan 2010). Such a shift has been accompanied by outsourcing in international production network facilitated by foreign multinationals. The unearthing of Sino-Korean product fragmentation throws new light on an evolving trade relation in North-East Asia. Given their geographical proximity and cultural affinity, the Korea-China case offers a new dimension. Korea exhibited increasing trend in offshoring to China since the 1990s and 2000, especially in textiles, machinery and electronic parts, metal work, and petrochemicals.

China's emergence as assembly base for processing exports led to renewed interest in exploring her economic cooperation with Korea on the one hand, and Japan, on the other hand. We find that despite Japan being the steady supplier of middle products to Korea, other East Asian countries including China had made rapid progress in exporting to Korea's market. In fact, China's assembly and reexports to Korea has increased while Japan experienced a relative fall. Apart from arm's length trade between nonaffiliated subcontractors, the dominant mode of offshoring is via multinationals or foreign-invested enterprises promoting intrafirm trade. According to our analysis, since 2000 Korea has emerged as a net exporter of intermediate goods, P&C, and capital goods to other East Asian countries including China, and also to the world market. Also, foreign-owned firms' trade in China's total trade expanded as Korean and Japanese multinationals spread their arms in offshoring to affiliates in China's local market. Given China's export sophistication owes to East Asian neighbors' supply of processed imports, a post-crisis business-cycle pass-through is possible for Korea and Japan as negative export demand shock could have ripple effects for such imported inputs.

Also, established evidence confirms that participating in this dominant triangular mode of value-chain slicing could have an effect on wage gap among the pairs. In case of Korea-China, given the nature of trade in goods-in-process dice are loaded in favor of the skilled workers at the expense of the unskilled workers with adverse effect on wages and employment. In this context, the government's role can in no way be ignored. Education, training, and a safety net are necessary to counter the adverse effects.

NOTES

1. Corresponding author, email: dasgouranga@gmail.com.
2. The phenomenon is so significant that, no wonder, whole issues of some prominent journals have devoted attention on it—for example, *North American Journal of Economics and Finance* (2001, vol. 12) and *International Review of Economics and Finance* (2005, vol. 14), among others. The paramount importance of such issue is felt more intensely after the financial debacle has shaken the Western world.
3. IT-enabled services trade is primarily of this nature—export-oriented FDI—via organizing production, sourcing, marketing and financing of sub-activities in stages on an international basis.
4. According to Yi (2003), the term "VS" was coined by Balassa (1967) for the first time.
5. In the literature, divergences in definition often lead to differences in measurement. Fragmentation broadly implies slicing integrated production process into fragments while outsourcing is a narrower term meaning these fragmented parts is sourced outside the parent firm—either locally or globally. Amiti and Wei (2004) used the term in-sourcing for *local* outsourcing.
6. Due to rise of the service links thanks to IT sector, such IIT is also temporal or periodic, as it takes advantage of time differences of geographically separated regions (say, West and the East).
7. It is hard to distinguish "true" intermediate goods from P&C. In this chapter, in order to avoid confusions regarding domain of such products, we adopt a broader one to cover both middle products and intermediates: "middle products" are P&C (goods-in-process) and "intermediate goods" are either assembled or, produced from the middle products resulting in some semifinished goods requiring further assembly or value-addition in final stage to give final shape.
8. GTAP is a large-scale multisectoral, multicountry Computable General Equilibrium global trade model housed in Purdue University, United States, and Monash University, Australia (Hertel 1997). CGE is based on input-output database in a multilateral framework.
9. Often, this is called flying geese to leading dragons especially in the context of PRC.
10. This has been called "substitution effect" between Japan and Hong Kong vis-à-vis South Korea (Li et al. 2010).
11. Recently, in order to avoid the conflicting political-economic relations rooted is history in North-East Asia, a Trilateral Cooperation Secretariat involving Japan-Korea-China has been launched by the Korean government (see *Korea Times*, June 4–5, 2011, 2). This could initiate a trilateral FTA and hence, more mobility of human capital as well as trade in goods and services.
12. This is from the *Korean Herald*, April 2011. Almost all companies like Samsung, LG, and Daewoo rely heavily on imports of microcontrollers from Japan for meeting their demands.
13. These are from world electronics dataset comprising: electronic data processing, office equipment, control and instrumentation, audio-video equipment, personal consumer equipment, X-ray and medical equipment, etc.
14. Usually, FDI from source to host country causes exports of intermediates and/or, capital goods to increase as production sites are delocalized to separate location. Concurrently, imports by FDI source country increases as affiliates in host increase exports of finished products (post assembly or processing) back to source.

15. KOTRA (2009).
16. Given the fact that India and China are emerging southern engines of growth, the dice are loaded in favor of India more. Given large English-speaking population, largest democracy, enormous market size, dynamic youth population, better rule of law, and skilled professional with superiority in ICT-enabled services, the elephant scores over the dragon to attract FDIs from Korean conglomerates.
17. A regression analysis is not mounted in this preliminary version; however, given the profusion of literature on such issue, running regression is more routine than offering a qualitative insights at this stage.For example, one could specify degree of outsourcing between "I" and "j" (OSij) as dependent variable such that: $OS_{ij} = F(GDP_i, GDP_j, V_{ij})$, where V_{ij} is binary vector of factors such as, FDI, institution, geography, trade policy, wage differential, telecommunication and transport cost, political-economic stability, etc.
18. One example is: use of similar keyboard character set like Korea and Japan using unique "double-byte system" for generating the character set of these countries. Chinese programmers familiarity with them is also conducive. Not only that, anchor *outsourcing Northeastern cities* like Tianjin, Beijing, Guangzhou, Shenyang, or Dalian have Korean (and Japanese) speaking population which offers incentives for Korean firms to relocate for better coordination and management.
19. According to Tholons (2010: 8), "China offers offshore rates because of significant cost-savings it generates for MNCs outsourcing to China. Moreover, geographical proximity allows Japanese and Korean clients the benefit and ability of employing a 'hands-on' management model because of the distance (or lack of)—a factor that high level management values. [Because] of two coexisting conditions—cultural affinity and geographical proximity—that Japan and Korea will continue to prefer China over neighboring countries such as Singapore, Malaysia, Philippines, Vietnam, and India. The majority of China's outsourcing industry capture in Japan and Korea lies in three industries, namely, the electronics industry, banking and finance services industry and chemicals industry (supporting software development, engineering, research and development, supply chain management, bioinformatics outsourcing, others). With inherent advantage in Korean markets, China has the opportunity to increase market scale by expanding to include other verticals such as electronics, automotive, and animation/game development industries from these client nations."
20. See www.forbes.com accessed on April 27, 2011. See Tholons (2010): China graduates more than four million students per year with 700, 000 IT professionals. See http://www.theoutsourceblog.com/2011/03/japan-and-korea-driving-it-outsourcing.
21. Tholons (2010).

References

Ahn, H., and H. Bang. 2007. "The Division of Labor among the Triad of Korea-Japan-China and Policy Implications" (Korean). World Economy Update 07-46, 5, Seoul: Korea Institute for International Economic Policy.

Ahn, S., K. Fukao, and K. Ito. 2008. "Outsourcing in East Asia and its Impact on the Japanese and Korean Labor Markets." OECD Trade Policy Working Papers, no. 65. Paris: OECD.

Amiti, M., and S.-J. Wei. 2005. "Fear of Service Outsourcing: Is It Justified?" *Economic Policy* 20 (42): 308–347.

Arndt, S. W., and H. Kierzkowski (eds.). 2001. *Fragmentation: New Production Patterns in the World Economy.* New York: Oxford University Press.

Assche, A. van, and B. Gangnes. 2010. "Electronics Production Upgrading: Is China Exceptional?" *Applied Economics Letters* 17 (5), 477–482.

Athukorala, P. 2005. "Product Fragmentation and Trade Patterns in East Asia." *Asian Economic Papers* 4 (3): 1–27. Originally issued as a Trade and Development Discussion Paper 2003/21, Division of Economics, Research School of Pacific and Asian Studies, Australian National University.

Athukorala, P. C., and J. Menon. 2010. "Global Production Sharing, Trade Patterns, and Determinants of Trade Flows in East Asia." ADB Working Paper, no. 41. Manila, Philippines: Asian Development Bank.

Athukorala, P., and N. Yamashita. 2006. "Production Fragmentation and Trade Integration: East Asia in a Global Context," *North American Journal of Economics and Finance* 17 (3): 233–256.

Balassa, B. 1967. "Trade Liberalization and 'Revealed' Comparative Advantage." *Manchester School of Economic and Social Studies* 33 (2): 99–123.

Baldwin, R., and F. Robert-Nicoud. 2007. "Offshoring: General Equilibrium Effects on Wages, Production and Trade." NBER Working Paper, no. 12991. Cambridge, MA: National Bureau of Economic Research.

Bardhan, A. D., and D. Jaffe. 2005. "Innovation, R&D, and Offshoring." Research Report of the Fisher Center for Real Estate and Urban Economics, Paper 1005, 1–20. Berkeley: University of California.

Chen, H.-Y., and Y.-M. Chang. 2006. "Trade Verticality and Structural Change in Industries: The Cases of Taiwan and South Korea." *Open Economies Review* 17 (3): 321–340.

Cheng, L., and Henryk Kierzkowski (eds.). 2001. Globalization of Trade and Production in South-East Asia. (Kluwer Academic Press, New York)

Das, G. G. 2007. "Does Trade and Technology Transmission facilitate Inequality Convergence? An Inquiry into the Role of Technology in Reducing the Poverty of Nations." Working Paper, WP/07/16. Washington. DC: International Monetary Fund.

———. 2009. "A Hybrid Production Structure in Trade: Theory and Implications." *International Review of Economics* 56 (4): 359–375, December. Online version: DOI 10.1007/s12232-009-0082-9.

Dean, J., M. Lovely, and J. Mora. 2009. "Decomposing China-Japan-U.S. Trade: Vertical Specialization, Ownership, and Organizational Form." *Journal of Asian Economics* 20: 596–610.

Deardorff, A. V. 2005. "A Trade Theorist's Take on Skilled-labor Outsourcing." *International Review of Economics and Finance* 14 (3): 259–271.

Dixit, Avinash K and Gene M. Grossman. 1982. "Trade and Protection with Multistage Production," *Review of Economic Studies* 59: 583–594.

Feenstra, R. C., and G. H. Hanson. 1996. "Globalization, Outsourcing, and Wage Inequality." *American Economic Review* 86(2): 240–245.

———. 2003. "Global Production Sharing and Rising Inequality: A Survey of Trade and Wages." In *Handbook of International Trade*, edited by E. K. Choi and R. J. Harrigan, 146–185. Oxford: Basil Blackwell.

Feenstra, R. C., andS.-J. Wei (eds.). 2011. *China's Growing Role in World Trade.* Chicago: University of Chicago Press.

Grossman, G. M., and E. Rossi-Hansberg. 2006b. "Trading Tasks: A Simple Theory of Offshoring." NBER Working Paper, no. 12721. Cambridge, MA: National Bureau of Economic Research.

Grossman, G. M., and E. Helpman. 2002. Outsourcing in a Global Economy. NBER Working Paper, no. 8728. Cambridge, MA: National Bureau of Economic Research.

Grubel, H. G., and P. J. Lloyd. 1975. *Intra-Industry Trade: The Theory and Measurement of International Trade in Differentiated Products*. London: John Wiley & Sons.

Ha, B., and S. Lee. 2011. "The Structure of Intra-Firm Trade by Manufacturing Affiliates of Korean Firms" (Korean). *Korean Economic Analysis* 17 (1): 133–175.

Harrigan, J., and H. Deng. 2011. "China's Local Comparative Advantage." In *China's Growing Role in World Trade*, edited by R. C. Feenstra and S.-J. Wei, 109–135. Chicago: University of Chicago Press.

Hertel, T. W. (ed.). 1997. *Global Trade Analysis: Modeling and Applications*. Cambridge, MA, Cambridge University Press.

Horgos, D. 2007. "International Outsourcing, Some Measurement Problems: An Empirical Analysis of Outsourcing Activities in Germany." IZA Working Paper.

Hummels, D., D. Rapoport, and K.-M. Yi. 1998. "Vertical Specialization and the Changing Nature of World Trade." *Federal Reserve Bank of New York Economic Policy Review* 4 (2): 79–99.

Hyun, H. 2008. "The Expansion of Gobal Outsourcing and Policy Implications" (Korean). World Economy Update 08-03, 5. Seoul: Korea Institute for International Economic Policy.

Institute for International Trade (IIT). 2008. "Trend of Korea's Trade." Mimeograph, IIT internal report.

Jones, R. W., and H. Kierzkowski. 2001, A Framework for Fragmentation." In *Fragmentation: New Production Patterns in the World Economy*, edited by S. W. Arndt and H. Kierzkowski, 17–34. New York: Oxford University Press.

———. 2005. "International Fragmentation and the New Economic Geography." *North American Journal of Economics and Finance* 16 (1): 1–10.

Jones, R. W., H. Kierzkowski, and L. Chen. 2005. "What Does the Evidence Tell Us about Fragmentation and Outsourcing?" *International Review of Economics and Finance* 14 (3): 305–316.

Kang, D., S. Lee, and S. Hwang. 2011. "Korea's Post-crisis Economic Reliance on China and Policy Suggestions." *Korea Focus* 19 (1): 106–115.

Kim, T., and K. Ju. 2007. "Korea's Horizontal and Vertical Intra-Industry Trade and FDI in Trade with East Asian Countries" (Korean). *Journal of International Economic Studies* 11 (1): 29–55 (June).

Kim, W. 2006. "Impacts of Offshoring on Productivity and Employment." e-KIET Industry Information Report, South Korea, no. 321, 5–7.

Kimura, F., and M. Ando. 2005. "Two-dimensional Fragmentation in East Asia: Conceptual Framework and Empirics." *International Review of Economics & Finance* 14 (3): 317–348.

Kimura, F., Y. Takahashi, and K. Hayakawa. 2007. "Fragmentation and Parts and Components Trade: Comparison between East Asia and Europe." *North American Journal of Economics and Finance* 18 (1): 23–40.

Korea Institute for International Economic Policy (KIEP). 2010. "Trends of FDI in Korea, Japan and China and Policy Implications" (Korean). Mimeograph, KIEP Policy Analysis, 49–51. Seoul: Korea Institute for International Economic Policy.

Korea Trade-Investment Promotion Agency (KOTRA). 2009. "Grand Survey of China" (Korean).

Krugman, P. 1995. "Growing World Trade: Causes and Consequences," Brookings Papers on Economic Activity, 1: 327–362.

Lall, S., M. Albaladejo, and J. Zhang. 2004. "Mapping Fragmentation: Electronics and Automobiles in East Asia and Latin America." *Oxford Development Studies* 32 (3): 407–432.

Lee, K., M. Park, and I. Kim. 2010. "The Impact of Off-shoring on Productivity and Labor Market and Policy Implications" (Korean). Korea Institute of Economics and Technology (KIET) Report, 2010-579, 107–111.

Lee, S. 2008. "Trends of Korea-China Trade Structure and its Macroeconomic Implications" (Korean). Seoul: KDI Policy Analysis, 2008-15, 23.

Lee, S., and G. Lim. 2007. "The Impacts of Firm's Globalization on Exports with Emphasis on Intra-firm Trade" (Korean). Seoul: KDI Economic Prospects, 158–167.

Lee, Y., I. Soe, and H. Seo. 2008. "A Study on the Contribution of Outsourcing to the Total Factor Productivity" (Korean). *Journal of Industrial Oraganization* 15 (4): 55–82.

Li K., L. Song, and X. Zhao. 2010. "Component Trade and China's Global Economic Integration." In *The Rise of China and India: Impacts, Prospects, and Implications,* edited by A. Santos-Paulino and G. Wan, 241–261. Basingstoke: Palgrave Macmillan.

Liang, M.-Y. 2010. "Confucianism and the East Asian Miracle." *American Economic Journal: Macroeconomics* 2 (3): 206–234.

Ma, A., A. V. Assche, and C. Hong. 2009. "Global Production Networks and China's Processing Trade." *Journal of Asian Economics* 20: 640–654.

Marjit, S., and R. Acharyya. 2003. *International Trade, Wage Inequality and the Developing Economy: A General Equilibrium Approach.* Heidelberg: Springer Physica-Verlag.

Nahm B. T. 2010. "The Effect of Global Outsourcing on Wage Inequality in Manufacturing," *Kyungjehak Yeon-gu* [Journal of Economic Studies] 58 (4): 133–156

Ng, F. and Yeats, A. J. 2001/2003. "Production Sharing in East Asia: Who Does What for Whom, and Why?" Policy Research Working Paper Series 2197. Washington, DC: World Bank.

Oh, Y., Y. Cho, B. Ha, M. Lee, M. Saking, and S. Lee. 2010. "Analysis of the International Division of Labor among Korea,China, and Japan, and Promotion of its Cooperation" (Korean). Korea Institute for Economics and Technology (KIET) Policy Analysis, no. 583, 73.

Ok, W., S. Jung, and Y. Oh. 2007. "The Effect of Trade Structure on International Division of Labor, Labor Demand Structure and Wage Gap: with emphasis on Korea-China Intra-industry Trade," *Korean Economic Analysis* 13 (3): 40–42.

OECD (Organisation of Economic Co-operation and Development). 2005. *Science, Technology and Industry Scoreboard 2005.* Paris: OECD.

———. 2007a. *Moving Up the Value Chain: Staying Competitive in the Global Economy.* Paris: OECD.

———. 2007b. *Offshoring and Employment: Trends and Impacts.* Paris: OECD.

Park, B.-S., H.-N. Kim, H.-J. Kwon, and C.-S. Park. 2011. "Korea-China FTA: Its Meanings and Major Issues." *Monthly Focus* 6 (June). Samsung Economic Research Institute (SERI).

Park, S. 2009. "The Impact of Service Offshoring on the Korean Manufacturing Sector" (Korean). *Journal of International Economic Studies* 13 (2): 175–202.

Sanyal, K. K., and R. W. Jones. 1982. "The Theory of Trade in Middle Products." *American Economic Review* 72 (1), 16–31.

Sinn, H.-W. 2003. *Der kranke Mann Europas: Diagnose und Therapie eines Kathedersozialisten.* Neuhardenberg: Institut und Ludwig-Maximilians-Universität Stiftung Schloß.

Suh, J., H. Lee, S. Park, and W. Kim. 2008. "The Impact of Market Liberalization and Global Outsourcing on Employment" (Korean). KIEP Long Term Study on International Economic Strategy 2008-04, 73–79. Seoul: Korea Institute for International Economic Policy.

Szirmai, A. 2009. "Industrialization as an Engine of Growth in Developing Countries." United Nations University (UNU)-MERIT Working Paper, no. 2009-010.

Taegi K., and J. Kyungwon. 2007. "Korea's Horizontal and Vertical Intra-Industry Trade and FDI in Trade with East Asian Countries" (Korean). *Journal of International Economic Studies* 11 (1) (June): 40–41.

Tholons. 2010. "China in the Asian Outsourcing Market." Tholons Advisory, Investments, and Research Services, February, 1–17.

Yang, P. 2007. "Analysis of Korea-China trade pattern and its implication on Korea-China FTA negotiation" (Korean). KIEP Policy Analysis, 2007-08, 64–72. Seoul: Korea Institute for International Economic Policy.

Yeats, A. J. 1998. "How Big is Global Production Sharing?" Policy Research Working Paper Series, no. 1871. Washington, DC: World Bank.

Yi, K.-M. 2003. "Can Vertical Specialization Explain the Growth of World Trade?" *Journal of Political Economy* 111 (1): 52–102.

CHAPTER 13

Offshoring, Inward Investment, and Export Performance in Ireland

FRANK BARRY AND ADELE BERGIN

Introduction

Ireland is one of the most FDI-intensive economies in the Organisation of Economic Co-operation and Development (OECD) and beyond. Foreign affiliates account for almost 50 percent of manufacturing employment and 80 percent of manufacturing value added, around twice the equivalent European Union (EU) shares. Though services are much less foreign direct investment (FDI) intensive, in this case also the Irish proportions are around twice the EU average (OECD 2010). McKinsey Global Institute (2003) ranked Ireland, with 8.3 percent of the global market, above India, with 7.7 percent, as the most popular destination for offshored business services, comprising both information technology and other business processes. Within information technology (IT), Ireland is reported to be one of the world's largest exporters of computer software. Foreign affiliates, furthermore, account for almost 80 percent of Irish exports. These various characteristics highlight Ireland's claim to attention in any discussion of globalization, offshoring and export-platform foreign investment.

Ireland was one of the first countries to adopt a development strategy that would lead to its emergence as a significant export platform for foreign multinational corporations (MNCs). The move to attract outward-oriented FDI dates back to the 1950s, even before protectionist tariff barriers began to be dismantled. The Industrial Development Authority (IDA) began in the early years of that decade to establish contacts with UK, Continental European, and US firms with a view to attracting them to Ireland. Extensive capital grants and corporation tax concessions for exporting activities were introduced in 1956, and a low corporation tax regime remains to this day one of the cornerstones of the country's inward FDI strategy.

Export platform investments boomed upon Ireland's accession to the EU in 1973 and again in the "Celtic Tiger" era of the 1990s. Globalization and the Single European Market saw US investments in Europe increase substantially in the latter period (Barry 2004). The outlawing of restrictive public procurement policies under the Single Market Initiative leveled the playing field for smaller export platform locations (MacSharry and White 2000), allowing Ireland to capture a sharply increased share of FDI inflows.

The increased globalization of recent decades is manifested in various ways, each of which is mirrored in the Irish experience. The number of transnational companies across the globe doubled to 70,000 between 1990 and 2005, the number of TNC affiliates grew more than fourfold, and the number of countries in which the average TNC operated increased from four to ten (UNCTAD 2006). Developments in Ireland in these respects are analyzed by Pavelin and Barry (2005). The inward FDI stock in Ireland increased fivefold over the twenty-year period from 1987, though this was less than the increase in the global FDI stock, which was increasingly drawn to emerging markets.

Technological change in air shipping and the declining cost of rapid transit have seen parts and components grow as a share of international trade (Hummels 2007; Yeats 2001; OECD 2010). Evidence on the extent and growth of vertical fragmentation in Irish trade is provided by Görg (2000), while Ruane and Görg (2001) trace the growth of fragmentation within the Irish computer hardware sector.

Advances in information technology have seen formerly non-tradable services become increasingly tradable, as reflected in services offshoring and the emergence of "trade in tasks" (Baldwin 2006). World services exports as a share of all exports grew from 15 percent to 19 percent between 1980 and 2005. Ireland's share of world services exports increased from 0.36 percent to 2.2 percent over the period, making Ireland the thirteenth-largest exporter of services in the world. Services as a share of Irish exports increased from 22 percent to 35 percent between 2000 and 2005 alone. In Ireland, as elsewhere, the increase was driven by computer and information services and finance and insurance (Forfás 2006).

A further component of the globalization of recent decades has been the increased offshoring of R&D functions by multinational companies (UNCTAD 2005). Foreign corporations account for some 70 percent of business expenditures on R&D in Ireland, and both gross expenditures and business expenditures on R&D in Ireland have increased far more rapidly than in the case of Western Europe or the OECD since the late 1980s (Barry 2008).

The present study is structured as follows. Section 2 focuses on Ireland's emergence and evolution as a manufacturing export platform and includes case studies of three of the most important FDI-intensive manufacturing sectors of recent times: ICT, pharmachem, and medical devices. Section 3 focuses on foreign-owned internationally traded services, which are of more recent provenance, and includes case studies of software and IT services and international financial services. Section 4 analyzes how Ireland's inward FDI sectors have fared over the course of the current global recession and the chapter concludes with a discussion of the factors that account for Ireland's success in attracting FDI.

2 Ireland as an Export Platform for Foreign-Owned Manufacturing MNCs

Though it remained protectionist into the 1960s, substantially later than most of the rest of Western Europe, Ireland began to attract export-oriented FDI from the mid-1950s, when generous tax relief for profits derived from increased manufacturing exports was introduced. Foreign firms—initially British and German—began to adopt Ireland as an export platform. With time, US firms became increasingly important, and these tended to be larger than firms of other nationalities. The total stock of US FDI in Ireland was US$6 million in 1958, with over 80 percent of it located in the petroleum sector and none in manufacturing. By 1973, when Ireland joined the EU, the stock had risen to US$269 million (in nominal terms), of which 90 percent was in manufacturing, with the bulk of output exported (Lipsey 2003b).

As Ireland at the time was a low-wage country with relatively poor educational attainment levels by Western European standards, it is not surprising that employment in the new export-oriented foreign firms attracted prior to 1973 tended to be in traditional or low-tech sectors such as textiles and clothing, metals industries (such as aluminum extrusions, shipbuilding, and cranes), pulp and paper, and rubber and plastics (O'Hearn 1987). FDI inflows also however led to rapid output growth in the chemicals sector, whose share of exports grew from less than 0.5 percent at the end of the 1950s to 6 percent at the time of EU entry (Lipsey 2003b).

The growth in foreign industry also contributed to a substantial diversification of Irish exports away from the UK market, with the then six-country EEC share of manufacturing exports rising by 10 percentage points between the late 1950s and the early 1970s.

Table 13.1 Sectoral allocation of manufacturing-sector foreign-firm employment (%)

	1973	1987	2000
Food, beverages, and tobacco	24	18	11
Textiles, clothing, and footwear	19	14	3
Chemicals (excluding pharmaceuticals)	6	7	5
Pharmaceuticals	2	6	11
Machinery and equipment	4	6	5
Office and data-processing equipment	1	7	19
Electrical and electronic components	4	10	14
Medical and optical instruments	4	8	11
Transport equipment	11	7	7
Remainder	24	17	12

Note: Remainder comprises Wood, Pulp, Paper and Printing; Rubber and Plastics; Non-Metallic Materials; Basic and Fabricated Metals; Coke and Refined Fuels, and Miscellaneous Manufactures.

Source: Forfás. (Totals may not sum to 100 due to rounding errors).

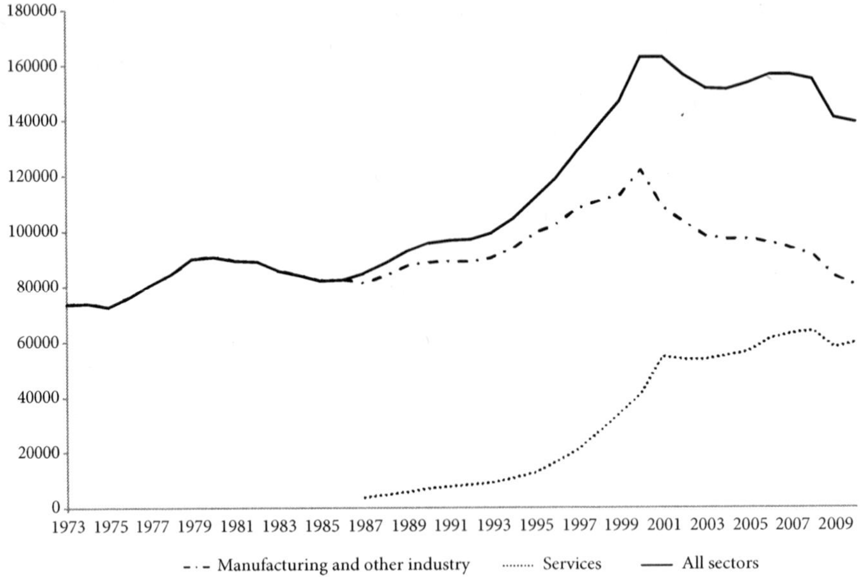

FIGURE 13.1 Employment in foreign-owned internationally-tradable manufacturing and services sectors.

Source: Forfás Annual Employment Surveys (various years); full-time employment. Note: there was a substantial reclassification of employment from manufacturing to services in year 2000.

Figure 13.1 plots developments in foreign-owned manufacturing firms and in all foreign-owned exporting firms from EU accession to the present. The broad parameters of the trends can be understood as follows. The growth in employment consequent upon EU entry was reversed by the deep fiscal and debt crisis of the 1980s. The Single Market programme of the 1990s and the confluence of factors that ushered in the "Celtic Tiger" era saw a massive increase in foreign-sector employment. This was partly crowded out by the property and construction bubble of the early years of the new millennium, however, while employment in these sectors, as in the economy at large, went into decline over the course of the current global crisis.

The employment data from 1973 onwards show a progressive movement into higher-technology sectors such as computers and electronic components, pharmaceuticals, and medical and optical devices, driven by continuing decline in British protectionist-era firms as well as expansion in newer firms which came primarily from the US (see Table 13.1).

The movement into higher technology sectors reflects the changing comparative advantage of the country, driven not just by the entry into the global economy of the lower-wage regions of East Asia and Central and Eastern Europe but also by the increasing educational attainment of the Irish workforce. Over the decades this converged on and eventually surpassed that of the rest of Western Europe. Ireland now has one of the highest proportions of the twenty-five- to thirty-four-year-old population in the OECD with a third-level educational qualification and a very high proportion of these have science and engineering degrees (Barry 2007).

Table 13.2 Sectoral allocation of manufacturing-sector foreign-firm employment (%)

	2001	2010
Food, beverages, and tobacco	13	11
Textiles, clothing, and footwear	3	0
Chemicals (including pharmaceuticals)	18	24
Machinery and equipment	7	5
Computer, electronic, optical, and electrical equipment	26	21
Medical and dental instruments and supplies	14	25
Transport equipment	5	3
Remainder	13	11

Source: Forfás Annual Employment Survey (2010). Totals may not sum to 100 due to rounding errors.

Table 13.2, which uses slightly different aggregates from the Table 13.1, shows that the restructuring of foreign-firm employment into higher-technology sectors has continued into the current millennium.

These inflows of export-oriented foreign investment have had a strong impact on Ireland's measured comparative advantage. Revealed comparative advantage (RCA) indicators for manufacturing showed Ireland in 2000–2004 to have a strong RCA in pharmaceuticals and other chemicals, medical and surgical equipment, office and computing machinery, a number of food and drink subsectors, and recorded media (Amador et al. 2007). Other than some of the food and drink subsegments, these other sectors are all FDI-dominated.

2.1 Manufacturing sector case study: information and communications technology

By the late 1990s, Ireland had become one of the major European centers of computer hardware production, accounting for 5 percent of global computer exports and about one-third of all personal computers sold in Europe. Ireland at this stage also accounted for around 6 percent of global exports of electronic components. Employment in computers and components hit a high of around 30,000 in the year 2000. The sector has experienced a sharp decline since then as production relocated eastwards to China and Central and Eastern Europe.[1]

Barry and Curran (2004) provide data on the evolution of world computer-hardware exports, charting the decline in importance over the 1990s of the more advanced countries in each of the triad regions (Europe, Asia, and the Americas) and the increase in export shares emanating from the periphery. Ireland's share of world exports more than doubled before declining again over the new millennium. Even over this latter period, however, its share of high-value digital integrated circuit exports (of the type produced by Intel) expanded.

In 1971 Digital Equipment Corporation, one of the pioneers in the minicomputer industry, set up a large-scale manufacturing plant in Ireland. This was followed by a number of other minicomputer and mainframe assemblers, which were replaced in the 1980s by PC manufacturers, beginning with Apple in 1980. Digital closed its Irish assembly operations in 1993 but associated job losses were more than offset by the arrival of three new PC assemblers, including Dell.

The closure, furthermore, did not lead to the dissipation of the skills pool. Several successful indigenous firms were established by former employees, existing firms such as Nortel and Compaq—which absorbed the software and computer engineering areas of Digital—expanded their operations, and the talent pool contributed to the emergence in the region of Europe's leading medical devices cluster. A year after the closure of its manufacturing operations, Digital opened a PC support center and a multimillion euro call center at new sites in the country.

By 2001, fewer than 400 of Apple's Irish workforce of 1,200 were involved in manufacturing. European customer support services and finance functions had been recently transferred to Ireland and the company's facilities in the south of the country had been transformed from a manufacturing base to a services campus. Local management had responsibility for sourcing and logistics and acted as landlord for R&D groups engaged in localization and software, with the latter managed from the US.

Similar processes operated in the case of Dell. Production was shifted out of Ireland in 2009, with the loss of around 2,000 jobs. Crucially, however, the company was to maintain its Global Innovation Solutions Center, its European Command Center, and its sales and marketing support functions in the country, retaining a further 2,000–2,500 jobs. According to the company, its Irish operations would "continue to co-ordinate EMEA manufacturing, logistics and supply-chain activities across a range of functions including product development, engineering, procurement and logistics" (Dell 2009).

Apple, Digital, Dell, and IBM had hence all followed similar paths, remaining in the country and upgrading from hardware assembly into higher-value services.

The computer components and peripherals sectors in Ireland experienced similar churning. IDA-Ireland in the mid 1990s began to discourage large companies from locating certain manufacturing operations in Ireland due to increasing competition from low-wage economies. New subsectors that began to be targeted included software development, contract manufacturing and computer networking/data communication.

A major breakthrough in ICT hardware came in 1989 with the decision of Intel to invest in a sophisticated microprocessor wafer manufacturing plant as well as a PC and motherboard assembly plant. In line with the rest of the sector, the labor-intensive assembly activities were later shifted to Puerto Rico and the Far East, and the Irish plant was refitted for much higher-level wafer production. The company has by now invested over $7 billion in its Irish plants, which have strong records within the company in terms of process development, compliance auditing etc. Barring some unanticipated firm- or sector-specific shocks, Intel's continuing presence in Ireland into the medium term seems secure.

2.2 Manufacturing sector case study: pharmaceuticals

The pharmaceutical industry has been one of the strongest-performing sectors of the Irish economy over recent decades, and is one of the highest-skill sectors within Irish manufacturing, whether proxied by the share of third-level graduates in sectoral employment or by wage levels per employee. Subsidiaries of foreign companies account for more than 90 percent of employment in the sector.[2]

Until the 1960s there was virtually no pharmaceutical industry in Ireland (Galvin 1998). The sector really took off in the 1970s following the IDA's adoption of fine chemicals as one of its target sectors (Childs 1996). Pfizer had established a plant in Ireland the previous year. It was followed within a short period of time by Merck Sharpe and Dohme and the forerunner of GlaxoSmithKline (MacSharry and White 2000).

Henceforth, Irish employment grew strongly, from just over 1,300 in 1972 to 4,500 in 1985, to over 20,000 in 2006, by which time pharmaceuticals had become one of the country's leading industrial sectors. The increased harmonization of regulatory regimes and reduction in other non-tariff barriers facilitated the offshoring of the industry from the former major drug-producing countries.

While the shares of world exports accounted for by traditional pharma exporting countries such as the United States, the United Kingdom, Switzerland, and Germany all shrank substantially since the mid-1960s, Ireland's market share in pharma has grown to now account for around 7 percent of world exports. The shares of India, China, Israel, and Singapore, by contrast, each stand at 1 percent or less of the world market.

A basic model of the value chain of the pharmaceutical industry includes: discovery, product development or clinical trials, process R&D, active ingredient manufacturing, drug product (formulation) manufacturing, sales and marketing, and corporate functions. Discovery covers the initial product R&D activities, that is, research into the causes of diseases and the identification of compounds that have a pharmacological effect. Product development includes the further development of these compounds, and notably their testing in pre-clinical and clinical trials. Process R&D is concerned with the development of safe and efficient manufacturing processes at commercial scale. Manufacturing encompasses the production of raw materials, intermediates, active ingredients, and drug products (formulations). All of these activities are in turn supported by corporate functions such as strategic management, finance, supply chain management, and so on.

Discovery, clinical trials, and corporate functions are generally considered to be high value added activities (Forfás 2003). Manufacturing is seen as a lower–value-added activity, though the level of value-added in active ingredients is higher than in drug formulations. Process R&D and sales and marketing are in turn generally characterized as medium level.

The available data allow us to explore the qualitative changes in the types of activities that are conducted in Ireland, within both manufacturing (active ingredients and drug formulations) and R&D (discovery, clinical trials, and process development).

Within manufacturing, there has been very little growth in the (relatively) low-value-generating activity of basic chemicals. Employment growth instead occurred mainly in drug formulation and the higher-value-generating active ingredients subsector. Alongside this, Irish plants have assumed a greater role in launch activities, an increased focus on the later stages of the chemical synthesis cycle, and a geographical widening of product mandates. All these developments have substantially increased the level of value creation.

Ireland's role in pharmaceutical R&D differs considerably from activity to activity. Notwithstanding recent developments in Irish third-level institutions and the growing number of indigenous research-based companies, Ireland's role in the high-value-generating drug-discovery field remains limited. Similarly, in spite of efforts to upgrade the necessary infrastructure, high value generating clinical trials activities remain underrepresented in Ireland. Ireland's role in medium value process R&D activities has increased substantially however, with a doubling of the number of people involved over the period 2000–2006, though even in this area, Ireland's involvement is concentrated in the (relatively) lower-value-generating downstream phases of the cycle.

Although the picture is complex and differentiated, it is clear that the level of value creation in the Irish pharmaceutical industry has increased substantially over recent decades.

2.3 Manufacturing sector case study: medical devices

The first wave of medical devices companies, including Abbott Laboratories, came largely from the United States in the early 1970s. Several further important companies, including CR Bard, arrived in the 1980s. One of the coups of the 1990s was the attraction of US company Boston Scientific in 1994, while another leading American MNC, Medtronic, took over the CR Bard subsidiary in 1999.[3]

Boston Scientific is the largest medical-device company in Ireland, employing almost 5,000 people in four manufacturing sites. In 2008 it announced a €50 million strategic R&D investment at its main Irish facility. Medtronic employs over 2,000 people in Ireland, including over 100 dedicated to research and development. Its main Irish site is a center of excellence for the development and manufacture of a number of the company's key medical technologies. The company also has a sales and shared services office elsewhere in the country.

Fifteen of the world's top twenty-five medical technology companies now have operations in Ireland and these, together with a smaller base of indigenous companies, employ an estimated 25,000 people in approximately 250 companies.[4] Among the other world-class firms with Irish operations are Johnson & Johnson, Stryker, Vistakon, and Tyco Healthcare. Ireland is now the second-largest exporter of medical products in Europe, after Germany, and records the highest employment level in the industry in Europe per head of population. The sector is now developing beyond manufacturing and becoming more R&D driven.

3 Ireland as an export platform for foreign-owned tradable services MNCs

The increasing relative and absolute employment levels of internationally tradable services within the foreign-owned export sector in Ireland are apparent in Figure 13.1. From providing very few jobs in the early 1980s, tradable services now represent more than 40 percent of the total.

Services data are of course more difficult to categorize than those pertaining to manufacturing.[5] We provide case studies below on IT services and international financial services, but many services activities defy straightforward sectoral classifications. Such activities might include call centers, shared services, supply chain management, sales and marketing, intellectual property licensing, professional consulting and internet-based business. We begin by saying a little about some of these activities before turning to the sectoral case studies.

UNCTAD (2004: 161) assesses Ireland to be the leading location for shared service centers among developed countries. Shared services centers (known as "managed services centers" in the United States) perform key functions for global corporations. They deal with technical support for staff and business customers as well as human resources, payroll, accounting, insurance and legal services, and internal communications (such as running companies' internet and intranet sites). Some are operated by outsourced suppliers, but most in Ireland are managed by the companies they serve.

The IDA has promoted the low-level call center sector in order to encourage firms which have established such operations in Ireland to add on additional functions such as financial management and software development. Already Ireland has achieved some substantial success in these "shared services" back office activities.

The term "call center" generally embraces sales and marketing shared services and IT shared services such as online technical assistance. Among the major firms that have established call centers in Ireland (in areas outside finance and sales and marketing of IT) are American Airlines, Best Western, ITT Sheraton, Global Reservations, Korean Air, Radisson Hotels, Rand McNally, and UPS. Among companies that have located elements of their financial administration in Ireland are Merrill Lynch, Microsoft, Morgan Grenfell, National Instruments, Novell, Scottish Amicable, advanced storage and retrieval firm EMC, and home-appliances firm Whirlpool.

Call center employment in the early years of the new millennium stood at a level somewhere between 12,000 and 19,000. On the basis of the latter number, CM Insight (2004) calculates that Ireland has the highest proportion of call center staff of any European

Table 13.3 Sectoral breakdown of firms in the Irish call center industry

Sector	%
Technology	35
Travel and tourism	16
Financial services	12
Outsourcing bureaus	12
Other	25
Total	100

Source: TMA (2002), from Datamonitor (November 2002).

country as a proportion of its working population, at 3.6 percent, compared to its nearest competitors, the United Kingdom at 2.8 percent and the Netherlands at 2.5 percent.

The breakdown of the Irish call center sector at the beginning of the millennium is shown in Table 13.3.

The educational requirements of the various segments of the call center sector differ substantially. The low-skill segments of telebusiness activities are in reservations and financial services. These comprise less than one-third of firms in the Irish sector however. The other two segments—comprising telebusiness in the computer and professional services sectors—are, on the basis of the available evidence, more high-skill than the average for the economy. Given the make-up of Irish call centers, there is a possibility that even within this globally fairly low-skill sector, the Irish segment may be more education-intensive than the average for the entire economy.

CM Insight (2004: 160) concludes that Ireland attracts more high-value, less price-sensitive contact center activity than other offshore locations. The report remarks on the substantial element of technical and software support in the Irish sector as well as a relatively high ratio of team leaders to agents, suggestive of a focus on quality and on more complex and less scripted contact center functions.

Turning now to the sectoral case studies, Siedschlag's (2008) estimates of RCA in services, based on 1998–2006 data, show Ireland developing a strong and increasing RCA in computer and information services (into which "recorded media" has merged) and in insurance and financial services. About one quarter of tradable services employment in foreign-owned firms in Ireland is in international financial services and the remainder of the jobs are divided between various forms of IT services, whether directly in the IT industry—in firms such as Apple, IBM, Microsoft, Google, among others—or in IT-enabled business process services.

3.1 Services sector case study: software and IT services

Software and IT services are quite distinct sectors though they are grouped together here because the Irish employment data do not allow us to distinguish between them.

Employment in foreign software firms was recorded as rising from around 4,000 in 1991 to some 16,000 in 2000, while employment in all foreign-owned computer and IT services activities hovered around 46,000 from 2001 to 2008 before declining somewhat over the global financial crisis.[6]

Within the narrow software component, around half of the jobs in the foreign-owned segment are in manufacturing, localization, and distribution (MLD) activities, while the other half are in software development, which is much more highly skilled.

Most of the localization of mass-market software for the EMEA region takes place in the country, while Singapore has traditionally performed a similar function for the Asian market (Coe 1999).[7] While the figures for Irish output are arguably inflated by the transfer pricing practices of multinational corporations, even in employment terms the mass market software sector has long been more important in Ireland than in other EU economies (Barry and Curran 2004).

The key players in the software sector (including Microsoft, Lotus, Oracle, Symantec, Informix, and Corel) first established software manufacturing facilities in Ireland around the mid-1980s, duplicating and shrink-wrapping disk copies of the software programmes developed by the parent company and arranging for the printing and assembly of manuals. This work was not in general very highly skilled, though the sector has moved up the value chain over time. The second phase, again beginning with Lotus and Microsoft, saw these companies adding localization to the process. This involves translating the original products into other languages and different cultural and technical formats appropriate to the destination markets. There is some programming involved in preparing the text to be translated and then reincorporating it back into the programme. The third phase of the sector's development saw the transfer of the responsibility for distribution, which had previously been handled by local distributors, to the Irish operations themselves. Thus Ireland became an operations hub; Ó'Riain (2004).

Many of the remaining jobs in the broader software and IT services sector are in what have traditionally been thought of as computer hardware firms. In the earlier discussion of the computer hardware sector, it was pointed out how most of the key international firms remained in Ireland, switching their Irish operations to IT-services delivery as the country transitioned out of hardware production.

IBM represents an interesting case study as the entire company has shifted its focus globally from products to services and solutions. It was one of the first companies to establish an international software facility in Ireland in the early 1980s but its acquisition of Lotus in 1995 (with the Irish facility renamed the Dublin Software Lab) added a significant software development component to its portfolio. The company started to invest heavily in Ireland from that point as EU developments allowed it to rationalize its European operations. It first opened a PC customer-support center, catering for twenty-nine countries (including the United States). The same year it began to develop a technology campus in Ireland with some high-end manufacturing operations, including the manufacturing and testing of logic chips, production of disc drive platters in a clean room environment, and production of customized high-end network servers.

In 2001, part of IBM's manufacturing operations was relocated from Ireland but there was new investment in areas such as supply chain management. Call center support for personal computers relocated to lower-cost regions and the technical support call center was transformed into a "dot-com center" with staff selling services directly to clients rather than simply offering support. The Dublin Software Lab has been expanded and in 2004 the Dublin Centre for Advanced Studies, one of seven such centers run by IBM worldwide, was launched. Most recently the company established three Competency Centres, developing software in areas such as biomedical search and service-oriented architecture, an IBM Business Incubation Centre, a European Venture Capital Centre, an Innovation Centre, and new supply chain operations.

As Barry and Van Egeraat (2008) show, the decline in computer hardware jobs in Ireland since the late 1990s has been associated with a progressive increase in jobs in business process export activities.

3.2 Services sector case study: international financial services

The International Financial Services Centre (IFSC), established in Dublin in 1987, has achieved notable success in attracting financial services FDI to Ireland. As MacSharry and White (2000: 318) note, "a combination of factors created an opportunity for a regional location like Ireland to become a player in the international financial services industry. First, world financial markets had become highly interdependent and operated on a round-the-clock basis. Second, the technology to set up and run international data- and fund-management centres was, in turn, creating an electronic market place, thanks to improvements in international telecommunications. And, third, global deregulation of financial services meant that an increasing range of these services were provided from beyond national boundaries."[8]

In response to these developments, the Irish government in 1987 launched the IFSC. Licensed companies were initially subject to a special low rate of corporation tax of 10 percent but from 2003 corporation tax rates were harmonized across the economy at 12.5 percent.

Around 450 international financial institutions now operate from Dublin, including half of the world's top fifty banks and half of the top twenty insurance companies. Over 80 percent of the financial institutions are non-Irish, with American companies representing the largest segment. The sector pays an estimated 15 percent of all corporation taxes collected.

Dublin specializes in back office activities, and has a particular specialization in four niche areas—fund administration, treasury operations, corporate banking, and insurance. While the marketing and management of funds is handled from the world's major financial centers, the associated administration is frequently offshored. Ireland now rivals Luxembourg in the area of fund administration, while FÁS (2005) reports a slow movement up the value chain towards fund management.

Similar to fund administration, treasury management involves routine back office tasks like handling payments and receipts and coordinating lending and borrowing between different divisions of a company. Many IFSC-based treasury operations are recognizable names in other industries, for example, companies such as Bristol-Myers Squibb, Ericsson, and Volkswagen. The Netherlands and Belgium are seen as the main competitors in the area of treasury operations

The IFSC is also a corporate banking center, providing loans to corporations and governments for very large purchases. Here Ireland competes with Luxembourg, the Isle of Man, and Jersey, while Dublin has come to rival London as a leading center for aircraft leasing.

Finally, the IFSC houses a significant number of life and nonlife insurers. EU regulatory changes enacted during the mid-1990s allowed life insurers headquartered in one EU country to sell insurance elsewhere in the EU. This provides the IFSC with an advantage over other offshore centers such as Guernsey and the Isle of Man, which also specialize in insurance, since these are not within the EU. Ireland's international life-insurance sector in 2001 overtook Luxembourg in terms of gross premia written, while recent statistics indicated that it may now also have overtaken the Isle of Man. In spite of this strong recent growth in life insurance, nonlife insurers remain more prevalent in the IFSC.

A recent breakdown of employment and activities in the international financial services sector in Ireland is provided in Table 13.4 below.

Table 13.4 Irish international financial services activities

Sector	Activities	Employment (2007)
Banking and capital markets	Corporate finance Structured finance Investment banking Securitization Treasury management. Asset financing/leasing	10,000
Investment management	Discretionary fund management Nondiscretionary fund management. Fund servicing Trustee and custodian servicing Transfer agency services Asset management	9,000 (Administration: 6500; Management: 2500)
Insurance	Life Captive Nonlife Reinsurance	3,000

Source: Expert Group on Future Skills Needs (2007).

4 Inward FDI and the Foreign Affiliate Sector over the Global Financial Crisis

Having reached an all-time high of almost $2 trillion in 2007, worldwide FDI flows collapsed over the following two years. Flows in 2009 were down almost 40 percent on those seen two years earlier. Developed countries were hit particularly hard, with 2009 inflows down over 50 percent on 2007 levels.

The extent of Ireland's FDI intensity might be thought to have left the country particularly vulnerable to the collapse in international FDI flows that occurred over the course of the global financial crisis. Ireland ended up bucking this trend however. Though inflows turned negative in 2008, 2009 inflows surpassed those achieved in 2007 and were not far off the Irish peak achieved in 2002.[9]

It is important to note though that FDI data of this type bear very little relationship to the real foreign MNC activities that are the main focus of attention.[10] The foreign-affiliate employment data used in this chapter, for example, refer only to export-platform FDI, while FDI stock and flow data from the balance of payments pertain to all sectors, including nontradables. A second reason is that the inward FDI data aggregate both IFSC and non-IFSC FDI, while, as UNCTAD (2004: 104) notes, "a good deal of services FDI—notably that in holdings and financial affiliates—involves activities with little value added, employment, sales or investment expenditure on fixed capital." A third reason is that the FDI data include only a subset of the forms of investment finance employed by MNCs, specifically inward equity flows, intracompany loans, and reinvested earnings. Barry and O'Mahony (2005) and Griffith (1999) show that FDI inflows in particular sectors are typically lower and much more volatile than measures of real foreign-MNC investments in plant and equipment.

The fact that gross FDI inflows to Ireland were negative over several recent years—indicating that interaffiliate loan advances and repayments from resident foreign-owned enterprises exceeded inward equity flows and reinvested earnings—is indicative of the complexity of MNC financing decisions. For some years, IFSC transactions were responsible for the negative aggregate; for other years, it was driven by non-IFSC inflows (Barry and Bergin 2010). For all of these reasons, our focus remains on real MNC activities such as exports and employment.

Total Irish exports remained relatively flat in 2008. There was a dramatic fall in 2009, while 2010 and 2011 witnessed a return to growth. As seen in Figure 13.2, these broad developments largely mirrored those in the other European economies—the EU27, the Western European EU15, France, Germany, and the United Kingdom—against which we benchmark Irish performance.

By 2011, the increase in Irish exports on 2007 levels, though lagging behind Germany, exceeded that for Western Europe overall and for the other Western European economies shown (Table 13.5).

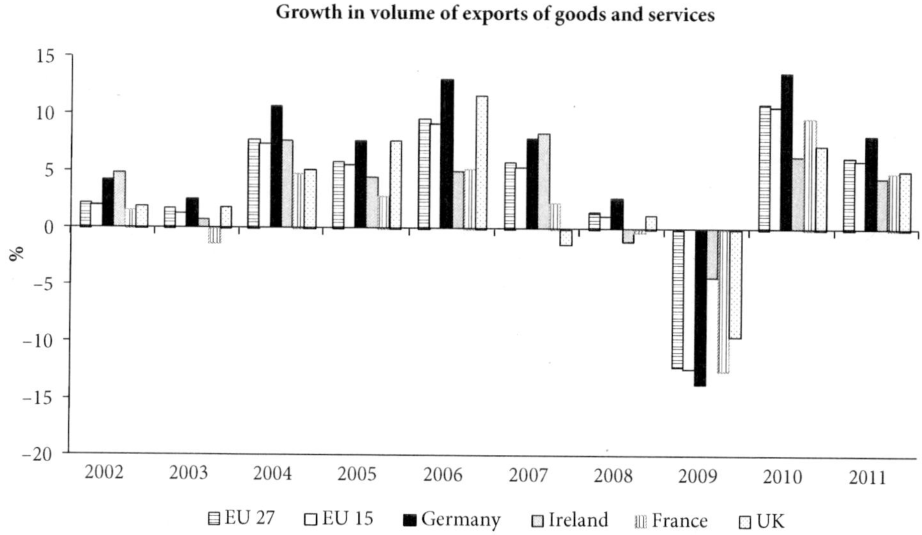

FIGURE 13.2 Growth in volume of exports of goods and services: various countries.

Source: Eurostat: Exports and imports by EU countries and third countries—volumes.

To what extent are these outcomes due to differing sectoral export compositions within manufacturing and services? As mentioned earlier, based on 2000–2004 export data Ireland had a strong revealed comparative advantage (RCA), among manufacturing sectors, in pharmaceuticals and other chemicals, medical and surgical equipment, office and computing machinery, a number of food and drink subsectors, and recorded media.

Ireland is likely to have lost its RCA in office and computing equipment more recently, particularly with the closure of Dell's manufacturing facilities, though the sector had been migrating out of Ireland over the last decade. Siedschlag's (2008) recent estimates of RCA in services, based on 1998–2006 data, show Ireland developing a strong and

Table 13.5 Export Volumes

	2011 outcome: % increase on 2007 outcome			Share of services in total exports
	Total	Goods	Services	2007
EU27	5	5	5	24
EU15	4	4	5	24
Germany	9	8	18	16
Ireland	5	4	7	33
France	1	1	−1	19
UK	3	5	2	39

Source: Eurostat: Exports and imports by EU countries and third countries—volumes.

increasing RCA in computer and information services (into which "recorded media" has merged) and in insurance and financial services.

Pharmaceuticals and chemicals have increased as a share of EU15 manufactured exports over the downturn, as have medical devices, suggesting—unsurprisingly—that these sectors are less vulnerable to recession. Ireland's RCA in these sectors has helped to stabilize the economy. Correspondingly, the fact that Ireland does not have an RCA in transport equipment will have helped to insulate the economy since this sector—globally and at the EU level—performed poorly over the downturn. In terms of services, computer and information services increased as a share of EU15 services exports over the period, suggesting that Ireland's revealed comparative advantage in this sector has also helped to stabilize the economy.[11]

Figures 13.3 and 13.4 chart the contributions of these and other sectors to Irish manufacturing and services export growth over the period 2001–2010. Pharmaceuticals and medical-devices exports helped to prop up the economy, while the performance of office machinery had an opposite effect.

Within services, computer and information services exports also had a beneficial effect (Figure 13.4).

While financial services and insurance made a negative contribution to export growth over 2008 and 2009, job numbers remained largely stable over the downturn (Figure 13.5). Within the banking and capital-markets segment, the employment fall in securitization activities was partly offset by an expansion in aircraft leasing, in which activity the IFSC is a major international player.[12] The IFSC also benefitted from the Foreign Account Tax Compliance Act introduced in the United States in 2009, which targeted Caribbean tax-haven jurisdictions. A number of US companies responded by moving

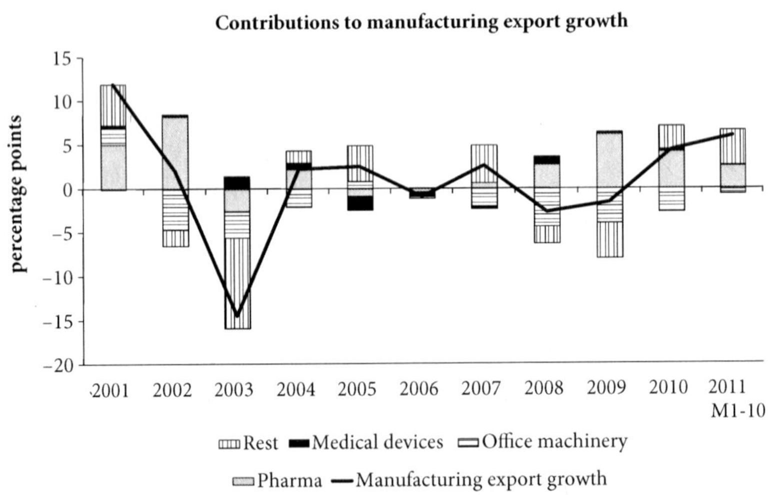

FIGURE 13.3 Sectoral contributions to Irish manufacturing export growth (€ millions).

Source: CSO External Trade Statistics. Note: The graph shows the growth in manufacturing exports in the first 10 months of 2011 compared to the first 10 months of 2010.

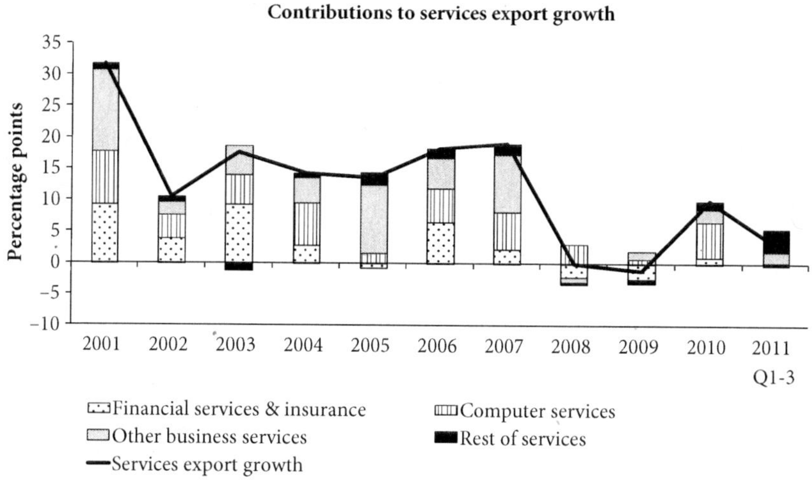

Figure 13.4 Sectoral contributions to Irish services export growth.

Source: CSO Balance of Payments.

their corporate headquarters from locations such as Bermuda and the Cayman Islands to Dublin.

We next turn to aggregate employment developments across the economy over the bubble period and the downturn. Table 13.6 shows the massive cyclical fluctuations in construction-sector employment, while employment in the tradables sectors is seen to have fluctuated less than for the overall private sector.[13]

Employment prospects for the future depend, on the demand side, on a resumption of growth in Irish export markets, and on a more diverse range of factors operating on the supply side. Barry and Bergin (2010) offer an optimistic assessment of Ireland's

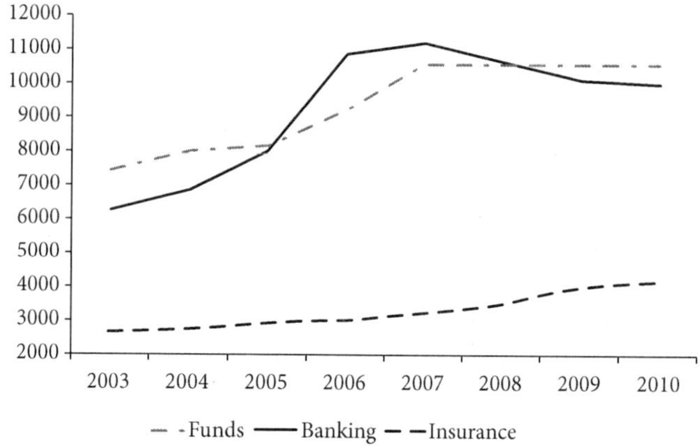

Figure 13.5 Employment in international financial services.

Source: Finance Dublin Yearbook.

Table 13.6 Employment in tradables and in the public and private sectors (thousands)

	2000	2007	2008	2009	2010	% change 2000–07	% change 2007–10
Private sector	1,354	1,665	1,628	1,446	1,358	23	−18
of which							
Foreign-owned tradables	182	174	170	154	155	−4	−11
Indigenous tradables	168	183	177	159	155	9	−15
Construction	166	267	236	156	120	61	−55
Public sector	343	457	472	483	490	33	7
Total	1,697	2,123	2,100	1,929	1,848	25	−13

Sources: Forfás (1997, 2010, AES) for total employment in tradables sectors; ESRI databank and Central Statistics Office, Dublin (Quarterly National Household Survey) for aggregate economy; CSO (2006, Construction and Housing in Ireland) for employment in construction in 2000.

attractiveness to FDI inflows over the medium term. Employment prospects will be enhanced by the reversal in the crowding out of the traded sector entailed by the collapse of construction, much slower (if not negative) growth in the public sector over the medium term, and the recent substantial improvement in Irish cost competitiveness associated with the downturn. This is likely to prove a greater stimulus to the indigenous than to the foreign sector, since the former is both more cost sensitive and more employment intensive.

Indirect employment effects of the foreign-affiliate sectors arise through wage expenditures (which in turn depend on job quality), total taxes paid, linkages, productivity spillovers, and other beneficial effects on the innovativeness of the enterprise environment. Foreign affiliates dominate indigenous firms on most of these fronts (Barry 2004). They pay higher wages and spend much more per job on training and on research and development.

Though indigenous firms purchase more materials in Ireland, foreign affiliates spend significantly more on Irish services, which are particularly employment intensive. It is notable that the bulk of Irish services purchases are made by the growing services segment of the foreign-affiliate sector (Table 13.7).[14]

Spillovers are another channel through which the foreign sector can benefit the economy. Though the international econometric evidence on productivity spillovers from foreign affiliates is mixed, the effects are generally found to be positive for Ireland (Görg and Greenaway 2004). The case study evidence supports this. Giblin and Ryan (2010) find evidence of beneficial intraindustry spillovers from the presence of the leading foreign medical devices firms in the west of Ireland, while Barry (2011) argues that the variety of FDI firms and sectors in Ireland in the 1970s and 1980s created an environment conducive to the emergence of a successful indigenous IT software export cluster, which was in turn the only significant source of export growth during the export downturn of 2009.

Table 13.7 Materials and services purchases in Ireland (€k)

	Raw materials purchased in Ireland, 2009	Services purchased in Ireland, 2009
Indigenous	8,465,137	4,493,298
of which		
Manufactures	7,953,974	3,665,906
Services	511,163	827,392
Foreign	2,494,805	9,106,688
of which		
Manufactures	1,882,450	2,733,417
Services	612,355	6,373,272

Source: Forfás *ABSEI* (2009).

Concluding comments: Ireland's success as an export platform

A cross-country study by Slaughter (2003) on the determinants of US FDI in Europe helps us to pinpoint some of the key factors behind Ireland's success in attracting export-platform FDI.[15] He finds geographic proximity to the United States to be a significant determinant of the overall level of FDI attracted, while EU membership is found to be particularly significant for FDI in manufacturing and financial services. Smaller markets unsurprisingly attract export-platform activity rather than production for local markets, and US affiliate production tends to be concentrated in low-tax countries.

The importance of Ireland's low corporation tax regime in kick-starting FDI inflows has already been alluded to. The country's corporation tax regime has remained amongst the most stable in Europe since the adoption of the low-tax strategy in the late 1950s, and according to Padraic White, a former managing director of the IDA, it remains "the unique and essential foundation stone of Ireland's foreign investment boom" (MacSharry and White 2000: 250).[16]

Most manufacturing industry had been taxed at a special rate of 10 percent from 1978, while the rate on services was substantially higher. From 1987, the special rate was extended to qualifying activities carried out at the recently established International Financial Services Centre in Dublin. In the face of European Commission pressure to harmonize rates across sectors, the government chose a low harmonized rate of 12.5 percent to apply across all sectors from 2003.

Another factor widely regarded as important in attracting FDI to Ireland has been the effectiveness of the state agency IDA-Ireland. MacSharry and White (2000)—the former an erstwhile finance minister and EU commissioner and the latter a former managing director of the IDA—describe how the organization in the wake of the oil shocks of the 1970s began to focus on sectors that would be more insulated from competition from lower wage locations, and on job creation through backward linkages rather than labor-intensive processes.

They summarize the modus operandi of the IDA as follows. First, the sectors and subsectors experiencing international growth—and that are thought to provide a good fit for Ireland's resources and development aims—are identified. Having attracted several computer and components firms in the 1970s, for example, and being favourably impressed by their performance in situ, electronics and computer software were among the industries listed as meeting these criteria in 1983, when an all-out campaign to develop Ireland as a major European location for the industry began.

In other cases, the identification of target niches appears prescient. The establishment of the IFSC in the late 1980s has been discussed earlier. Though the commercial development officer of the Isle of Man, which had a long-established reputation as an offshore financial center, cautioned that "Dublin would be better building on its own resources, which do not particularly include financial services," a little over a decade later the IFSC had grown to become a significant European offshore financial center itself.

After the identification of target niches, the IDA establishes contact with the strongest companies in these subsectors. The agency had been interacting with Intel and IBM for over a decade before these firms ultimately chose to locate in Ireland.

The IDA and its sister agencies also have an influence in the development and upgrading of the human capital and physical infrastructure required to facilitate the country in climbing the ladder of comparative advantage. This brings them into policy areas not traditionally recognized as lying within the industrial promotion remit. In Ireland, they played a major role in forcing through the modernization of the country's telecommunications infrastructure in the late 1970s to early 1980s and in convincing the government to use part of its EU regional aid allocations to institute conversion courses to furnish science graduates with electronics qualifications. The tertiary education system in Ireland has over recent decades become more tightly integrated into the country's economic development strategy through an agency known as the Expert Group on Future Skills Needs (Barry 2007).[17]

Agglomeration and demonstration effects have also been found to have played a role in enhancing Ireland's attractiveness as an export-platform location. Barry and Bradley (1997) noted that surveys of executives of newly arriving foreign companies in the computer, instrument engineering, pharmaceutical, and chemical sectors indicated that the presence of key market players in Ireland strongly influenced the location choice of the newcomers, for which Barry et al. (2003) subsequently provided empirical support.

It is clear that nonpolicy reasons have been important as well. That Ireland and the United Kingdom are particularly attractive locations for US corporations presumably reflects strong cultural connections, including a shared language and shared common-law traditions.[18] Proximity between FDI home and host locations remains a statistically significant determinant of FDI inflows, as seen in the gravity modeling of Slaughter (2003) for example. It is clear also that for many economic activities the overall "ease of doing business," which tends to change only slowly, insulates advanced EU countries from global competition in the market for inward FDI.

NOTES

1. This account is based largely on Barry and van Egeraat (2008).
2. This account is drawn largely from Van Egeraat and Barry (2008).
3. Much of this material is based on Giblin and Ryan (2010).
4. http://www.imda.ie/Sectors/IMDA/IMDA.nsf/vPages/About_us~sector-profile?OpenDocument.
5. The distinction between manufacturing and services is becoming increasingly blurred. In Ireland, over 30 percent of workers employed in the manufacturing sector are engaged in services-related activities, and this percentage is increasing over time (Forfás 2006).
6. Sources: National Software Directorate for the early years; Forfás Annual Employment Survey for the more recent period.
7. Ireland and Singapore share many similarities as advanced export platforms, though the state plays a more active role in enterprise in the latter case (Low 2005). Ó'Riain (2004) characterizes Ireland as a developmental network state and Singapore as a developmental bureaucratic state.
8. Even before the establishment of the IFSC, Ireland had drawn sixteen major international banks to its shores, as they entered to service the needs of the large multinational manufacturing corporations which had chosen Ireland as an export platform to serve the broader EU market (Reddan 2008: 59–62).
9. Data from UNCTAD online statistics.
10. See Lipsey (2003a) and, for the Irish case, Barry and O'Mahony (2005).
11. See Barry and Bergin (2010) for data on the aggregate performance of specific sectors at the EU level.
12. Aircraft leasing is countercyclical, in that many airlines opt to lease rather than buy during a downturn, while leasing companies benefit further from the better aircraft prices on offer.
13. The large decline in indigenous tradables employment is related to the collapse in construction in both Ireland and the United Kingdom (which is the most significant market for indigenous exports), as much of the output serves as an input to construction activities.
14. Services purchased in Ireland by foreign manufacturing and services affiliates both peaked in 2003, while total global services purchases continued to grow. Irish services purchases may have been damaged by the reduction in Irish competitiveness over the period of the property bubble.
15. This section draws substantially on Barry (2004).
16. Financial incentives in the form of grants to firms had been substantial in earlier years but have been scaled back significantly in line with EU restrictions on state aids to industry.
17. The Irish system offers a finite number of places in most third-level courses. These numbers are decided within the third-level institutions but are subject to government influence as the latter provides the bulk of educational funding. As Ó'Riain (2004) points out, this gives the Irish state a much greater capacity to mould the labor market for specific economic sectors than is the case in many other countries.
18. Kraemer and Dedrick (2002) point out that when Dell Computers first moved into Europe, the company was attracted by locations that were similar to the United Stated in terms of language and business culture.

References

Amador, J., S. Cabral, and J. R. Maria. 2007. "International Trade Patterns over the Last Four Decades: How Does Portugal Compare with other Cohesion Countries?" Bank of Portugal Working Paper, 14/07.

Baldwin, R. 2006. "Globalization: The Great Unbundling(s)." Economic Council of Finland.

Barry, F. 2004. "Export Platform FDI: the Irish Experience." *EIB Papers* 9 (2): 8–37.

———. 2007. "Third-Level Education, Foreign Direct Investment and Economic Boom in Ireland." *International Journal of Technology Management* 38 (3): 198–219.

———. 2008. "Some Issues Concerning Future Irish Growth." *Administration* 56 (1): 1–18.

———. 2011. "FDI, Inter-Industry Linkages and the Emergence of an Irish Indigenous Software Export Cluster." Paper presented to the Annual Conference of the Irish Economic Association, Limerick.

Barry, F., and A. Bergin. 2010. "Ireland's Inward FDI over the Recession and Beyond." IIIS Discussion Paper, no. 321, Trinity College Dublin.

Barry, F., and J. Bradley. 1997. "FDI and Trade: The Irish Host-Country Experience." *Economic Journal* 107: 1798–1811.

Barry, F., and D. Curran. 2004. "Enlargement and the European Geography of the Information Technology Sector." *World Economy* 27 (6): 901–922.

Barry, F., H. Görg, and E. Strobl. 2003. "Foreign Direct Investment, Agglomerations and Demonstration Effects: an Empirical Investigation." *Weltwirtschaftliches Archiv* 139 (4): 583–600.

Barry, F., and C. O'Mahony. 2005. "Making Sense of the Data on Ireland's Inward FDI." *Journal of the Statistical and Social Inquiry Society of Ireland* 34: 28–65.

Barry, F., and C. van Egeraat. 2008. "The Decline of the Computer Hardware Sector: How Ireland Adjusted." *ESRI Quarterly Economic Commentary* Spring: 38–57.

Childs, P. 1996. "The Chemical Industry in Cork." *Chemistry in Action* 47.

CM Insight. 2004. "The UK Contact Centre Industry: A Study." Report to the UK Department of Trade and Industry.

Coe, N. 1999. "Emulating the Celtic Tiger? A Comparison of the Software Industries of Singapore and Ireland." *Singapore Journal of Tropical Geography* 20 (1): 36–55.

Datamonitor. 2002. "Call Centres in EMEA to 2007." http://www.datamonitor.com/

Dell. 2009. "Dell to Migrate Manufacturing Operations from Ireland to Poland and Partners by Early 2010." Press Release, January 8. http://content.dell.com/us/en/corp/d/press-releases/2009-01-08-01-manufacturing-migration.

Expert Group on Future Skills Needs. 2007. *Future Skills and Research Needs of the International Financial Services Industry*, Dublin: Forfás.

FÁS. 2005. "Skill Shortages in the Financial Services Sector." Report prepared for the IFSC Clearing House Group, Department of the Taoiseach, subcommittee on Education Issues. Dublin: FÁS.

Forfás. 2003. *The Supply and Demand for Skills in the Biotechnology Sector*. Dublin: Forfás.

———. 2006. *The Changing Nature of Manufacturing and Services: Irish Trends and International Context*. Dublin: Forfás.

———. [various years]. *ABSEI: Annual Business Survey Of Economic Impact*. Dublin: Forfás.

Galvin, S. 1998. "The Chemical Industry in Ireland." *Chemistry in Action* 54: 9–16.

Giblin, M., and P. Ryan. 2010. "Tight Clusters or Loose Networks? The Critical Role of Inward FDI in Cluster Creation," CISC Working Paper, no. 35.

Görg, H. 2000. "Fragmentation and Trade: US Inward Processing Trade in the EU." *Weltwirtschaftliches Archiv* 136 (3): 403–422.

Görg, H., and D. Greenaway. 2004. "Much Ado about Nothing? Do Domestic Firms Really Benefit from Foreign Direct Investment?" *World Bank Research Observer* 19 (2): 171–197.

Griffith, R. 1999. "Productivity and Foreign Ownership in the UK Car Industry." Institute for Fiscal Studies Working Paper Series no. W99/11, http://www.ifs.org.uk/staff/rachel_g.shtml.

Hummels, D. 2007. "Transport Costs and International Trade in the Second Era of Globalization." *Journal of Economic Perspectives* 21 (2): 131–154.

Kraemer, K., and J. Dedrick. 2002. "Dell Computer: Organisation of a Global Production Network." Center for Research on Information Technology and Organizations, University of California, Irvine.

Lipsey, R. E. 2003a. "Foreign Direct Investment and the Operations of Multinational Firms: Concepts, History and Data." In *Handbook of International Trade*, edited by E. K. Choi and J. Harrigan, 287–319. Oxford: Basil Blackwell. Also available as NBER Working Paper, no. 8665. Cambridge, MA: National Bureau of Economic Research.

———. 2003b. "Discussion of 'EU Accession and Prospective FDI Flows to CEE Countries.'" In *Foreign Direct Investment in the Real and Financial Sector of Industrial Countries,* edited by H. Herrmann and R. Lipsey, 209–213. Berlin: Springer.

Low, L. 2005. "Entrepreneurship Development in Ireland and Singapore." *Journal of the Asia Pacific Economy* 10 (1): 116–138.

MacSharry, R., and P. White. 2000. *The Making of the Celtic Tiger: The Inside Story of Ireland's Booming Economy*. Dublin: Mercier Press.

McKinsey Global Institute. 2003. *Offshoring: Is It a Win-Win Game?* San Francisco: McKinsey.

OECD (Organisation for Economic Co-operation and Development). 2000, 2002. *Information Technology Outlook*. Paris: OECD.

———. 2010. *Measuring Globalisation: OECD Economic Globalisation Indicators*. Paris: OECD.

O'Hearn, D. 1987. "Estimates of New Foreign Manufacturing Employment in Ireland, 1956–72." *Economic and Social Review* 18 (3): 173–188.

Ó'Riain, S. 2004. *The Politics of High-Tech Growth: Developmental Network States in the Global Economy*. Cambridge: Cambridge University Press.

Pavelin, S., and F. Barry. 2005. "The Single Market and the Geographical Diversification of Leading Firms in the EU." *Economic and Social Review* 36 (1): 1–17.

Reddan, F. 2008. *Ireland's IFSC: A Story of Global Financial Success*. Cork: Mercier Press.

Ruane, F., and H. Görg. 2001. "Globalisation and Fragmentation: Evidence for the Electronics Industry in Ireland." In *Fragmentation: New Production Patterns in the World Economy*, edited by S. W. Arndt and H. Kierzkowski, 144–164. Oxford: Oxford University Press.

Siedschlag, I. 2008. "Making the Best of Globalisation." Unpublished presentation, Economic and Social Research Institute, Dublin.

Slaughter, M. 2003. "Host-Country Determinants of US Foreign Direct Investment into Europe." In *Foreign Direct Investment in the Real and Financial Sector of Industrial Countries*, edited by H. Herrmann and R. Lipsey, 7–32. Berlin: Springer.

Tom Martin & Associates. 2002. "Foreign Language Skills Requirements in Call Centres." Report to the Expert Group on Future Skills Needs (Forfás) and the Tele-Services Federation of Ireland, Dublin.

UNCTAD (United Nations Conference on Trade and Development). [various years]. *World Investment Report*. New York and Geneva: UNCTAD.

Van Egeraat, C., and F. Barry. 2008. "The Irish Pharmaceutical Industry over the Boom Period and Beyond." *Irish Geography* 42 (1): 23–44.

Yeats, A. 2001. "Just How Big is Global Production Sharing?" In *Fragmentation: New Production Patterns in the World Economy*, edited by S. W. Arndt and H. Kierzkowski, 108–43. New York: Oxford University Press.

CHAPTER 14

Offshoring Higher Education

The Australian Experience

CHRISTOPHER ZIGURAS

Introduction

Since the late 1980s, Australian higher-education providers have been venturing abroad to establish teaching partnerships and branch campuses. Along with the United States and the United Kingdom, Australia is one of three large-scale providers of programs to students based in other countries, with around 150,000 students enrolled in Australian programs taught offshore in 2010. In absolute terms the United Kingdom has more students, with around 201,000 registered in its offshore programs in 2009–10 and a further 208,000 studying toward a UK degree in a program that is validated by a UK university (HESA 2011). The other large provider, the United States, does not collect any data on offshore programs and campuses. Relative to the size of the domestic student population, Australia's international operations both onshore and offshore constitute a larger part of the tertiary education system than in any other country. International students comprise 27 percent of all students in Australian universities—21 percent in Australia on a student visa and a 6 percent studying offshore through a partner institution or branch campus (DEEWR 2011). As a result of the relative importance of offshore international education, there is now an unrivalled body of statistical data and research literature on Australian offshore provision, making it an obvious choice for a volume such as this.

The most obvious mode of supply of trade in educational services is "consumption abroad," to use the terminology of the World Trade Organization's General Agreement on Trade in Services (WTO 1995). This involves a student from one country traveling to attend an educational institution in another country, financed with funds from the student's home country. In this chapter we consider three other modes of supply that involve the education provider delivering education in the student's home country.

"Cross-border supply" involves an educational institution in one country teaching a student who is resident in another country through distance or online education, or through collaborative provision with a local partner institution. "Commercial presence" involves an educational institution based on one country establishing a branch campus in another country. "Presence of natural persons" involves staff of an educational institution (teachers, administrators, or marketing staff) traveling to provide educational services in another country.

Since the mid-1980s Australia has been a pioneer in providing education offshore to students who for various reasons prefer not to (or cannot) study in national institutions or travel overseas to study. Students in many cities in Asian cities are able to obtain Australian qualifications at a much lower price without the need to leave home. And while Australia is one of the world's major education exporters, it also imports education, but on a much smaller scale, when Australian students travel overseas to undertake degree studies abroad (typically at graduate level) and when Australian students enroll in foreign programs in Australia. Later in the chapter we consider the establishment of foreign campuses in Australia.

The offshore outsourcing of business processes by Australian education institutions has been relatively minor when compared with other services industries such as banking and telecommunications. Some institutions have outsourced aspects of their information technology support services or printing, but these initiatives have generally not aroused much interest beyond the service units directly involved. One way in which educational institutions outsource some of the core services they provide to their home-country students is by establishing study-abroad centers where their students can undertake some of their studies in a remote location. These are a common feature of the international operations of leading US universities, providing a focal point for area studies and languages, as does, for example, the University of Texas at Austin's Center for Arabic Study Abroad, which is located on the Tahrir Square campus of the American University in Cairo. Such offshoring is not an effort to cut costs, but a means of delivering a niche educational service in a location that provides students from the university's home country with first-hand experience of another society, culture, and language. These are not common in Australian universities, with one of the few examples being Monash University's center in Prato, Italy, where Monash students can take intensive courses in humanities, the arts, social sciences, business, and law for credit toward their degree.

Almost all of Australian higher education's offshore expansion has been directed at developing new services for students abroad rather than relocating services provided to Australian students. For that reason, the term "offshore education" is in many countries used interchangeably with "transnational education," referring to "all types of higher education study programmes, or sets of courses of study, or educational services (including those of distance education) in which the learners are located in a country different from the one where the awarding institution is based" (Council of Europe 2001).

The development of Australian offshore education has followed a pattern of development typical of export industries. Universities were initially developed to serve a domestic market, and in Australia nearly all of the universities are public institutions.

In the period after the Second World War they began to also export their services, firstly as official development assistance and later to fee-paying students. Between 1950 and 1975, Australia sponsored around 18,000 students on development scholarships, with the largest numbers of students coming from Indonesia, Malaysia, South Vietnam, and Thailand. Australia also hosted an increasing number of private international students, totaling 45,000 between 1950 and 1975, with the largest numbers from Malaysia, Hong Kong, and Singapore. By 1975, less than a quarter of the 12,500 international students in Australia were in government-sponsored programs (Cleverley and Jones 1976: 26–29). In the mid-1980s, Australia, like the United Kingdom and New Zealand, shifted from an aid to trade orientation, which involved removing government subsidies for private international students so that they would now pay the full cost of their education and allowing institutions to autonomously determine international student numbers and tuition fees. A shift towards a user-pays approach to tertiary education has been underway globally for several decades and it has proved much easier politically to introduce full fees for international students, who don't vote and to whom nation states feel little responsibility, than it has for domestic students, most of whom remain subsidized to some extent in most higher education systems.

The number of international students studying onshore has grown steadily since the mid-1980s, from around 20,000 in 1988 to around 617,000 in 2010, with around one-third in universities, one-third in vocational education and training, and the remaining third spread across intensive English language programs, semester exchange, schools and foundation programs (AEI 2011). The scale of student mobility has to be considered in relation to the size of Australia for its significance to be understood. At the highpoint, August 2009, there were 442,009 people in Australia on student visas, in a population of 22,065,700, so at that time one in every fifty people in Australia was an international student (ABS 2009; DIAC 2011). Tuition fees and living expenses of international students resulted in export income of A$18.5 billion (US$16.2 billion) in 2009–10 (DFAT 2011), making education Australia's third most-valuable export, behind coal and iron ore. This flow of students has had far broader consequences than merely the generation of export income. The presence of large numbers of international students has transformed the youth demography of the large cities, and those who stay in Australia have come to make up one of the largest sources of migrants to the country. Australia's universities are active throughout the region and have extensive alumni networks throughout Asia. Australian graduates, even if they have never traveled abroad, have learned alongside students from many countries and have often been taught by academic staff from an equally diverse range of backgrounds (Davis and Mackintosh 2012).

Many of the universities that were most active in establishing early offshore programs had been funded by the Commonwealth government between 1988 and 1994, to establish national Distance Education Centers. Their primary purpose was to develop correspondence programs for rural and remote students and "second chance" students who had missed out on undergraduate places (DEET 1993). These universities developed extensive resources for distance-education students, including bound collections of readings with commentaries, lecture slides and notes, focus questions, and activities. However, the export possibilities enabled by these centers soon became apparent. When the government's economic advisory agency, the Industry Commission, discussed the possibility of establishing offshore programs in its 1991 report, *Exports of Education Services*, it observed that the eight Distance Education Centers allowed these universities to provide "correspondence courses for overseas students, the electronic transmission of lectures and courses overseas, and Australians traveling overseas personally to provide various forms of education" (Industry Commission 1991). The following year the education minister similarly encouraged universities to "build on expertise in National Distance Education Centers to deliver education to students internationally" (Beazley 1992, 15).

Packaged "courseware" could be sent either to individual distance education students studying in Australia, or to a local partner institution overseas who would distribute the materials to a cohort of students. Local students in Australia and international students overseas would study the same materials, but offshore students would benefit from face-to-face classes, library facilities, and campus services often unavailable to distance-education students in Australia. While many partner-supported programs were initially based on distance-education materials, few students are enrolled in "standalone" distance-education or fully online programs.

Australian Universities Abroad: From Transnational Pathways to Branch Campuses

One feature of international education in Australia that was critical in the growth of offshore programs is the use of "pathways," in which students undertake a sequence of programs. A student who has completed secondary school in Hong Kong may for example undertake an intensive English language program of several months followed by a one-year foundation program or a vocational diploma before transferring to an undergraduate degree program. Around one-third of international students in Australia are enrolled in successive programs (AEI 2008), and this movement between programs partly explains why the number of international enrollments exceeds the number of international students in a given year. In recent years there has been a greater focus on tracking the academic performance of students who enter through various programs to ensure that equivalent entry standards are maintained (Lai et al. 2008).

Starting in the 1980s, Australian universities partnered with private colleges and professional associations in Singapore, Hong Kong, and Malaysia who were able to offer preparatory and diploma programs but not degrees. By linking these programs to the possibility of credit toward a subsequent degree in an Australian university, extensive transnational pathway networks were laid across the region. These arrangements benefited students, offshore partners, and Australian universities. By doing some of their studies close to home, students could shorten the duration of the expensive overseas component of a foreign degree. Offshore partner institutions could recruit students more readily, thanks to the halo effect of association with international universities and the promise of degree options for their graduates. Australian universities could rely on a steady stream of students recruited by their partners and could work with the partners to ensure that students were adequately prepared for their subsequent studies. British universities established the same articulation arrangements during this period, but US universities were much less active. One reason for this is the tighter regulation of credit for prior study in US universities. In response, some offshore partner institutions sought US regional accreditation while others established dedicated pathways overseen by resident academic directors seconded from the US partner.

One of the limitations of articulation programs is that students must apply upon completion of the first program for entry to the second. Entry to the desired degree is not guaranteed and it is unlikely that the curriculum of the two programs will align perfectly, further complicating the transition to study in Australia, with students often joining year two of a three-year degree program and possibly having missed some vital introductory studies. A solution to this limitation is for a university to outsource teaching of the first year of studies to the offshore partner. Students in these 1 + 2 programs would be enrolled with the Australian university from the beginning of their studies and would be studying first-year units from the Australian degree from the outset. They are typically taught predominantly by staff employed by the offshore partner college with curriculum provided by the Australian university, supplemented perhaps by fly-in fly-out lecturers and with assessment that is moderated by the Australian university. These "twinning" programs, as they came to be called in Southeast Asia, share many of the features of articulation arrangements but with the added benefit of certainty for students as well as curriculum alignment and quality assurance overseen by the Australian university. Students' tuition fees for the offshore component of the program are shared between the offshore partner and the Australian university. In the early days distance-education materials often formed the backbone of offshore course materials, and today online learning environments play that role, supplemented with locally employed teachers and fly-in fly-out visits by Australian teaching staff. Offshore teaching staff and infrastructure costs are considerably lower than in Australia, and as result tuition fees for offshore programs are typically less than half of the fee for the same program in Australia. When coupled with the higher cost of living in Australia, the price difference for the student is considerable.

Over time some of these 1 + 2 programs morphed into 2 + 1 programs, allowing students to complete two years offshore followed by one year in Australia, as the relationship matured and the capacity and capability of offshore partners developed. Between the late 1980s and late 1990s, the number of these Australian university offshore programs grew by around fifty per year. By 1997, thirty-five of the thirty-eight universities in Australia were offering programs offshore, with 493 offshore programs in total, across in twenty-four countries, but with three-quarters of these located in Malaysia (174),

Singapore (116), and Hong Kong (110) (Adams 1998). In the aftermath of the 1997 Asian financial crisis many students were unable to afford to study abroad; in response the Malaysian government granted approval to 3 + 0 programs, which allowed students to complete the whole of a foreign degree program at a college in Malaysia. Australian universities responded to the crisis by rapidly expanding the range of programs they offered in Asia and new programs were developed very rapidly, so that the total number of programs had increased fivefold to 1569 by 2003 (Universities Australia 2009).

The boom in partner-supported transnational education was concentrated in Asian cities—Singapore, Kuala Lumpur, and Hong Kong—that were experiencing rapid economic growth resulting from trade and investment liberalization. Demand for higher education rose quickly, especially demand for studies that would position graduates in the most lucrative sector of the economy, namely business administration courses taught in English. These global economic and linguistic developments influence students worldwide in an era of rapid economic globalization and the dominance of global English, but nowhere more than in these three trade and investment hubs. There were also local factors at play in each place. In Hong Kong, families invested in internationally portable qualifications around the time of the city-state's transfer of sovereignty to China in 1997. In Malaysia, many ethnic Chinese students were unable to access places in public universities due to racial quotas that aimed to equalize participation rates for previously underrepresented ethnic groups. In Singapore, entry into the small number of quality local universities was highly selective despite the widespread aspiration of families for their children to obtain tertiary qualifications.

In their account of the transnational education boom among Persian Gulf states in the 2000s, Miller-Idriss and Hanauer (2011) observe that along with global and local/national influences on policy, there are significant regional factors that explain the striking similarity in these governments' encouragement of foreign providers. They argue that, "neither neoinstitutional theories about global norm diffusion nor culturalist theories about the local politics of educational borrowing and transfer sufficiently explain this phenomenon, and call instead for a regional approach" (181). Persian Gulf states share common linguistic, cultural, and political features that foster policy borrowing. They also share conditions that make transnational programs and campuses attractive to governments: the need to invest the benefits of the current natural resources boom in long-term economic development; the presence of a large expatriate labor force; inadequacies in local higher education systems; a reluctance to allow daughters to study overseas; and the difficulty for students from these countries in obtaining student visas in the wake of the September 11 attacks in the United States.

A decade earlier in Singapore, Malaysia, and Hong Kong, a similar set of regional characteristics were at play. These three states were tied together by their British colonial foundations, with similar legal institutions and high levels of English language proficiency, and they continued to have strong political and social connections with Britain. These long-standing historical connections were reconstructed in the aftermath of the Second World War with the help of the Colombo Plan for Cooperative Economic Development in South and Southeast Asia, established by British Commonwealth states in 1950. One of the key features of Australia's involvement in the Colombo Plan was the sponsorship of thousands of students from British Commonwealth countries to study in Australia between the 1950s and the 1980s (Auletta 2000). Many of these students returned to take up prominent roles in the political and business elites of the region, and they maintained ongoing links with Australia through the many forms of cultural diplomacy wrapped around the scholarship program (Lowe 2010). These relationships paved the way for the establishment of dense connections between educational institutions, governments, and business leaders in subsequent decades. Political and business leaders in each of these states were very conscious of developments in the others and tended to emulate strategies that had proved effective in the others.

Definitions of what constitutes a "campus" vary widely, leading to much disagreement. A 1996 Australian government report on the internationalization of higher education reported that at that time seven universities reported having offshore campuses, while at the same time RMIT University was claiming that its new campus in Penang was Australia's first one overseas (Back et al. 1996). This chapter will use the Observatory for Borderless Higher Education's very useful definition of a branch campus as, "an entity trading directly as a branch of the parent institution, recruiting primarily local students, and attempting to replicate breadth of function of the parent institution (e.g., research as well as teaching)" (Becker 2009; Verbik and Merkley 2006). An international branch campus thus involves a bricks-and-mortar presence in the host country, fully or jointly owned by the foreign university. Courses are taught in a similar manner to other campuses of the institution and usually involve higher proportions of face-to-face teaching from more highly qualified teaching staff than is the case in partner-supported programs. The Observatory identified 162 such international branch campuses globally in 2009, double the eighty-two identified in 2006. Only thirty-five (22 percent) of the currently existing branch campuses have been in operation for more than a decade, indicating a very rapid rate of growth. Their locations are concentrated in the Middle East and Southeast Asia, with more being developed currently in India, China, and Central Asia. United States and Australian universities have the largest number of branch campuses, with smaller numbers operated by institutions based in the United Kingdom, Malaysia, and Singapore (Becker 2009). Eleven of Australia's thirty-nine universities, a quarter, have established offshore campuses and three of those have established a second offshore campus. Some have not withstood the test of time and currently seven universities operate ten offshore campuses (see Table 14.1).

Some Australian universities, particularly those based in regional centers, have branch campuses in Australian capital cities also, which resemble offshore branches in many respects (Baird 2009). The city campuses were developed to suit international students who prefer to live in cities, and they were able to price themselves below the established universities in those cities by setting up teaching-only centers with minimal facilities. Central Queensland University's "international" campuses in Melbourne, Sydney, and Brisbane enroll far more students than their now-closed Suva, Fiji, campus did. Curtin University, based in Perth, similarly operates branch campuses in Sarawak, Singapore, and Sydney. Unlike these metropolitan "international" teaching centers, one of the key

Table 14.1 Australian universities' offshore branch campuses

University	Location	First Intake	Current Status
Central Queensland University	Suva, Fiji	1998	Closed 2007
Monash University	Petaling Jaya, Malaysia	1998	Ongoing
University of Wollongong	Dubai, United Arab Emirates	1999	Ongoing
Curtin University	Miri, Sarawak, Malaysia	1999	Ongoing
Swinburne University	Kuching, Sarawak, Malaysia	2001	Ongoing
Monash University	Johannesburg, South Africa	2001	Ongoing
RMIT University	Ho Chi Minh City, Vietnam	2001	Ongoing
James Cook University	Singapore	2003	Ongoing
RMIT University	Hanoi, Vietnam	2004	Ongoing
Charles Sturt University	Burlington, Ontario, Canada	2005	Ongoing
University of New South Wales	Singapore	2007	Closed 2007
Curtin University	Singapore	2008	Ongoing

motivations of the overseas branches was conversely to replicate the full range of university functions offshore, which partner-supported programs cannot do. The limitations of partner-supported programs were highlighted by critics such as Philip Altbach who argued that transnational education does not represent true internationalization; "Knowledge products are being sold across borders, but there is little mutual exchange of ideas, long-term scientific collaboration, exchange of students or faculty, and the like" (Altbach 2000: 5).

Some universities that had been leading players in Southeast Asia were acutely aware of such shortcomings. Within a few months of the Malaysian prime minister's 1991 announcement that foreign universities might be allowed to establish campuses in the country, Monash University had presented a proposal to the Malaysian government to establish:

> [a] complete campus of Monash University, Australia, offering a broad range of undergraduate, graduate and research programs of relevance to Malaysia. The language of instruction will be English. The campus will be a truly international university, involving a partnership of Australian and Malaysian scholars, teachers and researchers. (quoted in Dyt 2007)

The enabling legislation, the Malaysian Private Higher Education Institutions Act, was passed in 1995, establishing key features of the regulatory frameworks for foreign university branch campuses and local private universities. Within six years, Malaysian campuses of Monash, Curtin, and Swinburne universities had been established.

When compared with large multinational corporations, even those universities with the largest transnational operations remain overwhelmingly based in their country of origin. The United Nations Conference on Trade and Development's transnationality index provides a means of quantifying the degree of internationalization of a company, measuring the share of an entity's operations that are located outside its home country. The index is determined by averaging the following three ratios: foreign assets/total assets, foreign sales/total sales, and foreign employment/total employment. This is very difficult to apply to a university. Universities' annual reports provide excellent data on total assets but such data is difficult to obtain for offshore subsidiaries. Similarly, employment data for Australian operations in readily available but not for offshore operations. The one indicator that is readily available for both onshore and offshore operations is enrollments, as illustrated in Table 14.2, although income to the university from these enrollments is not published. Connelly et al. (2010) devised a very interesting transnationality index that allows educational institutions to self-assess their degree of offshore activity using standard criteria and scoring.

The ten largest providers of transnational education, a quarter of Australia's universities, between them enroll three-quarters of the country's offshore students. These ten institutions between them have 17 percent of their students offshore, while only 2 percent of students in the remaining twenty-nine institutions are offshore (DEEWR 2011). These universities account for nine of Australia's ten offshore campuses and most have experienced continued growth in their offshore operations over more than two decades.

In addition to the figures quoted in Table 14.2, there are around 10,000 further offshore students classified as studying by "distance education" are, curiously, included in onshore numbers in government statistics (Banks et al. 2010). For example, the University of Southern Queensland has around 4,000 students who are studying offshore, but as they are considered distance-education students in the university's students records system, these are all reported inaccurately as onshore students. This is also the case for several other universities, and the total offshore is closer to 86,000.

Table 14.2 Australian universities' offshore Enrollments, 2010

	Offshore students	All students	Percentage offshore
RMIT University	16,089	51,865	31
Curtin University	9,111	45,884	20
Monash University	8,938	62,550	14
University of South Australia	6,002	35,940	17
University of Wollongong	4,289	27,127	16
Swinburne University	3,020	23,216	13
Murdoch University	2,932	18,101	16
Edith Cowan University	2,822	27,622	10
University of Tasmania	2,570	23,354	11
James Cook University	2,543	18,835	14
Other institutions	18,130	858,163	2
Total	76,446	1,192,657	6

Source: DEEWR 2011.

Australian Vocational Education and Training Providers Abroad: Catching Up Fast

It is likely that Australia's first transnational program was a diploma program offered by a vocational distance-education provider and its story reveals much about the way in which institutions were being held back from providing transnational education by Australian regulatory agencies before the policy changes of the mid-1980s (Brimblecombe 1996). The Darling Downs Institute of Advanced Education's External Studies Department was a UNESCO-appointed demonstration unit which showcased innovations in open and distance learning for visiting educators from Asian countries. In 1981, it commenced a collaborative program with the University of the South Pacific offering associate diploma courses in engineering to provide technician training in the South Pacific region (Clarke and McDonald 2007). However, the Queensland government's Board of Advanced Education ordered the program be terminated in 1984 on advice from the state's solicitor-general.

After the liberalization of international education in Australia in the mid-1980s, offshore activity of vocational education and training providers grew more slowly than did universities. In several states, specialized international units within government education departments worked with public providers (called Institutes of Technical and Further Education, or TAFEs) to strategically support the development of their international activities, including the offshore initiatives. This sometimes involved government staff based in key offshore markets assisting with commercial developments, and in other cases involved negotiating government-to-government projects (see Clayton and Ziguras 2012).

In Victoria, where TAFE institutions operate more autonomously, offshore operations were less influenced by government and individual institutions initiated significant activity in a wide range of offshore locations. Box Hill Institute began operating offshore in 2000 and by 2010 had over 2,000 students studying its programs through twenty partnerships in ten countries. It focuses on delivering practical training through well-matched local partners in areas of workforce need in particular locations. Australian universities have teamed up with public vocational education and training providers to establish offshore articulation pathways into their degree programs. This has been most noticeable in China, where the national Ministry of Education has exercised increasing levels of scrutiny over transnational higher-education programs, while provincial authorities responsible for vocational education and training have been less restrictive. As a result, the lion's share of the growth in offshore VET enrollments in the 2000s was in China, which by 2009 accounted for two-thirds of all offshore VET enrollments, while Australian university enrollments in China declined during the same period. Now far more students in China are enrolled in Australian diploma programs than in degree and graduate studies (Banks et al. 2010).

Private vocational education and training providers have become increasingly active in recent years. One form is the small private college, usually specializing in a single discipline, that has spread its operations to a handful of overseas sites. An example of these is the Kent Institute of Business and Technology, which was established in Sydney in 1989 and now in addition to its Sydney CBD campus it operates Kent International College in Ho Chi Minh City, Vietnam, as well as operating in partnership with a range of other private colleges in several Southeast Asian cities. The most successful Australian niche provider going global is SAE College, which started out in 1976 as an audio-engineering school and by 2011 had grown to encompass fifty-three campuses across nineteen countries, enrolling 8,500 students. In a sign of the times, it was acquired in 2010 by Navitas, Australia's largest for-profit education provider. Navitas also operates university pathway programs (foundation and diploma programs) at around thirty sites in Australia, the United Kingdom, United States, Canada, Singapore, Kenya, Sri Lanka, and Indonesia. It also manages and operates Curtin University's Singapore campus (Navitas 2011).

Data on offshore provision by public vocational education and training institutions have been collected since 2003, and since that time enrollments of international students have grown rapidly both onshore and offshore (NCVER 2010b, 2010a, 2011). As Table 14.3 illustrates, public vocational education and training providers have been much more successful enrolling international students offshore, particularly in China where universities face significant regulatory barriers. The decrease in the number of students from 2009 to 2010 does not represent a change of fortune for the sector; it was caused by a change in the way one institution counts students who are enrolled in a year-long program that extends across two calendar years, now counting them in one calendar year rather than both. Private providers grew their onshore international enrollments very rapidly in the late 2000s but their offshore operations remain dwarfed by public universities and TAFE institutes which between them account for 95 percent of Australia's offshore activity.

Table 14.3 International enrollments in Australian vocational education and training

	Onshore		Offshore	
	Government	Nongovernment	Government	Nongovernment
2003	12,403	33,589	18,291	-
2004	12,380	33,177	23,586	-
2005	13,934	37,061	27,842	-
2006	16,318	50,844	30,894	-
2007	20,694	81,651	43,953	-
2008	25,001	129,374	55,332	-
2009	30,181	178,011	64,813	8,452
2010	29,756	176,026	62,307	-

Source: DEEWR 2011; NCVER. 2010a, 2010b, 2011.

Foreign providers in Australia

The South Australian government has been keen to establish Adelaide as an international education hub and has recruited three foreign university campuses in an effort to lure a greater number of international students. This strategy has also been used by Singapore and Dubai over the past decade. Adelaide attracted small subsidized branch campuses of two prestigious schools—Carnegie Mellon University, which offers graduate programs in public policy and information technology, and University College London, which offers gradate energy and resources and PhD programs. A campus of UK-based Cranfield University was announced in 2007 but was abandoned in 2010 without enrolling any students (*Adelaide Now* 2010). More recently a new private university, with the working title Torrens University, has been approved to commence operations in 2013, owned by the US-based Laureate International Universities group (Laureate International Universities 2011). This will be Australia's third private university, and the first for-profit university. Another large US-based for-profit education conglomerate, Kaplan, in 2011 abandoned its plans to develop a campus in Adelaide, but will continue its diploma and university pathway programs through its Carrick Education brand, which operates campuses in Adelaide, Melbourne, Sydney, and Brisbane (Trounson 2011).

The increasing cross-border activity of for-profit providers, both into and out of Australia, is notable, and follows quite a different pattern. Whereas public providers tend to operate in partnership and are not able to invest large sums in offshore activities, private providers tend to purchase providers who are accredited to operate in the host country as local institutions, and so are not counted in transnational enrollment data. UNCTAD estimates the world inward foreign direct investment stock in education grew from just US$100 million in 1990 to US$8,755 million in 2009 (UNCTAD 2011: annex table 24). The vast majority of this investment is conducted by private firms moving between developed economies.

Impact on employment in Australia

There has been considerable discussion in Australian higher education about the qualitative impacts of transnational education on work in universities but little discussion of the quantitative impact. It is clear that many staff in Australian educational institutions are employed to service offshore students in a wide range of ways—developing curriculum materials, flying offshore to deliver lectures, setting, marking and moderating assessment, administering programs, and managing relationships with partner institutions. A significant proportion of the staffing of transnational programs is located where the student is, and the division of labor between onshore and offshore staff varies widely. Transnational education thus has a positive effect on the scale of employment in higher education in Australia.

One argument that is sometimes heard is that offshore programs divert students who may have studied in Australia into Australian programs in the home country, and the benefits to Australia are significantly reduced as a result. Not only is the income to the university considerably less, but also lost are the other expenditure and paid employment in Australia which would benefit the wider economy, and half of the work that would have been performed in Australia to service this student is now instead performed offshore. It appears unlikely, though, that a significant number of students who could study in Australia would elect instead to undertake a program offshore. There is a clear preference for study in Australia among students who are able to do so, and those who enroll in offshore programs are usually prevented from undertaking a program in Australia due to the cost involved or work or family commitments that prevent them from traveling for a prolonged period.

One effect of the blurring of staffing for offshore programs is that it becomes difficult to calculate the student-to-staff ratio within institutions. We know fairly accurately how many students there are enrolled in an institution and whether they are located onshore or offshore but it is very difficult to estimate how much of the teaching for offshore programs is done by staff of partner institutions who are not reported in the university's staffing records. The universities' peak body, which monitors student-to-staff ratios, now reports two sets of figures, one including and one excluding offshore students. In 1990, when offshore enrollments were negligible and institutions were better funded, the student-to-teacher ratio nationally was 12.9. By 2008, it had increased to 19.8, if only onshore students are included, and to 21.1, if offshore students are also included (Universities Australia 2010), with the actual figure somewhere between the two, if offshore teaching staff are factored in.

Teaching staff from Australian institutions who teach overseas for the first time often find the experience challenging. On top of the planning, preparation, and logistics of teaching far from home, teachers are put into an unfamiliar learning environment in which they are the outsiders. Students and the locally employed staff they are teaching alongside may have quite different expectations of them as teachers and professionals compared with students and colleagues back home. Transnational classrooms are invariably culturally hybrid learning environments, in which the teaching staff and students need to understand each others' expectations and norms to be able to accommodate them effectively (Chambers 2003; Dunn and Wallace 2006; Debowski 2008; Hoare 2006). Over time some teaching staff become adept at managing these challenges, often developing personally and professionally through their cross-border and cross-cultural experiences, while others move into roles that do not require them to teach offshore (Smith 2009a). Academic unions have been particularly vocal in drawing attention to the stresses and strains offshore teaching can impose (NTEU 2004a, 2004b). Although induction and ongoing professional development for staff teaching offshore still appear to be lacking in many institutions, the International Education Association of Australia has recently published a handbook for institutions that sets out extensive advice for selecting and supporting staff for offshore education (IEAA 2008).

Schapper and Mayson (2004) observe that the "packaging of curriculum" that was pioneered in the development of distance education through the 1980s in many institutions has been of enormous significance in facilitating the growth of transnational delivery:

> it can offer guarantees of standardised curriculum, standardised assessments and the reassurance to students and employers of the consistency of the degree irrespective of where that degree is completed. Efficiencies can be expected with the standardisation of courses—only one set of materials are required, the longer life of materials allow larger print runs of print materials and other materials can be made available electronically. (197)

While they accept that the productivity gains of such an approach are obvious, Schapper and Mayson see such standardization as an "assault on the professionalism of academic staff," arguing that "standardised courses rob academics of professional autonomy, professional judgment and intellectual engagement" (198). This echoes broader critiques of the commodification of higher education (Hayes and Wynyard 2002; Mok 1999; Ritzer 1993). In the United States, the University of Phoenix has used a similar low-cost model of "second chance" education, growing into one of the country's largest higher-education providers (Farrel 2003). In transnational education and multicampus for-profit colleges, we can observe a similar disembodiment of the curriculum. Previously, the knowledge and skills embodied in the lecturer provided the core of the teaching experience, but in these programs a set of digitally reproducible resources constitutes the "courseware" that is designed to be delivered by many different teachers interchangeably. Such packaging allows education to be traded across borders as a standardized product, facilitating the massification of international education.

Impact on Employment in Host Countries

Governments in Australia's key transnational education host countries allowed institutions to partner with foreign universities as a way to quickly grow the capacity of the higher-education system and respond to student demand that could not be met by existing local institutions. The presence of foreign branch campuses and partnerships has clearly increased and has not only benefited students but has also served to grow the size of the academic workforce. Teaching staff are typically recruited locally, from neighboring countries, and from the foreign institution's home country. Academic staff from many places come to work alongside one another, and over time the capacity and capability of the academic and administrative workforce is built up (Vincent-Lancrin 2007). Local providers benefit from these relationships and after a while are able to apply for degree-awarding status and develop their own programs. Singapore and Malaysia have used transnational programs in this way to profoundly develop the scale and quality of local private institutions, which now not only deliver a large number of programs to domestic students but also play a pivotal role in recruiting international students from many countries to study in both Malaysian and Singaporean accredited programs but also British and Australian programs closer to home.

The lower cost of locally employed academic and support staff in the offshore setting is one of the most significant advantages of transnational provision, allowing Australian institutions to deliver programs to students at much lower cost and in a more convenient location than the home campus (Edwards and Edwards 2001: 80). Weighing against this is students' and parents' expectation that if they enroll in a foreign program they will be taught by teachers from that country and preferably from that institution's home campus. After all, this is one of the features that would distinguish a transnational program from its domestic competitors.

The profile of an average locally employed teacher in a transnational program is quite different from that of a traditional academic in a conventional university. He or she may not be expected (or allowed the opportunity) to conduct research, will be more likely to need a teaching qualification and/or practical experience in their field, will probably be engaged on a casual or part-time basis, and may have little interaction with academic colleagues (Cunningham et al. 2000: 117–22). As well as the separation of teaching from research, there is often a separation of other tasks into specific components. In terms of education functions, curriculum development, production of learning materials, delivery, support and assessment can each be handled by separate individuals. The staff member may concentrate on only one of these.

Several recent studies have pointed to concerns among staff at offshore campuses (Dobos 2011; Pyvis 2008). While staff at the Australian campus may be concerned about deskilling and the challenges of frequent travel and unfamiliar educational cultures, staff offshore report serious status and power imbalances with their Australian colleagues. Many staff in transnational programs and at international branch campuses have never visited the "home" campus of the institution whose programs they teach. In a transnational institution where there is a clear power hierarchy between what are seen as the central and the remote operations, relationships are often fraught (Smith 2009b). For example, the ability to travel between sites, a privilege often reserved for those from the home campus, can mark a profound disparity between staff at different locations.

As well as its effects on employment in the education sector of host countries, transnational education has a significant effect on the development of the broader workforce. We know that private providers in Malaysia, after decades of partnering with foreign universities, now enroll more students than Malaysian public universities, making a huge contribution to increasing the graduate workforce. We know that in theory transnational programs are very responsive to market conditions, and where there is student demand, partnership arrangements are able to be established by drawing on an existing program abroad much more quickly than establishing an entirely new program from scratch at a local university. However, little is known about the impact that transnational programs have on labor markets or workforce productivity. The Australian Graduate Survey, which tracks graduate outcomes, is administered to all graduates who have completed programs in Australia but, sadly, not to those who have completed programs abroad. One recent study, which followed graduates of an Australian program delivered in Singapore, paints a positive picture of the transformative possibilities of such programs. Students who missed out on places in local universities and who sought out "second chance" foreign programs found that the skills they acquired proved highly beneficial in their career development, despite this not being obvious to participants at the time of their studies (Hoare 2011).

Conclusion

Educational trade has over the past several decades knitted together the social fabric of Australia and many Asian countries far more than any other form of cultural or economic exchange. The effects are noticeable across the region with the presence of hundreds of thousands of Australian alumni occupying positions in corporations, governments, schools, and hospitals. Most have studied in Australia, but an increasing proportion have earned their qualifications in an Australian program or campus in their own country. The broader consequences for the region and for Australia's relationship with the region are impossible to quantify. Easier to measure are the jobs created in the education sector supporting the delivery of Australian programs, either in a partner institution, an offshore campus, or at the institution's home campus in Australia. Clearly, offshore programs tend to create employment opportunities abroad while students traveling to Australia to study tend to create jobs in Australia.

Offshore programs could be seen as merely shifting the location of international education, and therefore jobs, offshore. In practice there appears to be little competition between these modes of supply, for two reasons. First, most students who seek an overseas qualification would rather study in the institution's home country, whether it be Australia, France, the United States, or Japan, and it tends to be those who cannot travel due to cost, family, or work obligations who study in offshore programs. Nevertheless, there are clearly some students who may have traveled to Australia who instead choose to study in an Australian program in their home country. Australian institutions do not appear too concerned by this; over time the range of options for students in their home country will expand considerably and Australian institutions are keen to be key participants in that growth rather than be threatened by it. The second reason why offshore delivery is not seen to be cannibalizing onshore study is the tendency for offshore programs to be used by students and education providers as pathways to study in Australia. Students in many cities in Asia can choose to access some foreign qualifications at home and others abroad, and will often combine these. For example, one student might study at an international secondary school, complete an undergraduate degree at an Australian campus, and undertake graduate study in Australia, while another student might, after completing secondary school, enroll in an English language school, then gain an offshore diploma through a private college, and then transfer to a degree program in Australia.

Offshore delivery of education is one of the ways in which many Australian universities and vocational colleges have sought to position themselves as providers of education and training for the Asia Pacific region rather than their home city. While the elite universities have been content to draw large numbers of students to their home campuses, institutions in the next tier have been keen to also take their programs offshore to meet the demand from a larger pool of students. We are likely to see a significant increase in offshore activity in coming years now that institutions have become more adept at implementing sustainable models of offshore. They are being pushed along by a decline in onshore enrollments due to the high Australian dollar and they are being pulled by the prospect of being a part of future decades of growth in Asia's emerging cities.

References

ABS (Australian Bureau of Statistics). 2011. *September Key Figures*. Australian Bureau of Statistics 2009 [cited October 28, 2011]. http://www.abs.gov.au/AUSSTATS/abs@.nsf/allprimarymainfeatures/8DEB63C39D475D4BCA25774B0015F48E?opendocument.

Adams, T. 1998. "The Operation of Transnational Degree and Diploma Programs: The Australian Case." *Journal of Studies in International Education* 2 (1): 3–22.

Adelaide Now. 2011. "'Lauded' UK-based Cranfield University closes Adelaide base." November 23, 2010. http://www.adelaidenow.com.au/news/south-australia/lauded-uk-based-cranfield-university-closes-adelaide-base/story-e6frea83-1225959509323.

AEI (Australian Education International). 2008. *Study Pathways of International Students in Australia*. Canberra: Department of Education, Employment and Workplace Relations.

———. 2011. *International Student Data*. Canberra: Department of Education, Employment and Workplace Relations. http://www.aei.gov.au/research/Pages/AEI%20Research.aspx.

Altbach, P. G. 2000. "The Crisis in Multinational Higher Education." *International Higher Education* 21 (Fall): 3–5.

Auletta, A. 2000. "A Retrospective View of the Colombo Plan: Government policy, Departmental Administration and Overseas Students." *Journal of Higher Education Policy and Management* 22 (1): 47–58. doi: 10.1080/713678129.

Back, K. J., D. M. Davis, and A. Olsen. 1996. *Internationalisation and Higher Education: Goals and Strategies*. Canberra: IDP Education Australia, Evaluations and Investigations Program Higher Education Division, Department of Employment Education, Training and Youth Affairs.

Baird, Jeanette. 2009. "When 'Onshore' Looks Like 'Offshore': Quality Assurance with Onshore Partner Providers." In *20th ISANA International Education Association Conference*, edited by F. Fallon. Canberra: ISANA International Education Association.

Banks, M., P. Kevat, C. Ziguras, A. Ciccarelli, and D. Clayton. 2010. *The Changing Fortunes of Australian Transnational Higher Education*. London: Observatory on Borderless Higher Education.

Beazley, Hon. K. 1992. *International Education in Australia through the 1990s*. Canberra: Australian Government Publishing Service.

Becker, R. 2009. *International Branch Campuses: Markets and Strategies*. London: Observatory on Borderless Higher Education.

Brimblecombe, E. 1996. *Pheonix Rising: The First Twenty One Years of Darling Downs College of Advanced Education*. Toowoomba: University of Southern Queensland.

Chambers, E. 2003. "Cultural Imperialism or Pluralism? Cross-Cultural Electronic Teaching in the Humanities." *Arts and Humanities in Higher Education* 2 (3): 249–264.

Clarke, J, and A. McDonald. 2007. *USQ: The First 40 Years*. Toowoomba: University of Southern Queensland.

Clayton, D., and C. Ziguras. 2012. "Transnational Delivery." In *Making a Difference: Australian International Education*, edited by D. Davis and B. Mackintosh. Sydney: UNSW Press.

Cleverley, J., and P. Jones. 1976. *Australia and International Education: Some Critical Issues*. Hawthorn: Australian Council for Educational Research.

Connelly, S., J. Garton, and A. Olsen. 2010. *A Transnationality Index for Higher Education Institutions*. London: Observatory on Borderless Higher Education.

Council of Europe. 2001. "Code of Good Practice in the Provision of Transnational Education." http://www.coe.int/t/dg4/highereducation/recognition/code%20of%20good%20practice_EN.asp.

Cunningham, S., Y. Ryan, L. Stedman, S. Tapsall, K. Bagdon, T. Flew, and P. Coaldrake. 2000. *The Business of Borderless Education*. Canberra: Department of Education, Training and Youth Affairs.

Davis, D., and B. Mackintosh. 2012. *Making a Difference: Australian International Education*. Sydney: UNSW Press.

Debowski, S. 2008. "Risky Business: Effective Planning and Management of Transnational Teaching." In *Teaching in Transnational Education: Enhancing Learning for Offshore and International Students*, edited by L. Dunn and M. Wallace, 204–216. New York: Routledge.

DEET (Department of Employment, Education and Training). 1993. *National Report on Australia's Higher Education Sector*. Canberra: Department of Employment, Education and Training.

DEEWR (Department of Education, Employment and Workplace Relations). 2011. *Student 2010 Full Year: Selected Higher Education Statistics*. http://www.innovation.gov.au/HigherEducation/HigherEducationStatistics/StatisticsPublications/Pages/Student2010FullYearSelectedHigherEducationStatistics.aspx.

DFAT (Department of Foreign Affairs and Trade). 2011. *Analysis of Australia's Education Exports*. Canberra: Department of Foreign Affairs and Trade.

DIAC (Department of Immigration and Citizenship). 2011. *Student Visa Program Report: 2010–11 to December 31, 2010*. Canberra: Department of Immigration and Citizenship.

Dobos, K. 2011. "'Serving Two Masters': Academics' Perspectives on Working at an Offshore Campus in Malaysia." *Educational Review* 63 (1): 19–35. doi: 10.1080/00131911003748035.

Dunn, L., and M. Wallace. 2006. "Australian Academics and Transnational Teaching: An Exploratory Study of their Preparedness and Experiences" *Higher Education Research and Development* 25 (4): 357–369.

Dyt, K. 2007. *Monash University Sunway: Building on a Vision*. Clayton: Monash University.

Edwards, R., and J. Edwards. 2001. "Internationalisation of Education: A Business Perspective." *Australian Journal of Education* 45 (1): 76–89.

Farrel, E. F. 2003. "Phoenix's Unusual Way of Crafting Courses." *Chronicle of Higher Education* 49 (23): 10.

Hayes, D., and R. Wynyard. 2002. *The McDonaldization of Higher Education*. Oxford: Greenwood.

HESA (Higher Education Statistics Agency). 2011. Students in Higher Education Institutions 2009/10. UK: Higher Education Statistics Agency.

Hoare, L. A. 2006. *So Near and Yet So Far: An Ethnographic Evaluation of an Australian Transnational Education Program*. Melbourne: Faculty of Education, University of Melbourne.

———. 2011. "Transnational Student Voices: Reflections on a Second Chance." *Journal of Studies in International Education* 16 (3): 271–286. doi: 10.1177/1028315311398045.

IEAA (International Education Association of Australia). 2008. *Good Practice in Offshore Delivery: A Guide for Australian Providers*. Melbourne: International Education Association of Australia.

Industry Commission. 1991. *Exports of Education Services*. Canberra: Australian Government Publishing Service.

Lai, K., S. Nankervis, M. Story, W. Hodgson, M. Lewenberg, and M. MacMahon Ball. 2008. "Providing Transparency and Credibility: The Selection of International Students for Australian Universities." *Higher Education Research & Development* 27 (4): 331–344. doi: 10.1080/07294360802406809.

Laureate International Universities. 2011. *Laureate International Universities to Open New International University in Australia*. October 17, 2011. http://laureate.net/en/NewsRoom/PressReleases/2011/10/LaureateInternationalUniversitiestoOpenNewInternationalUniversityinAustralia.aspx.

Lowe, D. 2010. "The Colombo Plan and 'Soft' Regionalism in the Asia-Pacific: Australian and New Zealand Cultural Diplomacy in the 1950s and 1960s." *Alfred Deakin Research Institute Working Paper Series* 1: 1–19.

Miller-Idriss, C., and E. Hanauer. 2011. "Transnational Higher Education: Offshore Campuses in the Middle East." *Comparative Education* 47 (2): 181–207.

Mok, K. 1999. "The Cost of Managerialism: The Implications for the 'McDonaldisation' of Higher Education in Hong Kong." *Journal of Higher Education Policy and Management* 21 (1): 117.

Navitas. 2011. *Navitas Limited Annual Report 2011*. Mt Pleasant, Australia: Navitas Limited.

NCVER (National Centre for Vocational Education Research). 2010a. *Data Collection on VET Offshore by Public and Private Providers 2009*. Melbourne: National Quality Council.

———. 2010b. *Delivery of VET Offshore by Public Providers, 2009*. Adelaide: National Centre for Vocational Education Research.

———. 2011. *Delivery of VET Offshore by Public Providers, 2010*. Canberra: Department of Education, Employment and Workplace Relations and the National Centre for Vocational Education Research.

NTEU (National Tertiary Education Union). 2004a. *Excess Baggage: Australian Staff Involvement in the Delivery of Offshore Courses*. South Melbourne: National Tertiary Education Union.

———. 2004b. *Working Offshore: A Guide for Australian University Staff Working Overseas*. South Melbourne: National Tertiary Education Union.

Pyvis, D. 2008. "Transnational Education in Mauritius: Quality Assurance for Program Exporters." In *Teaching in transnational higher education: Enhancing learning for offshore international students*, edited by L. Dunn and M. Wallace. New York: Routledge.

Ritzer, George. 1993. *The McDonaldization of Society*. Newbury Park, CA: Pine Forge Press.

Schapper, J. M., and S. E. Mayson. 2004. "Internationalisation of Curricula: An Alternative to the Taylorisation of Academic Work." *Journal of Higher Education Policy and Management* 26 (2): 189–205.

Smith, K. 2009a. "Transnational Teaching Experiences: An Under-explored Territory for Transformative Professional Development." *International Journal for Academic Development* 14 (2): 111–122.

Smith, L. 2009b. "Sinking in the Sand? Academic Work in an Offshore Campus of an Australian University." *Higher Education Research & Development* 28 (5): 467–479. doi: 10.1080/07294360903154118.

Trounson, A. 2011. "Red Tape Cuts US Plan for Adelaide 'University City.'" *The Australian*, August 26, 2011. http://www.theaustralian.com.au/higher-education/red-tape-cuts-us-plan-for-adelaide-university-city/story-e6frgcjx-1226122417968.

UNCTAD (United Nations Conference on Trade and Development). 2011. *World Investment Report 2011: Non-Equity Modes of International Production and Development*. Geneva: United Nations Conference on Trade and Development.

Universities Australia. 2009. *Offshore Programs of Australian Universities*. Canberra: Universities Australia.

———. 2011. *Staff Characteristics, Teaching & Graduate Outcomes*. Cited October 28, 2011. http://www.universitiesaustralia.edu.au/page/australia-s-universities/key-facts—data/graduates—staffing/.

Verbik, L., and C. Merkley. 2006. *The International Branch Campus: Models and Trends*. London: Observatory on Borderless Higher Education.

Vincent-Lancrin, S. 2007. *Cross-border Tertiary Education: A Way towards Capacity Development*. Paris and Washington, DC: Organisation for Economic Cooperation and Development and The World Bank.

WTO (World Trade Organization). 1995. *General Agreement on Trade in Services*. Geneva: World Trade Organization.

SECTION III

THE BRIC COUNTRIES

CHAPTER 15

Employment Expansion in Globalization

How Is China Responding to the Change in Comparative Advantage?

Cai Fang, Du Yang, Wang Meiyan, and Qu Yue

1 Introduction

In the past thirty-two years of economic reform and opening-up, China has seen annual GDP growth of 9.9 percent, which is considered a miracle such as the one accomplished by Japan and the "Four Tigers." Such a rapid economic growth has been accompanied by a dramatic demographic transition, in which the fertility rate has fallen continuously. This has yielded a rise in the proportion of the working-age population (that is, aged fifteen to sixty-four) to the total population, providing a demographic dividend to economic growth (Cai and Wang 2010). Unlike what some observers (for example, Rawski 2001) describe as growth with zero employment, the Chinese economic growth has created an unprecedented amount of nonagricultural employment opportunities and formed the largest labor migration in human history in peacetime (Roberts et al. 2004).

Such rapid economic growth and employment expansion are undoubtedly related to China's active participation in the economic globalization. Actually, the biggest jump in its trade volume has happened since 2001, when China joined the World Trade Organization (WTO). However, there is a misunderstanding about the interrelation between employment and trade in China, which may mislead Western observers and political leaders into making decisions based on incorrect information.

A popular opinion is that Chinese employment is highly dependent on trade. On one hand, such an impression might come from the contrast between the stagnation of employment in Western countries, which is characterized by "jobless recovery" in the United States and high youth unemployment in Europe, and the rapid expansion of employment and roaring labor migration in China. On the other hand, such a notion tends to reinforce the disputes between China and its major trade partners. It seems to be helpful for the politicians in the West to attribute the unsatisfactory employment performance to China. In addition, such a misunderstanding is so persistent that many do not see what is happening in the supply of and demand for labor in the Chinese economy, which prevents people from fully understanding the future of both China and the world economy.

This chapter is mainly based on two data sets. The first is the data from two rounds of the National Economic Census from the *China Economic Census Yearbook*, published by the National Bureau of Statistics in 2007 and 2011. The Economic Census investigates all the incorporated companies and individual employers in the secondary and tertiary sectors. The information collected includes the basic firm information, financial statements, production capacity, R&D, and so on. The two rounds of the Economic Census were conducted in 2004 and 2008. The second data set comes from the National Survey on Manufacturing, conducted by National Bureau of Statistics. This data set includes all state-owned enterprises and non-state-owned enterprises with an annual revenue greater than 5 million yuan from 2000 to 2007. It covers the manufacturing enterprises in thirty-one provinces (cities and autonomous areas). The number of manufacturing enterprises is about 150,000 in 2000 and 2001, 160,000 in 2002, 180,000 in 2003, 250,000 in 2004 and 2005, close to 280,000 in 2006, and over 310,000 in 2007.

It is necessary to warn of the limitations of the data mentioned above. First, data used in the paper mostly end by 2007 or 2008. It is likely that the response of the Chinese economy to the labor shortage and wages inflation that first appeared in 2004 becomes tremendous after 2007 and 2008, which may not be revealed by the data available. Second, the Chinese economy was first hit by the global financial crisis in the middle of 2008, so the data collected in 2008 may include some cyclical disturbance deviating from normal. Third, while exploring the relationship between exports and employment, one can speak only of direct effect and may inadvertently overlook indirect effects induced by the exporting sector. Despite those flaws, most conclusions drawn from the data are in general valid in terms of features of employment expansion, changes in comparative advantage, and direction of adjustment in the economy in accordance with such characteristics and changes.

By using various sources of statistics, this chapter tries to reveal the growth of urban employment during the first ten years of the twenty-first century. We confirm that the employment expansion has synchronized with urbanization and economic growth in the period. In addition, we use data from two rounds of the Economic Census and the national survey of manufacturing enterprises to estimate the contribution of exports to employment growth. The findings show that while the opening-up has positively helped economic growth and increased employment, the overall employment expansion in China has been driven by domestic demand. This chapter shows the trend of wage inflation in recent years and it also explores the impact of the changing labor-market profile on labor-intensive industries and discusses how industries and enterprises have responded to such a change in the comparative advantage of the Chinese economy. Finally, it concludes by drawing some policy suggestions.

2 Global factors of Chinese employment

The employment expansion during the period of rapid economic growth is mainly manifested in massive labor migration from rural to urban sectors and the enlarged labor participation of urban residents. In order to provide a general, convincing picture that can help to understand the state of China's labor market, we try to list various components of labor demand and supply based on the available data. The demographic and economic trends have together changed the relationship between supply of and demand for labor. If we consider the annual increase of the working population aged between fifteen and sixty-four as labor supply and the annual increase of urban employment as labor demand, the comparison between the two trends can clearly show the changed situation of the labor market (Table 15.1). Since the number of laborers engaged in agriculture is in a declining trend, the nonagricultural sectors in rural areas are not expected to expand, so the increase of urban employees including migrant workers may well represent the overall demand of the Chinese economy for labor.

By combining various sources of employment data, we find that in 2009, 12.5 percent, or 39 million of 310 million reported urban employees, were migrant workers. That is, the urban employment statistics do not cover well the migrant workers. In fact, the total

Table 15.1 Changes in stock of labor force demanded and supplied (million, percent)

Year	Urban resident employment	Urban migrant workers	Employment elasticity of urbanization	Employment elasticity of growth	Employment elasticity of population
2000	231.51	75.04	-	-	-
2001	236.07	80.29	1.00	0.95	-
2002	240.91	100.09	1.04	0.99	-
2003	245.69	108.89	1.01	0.95	1.02
2004	250.03	113.03	0.99	0.93	1.01
2005	254.30	120.25	1.00	0.93	1.02
2006	259.47	126.31	1.00	0.91	1.02
2007	264.92	130.94	0.99	0.90	1.02
2008	268.48	134.23	0.99	0.93	1.01
2009	272.24	138.94	0.99	0.94	1.01
2010	272.30	146.27	0.99	0.92	1.01

Source: Calculated according to data from *China Statistical Yearbook* (various years), *China Rural Household Survey Yearbook* (various years) and *China Population Statistical Yearbook* (various years).

number of migrant workers, who are defined as out-migrants from their home townships for more than six months, amounted to 153 million in 2010, of which 95.6 percent migrated to cities. By making some assumptions, we exclude the number of migrant workers from urban employment in order to get a pure number of urban resident workers. The summation of urban resident employees and migrant workers can then be considered as total urban employment.

In the period of 2000 to 2010, the annual growth rate of urban employment was 3.2 percent. To compare the urban employment growth with the speed of urbanization, GDP growth, and increase in working-age population, we calculate and list three elasticities in Table 15.1, which are: (1) employment elasticity of urbanization—namely, the ratio of urban employment growth rate to growth rate of the proportion of urban population; (2) employment elasticity of GDP—the ratio of urban employment growth rate to GDP growth rate; and (3) employment elasticity of population—the ratio of urban employment growth rate to the growth rate of working age population. The calculated three elasticities show convincingly that employment growth has been consistent with the pace of economic growth and urbanization.

Since China's economic reform and opening-up policy initiated in the late 1970s, particularly after its entry to the WTO in 2001, its extraordinary performance in economic growth has benefited from its trade expansion. Correspondingly, strong export of labor-intensive commodities has made a reasonable contribution to China's employment expansion. In Figure 15.1, we compare the exporting share of manufacturing by subsector with the growth rate of employment and find that the more

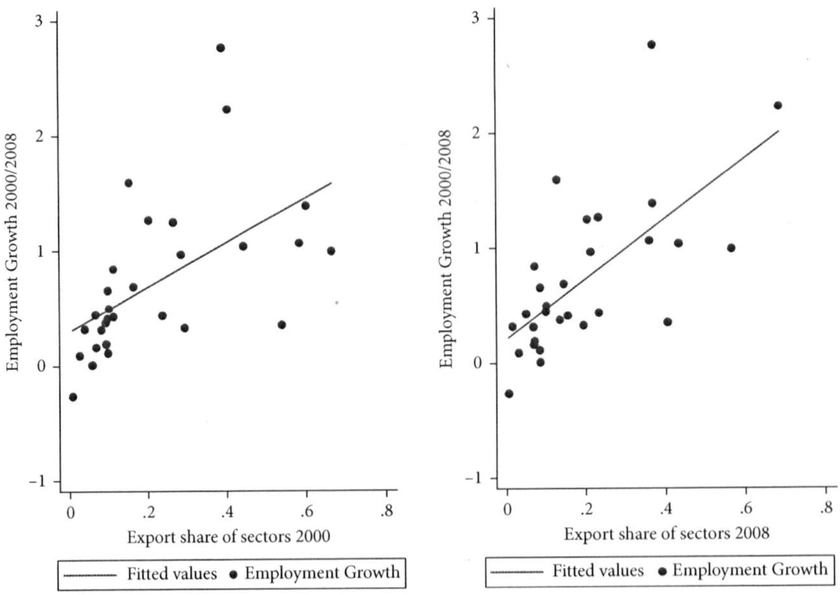

FIGURE 15.1 Exporting share of manufacturing and growth rate of employment by subsector.

Source: Authors' calculation.

export-led a subsector of manufacturing is, the faster growth of employment it has brought about.

However, one can hardly find convincing figures about how many Chinese workers actually work for exporting sectors. To look at the employment and wages in trade-related sectors we first need to identify the trade-intensive sectors.

Data from two rounds of the Economic Census provide information on the relative size of exports by subsectors in manufacturing in terms of total sales and value of exports. We define the share of the value of exports in total sales as an index to measure the degree of trade intensity in each subsector. According to this index, the thirty subsectors in manufacturing are grouped by quintile. The higher the share of exports in total sales, the more intensive the sector is trade related. Table 15.2 presents the information identifying the trade-related sectors. The most trade-intensive sectors include textile, electronic equipment manufacturing, and communication equipment manufacturing, among others.

Table 15.2 Trade intensity in manufacturing by quintile

Quintile	Average share of exports in sales (%)	Share in total production value (%)	Sectors
2004			
20–	3.1	19.0	Recycling and disposal of waste
			Tobacco manufacturing
			Processing of petroleum, coking, processing nuclear fuel
			Beverage manufacturing
			Manufacture of chemical fibers
			Smelting and pressing of ferrous metals
20~40	9.7	25.7	Manufacture of paper and paper products
			Printing, reproduction and recording media
			Raw chemical materials and chemical products
			Manufacture of transport equipment
			Manufacture of nonmetallic mineral products
			Smelting and pressing of nonferrous metals
40~60	12.8	16.1	Manufacture of medicine
			Food manufacturing
			Food processing from agricultural products
			Manufacture of special-purpose machinery
			Manufacture of general-purpose machinery
			Processing of timber, wood, bamboo, rattan, palm and straw products
60~80	27.6	19.6	Manufacture of rubber
			Manufacture of plastics
			Manufacture of electrical machinery and equipment
			Textiles manufacturing
			Manufacture of metal products
			Manufacture of artwork and other manufacturing
80+	56.9	19.5	Manufacture of measuring instruments and machinery for cultural activity and office

(Continued)

Table 15.2 (Continued)

Quintile	Average share of exports in sales (%)	Share in total production value (%)	Sectors
			Manufacture of textile wearing apparel, footwear, and caps Manufacture of furniture Manufacture of leather, fur, feather and related products Manufacture of communication equipment, computers and other electronic equipment Manufacture of articles for culture, education, and sports activities
All	23.9	100	- -
2008			
20-	3.0	22.7	Recycling and disposal of waste Tobacco manufacturing Processing of petroleum, coking, processing nuclear fuel Beverage manufacturing Smelting and pressing of nonferrous metals Smelting and pressing of ferrous metals
20~40	7.9	22.3	Manufacture of paper and paper products Manufacture of nonmetallic mineral products Food processing from agricultural products Manufacture of chemical fibers Raw chemical materials and chemical products Food manufacturing
40~60	12.7	19.9	Printing, reproduction of recording media Manufacture of medicine Processing of timber, wood, bamboo, rattan, palm and straw products Manufacture of special-purpose machinery Manufacture of general-purpose machinery Manufacture of transport equipment
60~80	23.9	20.5	Textiles manufacturing Manufacture of plastics Manufacture of metal products Manufacture of electrical machinery and equipment Manufacture of rubber Manufacture of textile wearing apparel, footwear, and caps
80+	46.8	14.6	Manufacture of furniture Manufacture of leather, fur, feather, and related products Manufacture of artwork and other manufacturing Manufacture of measuring instruments and machinery for cultural activity and office Manufacture of articles for culture, education, and sports activities Manufacture of communication equipment, computers and other electronic equipment
All	18.9	100	- -

Source: Authors' calculation from Economic Census data.

The last column in the table indicates small variations of the sector composition by trade intensity between 2004 and 2008. Although the total volume of exports in China has been increasing, it seems that the overall trade intensity in manufacturing declined in 2008. In 2004, the average share of exports in total sales was 23.9 percent and the share declined to 18.9 percent in 2008. The trade-intensive sectors are relatively small in terms of total production value. The most trade-intensive sectors accounted for 19.5 percent of total production value in manufacturing in 2004 and 14.6 percent in 2008. The trade-intensive sectors identified in this table are also characterized as labor intensive, which is analyzed in detail in what follows.

The features of employment and wages in trade-intensive sectors are of great interest in this chapter. Although there is no aggregate for all enterprises, information on employment of "enterprises with designated size" is available.

Table 15.3 shows the characteristics of employment in manufacturing by quintile of export share in total sales. The first column of Table 15.4 reports the employment in subsectors of manufacturing by quintile of export share. The second column indicates the employment associated with trade. As noted earlier, it is hard to separate trade employment from employment for domestic demand if the two types of employment are mixed at a micro level. Here we assume both domestic and export sectors have the same productivity and divide the employment according to the share of exports in total sales. Multiplying the export share by total employment, we get the number of employees associated with trade. The third column in this table reflects the share of manufacturing employment of the group. The last column is the ratio of employment to fixed assets, which refers to the number of workers employed per million of fixed assets.

The two rounds of Economic Census indicate rapid employment growth in manufacturing and in trade-intensive sectors. Employment in manufacturing increased

Table 15.3 Employment in manufacturing by quintile

Quintile of export share in sales	Employment (mln)	Trade employment (mln)	Employment share in manufacturing (%)	L/K
2004				
20–	4.92	0.25	8.7	3.86
20~40	14.04	1.39	24.8	8.38
40~60	10.62	1.52	18.7	12.97
60~80	15.30	4.77	27.0	17.85
80+	11.79	7.02	20.8	31.48
Total	56.67	14.95	100	-
2008				
20–	7.32	0.37	9.5	2.83
20~40	15.95	1.23	20.6	4.08
40~60	16.39	2.26	21.2	5.79
60~80	23.18	5.57	30.0	9.28
80+	14.48	7.82	18.7	13.87
Total	77.32	17.25	100	-

Source: Authors' calculation from Economic Census data.

Table 15.4 Breakdown of employment changes associated with trade

Codes	Changes in export share (%)	Changes in employment (1,000)	ΔEM*EX (1,000)	ΔEX*EM (1,000)	ΔEX*ΔEM (1,000)	Changes in trade empl (1,000)	Empl effect (%)	Export effect (%)	Structural effect (%)
1	−4.90	118.6	14.4	−9.63	−5.81	-1.04	-1387.9	928.0	559.9
2	−2.98	43.7	5.1	−3.30	−1.30	0.52	977.9	−629.8	-248.1
3	−1.43	29.1	1.3	−1.20	−0.42	-0.32	-412.2	380.3	132.0
4	−0.50	-0.1	0.0	−0.10	0.00	-0.10	1.1	99.5	-0.6
5	−10.63	64.1	19.3	−62.48	−6.82	-50.04	-38.5	124.9	13.6
6	−19.04	126.8	69.7	−63.20	−24.14	-17.62	-395.7	358.7	137.0
7	−21.16	62.1	36.1	−44.69	−13.14	-21.72	-166.2	205.8	60.5
8	−10.62	54.5	12.8	−8.16	−5.79	-1.19	-1075.9	687.8	488.1
9	−19.83	39.5	22.4	−12.88	−7.83	1.71	1313.6	−754.8	-458.8
10	−0.79	21.5	1.7	−1.04	−0.17	0.47	357.2	−220.8	-36.4
11	0.08	18.5	1.8	0.05	0.02	1.90	96.5	2.7	0.8
12	−12.94	25.2	17.5	−13.91	−3.26	0.37	4749.9	−3767.7	-882.2
13	−0.91	18.1	0.5	−0.62	−0.16	-0.32	-146.0	194.4	51.6
14	−1.32	103.3	10.2	−4.30	−1.36	4.59	223.3	−93.6	-29.6
15	−1.22	36.4	4.1	−1.39	−0.44	2.24	181.8	−62.1	-19.7
16	4.04	5.9	0.3	1.58	0.24	2.08	12.7	76.0	11.4
17	−2.84	16.5	4.3	−2.30	−0.47	1.53	280.4	−149.8	-30.6
18	−6.31	80.2	21.5	−11.06	−5.06	5.35	401.5	−206.8	-94.7
19	−3.33	83.4	8.7	−13.81	−2.77	-7.91	-109.8	174.7	35.1
20	1.16	36.2	2.1	3.22	0.42	5.70	36.1	56.5	7.4
21	−4.80	57.9	6.1	−6.11	−2.77	-2.82	-214.7	216.4	98.3
22	−9.68	114.1	35.1	−20.62	−11.04	3.45	1017.6	−597.7	-319.9
23	−2.44	149.5	25.1	−8.39	−3.65	13.09	192.0	−64.1	-27.9
24	1.24	88.5	10.9	2.73	1.10	14.69	73.9	18.6	7.5
25	5.50	131.8	13.2	18.77	7.25	39.18	33.6	47.9	18.5
26	−5.67	179.1	51.6	−19.77	−10.16	21.65	238.2	−91.3	-46.9
27	4.92	298.5	188.2	18.64	14.69	221.55	85.0	8.4	6.6
28	−11.74	32.1	17.6	-9.90	−3.77	3.97	444.3	−249.3	-95.0
29	−14.22	19.1	10.2	−17.66	−2.72	-10.19	-100.1	173.4	26.7
30	−0.13	−303.8	−1.8	−0.43	0.41	-1.81	98.9	23.6	-22.6
Average							225.6	−103.7	-21.9

from 56.7 million in 2004 to 77.3 million in 2008. Employment associated with exports increased from 14.95 million to 17.25 million.

A study shows that the actual share of the labor force engaged in agriculture was 24.7 percent in 2009 (Du and Wang 2010). That is, in total 587 million Chinese laborers were employed in nonagricultural sectors in the same year. Comparing with such a big number, the number of workers in export-related sectors is rather small. Despite the fact that export-related employment is underreported, it can be concluded that Chinese employment is not heavily dependent on exports. In a previous study, which was based on information of items and value of exported goods, and the ratio of value added to gross output by sub-sector, we estimate the value added of exports by subsector, which shows that the total value-added of exported goods accounted for 10.1 percent of GDP in 2007 (Cai, Du and Wang 2009). This is exactly identical to the finding of other research that suggests that in 2011, 11 percent of China's GDP growth can be attributed to external demand (Green and Shen 2011). All those are consistent with the conclusion in this chapter.

3 Impacts of the Changed Relationship between Labor Demand and Supply on Comparative Advantage

The change in employment associated with exports could be driven by various forces. As presented in the following equation, the change in employment from time $t-1$ to t can be separated into three components. The first part in the right side of the equation is the incremental effect of export change, that is, the impact of export share changes on employment even without total employment changes. The second item is the sectoral expansion effect, which refers to the effect of total employment changes in the sector without changes in export share. The last item is the effect of structural changes that are combined with the effect of export changes and total employment change in the sector.

$$\Delta TE_{i,t} = \Delta EX_{i,t} EM_{t-1} + \Delta EM_{i,t} EX_{i,t-1} + \Delta EM_{i,t} \Delta EX_{i,t}$$

We may separate the change of employment associated with trade into these three components in each sector of manufacturing. The results are presented in Table 15.4. The overall effect of employment expansion dominates the increase of employment associated with trade, and it accounted for 225.6 percent of trade employment. Meanwhile, the export changes actually play a negative role in employment changes associated with trade, accounting for −103.7 percent of net employment changes associated with trade. This trend implies that employment demand from the domestic market has played a more active role although overall exports have been increasing in China.

Thanks to the implementation of the one-child policy and to socioeconomic development, China has completed a demographic transition within a very short period of time compared to most developed countries. During the Chinese reform period, the stage of demographic transition was characterized by a deep drop in fertility, rapid decline in the proportion of youth, a slowdown of working-age population growth, and a quick increase in the proportion of elderly. When the pace of the decline in the proportion of youth exceeded the pace of increase in the proportion of elderly, China began to enjoy a sufficient labor supply, a result of productive population structure. As the demographic transition process continues to carry forward, the growth of working-age population becomes slower and slower, whereas population aging speeds up. Those changes raise many challenges to China's society.

Most predictions on China's population are based on the Total Fertility Rate (TFR) of 1.8 and the forecast that China would reach its population peak between 2025 and 2030, with a total population of between 1.40 and 1.44 billion (United Nations 2009; Hu 2009).[1] As the Chinese authority silently gives up a claim of 1.8 TFR—namely, the calculated TFR based on official population survey data published by National Bureau of Statistics has been lower than 1.5 for many years, the United Nations, in its newly published report *World Fertility Pattern, 2009*, revises China's TFR to be 1.4 in 2006, which places it on the list of low-fertility countries. Consequently, the declining labor supply caused by the change in population age structure may come sooner than anticipated.

The long-lasting low fertility has changed the population age structure. That is, since about 1980, the growth of the elderly population has accelerated, the growth of the working-age population has rapidly slowed down, and the growth of the youth population has shrunk. The implication of such a demographic dynamic is that the longstanding low fertility will lead to an inadequacy of labor supply as the working-age population first slows its growth and eventually stops growing. According to an updated prediction (United Nations 2009), the year 2015 is China's turning point, at which the population aged fifteen to sixty-four will stop increasing and begin shrinking.

According to a more detailed prediction (Hu 2009), which takes into account the impacts of rural-to-urban migration, the labor demand in the urban sector has been fulfilled by rural labor migration in recent years. By 2015, the increased number of the working-age population in urban area will be less than the reduction in working-age population in rural area, and the total working-age population will begin to shrink, the same conclusion drawn by the UN prediction. That implies that without substantial enhancement of wages and other incentives the migrant workers will not fill up the gap vacated by the rapid reduction in the urban labor force.

While labor supply diminishes, the demand of economic growth for labor remains strong. Based on the current employment elasticities of growth in secondary and tertiary sectors, we can predict a continued growth of employment in nonagricultural sectors. Under scenarios assuming 8 percent, 9 percent, 10 percent, and 11 percent of GDP growth rates, growths of employment will be fast in the coming years (Table 15.5). That will further tighten the labor market.

Table 15.5 Aggregate demand for labor in various scenarios of GDP growth

GDP growth scenario (%)	Secondary (%)	Tertiary (%)
8	3.74	6.06
9	4.21	6.82
10	4.68	7.58
11	5.15	8.34

Source: National Bureau of Statistics (2009), *Bulletin of the Second Economic Census, Statistical Bulletin of Economic and Social Development in 2009*, and *China Statistical Yearbook in 2009*.

The change of relationship between demand for and supply of labor has revised China's endowments of factors of production. As a result, marginal productivity of labor is not as low as what development economics alleges to characterize the dual economy, and wage rate is no longer determined at subsistence level but influenced by labor demand and supply. The labor shortage first appeared in the coastal areas in 2003 and has become widespread all over the country, since which time the wages of ordinary workers, notably of migrant workers, began to increase.

We have selected a set of wages, which include monthly wages of sectors such as manufacturing and construction, monthly wages of migrant workers, and the daily wages of selected agricultural sectors, to show the wages rise since 1998; the results are shown in Figure 15.2. In the following we explain the evidence and the changing trends.

First, we examine the increase of migrant workers' wages. When discussing the turning point of economic development characterized by a wages hike, Lewis (1972) emphasized that the wage increase matters only for unskilled workers, since there is always a scarcity in skilled workers at whatever stages of economic development. The wage data of urban formal employees in China's statistics are so aggregated and average that they are unable to reflect the status of unskilled workers, so it is best to take migrant workers' wages as proxy for those of unskilled workers.

There were no statistics distinguishing migrant workers' wages from those of urban workers before 2001, but it was commonly believed that the wage of migrant workers not only remained low but also had hardly witnessed any increase until 2003, when it began to increase at an annual rate of 10.8 percent in the period 2003 to 2010. Apart from the data shown in Figure 15.2, there are other individual surveys and new reports

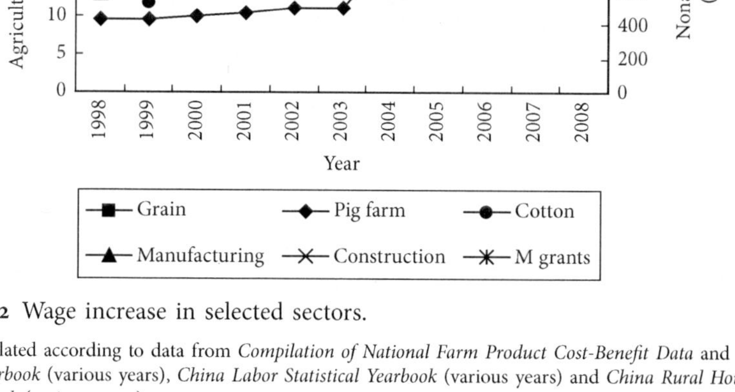

FIGURE 15.2 Wage increase in selected sectors.

Source: Calculated according to data from *Compilation of National Farm Product Cost-Benefit Data* and *China Statistical Yearbook* (various years), *China Labor Statistical Yearbook* (various years) and *China Rural Household Survey Yearbook* (various years).

that assert even higher levels and faster growth of migrants' wages. For example, a survey conducted by the People's Bank of China, the central bank, in early 2010, shows that the average wage of migrant workers was 1783.2 yuan in 2009, a 17.8 percent increase in real terms compared to the previous year (DSS-PBC 2010). It turned out that the real growth of migrant workers' wage was 19.3 percent in 2010.

In fact, to compare local and migrant workers' wages requires combining wage rates with working hours because the two groups work in different ways. According to a survey conducted in 2010 (called China Urban Labor Survey or CULS),[2] migrant workers work 27 percent more hours a week than do urban local workers. That is, migrants have to work longer in order to get higher monthly wages. As a matter of fact, the same survey shows that while migrants' wages were only 88.2 percent of those of local urban workers, the monthly wages of the former were slightly higher than those of the latter (5.6 percent higher) after adjusting the difference in weekly working hours between them. As the migrants' demographic characteristics change, the new generation of migrant workers tend to work fewer hours than did their older counterparts. The CULS results show that migrant workers worked nearly 12.4 hours less than did their predecessor in 2005. That is, the growth of migrants' wages and their convergence to urban locals' can imply a larger surge of actual wage rate (e.g., if measured by hourly wage rate).

Second, we examine the increase of wages in construction and manufacturing. Data on sectoral wages are collected from the reporting system, which requires all registered enterprises to report their total employment and wage expenses, and the data come together to the National Bureau of Statistics. While they mainly reflect wages of formal employees, the two sectors selected are characterized as employing unskilled workers. Therefore, they are representative to urban ordinary workers. In the period examined, the annual growth rate of wages was 19.5 percent and 9.8 percent, respectively in the two sectors. The two rounds of the Economic Census show that the workers' compensation in real tern increased from 14,200 yuan in 2004 to 23,900 yuan in 2008, an annual growth rate of 13.9 percent.

Finally, we look into wages of paid workers in selected agricultural sectors. If the currently observed labor shortage and resulting wages rise in nonagricultural sectors are the result of a substantial reduction of labor surplus in agriculture, one can anticipate an accompanying increase in wages in agriculture. Though hired workers are not used everywhere in Chinese agriculture, the published data on wages of agricultural paid workers allow us to distinguish labor compensation from the total revenue of agricultural production. For the selected agricultural sectors shown in Figure 15.2, whereas wages rates had stagnated in all agricultural sectors in the period 1998 to 2003, in the period 2003 to 2008, their annual growth rates went up substantially: 15.3 percent for hired workers producing grain, 11.7 percent for hired workers producing oilseed, and 19.4 percent for hired workers on pig farms with fifty pigs or more, which have in essence kept pace with the increase in migrant workers' wages, if not faster.

Not only is the labor supply becoming short, leading to an increase in wages, but policy is developing that supports further rises in wages. This policy includes components that aim at redistributing income and extending social security coverage to most of the population. For example, in 2009, the Chinese central government started a pilot program for pensions to cover rural residents. Premier Wen Jiabao set out on the ambitious task of covering 100 percent of the population with these benefits within the final year of his term.

Additionally, minimum-wage standards have increased in all cities, and the current twelfth Five-Year Plan has set up the goal to have a 13 percent annual minimum-wage increase for the next five years in real terms. That will also lead to an increase of the real wage rate. Labor-market institutions are also being promoted, such as collective bargaining for wages and labor-dispute settlements. The government tends to favor workers instead of employers when there is a dispute.

The result of these changes is multifold. First, an enterprise survey suggests that a 20 percent increase in labor costs will cause a decline in profit margin by 20–60 percent in competitive sectors. That is, wage inflation will increase the labor cost and reduce the profitability of most enterprises. Other research suggests that the demographic factor will contribute half to a reduction of the trade surplus. In about 2016, the surplus will no longer exist and a deficit will emerge. That is, a labor-cost increase will have a similar effect as Ren Min Bi (RMB) revaluation. While these are still only estimates, the numbers reveal the direction in which the Chinese economy is heading.

As for the manufacturing sector, unit labor compensation is one of the most important factors affecting the competitiveness of the industry. The determinants of unit labor compensation include wage rate, the benefit associated with labor, and working hours. In many cases, employers deal with variations of labor demand by adjusting working hours when facing an economic crisis or a labor shortage. For instance, when the impact of the global financial crisis was serious, the actual working hours per worker declined though the employer did not fire workers. With the reappearance of a labor shortage in 2009, the employers had to increase work hours. Average weekly working hours per worker in the manufacturing sector was 46.4 hours in 2003 and 50.4 hours in 2006, an increase of 8.6 percent per annum. The working hours have been decreasing since then.

Table 15.6 presents the hourly wage rates in manufacturing sectors. In China there are no official statistics reflecting the actual size of employment in manufacturing because the information on migrant workers is insufficient. To reflect the average wage level in manufacturing, we have estimated the average wages in manufacturing weighted by the size of employment of migrant workers and urban work unit employment. By considering the average weekly working hours and exchange rates, the hourly wage rates in US dollars are presented in the table too.

In addition to wages, the labor costs also include the other costs in labor compensation, which means that all the costs associated with labor use should be accounted in labor costs (Figure 15.3). In detail, labor compensation includes wages, bonuses, allowances, in kind transfers, free medical care, transport subsidies, and expenditure in social insurance. We have no direct data to calculate the other items of labor costs. According to Banister (2006), the ratio between labor compensation and wages is about 1.27 in China's manufacturing sector. Two factors might affect the adjustment ratio. First, migrant workers tend to have low levels of social protection, which implies that the ratio

Table 15.6 Nominal wage rates in manufacturing

	Monthly Wage (RMB)	Hourly Wage (RMB)	Hourly Wage (US$)
2001	760	3.97	0.48
2002	811	4.11	0.50
2003	882	4.44	0.54
2004	967	4.81	0.58
2005	1052	4.81	0.59
2006	1184	5.48	0.69
2007	1334	6.30	0.83
2008	1596	7.77	1.12
2009	1728	8.31	1.22
2010	2038	9.81	1.45

Source: Authors' calculation.

would be lower if migrants were included in employment estimates. Second, China has been increasing its labor protection in recent years, which means that the ratio is increasing over time. These two opposite forces make it possible to assume that the ratio of 1.27 is a reasonable adjustment.

Table 15.7 compares the hourly labor costs in manufacturing between China and other economies of interest. Among those economies, the developed countries and the neighboring economies are China's main trade partners. The developing countries with similar characteristics of endowment are competitors in trade. The following aspects are worth noting when evaluating the change in labor costs in China.

First of all, when passing through the Lewis turning point,[3] the changing relationship between labor supply and employment demand drive the increasing labor costs.

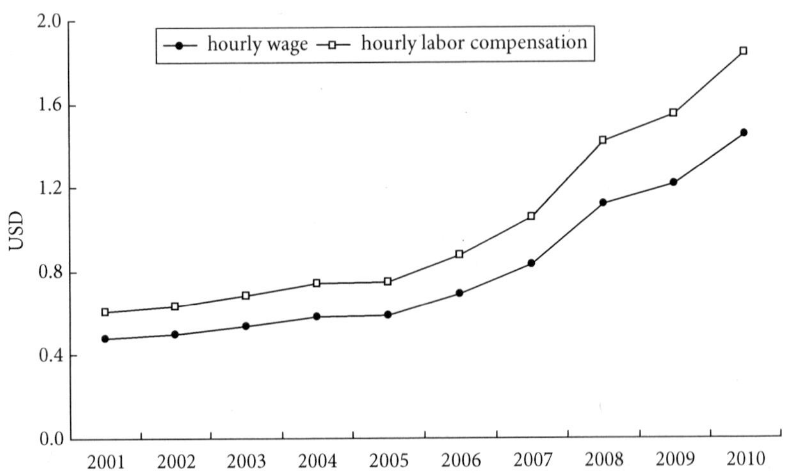

FIGURE 15.3 Average hourly labor cost per worker in manufacturing.

Source: Authors' calculation.

Table 15.7 Hourly labor costs in selected economies (US$)

	2003	2004	2005	2006	2006/2003
China (adjusted)	0.69	0.74	0.75	0.88	1.28
Main trading partners					
United States	22.48	23.13	23.81	23.82	1.06
Japan	20.32	21.95	21.54	20.2	0.99
Australia	19.79	23.38	25.11	26.14	1.32
United Kingdom	21.29	24.82	25.72	27.10	1.27
Canada	19.6	21.85	23.98	25.74	1.31
Euro Zone	24.55	27.57	28.24	29.21	1.19
Neighboring economies					
Korea	9.69	10.81	12.74	14.72	1.52
Singapore	7.23	7.47	7.30	8.55	1.18
Philippines	0.79	0.84	0.92	1.07	1.35
Hong Kong, China	5.54	5.51	5.65	5.78	1.04
Taiwan, China	5.69	5.98	6.42	6.43	1.13
Other emerging economies					
Brazil	2.74	3.14	4.16	4.91	1.79
Mexico	2.44	2.44	2.64	2.75	1.13

Source: The data on China are the same as Table 15.6 and the other countries are from Bureau of Labor Statistics, http://www.bls.gov/news.release/ichcc.t02.htm.

Meanwhile, the tendency of the RMB appreciation intensifies the labor cost increase when measured in US dollars. For instance, even the labor cost keeps constant in RMB; it still grew 4.6 percent in 2007 due to the appreciation of RMB. However, the impact of the labor-market transition on labor costs is just a small part of the matter. When facing a labor shortage, the employers tend to intensify their labor use first—for instance, increasing working hours—to deal with the growth of labor costs. It is obvious that this measure only works in the short run. With a small surplus of rural labor (Du and Wang, 2010), it is hard to depress the growth of labor cost by absorbing additional labor flow from rural areas. It is expected that the growth of labor cost will be a long-term trend in the Chinese labor market.

Second, China has an advantage when it comes to labor costs in terms of the absolute level of hourly labor cost when compared with developed countries. In fact, the level of hourly costs in developed countries is quite stable when measured in their own currency. In other words, most variations in labor costs come from fluctuations in exchange rates. Even so, China will keep its advantage in labor costs in the relatively long term.

Compared with the developing economies, China also has an advantage in labor costs. For example, the hourly labor costs in China are lower than Brazil and Mexico and similar to the Philippines. At the same time, the there has been a prominent growth of labor costs in other developing economies: 79 percent in Brazil and 35 percent in Philippines. It is unlikely, therefore, that China will lose competitiveness to those countries.

Finally, the comparison of hourly labor costs is just one side of the coin. The competitiveness in labor costs is determined by labor productivity too. The existing study has also shown growth in labor productivity in China (Du and Qu 2009). This may lessen the worry that China will lose competitiveness in manufacturing due to the growing labor costs.

4 How have enterprises responded to changes in comparative advantage?

The growing labor costs alter the relative price between labor and capital, which induces the employers to use labor-saving technology. When looking at the history of economic development in the Asian Tigers, it indicates simultaneity between industrial upgrading and labor-cost growth. As shown in Figure 15.4, the labor costs in manufacturing relative to the United States grew rapidly in the end of 1980s in the Asian Tigers. Since then, those economies have witnessed their economic structure upgrading significantly.

The changes in labor costs of manufacturing in those Tigers led to industrial transfers among Asian economies that is called a "flying geese" pattern (Okita 1985; Kojima, 2000). The rapid increase in labor costs in those four economies coincided with massive inflows of foreign direct investment in labor-intensive industries in China in the late 1980s and early 1990s. This shows the changed profile of the labor market in a significant sign of and useful viewpoint for observing changes in comparative advantages.

Under the conventional paradigm of the flying geese model, it is logical to predict a transfer of labor-intensive industries from China to neighboring countries endowed with cheap labor, as the demographic transition has altered the unlimited supply of labor

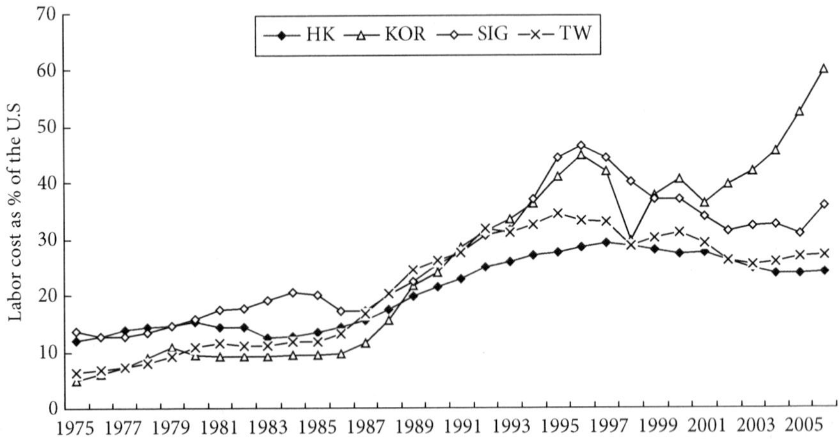

FIGURE 15.4 The Asian Tigers' labor cost in manufacturing relative to the United States.
Source: US Department of Labor, Bureau of Labor Statistics, March 2009.

and has caused wage inflation. It is true that the revision of comparative advantage at the macroeconomic level and the reduction of profit margin of labor-intensive enterprises at the microeconomic level have tended to raise the value chain of the Chinese industry.

The changing paths of comparative advantage and the form of the flying-geese model, however, are not the same between small and large economies. While for small economies, the flying-geese model is usually formed to transfer industries among countries, in a large economy the flying-geese model can be formed among domestic regions.[4] In their analysis of a small and large country, Chenery et al. (1975: chap. 4) noticed the difference in trade patterns. This can usefully be applied to explain the characteristics of China as a large economy—that is, highly outward-oriented and inward-oriented regions coexist, and given the differential endowments of production factors, it is divided into several smaller economies, among which flying geese–shaped developments can be accomplished.

We believe that it is more useful to observe the ongoing and forthcoming changes in the economic growth pattern of China in a domestic perspective than in an international perspective. The reason is threefold.

First, industrial relocation is more likely in the form of a domestic flying-geese pattern, because it will take a long time for neighboring countries to pick up labor-intensive industries. Since China makes up 40 percent of the working-age population of N-11 countries (plus India and exclude Korea), it tends to be the price maker instead of the price taker in the world's labor market. In sheer size, China is much too big to simply be replaced, and other countries need time to be able to take over its reins. In the meantime, the relocation of labor-intensive manufacturing is occurring, and will continue to occur, within China's own borders.

Second, we expect that the differentials of wages among regions will hold—namely, wages in the interior provinces will remain lower than those in the coastal provinces. As a result of faster economic growth in the central and western regions and labor-market integration, the wages of migrant workers have converged in recent years. For example, in 2003, wages in the central and western regions were about 75.0 percent and 73.7 percent respectively of wages in the eastern regions, whereas such percentages increased to 96.3 percent and 96.9 percent respectively in 2010. Having observed that, we still expect a faster increase in wages in the coastal regions, because enterprises in the coastal regions face a bigger pressure of wages increase than the central and western regions.

In 2009, 72 percent of labor disputes of the country were recorded in the eastern regions. Labor-dispute incidence—numbers of labor disputes reported per thousand workers—in the eastern regions was 1.6 times higher than in the central regions and 2.5 times higher than in the western regions. Since the main object of labor disputes is wages, the higher labor dispute incidence in the coastal regions implies that workers tend to be less satisfied with their compensation and such dissatisfaction will drive faster growth of wages rate in those regions. In contrast to that, the existing wages in the central and western regions are relatively attractive for local workers, especially for those rural laborers who are at their relatively older ages. Therefore, when labor-intensive industries move to those regions, the wage increase will be relatively moderate.

Third, since the Chinese economy and employment are not as export-dependent as commonly believed, one response to the weakening of international competitiveness caused by labor-cost increase should be that manufacturing becomes less export-oriented. While the next growth center is expected to be the fast urbanization and industrialization of the interior provinces, accompanied by a transfer of labor-intensive industries, it tends to be driven more by domestic consumption. This is confirmed by the fact that Chinese exports have become less labor intensive. The relationship between labor intensity and export orientation is shown in Figure 15.5. The horizontal axis is the share of exports in sales and the vertical axis is labor intensity, that is, the ratio of employment to fixed assets. The higher the ratio, the more labor intensive is the sector. Both panels indicate a positive relationship between labor intensity and export share.

Therefore, the response of Chinese industries and enterprises to the changes in comparative advantage can be examined through observing the industrial upgrading in the eastern regions, the industrial transfer from the eastern region to the central and western regions, and the related reallocation of the labor force among regions.

The reallocation of manufacturing among regions had already happened in 2004, when China witnessed a labor shortage for the first time. As is shown in Figure 15.6, the eastern region's shares of output value, total assets, and employment in manufacturing sector reached their peak in 2004 and have declined since then. Correspondingly, the central regions neighboring the coastal areas and endowed with massive experienced

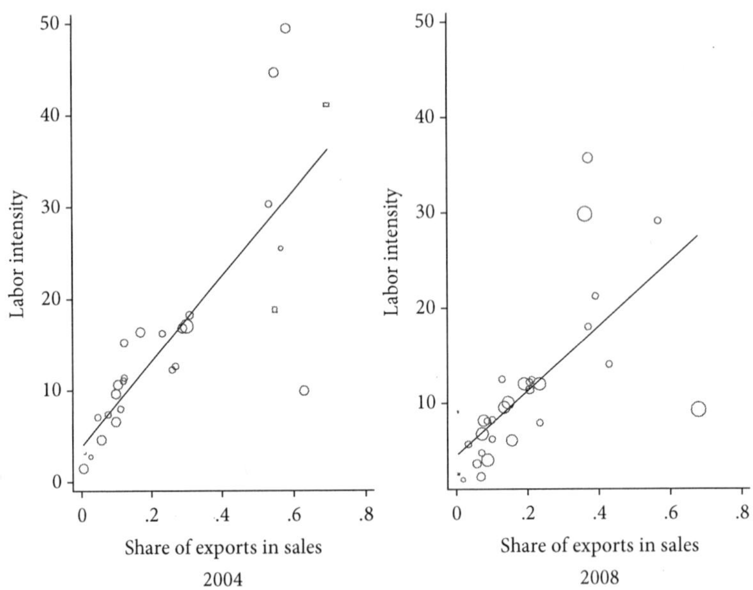

FIGURE 15.5 Export and employment intensity.

Note: Each bubble represents one subsector in manufacturing and the size of the bubble is weighted by employment in the subsector.

Source: Authors' calculation from Economic Census data.

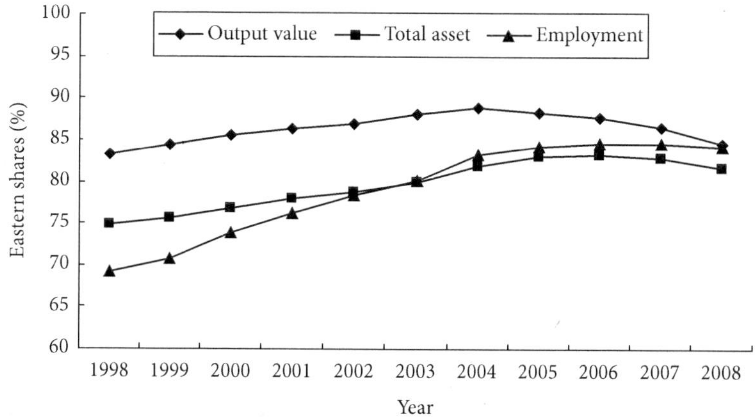

FIGURE 15.6 Eastern regions' shares in manufacturing sector.

Source: Calculation based on National Survey on Manufacturing.

workers, who previously were migrant laborers to the coastal factories, increased their related shares in the period.

Although such a trend can be considered as a response of the Chinese industries and enterprises to the changes in comparative advantage, it does not indicate the formation of a typical flying-geese pattern within China, for three reasons.

First, the industrial transfer observed has a significant tendency of consumption-oriented growth rather than a replacement of the central regions for the eastern regions in exporting sector. By processing the data of the National Survey on Manufacturing, we found that in the process of the decline in the proportion of export of Chinese manufacturing since 2004, while the eastern regions take the lead, the central and western regions have not played a role offsetting such a decline by increasing their proportion of exporting manufacturing goods. Thus, so far we cannot assert that the interior regions have carried on the comparative advantage in labor-intensive industries.

Second, the enhancement of the share of the central regions in manufacturing has not been mainly driven by the transfer of labor-intensive industries. Based on the manufacturing survey data, we calculated the average size and capital intensity for the eastern, central, and western manufacturers and find that in the period of 2000 to 2007: (1) the volume of value-added per firm in the eastern regions remained unchanged, whereas that in the central and western regions substantially increased and surpassed the eastern regions; and (2) the capital–labor ratio in the central and western regions increased and became higher than that in the eastern regions (Cai, Wang and Qu 2009).

Third, such a reallocation has not been accompanied by any significant rise up the value-added ladder in the eastern regions. By calculating the ratio of value-added to the total output value in manufacturing to denote the sector's relative status in the global value chain, we actually did not see an upswing of the eastern manufacturing in the value chain. Instead, the results show that such a ratio in the central regions experienced a jump in recent years (Figure 15.7).

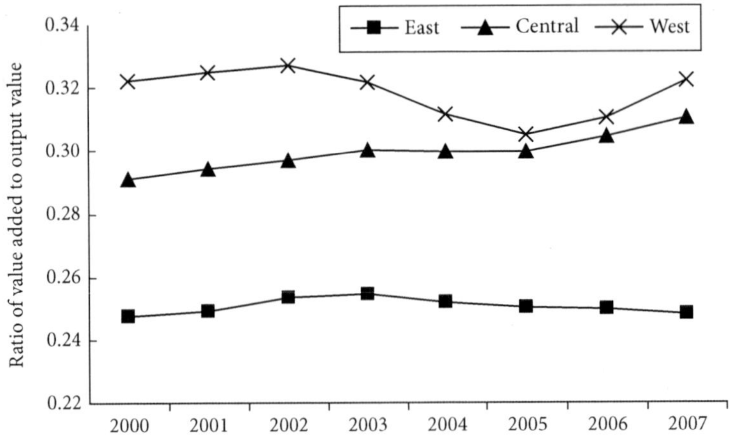

FIGURE 15.7 Changes in ratio of value-added of manufacturing by region.

Source: Calculation based on National Survey on Manufacturing.

In conclusion, while there has been a relocation of manufacturing among China's regions, it has not resembled what is expected in the hypothesis of the domestic flying-geese pattern, by which export-oriented and labor-intensive manufacturing agglomerate to the interior regions. This is more an outcome of region-biased investment and energy, chemicals, and other heavy industries-biased investment structure than a reflection on the process of central and western regions carrying on the transferred labor-intensive industries from eastern regions. In the period 1997 to 2007, the eastern province's share in total investment in fixed assets of the whole country declined from 61 percent to 56 percent, while the share of the central provinces increased from 22 percent to 24 percent and that of the western provinces increased from 17 percent to 20 percent. In 2007, of the sources of total investment in fixed assets, the part that came from the state budget accounted for 2.04 percent in the eastern regions, 4.72 percent in the central regions, and 6.37 percent in the western regions. In general, a larger proportion of government-supported investment in fixed assets can be observed in central and western regions.

5 Conclusion and Policy Implications

Consistent with other findings that the Chinese economy is driven more by domestic consumption than by export, this chapter confirms that the employment expansion accompanied by the rapid economic growth has also been induced by domestic production. Furthermore, in response to the newly emerged labor shortage, wages increase, and the consequent revision of comparative advantage since 2004, Chinese industries and enterprises have also adjusted their growth toward a pattern of domestic consumption.

Although this chapter concludes a less dependence of employment on export and a tendency of sectoral and regional adjustments toward further domestic consumption, it does not deny the significance of the involvement in economic globalization in spurring Chinese economic growth. China has been a significant producer of world manufacturing, and trade development has contributed a great deal to its employment expansion. More importantly, the close interplay between the world economy and domestic growth has provided a prices signal for the Chinese economy to follow its comparative advantage, which also benefits the domestic consumption-dominated sector by resources reallocation efficiency. It is also the close link between domestic and external economies that will guide the Chinese economy to adjust its industrial and regional structure in accordance with the dynamic comparative advantage.

First, such an adjustment requires getting rid of the conventional growth pattern, by which the government intervenes in the economic growth and heavily invests in regional development. Instead, the government role is to create a sound investment climate by correcting distortions in prices of production factors and providing a level playing field for all enterprises. While the comparative advantage in labor-intensive industries diminishes, the upgrading raising the Chinese industries to a higher position in the value chain is a gradual process. In order to maintain employment expansion and sustain economic growth, the adjustment should not take place in a radical way. Therefore, industrial transfer among the eastern and the central and western regions should carry on based on the regions' differential endowments of factors of production, so that China can gain more time to accomplish the adjustment.

Second, the structural adjustment requires China continue to be involved in globalization. Globalization is not only a process in which goods and services flow globally, but also, and more and more, a process in which ideas flow across national boundaries (Romer 2010). In the transition from its dual-economy development toward neoclassical growth, China is more and more dependent on globalization centered on idea flows in catching up in technological progress, strengthened ability of innovation, and accumulation of human capital. Particularly, as the Chinese industry climbs the ladder of the value chain, the development of human capital-intensive industries will provide more employment opportunities for skilled workers.

NOTES

1. The total fertility rate (TFR) of a population is the average number of children that would be born to a woman over her lifetime: (1) if she were to experience the exact current age-specific fertility rates through her lifetime, and (2) if she were to survive from birth through to the end of her reproductive life. This is obtained by summing the single-year age-specific rates at a given time.
2. China Urban Labor Survey, or CULS, is a series of surveys conducted by the Institute of Population and Labor Economics, Chinese Academy of Social Sciences in 2001, 2005, and 2010. It representatively sampled laborers in urban households and migrant households and surveyed both individual laborers and households in Shanghai, Wuhan, Shenyang, Fuzhou, and Xi'an.

3. According to Lewisian classical theory of economic development, those developing countries characterized by unlimited supply of labor are bound for a process of development of a dual economy. Namely, the modern sector can obtain an endless transformed labor force from the agricultural sector at constant wage rates and form its capital accumulation (Lewis 1954). When the development of the dual economy moves to a stage at which the labor demand of the modern sector exceeds the labor supply originating from the agricultural surplus labor force at the present wages rate, it reaches an important turning point—the Lewis turning point (Lewis 1972).
4. Here, we refer to a large economy in the sense of its regional diversity in terms of per capita GDP, education, infrastructure, and other factors like natural resources (see Cai et al. 2009).

References

Cai, F. and M. Wang. 2010. "Growth and Structural Changes in Employment in Transition China." *Journal of Comparative Economics* 38: 71–81.

Cai, F., M. Wang, and Y. Qu. 2009. "Industrial and Labor Relocations among Chinese Regions," *China Industrial Economics* 8: 5–16.

Cai, F., Y. Du., and M. Wang. 2009. "Crisis or Opportunities: China's Response to Global Financial Crisis." *Perspective of the World Review* 1 (1): 91–113.

Chenery, H., and M. Syrquin. 1975. *Patterns of Development, 1950–1970*. Oxford: Oxford University Press.

Du, Y., and M. Wang. 2010. "A New Estimation on Rural Surplus Labor." *Guangzhou University Journal* 4: 17–24.

Du, Y., and Y. Qu. 2009. "Labor Compensation, Labor Productivity, and China's Advantage in Manufacturing." *China Industrial Economy* 5: 25–35.

Department of Survey and Statistics, People's Bank of China (DSS-PBC). 2010. "The 5th Monitoring Report on Migrant Workers." In *Report on China's Population and Labor (No. 11): Labor Market Challenges in the Post-crisis Era*, edited by Cai Fang, Beijing: Social Sciences Academic Press (China).

Green, S., and L. Shen. 2011. "China: If Export Growth Rate Falls to Zero." Standard Chartered.

Hu, Y. 2009. "Predictions on Working Age Population of Rural and Urban China." unpublished memo.

Kojima, K. 2000. "The 'Flying Geese' Model of Asian Economic Development: Origin, Theoretical Extensions, and Regional Policy Implications," *Journal of Asian Economics* 11: 375–401.

Lewis, A. 1954. "Economic Development with Unlimited Supplies of Labour." *Manchester School of Economic and Social Studies* 22: 139–191.

Lewis, A. 1972. "Reflections on Unlimited Labour." In *International Economics and Development*, edited by L. Di Marco, 75–96. New York: Academic.

Okita, S. 1985. "Special Presentation: Prospect of Pacific Economies." In *Pacific Cooperation: Issues and Opportunities*, edited by Korea Development Institute, 18–29. Report of the Fourth Pacific Economic Cooperation Conference, Seoul, Korea, April 29 to May 1.

Rawski, T. G. 2001. "What's Happening to China's GDP Statistics?" *China Economic Review* 12 (4): 298–302.

Roberts, K., R. Connelly, Z. Xie, and Z. Zheng. 2004. "Patterns of Temporary Labour Migration of Rural Women from Anhui and Sichuan." *China Journal* 52: 49–70.
Romer, P. 2010. "Which Parts of Globalization Matter for Catch-up Growth?" NBER Working Paper, no. 15755. Cambridge, MA: National Bureau of Economic Research.
United Nations. 2009. "The World Population Prospects: The 2008 Revision." http://esa.un.org/unpp/.

CHAPTER 16

The Changing Character of Indian Offshore ICT Services Provision, 1985–2010

BALAJI PARTHASARATHY

1 Introduction

This chapter examines the emergence of India as the world's biggest exporter of information and communication technology (ICT) services (primarily software) (World Bank 2009). More specifically, the chapter examines the rise of India as an offshore production center for ICT services between 1985 and 2010 (Tables 16.1 and 16.2), especially with reference to the United States, which provided the market for 63 percent of India's ICT service exports in 2009–2010 (RBI 2011).[1]

Blinder (2006) offers two explanations for the emergence of a country such as India as an offshore producer of ICT services. First, improvements in technology, and their proliferation, ensure that anything which can be digitized and "delivered electronically over long distances with little or no degradation in quality" (114) will become tradable. This applies especially to impersonal services that do not require face-to-face contact, or do not involve issues of trust, or other location-specific attributes. Indeed, as section 2 describes, the origins of offshore development of ICT services in India can be traced to technological changes that led to growth in demand for software worldwide, and to the institutional conditions of software production, which led to the globalization of the software industry.

Second, offshoring is also a case of comparative advantage at work. Section 3 discusses how policy changes in the 1980s enabled India to capitalize on its low-cost but skilled labor to facilitate the enabled the country's entry into the international division of labor of the software industry. Initially, however, the industry in India was little more than

Table 16.1 India's information and communication technology services revenues and exports (in US$ millions) 1985–86 to 2008–09)

Year	Revenues in Millions of US$ (a)	Exports as % of Revenues	% Share of STPs	as % of all Exports
1985–86	81	29.63		
1986–87	108	36.11		
1987–88	130	40.00		
1988–89	160	41.88		
1989–90	197	50.76		
1990–91	243	52.78		
1991–92	304	53.95		
1992–93	388	57.99	8.0	
1993–94	560	58.93	12.0	
1994–95	787	62.13	16.0	1.9
1995–96	1253	60.18	29.0	2.4
1996–97	1841	59.75	46.0	3.2
1997–98	3011	58.42	54.0	4.9
1998–99	4069	63.90	58.0	7.6
1999–00	5611	70.61	68.0	10.6
2000–01	8386	74.14	70.7	13.8
2001–02	10073	76.79	80.9	17.0
2002–03	12324	79.29	80.7	18.0
2003–04	16700	77.25	88.4	20.2
2004–05	22500	78.67	92.3	21.2
2005–06	30300	77.89	97.0	22.9
2006–07	39300	79.13		24.6
2007–08	52000	77.69		
2008–09	58700	78.88		

Notes: (a) The export figures will differ from those in Table 1b since NASSCOM includes revenues of subsidiaries abroad in export income, whereas the Reserve Bank of India does not (see Note c in Table 1b).

Source: www.nasscom.org; National Association of Software and Service Companies (NASSCOM), *Indian Software Directory, 1993–94*. NASSCOM; National Association of Software and Service Companies (NASSCOM). 1992. *Indian Software Directory, 1992*. NASSCOM; STP data from www.stpi.soft.net.

"bodyshopping," the practice of providing inexpensive onsite (i.e., at customer locations overseas) labor on an hourly basis, for low value added programming services. But subsequent policy measures, especially the provision of data communication infrastructure, paved the way for organizational innovations and India's rise to prominence as a provider of low-cost but high-quality offshore software services in the 1990s.

The turn of the millennium witnessed a further transformation in the activities of firms in India, as section 4 points out. Thanks, ironically, to a global slump in demand for

Table 16.2 India's information and communications technology service exports (in US$ millions), with percentage break-up of subsectors, 2007–08 to 2009–10)

	Software Services	Product Development	Engineering Services (a)	BPO Services (b)	Total Exports	Subsidiaries abroad ©
2007–08	67.2%	9.4%	3.2%	20.2%	34,481	6,297
2008–09	64.0%	8.9%	4.1%	22.9%	36,636	8,835
2009–10	60.7%	8.2%	7.6%	23.5%	38,753	9,223

Note: (a) refers to Embedded Solutions; Product Design Engineering (mechanical and electrical but excluding software); Architectural and other technical services; any other services; (b) refers to Customer Interaction Services; Finance and Accounting, Auditing, Book keeping and Tax Consulting services; Human Resource Administration; Legal Services (including IP management); Business and Corporate research; Medical Transcription; Content Development, Management and Publishing; any other service:. (c) counted by NASSCOM as exports but not by the RBI under the General Agreement on Services

Source: RBI (2009, 2010, 2011).

ICTs, firms in India firms began to provide a wider range of ICT services than software services. Despite the slump, Indian ICT service exports grew as customers worldwide attempted to control costs by outsourcing not just software but a range of ICT-enabled services, ranging from research and development (R&D) and engineering services at one end of the skill spectrum to business processes at the other. This is also explained by Blinder (2009: 69) who, after constructing an offshorability index, to estimate the relative ease of offshoring 291 US occupations from 2004, declares that "contrary to conventional wisdom, the more offshorable occupations are not low-end jobs, whether measured by wages or by education. The correlation between skill and offshorability is almost zero."[2]

With offshorable jobs no longer corresponding to conventional distinctions between high-skilled and low-skilled work, conventional solutions, such as increasing investment in education, are no longer sufficient to deal with the employment challenge that offshoring poses to affluent countries (Blinder 2006). The policy uncertainty has, not surprisingly, generated rancorous political rhetoric in countries such as the United States, with calls for trade protection.[3] However, this chapter will argue that amidst the nationalist political rhetoric on one hand and calls by liberal economists, such as Blinder, to allow the benefits of comparative advantage to unfold, signs of other forces influencing offshoring are being overlooked. There are two aspects to this argument.

First, offshoring is not quite the zero-sum game that political rhetoric often makes it out to be. Although the OECD (2005) estimated that 20 percent of jobs were potentially vulnerable to offshoring in Europe, Australia, Canada, and the United States, a subsequent OECD (2007: 8) study concluded that, "in the service sector new job creation offsets job destruction from all causes combined, including offshoring."[4] Indian firms are also beginning to contribute to the job creation as the political barriers they face in their main markets are compounded by barriers at home, which inhibit improvements to the educational system and limit access to relevant skills, to expand their offshoring businesses. Such barriers have forced firms to explore diverse strategies, including locating in or near their main markets. Thus, instead of a unique spatial outcome, offshoring is leading to multiple trajectories.

These trajectories are explored in section 5 which presents the case of Infosys, a firm that was founded three decades ago and has since become India's third-largest ICT services exporter.[5] In many ways, Infosys exemplifies the rise of the Indian ICT services industry. For instance, as a firm that mostly offers labor-intensive custom software services, it relied on bodyshopping before shifting to offshore software development. The focus of this section is specifically on Infosys Labs, which was established in 2000 to create new markets based on new technologies. The means to do this is co-creation, or working with consortia of universities, research institutions, and other firms to identify how ICTs can be exploited to address problems of relevance to businesses. With co-creation, Infosys's emphasis has shifted from working with specific customers to integrating itself across an ecosystem. The formation of Infosys Labs notwithstanding, the ecosystem for a service provider which earns most of its revenues from non-Indian markets is global. This is reflected in an offshore development strategy that is no longer confined to India. The firm now has more global development centers overseas than in India, either close to or in its main markets.

The second aspect of the growth in offshoring is that it is not merely about the unfolding of comparative advantage provided by cost or skills as technological changes make more services tradable. New market opportunities, with characteristics that are unlike those in affluent countries, are emerging in India and in other locations where work is offshored, altering the raison d'être of offshoring. Meeting the product or service needs of hitherto neglected users and customers often demands spatial proximity to them and it entails working with partners. This aspect is the subject of section 6, and the case is Cisco Systems, a multinational corporation (MNC) from the United States, which first came to India in the mid-1990s seeking engineering talent to develop its networking products. Over time, however, the firm realized that to take advantage of rapidly growing markets in India and other emerging economies it had to create relevant products and services by forming local partnerships with domain experts and systems integrators. As a global Cisco evolved, the physical center of Cisco's expansion in India was a Cisco Globalization Center East in Bangalore that mirrored many headquarters functions. Thus, Bangalore is no longer only a place for software development or engineering, but it has grown to become a control center for global markets.

The chapter will conclude by drawing on the Indian experience as an ICT services exporter to emphasize the need for a nuanced, evolutionary understanding of offshoring, not least because the analytical and policy implications go beyond issues of skills and wages. Broadly, placing the burden of explanation for offshoring on arguments of cost minimization and the exploitation of low-wage, low-skilled labor unduly emphasizes absolute surplus extraction, ignoring that relative surplus extraction through technical innovation is the "general basis for accumulation in the capitalist mode of production" and consequently that, "relocation can be seen as a specific response which arises in circumstances when there are major obstacles to increasing relative surplus value" (Jenkins 1984: 43).

2 The technological context for India's emergence as a software producer[6]

The personal computer (PC), networking, and internet revolutions of, respectively, the 1970s, 1980s, and the 1990s led to a proliferation of computer usage in various economic sectors, creating a huge demand for software (Campbell-Kelly 2003). However, while automated, capital-intensive operations permit the mass production of high-quality hardware, software production, in comparison, has remained a craft-like, labor-intensive affair, plagued by uneven productivity and quality, relying more on trial and error to achieve its goals (Brooks 1995). The result is that software development is notoriously prone to "bugs," delays, and cost overruns.

To overcome this "software bottleneck," there has evolved a discipline of software engineering, along the lines of industrial engineering, to simultaneously automate and rationalize software development (Cusumano 2004). But the quality and productivity improvements delivered by software engineering have thus far been limited, supporting Brooks's (1995) contention that there is no "silver bullet" for the bottleneck. Further, Kraft's (1977) prediction that efforts to manage the software development process would lead to a division of labor between mental and manual labor has not quite happened. Thus, overcoming the bottleneck has required the deployment of more skilled software professionals.

Alongside the demand generated by the growing use of new software since the 1970s, there remained older software that demanded maintenance and reengineering.[7] Discarding older systems is often not easy as they embody years of valuable business information and experience. One aspect of maintenance and reengineering is format problems, such as those involving dates, of which the year 2000 (Y2K) problem received the widest publicity.[8] Many such time-specific, labor-intensive demands, and the general expansion in the use of software, created a huge demand for skilled labor in the 1990s, especially in advanced industrial countries that use ICTs extensively.

In the United States, for instance, the question of whether or not there was a shortage of skilled labor was controversial, though there was agreement about the shortage of people with specific skills, such as those familiar with old code written for mainframe systems (Koch 1998). Faced with a shortage of people with specific skills, and the pressure to limit the costs of labor-intensive projects, firms in the United States were forced to look elsewhere for the appropriate skill-cost combination. A 1992 survey sponsored by the World Bank found that US and European vendors ranked India as the top choice among the countries able to offer this combination for onsite and offshore software development, ahead of Israel, Ireland, Mexico, Singapore, China, Hungary, and the Philippines (InfoTech Consulting 1992: DA16).

Despite widespread illiteracy in the country, Indian education policies managed to create a large pool of skilled labor that, in a relatively slow-growing economy, suffered from underemployment if not unemployment, thus offering a ready resource. One indicator of skills availability is the annual output of graduates with a bachelor's degree in engineering. This output grew from 247 at the time of independence in 1947 to 237,000 in 2006 (Banerjee and Muley 2009: 9).[9] The colonial legacy also meant that this labor was mostly educated in English. India's most pointed advantage came, however, not merely from the availability of low-cost, English-speaking labor but from the skills embodied in it.

For reasons explained in the next section, access to computers until the 1980s was limited. With the growth in computer manufacture and usage in the 1980s, Unix became the operating system of choice. As the government undertook limited computerization of its activities, it played a role by encouraging the use of Unix. This emerging market encouraged innovations in the design of Unix-based hardware as firms obtained Unix source code and modified it to run on machines they designed (Heeks 1996). It is impossible to overemphasize the importance of familiarity with Unix. It was developed initially at AT&T Bell Labs in 1969 as a multiuser operating system to provide a comfortable programming environment, but its use spread rapidly as liberal licensing to universities led to the collaborative development of a truly open system, various versions of which were widely adopted by the world's leading computer vendors (Salus 1994). As circumstances forced Indian programmers to adopt Unix,

> India entered the 1990s in a position of special advantage. Indian programmers are not only well educated and English-speaking, but out of necessity they're keenly focussed on client/server or multiuser solutions for PCs running DOS (with Netware) or Unix—just the kinds of solutions that US and European companies are rushing to embrace. (Udell 1993: 56)

3 Responses to Global Opportunities: The Rise of Offshore Software Production

The availability of the necessary skill-cost advantage will not automatically guarantee the profitable exploitation of a global opportunity without a supportive socio-economic environment for firms. Thus, for instance, when India established the Department of Electronics (DoE; since November 2000 the Ministry of Information Technology, MIT) in 1971 to formulate electronics policy, India's electronics production was larger than that of South Korea (Sridharan 1996). But a decade later, Korean production and exports dwarfed India's. The DoE's domination by a scientific community committed to self-sufficiency and self-reliance, within a broader, state-dominated, autarkic, import-substitution-led industrialization (ISI) strategy pursued since the 1950s, proved inimical to innovation and entrepreneurship. Under this policy regime, there was no Indian software industry to speak of either (Subramanian 1992).

In the early 1980s, India's relatively poor economic record led to cautious efforts to liberalize the policy regime to encourage private investment and trade (Sridharan 1996). This opportunity was seized upon by a group of technologically and commercially pragmatic bureaucrats, who had taken leadership at the DoE and were keen that the globalization of the software industry did not bypass India. A consequence was the Computer Policy of November 1984, which, besides easing the local manufacture and availability of computers, recognized software as an "industry," making it eligible for investment allowance and other incentives. It also lowered duties on software imports and made software exports a priority.

The Computer Software Export, Development and Training Policy of December 1986 explicitly aimed at increasing India's share of world software production. The means to do this was the "flood in, flood out" feature: firms in India were provided liberal access to global technologies to encourage "thousands of small software companies in the country and thereby increasing export as well as local development" (Dataquest 1987: 87). Industry was to be independent, with the government stepping in only to provide infrastructure and to play a promotional role. Overall, this policy was an explicit rejection of Indian ISI and the ideology of self-reliance in the software sector.

Despite these policy initiatives, exporting in the 1980s typically involved little more than bodyshopping. The practice had its advantages and limitations. On one hand, it meant "input-less exports," requiring only a contact overseas, a little finance, and the names of local programmers who could be hired and sent onsite (Heeks 1996). The drawback, however, was an underutilization of the skills of well-trained engineers, many of whom tended quit to seek more challenging and better-paying jobs once sent overseas. The high turnover only reinforced the tendency of Indian firms to compete on low costs rather than being able to fall back on a repository of technical and managerial expertise acquired from previous projects.

Although bodyshopping seems like a quick-buck strategy, there were not too many other options for firms from a country that had hitherto not merited any consideration as a source of ICT products. Banerjee and Duflo's (2000) study of 230 projects across 125 firms in India shows that reputation matters in software contracting, even after controlling for project, firm, and client characteristics. While Indian engineers had the necessary technical skills, they were trained in a closed economy. Onsite services provided exposure to market trends, management processes, and socially specific communication protocols, besides emerging technologies.

The official encouragement given to bodyshopping reflected a limited understanding of the industry among policy makers: software was widely perceived as being "high tech" without adequate distinction made between the different stages of production or the corresponding value added. According to Sen (1994), amidst the euphoria following the growth in software exports in the 1980s, arrogance and ignorance encouraged the opinion that the software industry did not need much policy support.

Paving the way for a better understanding of the industry, and policy support, was a shift in approach to policy making. Based on inputs from the industry which, in 1988, formed the National Association of Software and Services Companies (NASSCOM), subsequent policy measures tried to promote the industry more proactively. The clearest instance of this was the establishment, in 1990, of the Software Technology Parks (STPs). As export zones dedicated to the software industry, the STPs offered data communication facilities and financial incentives, such as tax-free export earnings, that firms could use to offer offshore services—that is, service provision from India—instead of having to work at customer sites overseas.[10]

In 1991, the year after the STPs were established, a balance of payments crisis induced a major shift in economic policies, including devaluation of the rupee, trade liberalization and duty rationalization, openness to foreign investment, and a new industrial policy that removed entry barriers for new firms, a process that is still under way.[11] Even as these economy-wide changes benefited the software industry, many sector-specific policy changes also emerged from constant interaction with the industry, especially NASSCOM. Examples include income tax exemption on profits from service exports in 1992; elimination of import duties on software by 1997; and permission to grant employee stock options linked to American depository receipts (ADR) or global depository receipts (GDR) in 1998.

The shift to offshore services in a more liberal economic environment marked the beginning of a new relationship between the Indian software industry and global markets. According to Sen's (1994) analysis of quarterly export growth, between 1987 and 1992–93, a linear equation provides the best fit for the growth. From 1992–93 (until 1994, the last year for which Sen had data), however, an exponential equation provides a better fit. Although Sen had insufficient data to determine if it was a long-term trend, he projected that if exports maintained the exponential trajectory, they would reach $630 million by 1997. Since actual exports in 1996–97 were $1.1 billion (Table 16.1), there was clearly a change in the growth characteristics of Indian software exports.

The change in growth characteristics was a result of firms capitalizing on the policy changes since the 1980s, and the availability of the necessary skills and data communication facilities, to pioneer a "global offshore delivery model" in offshore development centers (ODCs). The ODCs replicated the infrastructure, technology, training programs, quality processes, productivity tools, and methodologies of the customer workplace and brought professionals under one roof, instead of having them scattered at customer sites across the world. For instance, firms adopted industry-wide certification norms, such as the ISO-9001/9000-3 standards prescribed by the International Standards Organization and the Software Engineering Institute's five-level Capability Maturity Model (SEI-CMM) to codify quality procedures in the development process. By June 2002, eighty-five firms were certified at level 5, the highest level of the SEI-CMM, compared with forty-two in the rest of the

Table 16.3 Sources of India's software export revenues, 1990–2003 (as a percentage of export revenues)

Year	Onsite services	Offshore services	Products and packages
1990	90.00	5.00	5.00
1993–94	62.01	30.05	7.94
1994–95	60.90	29.59	9.51
1995–96	60.32	31.63	8.05
1996–97	58.69	30.21	11.10
1997–98	59.00	32.20	8.80
1998–99	58.18	33.91	7.91
1999–2000	57.26	34.69	8.05
2000–01	56.09	38.62	5.29
2001–02	45.21	50.69	4.10
2002–03	38.95	57.90	3.15

Note: Data for 2002–03 is an estimate.

Source: www.nasscom.org; National Association of Software and Service Companies (NASSCOM). 2001. *Indian IT and Software Services Directory, 2001.* NASSCOM.

world, with Polaris Software being the first company in the world to obtain CMMi level 5 certification.[12]

According to Arora and Asundi (1999), following a well-defined and documented development process improves the ability of firms to estimate and manage the time and resources required for a project, helping them bid for larger projects, thereby expanding business. Although they conclude that the relationship between certification and better rates is not very robust, getting bigger projects is a route to obtaining turnkey contracts that are more profitable. Obtaining turnkey contracts forces firms to manage a wider range of tasks than just programming and take responsibility for the overall project schedule, quality, and productivity, in contrast to bodyshopping, which is little more than résumé selling. Further, by having most employees under one roof, offshore development also helped firms build a repository of knowledge to compete for subsequent projects.

Apart from the shift to offshore services by large Indian firms, the liberal economic climate of the 1990s also witnessed an influx of MNCs to establish ODCs to take advantage of the STPs and to capitalize on Indian skills. As ODCs proved popular among Indian firms and MNCs, the share of offshore services in software exports increased from 5 percent in 1990 to 38.62 percent in 2000–2001 (see Table 16.3). The popularity of STPs within the industry is also reflected in the growth of STP centers from three to forty-eight between 1990 and 2007; and the share of software exports passing through STPs increased from 8.0 percent in 1992–1993 to 97 percent in 2006–2007 (Table 16.1).

Table 16.4 International trade in software services (by mode of supply)

Year	Mode 1	Mode 2	Mode 3	Mode 4
2007–08	60.4%	0.6%	13.9%	25.1%
2008–09	56.3%	0.1%	16.8%	26.8%
2009–10	64.6%	0.0%	17.6%	17.8%

Notes: (a) Mode 1 refers to Cross Border Supply, Mode 2 to Consumption Abroad, Mode 3 to Commercial Presence, Mode 4 to Presence of Natural Persons (b) Mode 1 can be considered the equivalent of offshore service provision, Mode 3 as revenues from subsidiaries abroad, and Mode 4 as onsite service provision.

Source: RBI (2009, 2010, 2011).

4 The Limits of Organizational Innovation and the Broadening of Service Provision

Despite the organizational innovations and the transformations in the Indian ICT services industry in the 1990s, the industry was characterized by the dominance of exports and the near absence of innovative technical or product offerings. These two characteristics were intertwined. Although the availability of skilled labor, at relatively low wages, confers an advantage in terms of development costs, the distance from final markets meant that Indian firms were unable to react quickly with innovative products to meet the emerging needs of users. Despite the instantaneous access which modern data communication infrastructure provides to distant markets, the majority of Indian firms were stuck at the lower end of the business because the knowledge required to develop innovative products is often tacit and difficult to convey over long distances. Evidence from the US packaged-software industry shows how the local market matters. Over time, the industry has drifted gradually from regions where the computer manufacturing industry is dominant to regions with a concentration of the leading firms in user industries (Egan 1997).

In the case of the Indian industry, this was reflected in the slowdown in the shift to offshore services: while there was an increase in the share of offshore revenues in the early 1990s, from 5 percent to 30 percent, with the commissioning of the STPs, offshore revenues increased by just 8.41 percent between 1996–1997 and 2000–2001 (Table 16.3), despite the number of STPs doubling from six to a dozen. One factor that was crucial to this was access to the US market, especially through the H-1B visa program. This program was established by the Immigration Act of 1990 to enable the employment, for up to six years, of workers in a specialty occupation which requires the theoretical and practical application of knowledge requiring completion of a specific course of higher

Table 16.5 US admissions under temporary visas (H-1B and L-1), 1992–2009

	Worldwide admissions		Indian admissions (%)		India's global rank	
Year	H-1B	L-1	H-1B	L-1	H-1B	L-1
1992	110,193		7.48		3	
1994	104,889		16.16		1	
1996	144,458	140,457	20.24	1.61	1	13
1998	240,947	203,255	25.96	1.90	1	12
1999	302,326	234,443	28.12	2.63	1	10
2000	355,605	294,658	28.81	4.05	1	7
2001	384,191	320,480	27.19	4.85	1	7
2002	370,490	313,699	21.89	6.51	1	4
2003	360,498	298,054	21.07	7.30	1	3
2004	386,821	314,484	21.60	7.36	1	3
2005	407,418	312,144	25.13	9.12	1	3
2006	431,853	320,829	29.11	10.41	1	1
2007	461,730	363,536	34.14	14.16	1	1
2008	409,619	382,776	37.77	16.50	1	1
2009	339,243	333,386	36.26	16.36	1	1

Source: *Yearbook of Immigration Statistics*, US Department of Homeland Security, various years available at http://www.dhs.gov/files/statistics/publications/yearbook.shtm

education.[13] As the program was used extensively by Indian firms and the US ICT sector, Indians became the largest beneficiaries of H-1B admissions (and later L-1 too) (Table 16.5) and the program itself came to be widely identified as an "Indian program" (Alarcon 1998).[14]

The turn of the millennium, however, led to a qualitative transformation in the activities of firms in India. Facilitating this shift, ironically, was the global slump in demand for ICTs following overinvestment in the 1990s.[15] Despite this slump, the Indian ICT services industry and exports continued to grow after 2001 (Table 16.1 and 16.2) and there was also a gradual increase in offshore activity over the decade (Table 16.4). Enabling the growth were the efforts by firms worldwide to control costs by outsourcing not just software but also a range of ICT-enabled services, ranging from R&D and engineering services at one end of the skill spectrum to business processes, such as voice-based customer support centers (call centers) or medical transcription, at the other (Srinivas and Jayashankar 2002).

Facilitating the enhanced outsourcing in changed global economic conditions were changing technological and labor market conditions. For instance, one segment of R&D services that firms in India entered was embedded systems.[16] Despite the near absence of semiconductor manufacturing capabilities in India, the emergence of a new division of labor in the semiconductor industry made it possible for firms to offer their expertise globally in embedded systems. The vertically integrated firms that used to characterize the industry have given way to disintegrated firms occupying niches along a production continuum (Mathews and Cho 2000). This continuum ranges from the pure play foundries at one end, which offer contract manufacture, to design houses at the other, which rely on other firms to manufacture the chips they design. Firms in India took advantage of the changed organization of the industry by partnering with foundries elsewhere to produce their designs (Parthasarathy and Aoyama 2006).

Designing embedded systems requires engineers who are classically trained in the domain of application, say telecommunications. "It is very difficult to replicate a toll-quality speech codec or a radio modem with commodity programmers" (Lee 2000: 19). Obtaining more skilled labor became possible thanks to a deepening of the local labor market which helped firms in India seize the design opportunity. Following the demand slump in the United States in 2001, India's share of H-1B admissions declined (Table 16.5). Singh (2003) cites a NASSCOM estimate that 35,000 professionals returned to India, mostly from the United States. Of the returnees, an estimated 70 percent were H-1B visa holders, while another 10–15 percent had been abroad for at least ten years. These people returned not only because of shrinking international opportunities but also because they saw India as a place for innovation (Krishnadas 2003).[17] Even if they did not return permanently, many began to operate simultaneously from the United States and India, as "argonauts," to provide channels of technology and market access that did not exist previously (Saxenian 2006).

The growing importance of high-valued-added services, including segments such as embedded systems, is evident in the 15.8 percent contribution of product development and engineering services to exports in 2010 (Table 16.2). At the other end of the skill spectrum, BPO services grew to account for 23.5 percent of exports. It is against the backdrop of these changes to Indian ICT service exports, that the next two sections examine the evolution of Infosys and Cisco.

5 Infosys: from Services to Infosys Labs

Founded with US$250 in 1981 by seven people, the Bangalore-based Infosys grew to a US$4.8 billion firm in 2009–2010, employing 113,796 employees, mostly offering custom software development, maintenance, reengineering, ICT infrastructure services and business process outsourcing.[18] From relying on bodyshopping to enter the international division of labor to the subsequent shift to offshore development, from being the first Indian firm to list on NASDAQ in the United States in 1999, to being widely recognized and admired for its record, in many ways Infosys exemplifies the rise of the Indian ICT services industry.

But, since the 1990s, Infosys has faced the growth pressures of a ICT services firm that deployed labor-intensive processes in mature technologies and markets. As client-server technology gave way to internet technologies, customers began to ask how best they could take advantage of the new technologies rather than merely seeking help for something that they either already understood or were doing. In other words, while technology was available to anybody, the critical issue was how best to exploit it. As a firm that is in the business of helping customers exploit technology—believing that technology is the key differentiator, even if not the only one—Infosys had to identify emerging technologies, select the ones with promise, and devise innovative applications of those technologies for customers. Thus, there was a need to prepare for customers and their context with the necessary IP. In other words, instead of being a "reactive problem solver," the firm had to be a "proactive problem definer." It was such reasoning that led to Infosys Labs (until recently, Software Technology Labs, or SETLabs) being established in 2000, to focus on market creation based on new technologies instead of delivering products and services with existing technologies like the rest of Infosys. Infosys Labs aims to make itself an integral part of the service chain that firms depend to run more efficiently and to deploy new products and services.

There are three aspects to Infosys Labs' working with customers to help them reinvent themselves and stay competitive. One aspect is building "tomorrow's enterprise," which is about the changes that organizations should make as they decide on their strategies. The second aspect is operations, where Infosys Labs ensures the process efficiency of, say, BPO organizations, by linking business goals, predictive models, and day-to-day activities with real-time data.[19] The third aspect is innovation to help customers develop offerings with their clientele in mind. This is not merely about developing the products or the information systems that customers want; instead it is about "product engineering," or helping firms take a product from R&D to the market.

The technological underpinnings of product engineering at Infosys Labs are cloud computing, mobility, and business analytics.[20] These provide a horizontal foundation (middleware) on which diverse domains such as banking, insurance, retail, manufacturing, and healthcare can erect their layers. For instance, mobile banking[21] solutions are built on top of the platform mConnect, which is a context-aware, real-time enterprise middleware that enables mobile services for websites and eCommerce platforms.[22] The idea is that customers from domains such as banking should not spend their resources looking at mobility; rather, they are better off devising ways to exploit mobility in their business. While Infosys Labs provides the technology foundation, it works with consultants from the industry business units of Infosys for domain expertise.

In its efforts to build "tomorrow's enterprises," Infosys Labs has increasingly relied on the concept of "co-creation," whose premise is that "innovation is no longer possible within the four walls" of any organization but lies at the intersection of disciplines, technologies, domains, markets, and people.[23] As part of the co-creation process, Infosys Labs runs workshops with customers to identify problems of interest and to seek out new initiatives and product ideas. In other words, Infosys is increasingly trying to make innovation central to the conversations it is having with its customers. Indeed, while a majority of the 600 people with Infosys Labs are in India, in Bangalore, Hyderabad, and Pune, up to 25 percent of its staff is typically traveling to interact with customers on select projects that Infosys undertakes. The interaction is to understand the market and the issues that customers face, especially when they are doing something for the first time, and to identify possibilities for IP generation.

Co-creation is not merely a relationship between Infosys Labs and the customer, since it is often difficult for the firm to meet all the needs of a customer. Instead, it is also about working with universities, research institutes, and consortia to identify how ICTs can be exploited to address problems of relevance to businesses. One such consortium is the Indo-UK Advanced Technology Center, to establish next-generation networks, systems, and services, as the support infrastructure to enable the digital economy of both countries, in domains such as education, entertainment, and health.[24] The initiative brings together universities and industrial partners, including small and medium enterprises, in both countries. British Telecom is the lead industry partner on the British side, while it is Infosys for India.

Working in consortia helps address many challenges. In engineering terms, problems can be solved by combining various technologies to add value with new applications. Organizationally, what characterizes co-creation is that there is no template to define the roles of partners a priori. Instead, roles best suited to the context and effort are decided only after all the partners have had a say. This is a departure from arm's-length outsourcing, where a customer can adopt a take-it-or-leave-it attitude. With co-creation, all partners have a role to fulfill and the nonperformance of one partner affects everyone. Thus, for Infosys, the focus has shifted from the mere integration of applications within the firm, to the integration of applications with those of another firm, to integration across an ecosystem. It is developing the ability to nimbly address the needs of a dynamic ecosystem that Infosys Labs considers its ultimate goal.

The formation of Infosys Labs notwithstanding, the ecosystem for a service provider which earned 98.8 percent of its revenues from non-Indian markets in 2009–2010 is not confined to the country, much less Bangalore.[25] Thus, since the late 1990s, the firm's offshore development strategy has no longer been limited to India (Nair 1998). By 2010, Infosys and Infosys BPO had sixty-three global development and delivery centers of which only thirty were in India.[26] The others were distributed as follows: eleven in the United States, six in China, three in Australia, two each in Mexico and the United Kingdom, and one each in Brazil, Canada, the Czech Republic, France, Japan, Mauritius, Philippines, Poland, and Singapore. The opening of centers in countries such as Mexico or Poland can be viewed as "near-shoring," to be close to critical markets.[27]

The changing geography of Infosys's operations points to at least three changes to the nature and context of offshoring. First, opening centers in relatively high-cost locations, such as Europe, Japan, and North America, indicates that Infosys is no longer merely a provider of low-cost services. Further, the strategy of near-shoring indicates that outsourcing to a firm of Indian origin does not have to mean that work will be offshored to India. Second, the success of Infosys has attracted attention which, in the United States, has led to shrill political rhetoric and the tightening of immigration rules.[28] During the discussion to pass a Customs and Border Protection Law in August 2010,[29] Senator Charles Schumer referred to "chop shops that outsource good, high-paying American technology jobs to lower wage, temporary immigrant workers from other countries.

These are companies such as Infosys. But it will not affect the high-tech companies such as Intel or Microsoft that play by the rules and recruit workers in America."[30] Thus, opening development centers in its largest market is as much a means of coping with the political opposition to outsourcing as it is an economic decision.

A third reason has, ironically, to do with inadequate labor. Even as the direct employment provided by the Indian ICT services industry grew from 284,000 in 1999–2000 (DIT 2005: 2) to 2.26 million in 2009–10 (DIT 2011: 2),[31] it has had to contend with an education system that has emphasized quantity over quality. As a result, India's

> colleges and universities, with just a few exceptions, have become large, underfunded, ungovernable institutions. At many of them, politics has intruded into campus life, influencing academic appointments and decisions across levels. Underinvestment in libraries, information technology, laboratories, and classrooms makes it very difficult to provide top-quality instruction or engage in cutting-edge research. (Altbach 2005)

This is also an apt description of engineering education. Despite graduating a large number of engineers, the output is of uneven quality, and weak links between academia and industry limit the relevance of graduates' skills and market needs. This has forced many firms, especially in the ICT sector, to launch in-house training programs to provide new hires with the necessary competences for the job and to offer course material to colleges to enhance the relevance of their offerings for the industry (Froumien et al. 2007). Thus, in 2004, Infosys launched CampusConnect "to architect the education experience."[32] Another concern is that too few of India's engineers go on to obtain master's and doctoral degrees to support the research needs of the industry. For instance, in 2006, master's and doctoral degrees awarded were only 8.4 percent and 0.4 percent of the number of bachelor's degrees awarded; the corresponding figures for the United States were 52.6 percent and 11.3 percent (Banerjee and Muley 2009: 30).

Infosys is not alone is spatially reorganizing itself to deal with these issues. By 2010, Indian firms had more than 400 delivery/development centers outside India and a presence in more than 200 cities across 52 countries (DIT 2011: 2). A case in point is India's largest ICT services firm, Tata Consultancy Services (TCS), which also has delivery/development centers across the world.[33] For instance, in the United States, the firm has an innovation center in Cincinnati, working on product design and process modeling in close proximity to its large Midwestern clients. For TCS, the center represents "the bridgehead of its ambitions to go beyond being merely an outsourced back-office and coding shop and take on such consultancy giants as IBM, Hewlett-Packard (HP) and Accenture on their home turf" (*Economist* 2011b: 72). The center employs 450 (expected to grow to 1000), mostly US citizens, allowing the firm to skirt the difficulties of obtaining visas for Indians and to employ talented US graduates to overcome skills shortages. Similarly, by 2010–2011, 31 percent of the employees working across the more than seventy global delivery centers of Wipro, the second-largest Indian ICT service firm, were non-Indians, a share that is projected to rise to 50 percent by 2015.[34]

6 Cisco: Globalization Center East

Cisco first came to India in 1995 to establish a representative office to provide data communications solutions to customers.[35] In 1999, the firm established a Global Engineering Development Center in Bangalore with an investment of US$20 million to develop and test Cisco IOS(R) software, network management software, application specific integrated circuits (ASICs), and other technologies like VOIP (voice over internet protocol).[36] This center was in addition to the joint development centers established in partnership with Wipro and Infosys in Bangalore, HCL Technologies in Chennai, and Zensar Technologies in Pune. For Cisco, like most MNCs, India was, above all, a source of engineering talent to develop its products.

Over time, however, the firm realized that there were transitions taking place as its markets were growing primarily in Brazil, China, India, and other emerging economies. The firm also realized that if these were the markets of the future it had to create relevant products and services. Although Cisco was present in many of these countries, the pressure to understand what customers in new markets needed, and what would work for them, forced it to reconsider its globalization strategy. Cisco is not alone in this regard. As Aoyama and Parthasarathy (2012) point out, many other MNCs such as Microsoft and Hewlett Packard have also moved to India to seek and understand new markets.

Central to the "globalization vision" of Cisco was an effort to redefine itself as a provider of products and services of relevance to various markets by drawing on its strength which, as Gawer and Cusumano (2002) describe, is its platform leadership in networking technologies. Emblematic of this shift is the promotion of Smart + Connected Communities, a territorial concept that integrates various infrastructural and social functions:

> The foundation for the city of the future will be the network and the information it carries, enabling the delivery of vital services from transportation utilities and security to entertainment, education, and healthcare. Everything will be connected, intelligent, and green: from office buildings and appliances to hospitals and schools. Citizens and businesses will enjoy unprecedented levels of collaboration, productivity, and economic growth without compromising the environment. Managing and operating such a smart, connected community will be efficient, coordinated, and secure.[37]

The provision of such services on an open-architecture platform requires partnerships with both domain experts and systems integrators to tie together customer needs.

As the idea of a global Cisco evolved, CEO John Chambers announced an investment of US$1.1 billion in India over three years during a visit to the country in October 2005.[38] Of this, US$750 million was for R&D, training, staffing, and development; US$150 million was to provide leasing and financial solutions to customers and partners; US$100 million was venture capital directed at Indian start-ups; and US$100 million was for customer support operations including establishing spare parts depots and channel development. According to Chambers,

> Cisco chose India as the location from which to expand its globalization vision because India has a highly skilled workforce, supportive government, innovative customers and world-class partners that already have global capabilities.[39]

Typical of Cisco's partnerships in India is the one with Hindustan Construction Company, which is developing Lavasa, a 12,500 acre "live, work, play" city about a three-hour drive from Mumbai.[40] A third partner, Wipro, will use Cisco's platform to design the infrastructure for telecom services for governance and to provide solutions, such as integrated building management systems, physical security requirements, and other on-demand services, for resident and visitors. Similarly, a partnership with the Chennai-based Apollo Hospitals, Asia's largest healthcare provider, is to deliver health care in rural Raichur district, Karnataka, with the Cisco HealthPresence™ Extended Reach technology. The technology uses high-definition audio and video to facilitate end-to-end telemedicine and remote diagnostics.[41] Such partnerships also travel internationally. A case in point is Cisco offering Telepresence—a technology that provides high-definition audio and video conferencing facilities, allowing participants to meet their colleagues, customers, and business partners across a virtual table—to the Westin Tokyo and other hotels belonging to the Starwood Hotels and Resorts group.[42] This offering is made using the networks of Tata Communications.

The physical center of Cisco's expansion in India was a new US$50 million, million square foot campus in Bangalore to house 3000 employees.[43] The new facility was designated as Cisco Globalization Center East in December 2006 and it serves as a "mirror site" to many headquarters functions, including R&D, sales and customer support, and finance. The time difference of twelve and a half hours between San Jose and India allowed the firm to be run twelve hours out of the United States and twelve hours in India. In other words, Bangalore is no longer only a place for software development or engineering. It provides every other function as part of a global team, participating in global work. In the words of chief technology officer Padmasree Warrier, "The Globalization Center in Bangalore is not a center for [the] India market, it is a center for global markets."[44]

Cisco East was established under Wim Elfrink, the firm's first chief globalization officer. Elfrink has been based in India since 2007 and reports to John Chambers. In addition to his corporate role, Elfrink chaired the Confederation of Indian Industry (CII) Steering Committee on Intelligent Urbanization, which in May 2010 recommended a "framework for sustainable urbanization" for India. A number of senior executives moved from San Jose with Elfrink. While many have since returned, others have come to take their place, reflecting the intent of using Bangalore to offer an exposure to what doing business in new markets is about. In this regard, geography also played a role, as India is about a five-hour flight across a region covering a good portion of the firm's future market.

7 Conclusion

India found a place in the international division of labor of the ICT services industry in the 1980s for a combination of reasons. First, while technological changes fueled a demand for software, the labor-intensive character of software development also fueled a demand for skilled labor that advanced industrial economies could not meet. India could seize this window of locational opportunity for the ICT services industry primarily because its education policies had managed to create a large pool of skilled labor that also possessed the much-sought-after Unix skills. The ready availability of this labor pool was reinforced by policy changes in the 1980s that encouraged the growth of the software industry. Initially, however, the industry meant little more than the pursuit of practices of labor arbitrage, or bodyshopping. In the 1990s, policy initiatives in the form of STPs and economic policy changes encouraged offshore development. The economic policy changes since 1991 also made India a more attractive location for MNCs. The 1990s then witnessed the fashioning of a global delivery model, the adoption of which not only led to a growth in exports from India but also allowed firms to get larger and more profitable projects.

Despite the organizational innovations and the changed character of the ICT services industry, offshoring until the 1990s primarily meant that firms were producing *from* India, using factor inputs such as skilled but low-cost labor, infrastructure, and other financial incentives. Besides Infosys, which evolved from practicing bodyshopping in the 1980s, a firm such as Cisco came to India in the 1990s only for the engineering skills; that is, there was limited innovation *in* India. But the turn of the century witnessed a change in the roles as firms in India began to build on outsourcing capabilities to take advantage of a deepening labor market, shifts in the nature and geography of demand and in technology. Crucially, the opportunities for the provision of ICT services were no longer limited to software; instead, they expanded to include R&D and engineering services and BPO services.

Thus it was in 2000 that Infosys established Infosys Labs and Infosys BPO in 2002. Infosys Labs was established so that instead of remaining a builder of low-cost, high-quality software, the firm could be a "proactive problem definer." Although Infosys Labs is not necessarily the source of the technologies it uses, its role is to enhance the combinatorial possibilities of such technologies by working in consortia to help customers develop innovative offerings for their clients. This effort at co-creation not only underscored the idea that innovation is increasingly to be found at the intersection of disciplines, technologies, domains, markets, and people—that is, "innovation is no longer possible within the four walls" of any organization—but it also began to change the role of Infosys. From being just a provider of outsourced ICT services, with a specified role in a transaction, it was moving to become one of many partners in an ecosystem, collectively defining outcomes. Yet, working beyond the boundaries of the firm for a global market meant that the firm had to alter the geographical basis of its activities.

This is evident in the opening of development centers in both near-shore locations and in its main markets.

As a firm such as Infosys (or a Wipro) evolved to become a systems integration partner, it had implications for a Cisco. It facilitated the globalization and redefinition of Cisco as a provider of products and services, especially in emerging markets, by drawing on its strengths in networking technologies. The integration of functions on an open-architecture platform to provide relevant services requires partnerships with both systems integrators and domain experts. Instances of this are Cisco's partnership with the Hindustan Construction Company in the real-estate domain and the alliance with Apollo Hospitals to deliver rural health care. The implication of this shift in approach by Cisco meant that the firm could no longer view India merely as a source of engineering talent with which to address global markets. Thus grew Cisco Globalization Center East, as a functional equivalent, in the eastern hemisphere, of the global headquarters in the western hemisphere.

The Indian experience with ICT services shows that offshoring is an evolutionary phenomenon which does not have a teleological trajectory. India started offshoring in the mid-1980s using low-cost labor with the appropriate skills in a favorable policy environment. But, back then, offshoring to Indian firms meant bodyshopping. Following the availability of data communications infrastructure and the organizational innovation in the form of adopting global delivery models in ODCs, bodyshopping gave way to territorially grounded development of software in India. Subsequent changes in the labor market, and demand and technological conditions at the turn of the millennium, offered new opportunities. Firms in India embraced these opportunities to provide a broader range of ICT services than software.

Thus, Infosys built on its offshoring experience to offer BPO services on one hand, even as Infosys Labs became engaged in the co-creation of IP. But these changes, which demand either local language capability or interaction with customers and other consortia partners to innovatively address demands, require proximity to critical markets. Similarly, presence in major market also became imperative for an increasingly global firm that attracted unwanted political attention and simultaneously had to overcome a shortage of skills. Consequently, offshoring work to an Indian firm, such as Infosys, no longer implies that the work will necessarily travel to India. It can just as well stay either at home or close to home. At the same time, offshoring to India has changed in other ways. For MNCs such as Cisco, to create products and services for new markets, especially with the growth of markets in advanced industrial countries slowing, the availability of low-cost local skills was only a necessary condition to work in a country like India. The sufficient condition has increasingly become access to different markets, insights into customer needs, and access to partners.

Notes

1. According to the OECD (2007), outsourcing is the use of goods and services produced outside the enterprise, while offshoring is outsourcing abroad. Offshoring can take the form of either subcontracting to non-affiliated enterprises or relocation through the

enterprise's own affiliates. In this paper, the case of Infosys (see section 5) is an instance of the former, while the case of Cisco is an instance of the latter (see section 6).

2. Among the five leading occupations that are considered offshorable are Computer Programmers, Data Entry Keyers, and Computer and Information Scientists, Research. See the appendix in Blinder (2009) for the complete list.
3. See, for instance, http://www.ciol.com/News/News-Reports/Say-no-to-Bangalore-Obama/5509119200/0/. See section 5 for more examples of political rhetoric and protectionist initiatives.
4. Examining US employment data for the IT sector between 1994 and 2004, Bednarzik (2005) also concludes that offshoring is not occurring to "a great extent."
5. http://dqindia.ciol.com/dqtop20/2010/CompanyRanking/default.asp.
6. Sections 2, 3 and 4 have been abbreviated from "The Computer Software Industry as a Vehicle of Late Industrialization: Lessons from the Indian Case," *Journal of the Asia-Pacific Economy* 15 (3): 247–70.
7. Reengineering is a means of reducing and simplifying maintenance by essentially replacing the older software with equivalent new software i.e. changing its form without altering its function (Sneed 1995). The result is easier and more efficient data access by shortening access paths, providing better query facilities and distributing data among several servers. Other benefits include better security, elimination of bugs lurking in the older software, and laying the ground for functional enhancement. Typically, reengineering involves migration from a mainframe to a newer operating environment, such as Unix, and is likely to entail a language change. For example, C is upgraded to C++ or unstructured Cobol is upgraded to Object Cobol.
8. Jones (1998) points to many other format problems with older software that manifest themselves in the 1990s. One such was the shift to the Euro, which replaced twelve European currencies, from January 1, 1999.
9. The figure for the United States in 2006 was 104,200 (Banerjee and Muley 2009: 31).
10. For details of benefits offered by STPs, see www.stpi.soft.net.
11. For details of these policy changes, see Acharya (2002), and the essays in Oman (1996).
12. www.nasscom.org/artdisplay.asp?cat_id=205. Although SEI upgraded the CMM model to CMMi (Capability Maturity Model Integration) in 2000, the broad philosophy of the five-stage model remains the same. For details, see www.sei.cmu.edu/cmm/cmm.html.
13. Hira (2004) also emphasizes the importance of H-1B and L-1 (see note 13) visas for software firms in India. For instance, he attributes 52% of Infosys's revenues in 2002 to its use of these visas. The corresponding figures for Satyam and Wipro, two other software service firms, were 44% and 24%.
14. The L classification applies to intrafirm transferees who, within the three preceding years, were employed abroad continuously for one year, and who will be employed by a branch, parent, affiliate, or subsidiary of that same employer in the US in a managerial, executive, or specialized knowledge capacity for up to seven years. For information on visas, see http://www.dhs.gov/files/statistics/publications/yearbook.shtml.
15. For instance, spending on IT in the United States, after growing by 16% in 2000, fell by 6% in 2001 (*Economist* 2002) and, in aggregate terms, technology spending declined from nearly 5% of GDP in 2000 to about 4% by 2003 (*Economist* 2003).
16. An embedded system is any computer that is a component in a larger system and relies on its own microprocessor (Wolf 2002). The use of embedded systems has grown with more powerful microprocessors. They now find application in everything from consumer

goods to transport equipment and industrial process control systems. In these devices, embedded systems not only take over what mechanical and dedicated electronic systems used to do, but they increasingly connect to the Internet. It is the ability to digitally capture and simulate various mechanical or other functions that makes the globalization of R&D in various domains technologically feasible. Thus, for instance, automobile firms such as Mercedes-Benz have established R&D facilities in India. Embedded systems design is about adapting software abstractions, designed merely to transform data, to meet real-time constraints, power requirements and safety considerations in various domains while interacting with the physical world through sensors and actuators (Lee 2000).

17. On the domestic front, firms were helped by legal changes, important among which was the passage of the Semiconductor Integrated Circuits Layout-Design Act 2000, which provides for the registration and protection of IC layouts and designs for a ten-year period (Krishnadas 2000). While software patents are not permitted in India, on 27 December 2004, the GoI issued an ordinance to modify the Patent Act "to provide for patents when software has technical applications in industry in combination with hardware," i.e., embedded systems, effective 1 January 2005. See http://pib.nic.in/release/rel_print_page1.asp?relid=6074.
18. It was in April 2002 that the firm launched Infosys BPO (known as Progeon until August 2006). Unless otherwise mentioned, this section draws from www.infosys.com, and from interviews with representatives of Infosys Labs, Bangalore, in July 2010. The website also lists all the recognition and the numerous awards that the firm has won over the years.
19. http://www.infosys.com/investors/reports-filings/annual-report/annual/Documents/Infosys-AR-10.pdf.
20. Cloud computing is computing as a utility wherein computing capacity, whether it is hardware, or software and tools, moves from local computers to remote, centralized data centers (*Economist* 2011a). There are three distinct layers of cloud computing. The outer layer is SaaS (Software as a Service) which includes web-based applications such as Gmail. The second layer is PaaS (Platform as a Service), which refers to operating systems that reside in the cloud and allow developers to write applications for the web and mobile devices. The final layer is IaaS (Infrastructure as a Service) which is the provision of number crunching and data storage systems. Infosys Labs works with clients to build SaaS applications on various platforms.
21. http://www.infosys.com/finacle/solutions/solutions-mobile-bank-in-a-box.asp.
22. http://www.infosys.com/offerings/products-and-platforms/mconnect/pges/index.aspx.
23. http://www.infosys.com/innovation-co-creation/pages/index.aspx.
24. For more details, see http://www.iu-atc.com/.
25. Of the firm's sixty-four marketing offices, only four are in India, reflecting the extent of reliance on global markets. Of the sixty international marketing offices, nineteen are in the United States, four each in Australia and Germany, three each in Switzerland, the UAE and the United Kingdom, two each in Canada, the Czech Republic and France and one each in Belgium, Brazil, Denmark, Finland, Greece, Hong Kong, Ireland, Japan, Malaysia, Mauritius, Mexico, The Netherlands, New Zealand, Norway, Russia, Singapore, Spain, and Sweden.
26. Twelve of the sixty-three development centers are part of Infosys BPO and, of the twelve, seven are outside India. In the Americas the centers are in Atlanta, in the US, in Belo Horizonte, Brazil, and in Monterrey, Mexico. The Asian centers are in Hangzhou, China,

and in Manila, Philippines, while the European centers in Brno, the Czech Republic, and in Lodz, Poland. The centers provide services such as finance and accounting, procurement, logistics claims handling, and insurance support. All of them are multilingual. For instance, the Asian centers provide voice processes in Cantonese, Japanese, Korean, Mandarin, and Thai, with front-office and end-user interaction support in English.

27. Of course, offshore work still accounted for a majority of effort (73.9% of person-months) towards products and services (http://www.infosys.com/investors/reports-filings/annual-report/annual/Documents/Infosys-AR-10.pdf). Thus, while the role of the overseas development centers should not be overstated, their increasingly important role for the firm cannot be overlooked either.
28. For instance, in a Memorandum dated 8 January 2010 (available at http://www.uscis.gov/USCIS/Laws/Memoranda/2010/H1B%20Employer-Employee%20Memo010810.pdf), the US Citizenship and Immigration Services (USCIS) required all H-1B petitions to demonstrate a valid employee-employer relationship between the petitioner (employer) and the beneficiary (potential visa holder) on the grounds that H-1B visas were being misused. Since the USCIS spelt out the basis for determining a valid relationship, the H-1B petition represented an exception to the practice of relying on common law principles.
29. The law sought US$600 million to strengthen security along the Mexican border by increasing the "filing fee and fraud prevention and detection fee" by US$2,000 for H-1B and L-1 visa applications made by firms with more than fifty employees and with a US workforce in which more than fifty percent was on those visa categories. For details, see: http://www.gpo.gov/fdsys/pkg/PLAW-111publ230/pdf/PLAW-111publ230.pdf.
30. http://blogs.wsj.com/indiarealtime/2010/08/06/us-senator-infosys-is-a-chop-shop/.
31. Indirect employment in 2009–10 was estimated at 8.2 million.
32. For more details on CampusConnect, see http://campusconnect.infosys.com/WhoWeAre.aspx.
33. For a complete list of the TCS's delivery/development and innovation centers, see http://www.tcs.com/worldwide/Pages/default.aspx.
34. http://www.ciol.com/News/News-Reports/Wipro-to-hire-50-pc-staff-globally-by-2015/159309/0/.
35. Unless otherwise mentioned, this section draws on interviews with Cisco representatives in Bangalore, in July 2010.
36. http://newsroom.cisco.com/dlls/fspnisapi997f.html.
37. http://www.cisco.com/web/strategy/docs/scc/09CS2326_SCC_BrochureForWest_r3_112409.pdf.
38. http://newsroom.cisco.com/dlls/global/asiapac/news/2005/pr_10–19b.html.
39. http://newsroom.cisco.com/dlls/global/asiapac/news/2006/pr_12–06c.html.
40. http://newsroom.cisco.com/dlls/2010/prod_070710.html?sid=BAC-JsSynd The Lavasa project has become controversial following allegations that due procedure for land acquisition and environmental clearances were not followed (http://www.indianexpress.com/news/ building-blocks-before-hill-city/725830/0. But this controversy will not affect the analytical purpose of this paper.
41. http://newsroom.cisco.com/dlls/2010/prod_050710b.html?sid=BAC-JsSynd.
42. http://newsroom.cisco.com/dlls/2011/prod_012811.html?sid=BAC-JsSynd.
43. http://newsroom.cisco.com/dlls/global/asiapac/news/2005/pr_10–21.html.
44. http://www.forbes.com/2010/01/26/forbes-india-padmasree-warrior-cto-cisco-tech-with-business.html.

References

Acharya, S. 2002. "Macroeconomic Management in the Nineties." *Economic and Political Weekly* 37 (16): 1515–1538.

Alarcon, R. 1998. "The Migrants of the Information Age: Foreign Born Engineers and Scientists and Regional Development in Silicon Valley." PhD diss., University of California, Berkeley.

Altbach, P. G. 2005. "Higher Education in India." http://www.thehindu.com/2005/04/12/stories/2005041204141000.htm.

Aoyama, A., and B. Parthasarathy. 2012. "Research and Development Facilities of Multinational Enterprises in India." *Eurasian Geography and Economics* 53(6): 713–730.

Arora, A., and J. Asundi. 1999. Quality certification and the economics of contract software development: A study of the Indian software industry. NBER Working Paper, no. 7260. Cambridge, MA: National Bureau of Economic Research.

Banerjee, A. V., and E. Duflo. 2000. Reputation effects and the limits of contracting: A study of the Indian software industry, *Quarterly Journal of Economics* 115 (3): 989–1017.

Banerjee, R., and V. P. Muley. 2009. *Engineering Education in India*. Noida: Macmillan.

Bedzarnik, R. W. 2005. "Restructuring Information Technology: Is Offshoring a Concern?" *Monthly Labor Review* 128 (8): 11–21.

Blinder, A. S. 2009. "How Many US Jobs Might Be Offshorable?" *World Economics* 10 (2): 41–78.

Blinder, A. S. 2006. "Offshoring: The Next Industrial Revolution?" *Foreign Affairs* 85 (2): 113–128.

Brooks, F. P. 1995. *The Mythical Man-month: Essays on Software Engineering*. 2nd ed. New York: Addison Wesley Longman.

Campbell-Kelly, M. 2003. *From Airline Reservations to Sonic the Hedgehog: A History of the Software Industry*. Cambridge, MA: MIT Press.

Cusumano, M. A. 2004. *The Business of Software: What Every Manager, Programmer, and Entrepreneur Must Know to Thrive and Survive in Good Times and Bad*. New York: Free Press.

Dataquest. 1987. "The New Software Policy: Dr. Seshagiri Clarifies." January, 82–95.

DIT (Department of Information Technology). 2005. *Annual Report 2004–2005*. Government of India. http://www.mit.gov.in/sites/upload_files/dit/files/downloads/annualreports/annualreport2004-05.pdf.

———.2011. *Annual Report 2010–11*. Government of India. http://www.mit.gov.in/sites/upload_files/dit/files/annualreport2010–11.pdf.

The Economist. 2002. High-tech Companies: IT Grows Up." August 24, 45.

———.2003. "Spending on Information Technology: Some Like it Cold." October 4, 62.

———.2011a. "Tanks in the Cloud: Information Technology Goes Global." January 1, 42–43.

———. 2011b. "From Mumbai to the Midwest: Far from home: Tata Consultancy Services Strives to Move Upmarket." November 5, 72.

Egan, E. A. 1997. "The Spatial Dynamics of the U.S. Computer Software Industry." PhD diss., University of California, Berkeley.

Froumien, I., S. Divakaran, H. Tan, and Y. Savchenko. 2007. "Strengthening Skills and Education for Innovation." In *Unleashing India's Innovation: Towards Sustainable and Inclusive Growth*, edited by M. Dutz, 129–146. Washington, DC: World Bank.

Gawer, A., and M. Cusumano. 2002. *Platform Leadership: How Intel, Microsoft, and Cisco Drive Industry Innovation*. Boston: Harvard Business School Press.

Heeks, R. 1996. *India's Software Industry: State Policy, Liberalisation and Industrial Development*. New Delhi: Sage Publications.

Hira, R. 2004. "U.S. Immigration Regulations and India's Information Technology Industry." *Technological Forecasting and Social Change* 71, 837–854.

InfoTech Consulting. 1992. "India's Software and Services: Export Potential and Strategies." Report submitted in fulfillment of contract with the Government of India, Department of Electronics under World Bank Japan grant no. 2612.

Jenkins, R. 1984. "Divisions over the International Division of Labour." *Capital and Class* 22, 28–57.

Jones, C. 1998. "Bad Days for Software," *IEEE Spectrum* 35 (9): 47–52.

Koch, K. 1998. "High-tech Labor Shortage." *CQ Researcher* 8 (16): 361–384.

Kraft, P. 1977. *Programmers and Managers: The Routinization of Computer Programming in the United States*. New York: Springer-Verlag.

Krishnadas, K.C. 2000. "Indian Readies Laws to Protect IC Designs." www.eedesign.com/article/showArticle.jhtml?articleId=17405970.

———.2003. Indian EEs Show You Can Go Home Again." www.eetimes.com/article/showArticle.jhtml?articleId=18309505.

Lee, E. A. 2000. "What's Ahead for Embedded Software?" *IEEE Computer* 33 (9): 18–26.

Mathews, J. A., and D.-S. Cho. 2000. *Tiger Technology: The Creation of a Semiconductor Industry in East Asia*. New York: Cambridge University Press.

Nair, V. 1998. "Infosys Eyes Big, to Set up Three Software Centres Abroad." *Economic Times*, October 28.

NASSCOM (National Association of Software and Service Companies). 1992. *Indian Software Directory, 1992*. New Delhi: NASSCOM.

———. 1993. *Indian Software Directory, 1993–94*. New Delhi: NASSCOM.

———. 2001. *Indian IT Software and Services Directory, 2001*. New Delhi: NASSCOM.

Oman, C. (ed.). 1996. *Policy Reform in India*. Paris: OECD.

OECD (Organisation for Economic Co-operation and Development). 2005. "Potential Offshoring of ICT-intensive Using Occupations." Digital Economy Papers, no. 91. Paris: OECD.

———. 2007. *Offshoring and Employment: Trends and Impacts*. Paris: OECD.

Parthasarathy, B., and Y. Aoyama. 2006. "From Software Services to R&D Services: Local Entrepreneurship in the Software Industry in Bangalore, India." *Environment and Planning A* 38, 1269–1285.

RBI (Reserve Bank of India). 2010. "Survey on Computer Software and Information Technology Services Exports: 2008–2009." *RBI Monthly Bulletin* 64 (8): 1555–1577.

———. 2011 "Survey on Computer Software and Information Technology Services Exports: 2009–2010." *RBI Monthly Bulletin* 65 (6) (July): 941–959.

Salus, P. H. 1994. "Unix at 25." *Byte* 19 (10): 75–82.

Saxenian, A. 2006. *The New Argonauts: Regional Advantage in a Global Economy*. Cambridge, MA: Harvard University Press.

Sen, P. 1994. "Software Exports from India: A Systemic Analysis." *Electronics Information and Planning* 22 (2): 55–63.

Singh, S. 2003. "India Calling." www.businessworldindia.com/Nov1003/coverstory02.asp.

Sneed, H. M. 1995. "Planning the Reengineering of Legacy Systems." *IEEE Software* 12 (1): 24–34.

Sridharan, E. 1996. *The Political Economy of Industrial Promotion: Indian, Brazilian, and Korean Electronics in Comparative Perspective,* 1969–1994. London: Praeger.

Srinivas, A., and M. Jayashankar. 2002. "Hard Times, Hard Lessons: The New Software Solutions." *Business Worl* 25 (February): 24–29.

Subramanian, C. R. 1992. *India and the Computer: A Study of Planned Development*. New Delhi: Oxford University Press.

Udell, J. 1993. "India's Software Edge." *Byte* 18 (10): 55–60.

Wolf, W. 2002. "What Is Embedded Computing?" *IEEE Computer* 35 (1): 136–137.

World Bank. 2009. Press Release no. 2009/316/DEC, April 22. http://web.worldbank.org/WBSITE/EXTERNAL/NEWS/0,,contentMDK:22151486~menuPK:34463~pagePK:34370~piPK:34424~theSitePK:4607,00.html.

CHAPTER 17

Offshoring Strategy in Subsdidiaries of Multinational Corporations in Brazil

PAULO ROBERTO GIÃO AND
MOACIR DE MIRANDA OLIVEIRA JÚNIOR

Introduction

The growing importance of emerging markets can be perceived by the amount of investments multinational corporations (MNCs) have made in these countries (UNCTAD 1993–2009). In this respect, it is important to note the relatively small share of investments from MNCs attracted by developing countries in the early 1990s (Fig. 17.1). In 1987, 18 percent of all foreign direct investments (FDIs) were in developing countries. This figure changed significantly (though with fluctuations) to 39 percent of the total in 2008. Great emphasis should be given to the period before the 2009 crisis, because even with a reduction of $281 billion in the total amount of investment between 2007 and 2008, there was an increase of $121 billion in investments in developing countries in the same period.

The increase in the pace of FDI observed since 2003, as evidenced by the data of UNCTAD, practically coincides with the rise of the phenomenon called "offshoring." Lewin et al. (2009) defined offshoring as the process and coordination of activities (value chain/supply chain) or business functions across the national borders of a company, and they clarify that offshoring can be seen as a new form of globalization in which companies disaggregate their value chains to multiple locations, and it may also involve externalizing process-specific capabilities to others. Carmel et al. (2009), on the other hand, treat offshoring as a management innovation, using the term as it is defined by

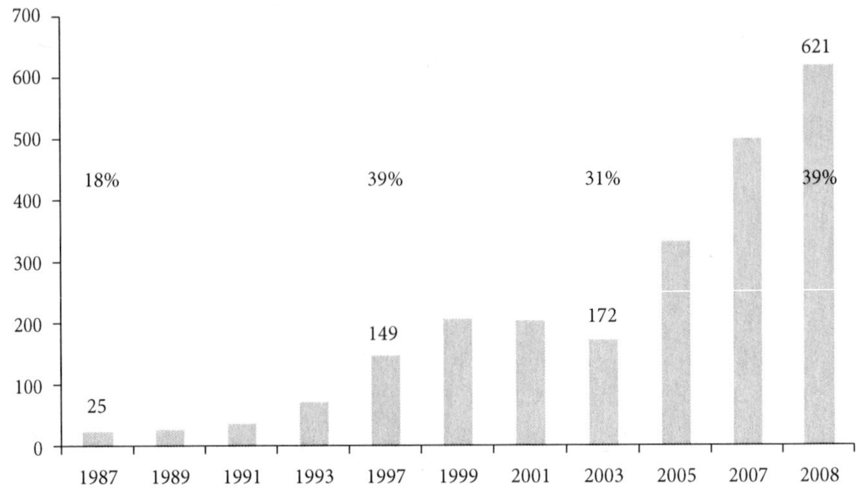

FIGURE 17.1 Foreign direct investments in developing countries (US$ billion).
Source: Prepared by the authors based on data from UNCTAD (1993–2009).

Birkinshaw et al. (2008), and which Abramovsky et al. (2004) had already suggested was about decreasing the activities of corporations.

The term offshoring can be represented in two ways: the offshore insource (OI), representing FDI in other countries (sometimes referred to as "in-house" or "captive" offshoring), and offshore outsource (OO), which would signify the contracting, purchasing, and importing of products and services from companies located in other countries. Outsourcing noncore activities has been studied for several decades. The hiring of other companies to perform various stages of production dates back to the 1960s, and more recently in the 1990s it also significantly reached the service areas of companies. This move has caused concern and even new expectations about the process of outsourcing (and also of offshoring) that jobs and competencies will be lost from developed countries to developing countries. While offshoring has the boundaries between countries as its major dimension, outsourcing has as the principal dimension the boundaries (or limits) of the organization.

Specifically analyzing Brazil: the investments of MNCs in the period 1990 to 2008 (UNCTAD 1993–2009) show a similar pace to investments in developing countries (Fig. 17.2). We can observe that the value of MNC investment in Brazil jumped from a value of about $990 million in 1990 (which represented 2.9 percent of investments in developing countries) to $45 billion in 2008 (7.2 percent of the total invested in developing countries). The highest percentage of investments in Brazil occurred in the period between 1998 and 2000, when the values ranged between $28.5 billion and $33.5 billion and accounted for 15.2 to 14.0 percent of the total investment in developing countries. That period coincided with the liberalization and privatization of some sectors in the country such as telecommunications, mining, and steel, which attracted new multinationals from different countries and generated billions for

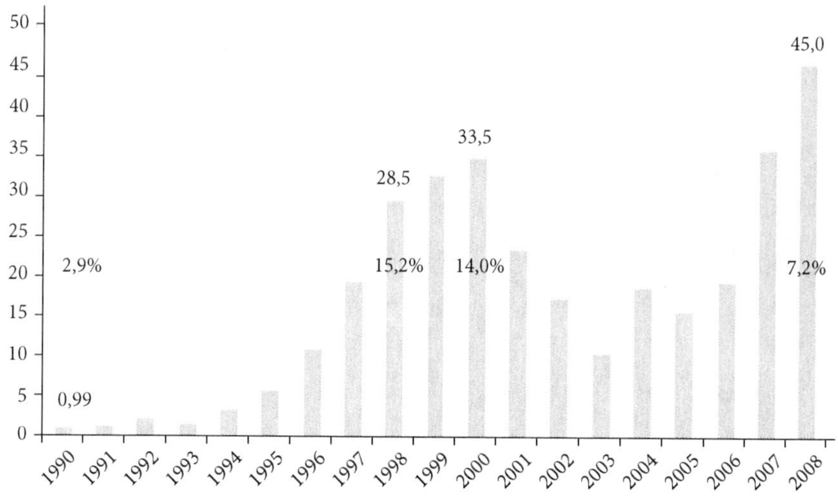

FIGURE 17.2 Foreign direct investments in Brazil.

Source: Prepared by the authors based on data from UNCTAD (1993–2009).

government coffers. MNCs had already been conducting offshore insource through their subsidiaries in Brazil for many years, but that intensified in the decades of 1990 and 2000.

Considering these global movements, their causes and consequences, it is important to assess how multinational corporations use their supply chains with regard to Brazil, through the deployment of subsidiaries. These production relationships are new, and the resulting opportunities, concerns, and strategic effects are still not fully determined and predictable, raising questions about the effects not only on companies but also on national economies. The concern of developed countries with the loss of jobs and training in various stages of production, including R&D, is one sensitive topic that has been studied and is addressed in other chapters in this book.

Bearing that in mind, this chapter seeks to answer the following questions: How do subsidiaries of MNCs operating in Brazil make use of offshore insourcing and outsourcing to get all the resources and competencies required, and how is a balance met between the two? In other words, within the interpretation of other concepts present in the study of international business (IB), this chapter aims to analyze the process of internalization of activities conducted by subsidiaries of MNCs operating in Brazil and how those subsidiaries interact with the environment in Brazil. This interaction is evaluated according to strategic and nonstrategic activities undertaken in the country. In 2009, a survey was carried out among 145 multinational subsidiaries located in Brazil to evaluate whether they developed both strategic and nonstrategic activities and, if so, what strategic activities they developed. The survey also looked at the role of outsourcing to Brazilian or from foreign companies located in Brazil.

Background

Offshoring and outsourcing have proven strategic options for many corporations, for different reasons and at various periods of time. The industry has practiced offshoring in the past fifty years involving work related to the manufacturing of products, or so-called blue-collar jobs (Lewin and Peeters 2006). Mol (2007) shows that outsourcing is similar in meaning to words such as subcontracting, contracting out, and contracting, and he says that outsourcing refers to those activities that are contracted from outside suppliers, to the transfer of activities and perhaps assets of a company to outside vendors, and to those activities that are undertaken by external suppliers and that can also be performed by the company itself.

Consideration of the issue of offshoring within the area of IB through an analysis of the *Journal of International Business Studies* (*JIBS*) shows that the first paper that presents the neologism appeared in 2005 and since then, forty-five references can be identified, with nineteen of them just for the years 2009 to 2010.

Jensen (2009) shows that offshoring of manufacturing activities from developed countries (high cost) to developing countries (low cost) has been reported in the IB literature for several decades. Particularly in the past decade, this phenomenon has reached the service sector as well, where it is called "globalization of services."

For decades, MNCs have been cutting costs by offshoring engineering and production activities to low-cost regions of the world (Lynn and Salzman 2007). They also have deployed development centers for global products suitable to the specific local markets. Nevertheless, the systems integration and the more valuable activities of the value chain were kept in the home countries or in countries that compose the triad of North America, Europe, and Japan. According to Coucke and Sleuwaegen (2008), phases of production that were typically less efficient or more costly were transferred to third parties in other countries. However, recent trends have shown that offshoring is not only about standardized and routine activities, but includes others that require a larger amount of embedded knowledge. To Bunyaratavej et al. (2007), while the whole process of manufacturing involves highly skilled workers, some separate functions, such as assembly, require workers with moderate skills.

However, offshoring has existed for such a short time that its concept is not yet fully stabilized (WTO 2005) and this creates inconsistencies in understanding among organizations, media, and academics. The various definitions of offshoring differ regarding focus and scope, presenting their authors' different interpretations and involving variables such as weather, jobs, type of activity, costs, limitations of the companies, and even an intricate and confusing synergy with the outsourcing process.

For the time variable, for example, Kedia and Mukherjee (2009) and Varadarajan (2008) argue that there is no need to limit the definition to "business functions that were previously performed internally." This is because new activities arise due to new products or services being developed and they are likely to be performed externally without a new name needing to be given. This consideration restricts the scope for a proper definition of offshoring. Regarding jobs (see, for instance, Stack and Downing 2005; Ellis 2004; Hatonen and Eriksson 2009), if an existing activity is transferred to a subsidiary in another country, it means that the organization is adequate internally and has just moved jobs from one place to another. If activities are transferred not to subsidiaries but to other companies (in the same country or another), jobs are not transferred but lost to the organization doing the transfer. However, what if one is dealing with new activities, products, or business? Jobs that did not exist will exist in the places chosen for deployment in accordance with the strategic intentions of the organization and these may be within the organization, either through its subsidiaries or through the use of subcontractors. So, including jobs in the definition of offshoring also limits the definition.

Considering offshoring only when a whole factory is transferred abroad, as presented by Friedman (2005) and OECD (2007), seems to be too extreme and would limit the number of cases of corporations using offshoring process. More reasonable is to consider offshoring as the realization of activities abroad, in any amount or of any quality (for example, call-center, design, or R&D).

The search for lower costs (e.g., OECD 2007; Lynn and Salzman 2007) also seems to be a limiting factor. Activities contracted abroad do not refer just to functions of low complexity, but also to the search for technologies or capabilities that do not exist either within the company or even in its home country. And thus, there may be even higher costs in the search for innovations, so the variable cost does not seem applicable in all cases. And companies located in or from developing countries would not go in search just of low costs, but of competencies, markets, products, or services that are not available in their countries of origin.

With regard to the limits of the company (e.g., Varadanjan 2008), contracting products and services only from company's subsidiaries in other countries also seems to limit the definition to a smaller number of situations. Why limit the definition to contracting only its own foreign subsidiaries when so many cases are reported of hiring other companies to perform activities? What name should then be given to this variant of internationalization? Therefore, in one way or another, these attempts at defining or characterizing offshoring limit what could be a more comprehensive and impartial definition.

The simplest and most direct approach seems to be that used by Lewin et al. (2009), which shows offshoring as the allocation of activities by organizations outside the borders of their country of origin. This definition does not take into consideration variables such as time, jobs, type, and amount of activities, but focuses only on the borders of the organization and country. Additionally, Massini and Peeters (2009) and Abramovsky et al. (2004) present a scheme to differentiate the possibilities in a supply chain value. The possibilities involving offshoring include performing certain operations abroad through subsidiaries (OI) and outsourcing to suppliers outside the corporate structure (OO).

The process of offshore insource (OI) is when organizations become more international through the establishment of subsidiaries ("greenfield"), through the acquisition of companies or through joint ventures with local companies. The process of offshore outsource (OO) occurs when an organization outsources activities to another company in another country.

From another point of view, the type of activity being offshored evolved from activities with low added value or more routine ones (call centers, ticket reservations) to strategic activities (design, R&D). Mudambi (2008) argues that the trend showed that high-value-added activities are performed in advanced market economies, while those with low added value are held in emerging economies. However, this situation is under pressure due to companies in emerging economies developing competencies in high-value-added activities and companies from developed countries getting rid of standard parts of their activities with high added value and reducing costs by reallocating to emerging economies.

In a short period of time, offshoring has changed and now encompasses not only activities with low added value but also other more strategic activities for organizations. According to OECD (2008), the traditional reason for FDI in R&D was to serve as a conduit for exploitation of intellectual assets developed by MNCs in their countries of origin. According to this view, the R&D centers from affiliates had the aim of customizing technology to the needs of local consumers. In recent years, this vision has been complemented with important adaptive innovative activities. The strategies in innovation have increased the use of global supply to meet and fulfill new markets needs and trends around the world. A change in the flow of knowledge is now seen, with greater quantity (and quality) of ideas and innovations flowing from R&D centers abroad to the headquarters of MNCs in developed countries. Also according to the OECD (2008), the internationalization of R&D is not something entirely new. In the 1980s, investments in R&D occurred mainly among developed countries and differed from those observed today in three characteristics: the rapid pace of internationalization, the dispersion to developing countries, and moving beyond the adaptation of products and technologies for local markets. While many R&D activities are still held in the MNCs' countries of origin, the companies have changed their process of innovation and have globally distributed networks of R&D and innovation (OECD 2008).

In continuing the process of offshoring and outsourcing as well, organizations have begun to identify advantages in applying them to activities with higher added value. Investment in R&D by MNCs has grown steadily as part of their global strategies of access to new technologies (OECD 2007). These strategies involve the construction of networks of R&D centers aiming to have access to local knowledge sources and to develop new technologies. In a survey on the topic of globalization of R&D, the Economist Intelligence Unit (2004) asked senior executives in which countries their companies planned to develop R&D over the next three years; the responses were in the following order: China (39 percent), United States (29 percent), India (28 percent), United Kingdom (24 percent), Germany (19 percent), and Brazil (11 percent).

Lewin and Peeters (2006) found in their research surprising results, since companies internationalize 44 percent of their engineering services and 32 percent of their implementations in research. Such activities may be regarded as critical to the competitiveness of enterprises, but even then the tendency is that they continue to be sent overseas. Also according to the Economist Intelligence Unit (2007), the traditional innovation process through which companies centralized their R&D centers is gradually being phased out. In its place, companies from a variety of sectors are breaking down their departments of R&D and delivering the innovation process through a network of external partners and locations abroad (offshoring). In recent years, innovation has been a major topic of study by many companies (Weeks and Feeny 2008).

Lewin et al. (2009) estimate that there is a trend of companies to increasingly globalize more complex and higher-value-added activities, to have access to expertise and to highly skilled workers. To Amos and Reitsperger (2004), moving core competencies to the periphery allows the company to benefit from the resources available outside the country of origin, creating, on the other hand, issues related to control and integration. Also, the Economist Intelligence Unit (2007) notes that a key feature of the global network of innovation is that it involves a variety of organizations and companies that have outsourced R&D or formed partnerships with other companies to share the work and the benefits of innovation.

Lynn and Salzman (2007) say that one of the most significant events of the last decade has been the offshoring of product development and technologies by MNCs to emerging economies (EE). This trend seems contrary to the history of large companies that evolved through the increasing integration of activities into their organizational structures followed by strategies to protect their core competencies and resources that provide sustainable competitive advantages. Lynn and Salzman (2005) argue that the past decade has witnessed the spread of essential activities by multinationals across the world. Mobile phone and telecommunications services advanced in China, software development and pharmaceutical research in India, and aerospace advances being made in Brazil show the emergence of highly specialized companies in developing countries to what might be called "new globalization of engineering."

Also noted in the continuing process of offshoring presented above is that not only are low-value or even routine (nonstrategic) activities or services being transferred to other countries, but also those that are sensitive (strategic) or of high added value to corporations. Broadly speaking, among the nonstrategic activities, we can mention call centers, back office, data entry systems, technical support, ticket reservations, and the setting up of equipment. Likewise, among the strategic activities we can mention research and development, design, new product development, engineering services, as well as specialized and accurate software.

Figure 17.3 shows the use of offshoring according to the boundaries of the company and of the activities it develops. A corporation with headquarters (H) in a given country and its subsidiaries (S) scattered over several countries is already practicing offshore insource (OI). If the headquarters or one of its subsidiaries contracts activities or services in countries other than where it is located, it is operating in offshore outsource (OO). Naturally, it is perfectly possible that a company operates in a hybrid form (DTT 2005), looking both ways. With respect to strategic and nonstrategic activities, the company may choose to develop the strategic activities within its boundaries and outsource the non-strategic ones, or even operate in a hybrid manner also according to the size of company boundaries.

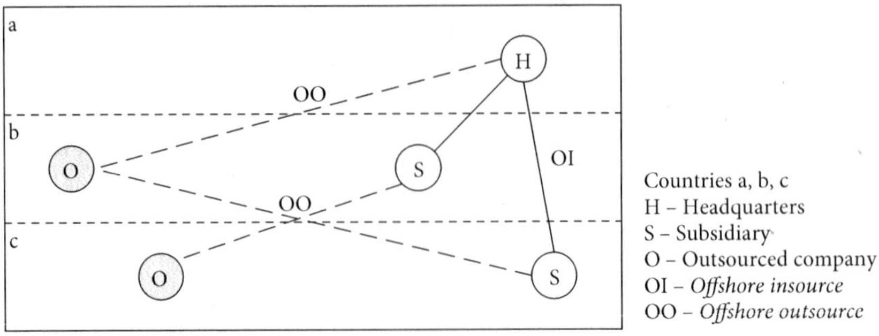

FIGURE 17.3 Offshoring of activities and the boundaries of the company.

Still in Figure 17.3, the circles on the company side (right, white circles) represent its parent and subsidiaries around the world and outside the company sphere (left, gray circles), the companies contracted (O).

Unlike offshoring, it does not seem difficult to identify a reasonable definition for outsourcing. The main point of consensus is hiring an external source to perform some type of activity (the production of something or a service). Daugherty (1988) defines outsourcing as the purchasing of products and services from external providers. Tayles and Drury (2001) explain that decisions on outsourcing are not confined to materials or components of a product. They also apply to activities not related to manufacturing, such as support services. This is important as it reflects that outsourcing is not necessarily related to products and offshoring to services, as considered by some authors. To McIvor (2005), outsourcing involves goods and services previously produced internally in the organization being provided by external suppliers and may involve the transfer of entire business functions (including people and physical assets) to a supplier.

According to Quinn and Hilmer (1994), companies can better leverage their resources through what they call "strategic outsourcing," and that can be achieved by selecting a few core competencies of relevance to consumers that can be best-in-world, focusing the investment and directing management attention on them, and outsourcing other activities in which are not or do not need to be the best. This is corroborated by Domberg (1998), who shows that among the strategic options that the company needs to define is the delimitation of its frontiers or, in other words, to define what to produce by itself and what to hire in the market.

To McIvor (2005), outsourcing evolved from peripheral business activities toward critical activities that contributed to the organization's competitive advantage, as businesses sought greater efficiency and cost reduction, and by outsourcing activities previously performed internally, businesses ended up ultimately redefining the boundaries of their organization. Similarly, Kedia and Mukherjee (2009) say that offshoring has emerged as an effective strategic practice with which companies can relocate their business functions (which were previously performed internally) in locations abroad.

What is strategic for companies that outsource can also be strategic for contractors who see an opportunity to improve their products and services and even learn new

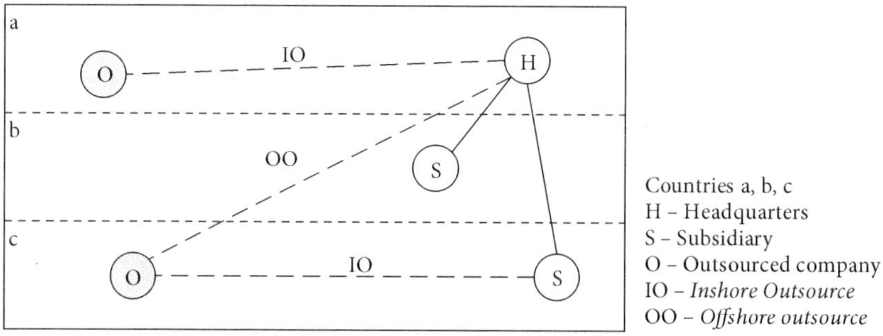

FIGURE 17.4 Outsourcing of activities and national boundaries.

activities. King (2005) says that outsourcing companies continue to evolve, upgrading their services to higher-value-added activities such as software development, integration of business processes, and software maintenance. This is complemented by Mol (2007), who argues that external providers are often highly specialized in the production of certain components and products, which enables them to produce at lower cost than the company that hires.

As with offshoring, it is also possible to graph the possibilities involving outsourcing and the activities involved with the main dimension, the boundaries between countries. In Figure 17.4, the various units of a corporation—its parent (H) and its subsidiaries (S)—outsource (O) to perform activities or services. When this contract is made within the home country of the unit of the corporation that hires, it is simply making an outsourcing operation. When a plant hires activities outside the borders where it is located, it would be operating in the offshore outsource (OO) mode. In Figure 17.4, outsourcing cases are represented by dashed lines between white and gray circles. Thus, as in the case of offshoring, the company may choose to hire outsourced strategic and nonstrategic activities from third parties within the countries in which the units operate or hire them from third parties in other countries, or even operate in a hybrid mode (DTT 2005) according to the dimensions of the countries.

With the foregoing, it may be asked whether the type of activity developed in a country by subsidiaries of MNCs surveyed can be classified only as nonstrategic or whether it is strategic as well. This situation characterizes the offshore insource (OI) activities with low or high added value. By classifying such activities and searching them in their subsidiaries, we attempt to verify the conditions found in the country that facilitate the development of certain activities. If only non-strategic activities are identified inside the subsidiaries, the country may show a low level of skilled labor in its various aspects, as well as of natural resources and probably the market demand (mainly selling its products and servces in this market) would be the reason for operating in the country. On the other hand, developing strategic activities shows that the country presents conditions for the development of such activities through internalization of human resources or contracting third parties for the realization of these strategic activities. In the first case, the subsidiary can minimize problems of low quality of workforce through internal training and, in the second case, already finds companies that have the quality of products or services at the level desired by the company.

From this point, the following can be defined as strategic activities (Si) performed by subsidiaries in the country: research and development; innovation; creating new products and services; and creating and modifying production processes (Hakansson and Henders 1994; Sturgeon, 2006; Lynn and Salzman 2007; OECD 2008; Lewin et al. 2009). The classification of these activities as strategic is in line with the literature and shows the close relationship between them, when functional areas overlap with the results expected of them. Additionally, the internal nonstrategic activities (Ni) are defined, as those relating to purchasing, to human resources, to production, and to marketing (Moxon, 1975; Lewin and Peeters 2006; Lyyn and Salzman 2007; Mudambi 2008; Jensen 2009). The denomination as nonstrategic does not mean they are unimportant in the context of the subsidiary, but of the corporation as a whole, which chose the country in which to develop them. For example, the activity of production at this site may be to supply the local market or even other countries and marketing may focus more specifically on the understanding, care, and communication with the local market. Thus the first hypothesis to be researched observes the internal development of nonstrategic activities and the strategic part of the subsidiaries that participated in the survey.

> Hypothesis 1: The higher the internal development of nonstrategic activities (Ni), the greater the development of strategic activities (Si) internally.

Based on the hypothesis that tries to identify the type of activity performed, the field of study now expands with the introduction of the possible use of outsourcing within the country by the subsidiaries surveyed. Regardless of whether the statement of hypothesis 1 is corroborated or not, the use of outsourcing opens new perspectives in the structuring of the company in the country and in how the company conducts its operations, with greater or lesser amount of activities carried out internally or externally.

Thus, differentiated from the concept of strategic activities developed internally (Si), strategic services outsourced (So) are similarly defined as those restricted to the activities of design and R&D contracted with a third party located in Brazil (for example, Economist Intelligence Unit 2007; Lynn and Salzman 2005; Lewin et al. 2009). Likewise, in addition to the nonstrategic activities performed internally (Ni) the nonstrategic services outsourced (No) are similarly defined as those that involve the assembly of equipment, component manufacturing, engineering services and IT and call centers, back office and help-desk (for example, based on Lewin and Peeters 2006; Bunyaratavej et al. 2007; Lynn and Salzman 2007; Cha et al. 2008; Coucke and Sleuwaegen 2008).

Thus, we propose Hypothesis 2A, in which even performing strategic activities internally, there is still a need for a company to contract strategic services with third parties to complement its operations (McIvor 2005; Economist Intelligence Unit 2007, Parkhe 2007). In other words, the subsidiary internalizes strategic activities, but not all of them necessary for their operations and thus requires new competencies and strategic resources from third parties.

> Hypothesis 2A: The higher the internal development of the strategic activities (Si), the greater the outsourcing of strategic services (So) by the subsidiaries of MNCs.

Similarly, Hypothesis 2B is constructed to investigate if the internal development of nonstrategic activities is supplemented by the contracting of strategic services. This could show that the subsidiary is unable or unwilling to internalize strategic activities and demonstrates that by hiring in the market.

> Hypothesis 2B: The higher the internal development of the nonstrategic activities (Ni), the greater the outsourcing of strategic services (So) by the subsidiaries of MNCs.

Finally, Hypothesis 2C shows an association between No and So, trying to check whether the majority of activities and services are performed externally to the subsidiaries.

> Hypothesis 2C: The higher the outsourcing of nonstrategic services (No), the higher the outsourcing of strategic services (So) by subsidiaries of MNCs.

In addition to Hypothesis 1, this set of hypotheses seeks to assess whether the effects of internal development activities are reflected in the environment external to the subsidiary, if internal activities (nonstrategic or strategic) are complemented by similar developments (nonstrategic or strategic services) contracted externally in the market.,.

Method

Several variables collected through the research strategy are interrelated and of sufficient quantity to meet the requirements of statistical analysis. The questionnaire was developed from a composite of several articles and publications in the literature. In part, it represents the second edition of the survey on subsidiaries of Brazilian-headquartered MNCs conducted by Oliveira Júnior and Borini (2003), based on Birkinshaw and Morrison (1995), Birkinshaw et al. (1998), with appropriate updates and with the inclusion of a specific section on offshoring and outsourcing and some other related topics. The part on offshoring and outsourcing was based on some international research on offshoring and internationalization strategy, drawing from the questionnaire presented in Kyostila and Cardwell (2005) on the impact of offshoring on IT companies in Finland and on a survey conducted by Couto et al. (2006) on the development of offshoring from 537 US and European companies (Lewin et al. 2009; A. T. Kearney 2007, 2009). These resources were important in developing a more structured, comprehensive and accurate survey and issues to pretended purposes.

Regarding the method of carrying it out, we chose a web-based application. Thirty-seven questions were arranged into five sections reflecting the interests of research, totaling seven pages in the paper version. The questions of this type made use of a Likert scale, with variations in the lower and upper levels according to the question being assessed. In some cases, they could range from "strongly disagree" to "strongly agree," in others from "bad" to "excellent" or even from "never" to "always."

Within this planning of research, we initially sought to stratify the sampling of the 1,200 largest companies (revenue criteria) provided by the *Gazeta Mercantil*. From this list, a first screening showed that the mailing list had not been updated and 200 companies were excluded, leaving 1,000 candidate companies. Later, due to the difficulty in obtaining a greater number of responses, we opted for a nonprobability sampling for convenience, using the contacts that, on other occasions, had been established for one reason or another or even used in previous research. Thus, the exact number of companies contacted was 1,030 subsidiaries of non-Brazilian MNCs and from different multinationals. According to UNCTAD (2009), there were 4,172 subsidiaries of MNCs in Brazil in 2009. If this UNCTAD number represents a subsidiary per MNCs (there is no information in the report) the sample represents at least 24.7 percent of all subsidiaries presented in Brazil. That stated, this research should then be considered as coming from a nonrandom convenience sample.

From the sample universe of 1,030 subsidiaries, only 172 agreed to participate in this survey. From this established base, 91.3 percent outsource some type of service or activity and the remaining 8.7 percent (15 subsidiaries) responded negatively to outsourcing. Of the 157 companies that responded to outsourcing, it appears that 92.4 percent of questionnaires (145) were answered by members of senior management of the subsidiaries, as was the goal of the research field. The sample considered for analysis now contains 145 questionnaires filled out by subsidiaries. Again, the database represents at least 3.5 percent of all subsidiaries installed in Brazil, according to UNCTAD (2009).

The sample base built consisted of 145 subsidiaries of MNCs from all continents and represented the most diverse sectors of the economy, as can be seen in Table 17.1.

Most companies surveyed came from Europe (83) followed by the Americas with 51 subsidiaries. Note that only 5.5 percent of MNCs subsidiaries came from the Asian continent. After this survey, several large Chinese companies, particularly in the automotive and electronic industries, settled in Brazil, which certainly would generate a database with higher percentage of Asian companies.

With respect to industries surveyed, the chemical/petrochemical and automotive sectors were the most representative, with 24 and 23 subsidiaries respectively. The large percentage observed in "Others" is composed of sectors that hardly participated in the survey, for example, hospitality, retailing, tobacco, among others. Additional descriptive material can be found in Table 17.8 below.

With the proposed hypotheses and structured database, dependent and independent variables were built to verify the goals of this chapter. The first dependent variable considered and used to test the hypothesis regarded the internal development of strategic activities (Si). The variable "internal strategic activities" (Si) involve high-value activities performed by subsidiaries in the country. More specifically, they consist of the research

Table 17.1 Brief description of database subsidiaries

	Percentage of subsidiaries	No. of subsidiaries
Origin		
America	35.2	51
Asia	5.5	8
Africa	0.7	1
Europe	57.2	83
Oceania	1.4	2
Industry		
Automotive	15.9	23
Building	2.8	4
Chemical and petrochemical	16.6	24
Electrical and electronics	7.6	11
Financial services	4.1	6
IT	4.8	7
Logistic	3.4	5
Machinery and equipment	10.3	15
Telecommunications	3.4	5
Others	31.0	45

and development (R&D), innovation, development of new products and services and production processes. The set of these variables showed a Cronbach's alpha of 0.687.

The second dependent variable used to verify Hypotheses 2A–C refers to the external development of strategic services through outsourcing, called "outsourcing of strategic services" (So). This variable consists of the strategic services contracted from third parties and encompasses the activities of design and R&D. The variable components showed a Cronbach's alpha of 0.684.

The models developed use different independent variables according to the objectives to which they refer. The verification of the internal performance of strategic and nonstrategic activities. "strategic services outsourced" (So) is modeled using the independent variables "strategic activities performed internally" (Si), "nonstrategic activities performed internally" (Ni), and "nonstrategic services outsourced" (No). Ni is modeled by using the variables related to the activities of marketing, production, human resources, and purchasing. The variable components showed a Cronbach's alpha of 0.756. No encompasses the variables that involve services/activities considered nonstrategic, such as assembly, manufacturing, call center, engineering services, and IT. These variables presented jointly a Cronbach's alpha of 0.684.

RESULTS AND DISCUSSION

The variable So is presented in Table 17.2, along with its component variables. It is observed that the frequency of outsourcing of service design and R&D (10.4 and

Table 17.2 Composition of the construct "strategic services outsourced" (So)

	Design	R&D	So
Low (%)	70.3	71.7	71.0
Intermediate (%)	19.3	15.2	17.3
High (%)	10.4	13.1	11.8
Median	2.0	2.0	2.0
Mean	2.07	2.11	2.1
Mode	1.0	2.0	1.5
Std. deviation	1.05	1.05	1.1

13.1 percent respectively) is relatively low, below both the Intermediate and the High percent.

Table 17.2 represents the 145 organizations considered: 19 of them had high scores, between 4 and 5, and 115 scored 1 or 2. This can be checked out through the mean, median, and modes presented. Jointly, this meant that 15 companies outsource services of design and 19 of them outsource R&D. It appears that strategic services (So), here considered as design and R&D, are at a **initial stage,** with only 19 of the 145 companies surveyed (13.1 percent) hiring such services. This may show either that they prefer carrying out the strategic activities internally or that they are not finding suppliers who can meet the needs required by the subsidiaries.

Apropos the internal development of strategic activities, Table 17.3 presents the frequency of distributions of the questionnaire questions that comprise the internal variable "strategic activities" (Si).

The last column on the right shows the total composition of variable Si prepared by transforming the sum of all the component variables divided by the number of variables (in this case six). After evaluating the variables that make up this construct, there is a high incidence of internal development of strategic activities. The six questions that formed the Si construct all showed positive bias of achievement by the subsidiaries in Brazil. The percentage of high achievement by the subsidiaries ranged from 43.5 percent for R&D to 72.4 percent for the implementation of innovation processes, with all questions presenting higher level of achievement than of the nonperformance (low-score responses).

The "innovation" component stands out positively, with the highest percentage of responses allocated to the concept of High, 72.4 percent, and even among the components with lower scoring, High was at 43.5 percent (R&D), still higher than the percentage allocated as Low in the conceptualization (35.9 percent). Also notable is that all those component variables considered have a percentage of the conceptualization High, higher than both Low and Mid, and also that all variables had the closest answer (mode) in four. Moreover, an important point stands out: that all variables showed a high percentage of response higher than the component R&D. This seems to indicate that these

Table 17.3 Composition of the construct "strategic activities performed internally" (Si)

	R&D	Innovation	New products and services development	New processes	Developed new products	Developed processes	Si
Low (%)	35.9	11.0	20.0	15.2	29.00	21.4	22.1
Intermediate (%)	20.7	16.6	12.4	21.4	24.10	27.6	20.5
High (%)	43.5	72.4	67.6	63.4	47.00	51.1	57.5
Median	3	4	4	4	3	4	3.7
Mean	3.01	3.82	3.26	3.63	3.26	3.33	3.4
Mode	4	4	4	4	4	4	4.0
Std. deviation	1.13	0.98	1.17	1.05	1.17	0.98	1.08

Table 17.4 Composition of the construct "nonstrategic activities performed internally" (Ni)

	Marketing	Manufacturing	HR	Procurement	Ni
Low (%)	29.7	24.8	33.8	35.9	31.1
Intermediate (%)	28.3	29.0	29.7	33.1	30.0
High (%)	42.1	45.5	36.5	31.0	38.8
Median	3	3	3	3	3.0
Mean	3.16	3.2	3.03	2.94	3.1
Mode	4	4	4	3	3.8
Std. deviation	1.04	1.05	1.01	0.99	1.0

other activities (innovation, developing new products and processes, etc.) are not necessarily developed in specific areas of R&D, but can be found scattered throughout other areas of the company. This could be explained by a bias introduced by the services sector embedded in the samples, but even considering only subsidiaries of the industrial sector, 45.9 percent of them develop R&D, while the percentage observed for innovation reaches 74.8 percent. Finally, the resulting variable Si reflects the above considerations and conceptualization High (57.5 percent), being greater than the sum of the percentages obtained for the concepts Middle and Low (42.6 percent).

The composition of the construct "nonstrategic activities performed internally" (Ni) and its component variables are presented in Table 17.4. There is in this case a difference among the variables marketing, production, and HR and the variable purchasing. The first three have a High concept higher than the concept Low, while for the variable purchasing, the bias is reversed, with the Low conceptualization being higher.

At this point, it is important to stress two points observed by referring to Table 17.3 regarding Si and Table 17.4 regarding Ni. First, we can already conclude that the

Table 17.5 Composition of the construct "nonstrategic services outsourced" (No)

	Assembly	Manufacturing	Call center	Engineering	IT	No
Low (%)	37.9	35.9	60.7	44.1	20.7	39.9
Intermediate (%)	18.6	19.3	12.4	29.0	29.0	21.7
High (%)	43.4	44.8	26.9	26.9	50.3	38.5
Median	3	3	2	3	3	2.8
Mean	3.12	3.14	2.48	2.82	3.31	3.0
Mode	4	4	1	3	3	3.0
Std. deviation	1.33	1.32	1.42	1.11	1.12	1.3

subsidiaries that comprise the database develop strategic activities in the target country, and second, the internal development of strategic activities presents higher scores (median and dispersion) than for nonstrategic activities carried out internally, showing that the subsidiaries, on average, develop more strategic activities than nonstrategic in the country.

The variable "nonstrategic services outsourced" (No) and the variables that comprise it are presented in Table 17.5. It is observed that with the exception of the variables call center and engineering services, the others showed a High score superior to the Low scores.

Comparing these frequencies with the strategic services outsourced, there is a substantial difference, showing, in general, that while on average 38.5 percent outsource No, 11.1 percent outsource So. Particularly on the engineering and IT services, it appears that 39 and 73 companies respectively outsource some work in these areas. We highlight these areas, since they seem to be a middle ground between what would be strategic and nonstrategic services and that could be allocated in either case depending on the macrosector (industry, services, etc.) or even the sector (automotive, construction, electronics, finance, logistics, and telecommunications, among others) of the economy. Just as an example, since it is not the aim of this work, in the macroservices sector, 60 percent of companies outsource IT services, this figure falls to 48 percent in macroindustry sectors within the subsidiaries surveyed.

Unlike the So, the amount of nonstrategic services outsourced (No) was more significant. Involving assembly, manufacturing, call center, IT, and engineering services, this high-concept construct obtained for 64 of 145 surveyed (44.1 percent), with engineering services and call center getting the lowest percentage, 26.9 percent, and IT services the highest percentage, 50.3 percent.

The correlation between the variables used in the event, according to the Pearson coefficient, as well as their significance, are presented in Table 17.6. According to the classification of Morgan et al. (2004), the correlation between the variable Ni and Si can be considered medium ($r = 0.446$, $p < 0.001$), very close to what could be considered strong (0.50).

This means that both variables vary together in the same direction, when one increases the other also increases and vice versa.

Table 17.6 Correlation between variables in Model A_x

	Ni	Si
Ni	1	
Si	0.446***	1

*** p < 0.001; N = 145.

Table 17.7 Correlation between variables in Model B_x

	So	Si	Ni	No
So	1			
Si	0.309***	1		
Ni	0.191*	0.446***	1	
No	0.226**	0.057	0.263***	1

***p < 0.001 **p < 0.01 *p < 0.05; N = 145.

The results obtained by the correlation of Pearson for the set of Hypothesis 2_x and also their significances are presented in Table 17.7. In general, according to the classification of Morgan et al. (2004), the correlations can be considered weak or medium. And in only one case was it not significant. Another four of the correlations were statistically significant at $p < 0.01$ and a correlation was shown for $p < 0.05$.

Evaluating each correlation, it appears that the variable So correlates positively with all other variables shown. Its highest correlation occurs with the variable Si ($r = 0.309$, $p < 0.001$); that is, upon the internal development and recruitment, the two move in the same direction. The same trend is observed in lower intensity with No ($r = 0.226$, $p < 0.01$) and Ni ($r = 0.191$, $p < 0.05$).

The Si variable correlates positively and moderately with the variable Ni ($r = 0.446$, $p < 0.001$). In this case the correlation shows that the higher the internal development of nonstrategic activities (Ni) the greater the possibility that strategic activities are being carried out internally (Si), showing joint positive changes among these variables. The internal development of nonstrategic activities (Ni) also correlated positively with No ($r = 0.263$, $p < 0.001$). That is, the development of Ni by the subsidiaries varies jointly with outsourcing strategic and nonstrategic activities. No statistical significance was found between Si and No.

In the proposed models, the following control variables were used: how long the subsidiary was established in Brazil (age: whether before or after 1990); the number of employees (size: if the subsidiary has more than 500 employees in the country or not); and the entry mode into the country (entry: whether through acquisition of existing company, greenfield, or joint venture). The percentages obtained in each case are presented in Table 17.8.

Table 17.8 Control variables

	Percentage of subsidiaries	Number of subsidiaries
Firm size (no. of employees)		
< 500	56.7	89
> 500	43.3	68
Entry mode		
Acquisition	31.2	45
Joint venture	11.5	17
Greenfield	57.3	83
Age		
< 1990	52.2	76
> 1990	47.8	69

Table 17.9 Regression models for internal strategic activities

	Models:	Control model	A1
Dependent variable: Si			
Variables:			
Constant		3.328	2.306
Independent	Ni	–	0.364***
Control	Age > 1990	−0.092	−0.030
	Entry	0.050	−0.040
	Size > 500	0.282*	0.048
	Adjusted R^2	0.038	0.193
	F	6.635	35.461***

***p < 0.001 **p < 0.01 *p < 0.05 stepwise.

The first regression analysis was done relating the internal development of strategic and nonstrategic activities (Hypothesis 1).

$$\text{Control Model} \rightarrow \text{Si} = \text{Age} + \text{Size} + \text{Entry}$$

$$\text{Model A1} \rightarrow \text{Si} = \text{Ni} + \text{Age} + \text{Size} + \text{Entry}$$

This assumption seeks to verify whether the subsidiaries surveyed find conditions in the country to develop both types of activities or only those of lower added value. As can be seen in Table 17.9, the Si variable correlates positively and moderately with the variable Ni ($r = 0.364$, $p < 0.001$). In this case the correlation shows that the higher the internal development of nonstrategic activities (Ni) the greater the possibility that strategic activities are being carried out internally (Si), showing joint positive variations among these variables.

That is, the results show that the explanatory power of the dependent variable "strategic activities performed internally" (Si) by the independent variable "nonstrategic activities performed internally" (Ni) is significantly positive ($r^2 = 0.193$), showing that the subsidiaries surveyed develop together both types of activities, thus confirming Hypothesis 1. This may show that the country is at a level at which companies develop internally (insource offshore) activities of both low and high value-added.

The results presented in this regression, associated with the internal development of strategic activities shown in Table 17.3, show that among the subsidiaries surveyed, quality workers who contribute effectively in activities of high added value are found. This shows that part of the investments made by multinationals in their subsidiaries in Brazil (UNCTAD 2009) occurred or developed to generate value (Hakansson and Henders1994; Lewin and Peeters 2006; Bunyaratavej et al. 2007; Lynn and Salzman 2007; Kedia and Mukherjee 2009; Jensen 2009) and not only for production (Moxon 1975; Lynn and Salzman 2007). They also show that ratings on the country's attractiveness for offshoring as presented, for example, by A. T. Kearney (2007, 2009) are a reality, whether their roles are either as predictive or as catalyst for this process.

Models B1 to B4 are designed for the analysis of Hypotheses 2A–C with the variable "outsourcing strategic activities" as a dependent,.

$$\text{Control Model} \rightarrow \text{So} = \text{Age} + \text{Size} + \text{Entry}$$

$$\text{Modelo B1} \rightarrow \text{So} = \text{Si} + \text{Age} + \text{Size} + \text{Entry}$$

$$\text{Modelo B2} \rightarrow \text{So} = \text{Si} + \text{Age} + \text{Size} + \text{Entry}$$

$$\text{Modelo B3} \rightarrow \text{So} = \text{No} + \text{Age} + \text{Size} + \text{Entry}$$

$$\text{Modelo B4} \rightarrow \text{So} = \text{Si} + \text{Ni} + \text{No} + \text{Age} + \text{Size} + \text{Entry}$$

The results for each model are presented in Table 17.10. Initially it appears that the introduction of control variables (age, mode of entry, and size) showed changes in the explanatory power of models.

The B4 model showed the best explanatory power of the dependent variable "outsourced strategic activities" (So), by the independent variables considered and significant ($r^2 = 0.181$). With the inclusion of predictive variables Si and No the control variables for companies established during the 1990s and employing over 500 employees plus exclusion (the ones not statistically significant) of the other variables, Hypothesis 2A is confirmed, nothing can be asserted on Hypothesis 2B, and Hypothesis 2C is also confirmed.

Hypothesis 2A questioned whether there would be a direct relationship between the internal development of strategic activities (Si) and the hiring of strategic activities with a third party (So). This was confirmed by the positive coefficient 0.374 ($p < 0.001$) presented in Table 17.2. Thus, it appears that the higher the internal development of

Table 17.10 Regression models for outsourced strategic activities

	Models:	Control model	B1	B2	B3	B4
Dependent variable: So						
Variables:						
Constant		1.845	0.656	1.846	1.296	−0.138
Independent	Si	-	0.358***	-	-	0.374***
	Ni	-	-	0.091	-	−0.044
	No	-	-	-	0.193*	0.197*
Control	Age > 1990	0.129	0.092	0.129	0.138	0.301*
	Entry	0.010	−0.044	−0.016	0.016	0.036
	size > 500	0.554***	0.453**	0.554***	0.490***	0.458***
	Adjusted R^2	0.082	0.14	0.089	0.105	0.181
	F	13.904	12.718	13.904	9.439	8.966***

***$p < 0.001$ **$p < 0.01$ *$p < 0.05$ stepwise.

strategic activities by the subsidiaries surveyed the larger the increase in the hiring of strategic services from third parties. This shows that companies cannot or do not intend to internalize all the functions needed to develop their operations.

Likewise, it shows that outsourcing remains a strategic tool (Insinga and Werle 2000; Cha et al. 2008) even for the subsidiaries in addition to internal strategic developments. Or even that what Mol (2007) says might happen, that external suppliers can be highly skilled and able to produce the desired services at lower costs. It is also worth noting that either lower costs are still being sought or companies are intending to have access to expertise and innovations (Domberg 1998; Chiesa et al. 2004; McIvor 2005) available on the market.

Hypothesis 2B stated that there would be a direct and positive relationship between the internal development of nonstrategic activities and the strategic activities with a third party. This cannot be verified statistically with the data obtained in the survey conducted. This could show that subsidiaries would have access to suppliers with great competence in contracted services (design and R&D, as proposed) and would internalize production (stage of assembly, for example) or even would dedicate themselves to marketing campaigns to provide products and services.

Finally, Hypothesis 2C, which focuses on the relationship between recruitment of strategic and nonstrategic activities with third parties. This proposition was confirmed by the positive coefficient 0.197 ($p < 0.05$) identified. However, the survey carried out does not indicate whether there has been a learning process, or evolution, beginning by outsourcing activities of lower value and then migrating to others of higher value. This hypothesis seeks to show that both strategic and nonstrategic services are available in the market, even though what might be occurring (or might occur in future) is what King (2005) identifies as contractors "upgrading" the services they provide, or what Sharma et al. (2007) present about India's TCS, which knew how to develop new competencies in which they could show a high degree of interdependence between tasks (Kumar et al. 2009).

It was also observed in Table 17.10 that the control variables "date of deployment since 1990" and "employing more than 500 employees" were also significant. In the first case, it may be related to an increased movement of opening national markets and privatization that occurred, starting in the 1990s, which can even be verified by a significant increase of direct investments in the country according to UNCTAD (1993–2009) and in globally, with the pace of the growing movement of offshoring. Also with regard to the size of the subsidiaries, which was fairly representative from the control model, a descriptive evaluation of the data shows that 63 percent of the subsidiaries with more than 500 employees employ strategic services from third parties, and of those, 85 percent carry out strategic activities internally. That seems to be an issue to be considered in the future.

Broadly speaking, these assumptions (Hypotheses 2A and 2C) show that even going across borders (offshore insource) in search of lower costs, according to some authors (Stack and Downing 2005; Lynn and Salzman 2007; Coucke and Sleuwaegen 2008), and internalizing them (strategic and nonstrategic services) through their subsidiaries, corporations continue to hire strategic and nonstrategic services from third parties (market).

The assumptions made and the statistical tests performed showed the following: first, the subsidiaries of MNCs installed in Brazil are able (or develop conditions to be able) to perform high-value-added activities; and second, even with these options, outsource activities of high and low added value for companies installed also in the Brazilian market. Otherwise, these subsidiaries internalize activities, but also need to outsource other activities in addition to their operations or to their business models. In this context, it is important to consider how these subsidiaries assess the remunerations offered internally and externally and also the quality of internal manpower and external.

The remuneration paid to employees at various levels is considered by many authors as the main component of offshoring operations costs. Initially, evaluating Figure 17.5, it is possible to identify three different clusters for the salaries of some occupations, enabling comparison between countries. The data presented refer to programmers with three years' experience. A first track of countries with salaries for programmers around US$10,000 annually. A second track around US$20,000 annually and, finally, a top banner with salaries above US$30,000. It is also possible to observe a great difference with the remuneration paid in the United States, surpassing US$60,000. It is possible to identify the track in which Brazil is positioned, in what could be classified as medium-cost countries.

This can also be verified when comparing other extreme occupations, such as call center operators and electronic engineers, using information obtained in Dedrick and Kraemer (2006) and Brazil (Wage Indicator 2011). In the first case, operators of call centers earn on average US$12.57 and less than US$1 per hour in the United States and India respectively. In Brazil, the average wage for that occupation in current values is around US$3.37 per hour. In the case of electronic engineers, comparing the studies of Dedrick and Kraemer (2006), the remuneration in Brazil also positions it in an intermediate position, with an average of just over US$23,000 per year, above Taiwan and China,

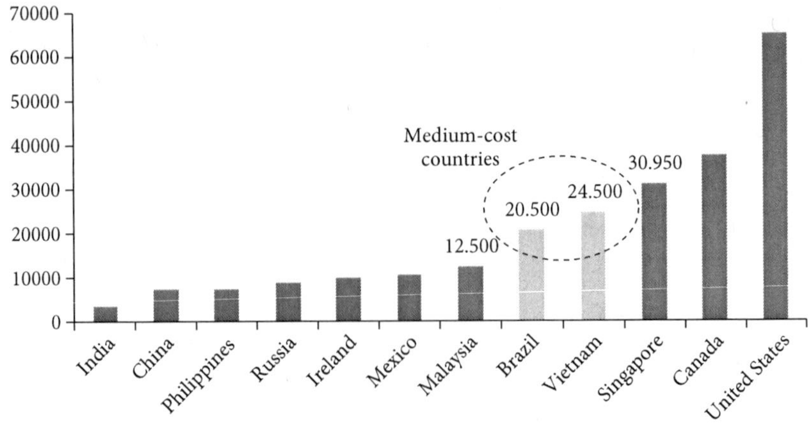

FIGURE 17.5 Remuneration for programmers (three years' experience) in developing and developed countries (in US$).

with US$10,000 and US$20,000 respectively, and well below Japan and the United States, with US$63,000 and US$78,000 respectively.

Once inside the country, it is still possible to identify another difference in remuneration. This is perceived by comparing remuneration paid by subsidiaries of multinationals in Brazil and by national companies (Wage Indicator 2011). It was noted that there is price premium of 25 to 40 percent paid by multinational employers, compared to Brazilian employers for occupations with similar characteristics. This may be an attempt to attract, internalize, and retain employees with the skills needed to maintain the companies' operations in the country, even though it is not able to take advantage of the entire remuneration gap in developed and emerging countries as it is in the case of Brazil. With this, the demand for external suppliers with the required quality and at lower cost is always a reality.

With respect to the quality of human resources, significant differences were observed in the surveyed subsidiaries point of view, with respect to internal and external labor force. This evaluation included administrative, operational areas, and areas of R&D and shows that the prospects are quite distinct. While the quality of internal human resources is considered high for 75 percent of the respondents, the quality of external labour is high only for 21 percent of respondents. In this case, internal human resources can involve expatriate employees from the different countries or Brazilian nationals working within the subsidiaries.

Such a situation may explain why subsidiaries prefer to perform most of their strategic activities internally and not pick them in the Brazilian market. To internalize their main activities, these companies can develop their human resources according to their philosophies, competencies, and purposes. In addition to this, our surveys have confirmed what has been identified by large companies and also by the government: there is a lack of qualified manpower in almost all sectors of the economy. This seems to have been detected recently, more specifically when Brazil began a cycle of growth above the world average and in line with the other BRIC countries or even from an opening of national borders as part of globalization.

Various associations of companies began to identify the lack of qualified professionals in their areas of expertise. Not only sectors that involve more advanced technologies, but also in others like construction and tourism. The number of job vacancies has been larger than the number of employees who apply, many of whom lack qualifications for the jobs. With this, the national economy seems to be encountering a noticeable bottleneck slowing down continuous growth and also suffering a significant loss in international competitiveness, when comparing to other countries, in attracting multinational companies. The situation also seems critical with respect to poor training in basic educational aspects such as knowledge in English, which will be necessary in the short term with the football World Cup in 2014 and the Olympic Games in 2016.

Alerted to these aspects, the government has sought to minimize this situation through specifying more flexible undergraduate course requirements that respond to the most urgent concerns of the market. All levels of government (municipal, state, and federal) have moved to reduce the gap between the needs of businesses and the manpower available in the market today. However, it is necessary that national and multinational companies are included in this process, showing what they need and the best way to prepare new professionals. In many cases this has been done through the constant presence of these companies in Brazilian universities, demonstrating opportunities and career plans, identifying the best possible future professionals and hiring them as trainees until they complete their courses.

Final considerations

It was found that the subsidiaries surveyed develop both strategic activities (Si) and nonstrategic (confirming Hypothesis 1), showing that conditions conducive to such achievements exist, in both material and human resources that are internalized and allow operation in the country. The set of activities examined encompassed strategic research and development, innovation, and development of new products and services, among others, so that the results may be considered significant for a broad range of activities.

However, it was found that the subsidiaries do not aim to internalize all activities, be they strategic or nonstrategic, and that outsourcing of both strategic activities (Hypothesis 2A) and nonstrategic (Hypothesis 2C) was confirmed. Regarding Hypothesis 2A, it was found that the higher the internal development of strategic activities, the greater the employment of external strategic services to complement their operations. For Hypothesis 2C, a similar situation occurred with respect to Hypothesis 1. Just as the internal development of nonstrategic activities and strategies are correlated, so does the hiring of third party strategic and nonstrategic service. This shows that the subsidiary both internalizes high- and low-value-added functions and outsources such functions as well, showing a business model in which internal and external environments are complementary. The possibility that the subsidiary would perform nonstrategic activities and capture strategic services from other companies (Hypothesis 2B) cannot be confirmed by information obtained in the survey conducted.

Multinational corporations make use of the process of offshore insource (OI) through its subsidiaries in Brazil for nonstrategic activities (Ni) but mainly for strategic activities (Si). Particularly in regard to strategic activities (or high added value), the consolidation of the activities shown in Table 17.2 and their components was quite significant, showing that, at least with the practice of offshore insource, the subsidiaries can select resources and talents to mold to their needs. Nevertheless, such an operation is complemented by contracting third parties for noncore strategic services.

For the academic studies, some relevant points deserve to be assessed (or reassessed) with greater attention. First, it needs to be verified that within the base of the surveyed companies the subsidiaries of MNCs operating in Brazil not only develop activities with low added value but find conditions to develop high-added-value activities. This situation seems to position the country not as a low-cost country but with competencies that, internalized by the subsidiaries, allow operation according to its business model and the strategy of the organization. The hybrid mode of operation, internalizing some activities and hiring others, shows what can be an intermediate step between the processes of offshore insource (OI) and offshore outsource (OO).

The survey results indicate that the subsidiaries of MNCs located or wishing to settle in a country can adopt more than one strategy toward developing strategic activities there. The internalization of these activities is possible if the MNC can identify and obtain resources (human or material) to the needs of its operations. Furthermore, these companies can benefit from outsourcing as a strategic move to that place because, as the research shows, many companies from different sectors are already doing this, showing that it is also possible to hire external strategic services in addition to their operations. The subsidiary can act as a scouting unit (Hansen and Birkinshaw 2007) in an organized or intuitive way, which can be beneficial to the corporation as a whole or even to the subsidiary's own strategic intentions in attracting new projects or activities to its borders, increasing its strategic importance within the MNC.

As for the contracted or the companies wishing to engage in this market, the opportunities are significant. In both cases there is the possibility of participating in the value chain of one or more of the MNCs that outsource and to learn as much as possible about the business, its processes, and its products and services. Having learned those things, the companies can perform the contracted services as efficiently as possible and with the best quality, so that they can effectively control what they do, and then what they have learned can become their own core competencies (Lynn and Salzman 2005, Mol 2007), allowing their portfolio of services to evolve so that they can even, depending on the goal, become a competitor in this sector of activity (e.g., the cases of Asustek companies, TCS and TPV [Gião, Oliveira Júnior, and Vasconcellos 2008; Gião, Oliveira Júnior, and Bhagat 2009]). This path has been followed by many companies that once were providers only of products and services to multinational companies.

For the government there is the opportunity to present the country, albeit tentatively, as already a host for the provision of strategic activities by companies, and naturally that would generate jobs. In this case, the quality ratings made by this research would need to be worked on to become an important pole of attraction for offshoring. The government could also act as a catalyst or facilitator to improve the quality of manpower in the country in different aspects or even by establishing incentives for companies that wish to operate in these areas. Above and beyond, the possibility of opening direct channels between foreign companies and suppliers located in Brazil (offshore outsourcing) through government actions and marketing (events, fairs, business meetings, etc.) would expand opportunities for businesses and could create jobs.

Directions for future reseach

First, as in part we have sought to do in this chapter, future research could identify settings and drivers that can be applied between developed countries and emerging countries. Many definitions of offshoring available in the literature have a low-cost bias that somehow restricts the movement of offshoring from developed countries to emerging countries. Such a situation does not seem appropriate and the search for a broader definition involving emerging countries moving toward developed countries must also be sought. Certainly when emerging companies such as Haier, Huawei, and ZTE (China), TCS and Wipro (India), Embraer, Petrobras, and Gerdau (Brazil) install subsidiaries in developed countries, with very varied purposes, ranging from sales and maintenance to research and development, they are going in search of low cost but also available skills. Moreover, a more thorough assessment shows that the first reason for offshoring is the search for competencies and not low costs. Developed countries have low cost as an additional aspect of this process, but because the cost is something that can be measured, it is soon considered as the main reason for offshoring. Therefore, the search for reasons, drivers, and broader definitions involving interactions between the various countries, both developed and emerging economies, should be the main issue in the future.

It was not the goal of the survey, but another interesting research topic could be to check whether these subsidiaries of MNCs installed in Brazil outsource to Brazilian domestic companies. This would show the competence and competitiveness of Brazilian companies in the provision of products and services in conducting strategic and non-strategic activities.

Since this chapter deals with activities developed by subsidiaries of MNCs installed in Brazil (offshore insource) and the services that these companies also hire already installed here (outsourcing), it remains to identify and map the situations in which companies (their headquarters or subsidiaries) located in other countries contract services or products directly from companies installed in Brazil (offshore outsourcing). Certainly, with the two ways studied, some traces or evidence can be identified about the types of activities contracted and their quality, and perhaps in the near future, subsidiaries of

MNCs can open canals or facilitate direct access of companies from outside those companies installed in Brazil.

A theme that seems to deserve special attention in future refers to the service sector. According to the information submitted by Sako (2006), this is the most representative within the economies of developed and developing countries, and current assessments seem to still refer to terms of production/manufacturing. To exactly which internal areas of the organizations in the sectors of services do terms such as research and development, design, product development, basic or applied research apply?

Offshoring and outsourcing allow greater competitiveness for organizations but also expose them to greatest risks. However, the risks for contracting companies can lead to great opportunities for the outsourced companies if they wish to move (if they have a strategic intention to move) across the value chain and increase their portfolio of services. With this in mind, a study that explores the outsourced company's point of view and the development of new skills and competences could be of great relevance. The articles about learning by Dodgson (1993), Anderson and Parker (2002), and King (2005) should also be considered from the perspective of contracted companies who are learning and may become more competent at what they do and may create innovations.

Even in respect of the risks, but now in relation to offshoring, many authors and organizations (Abramovsky et al. 2004; UNCTAD 2004; US Chamber of Commerce 2004; International Monetary Fund 2005) highlight the risk that this process can cause a loss of jobs in the corporations' countries of origin. If offshoring poses a threat to these countries, it can be of great value to the creation of job openings in emerging and developing countries. Therefore, a study that offers answers to this question of job creation due to internationalized services may be of interest both to the government and to enterprises throughout the country.

With the beginning of the great crisis of 2008–09, the Brazilian government sought to act proactively, accelerating internal investment, particularly in infrastructure, and to provide incentives for the population to continue buying, in particular through the reduction of taxes, which meant that the country did not suffer the crisis sharply. This proved significant in making sure that Brazilian GDP in 2009 showed only a 0.2 percent contraction, the sixth-best performance among the G20 countries and much better than countries such as United States (−2.4 percent), Japan (−5.0 percent), and the European Union (around −4.2 percent).

Already in 2011, the recovery could be perceived, with the country becoming the country that most attracted the fifth-largest investment, against a position lower than tenth place in 2009 (UNCTAD 2011). The value achieved in 2011 ($48 billion) was in excess of the $45 billion seen in the year preceding the crisis (2008), as shown in Figure 17.2. Among the BRIC countries, Brazil presented greater absolute value and percentage growth between 2009 and 2010 inflow FDIs.

Also significant are the prospects of the country in attracting FDI, as shown in research data in UNCTAD (2011), with Brazil occupying fourth position in better conditions for receiving of investment, behind China, the United States, and India. So, it looks like Brazil will remain a pole of attraction for MNCs for years to come, and further research, such as that shown in this chapter, can show this trend.

References

Abramovsky, L., R. Griffith, and M. Sako. 2004. "Offshoring of Business Services and Its Impact on the UK Economy." Advanced Institute of Management Research. Retrieved January 15, 2007, from http://www.aimresearch.org/uploads/Offshoring(2).pdf.

Amos, B., and W. D.Reitsperger. 2004. "Offshore Centers of Excellence: Social Control and Success." *Management International Review*, 44: 51–65.

Anderson, E. G., and G. G. Parker. 2002. "The effect of learning on the make/buy decision." *Production and Operations Management* 11 (3).

A. T. Kearney. 2007. *Offshoring for Long-term Advantage*. Chicago: A.T. Kearney.

———. 2009. *The Shifting Geography of Offshoring*. Chicago: A.T. Kearney.

Birkinshaw, J., G. Hamel, and M. J.Mol. 2008. "Management Innovation." *Academy of Management Review* 33 (4): 825–845

Birkinshaw, J. M., and A. J.Morrison. 1995. "Configurations of Strategy and Structure in Subsidiaries of Multinational Corporations." *Journal of International Business Studies* 26: 729–753.

Birkinshaw, J., N. Hood, and S. Jonsson. 1998. "Building Firm-specific Advantages in Multinational Corporations: The Role of Subsidiary Initiative." *Strategic Management Journal* 19 (3): 221–241.

Bunyaratavej, K., E. D. Hahn, and J. P. Doh. 2007. "International Offshoring of Services: A Parity Study." *Journal of International Management* 13: 7–21.

Carmel, E., J. Dedrick, and K. L. Kraemer. 2009. "Routinizing the Offshore Choice: Applying Diffusion of Innovation to the Case of EDS." *Strategic Outsourcing: An International Journal* 2 (3): 223–239.

Cha, H. S., D. E. Pingry, and M. E. Thatcher. 2008. "Managing the Knowledge Supply Chain: An Organizational Learning Model of Information Technology Offshore Outsourcing." *MIS Quarterly* 32 (2): 281–306.

Chesbrough, H. W., and D. J. Teece. 1996. "Organizing for Innovation: When Is Virtual Virtuous?" *Harvard Business Review* 74: 65–73.

Chiesa, V., R. Manzini, E. Pizzurno. 2004. "The Externalisation of R&D Activities and the Growing Market of Product Development Services." *R&D Management* 34 (1): 65–75.

Coucke, K., and L. Sleuwaegen. 2008. "Offshoring as a Survival Strategy: Evidence from Manufacturing Firms in Belgium." *Journal of International Business Studies* 39: 1261–1277.

Couto, V., M. Mani, A. Y.Lewin, and C. Peeters. 2006. *The Globalization of White-collar Work*. Duke University and Booz Allen Hamilton. https://offshoring.fuqua.duke.edu/pdfs/gowc_v4.pdf.

Daugherty, P. J. 1988. "Outsourcing Logistical Services: Firm-specific Usage Patterns." PhD diss., Michigan State University. AAT 8912566.

Dodgson, M. 1993. "Organizational learning: a review of some literatures." *Organization Studies* 14 (3).

DTT (Deloitte Touche Tohmatsu). 2005. *Global Financial Services Offshoring Report: Scaling the Heights*. Deloitte Touche Tohmatsu. http://www.deloitte.com/view/en_mk/mk/719264fe1a10e110VgnVCM100000ba42f00aRCRD.htm.

Domberger, S. 1998. The Contracting Organization: A Strategic Guide to Outsourcing. New York: Oxford University Press.

Economist Intelligence Unit. 2004. Scattering the Seeds of Invention: The Globalisation of Research and Development. London: Economist Intelligence Unit.

Ellis, W. 2004. "From Outsourcing to Worldsourcing." *Magazine of the International Trade Centre*, January.

Friedman, T. L. 2005. *O mundoé plano: uma breve história do século XXI*. Rio de Janeiro: Editora Objetiva.

Gião, P. R., M. M. Oliveira Júnior, and R. S. Bhagat. 2009. "Offshore Outsourcing of Services: Emerging Countries Point of View." Presented at the Third Annual Offshoring Research Conference and Paper Development Workshop, April.

Gião, P. R., M. M. Oliveira Júnior, and E. P. G. Vasconcellos. 2008. "Services Offshoring and Its Strategic Effects on Value Chains." *BAR, Curitiba* 5 (3): 193–209.

Hakansson, H., B. Henders. 1994. "International Co-operative Relationships in Technological Development." In *Managing Networks in International Business*, edited by M. Forsgren and J. Johanson. New York: Gordon and Breach.

Hansen, M. T., and J. Birkinshaw. 2007. "The Innovation Value Chain." *Harvard Business Review* 85 (6): 121–130.

Hatonen, J., and T. Eriksson. 2009. "30+ Years of Research and Practice of Outsourcing: Exploring the Past and Anticipating the Future." *Journal of International Management* 15: 142–155.

Insinga, R. C., and M. J. Werle. 2000. "Linking Outsourcing to Business Strategy." *Academy of Management Executive* 14 (4): 58–71.

IMF (International Monetary Fund). 2005. "Service offshoring, productivity, and employment: evidence from the United States." IMF Working Paper, Research Department, December.

Jensen, P. D. Ø. 2009. "A Learning Perspective on the Offshoring of Advanced Services." *Journal of International Management* 15: 181–193.

Kedia, B. L., and D. Mukherjee. 2009. "Understanding Offshoring: A Research Framework Based on Disintegration, Location and Externalization Advantages." *Journal of World Business* 44: 250–261.

King, W. R. 2005. "Outsourcing Becomes More Complex." *Information Systems Management Journal* 22 (2): 89–90.

Kotabe, M., and R. Mudambi. 2009. "Global Sourcing and Value Creation: Opportunities and Challenges." *Journal of International Management* 15: 121–125.

Kumar, K., P. C. van Fenema, and M. A. von Glinow. 2009. "Offshoring and the Global Distribution of Work: Implications for Task Interdependence Theory and Practice." *Journal of International Business Studies* 40: 642–667.

Kyostila, V., and W. Cardwell. 2005. "The Impacts of Offshoring on Value Creation in Finnish Venture-backed Software Companies." Helsinky University of Technology (May). http://www.sitra.fi/julkaisut/muut/Offshoring.pdf.

Lewin, A. Y. 2005. "An Emerging Challenge for IB Research—Editorial: Letter from the Editor." http://www.palgrave-journals.com/jibs/journal/v36/n5/full/8400163a.html; Accessed in: 10.05.2010.

Lewin, A. Y., S. Massini, and C. Peeters. 2009. "Why are Companies Offshoring Innovation? The Emerging Global Race for Talent." *Journal of International Business Studies* 40 (6): 901–925.

Lewin, A. Y., and C. Peeters. 2006. Offshoring Work: Business Hype or the Onset of Fundamental Transformation?" *Long Range Planning* 39: 221–239.

Lynn, L., and H. Salzman. 2005. "The 'New' Globalization of Engineering: How the Offshoring of Advanced Engineering Affects Competitiveness and Development." 21st European Group for Organizational Studies (EGOS) Colloquium "Unlocking Organizations," Berlin, Germany.

———. 2007. "'Innovation Shift' to the Emerging Economies: Cases from IT and Heavy Industries." Draft prepared for Sloan Industries Conference, April.

McIvor, R. 2005. *The Outsourcing Process: Strategies for Evaluation and Management*. Cambridge: Cambridge University Press.

Mol, M. J. 2007. Outsourcing: Design, Process, and Performance. Cambridge: Cambridge University Press.

Morgan, George A., N. L. Leech, G. W. Gloeckner, and K. C. Barrett. 2004. *SPSS for Introductory Statistics: Use and Interpretation*. New Jersey: Lawrence Erlbaum.

Moxon, R. W. 1975. "The Motivation for Investment in Offshore Plants: The Case of the U.S. Electronic Industry." *Journal of International Business Studies* 6: 51–66.

Mudambi, R. 2008. "Location, Control and Innovation in Knowledge Intensive Industries." *Journal of Economic Geography* 8: 699–725.

Neoit. 2005. "Mapping Offshore Markets." NeoIT. http://www.hca.org.vn/tin_tuc/tu_lieu_ts/nam2006/thang1/tulieunngoai2005/Mapping-Offshore-Markets2005.

OECD (Organisation for Economic Co-operation and Development). 2007. *Offshoring and Employment: Trends and Impacts*. Paris: OECD.

———. 2008. "Research and Development Going Global." Policy brief. Paris: OECD.

Oliveira Júnior, M. M., and F. M.Borini. 2003. "Relevância estratégica das subsidiárias brasileiras para as corporações multinacionais." In *Anais do Encontro Nacional da ANPAD*. São Paolo: Atibaia.

Parkhe, A. 2007. "International Outsourcing of Services: Introduction to the Special Issue." *Journal of International Management* 13 (1): 3–6.

Quinn, J. B., and F. G.Hilmer. 1994. "Strategic Outsourcing." *Sloan Management Review* 35 (4): 43–55.

Sako, M. 2006. "Outsourcing and Offshoring: Implications for Productivity of Business Services." *Oxford Review of Economic Policy* 22 (4): 499–512.

Sharma, R. S., A.Siddiqui, A. Sharma, R. Singh, R. Kumar, S. Kaushal, and S. Banerjee. 2007. "Leveraging Knowledge Management for Growth: A Case Study of Tata Consultancy Services." *Journal of Information Technology Case and Application Research* 9 (4): 29–65.

Stack, M., and R. Downing. 2005. "Another Look at Offshoring: Which Jobs are at Risk and Why?" *Business Horizons* 48 (6): 513–523.

Tadelis, S. 2007. 'The Innovative Organization: Creating Value through Outsourcing." *California Management Review* 50 (1): 261–278.

Tayles, M., and C. Drury. 2001. "Moving from Make/Buy to Strategic Sourcing: The Outsource Decision Process." *Long Range Planning* 34: 605–622.

UNCTAD (United Nations Conference on Trade and Development). 1993. "Transnational Corporations and Integrated International Production. World Investment Report 1993." New York: UNCTAD.

———. 1994. "Transnational Corporations, Employment and the Workplace. World Investment Report 1994." New York and Geneva: UNCTAD.

———. 1995. "Transnational Corporations and Competitiveness. World Investment Report 1995." New York and Geneva: UNCTAD.

———. 1996. "Investment, Trade and International Policy Arrangements. World Investment Report 1996." New York and Geneva: UNCTAD.

———. 1997. "Transnational Corporations, Market Structure and Competition Policy. World Investment Report 1997." New York and Geneva: UNCTAD.

———. 2003. "FDI Policies for Development: National and International Perspectives. World Investment Report 2003." New York and Geneva: UNCTAD.

———. 2004. "The Shift towards Services. World Investment Report 2004." New York and Geneva: UNCTAD.

———. 2005. "Transnational Corporations and the Internationalization of R&D. World Investment Report 2005." New York and Geneva: UNCTAD.

———. 2009. "Transnational Corporations, Agricultural production and Development. World Investment Report 2009." New York and Geneva: UNCTAD.

———. 2011. "Non-Equity Modes of International Production and Development. World Investment Report 2011." New York and Geneva: UNCTAD.

US Chamber of Commerce. 2004. "Jobs, trade, sourcing, and the future of the American workforce." Washington, DC.

Varadarajan, R. 2008. "Outsourcing: Think More Expansively." *Journal of Business Research* 62 (11): 1165–1172.

Wage Indicator. "Pesquisa Salarial." http://meusalario.uol.com.br/main/ [accessed October 1, 2011].

Weeks, M. R., and D. Feeny. 2008. "Outsourcing: From Cost Management to Innovation and Business Value." *California Management Review* 50 (4): 127–146.

WTO (World Trade Organization). 2005. *World Trade Report 2005. Exploring the Links between Trade, Standards and the WTO.* Geneva: World Trade Organization.

CHAPTER 18

Evaluation of Russia's Attractiveness as an IT Offshoring Destination

JULIA KOTLARSKY, NATALIA LEVINA, AND EKATERINA KURAKSINA

Introduction

With increasing globalization and technological developments that facilitate fast information exchange and enable location-free business processes, many countries around the world have become attractive locations for Western companies to relocate their processes and functions (Hahn et al. 2009) as they seek to capitalize on lowering business process costs following the global economic downturn. This movement, widely known as *offshoring*, embraces *offshore outsourcing* and *captive offshoring* trends (e.g., Lewin and Peeters 2006). In this regard, *offshore outsourcing* implies contracting work for a specified length of time, cost, and level of service to a third party (vendor) that is based at an offshore location, which usually means the vendor is located in a developing country and separated from the client by an ocean (Carmel and Tjia 2005). *Captive offshoring*, on the other hand, implies that the work is delegated to an internal entity (i.e., a captive facility) located offshore (Oshri 2011).

Beyond cheap labor, which was one of the main drivers for offshoring in the late 1980s and early 1990s, emerging markets today compete on availability and scalability of skills (e.g., in math, engineering, computer sciences, finance) and domain expertise (e.g., in specific business processes and markets). Beyond Tier 1 BRIC countries (Brazil, Russia, India, and China), there are more than 125 developing countries that try to find their niche and attract foreign investments, whether in the form of offshore captive centers, delivery center of world-leading suppliers, or through services provided by local suppliers. This puts pressure on BRIC countries, India in particular, that are already experiencing upward pressure on wages and high attrition rates.

In today's environment, skills and scale are becoming the most important factors that clients consider in their assessment of attractive locations. In this regard, Brazil has the advantage of a large population, the innovative creativity of its engineers, and government programs supporting the outsourcing industry. The Chinese government is investing heavily in Information and Communication Technologies (ICT) and English language training to improve China's competitive position (Oshri et al. 2011). Indian suppliers that have become world-leading Information Technology Outsourcing (ITO) providers, such as Infosys, Tata Consultancy Services (TCS), and Wipro, are increasingly expanding to developed as well as developing countries around the world. They locate offices in Western countries to be closer to their clients (i.e., for sales and marketing and for onshore development and support facilities), as well as offices in developing countries to gain access to diverse skill pools, to be closer to certain clients (e.g., Eastern Europe for Western Europe), and to explore opportunities to sell in local markets where demand for IT services is growing.

Among the four Tier 1 nations, Russia lags behind its rivals. In particular, as India has taken leadership in terms of market volumes, reaching over US$40 billion in software export value, and China is coming in second with US$5 billion, Russian sales have reached only US$3.65 billion (Willcocks and Lacity 2009). Recently there were several discussions in various outsourcing-related communities and professional magazines regarding removing Russia from the Tier 1 league (e.g., articles from *Business Insider*,[1] *Telegraph*,[2] *Foreign Policy*[3]).

In response to these views challenging Russia's current position among the Tier 1 sourcing destinations, the aim of this chapter is to objectively evaluate the extent of Russia's attractiveness in the global IT offshoring market. Our analysis relies on frameworks and factors for country selection suggested in the existing literature (e.g., Farrell 2006; Carmel and Tija 2005). In particular, we discuss the specifics of the IT offshoring market in Russia and assess its strengths, weaknesses, opportunities, and threats (SWOT). The chapter concludes with a discussion of Russia's major competitors in the global IT offshoring market, and we highlight key areas where Russia is likely to attract offshoring business in the future.

Russia's IT offshoring industry: background

In contrast to India, which has received significant attention among researchers focusing on topics related to offshoring (e.g., Rajkumar and Mani 2001; Joshi and Mudigonda 2008; Kotlarsky and Oshri 2008; Vlaar et al. 2008), there are only a few academic papers that discuss Russia from an offshoring perspective.[4] Earlier articles argued that doing business in Russia is risky, and the country in general represents a developing market with a high degree of instability (McCarthy et al. 1993; Kripalani 1997; Puffer et al.

1998). More recently, several authors have recognized the potential of the Russian IT offshoring industry (e.g., Dyker 1996, 2001; Carmel 2003; Palvia 2004; Adelakun 2008; Levina and Vaast 2008; Cusumano 2006). Palvia (2004), for example, refers to Russia as an emerging offshoring destination and argues that it has the capability to compete with India in terms of costs. Levina and colleagues (Levina and Su 2008; Levina and Vaast 2008) studied offshoring to Russia as a part of research that included Indian, Russian, and US-based teams. Their findings reflect on the cultural and organizational factors involved in offshoring to Russia (Levina and Vaast 2008) and the importance of considering Russian firms in multivendor outsourcing arrangements (Levina and Su 2009).

While many academic articles refer to Russia as a rising offshoring destination, only a few are fully devoted to analyzing the Russian IT offshoring industry. Among those, Hawk and McHenry (2005) measure the maturation of the Russian offshore software industry by analyzing what the industry has achieved so far and what obstacles stand in the way of future growth. Bardhan and Kroll (2006) apply Porter's (1990) framework to assess the underlying sources of Russia's competitive edge in the IT sector, such as the country's scientific background, education system, and low costs. They also provide a comprehensive comparison with the Indian software industry. However, taking into account the unprecedented growth of the Russian and Indian software industries, most of those finding have become somewhat dated.

Country Attractiveness Framework

We compared and combined factors identified in several offshore destination evaluation frameworks, primarily developed in practitioner-oriented literature, to define criteria we will use for evaluating Russia. These factors are described in Table 18.1.

Methodology

Data collection

The study uses qualitative methods to understand this emergent, contextually embedded phenomenon (Eisenhardt 1989; Yin 1994). The primary sources of data were archival records, which were supplemented by qualitative interviews. The archival data collection sources include a variety of academic and professional articles, industry reports, press releases, and reliable internet sources (such as official websites). While most of data presented in this chapter comes from these archival sources, interviews (Myers and Newman 2007) are used to interpret and expand on the archival data and to validate the findings. Interviews included: (1) individuals who provide

Table 18.1 Factors for evaluating attractiveness of offshore destination

Factor	Description	References
Cost	• labor costs (average wages for skilled workers and managers) • infrastructure costs (unit costs for telecom networks, internet access and power, and office rent) • corporate taxes (tax breaks, regulations and other incentives for local investment)	Carmel and Tija (2005) Doh et al. (2009) Farrell (2006) Bardhan and Kroll (2006) Heeks and Nicholson (2004)
Skills	• skill pool (the size of the labor pool with required skills). Required skills may include technical and business knowledge, management skills, languages and the ability to learn new concepts and innovate. The scalability of labor resources in the long term (that is, the ability to supply sufficient labor resources to handle growing demand) is a major issue to consider when choosing a sourcing destination. An indication of the scalability of labor resources in a country is the growth in the number of graduates with desired skills that it is able to demonstrate year to year. Countries that offer scalability of labor resources are also more likely to keep wages relatively low due to the constant supply of new graduates • vendor landscape (the size of the local sector providing IT services and other business functions). For clients looking to outsource IT or business processes, it is imperative to evaluate the vendor's landscape in terms of the general skills-set (or capabilities) and competencies of vendors.	Carmel and Tija (2005) Doh et al. (2009) Bardhan and Kroll (2006) Farrell (2006) Zaheer et al. (2009) Heeks and Nicholson (2004)
Environment	• government support (policy on foreign investment, labor laws, bureaucratic and regulatory burden, level of corruption) • business environment (compatibility with prevailing business culture and ethics) • living environment (overall quality of life, prevalence of HIV infection, serious crime per capita) • accessibility (travel time, flight frequency and time difference)	Carmel (2005) Hahn et al. (2009) Farrell (2006) Bardhan and Kroll (2006) Zaheer et al. (2009) Heeks and Nicholson (2004)
Market potential	• attractiveness of the local market (the current gross domestic product and its growth rate) • access to nearby markets (adjacent region)	Farrell (2006)
Risk profile	• security issues (that is, risks to personal security) and property-related issues, such as fraud, crime, and terrorism • disruptive events (including the risk of a labor uprising, political unrest and natural disasters) • regulatory risks (the stability, fairness and efficiency of the legal framework) • macroeconomic risks (such as cost inflation, currency fluctuation and capital freedom) • intellectual property (IP) risk (strength of the data and IP protection regime)	Doh et al. (2009) Hahn et al. (2009) Farrell (2006) Bardhan and Kroll (2006) Zaheer et al. (2009) Heeks and Nicholson (2004)

(Continued)

Table 18.1 (Continued)

Factor	Description	References
Quality of infrastructure	• telecommunication and IT (that is, network downtime, speed of service restoration and connectivity) • real estate (both the availability and quality) • transportation (the scale and quality of road and rail networks) • power (the reliability of power supply)	Carmel and Tija (2005) Doh et al. (2009) Farrell (2006) Bardhan and Kroll (2006) Zaheer et al. (2009) Heeks and Nicholson (2004)
Cultural compatibility	• key characteristics of the national culture (how they are similar of different to the cultures of the target markets) • business culture (expectations and behaviours at a workplace and employee-worker relationships)	Carmel and Tija (2005) Hahn and Bunyaratavej (2010) Farrell (2006) Hahn et al. (2009) Bardhan and Kroll (2006) Zaheer et al. (2009) Heeks and Nicholson (2004)

advisory services on offshoring to Russia, (2) senior executives of Russian IT services firms, and (3) senior executives of several Russian captive centers, as summarized in Table 18.2.

The combination of interviews and information collected from published sources (listed earlier) enabled triangulation of data collected from multiple sources, which was important for studying the phenomenon from different angles and for increasing the validity of the research findings. The interviews were recorded and transcribed.

Table 18.2 Interviewees

Interviewee	Organizational Background
BLP experts (3 interviewees)	Berwin Leighton Paisner (BLP), a UK-based law firm that has one of the largest outsourcing practices in the UK. The interviews were conducted with the company's experts, both at BLP head office in London and its international office in Moscow, Russia, known as Goltsblat BLP. This enabled us to compare perspectives on Russia's attractiveness from Russian, as well as foreign, experts.
Paul Tjia	Founder of GPI Consultancy based in the Netherlands and coauthor of the book Offshoring Information Technology—Sourcing and Outsourcing to a Global Workforce, focused on issues related to the Dutch market perception and trends of IT offshoring to Russia.
Valentin Makarov	President of Russoft Association—the nationwide association of software developing companies that provides analytics and other relevant information about the Russian software market—was interviewed about a wide range of aspects related to the attractiveness of Russia, in line with the theoretical framework adopted.
5 captive interviews	Five senior executives from two firms involved in creating and running software development-focused captive centers in Russia.
11 vendor interviews	Eleven senior executives from seven firms involved in running Russian vendor companies.

Data analysis

The attractiveness of Russia as an IT offshoring destination was evaluated based on seven factors included in the theoretical framework. The framework guided the analysis as we analyzed data collected from the various academic and industry sources, as well as the results of the interviews, and synthesized the findings related to each factor. These findings are used further for conducting SWOT analysis of Russia's attractiveness for IT offshoring.

Evaluation of Russia's attractiveness for IT offshoring

Factor one: costs

This factor includes labor and infrastructure costs as well as corporate taxes (see Table 18.1).

Labor costs

While labor costs in Russia are significantly lower than in the United States or Western Europe, they are higher than in India or China (see comparison of starting salaries in Table 18.3), which makes Russia somewhat less favorable for companies interested purely in reducing costs.

The average salaries in the Russian Federation overall and the IT industry in particular have grown in past years. For example, for several years, average salaries of software developers have increased by 20–30 percent per year. According to analytics, this tendency is partly due to ruble devaluation (by 25 percent) at the end of 2008 (Russoft 2008). Salaries decreased slightly from 2008 to 2009 and 2010 because of the global

Table 18.3 Starting salary and net availability (based on Joshi and Mudigonda 2008)

Country	Average annual starting salary (US$)	Yearly availability (thousands)
Vietnam	3,150	85
Indonesia	3,500	228
China	5,370	714
India	5,400	1,770
Philippines	8,150	514
Russia	11,700	657
Malaysia	12,400	142
Poland	15,925	285

economic crisis. As of 2009, based on the latest Russoft survey, the highest salaries were paid in Moscow (US$1,604 per month) and St. Petersburg (US$1,460 per month), and slightly below US$1,000 in other areas (Russoft 2010). While the official numbers for 2010 are not released yet, some evidence suggests they have recovered to precrisis levels (Russoft 2010).

It is no secret that the main part of Russia's economy is "gray"; that is, it combines both officially reported "white" accounting with unreported "black" accounting (Busovikova 2002; Butrin 2002). Typically, Russian companies go for such "black" accounting to reduce their tax burden. According to the survey results reported by Busovikova (2002), the majority of people believe that in Russia, the gray economy will live forever. However, despite this pessimistic opinion, after the reduction of income tax rates to 13 percent in 2001, salaries in Russia started to become "whiter" and are increasingly paid legally (Butrin 2002). Moreover, the economy is becoming more stabilized and the government is strengthening control over financial reporting. In addition, some Russian employees now prefer "white" salaries, as they believe having a higher officially reported salary means increased creditworthiness. Many Russian companies (especially ones based in Moscow) are reluctant to discuss and reveal their price lists in order to maintain their image as low-cost providers (Hawk and McHenry 2005). Therefore, it is important to note that actual labor costs in Russia might be higher than the numbers reported officially.

While global financial and Russian currency crises led to salary declines in 2008–10, overall most reports predict a significant salary growth in major Russian cities in the future (Hawk and McHenry 2005; Russoft 2010). Thus, it is becoming more and more difficult for Russia to keep up with BRIC and many Tier 2 non-BRIC emerging sourcing destinations, such as Vietnam, the Philippines, and others (Oshri et al. 2011), where labor, real estate, and infrastructure costs are significantly lower than in Russia. To respond to cost pressures, some of the larger Russian outsourcing vendors have expanded to lower-cost locations. For example, Luxoft has built a development center in Dubna and DataArt set up its center in Novgorod and Voronezh. Russian software firms are also opening offices in other CIS countries with lower costs. For example, Lizatec opened a second office in Kyrgyzstan and Luxoft and DataArt have opened offices in Ukraine.

Infrastructure costs

With respect to real estate, Moscow is one of the world's most expensive cities. This has stifled the growth of delivery centers in the city, where office rentals can be as high as US$2,000 per square foot per year for class-A office space. Conversely, the costs of telecommunication and personal transportation in Russia are quite low. Due to an excellent public transportation system, private transportation arrangements, which are often involved in sourcing work to India, can be avoided.

Corporate taxes

Until recently, Russia was criticized for the lack of incentives within the software industry and relief on foreign capital (Bardhan and Kroll 2006). However, Russian government has recently adopted several initiatives aimed at improving the taxation system for software development companies. First, in 2001, the taxation system in Russia underwent comprehensive reform, designed to ease the tax burden on individuals and companies. As of 2011, the standard rate of Russian corporate profit tax is 20 percent, lower than in the other BRIC countries. Companies also pay 9 percent tax on dividend income. Some regions have an additional incentive reduction. Under certain conditions, companies with holdings of 50 percent or more are entitled to a participation exemption on dividend income.[5] In July 2005, Vladimir Putin signed a federal law creating new special economic zones (SEZs), four of which are technical/innovation zones (Shapovalov 2006). Companies within these four zones are provided customs and tax breaks for periods of up to twenty years. However, according to business analyst reports, leading foreign high-tech firms have yet to invest in Russian SEZs.

Factor two: availability of skills

This factor includes the size of the labor pool with required skills and the vendor landscape.

Skills pool

The availability of skills is increasingly one of the most crucial factors when choosing an offshore location, often overshadowing the importance of lower costs (Bardhan and Kroll 2006; Czaja 2009; Kennedy 2009). In this area, Russia's main strength is the availability of its large pool of well-qualified technical specialists and low turnover compared to other BRIC countries like India.

Education system

To some extent, Russia benefits from the fact that it has the largest territory in the world—and the largest population in Europe—with an almost 100 percent literacy rate. Russia has a strong educational system that historically has prepared highly skilled professionals to tackle nonstandard tasks, particularly in such disciplines as mathematics and engineering (Prencipe 2001; Kolding and Kroa 2007). It has the highest rate of people with doctorate degrees in the world (Gartner 2009).

The Russian education system relies on a large number of universities, institutes, and colleges, which have focused on the technical sciences since the Soviet era. According to the World Bank, Russia has the third-highest number of scientists and engineers per capita in the world (Trombly 2003), well known for their creativity, innovative natures, and assiduousness (McCue 2007; Gibson 2006; Prencipe 2001). Fifty percent of students major in technology, science, or engineering—far more than in China, India, Japan or the United States.[6]

There are, however, some disturbing signals indicating a potential deterioration of the educational system and institutional infrastructure. Some analysts (e.g., Grishina

2009; Terekhov 2001) note that since Russia's transition to a market economy, there has been a steady decline in government spending on the sciences. The number of scientific centers and working scientists in Russia has decreased significantly over the years (from 4,646 scientific centers employing 1,943,110 scientists in 1990 to 3,559 centers with 820,470 scientists in 2005). Moreover, the Ministry of Education recently claimed that only 10–20 percent of higher-education institutions maintain the high educational standards set during the Soviet era (Gartner 2009). The Russian economy has yet to realize the effects of any real decline in its educational system. Soviet-era specialists are still a major part of the workforce. With time, however, a decline in technical skills may become more apparent.

The production of a skilled Russian labor pool also has been limited by the population decline in Russia between the early 1990s and 2009. There is some room for optimism here, however, as 2009 showed a slight population increase (23,300) after fifteen years of steady decline.[7]

Another factor to consider is that technical graduates in Russia lack an understanding of Western business processes and culture, making it difficult to employ them in the offshore software industry. In an effort to mitigate this factor, many companies partner with universities and colleges to create training programs and internship opportunities targeted at closing this skills gap (Russoft 2010).

Management skills

Russian managerial skills in the IT services industry have been hailed as both good and bad over the last decade of offshoring. On the one hand, managerial knowledge in the IT industry is relatively new to Russian managers. Mark Lewis (head of outsourcing, BLP) explained that, "Western management skills have been developing for many years and Russian management exists only for about twenty years." The small number of relatively recent business schools is unable to deliver the volume of managerial skills required to address this gap. Modern sales and marketing knowledge is particularly difficult to find. Some argue that Russian enterprises have inherited the poor managerial habits of the Soviet era, stifling initiative and productive debate. This criticism, however, does not seem to be prevalent within the IT services industry, which is dominated by the highly trained technical elite of Russian society, who have been criticized as being too assertive and vocal. Many studies of IT offshoring to Russia document client frustration with Russian specialists' desires to get involved in strategic project decision making and to, at times, circumvent client authority with respect to deadlines, priorities, and technical architecture (Weinert et al. 2008; Hawk and McHenry 2005; Levina and Vaast 2008).

Yet, some clients have found Russian initiative and dissent to be refreshing and useful. Not only can Russian developers provide deep technical insight but they provide a fresh perspective with respect to managerial decision making (Levina and Vaast 2008). Companies that perceived value in nurturing this approach also learned to mitigate the downside by training more senior delivery managers to adjust to Western management styles and create close monitoring of "runaway" programmers. They also engaged in close monitoring on the client's end without necessarily killing innovation and diversity (Levina and Vaast 2008).

Language skills

Companies planning to offshore to Russia may face relatively poor English competency (Trombly 2003; Gibson 2006). During the Soviet era, foreign language instruction was limited to reading texts, with limited exposure to spoken language. Travel opportunities and exposure to foreign media were few and far between. Only after the collapse of the USSR has the practice changed as more spoken language courses and native English teachers were introduced in the education system (Cherednichenko 2009). Older workers, therefore, are rarely proficient in English or other foreign languages.

However, the number of Russian students studying abroad has grown in recent years. In 1999, there were approximately 10,000 Russians studying abroad, 30 percent of whom studied in the United Kingdom (Popovich 1999). In 2009, the number of students studying abroad tripled, with the United Kingdom and the United States being the most popular destinations (Khomutsky 2007). Experts forecast that this number will double again in the near future. The perceived language barrier has less of an impact on the Russian IT outsourcing sector. Russoft (2010) estimates that, on average, 65 percent of employees in Russian IT services firms are fluent in English. Our qualitative data analysis confirms that senior, delivery, and project managers working for export-oriented firms are indeed fluent (e.g., they did not care which language they were interviewed in and were able to answer questions equally in Russian or English). However, lower-level employees, including team leaders, are usually fluent in writing skills but rather weak in oral communication, preferring to communicate via email or text messaging. With the rapid increase in the country's English-language skills, it is likely language barriers will not have a profound or lasting effect on the Russian IT offshoring climate.

Employee turnover

One of the major selling points within the Russian software industry is the relatively low rate of employee turnover. According to Russoft (2010), the voluntary and involuntary turnover combined was 2–5 percent in Moscow and Siberia and 11 percent in St. Petersburg, with export-oriented companies experiencing even lower levels of turnover. While one can argue that such low levels are associated with industry decline and lack of worker mobility, figures show that even during the boom years, Russian providers experienced only 6–8 percent staff turnover levels. In this respect, Russia has a clear advantage over countries like India, with high attrition rates.

A bigger threat to workforce stability is the opportunity for English-speaking, "Westernized" technical specialists to leave Russia altogether for better pastures abroad. Brain drain to the United States, Israel, and Western Europe is significant. One interesting factor that came out of our analysis, however, is that many of the people we interviewed in more senior positions within the Russian IT industry were returnees—people who had already explored opportunities abroad and had decided to return to Russia for family or other social reasons. They brought with them valued business knowledge from abroad (Filatotchev et al. 2009).

Vendor landscape

This section provides an overview of the companies operating in the Russian IT offshoring market, in particular major software development vendors.

Main local IT providers

Arguably, as of 2008, the majority of the Russian IT providers are small and medium-sized companies that employ fewer than 50 people (59 percent) or between 50 and 100 people (12 percent). Only 10 percent of local vendors employ more than 300 people. Weinert et al. (2008) predict that a majority of Russian companies will be reluctant to employ more than 400–500 people, as most of them are niche players not seeking rapid growth. Luxoft continues to be the largest vendor with headquarters in Russia and operations in Ukraine and other regions. Other major vendors perceived as "Russian" include EPAM and IBA, each employing 2,000–4,000 staff. Other notable players include DataArt, Exigen Services, MERA Networks and Reksoft, Auriga, and AT Software. Most have a major presence in Moscow (nearly 40 percent), St. Petersburg (26 percent), or Novosibirsk (approximately 10 percent) (Weinert et al. 2008).

Technical skills of Russian IT vendors

According to the survey conducted by Kolding and Kroa (2007), technical skills and software development methodologies are key strengths in the Russian software and services industry. Russian IT companies provide multiple IT services (see Figure 18.1), with high-end and complex systems design and development being the most popular. These areas directly affect clients' core business processes (Weinert et al. 2008; Levina and Vaast 2008).

Repetitive and low-end tasks such as coding, systems maintenance, and customer support are not popular among Russian IT providers. According to Weinert et al. (2008), the work of Russian programmers can be characterized as "technology problem-solving rather than simple low-cost programming." Typically, Russian programmers strive to work on projects that require creativity and innovation, and they are rarely interested in simple coding or maintenance (Gibson 2006).

Clients of Russian IT Vendors

Hawk and McHenry (2005) emphasize that a majority of Russian IT clients are technology firms that place demanding requirements on Russian engineers for scientific knowledge or advanced computer science and software engineering skills. The majority of Russian vendors are still SMEs and their services are built around strong technical skills and low turnover rates.

In geographical terms, the United States and Canada remain primary foreign target markets for Russian vendors and are the primary sources of FDI into Russian captive centers. There is a large presence of such American companies as Microsoft, IBM,

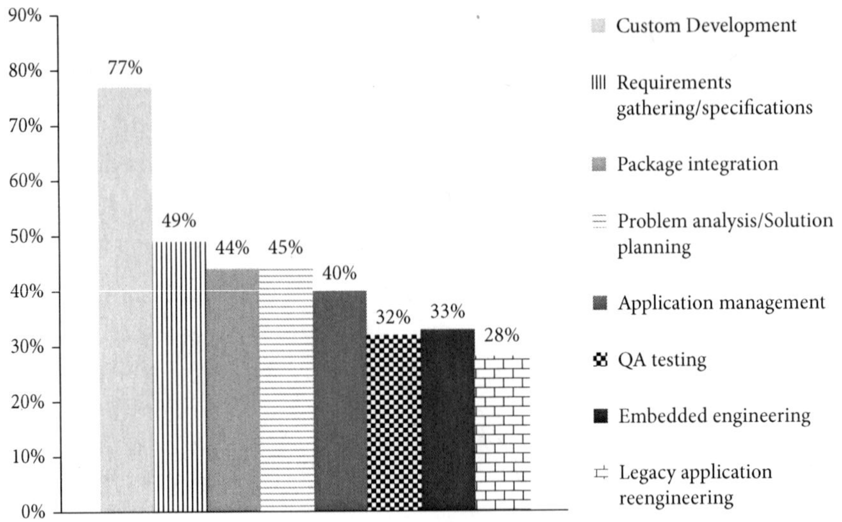

FIGURE 18.1 Figure Kotlarsky.1: Services offered by Russian IT providers (based on Weinert et al. 2008).

Oracle, SAP, Intel, Yahoo!, Google, and many others in Russia, mainly in the form of captive R&D centers (King 2009), which constitute 55 percent of software export in Russia (Russoft 2009). The United States and Canada are followed by Ukraine, Western Europe, Germany, and Scandinavia (see Figure 18.2).

Factor three: environment

This factor covers government support, business and living environment, and accessibility.

Government support

Despite the critique, between 2002 and 2007, the Russian government appeared to understand the strategic potential of the software development industry. Putin claimed there was a need to diversify the economy from its heavy dependence on natural resources and to take advantage of the large pool of highly trained programmers and scientists.[8] However, actual support has lagged far behind government promises.

The E-Russia program aimed to improve use of ICT across the country (e.g., to facilitate electronic circulation of documents and to promote a "computer for every home"), as well as improving the offshore programming sector (King 2009). E-Russia was supposed to be implemented by 2010, with a goal of increasing software export to US$1.5–2 billion.[9] However, this turned out to be overly optimistic considering the limited budget, which accounted for only 20–25 percent of the initially planned investment of US$2.6 billion (Hawk and McHenry 2005).

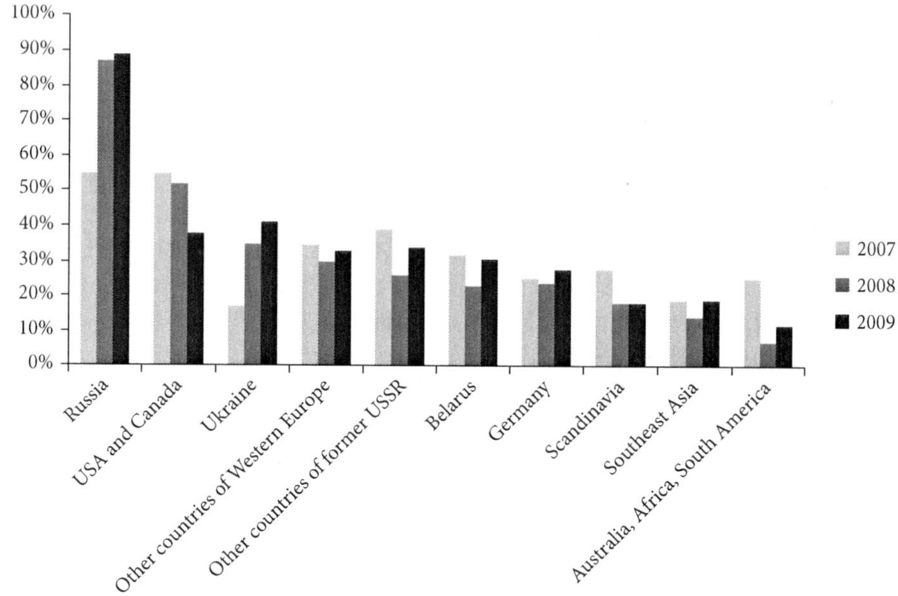

FIGURE 18.2 Figure Kotlarsky.2: Key markets of Russian IT vendors (based on Russoft 2010).

In 2006, the government approved a plan to develop techno-parks in seven regions, including Moscow and St. Petersburg.[10] The goals were ambitious: overall investment of US$985 million (US$75 million from the federal budget), techno-park revenues of US$4.4 billion by 2011, and 75,000 new jobs (King 2009). To date, however, these projects have fallen far short of their goals. For instance, of the seven parks planned, only the one in St. Petersburg has reached a significant size and is approaching completion (King 2009).

On a positive note, city governments sometimes take leadership. St. Petersburg's administration, for example, has worked to make the city a leading worldwide high-tech center. One recent program with a budget of 10 billion rubles aims to increase the share of innovative products in city production to 10.3 percent.[11] This has convinced many foreign firms to set up captive centers in St. Petersburg over Moscow.

Bureaucratic and excessive administrative controls are serious barriers to any business in Russia, not just the IT industry. They result in higher accounting and legal costs for businesses (Bardhan and Kroll 2006). This problem is especially relevant for the small and medium-sized companies that comprise the majority of the Russian IT industry. These companies lack substantial resources to overcome bureaucratic barriers. Corruption is widespread in Russia. Officials demand bribes in exchange for regular government services, such as business registration, utility hook-ups, and development permits. However in recent years, fewer small and medium-sized businesses reported difficulties in this regard, especially in the Moscow region.[12] While the government has made an effort to fight corruption, lack of enforcement remains a problem.

Living environment

The quality of life in Russia is relatively favorable. Since Putin's economic restructuring, living standards have improved and a sizeable middle class has emerged in Russia.[13] However, with improved living standards, the price of living has increased as well. According to Mercer's 2010 *Worldwide Cost of Living Survey*, Moscow is the most expensive city in Europe and also has the largest number of billionaires among all the cities in the world.[14]

Outside of Moscow, Russia is not an expensive country to live in, especially after the currency falls in Eastern Europe. In particular, cities such as St. Petersburg and Novosibirsk are very attractive for offshoring as high-tech clusters and for the lower cost of living. Although the crime level in Russia is still quite high, particularly in the larger cities, the threat is probably no greater than in most big cities around the world. As violent crime becomes less problematic, there are still very high levels of various forms of fraud: corruption, counterfeiting, financial frauds, and computer hacking are still common.

In spite of these problems, our interviews with Russian firms and their clients indicate that foreigners generally find it desirable to visit St. Petersburg and Moscow. Often, up to half of onshore team members have visited Russia during multiyear projects to establish business, intellectual, and social ties.

Accessibility

Face-to-face meetings are unavoidable in successful outsourcing and offshoring relationships. Most popular offshoring destinations in Asia are far from their main clientele based the United States and Western Europe. In comparison, Russia benefits from greater proximity to its main clientele. Captive R&D centers in Moscow and St. Petersburg are only a two- to three-hour flight from most European capitals, making Russia a "nearshoring" location rather than "offshoring" (or "farshoring") option. The nine-hour flight from North America to Russia is far shorter than fifteen hours to India or China. Shorter travel time helps reduce the costs, and the decreased time-zone difference supports more effective management activities, communication, and coordination in real time (Kolarova et al. 2006; Bardhan and Kroll 2006).

Because of the time difference with the United States, Russian companies follow their Indian counterparts in promoting the twenty-four-hour development cycle, where Russian developers work while US developers are still asleep (Kolarova et al. 2006; Bardhan and Kroll 2006). This enables a company to reduce time to market by shortening the overall project timeline (Weinert et al. 2008).

There are, however, several accessibility obstacles to consider. First, the procedure to obtain a visa or work permit is expensive and time consuming, due to the complexities involved (Filimonov 2001). Second, there is a shortage of reasonably priced business-class hotels in the main Russian outsourcing centers. Moscow and St. Petersburg have either luxury hotels that are very expensive or cheap hotels that are in extremely poor condition (Filimonov 2001).

Factor four: market potential

This factor considers the attractiveness of the local market and markets in the neighboring countries.

Some large Western multinational companies see a potential for the local market to become a consumer of their products and services in the near future. Typically, such companies decide to make an investment early on and use their presence in Russia to develop relationships with local businesses and governmental bodies that may become their consumers or may influence the extent to which they are able to enter the Russian market. For example, one Russian interviewee working for a large American corporation explained that his company opened a site in Moscow for political reasons, to demonstrate that the company does consider Russia an important market and partner.[15] This may explain the presence of large multinationals in strategic cities, such as Moscow and St. Petersburg, despite high salaries and cost of living in these cities.

Due to the large size of the Russian market, there may not be significant additional value in setting up presence in Russia for its proximity to the potential markets for selling products and services of its neighboring Central and Eastern European (CEE) and Asian countries. On the contrary, establishing a presence in other CEE countries may help Western firms to explore proximity to Russian in order to access the local Russian market.

Factor five: risk profile

This factor includes disruptive events, security issues, regulatory, macroeconomic, and IP risks.

Disruptive events and security

Overall, unlike countries in the Middle East, Africa, and Asia, most of the CEE countries are quite safe for living and travelling (Oshri et al. 2011). In terms of terrorism, however, there are still threats to Russian security because of the situation in Chechnya. In 2009, an attack on the Nevsky Express killed twenty-seven people. In March 2010, a bombing in a Moscow metro station killed twenty-nine people. These are just two of the most recent violent attacks in Russia's recent history.[16] However, unlike India, there was no Russian city included in the twenty-five "most dangerous outsourcing locations" for 2010.[17] Since Russia has achieved greater political stability under Putin's leadership, political instability does not currently factor as significantly into the risk profile. The country's economy grew significantly due to initiated reforms in banking, labor, private property, and mainly as a result of the increase in oil prices.[18] This current political stability is likely to continue for the foreseeable future.[19]

Regulatory risk

According to legal experts from Goltsblat BLP we have interviewed, all necessary legal conditions for outsourcing to Russia, as well as within Russia, are present. However, past research reported numerous problems experienced by foreign companies interested in setting up facilities in Russia. These included unclear legal systems, intellectual property rights, export and import legislation, complicated taxation, labor and currency laws, company accounting rules, bureaucracy, restrictions on international businesses, and lack of supportive government policies toward businesses (Filimonov 2001; Mills et al. 2007).

Intellectual property risk (IPR)

Recently, Russia has made considerable improvements in the IPR-protection field. According to a 2008 Russoft report, government and business associations initiated antipiracy campaigns that resulted in increased IP security. The annual BSA/IDC Global Software Piracy Study reported continuous improvement in software piracy levels that dropped from 80 percent in 2006 to 65 percent in 2010. This compares favorably to China, where piracy rates were 78 percent in 2010, and is similar to India (64 percent piracy rate).[20]

Despite significant improvement, many challenges remain. Enforcement is lax, as judges often lack IPR expertise or they simply refuse to consider such cases as serious crimes. Moreover, corruption continues to be a problem. The law experts from Goltsblat BLP we have interviewed emphasized this problem. As one interviewee put it, "We have all the appropriate laws in place and court practice. The problem is that people do not respect intellectual property." In his opinion, the low level of income prevents many people from buying costly licensed software. However, enforcement may increase as a result of the government's attempts to enter the World Trade Organization (WTO) (King 2009).

Macroeconomic risk

The macroeconomic climate in Russia has been rather positive and stable recently, which has increased the country's credit rating (Mills et al. 2007). Russia's GDP grew between 1998 and 2007 but declined slightly from 2008 to 2010 due to the global economic crisis, not unlike other countries around the world. Russia's economy depends heavily on such sectors as fuels, energy, and metallurgy, which account for about 35 percent of industrial output, and electricity and food sectors account for another 25 percent. This leaves the economy quite vulnerable to world oil prices. This factor might be a threat to the overall country's stability. Diversifying the economy by increasing support to the country's IT services industry could help reduce its dependency on nonrenewable resource exports and create a more stable, modern global economic foundation.

Furthermore, inflation has been one of the main issues affecting Russia's overall economic stability.[21] From 2000 to 2007, the level of inflation fell from 20 percent to a record low of about 9 percent. However, in 2008, inflation increased dramatically by about 52 percent as a consequence of buoyant energy prices, rising global food prices, and the global financial crunch.

Factor six: quality of infrastructure

This factor considers IT and telecom, real estate and transportation infrastructures in the country.

Telecoms and the Internet

Past research emphasized that Russia suffers from inadequate telecommunications and technological infrastructure (Goolsby 2001; Trombly 2003). However over the last ten years, the situation has improved as new communication channels have been developed. The telecoms sector grew dramatically, especially in the cities with the large populations. Sixty percent of regional cities have modern digital infrastructures. In rural areas the telephone services are still quite outdated, and there are only 30 fixed lines per 100 households across the country.[22] The number of Internet users in Russia has increased dramatically between 2005 and 2010, reaching 42 million people (30 percent of the population); about one-quarter of these users are in Moscow and St. Petersburg (Gartner 2010). Similar to other CEE countries, ICT infrastructure in Russia is fragmented (Oshri et al. 2011; Kolarova et al. 2006). World-class infrastructure is available in major cities, SEZs and techno-parks, whereas the rest of the country suffers from limited access to IT and telecom services. Although the government has started to address this problem through one of the E-Russia program initiatives (Kolarova et al. 2006), a lack of funding has undermined the development of this initiative.

Real estate and transportation

Physical infrastructure, including real estate and transportation routes, in Russia is improving as well, as modern business centers and new roads are built (Russoft 2009). While over 500,000 square meters of new office space is put on the market annually,[23] the lease rates and prices for commercial property are growing as demand continues to increase. Moreover, according to Hawk and McHenry (2005), it is very difficult for companies to expand their office space to accommodate growth due to the high occupancy rates in main centers. This problem, however, is not specific to Russia as many other big cities, such as London and New York, face similar issues. Transport infrastructure (i.e., the quality of roads, the quality and availability of public transport) is adequate in large cities and relatively poor in rural areas, and safety is an issue. Domestic airlines traditionally have been considered low quality (Hawk and McHenry 2005), but national air transport has experienced considerable growth in the post-Soviet era. Both airlines and railway networks require significant modernization.[24]

Factor seven: cultural compatibility

This factor assess compatibility between Russian and Western cultures and how it may impact business relationships between Russian and foreign firms.

Main cultural dimensions

According to Bradley (1999), Russian culture is characterized by a moderate level of individualism, high level of power distance, a high degree of uncertainty avoidance, and low masculinity value. Employees in Russia require a highly cooperative environment, external benefits provided by the company, clear plans for the future, and security. Employees feel managers are responsible for providing such things, and a top-down management approach is highly undesirable.

Business culture of Russian IT providers

Overall, Russian specialists are curious and want to know all the specifications and details about the project and its purpose. They work on a task until the result is perfect. They are innovative and offer alternatives, options, and fresh ideas. Russian employees are flexible with respect to long hours or weekends, similar to Indian culture, but very different from most Western cultures where 5 p.m. constitutes the end of the work day, regardless of whether the work has been completed. According to Makarov, most foreign customers admire several of the distinctive characteristics of Russian business culture: a high degree of responsibility, problem-solving skills, flexibility, ability to innovate, top technological skills, and company loyalty.[25]

Some characteristics have their drawbacks. Typically, Russian specialists are very straightforward in their opinions of management ideas. While openness and active engagement fosters creativity, this may have a negative impact on authority distribution. Allowing Russian specialists to interfere in project management and planning may have disappointing results, as Russian project management skills are not well developed. However, it is important to note that in comparison to other BRIC countries, it is commonly accepted that Russia has the advantage of cultural proximity to the United States and Europe (Levina and Su 2008; Russoft 2009; Kolarova et al. 2006; Weinert et al. 2008; Filimonov 2001).

Conclusions

In this section we present SWOT analysis of Russia's attractiveness as an IT offshore destination based on the seven factors discussed earlier.

SWOT analysis

SWOT analysis remains a major analytical tool, typically used for evaluating the internal core competencies and main problems of an organization (strengths and weaknesses) and the external environment (opportunities and threats) surrounding it (Coman and Ronen 2009). In this paper we use the SWOT analysis tool to assess Russia's attractiveness in the IT offshoring industry, based on the seven factors discussed earlier. Table 18.4 summarizes the strengths and weaknesses of the Russian IT offshoring industry,

Table 18.4 SWOT analysis of the Russian IT offshoring industry

Strengths	Weaknesses
• Excellent IT human resources with highly developed technical skills, ability to perform non-standard tasks and experience with complex projects • Strong fundamental education system with focus on math, sciences and engineering • Scalability of resources in terms of annual number of graduates in math, sciences and engineering • Russia has closer cultural proximity with the West than most other popular offshoring destinations, including other BRIC countries • Low attrition rate • Nearshoring rather than far-shoring destination for European and US (east coast based) companies • Time zones are better synchronized with the US and Europe than other countries (India and China) to allow real-time communications (with Europe) and 24-hour working days (with US) • Low labor costs (compared to Western countries) • Country's increasing political and economic stability • Relatively low corporate tax and positive dynamic in overall taxation policy • Improvements in physical and ICT infrastructures in Russia over the last 10 years, particularly in large cities	• Poor understanding of western business practices and poor project management skills among Russian software companies • Management style and culture are different from Western ones (although culture is closer than India, China or Brazil) • English language skills are less developed than in other popular offshoring destinations, such as India and some CEE countries • Difficulty visiting Russia due to visa requirements • Highly fragmented ICT and transport infrastructure between large cities and rural areas • Lack of marketing activities and administrative bodies responsible for marketing activities and promotion of the Russian IT offshoring • Lack of certification authorities and, as a result, lack of CMM certified IT firms • Lack of sufficient government support • High level of corruption and bureaucracy • Relatively high level of piracy • Legal challenges (mostly related to foreign companies planning to set up a presence in Russia rather than software export activities)

Opportunities	Threats
• Growth of nearshoring trend • Growth of multi-sourcing trend • Russian IT outsourcing industry is dominated by medium-sized companies. However, their growth is extremely high and so the number of large companies is expected to increase in the future. • Potential to attract more foreign companies to set up R&D centers • Potential for domestic IT outsourcing market development • Large Russian diasporas present in many countries have an opportunity to create international links beneficial for the industry and to attract new capital • Growing interest in the IT industry from the Russian government and recognition of the sector as strategically important	• Growing competition from non-BRIC countries, in particular, other CEE countries • Growing threat of the future deterioration of the educational system and institutional infrastructure due to lack of financial support and the decreasing prestige of scientific work • Growing costs of living in the main business centers, such as Moscow and St Petersburg • Continued brain drain • Declining population • Increasing competition for talent • Overall perception of Russia as a difficult place to do business • Terrorist activities that continue to hit Moscow

opportunities the industry should exploit in the future, and threats that might undermine its further development in the global IT offshoring market.

Analysis of Russia's overall attractiveness as an outsourcing destination

Academic literature (e.g., Bardhan and Kroll 2006; Hawk and McHenry 2005; Carmel 2003; Gibson 2006) as well as the industry reports (e.g., Terekhov 2001; Trombly 2003; Sayfutdinova 2009; King 2009; Russoft 2010), commonly name other BRIC countries, notably China and India, as Russia's main competitors. If we compare Russia with these other countries in terms of the amount of revenue and volumes of service, India and China outpace Russia simply due to larger populations and lower quality and cost of living. Owing to the population numbers and well-run systems of personnel preparation, no country can currently compete with India and China in terms of the sheer volume of outsourcing services provided. According to Valentin Makarov (as explained during the interview):

> In [the] long term, Russia will inevitably be behind India and China in the field of outsourcing because of the resource difference. Population of Russia is approximately ten times less than that of India and China. Russia will continue to keep its niche of high-tech development but will not compete in the mass routine IT-outsourcing and BPO.

Therefore, the question is whether it is valid to name India and China as Russia's main competitors when those countries do not compete on the same scale. Leon (2009), for example, has noted that Russia cannot compete with China either in terms of the size of the skill pool, as the population of China is many times larger, or on costs, as China has become even cheaper than India. According to Ulfelder (2003), China is best suited for low-tech, routine IT work that includes maintenance of old legacy systems, which may no longer interest even Indian firms. In this regard, Russian providers typically focus on complex engineering work and R&D activities that are different from services delivered by either China or India.

On the other hand, while many Indian companies still specialize in low-tech routine tasks, such as back office support, large Indian vendors like Infosys, TCS, and Wipro, who dominate the Indian IT outsourcing industry, have moved up the value chain and offer support for high-value, complex, and knowledge-intensive tasks and strategic systems to Western clients. They have accumulated considerable experience working with Western companies and they actively participate in joint ventures. Such companies truly constitute the main competitors of large Russian vendors in the high-tech software services market. According to the Russoft survey (2009), large Russian IT vendors often compete against rival Indian vendors when they participate in international tenders. However, since the Russian IT outsourcing industry is dominated by SMEs, the number of large outsourcing providers in Russia is limited. Therefore, a majority of Russian vendors compete in their niche market mainly against small and medium-sized vendors from other CEE countries.

Overall, Russian IT providers see their niche in the global outsourcing market of software development services as "specialization in the implementation of complex science intensive projects, requiring deep mathematical knowledge from the contractors" (Russoft 2008). This is the area where Russia holds a competitive advantage in terms of employment and industry growth, and companies should continue to sustain and develop it further. Since other CEE countries compete in the same niche (Tromby 2003; Russoft 2009; Willcocks et al. 2009), in particular Poland and the Czech Republic (Russoft 2008), analysts should take a close look into those countries as Russia's real main competitors. As of 2009, IT spending in Russia was higher than in other CEE countries;[26] in the future, these rising offshoring destinations may constitute a significant threat for Russia, in particular as many of them have become part of the European Union, making it easier for Western companies to travel to and conduct business in these countries. CEE countries may become an attractive alternate destination for Russia's technical skill pool, with the cost of living lower than in the United States or Western Europe and a legacy culture that is more similar than Western countries. CEE countries also offer proximity to the "home" country.

Russia's attractiveness as a captive offshoring destination

Due to Russia's intellectual potential, it has established itself at an attractive destination for captive R&D centers, as the Russian engineering abilities are recognized worldwide (Leon 2009). According to Dyker (2001), R&D services in Russia are potentially the strongest among other popular outsourcing destinations, as Russian scientists are often recognized to have a great potential for creating innovative products and solutions. According to Zinnov Management Consulting,[27] in 2008 Russia's IT offshoring market, which includes the export of software and IT services, is at least four times as high as the largest CEE market (Ukraine) at US$2,500 million,[28] compared to Ukraine at US$566 million, Poland US$478 million, followed by the Czech Republic, Belarus, Hungary, Romania, Bulgaria, and Slovakia, in decreasing order. During the last few years, the Russian IT offshoring market grown at a rate that is the highest in the world (see Figure 18.3).

Many large Western companies, mainly MNCs that opened their R&D centers in Russia prior to 2000, used Russian R&D to support their production units. Late entrants, however, are now opening independent R&D centers to undertake emerging research and innovation activities in high-tech, high-value areas of business. This trend is expected to continue, as more Western companies realize the potential of Russia's technologically skilled labor pool to innovate and develop new products and solutions and to further take advantage of these unique resources. The increasing popularity of the nearshoring trend makes Russia even more attractive for Western European companies considering setting up a captive facility.

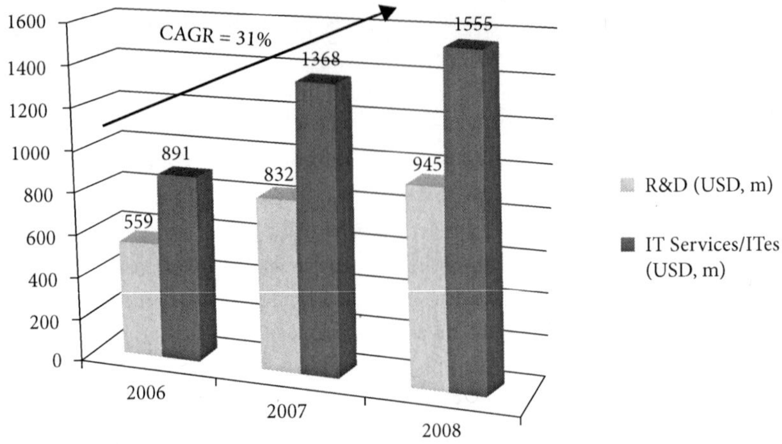

FIGURE 18.3 Figure Kotlarsky.3: Russia's IT offshoring market (based on Zinnov Management Consultancy 2009).

Developing and strengthening the IT services sector can offer excellent opportunities for growing employment and diversifying Russia's economy, decreasing its economic reliance on nonrenewable resources. It is critical to Russia's success that government and business work to increase its service-sector offerings to compete in a modern global economy. As shown, it is unlikely that Russia can compete in the near term in the large company IT service sector, as China and India prohibit Russia from competing simply in terms of population in resources. Russia's advantage in the IT services market lies mainly in developing small and medium-sized niche specialist companies that provide high-tech, complex solutions for clients interested in nearshoring opportunities with businesses who are more culturally compatible with Western business ideals.

Notes

1. www.businessinsider.com/its-time-to-remove-russia-from-the-brics-2009-8+removing +russia+from+bric&cd=2&hl=en&ct=clnk&gl=uk; August 11, 2009.
2. "BRIC: Russia is the Underdog," *The Telegraph*, June 1, 2010; http://www.telegraph.co.uk/finance/personalfinance/investing/7790010/BRIC-Russia-is-the-underdog.html.
3. A. Åslund, "Take the R out of BRIC," *Foreign Policy*, December 2, 2009; http://www.foreignpolicy.com/articles/2009/12/02/kick_russia_out_of_bric.
4. Taking into account that the term "offshoring" include both "offshore outsourcing" and "captive" sourcing models, in our literature review we included articles that discuss both types of arrangements and refer to either of them as "offshoring."
5. World-tax.com.
6. Outsourcing-Russia.com.
7. BBC news, 2009.
8. CNews, December 12, 2007.

9. Cinfo.ru (2003).
10. CNews, December 12, 2007.
11. CNews, January 24, 2008.
12. *Political Risk Yearbook: Russia Country Report*, 2009.
13. *Economist*, 2006.
14. Based on C. Vorasarun, "Cities of the Billionaires," Forbes.com, April 30, 2008; http://www.forbes.com/2008/04/30/billionaires-london-moscow-biz-billies-cz_cv_0430billiecities.html.
15. The name of the interviewee and the company (s)he works for is kept anonymous.
16. See P. Bhattacharji, "Chechen Terrorism (Russia, Chechnya, Separatist)," Council on Foreign Relations, April 8, 2010; http://www.cfr.org/publication/9181/chechen_terrorism_russia_chechnya_separatist.html#p6.
17. S. Overby, "The 24 Most Dangerous Cities for Offshore Outsourcing," CIO.com, February 26, 2009; http://www.cio.com/article/482404/The_25_Most_Dangerous_Cities_for_Offshore_Outsourcing.
18. *Notes on Countries of the World: Russia* (2008).
19. *Political Risk Services, Country Forecast* (2008).
20. The piracy rate is calculated as the total number of units of pirated software deployed divided by the total units of software installed. See explanation of the methodology in BSA/IDC Global Software Piracy Study (2010) report, available from http://portal.bsa.org/globalpiracy2010/.
21. Country Profile-Russia (2008).
22. Country Profile Russia (2008).
23. Country Profile Russia (2008).
24. Country Profile Russia (2008).
25. CNews, April 19, 2007.
26. PR-inside.com, 2009.
27. Presentation of April 2009; www.zinnov.com.
28. Russoft survey (2009) reported US$2,650 million in 2008.

REFERENCES

Bardhan, A., and C. A. Kroll. 2006. "Competitiveness and an Emerging Sector: The Russian Software Industry and its Global Linkages." *Industry and Innovation* 13 (1): 69–95.

BBC News. 2010. "Russia Sees the First Population Increase in 15 Years." January 19. http://news.bbc.co.uk/1/hi/world/europe/8468185.stm.

Bradley, T. L. 1999. "Cultural Dimensions of Russia: Implications for International Companies in a Changing Economy." *Thunderbird International Business Review* 41 (1): 49–67.

Busovikova, Y. 2002. "What Role Does the Black Economy Play in Society's Development?" *Russia Journal* 405: 17–23.

Butrin, D. 2002. "2001: The Year of the White Salary." *Kommersant*, March 5.

Carmel, E. 2003. "The New Software Exporting Nations: Success Factors." *Electronic Journal on Information Systems in Developing Countries* 13 (4): 1–12.

Carmel, E., and P. Tjia. 2005. Offshoring Information Technology. Sourcing and Outsourcing to a Global Workforce. Cambridge: Cambridge University Press.

Cherednichenko, G. A. 2009. "The Study of Foreign Languages Abroad." *Russian Education & Society* 51 (4): 29–49.
CNews. 2008. Six Russian IT Outsourcers in Global Top-100." April 14. http://www.russoft.com/docs/?doc=1468.
———. 2007. "West Prefers Russian Programmers to Indian Ones." April 19. http://www.russoft.com/docs/?doc=1352.
——— 2007. "2008: Seven New Russian Techno Parks to be Launched." December 12. http://www.russoft.com/docs/?doc=1444.
——— 2007. "RF Government Adopts Accreditation Standards for IT Companies." November 9. http://www.russoft.com/docs/?doc=1424.
Coman, A., and B. Ronen. 2009. "Focused SWOT: Diagnosing Critical Strengths and Weaknesses." *International Journal of Production Research* 47 (20): 5677–5689.
Cusumano, M. A. 2006. "Where Does Russia Fit into the Global Software Industry?" *Communications of the ACM* 49 (2): 31–34.
Czaja, J. 2009. "The Nearshoring Bug: Why It's Catching." *Russian IT Quarterly* July: 7–8.
Doh, J. P. 2005. "Offshore Outsourcing: Implications for International Business and Strategic Management Theory and Practice." *Journal of Management Studies* 42 (3): 695–704.
Doh, J. P., K. Bunyaratavej, and E. D. Hahn. 2009. "Separable but not Equal: The Location Determinants of Discrete Services Off Shoring Activities." *Journal of International Business Studies* 40: 926–943.
Dyker, D. 2001. "Technology Exchange and the Foreign Business Sector in Russia." *Research Policy* 30: 851–868.
Eisenhardt, K. M. 1989. "Building Theories from Case Study Research." *Academy of Management Review* 14 (4): 532–550.
Farpost. 2009. "Investment in Russia vs. Investment in India: The Pros and Cons." http://www.farpost.com/outsourcing/Investment_in_Russia_vs_Investment_in_India.php; accessed October 20, 2012.
Farrell, D. 2006. "Smarter Offshoring." *Harvard Business Review* 84 (6): 84–92.
Filatotchev, I., X. H. Liu, T. Buck, and M. Wright. 2009. "The Export Orientation and Export Performance of High-technology SMEs in Emerging Markets: The Effects of Knowledge Transfer by Returnee Entrepreneurs." *Journal of International Business Studies* 40 (6): 1005–1021.
Filimonov, A. 2001. "The Advantages and Disadvantages of Russia as an Outsourcing Partner." October 3. http://www.russoft.org/docs/?doc=734.
Garrett, J. 2009. "Outsourcers ask for Russian Government Support." *Russian IT Quarterly* July: 9.
Gibson, S. 2006. Russia Revealed." *EWeek* 12: 22–27.
Goolsby, K. 2001. "Nobody Does it Better: Russian and Ukrainian Skills Valued in Outsourcing." April 1. http://www.outsourcing-journal.com/apr2001-globalview.html.
Grishina, E. A. 2009. "The Scientific Intelligentsia: Contradictions of Social Identity." *Russian Education & Society* 51 (6): 31–51.
Hahn, E. D., and K. Bunyaratavej. 2010. "Services Cultural Alignment in Offshoring: The Impact of Cultural Dimensions on Offshoring Location Choices." *Journal of Operations Management* 28 (3): 186–193.
Hahn, E. D., K. Bunyaratavej, and J. P. Doh. 2010. "Impacts of Risk and Service Type on Nearshore and Offshore Investment Location Decisions: An Empirical Approach." *Management International Review* 51 (3): 357–380.

Hahn, E. D., J. P. Doh, and K. Bunyaratavej. 2009. "The Evolution of Risk in IS Offshoring: The Impact of Home Country Risk, Firm Learning and Competitive Dynamics." *Management Information Systems Quarterly* 33 (3): 597–616.

Hatonen, J. 2009. "Making the Locational Choice: A Case Approach to the Development of a Theory of Offshore Outsourcing and Internationalization." *Journal of International Management* 15 (1): 61–76.

Hawk, S., and W. McHenry. 2005. "The Maturation of the Russian Offshore Software Industry." *Information Technology for Development* 11 (1): 31–57.

Heeks, R., and B. Nicholson. 2004. "Software Export Success Factors and Strategies in 'Follower' Nations." *Competition & Change* 8 (3): 267–303.

Hodge, S. A. 2008. "Russia to Cut Corporate Taxes." *Washington Dithers*, November 20. http://www.taxfoundation.org/blog/show/23949.html.

Hudson, W. 2008. "From Russia with Cash." *Forbes* 182 (3).

Internet Access Industry Profile: Russia. 2009. Mississippi State: Datamonitor.

ITAR-TASS. 2007. "RF Should Be One of Global Info Leaders by 2015—Putin." July 26. http://www.russoft.com/docs/?doc=1394.

——— 2009. "Russia IT Market Volume Reaches $1 Bln—Medvedev." February 12. http://www.russoft.com/docs/?doc=1633.

ITONews.eu. 2009. "CEE Strengthens Its Position in IT Outsourcing Market." July 24. http://www.russoft.com/docs/?doc=1726.

Joshi, K., and S. Mudigonda. 2008. "An Analysis of India's Future Attractiveness as an Offshore Destination for IT and IT-enabled Services." *Journal of Information Technology* 23 (4): 215–227.

Kennedy, R. 2009. "The Game You Have to Play." *Financial Executive* 25 (4): 23–26.

Khomutsky, D. 2007. "Russians Are Willing to get European Education." *Baltic Course* 27, Autumn. http://www.baltic-course.com/eng/round_table/?doc=41.

King, R. 2006. "Outsourcing: Beyond Bangalore." *Business Week Online*, December 11. http://www.businessweek.com/stories/2006-12-11/outsourcing-beyond-bangalorebusinessweek-business-news-stock-market-and-financial-advice.

Kolarova, D., A. Samaganova, I.Samson, and P. Ternaux. 2006. "Spatial Aspects of ICT Development in Russia." *Service Industries Journal* 26 (8): 873–888.

Kotlarsky, J., and Oshri, I. 2008. "Country Attractiveness for Offshoring and Offshore-Outsourcing: Additional Considerations." *Journal of Information Technology* 23 (4): 228–231.

——— 2005. "Social Ties, Knowledge Sharing and Successful Collaboration in Globally Distributed System Development Projects." *European Journal of Information Systems* 14: 37–48.

Kripalani, M. 1997. "Investing in India: Not for the Fainthearted." *Business Week*, August 10, 46–47.

Leon, P. H. 2009. "Outsourcing: China's Competitive Edge over Russia, Marchmont News." July 13. http://www.russoft.org/docs/?doc=1718.

Levina, N., and J. W. Ross. 2003. "From the Vendor's Perspective: Exploring the Value Proposition in IT Outsourcing." *MIS Quarterly* 27 (3): 331–364.

Levina, N., and N. Su. 2008. "Global IT Multisourcing Strategy: Understanding Supplier Structure, Decision Process and Evolutionary Dynamics." *Decision Sciences*, May 21.

Levina, N., and E. Vaast. 2008. "Innovating or Doing as Told? Status Differences and Overlapping Boundaries in Offshore Collaboration." *Management Information Systems Quarterly* 32 (2): 307–332.

Lewin, A. Y., and C. Peeters. 2006. "Offshoring Work: Business Hype or the Onset of Fundamental Transformation." *Long Range Planning* 39 (3): 221–239.

McCarthy, D. J., S. M. Puffer, and P. J. Simmonds. 1993. "Riding the Russian Roller Coaster: US Firms' Recent Experience and Future Plans in the Former USSR." *California Management Review* 36 (1): 99–115.

McCue, A. 2007. "Bad Image Hurts Russian IT Outsourcing." *Business Week*, February 16. http://www.businessweek.com/globalbiz/content/feb2007/gb20070216_283171.htm.

Mills, T., I. Dukeov, and C. F. Fey. 2007. "Russian Competitiveness in the Global Economy." *Journal of East-West Business* 13 (4): 97–138.

Moscow News. 2008. "'Over the Counter' Wages Rise in Russia." July 24. http://www.themoscownews.com/realestate/20080724/55338932.html.

Myers, M., and M. Newman. 2007. "The Qualitative Interview in IS Research: Examining the Craft." *Information & Organization* 17: 2–26.

Oshri, I. 2011. *Offshoring strategies: Evolving captive center models*. The MIT press.

Oshri, I., J. Kotlarsky, and L. P. Willcocks. 2007. "Global Software Development: Exploring Socialization in Distributed Strategic Projects." *Journal of Strategic Information Systems* 16 (1): 25–49.

———2011. *The Handbook of Global Outsourcing and Offshoring*. 2nd ed. London: Macmillan.

Palvia, S. C. J. 2004. "Global Outsourcing of IT and IT Enabled Services: A Framework for Choosing an (Outsourcee) Country." *Journal of Information Technology Cases and Applications* 6 (3): 1–20.

Porter, M. E. 1990. *The Competitive Advantage of Nations*. New York: Free Press.

Rai, A., L. M. Maruping, and V. Venkatesh. 2009. "Offshore Information Systems Project Success: The Role of Social Embeddedness and Cultural Characteristics." *Management Information Systems Quarterly* 33 (3): 617–649.

Rajkumar, T. M., and R. V. S. Mani. 2001. "Offshore Software Development: The View from Indian Suppliers." *Information Systems Management* 18 (2): 63–73.

Russoft. 2008. "Russian Software Developing Industry and Software Exports." Russoft Association Fifth Annual Survey 2008.

———2010. "Russian Software Developing Industry and Software Exports." Russoft Association Seventh Annual Survey 2010.

Sayfutdinova, G. 2009. "Looking for Outsourcing Alternatives." *Russian IT Quarterly* 20: 2.

Shapovalov, A. 2006. "Who Will Get Tax Incentives?" *Kommersant*, May 25.

Shifrin, T. 2005. "India Is the Best Bet for Offshore IT Outsourcing, Advises Gartner." *Computer Weekly*, September 27, 18.

Skoblo A. 2002. "Copyright Law—Russian Federation: Recognition and Protection of Copyright in Computer Software and Databases on the Territory of the Russian Federation." *Computer Law and Security Report* 18 (1): 48–52.

Tamazian, A., J. P. Chousa, and K. C. Vadlamannati. 2009. "Does Higher Economic and Financial Development Lead to Environmental Degradation: Evidence from BRIC Countries." *Energy Policy* 37: 246–253.

Terekhov, A. 2001. "The Russian Software Industry." *IEEE Software* 18 (6): 98–101.

Trombly, M. 2003. "Russia and Eastern Europe." *Computerworld*, September 15. http://www.computerworld.com/s/article/84874/Russia_and_Eastern_Europe?taxonomyId=060.

Ulfelder, S. 2003. "China: Low-level Work at Lower-than-average Cost." *Computerworld*, September 15. http://www.computerworld.com/s/article/84863/China?taxonomyId=060.

Vlaar, P. W. L., P. C. van Fenema, and V. Tiwari. 2008. "Cocreating Understanding and Value in Distributed Work: How Members of Onsite and Offshore Vendor Teams Give, Make, Demand, and Break Sense." *Management Information Systems Quarterly* 32 (2): 227–255.

Weinert, S., M. Weber, and D. Vasak. 2008. "Offshore Outsourcing to Russian IT Providers: Opportunities, Risks and Best Practice Procedures." Schumpeter Discussion Papers, Schumpeter School of Business and Economics, University of Wuppertal, Germany.

Willcocks, L. P., and M. Lacity. 2009. *The Practice of Outsourcing: From ITO to BPO and Offshoring*. London: Palgrave.

Worldwide-tax.com. 2009. "Russia Income Taxes and Tax Laws." http://www.worldwide-tax.com/russia/russia_tax.asp (accessed July 19, 2009).

Yin, R. K. 1994. *Case Study Research: Design and Methods*. Newbury Park, CA: Sage.

Zaheer, S., A. Lamin, and M. Subramani. 2009. Cluster Capabilities or Ethnic Ties? Location Choice by Foreign and Domestic Entrants in the Services Offshoring Industry in India." *Journal of International Business Studies* 40 (6): 944–968.

SECTION IV

OTHER PARTS OF THE DEVELOPING WORLD

CHAPTER 19

Job Quality in Offshored Business Services

NAJ GHOSHEH AND JON MESSENGER*

1 Introduction

Global interconnectivity in the trade of goods is an old phenomenon in the history of the world, but its pace has been determined by factors such as technology and economic cost. In recent years there has been a rapid acceleration in the interdependence of economies around the world as production, transportation, and communications costs have systematically declined over recent decades. As the capacity to produce goods and services of improved quality continues to gather pace around the world, heightened demands on organizations to maximize production and profits will continue. Meanwhile policy makers at national level will simultaneously face pressures to improve the conditions for markets, including labor markets, in order to continue economic development within the country. Thus, in an organic sense, offshoring is a process that has now taken root and, given the above factors, will likely grow for some time to come.

The principle of offshoring is, in itself, neither new nor particularly innovative. In strict definitional terms, the offshoring of a business production function takes place when a production process is located in a country other than the country where the initial business is located. With advances in transportation and communication that have reduced their costs, goods and components could be moved quickly and inexpensively to external suppliers and thus benefit from lower costs or specific circumstances by relocating activities there (Bottini et al. 2007). For some organizations the manufacturing of products in other countries was the only outcome, but for others offshoring also meant the establishment of global supply chains in different countries in which integration of value-added functions can lead to greater flexibility and profitability. While offshoring has been more common in manufacturing, as technological costs have come down and quality has improved, it has in recent years become a much more important phenomenon in the services sector, as businesses seek to streamline organizational functions to improve profitability.

The emphasis of this chapter will be on the offshoring of services, namely business services. The chapter will examine the recent burgeoning of offshoring of services, what type of industry this encompasses, who works in the industry, and the reasons it has been growing in many developing countries. It will also delve into an evolving literature in this field, namely studies regarding the quality of those jobs that exist in offshored business services. Specifically, the chapter will review these job quality factors that need to be considered when examining service sector outsourcing. Finally, the chapter will consider what measures are necessary to ensure that these jobs do not become the feared "electronic sweatshops" (a term used by a number of authors), but rather good-quality jobs in the countries where they are found. Recommendations will be made regarding how policymakers can create national policies to improve job quality in offshored services, as well as those practices which organizations can implement to provide for better quality jobs and working environments.

2 What are offshored business services? Defining and understanding the industry

2.1 Defining the terms

There is a vast literature that has attempted to distinguish the sometimes complex issues that need to be considered when examining offshoring of services. As Javalgi et al. (2009) have pointed out, the academic literature has defined offshoring as meaning anything from "outside a country's boundaries" (Monczaka and Thomas 1995), to not domestic nor a bordering country (Shamis et al. 2005) to remote, low-cost locations (Robinson and Kalakota 2004) or geographical relocation of business functions abroad, irrespective of whether or not such functions continue to be performed by a subsidiary of the firm or are contractually outsourced to an independent party (Prasad and Prasad 2007). While taking this range of potential definitions into account, Table 19.1 below summarizes some key terms regarding the offshoring of business services. These definitions will provide the foundation for the discussion in the remainder of the chapter.

According to Minevich and Richter (2005), the business process outsourcing (BPO) industry was expected to continue growing due to the expansion of services provided via technology and the emergence of a multitude of remote work arrangements in the BPO "industry," the best known being call and contact centers. This industry has taken on different forms in countries around the world where they have been located, notably in Asia, Central Europe, Latin America, and North Africa. A range of other BPO

Table 19.1 Key definitions related to the offshoring of business services

Business process services (BPS): Services that involve the processing of business transactions, such as insurance, credit card claims, and payroll. There is nothing particularly new about these business functions; the "new" aspect is that many of these services are now *IT-enabled* (see the definition below)—which means that they can now be "outsourced" or even "offshored" (see the definitions below) with relative ease via ICTs.

Information technology-enabled services (ITES): a form of BPS which is made possible by the use of advanced Information and Communications Technologies (ICTs). ICTs are the *essential enabler* of the remote delivery of BPS. ITES is used in various industries, such as finance, insurance, telecommunications, etc. Examples are legal and medical transcription, accounting, insurance claim handling, credit card processing, etc.

Remote work: A more common name for business services provided at a distance using ICTs. Essentially, remote work is a synonym for ITES, although in this volume, we will use the term mainly to describe those jobs that involve providing ITES to customers across the world.

Business process outsourcing (BPO): The name of the "industry" which provides ITES functions and processes, along with the associated operational activities and tasks. The use of quotation marks around the term "industry" is meant to signify that BPO actually consists of the ITES segments of *other* industries, such as finance and telecommunications.

Outsourcing: the subcontracting a process, such as product design or manufacturing, to another company—called a third-party provider. Outsourcing may occur within a country or outside of the country—in the latter case, it is termed "offshoring" or, if a nearby country, "nearshoring."

Offshoring: The phenomenon of locating IT-services and business process services in locations outside of the source country, largely enabled through recent advances in ICT's, to leverage differences in wage levels and the availability of skilled labour across borders.

Nearshoring: This term refers to sourcing ITES to a country that is relatively close to the source country in terms of geographic distance, time zone, or both (also called "nearsourcing" and "nearshore outsourcing").

In-house or "captive" unit: the situation in which companies set up their own, wholly-owned *offshore* subsidiary to provide ITES to its customers.

Third-party provider: a company that is paid, usually based on the number of calls taken or quality assurance measurements, to provide ITES for another company. A third-party provider will generally handle several different contracts from different companies at the same time.

Source: Messenger and Ghosheh (2010: 2).

"industry" studies have made optimistic forecasts for future growth (e.g., A. T. Kearney 2007). Nevertheless, even allowing for a certain amount of marketing hyperbole, the reality is that BPO has been growing at extremely rapid, and in some cases, even exponential rates (Messenger and Ghosheh 2010).

The dramatic growth in the BPO industry has been based on the diffusion and costs of information and communication technologies (ICT). The importance of ICTs to BPO growth cannot be overstated. They are essential in enabling the delivery of business process services (BPS) from remote or distant locations vis-à-vis the ultimate customer. ITES, or information technology enabled services, is a short hand for the relationship that refers to the business services that are delivered to customers from different locations by means of ICTs (Messenger and Ghosheh 2010).

According to a study by A. T. Kearney, the distribution of ICTs in a country can be measured by three components: (1) the number of telephone lines, (2) the number of personal computers, and (3) the number of internet users (A. T. Kearney 2007). The growth in this industry has been most pronounced where the modernization of the telecommunication infrastructure, the deregulation of telecommunications to lower costs, the construction of networked free zones and the expansion of the internet or some combination of these factors exists. This has played an important role in the growth of ITES in countries with established industries, such as India and the Philippines, and also the development of a nascent industry in other parts of the world, particularly countries in Latin America and North Africa.

Pundits in the industry, seeing the growth of the industry in established countries and its rapid development in many others, have over the years predicted high levels of growth and employment opportunities, though recent global realities have challenged these expectations. The global financial crisis of 2009 had a significant impact on the global services outsourcing as many large financial services firms were the biggest customers of BPS services. As the most recent A. T. Kearney study has suggested, the global business environment has been profoundly impacted by the crisis for a variety of reasons including: contrasting and conflicting recovery and post-recovery strategies; asymmetrical rates of recovery between industrialized and developing countries; questions about economic conditions in the United States and in Europe; and concerns regarding the G20 countries' ability to develop a unified response to their various economic challenges (A. T. Kearney 2011: 3). The earthquake and tsunami in Japan will no doubt compound economic concerns regarding the Japanese economy and its place in the world. Also, owing to poor jobs markets in many industrialized countries after these financial and natural calamities, there has been a push in industrialized countries to repatriate jobs that have been offshored. In addition to these variables, other tests to the ITES industry in developing countries have also been taking place. For example in countries with significant established ITES-related industries, notably India, issues such as currency fluctuations (notably with the US dollar), corporate scandals (such as the Satyam accounting debacle), and geographic position in proximity to turbulent neighbours have highlighted that the industry is not invulnerable (A. T. Kearney 2009). In Arabic speaking countries where growth in ITES has been taking place, such as Egypt and Tunisia, as well as parts of the Middle East, the protests and changes in government have created concerns for decision makers who were considering offshoring of services to these countries. The factors that will stimulate or slow the growth of ITES remain to be seen, but it is highly unlikely that the industry will diminish so long as organizations believe competitive advantages can be obtained by offshoring services.

2.2 Background of offshoring

Prior to the development of call centers and other forms of offshored work, businesses and other organizations that had offices outside of their home country did not have an intentional globalized communication supply chain.[1] Organizations that had offices in other countries only did so to access local customers and knowledge, not as "one node in a global value chain" (Gereffi et al. 2005; Dossani and Kenney 2007). In the old model, labor costs in a particular country were not the key factor in the location decision, and the host country organization did not learn significantly from their offshore subsidiary (Dossani and Kenney 2007). These are important points to bear in mind in order to better understand the factors that have led to the development of the business services industry and efforts to offshore and outsource it.

As noted earlier, offshoring and outsourcing are not particularly new concepts, having been utilized in manufacturing sectors for many decades. In fact, contrary to popular belief, they are not really "new" even in the services sector, as they have been developing over the course of the last 35–40 years. Some dimensions of service sector outsourcing, such as call centers, have been a significant segment of other industries in some developed countries such as the United States, United Kingdom, Canada, Australia, and even Spain. It is only within the last twenty years that these call center services, and BPO work more generally, have been offshored to developing countries.

The spatial relocation of services based on geographical repositioning of service functions, attributes, and tasks first took place *within* the developed countries (Richardson et al. 2000: Dossani and Kenney 2007). The transformation in the configuration and location of the business service industry happened in call centers in the telecommunications industry in the United States (Batt and Monihan 2002). In their early stages, call centers were located regionally and often in suburban or rural areas of developed countries to keep down costs (Bain and Taylor 2002). As time passed, the typical call center began serving national markets rather than just local or regional markets. However, beginning in the 1990s a number of factors began to undermine the call center model that had existed. While there was considerable cost savings in rural areas, there was also a lack of highly skilled workers that limited the scale of operations and their growth (Dossani and Kenney 2007). In addition, the dot-com collapse in the early 2000s compelled companies to further reduce labor costs. This led companies to experiment with so-called nearshoring. With nearshoring, organizations could relocate outside of the United States to a geographically close neighbor (e.g., Canada and Mexico), to diminish costs through exchange rates and lower labor costs and keep operations in a similar zone. While this strategy did lower costs, it met with mixed success. What made it important, however, was that as this experimentation was taking place other developments in business management systems were occurring that would lead to an expansion of service functions, activities, and tasks that might be performed abroad, which in time would become the global BPO industry.

Telephone call centers were viewed as a model of efficiency by managers who thought about how this model could be replicated in order to deliver services. This model helped drive the expansion of the business process reengineering movement in management and business in the 1990s, which focused on how cost savings could be achieved through the reorganization of business processes. One way was to decompose, examine, and standardize the activities necessary to complete a business process (Hammer and Champy 1993; Cole 1994). The result was standardization of activities to create "pinch points" through which handoffs would allow the separation of work geographically, organizationally, or both. This approach included the digitization of work tasks or entire processes through which cost-effective ways to complete an activity could be determined by managers. These considerations were revolutionary in the development of offshoring/outsourcing of BPO. Prior to the 1990s there was little or no precedent for offshoring business services, although there were some limited activities in software development in India, Ireland, and Israel, and in call centers and data-processing facilities for credit cards (with workers performing low-skill data entry tasks) in Latin America and the island countries of the Caribbean (Dossani and Kenney 2007).

ICTs played an important role in the development of offshored and outsourced services, but it was not the only reason for the development of these services abroad. The expansion of voice over internet protocol (VOIP) and automated call distribution systems in the late 1990s and early 2000s radically improved business processes essentially erasing geographical boundaries and opening up a new way to offshore/outsource service sector work. Yet, while these technological advances were necessary, they alone did not provide sufficient reason for firms to offshore service work. In addition, managers in the headquarters upstream in developing countries had to be convinced that offshoring was acceptable as a "legitimate" strategy (Dossani and Kenney 2007). These strategic rationales for offshoring will be explored more in section 2.3.

The offshore locations of many of these service providers were chosen for different reasons. While wage costs are always a strategic business consideration, including the offshoring decision, other issues have been important as well. Most organizations in North America and Europe that considered offshoring ITES functions chose locations in Asia. Most prominently, India and the Philippines have established themselves as cost-effective locations for the provision of ITES. An obvious concern of such an arrangement, however, is the time zone differences vis-à-vis BPS customers (which indeed has played a role in the location of the industry, especially for the nearshoring of services). Offshore service providers in both India and the Philippines have adapted their workplaces by extensively scheduling work at night (especially in voice services) to meet the needs of North American and European customers, but this strategy has also created one of the most problematic working conditions for workers in the BPO industries in these countries (Messenger and Ghosheh 2010). Language is another important variable that for example has led to a growth in the offshoring of service work for Spanish speakers to Latin America. In Latin America there is some night work (mainly for some customers of Spain and other parts of Western Europe), but most of the work for US markets takes place roughly in the same time zone. The growth of the BPO in Latin America has also been facilitated by the growth in the number of university educated graduates in that region. Similarly, until the political upheaval in early 2011, North Africa and the Middle East provided services to European markets based on language (French and English), cost, and proximity to these markets.

As pressures on national policymakers grow for economic development in a globalized world, there will be more countries looking at the ways and means to bring offshored/outsourced work to their country. Two actions would appear to play an important role in this process. First, although governments in different countries have chosen different policies and legal activities to stimulate the development of the BPO industry, one important policy has been to deregulate the telecommunications industry. This has helped to attract ITES work because it has opened up new possibilities for telecommunications activities and generally lowered infrastructure costs for line use in the industry. Second, the location of the BPO industry has been historically important. As noted earlier, as multinational organizations had originally located in some countries for the available customer and market potential, it is not surprising that major cities or nearby areas were the main locations for these growing services industries. More recently, national, state, and local governments have offered incentives for BPO companies to locate to a particular region of a country. There is a certain amount of irony in this approach, as the whole idea of the provision of services from a distance would in theory mean that such geographic clustering would be superfluous, but in many countries that is exactly what is taking place. In one further irony, this has also meant that patterns of similar work and employment for workers in BPO industry have developed in geographic clusters and may in fact contribute to the fluidity of the labor market in this industry in developing countries.

2.3 Rationales and management issues when organizations consider offshoring

At first glance, the ambition for organizations that offshore business services is to enhance their competitiveness by achieving a higher return on investments through less capital commitment and the increasing ability to adjust to a changing business environment or, in the vernacular, "do more, with less" (Insinga and Werle 2008: 58). This form of strategic thinking has compelled many organizations, including those in the public sector, to examine all of their operations to determine those costs that must be borne, those that can be minimized, and those that can be avoided by going offshore.

The strategic management literature has identified two preliminary dimensions that must always be accounted for when considering offshoring. Porter and Millar differentiate between primary (or essential activities) and nonessential activities, suggesting that essential activities create products and services and nonessential activities provide the necessary inputs and infrastructure to conduct essential ones (Porter and Millar 1985). The seminal and perhaps most influential work on this topic was the analysis by Prahalad and Hamel. In their assessment, organiszations must be certain that they protect their core competencies, which are defined as those functions that, if lost, could compromise the viability of the organization as a whole (Prahalad and Hamel 1990). Organizations therefore need to consider and develop a strategy that distinguishes core functions that must remain within the organization from those that can be done more cost effectively and efficiently by service providers outside of the organization.

Several theoretical conceptions have evolved that have suggested just what types of criteria should go into decision making about core versus noncore functions of the firm. The two main theories are the resource-based view of the firm (RBV) and the use of transaction cost economics (TCE). RBV was a framework developed by Edith Penrose (1959). It emphasizes that nonsubstitutable strategic functions should remain within the organization, while other functions that could be done more cost effectively by others should be outsourced (Willcocks and Lacity 2006). This framework retains the advantage of extending learning and innovation and developing capabilities that can benefit the organizations that take on the offshored function and which can then be transmitted back to the organization making decisions upstream. By contrast, the TCE theory was developed by Oliver Williamson, based on the initial research by Ronald Coase (Williamson 1975; Coase 1937). According to this framework, the functions in a company or other organizations that tend to be very specific, very uncertain, or frequently taking place should be managed by the organization, but those not meeting these criteria may be more cost effectively performed by other firms or by extension offshore (Willcocks and Lacity 2006).

While such a decision would seem to be quite simple or self-evident, organizations often suffer the consequences of not making a careful and thoughtful evaluation of how they proceed to offshore work. This is especially true if the work is offshored and outsourced to another firm. The lure of substantial cost savings can be exceptionally enticing, yet if the expectations regarding cost reductions are too optimistic they can lead to a "cost savings mirage" in which savings are lost due to a lack of the foresight to address management processes and unrealistic expectations (Shi 2007). Aron and Singh have pointed out that if organizations are not systematic in their decision making with regard to offshoring, three fundamental mistakes can take place (Aron and Singh 2005). The first mistake is focusing on the location and price rather than an evaluation of the processes that will be offshored/outsourced. The second mistake is when management uses cost-benefit analysis to make decisions rather than considering the potential risks that can result from the offshoring process (e.g., the third-party provider holding the organization to "ransom"). The third mistake is when organizations view offshoring/outsourcing as a false dichotomy: an "all or nothing" proposition rather than as one choice from a range of options. These organizational considerations are not only important for organizational strategy, they also have consequences for the working conditions in offshore/outsourced workplaces (which will be explored further later in this chapter).

Different factors have been suggested to improve organizational decision making when considering the possibility of offshoring. Aron and Singh suggest that organizations first need to rank their processes in hierarchical terms to determine which ones can be offshored (Aron and Singh 2005). There are two forms of risk that then need to be determined: operational and structural risks. Operational risks consist of two components: first, acknowledgment that initially offshored and/or outsourced service providers will not be as fast as in-house providers; and, second, that the metrics to measure offshore processes might not all be the same. Structural risks are those based on organizations relying on service providers to act in certain prescribed ways, perhaps reflecting organizational culture. This can become problematic due to unrealistic upstream expectations, changes in the demands downstream, or unrealistic promises made by the downstream provider. What is important to acknowledge is that the structural risks are based on the behavior of the organization managers upstream and the managers and workforce downstream.

Another very important structural concern involves the technological compatibility in ITES provision offshore. In this case the structural risk is the synchronicity of technology between the upstream organization and downstream provider. As Shi (2007) points out, asynchronous technology can result in higher costs or lower quality delivery of services. Two ways to overcome this problem are, first, for organizations to make sure that services that are offshored, and especially outsourced, are contracted to service providers who can work with their technological architecture and, second, to modularize the services provided to ensure that work activities and tasks are more standardized (Shi 2007). These practices can help to improve working conditions for the offshored/outsourced workplace in that the focus of the service provider is on the work activities rather than being additionally concerned about the work processes and delivery mechanisms, which add time and stress to the service provider's workplace.

How organizations engage the services they choose to offshore or outsource can also have vast implications beyond strategy, impacting the workplace and workforce that perform the services. If the organization is engaging in financial arbitrage or attempting to establish a global supply chain from within their organization, then clear organizational rules and procedures will need to be put into place so that services can be efficiently provided from offshore to the main office. On the other hand, if the services are both offshored and outsourced then organizations need to negotiate contracts with the service providers called "service agreements" (Holman et al. 2007). These agreements take four general forms: (1) a standard form with the client signing a standard agreement created by the firm for the sourcing of functions; (2) a detailed contract that establishes specific guidelines; (3) a loose or task-based contract in which the vendor agrees to complete a set of tasks set out in the contract; or (4) a mixed contract with loose provisions (Willcocks and Lacity 2006: 20). Signing a contract is only the beginning of the relationship, however, not the endpoint. The contract often sets the boundaries of the relationship but not the day-to-day context of it. As organizations are looking to save money and engage their management structure in another country and potentially another firm, both parties need to manage the relationship or risk the possibility of disappointment and lost economic efficiency. For this reason, the organization needs to also factor in the cost of assigning a contract manager to manage the relationship with the offshore service provider. The designated persons on both sides can then help the parties address the smaller issues so that they don't become bigger issues that overwhelm, damage, or ruin the relationship.

Once the contract managers are designated by the organization and the offshore service provider, they need to communicate regularly regarding how work is performed, the results delivered, and also to sort out the day-to-day problems. For firms that are merely offshoring services, this can be addressed by internal structures of the organization. However, for organizations that outsource the work to an offshore third-party service provider, it means that a number of social and organizational boundaries will be crossed, often simultaneously (Espinosa et al. 2003). These include national culture, organizational culture, and various operational boundaries. Under these circumstances, unclear communications from either side can complicate the relationship and contribute to jeopardising the offshoring/outsourcing exercise.

The key ingredient in making the offshoring relationship between the parties work is trust. Trust is not solved by the contract, but it is an important element for the contract to function between the parties. The organization engaging in offshore outsourcing must at least trust a service provider's competence and willingness to keep its agreements, usually based on the service provider's record and reputation (Hoecht and Trott 2006). However, that alone may not be enough. Once disagreements and tensions set in between the parties, it can be difficult to resolve problems and find mutually beneficial solutions on the basis of trust (Sitkin and Strickel 1996; Hoecht and Trott 2006). Therefore, the parties need to find a way to develop trust, and different mechanisms can help to achieve this end. For example, the contract itself can include provisions that encourage trust between the parties, through trust-enabling governance structures and management control approaches such that flexible decision making can take place between the parties, with outcome-based rewards that focus on the recognition of priorities to meet dynamic goals rather than static contractual obligations (Dekker 2001; Hoecht and Trott 2006). The agreement may include provisions suggesting how often communication takes place between the upstream and downstream managers. It might also involve longer-term contracts to provide the opportunity to develop deeper relationships that can help in the management of the work and relationship between the parties. As the relationships develop, strains that might otherwise unravel the arrangements can be dealt with in a timely and professional manner.

Beyond the contractual issues, the BPO "industry" has certain working conditions that are inherent to the types of work in the industry. Recent research has identified a few key conditions that are impacted by this type of work and its location offshore. Pay is a key issue in the BPO industry, with compensation being an important reason many people chose this type of work (Messenger and Ghosheh 2010). Working time is also a factor with night work, scheduling concerns (including breaks), and irregular and unpredictable schedules all quite common in the industry. While scheduling issues are local management issues, night work is a core function of serving distant customers not located within the same region and can result in difficult adjustments for workers due to the fact that it requires them to work in opposition to their biological clocks. Work organization issues can also be a factor with industry workloads often being high, underpinned by strict performance targets, but with relatively low levels of discretion regarding how to handle the work (notably in call centers). Relating to work organization, ergonomics can be an issue, with workers spending long hours looking at computer screens, repetitive stress injuries from extensive time spent typing, and vocal and auditory fatigue (i.e., voice and hearing problems) from long hours listening and talking to clients. Finally, turnover in the BPO industry is relatively high, due to the lack of skilled workers in the industry in developing countries. If workers feel that any of the preceding working conditions are not satisfactory they can rapidly change firms, which can be costly for the employer in terms of training and recruitment costs (Messenger and Ghosheh 2010).

To a certain extent, the working conditions in the BPO industry are quite intrinsic to the type of work being done and the geography of where the work is being performed, but certain factors can make these conditions worse. Problems due to the absence of organizational strategy, appointing contract managers, and the development of trust mechanisms in the relationship can have a profoundly negative impact on the working conditions that exist in the offshored/outsourced workplace. For example, in the absence of communication on business functions and products for delivery, a manager may be inclined to demand greater efforts from the workforce in the form of long hours, limited breaks, or some form of mandated overtime. If this ambiguity permeates to the workforce it can also create what is called "role ambiguity," which takes place when workers struggle to provide effective responses to unpredictable circumstances or lack certainty regarding the consequences of performing their work tasks (Pearce 1981; Messenger and Ghosheh 2010). The lack of communication between core organization and offshored/outsourced workplace might also result in increased workloads or greater monitoring (a notorious issue in this industry) in an attempt to address unrealistic expectations by managers, resulting in greater stress for workers (which will be discussed in section 3). The importance of mechanisms to improve communication and trust between the organizational or contractual parties thus becomes heightened, not only for strategic interest of the organization, but also to ensure that cost-efficiencies and reasonable productivity can be achieved in the offshored/outsourced location.

3 Job quality in the offshored/outsourced BPO industry

3.1 Categorizing types of offshored/outsourced business process services (BPS)

The BPO industry can be divided into two main categories. The first category is the call/contact center arrangement that primarily focuses on voice-based ITES, such as inbound customer service, outbound sales, and technical support. The second category is IT-enabled back office services that include a variety of nonvoice ITES, ranging from basic data entry/processing (e.g., credit card processing, payroll processing, etc.) to professional business services (e.g., accounting, human resource administration, engineering, etc.). It is likely that there are important job quality differences within these two broad categories, mainly due to the nature of the work being performed and how it is handled by the offshored/outsourced workplace. The limited evidence to date suggests that technical call center positions are typically of higher quality than inbound and outbound call center jobs, particularly in terms of factors such as task complexity, task variety, and job discretion/autonomy (D'Cruz and Noronha 2007). Back office services are broader in scope, though mainly focused on business process services; however, they can include knowledge process outsourcing which provides services requiring domain-specific knowledge (e.g., market analysis).

The jobs in the BPO industry provide important employment opportunities for people in developing countries, certainly as compared to those jobs that have been available in the recent past in these same countries. However, to consider this basic reality and nothing else would be to look at only part of the picture. As noted above, certain factors are important for emerging industries to locate in a country, such as the loosening of telecommunications laws and the availability of a skilled workforce, but other factors play an important role in completing this picture. National legal frameworks and labor market policies have implications for working and employment conditions in the BPO industry and help to determine the quality of job.

3.2 Job quality in the BPO industry: theoretical considerations

When considering the quality associated with the BPO industries in developing countries, it is not enough to suggest that the level of compensation is the only criterion. There are a number of factors that can be taken into account to help with such a determination. The aim of this analysis will be to put together the available evidence to answer two principal questions: (1) To what extent can offshore positions be considered "good" or "bad" jobs? and (2) How does the quality of jobs vary between different types of BPO position?

In order to conduct this analysis a brief review of some key pieces of literature on job quality will be required. The literature on job quality is vast (exceptionally so if "quality of working life" or "QWL" is included) and, as such, the emphasis will be on comparatively recent and/or influential articles, as well as information from the very limited number that have used concepts of job quality as a lens to examine jobs in the BPO industry.

The concept of "job quality" refers to the extent to which the characteristics of a particular job are considered to be positive or negative in different dimensions and as an overall package. The concept raises questions regarding what characteristics should be considered in the evaluation of job quality and what specific factors should be considered in order to make a determination as to whether a job is "good" or "bad" on a particular dimension, or even overall. Generally, job quality can be viewed from either a subjective perspective based entirely on the view of the employee (e.g., job satisfaction) or alternatively, from a more "objective" perspective, which is the more typical approach and places the focus on a set of criteria for evaluation.

The criteria used to evaluate job quality vary widely across research disciplines and studies. In fact the question of defining a good or bad job remains unresolved as the concept is dependent on the perspective from which the analysis is conducted. A job may be considered a good job in a particular country or labor market, but at the same time may be classified as a bad job if is compared with jobs in other countries or other labor markets. For instance, the wages of a BPO industry worker in India or the Philippines may be considered poor by the standards of industrialized countries, though in their respective labor markets they are quite generous. In addition, the quality of the same type of job can be very different even in the same country, since specific circumstances in the workplace may vary widely across organizations that employ such workers. The specific criteria used to evaluate jobs can help to determine what the quality outcomes could be, though the criteria used to determine the quality in research has been based on the social science (including management) disciplines forming the basis of the job quality study. Kalleberg and Viasey's view saliently captures this formulation:

> Social scientists approach the study of job quality in different ways. Economists tend to focus on aspects of economic compensation such as wages or fringe benefits [...]. Sociologists generally study occupational prestige within a system of social stratification as well as the degree of autonomy and control that workers have over their jobs. Psychologists more often emphasize the non-economic aspects of work [...] and assess the variety of psychological sources of job satisfaction. Each of these perspectives is useful but only partially so: understanding job quality requires a multi-dimensional approach that takes into account economic as well as non-economic sources of variation in the goodness of jobs; these components of job quality all constitute significant foci for research (Kalleberg and Viasey 2005: 432).

It is clear that in order to obtain more complete and substantive results, a more multidisciplinary approach to job quality analysis is needed. Recently, some researchers have proposed developing mechanisms that take such an approach. British economist Professor Francis Green has taken a multidisciplinary approach in his book entitled *Demanding Work*, where he has examined job quality in industrialized countries (Green 2006). Green's approach to job quality examined a range of different dimensions, including wages, skills, job discretion, job security, workload/work intensification, and worker well-being. Similarly, Davoine provided criticism of the European Union Job Quality indicators (or the "Laeken indicators") and further emphasized the importance of a multidisciplinary approach (Davoine et al. 2008). Davoine recommends a multidisciplinary approach, and suggests a set of indicators emphasising four main aspects of job quality: socioeconomic security, including decent wages; skills and training; working conditions; and the ability to combine work and family life.

While the literature on job quality in many other industries has been abundant, it is perhaps surprising that studies applying job quality principles to the BPO industry in developing countries are so rare. The few studies that exist are found mainly in research on call centers. The seminal study of this type was *The Global Call Centre Report*, which examined job quality as one small component of a large-scale, comprehensive study examining management strategies and human resource practices in call centers (Holman et al. 2007). Possibly due to the emphasis of the overall study, job quality was defined in strict terms as "a high quality job which combines high job discretion with low performance monitoring." Using this definition, the report stated that about one-third of all call centers studied had high- or very high-quality jobs and slightly more than one-third had low- to very low-quality jobs. Those in the mainly lower-quality jobs tended to be in larger call centers.

In other parts of the world, job quality is also being used to assess BPO work. In Australia another significant study on job quality in the BPO industry was undertaken around the same time. Hannif et al. examined job quality in company based case studies in Australia. In their assessment of job quality they used four main categories with sub-categories as follows: job functions (aspects of job and identification with work); work organization (income, working hours, work-life balance, and employment status); workplace relationships/initiatives (relationships with coworkers, managerial style, training and development opportunities); and protective mechanisms (occupational safety and health, unionization) (Hannif et al. 2008). Similarly, Valverde et al. (2007) suggested a classification of factors to define job quality in their study of call centers in Spain. These factors include: the characteristics of the contract (percentages of temporary employees who become full-time, permanent employees, and the percentage of employees with a permanent contract versus those with a temporary contract); job stability or security; access to training and career development opportunities; and gross salary and benefits. These factors were then converted into an index which indicated that call centers in Spain were at the lower to middle levels of job quality. While the findings of these studies are themselves important, they also demonstrate that the view of the importance of job quality in the BPO industry is becoming a global research and policy concern that is not restricted by geography.

One of the more recent works that has examined the job quality issue in BPO in more detail has been the book *Offshoring and Working Conditions in Remote Work* by Messenger and Ghosheh (2010). In this edited volume, Messenger and Ghosheh use a variant of the above job quality indicators to frame the analysis of job quality in the BPO industry in India, the Philippines, Argentina and Brazil. These job quality indicators included a mix of "hard" (objective) and "soft" (subjective, self-reported) measures, but the main focus is on working and employment conditions, occupational health and safety, and work organization and control issues, the last being key issues in the BPO industry. The resulting measures were as follows: average wages and employee nonwage benefits; hours of work, work schedules, and work-life balance; job stability (length of time in current job) and job security (characteristics of the employment contract); various aspects of physical work environment and workers health concerns; and work organization, workload, and job discretion (notably the use of electronic monitoring and performance targets for work control, and aspects of self-reported employee stress). These measures were also applied to both male and female workers, in order to determine gender differences in job quality based on the available data.

With regard to the working conditions in the BPO industry there is evidence that while some conditions are better than can be found in the local labor market, there are others that are less desirable. For example, the wages of BPO employees are generally higher than average wages in developing countries. According to Messenger and Ghosheh, in countries such as the Philippines the average monthly salary of a typical BPO worker was US$413, but that was 53 percent higher than the prevailing wage paid to workers the same age in other Filipino industries (Messenger and Ghosheh 2010). Similarly, in Argentina back office employees earned between US$1,374 and US$1,405 per month, which was more than the average monthly wage of US$368. However, in Brazil higher wages were based on being multilingual, as a multilingual telemarketer could earn between US$450 and US$562, whereas a Portuguese-only speaker earned only about US$314 per month, which was below the average monthly wage of US$450. Overall, it is not a surprise that the compensation for such jobs attracts workers to the BPO industry.

Besides wages, working time and how that time is organized was another important feature of the BPO industry considered in the study. Working time, which includes the number of hours worked and the work schedules, has significant consequences for the quality of this BPO work. The average weekly working hours in India and the Philippines are typically between forty and fifty. However, as Table 19.2 indicates, the hours are higher in the BPO industry in the Philippines, but not in India. An important factor is that night work is relatively common in the BPO industry, affecting between one-third and one-half of all BPO employees in India and the Philippines, particularly those in call centers (Messenger and Ghosheh 2010). Sleeping disorders are generally frequent among these workers. In addition, work schedules in the BPO industry can be quite variable, but this is more common in call centers that in back-office work.

Job tenure is generally quite short in this industry according to the study. Average job tenure is 15.8 months in India, 17.0 months in the Philippines, and 2.4 years in Brazil, though in the Brazilian context most BPO employees only have less than one year with their current employer (Messenger and Ghosheh 2010). While such short tenure might suggest job insecurity, there are several reasons why average tenure is so low. One factor is that the work done in some parts of the BPO industry is project-based, which can have implications for job tenure. Another factor is that staff turnover in the BPO industry is high, which is endemic across national borders. The BPO industry tends to hire younger workers who are more willing to change jobs to secure higher salaries, promotions, or better conditions. As the BPO industry in most developing countries is dependent on educated workers and the supply of such workers does not meet the demand, workers that are not satisfied can generally switch employers. Thus, low level of job stability has more to do with the nature of the industry rather than poor quality of the jobs per se (Messenger and Ghosheh 2010).

Table 19.2 Weekly hours in the BPO industry by gender and type of arrangement

	India				The Philippines			
	Work hours	Mean BPO	Back office	Call center	Work hours	Mean BPO	Back office	Call center
Total	47.2	46.49	45.64	47.02	41.7	44.70	43.55	44.98
Men	47.1	46.64	45.75	47.22	41.4	44.70	46.77	44.86
Women	46.9	46.03	45.22	46.45	42.1	44.67	43.30	45.07

Source: Messenger and Ghosheh (2010: 220).

The Messenger and Ghosheh study also identified work organization within BPO firms is as a key element that affects job quality. The BPO industry, particularly call centers, has been characterized as "Taylorized," a mass-production model of work. Two key work organization factors affect job quality for workers in the BPO industry: employee workloads (i.e., job demands) and employees' discretion in responding efficiently and effectively to those demands (i.e., job control). The study concluded that workloads in the industry are generally high, and backed by performance targets. However, as Table 19.3 indicates, BPO employees reported mid-to-low levels of job discretion on most work-related activities, likely due to highly standardized procedures enhanced by electronic monitoring. Thus, while the BPO industry is characterized as using advanced technologies that permit sophisticated electronic tracking and monitoring of work activities, this same technology can be used to implement and enforce tightly controlled work processes (Messenger and Ghosheh 2010). When combined with high workloads and constant time pressures these factors can raise stress levels for BPO workers.

Overall, the Messenger and Ghosheh study found that jobs in the BPO industry in developing countries, and especially the working and employment conditions that exist, are generally of better quality than typical jobs in the same countries. This is not to suggest they are perfect, however, as there are significant negative aspects to the jobs, such as high levels of stress in call center work. However, there were differences in the job quality among workers in different types of BPO work. Back office workers generally had better working conditions that call center workers, based on the higher qualifications required for many back office positions, higher levels of job discretion, and minimal use of night work. Job quality in "captive units" (in-house) were typically superior to similar positions in "third-party providers" (outsourced firms), which was similar to the findings in the *Global Call Centre Report* (Holman et al. 2007). This was likely due to the contractual arrangements between companies with ITES functions and third-party offshore

Table 19.3 Job discretion (five-point Likert scale: 1 = not at all, 5 = a great deal; with mean scores for BPO employees surveyed)

	India (N = 710)	The Philippines (N = 298)
Setting daily work tasks	2.61	3.15
Pace or speed of work	3.36	3.28
Setting breaks	2.60	2.60
Revising work methods	3.15	2.65
Handling additional requests	2.34	3.05
Settling customer complaints	2.43	3.10
Plan the work	2.89	-
Set work targets	2.63	-
Work overtime when wanted	1.93	-
Design and use technology	-	2.87
Tools, methods, and procedures to use	-	3.02

Source: Messenger and Ghosheh (2010: 228).

providers and the associated management issues (which were raised earlier in this chapter). Also, many of the jobs that had a corresponding international market that they "faced" also had higher-quality jobs, likely based on the fact that the job skill requirements for employment in those firms (e.g., being multilingual) was relatively high.

4 LINKING JOB QUALITY AND OFFSHORED BPO: ISSUES FOR NATIONAL AND WORKPLACE POLICIES

4.1 Growing questions regarding the ad hoc development of the BPO industry

Offshoring and outsourcing of BPO functions will no doubt continue in the future as organizations continue to look for ways to lower costs and maintain or increase productivity. In spite of the economic crisis that began in 2008, and whose aftermath continues to affect economies around the globe, the underlying fundamentals that have driven the growth of the BPO industry (e.g., reduced costs; the availability of skilled workers at lower salaries; and organizational desire for access to developing countries' markets) remain in place and will likely grow should economic conditions improve globally. However, as the BPO industry becomes more entrenched in developing economies around the globe, it will be important to recognize the issues that affect the job quality in the industry and consider what can be done to ensure decent quality jobs for the BPO workforce.

An important issue that has been raised as this industry has grown is what do jobs in the BPO industry mean for different parts of the workforce? For example, in line with the research questions highlighted earlier in this chapter, what is the impact of the offshoring of BPO work on women's employment in the industry? Mainstream literature is rather quiet on the subject, in spite of the fact that women form a large proportion of the workforce employed in call centers in many countries including India and the Philippines. As many of these countries still view family responsibilities as mainly a woman's concern, national and workplace policies that take into account the work and family needs of workers become very important.

Another issue of concern is how many jobs can the BPO industry create? While statistics indicate a growth of employment in BPO-related work in many developing countries, there is concern that it may not offer enough jobs to satisfy national labor market needs. For example, growth in the BPO industry in India has meant a huge growth of employment in the industry but arguably a relatively minor growth in the Indian labor force overall (Bottini et al. 2007). As Bardhan has noted, while the benefits of job creation in developing countries due to BPO offshoring are irrefutable, other factors to be considered include the geographic and social distribution of economic gains, the spill-over effects for the rest of the economy, and the sustainability of the offshoring model

(Bardhan 2006). Of particular concern are generally high entry barriers that may need to be surmounted in countries, including gender and ethnic discrimination and limited educational opportunities. One of the big problems of the industry is finding workers whose skill sets meet the needs of the BPO workplace, with insufficient language proficiency, cultural barriers, and inadequate educational standards and capacity among the main problems. These socioeconomic problems in countries and organizations create the paradox in the BPO industry that, even though the jobs in the industry are considered to be of "good quality" compared to the other jobs in the economy, the conditions of employment may mean that only certain social groups benefit from the BPO work and the conditions of work in the workplaces may not be "good quality" because the numbers of people applying for jobs are high and managers feel little or no pressure to ensure decent working conditions.

One issue that has not received any real attention with regard to the development of the BPO industry in developing countries is the amount of resources expended versus the value added to the country's development. Most of the workers hired in the BPO industry represent generally those in the population who are more highly educated. They are usually university graduates and in addition to a particular skill set, may also be multilingual. Developing countries encourage the development of the BPO industry in part because it allows these educated people to move upward economically, enabling them to enter into the middle class. It is a fairly quick and painless way to economically improve conditions for a country's citizens. In spite of these important benefits, the vast majority of these jobs are part of global value chains in which the main beneficiaries remain organizations upstream. Most BPO jobs do not really allow for development or innovation, which is where the value added comes from in many cases. Thus, while the BPO industry is an accelerated way to improve economic conditions and technological availability for a segment of the workforce within the country, it is not a replacement for the development of local organizations that may attempt to compete at national, regional, and international levels.

The need to ensure good-quality work in the BPO industry and the importance for organizations to find the best people mean that the industry cannot go on developing in an ad hoc manner. Greater attention to national policies and workplace practices that improve the skills of workers and the quality of the jobs will be important. The remainder of this chapter will suggest some policies and practices that could contribute improving employment opportunities and job quality in the BPO industry.

4.2 National policies and workplace practices to improve working conditions in the BPO industry

The BPO industry is not without its redeeming qualities. As Messenger and Ghosheh point out, wage levels typically far above the minimum wage and reasonable weekly working hours are a couple of the positive practices that can be found in the BPO industry in some developing countries (Messenger and Ghosheh 2010). Nevertheless, as noted

Table 19.4 Job-quality criteria in BPO industry

Criteria	"Good" job	"Bad" job
Wages and benefits	Generally higher than national average wage; non-wage benefits also better	Wages below national average; little to no associated benefits
Working time (including hours of work, scheduling, and work-life balance)	Predictable hours of work and overtime; flexible schedules; schedule for workweek negotiable; recognition of life beyond workplace	Long hours; unpredictable schedule (especially overtime); no flexibility in work schedule; only work at night with no protections; no recognition of life beyond workplace
Job stability/security	Good security of work; transferable skills with training and room for advancement or growth	No security or stability in work; skills are firm dependent with no possibility of advancement or growth
Work environment and health concerns	Workplace takes into account work strains and provides appropriate equipment to address workers' needs; regular breaks are provided to improve morale and productivity	Workplace does not provide any equipment to address workers' needs; minimal or no rest breaks for workers
Work organisation (including workload and job discretion)	Manageable workload within established deadlines; greater discretion to deal with problems/customers (including flexibility to problem solve in the workplace)	Unmanageable workloads; minimal discretion to perform the work

Source: Based on Messenger and Ghosheh (2010).

above, many positions in the industry have certain aspects that can have negative implications for working and employment conditions. Government policies and employment practices designed to address these issues hold the potential not only to improve working and employment conditions in the BPO industry, but might also serve as a models of good practice for the service sector in developing countries more generally.

Government policies may help to make the BPO industry more effective and productive in developing countries by promoting better working conditions. One of the key employment issues in the BPO industry in many developing countries is the high rate of attrition among workers. This has been a particular "Achilles' heel" of the industry, as workers often leave firms for better opportunities elsewhere because of the general lack of skilled workers in countries with large BPO industries. Some of these skill shortages may be attributable to government policies that promote the "clustering" of the industry in certain geographic areas through tax or other incentives. This creates BPO "hubs" within particular countries. The costs of relocating to these hubscan create problems for workers if they are not from the area or the hubs are not close to large metropolitan areas. Ironically, because of the clustering of BPO organizations, once workers are in the area, if they don't like the working or employment conditions in one firm, they can easily switch to other firms. This also raises the recruitment and training costs for firms, but such conditions can exist as long as the need for skilled workers is so high (in the short term workers are in a uniquely favourable position, but long term this might not be the case). Owing to the nature of this type of work, governments should be open to having firms locate in different areas and perhaps closer to areas where recruits can get to BPO organizations more easily (e.g., near universities or larger metropolitan areas). This would create greater awareness of the industry outside the BPO hubs, and allow potential new recruits to observe such opportunities from a much closer position.

The declustering of the industry by governments might also help with another issue for the BPO industry, which is skills development. One of the biggest complaints in certain segments of the industry, especially call centers, is the problem of a lack of training and skill development opportunities to advance beyond the initial task a worker is hired to perform. Governments' assumption that workers in the industry are well-educated does not take into account the need for further development of these workers' skills. The BPO industry and governments need to work together to help create training opportunities that provide career ladders for workers, which will in turn allow workers to advance in the industry and also create "home grown" managers for the industry. Such training initiatives would help to reduce staff turnover and strengthen the industry as a whole, which would benefit both the BPO industry and government coffers. Governments will also need to work with the industry to ensure both that training is relevant to industry needs and that the benefits and opportunities offered by the industry are spread more widely throughout the country.

High turnover in the BPO industry in many countries is also linked with a lack of worker "voice" in the workplace. Yet at the same time there is generally a negative view toward trade unions in the BPO industry (Messenger and Ghosheh 2010). This is ironic, as research in countries such as Brazil (Oliveira Júnior et al. 2005) and South Africa (Benner et al. 2007) have suggested that greater levels of unionization in the BPO industry in those countries may actually be associated with lower levels of turnover. The lack of organizational mechanisms in BPO countries to facilitate employee participation in firm's decision making, such as problem-solving groups, has been identified as a problem in India and the Philippines (Noronha and D'Cruz 2010; Amante 2010). While BPO workers are generally well educated, the BPO companies and workplaces often employ top-down methods of management, which can impair the working environment and reduce workers job discretion—limiting their ability to use or apply their skills. Thus, there is a clear need for policies aimed at improving workers' collective voice and promoting forms of dialogue between workers and employers in the industry.

Some practices to improve the working and employment conditions in the BPO industry need to be engaged in the workplace through managerial or organizational initiatives. As noted before with regard to offshore outsourced BPO services, the need for regular communication between the organization upstream and in the developing country cannot be overstated. Contracts that are overly restrictive, upstream organizations that demand more than what is in the contract, or problems of trust that are not resolved early in the process can create enormous problems for managers and workers downstream. Appointing people with the professional skills to manage the downstream and upstream expectations of the offshore outsourced BPO relationship is critical to help ensure that workers are not asked to compensate for managerial miscommunication. Research has found that unscheduled overtime, irregular long hours, lack of overtime compensation, transport problems between home and the workplace, greater workplace monitoring, lack of breaks for food or to go to the toilet, and poor work-life balance are some of the problems that can result for workers in the absence of a sound managerial strategy for dealing with the upstream-downstream relationship between the source organization and the BPO workplace in the developing country (Messenger and Ghosheh 2010).

One of the consistent concerns in the offshore BPO industry is work-related stress. As noted above, if there is a lack of communication between the upstream organization and downstream service provider, the result can be local management attempts to increase workloads that cause workers stress. The effect is worse if the work being asked is unrealistic within a time frame or targets fluctuate so much that workers are unable to predict when their work will need to be done. Another more consistent concern is workplace monitoring, in which managers electronically monitor workers in the workplace to determine the pace at which they are working (e.g., how many calls are answered per hour in call centers) or whether they are following standard procedures (e.g., scripts). This type of monitoring increases the pressure to meet targets without considering the stress that is being imposed on the worker (especially if breaks are restricted or not allowed). There is also the emotional stress that is linked with two other factors, especially in call or contact centers. First is the need to change accent when speaking with customers from the client country, which can cause problems for workers in adapting between work and personal life. Another stress concern can come from the verbal abuse taken by workers from customers in the client's country. This emotional abuse, often again in call centers, increases the stress of the workplace and, when coupled with regular monitoring and limited breaks, can turn an otherwise "good" job into a "bad" one very quickly. Managers need to be aware of the stress involved in BPO work and develop stress-release mechanisms for their workforces. Whether allocating sufficient break time, time for a meal, or a room to relax, such measures are key to improving the quality of work that can easily be achieved by BPO organizations and that will also benefit them via improved productivity and reduced turnover.

In addition to the work organisation, perhaps the key issue for the BPO industry in developing countries (which relates to stress as well) is the organization of working hours (i.e., work schedules). Problems with work schedules have been found to be one of the key factors affecting job quality in BPO firms (Messenger and Ghosheh 2010). The most significant work-scheduling issues can be classified into three groups: night work, infrequent or irregular rest breaks (noted above), and irregular (variable) work schedules. Night work can have significant negative effects on workers' health, including sleep-related disorders, and on workplace safety (Spurgeon 2003). The reason for the extensive use of night work in the BPO industry is that the developing countries where such downstream workplaces are located are not always in the same time zone as

BPO customers (e.g., India or the Philippines serving customers in the United States). As avoiding night work is not always feasible, especially for voice services provided to customers in real time, managers need to consider measures that would help to mitigate the problems that can result from night work. Many of the measures that can help to improve the working conditions for night workers can be found in the ILO Night Work Convention (No. 171) and accompanying ILO Night Work Recommendation (R178). Strong measures within the industry and improved company practices regarding night work can help to improve the quality of the jobs immensely and increase the productivity of a workforce that is less fatigued.[3]

With regard to work scheduling, recent research has suggested that a substantial proportion of BPO workers have reported moderate or frequent changes in their work schedules, which as noted above can cause significant interference between work and personal life (Messenger and Ghosheh 2010; Fagan 2004). In order to improve workers' work-life balance, a range of good practices might be adopted, including flexible working time arrangements with some degree of choice regarding work schedules. This might include assigning shift schedules based on worker preferences' to better accommodate their personal needs (Boulin et al. 2006). Similar to overtime concerns, it is important for workers to have advance notice of work schedules in order to have sufficient time to plan how to handle their family responsibilities. This is especially important if the workplace is in a remote location requiring extended planning and travel time on public transport or even in the instance where employers may provide periodic transport to workers.[3]

A critical health and safety issue that is often, ironically, ignored in service-sector workplaces (whether they are in industrialized or developing countries) is ergonomics. Workers in the BPO industry note significant physical problems associated with the work performed, especially if it is done for long hours or without adequate breaks (Messenger and Ghosheh 2010). Among the issues of concern are visual fatigue (eye strain) from hours in front of video display monitors; musculoskeletal complaints (e.g., back, shoulder, and neck problems) from sitting upright in the same position for extended periods of time; vocal and auditory fatigue (e.g., voice problems) from speaking and listening nonstop during the workday; and repetitive strain injuries (such as carpel tunnel syndrome) from typing at computer keyboards over long periods. Addressing these issues may not require much money and may be as simple as changing the layout of the work stations or adapting existing ones to minimize or eliminate the underlying factors affecting the workers' health. Other equipment that can help improve this situation might include ergonomic chairs, tables, keyboards, and computer video screens. Such measures improve the job quality at relatively low cost and will provide much higher returns in productivity terms to managers and the organization.

The measures suggested here are by no means the only measures that can be taken to improve the job quality of workers in the BPO industry. Many innovative practices and policies adopted by multinational organizations in their headquarters in industrialized countries could, if properly applied, improve substantially the working conditions in BPO workplaces in developing countries. What is essential to the process of improving working and employment conditions in the BPO industry, and by extension the quality of BPO jobs, is good and consistent communication between workers and employers in the developing-country workplace, and the acknowledgement from organizations in industrialized countries that a similar form of communication is required from them. If, as the management literature suggests, communication is important for product development, why would it not be equally important for those workers handling, developing, or solving product-related issues for an organization?

Notes

*. The views expressed in this chapter are the views of the authors alone. They do not represent the explicit or implicit views, opinions, or policies of the International Labour Organisation (ILO), its constituents, or any affiliates.

1. In modern terms, many companies have strategically looked at how to establish global supply chains in everything from manufacturing to service provision. In this context, the global supply chain is about providing a seamless system of production from one place to another to complete the final product or the provision of services. The reference here is that in the past, before advanced ICT's, firms established themselves in foreign markets mainly to compete in the respective markets rather than cut costs for organisational operations.
2. Government action in the form of legislation regarding night work can provide important support to the industry and workers.
3. For example, owing to night shifts for call centre workers in the Philippines, workplaces will arrange transport for the workers due to the fact that their homes may be in remote locations, the public transport schedule does not function at the times the workforce needs them, and to provide security against possible violence for the women working in these locations (Messenger and Ghosheh 2010).

References

Amante, M. S. V. 2010."Offshored Work in Philippine BPO's." In *Offshoring and Working Conditions in Remote Work*, edited by J. M. Messenger and N. Ghosheh, 101–134. Basingstoke: Palgrave-Macmillan.

Aron, R., Singh. J. V. 2005. "Getting Offshoring Right." *Harvard Business Review* 83 (12): 135–143.

A. T. Kearney. 2007. *Destination Latin America: A Near-shore Alternative*. Chicago: A.T. Kearney.

Bain, P., and P. Taylor. 2002. "Ringing the Changes? Union Recognition and Organisation in Call Centres in the U.K. Finance Sector." *Industrial Relations Journal* 33 (2): 246–261.

Bardhan, A. 2006. "Globalisation, Job Creation, and Inequality: The Challenges and Opportunities on Both Sides of the Offshoring Divide." Mimeograph, University of California, Berkeley.

Batt, R., and L. Monihan. 2002. "The Viability of Alternative Call Centre Production models." *Human Resource Management Journal* 12 (4): 14–34.

Benner, C., C. Lewis, and R. Omar. 2007. *The South African Call Centre Industry: A Study of Strategy, Human Resource Practices and Performance*. Johannesburg: Link Centre and the Sociology of Work Unit, University of Witwatersrand.

Bottini, N., C. Ernst, and M. Luebker. 2007. "Offshoring and the Labour Market: What Are the Issues?" International Labour Organization Working Paper, Economic and Labour Market Analysis Department, 2007/11.

Boulin, J. Y., M. Lallement, J. Messenger, and F. Michon (eds.). 2006. *Decent Working Time: New Trends, New Issues*. Geneva: International Labour Organization.

Coase, R. H. 1937. "The Nature of the Firm." *Economica* 4 (4): 386–405.

Cole, R. E. 1994. "Reengineering the Corporation: A Review Essay." *Quality Management Journal* 1 (4): 77–85.

Davoine, L., C. Erhel, and M. Guergoat-Lariveire. 2008. "Monitoring Quality in Work: European Employment Strategy Indicators and Beyond." *International Labour Review* 147 (2–3): 163–198.

D'Cruz, P., and E.Noronha. 2007. "Reconciling Dichotomous Demands: Telemarketing Agents in Bangalore and Mumbai, India." *Qualitative Report* 12 (2): 255–280.

———. 2010. "Employee Dilemmas in the Indian ITES-BPO Sector." In *Offshoring and Working Conditions in Remote Work*, edited by J. M. Messenger and N. Ghosheh, 60–100. Basingstoke: Palgrave-Macmillan.

Dekker, H. C. 2001. "Control of Inter-organisational Relationships: Theoretical Frameworks and an Empirical Investigation." ARCA Research Memoranda, ARCA-RM 01–12, Vrije Universiteit Amsterdam.

Dossani, R., and M. Kenney. 2007. "'The Next Wave of Globalisation' Relocating Service Provision to India." *World Development* 25 (5): 772–791.

Espinosa, J. A., J. N. Cummings, J. M. Wilson, and B. M. Pearce. 2003. "Team Boundary Issues across Multiple Global Firms." *Journal of Management Systems* 19 (4): 157–190.

Fagan, C. 2004. "Gender and Working Time in Industrialised Countries." In *Working Time and Workers' Preferences in Industrialised Countries: Finding the Balance*, edited by J. C. Messenger, 108–146. London: Routledge.

Gereffi, G., J. Humphrey, and T. Sturgeon. 2005. "The Governance of Global Value Chains." *Review of International Political Economy* 12 (1): 78–104.

Green, F. 2006. *Demanding Work: The Paradox of Job Quality in the Affluent Economy*. Princeton: Princeton University Press.

Hammer, M., and J. Champy. 1993. *Reengineering the Corporation: A Manifesto for Business Revolution*. New York: HarperCollins.

Hannif, Z., J. Burgess, and J. Connell. 2008. "Call Centres and the Quality of Work Life: Towards a Research Agenda." *Journal of Industrial Relations* 50 (2): 271–284.

Hoecht, A., and P. Trott. 2006. "Innovation Risks in Strategic Outsourcing." *Technovation* 26: 672–681.

Holman, D., R. Batt, and U. Holtgrewe. 2007. *The Global Call Centre Report: International Perspectives on Management and Employment*. Sheffield: Global Call Centre Research Network.

Insinga, R. C., and M. J. Werle. 2000. "Lining Outsourcing Business Strategy." *Academy of Management Executive* 14: 58–70.

Javalgi, R. G., A. Dixit, and R.Scherer. 2009. "Outsourcing to Emerging Markets: Theoretical perspectives and policy Implications." *Journal of International Management* 15: 156–168.

Kalleberg, A., and S. Viasey. 2005. "Pathways to a Good Job: Perceived Job Quality among Machinists in North America." *British Journal of Industrial Relations* 43: 431–454.

Messenger, J. M., and N. Ghosheh (eds.). 2010. *Offshoring and Working Conditions in Remote Work*. Basingstoke: Palgrave-Macmillan.

Minevich, M., and F.-J. Richter. 2005. *Global Sourcing Report 2005*. New York and Geneva: Going Global Ventures and Horasis.

Monczaka, R. M., and J. C. Thomas. 1995. "Predictors of Relationships among Buying and Supplying Firms." *International Journal of Physical Distribution and Logistics Management* 25: 45–59.

Oliveira Júnior, M. M., A. J. de Hoyos Guevara, L. Nelmi Trevisan, A. J. F. M. Nogueira, P. R. Gião, M. de Fatimá Silva, P. L. de Resende Melo. 2005. *Brazilian Call Centre Industry Report 2005* (The Global Call Centre Industry Project). São Paulo: Pontifícia Universidade Católica de São Paulo.

Pearce, J. 1981. "Bringing Some Clarity to Role Ambiguity Research." *Academy of Management Review* 6 (4): 665–674.

Penrose, E. 1959. *The Theory of the Growth of the Firm*. Chichester: John Wiley.

Porter, M. E., and V. E. Millar. 1985, "How Information Gives You Competitive Advantage." *Harvard Business Review* 63 (4): 149–160.

Prahalad, C. K., and G. Hamel. 1990. "The Core Competence of the Corporation." *Harvard Business Review* 68 (3): 79–91.

Prasad, A., and P. Prasad. 2007, "Moving Out: Towards Understanding the Complexity of Outsourcing in the Age of Globalization." *Business Renaissance Quarterly* 2: 67–91.

Richardson, R., V. Belt, andN. Marshall. 2000. "Taking Calls to Newcastle: The Regional Implications of the Growth in Call Centers." *Regional Studies* 34 (4): 357–369.

Robinson, M., and R. Kalakota. 2004. *Offshore Outsourcing: Business Models, ROI, and Best Practice*. Alpharetta, GA: Mivar.

Shamis, G. S., M. C. Green, S. M. Sorensen, and D. L. Kyle. 2005. "Outsourcing, Offshoring, Nearshoring: What to Do?" *Journal of Accountancy* 199: 57–61.

Shi, Y. 2007. "Today's Solution and Tomorrow's Problem: The Business Process Outsourcing Risk Management Puzzle." *California Management Review* 49 (3): 27–44.

Sitkin, S., and D. Stickel. 1996. "The road to hell: the dynamics of distrust in an era of quality." In *Trust in Organizations. Frontiers of theory and Research*, edited by R. Kramer and T. Tyler, 196–215. Thousand Oaks, CA: Sage.

Spurgeon, A. 2003. *Working Time: Its Impact on Safety and Health*. Geneva: International Labour Organization.

Valverde, M., G. Ryan, and M. T. Gorjup. 2007. "An Examination of the Quality of Jobs in the Call Centre Industry." *International Advanced Economic Research* 13: 146–156.

Willcocks, L. P., and M. C. Lacity. 2006. *Global Sourcing of Business and IT Services*. Basingstoke: Palgrave Macmillan.

Williamson, O. E. 1975. *Markets and Hierarchies: Analysis and Antitrust Implications*. New York: Macmillan Free Press.

CHAPTER 20

DOES INDUSTRIAL UPGRADING GENERATE EMPLOYMENT AND WAGE GAINS?

THOMAS BERNHARDT AND WILLIAM MILBERG[1]

1 INTRODUCTION

As the production of goods and services in the late twentieth century increasingly became organized within international networks—with lead firms coordinating suppliers, logistics, and marketing in multiple locations—the path of economic development changed. Economic development became associated with "industrial upgrading" within these networks, sometimes called "global value chains" (GVCs). The internationalization of production brings new opportunities and new challenges for the improvement of living standards in low- and middle-income countries.

Gereffi (2005: 171) defines economic upgrading as "the process by which economic actors—firms and workers—move from low-value to relatively high-value activities in global production networks." Economic upgrading has been studied in hundreds of country cases, ranging from Brazilian shoe production, Kenyan green beans, and Mexican blue jeans and computers to Mauritian t-shirts and Chinese auto parts.[2] This case study literature identifies many successes and some failures of economic development within this new global production structure. It also shows that economic upgrading is a multifaceted and complex process involving changes in business strategy, production structure and technology, policy, and the organization of markets.

The case studies raise a number of questions. The first is simply how widespread is economic upgrading? The case study literature possibly suffers from a bias toward examples of successful upgrading. Such a selection bias problem would skew any general conclusion from the case studies. It would also indicate a lack of analysis of failed efforts at upgrading.

A second question—and the main focus of this chapter—is about the social consequences of economic upgrading. Does economic upgrading necessarily and quickly translate into improvements in employment, wages, and labor standards? Simply raising productivity or value added per person in a sector says little about how the gains from economic upgrading are distributed and thus how social welfare and, ultimately, economic development are affected. Barrientos, Gereffi, and Rossi (2011) refer to the distribution of gains from industrial upgrading in global production networks as "social upgrading" and they ask, similarly, what the connection is between economic upgrading and social upgrading. While most research presumes that economic upgrading leads directly to social upgrading, this connection has not generally been analyzed in a systematic fashion and there is ample evidence that there is considerable slippage between the "cup" of economic upgrading—gains in productivity or exports—and the "lip" of social upgrading—wages, labor standards, and environmental standards. Milberg and Winkler (2011) present aggregate data for thirty developing countries and find a fairly weak link between economic and social upgrading. In addition, they find that economic upgrading is not the norm in most countries, and that there are clear cases of economic and social "downgrading" associated with participation in global value chains. Others have documented cases where economic downgrading is associated with some social upgrading.[3]

The globalization of production within global value chains has raised the volume of international trade relative to economic activity and especially of trade in intermediate goods and services.[4] Thus our analysis connecting economic and social upgrading raises the additional question of how improved international trade competitiveness of a sector translates into social gains. That is, does improved export performance drive social upgrading?

In this chapter we begin to address these issues by taking a parsimonious and operational approach to economic and social upgrading. The goal is to get an idea about whether selected developing countries experience economic and social upgrading or downgrading in selected sectors of their economy and whether there is a connection between developments in the economic sphere on the one hand and the social sphere on the other. An objective of this parsimonious approach is to begin to fill in a gap identified by Sturgeon and Gereffi (2009: 5), namely that "[t]he GVC framework provides a conceptual toolbox, but quantitative measures are lacking."

As part of the "Capturing the Gains" research project,[5] we focus on four sectors—apparel, horticulture, mobile telecommunications, and tourism—and on eight to ten developing countries that operate in each of the sectors. Our analysis of economic and social upgrading relies entirely on published data on trade and labor markets for the period 1990–2009. Published data are not always adequate for our purposes. First, data are scarce, especially for social upgrading indicators where time series often have quite substantial gaps. Second, in various cases time series include outliers and jumps, raising questions about the consistency of data. Third, drawing on different data sources affects the comparability of data and the results based on them. All this somewhat limits our ability to make robust inferences from our analysis and, thus, calls for a note of caution when it comes to interpreting our findings. It also indicates the need for a rethinking of data collection in a world economy effectively organized in global value chains.

We define economic upgrading in terms of trade performance and social upgrading in terms of employment and wage growth. While these are admittedly narrow definitions, we nonetheless generate a set of rich findings. Regarding economic upgrading we find that in all sectors except apparel, positive growth in world export market share was generally associated with economic upgrading. However, export market share growth was generally associated with less-than-proportional growth or declines in export unit values. Regarding social upgrading, the general pattern was of employment growth and considerably less growth of real wages.

Our analysis, which relies entirely on published data and an admittedly parsimonious definition of upgrading, shows that economic downgrading and social downgrading are both fairly regular occurrences, with social downgrading more common in particular because of stagnant real wages. This contrasts with the findings of many published case studies of global value chains, which tend to focus on success stories.

Contrary to standard economic theory on the relation between productivity growth and wage growth, we found that there is a variety in the pattern observed across GVCs in the relation between economic and social upgrading: In apparel and horticulture we generally find a positive correlation between economic upgrading and social upgrading. In mobile telecommunications there is widespread economic upgrading without social upgrading. And in tourism we found many cases of social upgrading with less economic upgrading. Overall, economic and social upgrading occurred together in only 15–17 out of 30 cases. We also find that in almost all cases, social upgrading does not occur in the absence of economic upgrading. These results were found to be generally robust across a few alternative techniques for measuring upgrading and downgrading. The robustness of these results will depend crucially on a more detailed analysis of institutions and regulations in place in the different locations and especially on the private sector governance structures that regulate each of the global value chains.

This chapter has six sections. In section 2, we define economic and social upgrading and describe the general framework for mapping their relation to each other. In section 3 we summarize the evidence on economic upgrading and downgrading, and in section 4 we do the same for social upgrading and downgrading. In section 5 we present the evidence on the interrelation between the economic and social realms, and section 6 concludes with a summary of our findings and a note of caution about interpreting the results, given the problems with data on international trade and labor markets at this detailed level of analysis.

2 A Parsimonious Approach to Economic and Social Upgrading in Global Value Chains

Social upgrading can be understood as a process of improvement in the entitlements and rights of workers as social actors, which enhances the quality of their employment (Sen 1999, 2000). From this perspective, social upgrading involves the advancement of employment based on decent work and respect for labor standards. At the same time, access to better work as just described might actually result from economic upgrading (Barrientos et al. 2011). These are very broad definitions. To operationalize these concepts, given available data, we propose a parsimonious approach to the study of economic and social upgrading, as follows: A country is said to experience *economic upgrading* in a given sector when the following two necessary conditions are fulfilled:[6]

(1) There is an increase in the world export market share (i.e., its exports are internationally competitive);
(2) There is an increase in the export unit value, implying the production of higher-value products in the sector concerned.

According to the typology developed in the recent research on global value chains (see, for example, Humphrey and Schmitz 2002; Humphrey 2004; Gereffi et al. 2005; UNIDO 2011), progress on these two indicators reflects "product upgrading" or "functional upgrading." In any case, it is important to include both dimensions in our analysis to adequately capture economic upgrading. Export unit values measure the average monetary value of one unit of export and are calculated by dividing the total value of a country's exports (of a certain commodity class or product group) in a given period by the quantity or volume of these exports. Export unit values are often used as proxies or surrogates for price indices (see IMF et al. 2009, for example). A number of recent studies of global value chains have argued for using export unit value data to capture upgrading. Evgeniev and Gereffi (2008) use export unit values to distinguish between "up-market," "middle-market," and "down-market" exports in a study of Turkish and Bulgarian textiles and apparel, illuminating "the possibilities for particular countries to upgrade and climb the industrial ladder of export roles."[7] Li and Song (2011) use export unit value data in their study of Chinese trade and point out that "we can use the price of a product as a proxy to evaluate its quality. In the international market, for the same kinds of products coming from different countries, the ones with higher prices are often of relatively higher quality."[8] Similarly, Aiginger (1997) writes that,

> A country with a higher [export] unit value will in some sense supply more quality, perhaps owing to its ability to sell an identical product at a higher price [...], or by specializing in a more highly-priced product segment. [...] The unit value is an indicator which can be used to provide complementary information on the competitiveness of firms and industries. (Aiginger 1997: 574, 586)

In principle, an increase in the unit values of a given country's exports can reflect either a shift in the composition of the sectoral export basket away from lower-value towards higher-value products or a general (i.e., across-the-board) increase in unit values of given product categories (as a result of higher quality, an increase in global demand relative to supply, or increased market power), or a combination of both. It is important to note that greater competitiveness in international trade is typically associated with lower costs and thus lower unit values. Upgrading, then, hinges on the simultaneous maintenance of international competitiveness (world export market share) and the attainment of higher export unit values. Thus, according to Kaplinsky and Readman (2005: 682): "Firms which engage in successful product innovation [...] can expect to receive relatively higher prices for their output. [...] Higher prices may also reflect inefficiencies in production, suggesting a decline in innovative performance, but in this case with regard to process innovation. Therefore we need an indicator of cost competitiveness." For this purpose, they suggest the use of export market shares which, in combination with the first indicator (export unit values), gives a more complete and reliable picture about whether a sector experiences upgrading or not.

An alternative to export unit values as an indicator of economic upgrading is to use a direct measure of value added per worker or productivity growth. This has been adopted in a number of studies of global value chains. We opt for the export unit value approach here because it retains the connection to international trade (which is of relevance given that *global* value chains involve cross-border transactions) and because a number of the most recent studies (discussed above) also use this measure. For a discussion of the wide variety of measures that have been adopted in the value chain case study literature, see Milberg and Winkler (2011).

As for the second part of our parsimonious approach, *social upgrading* is defined as occurring in a given sector when the following two necessary conditions are fulfilled:

(1) There is an increase in employment;
(2) There is an increase in real wages.

The motivation for the choice of these indicators is straightforward: The major contribution a sector of production can make to social well-being is the creation of jobs, thereby giving labor the possibility to earn income. However, such a quantitative treatment of social upgrading in terms of employment generation alone is not enough. What also matters is the *quality* of jobs (created or retained). This is to be captured by including real wages in our analysis. In a sense, their remuneration is a measure of how much workers benefit from the value created by economic activity in the different sectors. It gives an idea of how much of the (sectoral) value added generated is appropriated by workers.[9] Other sensible options, to be explored in future research, would be to use changes in the sectoral share in total employment, or changes in sectoral employment relative to population growth instead of nominal growth in sectoral employment as indicator for social upgrading. An even more nuanced picture of social upgrading would require the inclusion of labor standards into our analysis. However, given that published data on this issue are hardly available (particularly at the sectoral level), this is also an endeavor that we leave to future research.

3 Economic upgrading in the four sectors

In this section we provide an overview of economic upgrading over the last twenty years in the four sectors under study. In the next section we turn to social upgrading. The complete time series for all the component variables in economic and social upgrading are reported in Bernhardt and Milberg (2011: appendices 2 to 5). In this section we present the data for the two economic upgrading indicators and highlight important patterns and trends. We consider each sector separately.

Sector selection was guided by the desire to have variety in terms of technological intensity. The four sectors and their technological profile are as follows:

- Horticulture (as an example of a commodity-based, low-tech sector);
- Apparel (as an example of a medium-tech and labor-intensive sector);
- Mobile telecom (as an example of a high-tech sector);
- Tourism (as an example of a service sector).

We should also note that the nature of the value chain is different across our sample, not only in terms of the technological content of the final and component products, but also in terms of the functioning of the chain, as first discussed by Gereffi (1994). Apparel is a classic "buyer led" chain, in which lead firms—both retailers such as Walmart and designers/retailers such as The Gap—source globally.[10] The mobile telecom industry is more of a "producer led" chain, in which technology development and design companies (e.g., Apple, Nokia) source parts and assembly.[11] Agro-foods are closer to the buyer-led model, particularly in the case of the products on which we will focus, fruits and vegetables. Nonetheless there are clear prospects for upgrading—both economic and social—in this sector, as developing country firms can seek to engage in more processing of the good. The case of green beans in Kenya, studied by Dolan and Humphrey (2004), is a good example, where packaging and canning is a higher-value segment of the chain that Kenyan producers sought to capture from their retail buyers in the United Kingdom. Tourism has increasingly become a producer-led sector, as multinational firms have gained control of local tourist services. Economic upgrading in tourism would involve increased control over the management and design of tour packages and operations rather than just the provision of labor in a local hotel or tour sector.[12]

In each of these sectors, we analyzed a slightly different set of developing countries. The selection of countries was guided by the idea of including the major developing countries for each sector and for each continent, such as China, India, Mexico, or South Africa. The other countries were chosen to reflect a balanced regional distribution with a certain emphasis on countries that have an established link with the lead firm or key supplier firms in the global value chain. A full overview of the countries in the sample is provided in Table A1. In Table A2 we give the precise definition of each of the sectors in terms of product coverage/product categories. The analysis draws on the following international data sets:

- UN Comtrade (exports, unit values);
- UNCTAD Handbook of Statistics (tourism exports, unit values);
- UNIDO INDSTAT4 (employment, earnings);
- ILO Laborsta and ILO KILM (earnings);
- World Travel & Tourism Council (WTTC) Economic Data Search Tool (tourism employment).

As noted above, a country is considered to experience economic upgrading in a given sector when two conditions are fulfilled: (1) there is an increase in the country's world export market share; and (2) there is an increase in the export unit value. Looking at changes over time ensures that the dynamic nature of upgrading (or downgrading) as a *process* is captured, as opposed to earlier practices using static indicators of innovative progress (i.e., up- or downgrading) (Kaplinsky and Readman 2005: 680). Below, we present the percentage change from 1990 to 2009 in both the world export market share and the export unit value for all the countries in our sample and for each of the four sectors, beginning with the horticulture sector.

3.1 Horticulture

The top three horticulture exporters in terms of world export market share are all developed countries but about half of the top fifteen exporters come from the developing world. Latin America plays a dominant role in this regard: one-third of the top fifteen horticulture exporters are either Central or South American economies, the most important being Mexico, followed by Chile, Ecuador, Colombia, and Costa Rica. Other important horticulture exporters from the developing world include China (with the fifth-largest export market share) and Turkey (tenth).

None of the African countries in our sample plays a really important role in the horticulture sector. The most competitive exporter is Kenya with a market share of 0.44 percent in 2009 (up from 0.19 percent in 1990 but down from 0.72 percent in 2008). Among the Asian countries in our sample, Thailand and Viet Nam are significant players in the horticulture sector with both accounting for more than one percent of the global export market in 2009. However, while Viet Nam was able to increase its world export market share from 0.13 percent in 1990 to 1.10 percent in 2009, Thailand lost 0.83 percentage points in the same period of time (from 2.66 percent in 1990 to 1.83 percent in 2009). Five of the selected Latin American economies had an export world market share of more than 1 percent in 2009: Mexico (5.32 percent), Chile (3.67 percent), Ecuador (3.12 percent), Colombia (2.40 percent), and Costa Rica (2.32 percent). Moreover, all of them succeeded in increasing their market share since 1990, some of them even substantially.

When using UN Comtrade data, export unit values can only be calculated at a higher (four-digit) level of product disaggregation. To give a first example of a horticulture product, export unit values of *cut flowers and dried flowers for bouquets* (HS code 0603) have increased for two-thirds of the countries in our sample during the last twenty years. All the African countries in our sample saw an increase in the unit values of their flower exports between 1990 and 2009 while all the Asian countries experienced a decline. Moreover, there are large differences in unit values across countries. While, in 2009, Uganda and Panama sold their flowers abroad for more than US$9 per kilogram, Bangladesh and Honduras got less than US$1 per kilogram of flower exports.

For *fresh and chilled vegetables* (HS code 0709), however, only one-third of the countries in our sample succeeded in increasing their export unit values while the rest saw stagnating or declining unit values. African countries, again, have been performing quite well, with three out of four (Kenya, Tanzania, and Uganda) managing to raise their export unit values while three of the four South American countries in our sample (Brazil, Chile, and Ecuador) experienced declining unit values (the only exception was Colombia) and only one of the three Asian countries in our sample (Bangladesh) succeeded in increasing its export unit values. *Fresh or dried citrus fruits* (HS code 0805) are exported by all the countries in our sample. While all Asian countries and three out of four African countries in our sample could lift the unit values of their citrus fruit exports, all Central American countries (except for Panama) and half of the South American countries saw their export unit values deteriorate. In general, Central American countries sell their citrus fruits very cheaply: In 2009, Nicaragua, Costa Rica, and Honduras earned a mere US$0.07/kg, US$0.12/kg, and US$0.16/kg, respectively. Other low earners include Ecuador (US$0.13/kg) and Kenya (US$0.19/kg). Their revenues contrast with those of Bangladesh, Ethiopia, and Uganda that, in 2009, exported their citrus fruits for more than US$2.0/kg.

According to our definition of economic upgrading, six out of nineteen countries managed to upgrade in the horticulture sector between 1990 and 2009 (see Table 20.1). Among them, Uganda is the most impressive success story, multiplying its market share by 78 (albeit from very low levels in the early 1990s) and its export unit values by six during the last twenty years. Two other African countries also stand out as excellent performers: Ethiopia and Kenya. Both were able to more than double the unit value of their horticulture exports while increasing their market shares more than sevenfold and threefold respectively. In Latin America, Chile and Ecuador were the only clear economic upgraders from 1990 to 2009, the latter recording an impressive growth in the unit values of its exports of 150 percent during this period. However, looking at a shorter and more recent time period (2000–2009) reveals that Brazil, Mexico and Nicaragua also experienced clear economic upgrading during the last decade.

For the longer time period, the only country whose horticulture sector experienced clear economic downgrading was Thailand, losing almost 40 percent of its market share and seeing its export unit values decrease by a quarter over 1990–2009. Interestingly, in the 2000s, Thailand experienced clear economic upgrading, increasing both its market share and its export unit values by more than 10 percent, so it seems that the Thai

Table 20.1 Economic upgrading in horticulture, 1990–2009

	Growth (%) in market share	Growth (%) in unit value
Economic Upgraders		
Bangladesh	276.04	47.32
Chile	23.06	53.87
Ecuador	13.59	149.99
Ethiopia	656.11	176.28
Kenya	228.39	113.44
Uganda	7,835.38	529.47
Economic Downgraders		
Thailand	−39.93	−24.52
Intermediate Cases		
Belize	2,148.48	−42.66
Brazil	71.08	−29.25
Colombia	7.45	−26.76
Costa Rica	15.66	−24.02
El Salvador	−24.95	86.14
Guatemala	48.59	−40.19
Honduras	−53.40	5.21
Mexico	42.97	−30.90
Nicaragua	−2.26	93.29
Panama	−70.03	20.26
Tanzania	5.39	−82.90
Viet Nam	549.93	−75.09

Source: Authors' own calculations based on data from UN Comtrade.

horticulture sector suffered during the 1990s but recovered during the last decade. Among the Asian countries in our sample, only Bangladesh established itself as a clear "upgrader" in the horticulture sector. Viet Nam, on the other hand, impressively managed to more than sextuple its market share—albeit at the cost of declining export unit values (−75 percent). It is therefore an intermediate or mixed case, having done well on one front (export market share) but rather poorly on the other front (export unit values).[13] At the same time, the Central American countries El Salvador, Honduras, Nicaragua, and Panama lost market shares but increased their export unit values, while Brazil, Colombia, Costa Rica, Mexico, Tanzania, and Viet Nam had market share gains but export unit value losses.

3.2 Apparel

Apparel production has been much debated as a catalyst for economic development and developing countries are among the major exporters of apparel products. Four of the top five (China, Bangladesh, Turkey, and India) and nine of the top fifteen apparel-exporting countries in terms of world export market share are developing countries. Almost all of them are Asian: Besides the four economies already mentioned, the ranking also includes Viet Nam, Indonesia, and Sri Lanka. The only other developing countries that made it into the top fifteen exporters ranking are Mexico (with the eleventh-largest export market share) and Tunisia (the world's number thirteen).

None of the African countries has succeeded in establishing itself as major exporter in the apparel sector. The most competitive African exporter in 2009 was Mauritius, with a market share of 0.31 percent (yet down from 0.33 percent in 1990). The remaining three African economies in our sample have gone through opposing experiences: While South Africa has dramatically lost market share (from 0.20 percent in 2000 to 0.03 percent in 2009), Kenya (up from 0.001 percent in 1990 to 0.085 percent in 2009) and Lesotho (up from 0.08 percent in 2000 to 0.12 percent in 2009) have been among the biggest winners. As already mentioned, all the Asian countries in our sample are important players in the apparel sector; even Cambodia, the only Asian economy that did not make it into the top fifteen, has a market share of 1.3 percent. Strikingly, all of them have continuously increased their market shares, both in the 1990s and in the 2000s. Meanwhile, apparel exports of the Latin American and Caribbean countries in our sample have also gone up significantly, even though none of them (except for Mexico) has a market share above 1 percent. However, considering their (economic) size, several Central American and Caribbean countries had quite impressive export market shares in 2009: El Salvador (0.57 percent), Guatemala (0.50 percent), Nicaragua (0.39 percent), the Dominican Republic (0.27 percent), and Haiti (0.23 percent), all of them up from extremely low levels.

As with the horticulture sector, it is hard to make general observations on export unit values. Bernhardt and Milberg (2011: appendix, table 20.A.3.2) report how export unit values have changed between 1990 and 2009 for each country's top ten apparel products at the four-digit level of product disaggregation. In the apparel sector generally speaking there has been much more market share growth than export unit value growth. One interpretation would be that low unit values are required for gains in market share—a downward sloping product demand curve. In any case, more than half of all the countries in our sample (nine out of sixteen) experienced clear economic upgrading from 1990 to 2009 (see Table 20.2). The most outstanding cases are Cambodia, Kenya, and Viet Nam, which have multiplied their export market shares by 55, 8, and 13, respectively. In this time period, Cambodia and Viet Nam managed to elevate their market shares to over 1 percent of world exports (1.3 percent and 3.3 percent, respectively) up from a low 0.02 percent and 0.20 percent, respectively. Cambodia was, moreover, able to combine this with a considerable rise in its apparel export unit value of 54 percent whereas Viet Nam's exports gained a mere 1.35 percent in value per unit between 1990 and 2009. In fact, the best performer in this regard has been Guatemala whose export unit values more than doubled during the last twenty years—allowing it to increase its world export market share by almost 40 percent, apparently in higher-value segments. Other unambiguous economic upgraders include the Asian powerhouses China and

Table 20.2 Economic upgrading in apparel, 1990–2009

	Growth (%) in market share	Growth (%) in unit value
Economic Upgraders		
Bangladesh	373.89	16.86
Cambodia	5,539.65	53.88
China	163.94	13.25
Guatemala	37.46	128.54
India	63.86	10.96
Kenya	791.80	35.40
Mexico	80.04	15.56
Sri Lanka	47.71	45.69
Viet Nam	1,307.10	1.35
Economic Downgraders		
-		
Intermediate Cases		
Dominican Rep.	−67.34	18.39
El Salvador	387.33	−27.62
Haiti	80.44	−20.42
Lesotho	−2.03	14.93
Mauritius	−15.60	12.71
Nicaragua	16,970.36	−15.86
South Africa	−67.31	82.95

Note: Time span covered is 2000–2009 for Lesotho and South Africa.

Source: Authors' own calculations based on data from UN Comtrade.

India as well as Bangladesh, Sri Lanka, and Mexico. Remarkably, a significant part of this overall upgrading of these countries over 1990–2009 seems to have occurred in the first half of this period, i.e. in the 1990s. Only four of the nine countries (Bangladesh, Cambodia, India, and Kenya) figure among the list of clear economic upgraders if one looks at the shorter and more recent time period, 2000–2009.[14] China, on the other hand, had a mixed experience in the 2000s with its market share still growing by 57 percent, yet its export unit values falling by 6 percent.

None of the countries in our sample experienced clear-cut economic downgrading in the apparel sector over the entire period. However, this is not true for the 2000s when El Salvador and Guatemala somewhat reversed their good performance from the 1990s and lost both export market shares and export unit values. Another notable case is Nicaragua whose export market share shot up by a stunning 17,000 percent from 1990 to 2009 (with a significant slowdown of market share gains in the second half of the period)—on the back of a simultaneous decrease in export unit values of 16 percent. What is also interesting to note is that, except for Kenya, all the African countries in our sample (Lesotho, Mauritius, and South Africa) are intermediate cases with a common pattern: While all of them succeeded in enhancing the unit values of their exports, they did so at the expense of markets shares, which dropped by 2 percent (Lesotho), 16 percent (Mauritius), and 67 percent (South Africa).

3.3 Mobile telecom

There are only four developing countries among the fifteen leading exporters in the sector. These four countries, however, occupy top spots, with China and South Korea ranking first and second while Mexico and Malaysia are the world's fifth- and ninth-largest exporters. Apart from these exceptions, the technology intensity of the mobile telecom sector guarantees that the world market is dominated by exports from the advanced economies, and the huge majority of the countries in our sample play very small roles as exporters. It is important to note that we have not included the raw materials such as coltan in our definition of the mobile telecom sector, thus understating the importance of developing countries within the global value chain.[15]

Changes in market shares over the last 20 years were relatively minor for most Latin American and Caribbean countries. The notable exceptions are the two most competitive exporters, Mexico and Brazil. Both have managed to increase their market shares quite substantively since 1990. Meanwhile, mobile telecom exports from almost all the Asian countries in our sample have gone up significantly, and today some of them are important players, as already mentioned. The stellar performer was, of course, China, which managed to ramp up its market share from 2.5 percent in 1990 to 37.4 percent in 2009. Viet Nam and the Philippines represent similar success stories, albeit at much lower levels (reaching export market shares of 0.18 percent and 0.39 percent, respectively, in 2009). The two Asian countries in our sample with the largest world export market shares after China, namely Thailand (0.88 percent in 2009) and India (0.77 percent in 2009), on the other hand, have experienced up-and-downs: While both gained export market shares in the 1990s, they lost market shares in the 2000s (see Table 20.3).

Two-thirds of the countries in our sample have recorded an increase in the unit values of their mobile telecom exports over the last decade.[16] However, interregional differences are quite significant. While 80 percent of the African countries in the sample succeeded in raising their export unit values since 2000, the same is true for only about half of the Asian and Latin American and Caribbean countries. In Asia, Bangladesh, China, Pakistan, and Thailand where those economies which managed to increase the unit values of their mobile telecom exports, while India, the Philippines, Sri Lanka, and Viet Nam saw their unit values decline. In Latin America and the Caribbean, in turn, winners in terms of export unit values included Brazil, Colombia, Costa Rica, Guatemala, Haiti, and Mexico, whereas losers included El Salvador, Honduras, Nicaragua, Paraguay, and Peru. We can also compare these changes to those experienced by some of the leading industrialized country firms in this sector. For example, the percentage increase in export unit values between 2000 and 2009 was 67 percent in Finland, 57 percent in Japan, and 9.5 percent in the United Kingdom.

Table 20.3 Economic upgrading in mobile telecom, 2000–2009

	Growth (%) in market share	Growth (%) in unit value
Economic Upgraders		
Brazil	619.77	918.94
China	418.82	646.93
Colombia	308.51	4.29
Costa Rica	223.85	980.57
Ghana	109.58	19.72
Guatemala	48.57	107.10
Haiti	987.15	20,325.01
India	226.49	207.30
Kenya	116.16	1,022.41
Mexico	53.87	1,636.72
Nigeria	193.06	894.21
Pakistan	237.59	587.40
Peru	568.11	108.65
Philippines	1,431.07	2,463.84
Rwanda	45.40	1,999.95
Sri Lanka	40.62	1,921.25
Viet Nam	4,836.63	143.36
Economic Downgraders		
Honduras	−3.32	−31.42
Nicaragua	−93.51	−26.64
Intermediate Cases		
Bangladesh	−92.39	754.66
Congo, Dem. Rep.	209.33	−45.06
El Salvador	244.93	−92.86
Ethiopia	−85.92	1,615.58
Mozambique	1,212.14	−2.40
Paraguay	1,064.76	-49.58
South Africa	−15.75	128.43
Tanzania	63.96	−9.22
Thailand	−20.08	601.89
Uganda	1,902.18	−3.34

Source: Authors' own calculations based on data from UN Comtrade.

Note: Given the rather recent emergence of the mobile telecom sector, this table concentrates on developments since the year 2000 (unlike Tables 20.1, 20.2, and 20.4, which report growth rates from 1990 to 2009).

More than 60 percent of the countries in our sample (eighteen out of twenty-nine) managed to economically upgrade in the mobile telecom sector during the last decade. Several stunning success stories stand out: Brazil, Haiti and the Philippines increased both their market shares and their export unit values almost or even more than ten-fold. Meanwhile, a number of other upgraders did particularly well on one of the two indicators: Peru and Viet Nam, on the one hand, could multiply their market shares by 20 and 108 respectively (while also approximately doubling the unit values of their exports), whereas on the other hand, China, Ghana, and the Philippines, multiplied their export unit values by 14, 26, and 21 respectively (while also gaining world export market shares). Interestingly, the upgraders include countries from all three (sub) continents.

Among the eleven intermediate cases, two countries' experiences are particularly striking. Paraguay succeeded to increase its share in the world mobile telecom market tenfold but saw its export unit values decline by 65 percent. Thailand, on the other hand, experienced the opposite: The almost ninefold rise in the unit value of its mobile telecom exports came at the expense of a market share loss of 27 percent. The only countries that experienced outright downgrading between 2000 and 2009 were Honduras and Nicaragua.

3.4 Tourism

On a global scale, developing countries do not (yet) play a leading role as exporters of tourism services. Among the top fifteen tourism exporters there are only three developing countries: China is ranked sixth while Turkey and Thailand have the tenth-largest and eleventh-largest world export market shares, respectively. The rest of the ranking is dominated by North American and European countries.

The countries in our sample are, thus, all rather small players in the global tourism industry. Among them, the most important exporter of tourism services is China, with a world market share of 4.5 percent in 2007. Its continuous gains in market share (up from a bit more than 1 percent in 1990) have actually earned China a place among the top six world exporters, only slightly behind the United Kingdom. India is the only other Asian country in our sample with a world market share exceeding 1 percent (namely 1.3 percent in 2007). After gaining market shares in the first half of the 1990s (from 0.97 percent in 1990 up to 1.03 percent in 1994), it dramatically lost market shares until the early 2000s (down to 0.64 percent in 2002) when it started to regain ground. The same pattern (with market share losses in the 1990s and gains in the 2000s) can also be observed for Brazil, Kenya, Jordan, and South Africa. Meanwhile, Costa Rica and Uganda steadily increased their export market shares whereas the tourism sectors of Indonesia, Jamaica, and Nepal were in continuous decline.

While the unit value measure is relatively straightforward for commodities, calculation of unit values is not as simple for services, and for tourism in particular. In view of the data that are available in UNCTAD's *Handbook of Statistics 2009*, we divided the value of tourism services exports by the number of arrivals of visitors in order to derive a measure for export unit values, namely "travel expenditures per visitor" (in US$). Using this measure of unit values in tourism exports, we find that more than half the countries in our sample experienced declines between 1990 and 2007. Among the African and Latin American and Caribbean countries in our sample, two out of three earned less in travel expenditures per foreign visitor in 2007 than in 1990 (namely Kenya and South Africa, and Brazil and Jamaica). In Africa, the exception to this downward trend is Uganda, while in Latin America the only country where visitors from abroad increased their expenditures is Costa Rica. Among the Asian countries in our sample, three countries experienced a decline in tourism export unit values (Indonesia, Jordan, Nepal) and three countries an increase (China, India, Viet Nam).

Travel expenditures per foreign visitor vary quite significantly across regions and countries. In 2007, India earned by far the most per tourist, about US$2,000. At the other extreme, in the same year an average visitor to China spent less than a mere US$300 on tourism services. Other countries with low export unit values (of below US$400) include Jordan, Kenya, and Nepal, where travel expenditures per visitor in 2007 were US$354, US$373, and US$380, respectively. High earners in the tourism sector, on the other hand, include Brazil, Indonesia, and South Africa where foreign visitors spent, on average, US$985, US$970, and US$917, respectively.

Strikingly, during 1990–2007 all countries in our sample experienced either clear economic upgrading or clear economic downgrading in their tourism sectors (see Table 20.4). Five countries experienced upgrading and seven experienced downgrading.

Table 20.4 Economic upgrading in tourism (1990–2007)

	Growth (%) in market share	Growth (%) in unit value
Economic Upgraders		
China	314.29	70.31
Costa Rica	37.68	34.53
India	33.14	124.11
Uganda	184.52	117.46
Viet Nam	64.27	54.95
Economic Downgraders		
Brazil	−30.74	−22.26
Indonesia	−51.98	−1.78
Jamaica	−50.97	−12.93
Jordan	−12.54	−60.38
Kenya	−62.19	−34.71
Nepal	−64.54	−11.27
South Africa	−11.04	−48.59
Intermediate Cases		
-		

Note: Time span covered is 1993–2007 for Uganda and 2003–2006 for Viet Nam.

Source: Authors' own calculations based on data from UNCTAD's *Handbook of Statistics*, 2009.

3.5 Economic upgrading: a summing up

Using a parsimonious and operational definition of economic upgrading reveals considerable variation across our four sectors. Economic upgrading is the norm in the apparel and telecom sectors: in the apparel sector there has not been a single case of clear-cut economic downgrading over 1990–2009, while in the mobile telecom sector there have been just two such cases. In horticulture and tourism, the picture is less rosy. In horticulture, while there has been only one case of unambiguous economic downgrading (and a few instances of clear-cut economic upgrading), the bulk of countries have not succeeded in advancing on *both* fronts (i.e., in terms of world market share *and* export unit values). Meanwhile, the tourism sector has offered the fewest prospects for economic upgrading for the developing countries in our sample over 1990–2007. The majority of sample countries experienced economic downgrading.

Variations in performance across sectors can also be observed for single countries that figure in the samples of various sectors. Brazil, for example, experienced clear-cut upgrading in the mobile telecom sector but clear-cut downgrading in the tourism sector (while being an intermediate case in horticulture). China and India, in turn, have succeeded in upgrading in *all* the sectors in which their performances were analyzed (apparel, mobile telecom, and tourism). The same is true for Bangladesh (in horticulture, apparel, and mobile telecom). Other general success stories include Mexico (clear-cut upgrading in apparel and mobile telecom and a mixed performance in horticulture) and Viet Nam (clear-cut upgrading in apparel, mobile telecom, and tourism and a mixed performance in horticulture). South Africa, on the other hand, has done rather poorly overall. While none of its sectors managed to upgrade, its tourism sector witnessed economic downgrading while its apparel and mobile telecom sectors were among the intermediate cases.

Looking at our two indicators of economic upgrading separately, it can be observed that, in general, achieving gains in export market share has been easier than achieving increases in export unit value. As a consequence, export market share growth has generally been associated with less-than-proportional growth or even declines in export unit values. In conclusion, it can be said that economic upgrading is not the norm and is more difficult to achieve than indicated by the case study literature, which often focuses on success stories (Milberg and Winkler 2011).

4 Social upgrading in the four sectors

We now turn to the issue of social upgrading and downgrading in the four sectors. According to our definition (outlined in section 2) a country experiences social upgrading in a given sector when two conditions are fulfilled: (1) there is an increase in employment; and (2) there is an increase in real wages. Depending on data availability, we calculated the percentage change in these variables from the early 1990s to the late 2000s for all the countries in our sample. Generally, analysis of social upgrading and downgrading is more difficult than the analysis of the economic realm due to significant data gaps. For various countries and years data are very scarce or not available at all. For the horticulture sector, for example, we did not find meaningful data on sectoral employment. Moreover, contingent on data availability, the time spans of data coverage vary across the countries in our sample, i.e. coverage is not identical across countries. The growth rates reported are therefore not always fully comparable, and thus inferences made here have to be interpreted accordingly. The same caveat must be applied to the analysis of the connection of economic and social upgrading undertaken in section 5.

4.1 Apparel

Social upgrading data are particularly scarce for Latin American and Caribbean economies. In fact, the only country for which data are available is Mexico. In 2003, the latest year for which data are available, the Mexican apparel sector employed 406,000 workers—an almost tenfold increase from 1994, the earliest year for which data are available. This figure falls well short of employment numbers for the Asian economies in our sample where the apparel sector appears to play a much more important role.

The Chinese apparel sector is the largest in terms of employment in our sample, employing almost 5.5 million people in 2007, up from 3.5 million in 2003. In Bangladesh, close to a million people were working in apparel production already in 1998 (the latest year for which data are available), up from 720,000 workers in 1993 (the earliest figure available). Most recent data show that the apparel sector gave employment to 706,000 people in Viet Nam (in 2007), 540,000 people in India (2005), 482,000 people in Sri Lanka (2006) and 169,000 people in Cambodia (2000). All of these countries actually registered quite significant increases in the number of jobs over the last ten to twenty years. This starkly contrasts with the experience of the African countries in our sample. Apparel sector employment in South Africa went down to 64,000 in 2007 from 109,000 jobs in 1993. In Mauritius, employment fell to 51,000 in 2007 from 67,000 ten years earlier. In Lesotho, employment fell to 27,000 from 51,000 over that same period. Interestingly, Lesotho still managed to increase its market share in world exports (see above)—whereas in Mauritius and South Africa the decline in employment occurred as world export market shares declined.

While total employment levels in apparel are lowest in the African countries in our sample, real wages are highest, as can be seen in Figure 20.1. An employee in the South African apparel sector, on average, earned US$6,100 a year in 2007, up from US$5,000 in 1993, while the average annual wage of his or her counterpart in Mauritius was US$3,600 in 2006, up from US$2,600 in 1997. The only exception in our sample to these high wages paid in African apparel production is Lesotho, where in 2007 an average worker earned merely US$1,300 per year, up from US$256 in 2001, but down from the

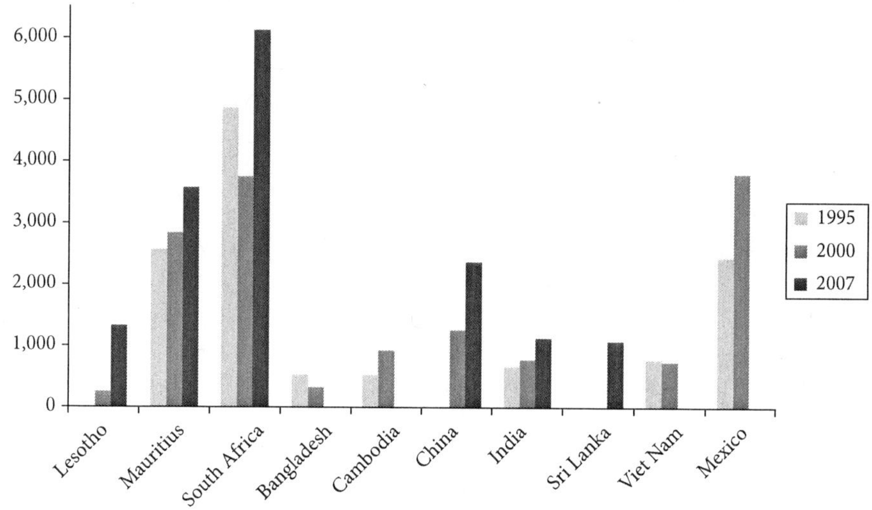

FIGURE 20.1 Average annual nominal wages (in US$) in the apparel sector, selected countries.

Note: For Lesotho, the figure for 2000 refers to 2001; for Mauritius, the figure for 1995 refers to 1997 while the figure for 2007 refers to 2006; for China, the figure for 2000 refers to 2003; for India, the figures for 1995 and 2007 refer to 1998 and 2005 respectively; for Sri Lanka, the figure for 2007 refers to 2006; and for Viet Nam, the figure for 1995 refers to 1998.

Source: Authors' own illustration based on data from UNIDO's INDSTAT4 database (2010 version).

peak of US$1,700 in 2005. However, this was still much more than the wages that were paid in various South Asian and Southeast Asian countries. The average annual remuneration was US$332 in Bangladesh (in 1998), US$734 in Viet Nam (in 2000), US$918 in Cambodia (in 2000), and US$1,133 in India (in 2005).[17] In the medium range, we find China, where the average annual wage in 2007 was US$2,400, and Mexico, where the average annual wage in 2003 was US$2,600. In terms of changes over time, most countries have witnessed an increase in average (nominal) wages since the 1990s, most notably Lesotho, China and India. In Mexico, on the other hand, a typical worker in the apparel sector in 2003 (the latest year for which data are available) earned less than in 2000 and also 1994 (but more than in 1995, as displayed in Figure 20.1)—even in nominal terms. Other countries in our sample where wages went down include Bangladesh and Viet Nam; although in these cases, due to a lack of data, the declines refer to time periods of only three and two years, respectively, and therefore cannot be fully compared to the figures for other countries which cover longer time periods. Overall, however, one can observe a slight upward trend in nominal wages in the apparel sector over the last ten to twenty years.

Combining data on employment and wage changes to assess social upgrading or downgrading, we find that clear-cut social upgrading in the apparel sector was rather scarce over the last two decades (see Table 20.5). There were, in fact, only two unambiguous cases of social upgrading, namely Cambodia and China. However, while

Table 20.5 Social upgrading in apparel, early 1990s to late 2000s

	Growth (%) in employment	Growth (%) in real wages
Social Upgraders		
Cambodia	5,824.69	84.53
China	54.81	66.70
Social Downgraders		
Mauritius	−29.11	−16.13
South Africa	−37.31	−43.82
Intermediate Cases		
India	52.02	−80.53
Lesotho	−60.56	190.53
Mexico	1,080.62	−78.99
Viet Nam	41.72	−5.22

Time spans covered are as follows: Lesotho (2001–2007), Mauritius (1997–2006), South Africa (1993–2007), China (2003–2007), India (1998–2005), Viet Nam (2005–2008), Mexico (1995–2003).

Source: Authors' own calculations based on nominal wage data from UNIDO's INDSTAT4 database, and inflation data from the IMF's International Financial Statistics (IFS) database.

China's improvements in terms of employment and real wages have been rather modest (around 60 percent each over a period of five years), Cambodia's performance has been extraordinary, with a doubling of real wages and an almost sixty-fold increase in employment.

At the other extreme, all the African countries in our sample recorded a decline in employment. In Lesotho this was accompanied by an increase in real wages (the largest in our sample, reaching an impressive +191 percent between 2001 and 2007). In Mauritius and South Africa, workers' remuneration went down too so that their apparel sectors experienced clear-cut social downgrading.

Besides Lesotho, there have actually been quite a number of other "intermediate cases," yet with exactly opposite developments on the two indicators (i.e., with employment up and real wages down). These include the two remaining Asian countries in our sample (India and Viet Nam) as well as the only Latin American country in our sample, Mexico. The latter has followed a quite peculiar trajectory, which featured a tremendous (tenfold) increase in employment at the same time as real wages went down by 79 percent.[18] Only India's apparel sector has witnessed a more dramatic fall in real wages (of −81 percent). Meanwhile, Viet Nam was very close to being categorized as a social upgrader, with a wage decline only slightly above zero and employment growth of 42 percent.

4.2 Mobile telecom

Data on wages and employment in mobile telecom are best for the Asian countries in our sample. China plays an outstanding role with 1.8 million employees in the mobile telecom sector in 2007 (up from 934,000 in 2003)—which also reflects its dominance as an exporter to world markets. Employment is also sizeable in Thailand and India, although the two countries have gone through opposing developments. While in Thailand the number of jobs in the mobile telecom sector grew from 44,000 to 59,000 between 1996 and 2006, in India employment fell from 90,000 in 1998 to 57,000 in 2005. In Latin America, Mexico's mobile telecom sector is by far the largest in terms of employment. In 2003, the latest year for which data are available, it gave work to 83,500 people—an astonishing increase compared to the 6,000 workers it had in 1994 (the earliest year for which data are available). In Brazil, employment figures have been much more stable: The 59,700 jobs that the mobile telecom sector offered in 2007 were only slightly less than the 61,000 jobs it offered in 1996.

The countries with the highest average annual wages are Brazil, South Africa and Mexico (see Figure 20.2). However, wages have developed quite differently in these three countries over the last decade or so. In Brazil, average annual wages decreased between the mid-1990s and mid-2000s (from US$28,100 in 1996 to US$17,400 in 2004) but increased again afterwards so that in 2007 (US$28,400, the latest figure available) they were slightly higher than in 1996. Wages in the South African mobile telecom sector actually went through a similar trajectory although the downward trend in the earlier years was less pronounced (from US$11,600 in 1993 slightly down to US$8,000 in 2002) whereas the upward trend in the later years was more pronounced (from US$8,000 in 2002 to US$20,500 in 2006). Meanwhile, Mexico experienced the reverse trends: the average pay went up from US$11,500 per year in 1995 to US$19,900 in 2000, and then down again to US$11,200 in 2003. In Colombia and China, in turn, workers' remuneration has continuously grown since the turn of the millennium so that by the end of the 2000s they had almost reached the Mexican wage level. In 2005, a typical Colombian employee in the mobile telecom sector earned US$10,500 per year while his or her Chinese counterpart received only a bit less than US$10,000 in 2007. A similar steady upward trend in workers' income (albeit at a lower level) was experienced in the Indian mobile telecom sector where annual average wages rose from US$3,400 in 1998 to US$6,000 in 2005. In the Philippines, Thailand and Viet Nam, on the other hand, wages developed in the opposite direction. They went down from a high US$8,900 a year in 1996 to US$5,400 in 2006 in Thailand, from US$3,800 per year in 1996 to US$2,000 in 2005 in the Philippines, and from US$3,300 a year in 1998 to US$3,000 in 2000 in Viet Nam. However, the lowest wages (in our sample) are paid in Bangladesh and Ghana where a typical employee in the mobile telecom sector earned a mere US$620 (in 1998) and US$1,970 (in 2003) per year respectively. Note that average wages are still much higher in the mobile telecom sector than in both the horticulture sector and the apparel sector.

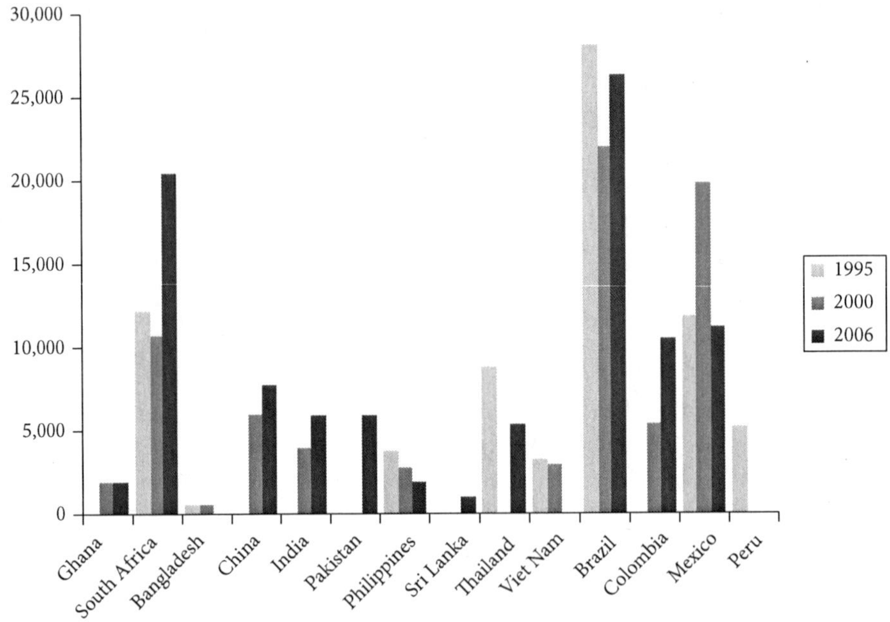

FIGURE 20.2 Average annual nominal wages (in US$) in the mobile telecom sector, selected countries.

Note: For Ghana, the figure for 2006 refers to 2003; for Bangladesh, the figure for 2000 refers to 1998; for China, the figure for 2000 refers to 2003; for India, the figure for 2006 refers to 2005; for the Philippines, the figures for 1995, 2000, and 2006 refer to 1996, 1999, and 2005 respectively; for Thailand, the figure for 1995 refers to 1998; for Brazil, the figure for 1995 refers to 1996; for Colombia, the figure for 2006 refers to 2005; and for Mexico, the figure for 2006 refers to 2003.

Source: Authors' own illustration based on data from UNIDO's INDSTAT4 database (2010 version).

Overall, in the mobile telecom sector social upgrading has been rare. This is largely because very few countries have experienced gains in real wages. The only unambiguous success story was China where employment doubled and real wages increased by 50 percent (see Table 20.6). On the other hand, a third of all the countries in our sample for which data were available have experienced plain social downgrading. The worst performer was South Africa where employment went down by 58 percent and real wages by 57 percent, respectively. The decline in real wages has actually been more dramatic in both Brazil and the Philippines, the two other clear-cut social downgraders, yet they have seen a less drastic reduction in employment (of −19 percent and −35 percent, respectively) as compared to South Africa. Most of the countries in the sample, in fact, have to be classified as intermediate cases. Among them, Mexico has again followed a very peculiar trajectory: its mobile telecom sector has combined impressive employment growth with a tremendous decline in real wages of −71 percent. In India real wages increased (by a decent 68 percent) whereas Thailand and Viet Nam registered growth in employment but a decrease in real wages.

Table 20.6 Social upgrading in mobile telecom, early 1990s to late 2000s

	Growth (%) in employment	Growth (%) in real wages
Social Upgraders		
China	97.95	47.38
Social Downgraders		
Brazil	−19.27	−63.85
Philippines	−34.59	−68.50
South Africa	−58.12	−56.67
Intermediate Cases		
Colombia	−88.15	11.72
India	−32.69	67.61
Mexico	2,822.86	−71.45
Thailand	45.44	−49.33
Viet Nam	4.70	−20.52

Note: Time spans covered are as follows: Brazil (1996–2007), China (2003–2007), Colombia (2000–2005), India (1998–2005), Mexico (1994–2003), Philippines (1996–2005), South Africa (1993–2006), Thailand (1996–2006), Viet Nam (1998–2000).

Source: Authors' own calculations based on nominal wage data from UNIDO's INDSTAT4 database, and inflation data from the IMF's International Financial Statistics database.

4.3 Horticulture

Data on employment in the horticulture sector are not available in international databases, only on wages, and here only at a very disaggregated level (namely for different *occupational groups* within the horticulture sector). In Bangladesh, one of the few countries for which longer time series evidence on wages are available, *monthly minimum wages* for farm supervisors increased from 800 Bangladeshi taka (= US$23) in 1990 to 4,700 Bangladeshi taka (= US$100) in 1998. Meanwhile, monthly minimum wages for plantation supervisors rose from 800 Bangladeshi taka to only 2,973 Bangladeshi taka (= US$62.6) in 1998. During the same period of time, plantation workers saw their monthly minimum wages increasing from US$14.5 in 1990 to US$46 in 1998.[19]

For Costa Rica between 2005 and 2008, *monthly wages* of farm supervisors and plantation supervisors rose from 168,573 to 293,466 Costa Rican colónes (from US$353 to US$559). In the same time period, monthly wages of plantation workers almost did not change in US dollar term (but stayed at around US$200) while monthly wages of field crop farm workers increased quite a bit (from US$181 to US$255).

Monthly average earnings for plantation and farm supervisors on the one hand and workers on the other hand rather diverged in Mexico. In 1999, a typical farm supervisor earned 2,673 Mexican pesos (= US$280) a month while a plantation supervisor, on

Table 20.7 Social upgrading in horticulture, 1990s to 2000s

	Real Wage % change
Bangladesh	145.09
Belize	1,295.26
Brazil	26.75
Costa Rica	15.72
El Salvador	25.01
Honduras	−55.33
Mexico	77.17
Nicaragua	−33.81

Note: Time spans covered are as follows: Bangladesh (1990–1998), Belize (1990–1995), Brazil (1999–2001), Costa Rica (2005–2008), El Salvador (2001–2008), Honduras (1990–1997), Mexico (1999–2008), Nicaragua (1993–2002).

Source: Authors' own calculations based on nominal wage data from the ILO's LABORSTA and KILM databases, and inflation data from the IMF's International Financial Statistics database.

average, earned 1,864 Mexican pesos (= US$195) per month. Farm workers and plantation workers, on the other hand, received average monthly wages of 1,137 Mexican pesos (= US$119) and 1,280 Mexican pesos (= US$134) respectively. By the late 2000s, this wage gap had widened. In 2008, a plantation supervisor's average monthly earnings were 6,536 Mexican pesos (= US$592.5) whereas farm workers and plantation workers' average monthly wages had only increased to 2,780 Mexican pesos (= US$252) and 2,641 pesos (= US$239), respectively. The latest year, for which income data is available for farm supervisors is 2004; in that year, their average monthly earnings were 4,672 Mexican pesos (= US$414).

In terms of real wages, only two countries, Honduras and Nicaragua, saw a decline (Table 20.7). On the other hand, three quarters of the countries in our sample have registered an increase in horticulture real wages, some of them even impressively so (most notably Belize, where real wages grew more than tenfold, and Bangladesh, where they more than doubled).

4.4 Tourism

Employment in the tourism sector increased in all the countries in our sample over the past two decades. In absolute terms, the two Asian giants, China and India, have the highest numbers of employees in the tourism sector. In 2009, the Indian tourism industry provided jobs for 18.4 million people while the Chinese industry employed 16.7

million people. Both figures have grown considerably since 1990 when tourism employment in both countries amounted to about 11.7 million. Brazil and Indonesia rank third and fourth in terms of the number of jobs; both had more than 2 million employees in the tourism industry in 2009. However, they have experienced much slower growth in tourism jobs than China and India.

One of the countries with the most rapid increase in tourism employment has been Uganda (up from 43,700 jobs in 1990 to 182,500 jobs in 2009). This contrasts with the experience of the two other African countries in our sample, Kenya and South Africa, where employment growth has been more moderate (from 151,000 to 197,000 and from 252,000 to 389,000, respectively, between 1990 and 2009).

Similar intraregional discrepancies can be observed in Latin America and the Caribbean where Brazil (up from 2.06 million to 2.18 million jobs) and Jamaica (up from 67,900 to 85,800 jobs) have experienced only sluggish job growth in the tourism sector whereas in Costa Rica employment has increased quite dramatically over the last twenty years (from 52,400 to 118,900 jobs). Meanwhile, in Asia, tourism employment growth has been significant in Jordan and Nepal (from 53,800 and 141,700 to 130,400 and 274,400 jobs respectively) but rather slow in Viet Nam (from 951,000 to 1.4 million jobs).

Wage data in the tourism sector are scarce. For the African countries in our sample, for instance, there are no income data available. By comparison, data availability is much better for Asia where we have wage data for four out of the six countries in our sample—which refer to different *occupational groups* within the tourism industry. Interestingly, nominal wages have risen in all these four countries since the early 1990s. In China, for example, between 1990 and 2006 *annual average wages* increased dramatically from 248 yuan to 24,700 yuan (US$52 to US$3,200) for cooks, from 165 yuan to 12,700 yuan (US$35 to US$1,700) for waiters, from 229 yuan to 11,400 yuan (US$48 to US$1,500) for room attendants and chambermaids, and from 299 yuan (in 1992) to 14,000 yuan (US$54 to US$1,800) for hotel receptionists.[20]

For India, data are only available for the 1990s, during which all occupations experienced real wage gains. In Brazil, we have the interesting situation that across all occupations nominal wages increased across in local currency terms but not if converted into US dollars. In Costa Rica, on the other hand, wages in the tourism sector grew quite considerably, both in local currency and US dollar terms. Hotel receptionists, for example, saw their *monthly wages* increase from 26,600 Costa Rican colónes (= US$187) in 1993 to 213,600 colónes (= US$407) in 2008. Room attendants and chambermaids, in turn, on average earned 73,900 Costa Rican colónes (= US$259) in 1999 and, after a steady increase, 154,300 colónes (= US$294) in 2008.

Analyzing social upgrading in the tourism sector is difficult because of the paucity of wage data. Among those countries for which data are available, three are unequivocal upgraders while two represent intermediate cases so there are no clear-cut downgraders (see Table 20.8). The stellar performer has been China's tourism sector where workers have seen an exceptional, twenty-fold increase of their real wages; yet employment has grown only by around 20 percent. Meanwhile, Costa Rica's achievements are also

Table 20.8 Social upgrading in tourism, early 1990s to late 2000s

	Growth (in %) Employment	Growth (in %) Real Wages
Social Upgraders		
China	18.10	1,962.29
Costa Rica	121.28	81.79
India	41.01	40.21
Social Downgraders		
-		
Intermediate Cases		
Brazil	15.00	−5.79
Jordan	64.40	−1.80

Source: Authors' own calculations based on employment data from the World Travel & Tourism Council's (WTTC) Economic Data Search Tool, wage data from the ILO's LABORSTA and KILM databases, and inflation data from IMF International Financial Statistics database.

impressive: Employment has more than doubled while real wages have gone up by 82 percent. In India, the number of tourism jobs has grown faster than in China (+41 percent) but the rise in real wages (+40 percent) has fallen short of that in the two other upgraders, China and Costa Rica. The remaining two "intermediate cases" have both seen an increase in tourism employment but a decrease in real wages. In both Brazil and Jordan real wage declines have, in fact, been quite small (−6 percent and −2 percent, respectively). With such an insignificant decrease in real wages and an increase in tourism employment of 64 percent, Jordan has actually come very close to be an upgrader. Brazil's growth in employment, in turn, has been much more modest (+15 percent).

4.5 Social upgrading: a summing up

As with economic upgrading, patterns of social upgrading or downgrading vary quite a bit across sectors. Social upgrading has been most difficult in the mobile telecom sector, where employment gains have been widespread but wage gains have occurred in only a few countries. By contrast, social achievements have been more widespread in the tourism sector (with no clear-cut "downgrader") and the apparel sector (where only a quarter of the countries in our sample have experienced unambiguous social downgrading). Yet, clear-cut social upgrading has been scarce even in the apparel sector (with solely two cases) while the tourism sector is the only sector where clear-cut upgraders constitute the majority (60 percent of the countries in our sample).

Overall, the bulk of countries in our sample have experienced ambiguous progress, with improvements on one front but deterioration on the other front, which makes them "intermediate cases" according to our categorization scheme. In this regard, looking at our two indicators of social upgrading separately reveals that, in general, achieving gains in employment has been more common than achieving increases in real wages. As a corollary, employment growth has generally been associated with less-than-proportional growth or even declines in real wages.

Interestingly, looking at the social performance of single countries across sectors shows much more consistent patterns as compared to the economic sphere. China, for example, has experienced clear-cut social upgrading in *all* the sectors where its performance was analyzed (namely apparel, mobile telecom, and tourism). Meanwhile, Mexico and Viet Nam have displayed mixed performances in all the sectors where they were included in the sample (being "intermediate cases" in the apparel and mobile telecom sectors) whereas India was classified as an "intermediate case" in two of three sectors (apparel and mobile telecom, while in tourism it qualified as upgrader). South Africa, on the other hand, has experienced social downgrading in *both* of the sectors where South African performance was analyzed (apparel and mobile telecom)—which, by the way, matches its overall poor performance in economic terms. The only slight inconsistency can be observed in the case of Brazil whose mobile telecom sector has experienced clear-cut social downgrading while its tourism sector's social performance has been ambiguous.

Compared to the economic realm, it seems that upgrading has been more tenuous in the social sphere while downgrading has been more common (although, interestingly, results are reverse in the tourism sector where economic downgrading has been widespread while there has not been a single case of social downgrading). This observation already gives a first hint on the possible relationship (or lack thereof) between economic and social up- and downgrading. Let us therefore now take a look at the two realms combined.

5 The Relation between Economic and Social Upgrading

A central purpose of this chapter is to analyze the relationship between economic and social upgrading. We have defined economic upgrading as a combination of changes in export market shares and changes in export unit values. Social upgrading is defined by changes in employment and changes in real wages. However, is improved export performance associated with better labor market conditions? To begin to address this question, we use the data presented above to create a single index of economic upgrading and a single index of social upgrading and plot them together. This allows an analysis of the relation between economic and social upgrading in a 2×2 matrix, a prototype of which is depicted in Figure 20.3. Of the four different scenarios, the northeastern and the southwestern quadrants represent the clear-cut cases. The northeastern quadrant includes those countries that combine economic upgrading and social upgrading

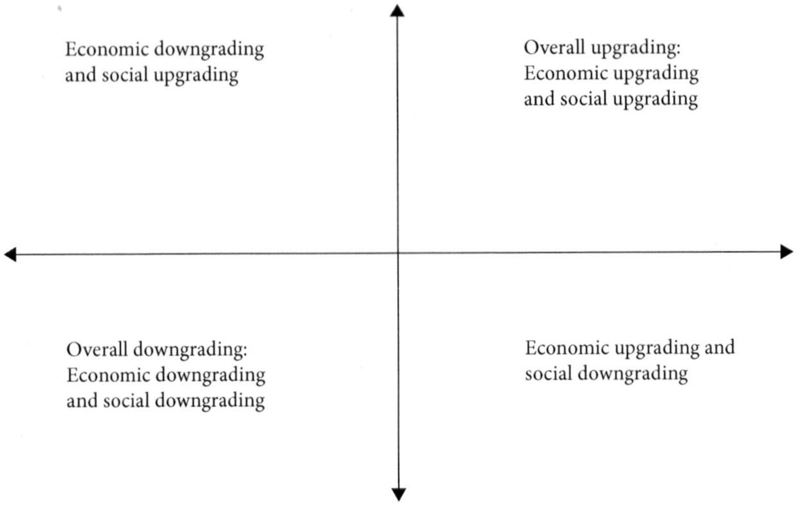

FIGURE 20.3 Prototype matrix of economic and social upgrading.

for "overall upgrading." In the southwestern quadrant, on the other hand, will be those countries that have experienced both economic and social downgrading and that, therefore, have to be called "overall downgraders." Countries falling in the remaining two quadrants are again intermediate cases, with success on one front (either economic or social) but lack of progress on the other front. Their experiences are, thus, harder to be interpreted as either clear "overall" upgrading or downgrading.[21]

We propose a simple method for combining the two variables in each realm which gives equal weight to each component. To get an indicator for economic upgrading, for example, a weight of 50 percent each is assigned to both the percentage change in export market share and the percentage change in export unit value. The underlying formulas for the calculation of upgrading are:

Economic Upgrading = 0.5 × (% change in market share) + 0.5 × (% change in export unit value)

Social Upgrading = 0.5 × (% change in employment) + 0.5 × (% change in real wage)

After we present the calculations using this method, we introduce two alternative algorithms for calculating upgrading/downgrading and we compare results across methods in order to provide a sense of the robustness of the results with any one of the methods.

5.1 Overall upgrading calculations

In **horticulture**, the majority of countries in our sample for which data are available (five out of eight) show up in the northeastern quadrant, that is having undergone both economic and social upgrading. The most outstanding performer has been Belize with impressive upgrading on both the economic and the social front. It is interesting to note that Bangladesh has been the second stellar performer, with significant improvements in both economic and social terms. Advances have been more modest in the remaining upgraders, namely Brazil, El Salvador, and Mexico, with the latter scoring high on the social front while recording only a very small improvement on the economic front. In the southwestern quadrant, Honduras figures as the only straightforward overall horticultural downgrader in our sample, with regress notably in the social sphere. The two intermediate cases in our sample, Costa Rica and Nicaragua, have had opposing experiences. While Costa Rica improved on the social front but did not manage to do so on the economic front (although only narrowly), Nicaragua has not been able to accompany its economic success with social progress. Overall, however, Figure 20.4 gives the impression that there has been a positive correlation between economic upgrading and social upgrading in the horticulture sector.

The **apparel** sector has also many cases of overall upgrading. Figure 20.5 shows that more than 60 percent of the countries in our sample for which data are available (five out of eight countries) appear in the northeastern quadrant of clear overall upgraders. Among them, Cambodia has clearly been the prime performer with formidable upgrading in both economic and social terms. Other outstanding performers include Viet Nam (on the economic front) and Mexico (on the social front). The remaining two upgraders' progress has been less pronounced but still decent, particularly China's (with respectable

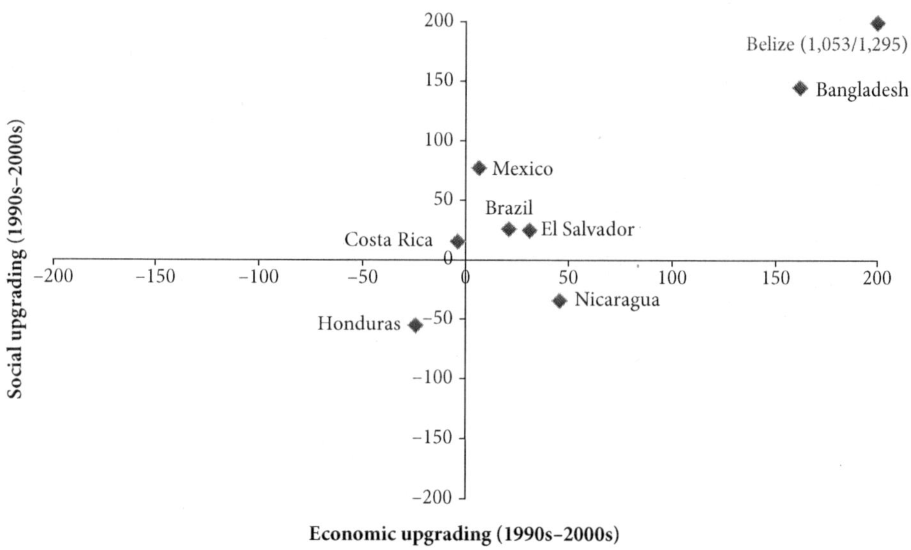

FIGURE 20.4 Economic and social upgrading and downgrading in horticulture, 1990s to 2000s.

Note: The measure for social upgrading includes only changes in real wages.

Source: Authors' own illustration based on data from UNIDO's INDSTAT4 (2010), ILO's LABORSTA and KILM, and the IMF's IFS databases.

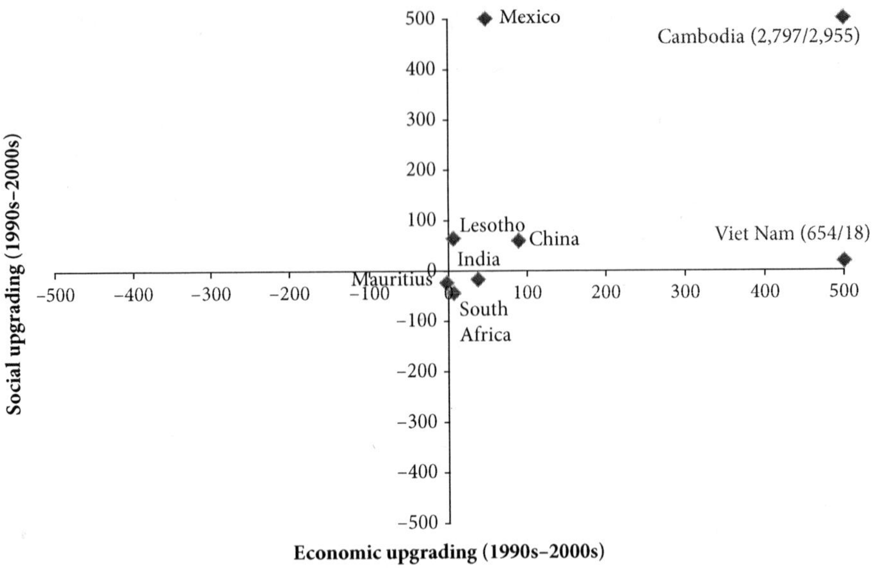

FIGURE 20.5 Economic and social upgrading and downgrading in apparel, 1990s to 2000s.

Source: Authors' own illustration based on data from UNIDO's INDSTAT4 (2010) and the IMF's IFS databases.

upgrading on both fronts, actually). Lesotho, in turn, has performed quite well in social terms but has not been able to match this with equal progress in economic terms. There is just a single case of full-fledged overall downgrading in the apparel sector, namely Mauritius. The remaining two countries in our sample, India and South Africa, are categorized as intermediate cases. Both have experienced upgrading in the economic sphere but downgrading in the social sphere. Overall, when judged by Figure 20.5, there seems to have been a positive relationship between economic upgrading and social upgrading in the apparel sector.

In the **mobile telecom** sector there has been ubiquitous economic upgrading but very little social upgrading. As can be seen in Figure 20.6, all of the countries in our sample are located to the right of the vertical axis, implying that there has not been a single case of economic downgrading. The best overall performer has clearly been Mexico with spectacular upgrading on both the economic and the social fronts. Mexico's social performance is particularly noteworthy, especially when compared to the sluggish or, even more often, entirely absent social progress in the other countries. In fact, the two Asian giants, China and India, are the only other countries that qualify as overall upgraders in the mobile telecom sector. Both have combined an excellent economic performance with weak social upgrading. All the remaining countries in our sample (i.e., almost 70 percent) are classified as intermediate cases—invariably because of a lack of social upgrading. These include some very strong economic performers, however, most notably the Philippines, Viet Nam, and Brazil. In fact, Viet Nam's—as well as Thailand's—social performance indicator falls only narrowly in the negative range, so that these two Southeast Asian countries have actually come very close to be overall upgraders. The

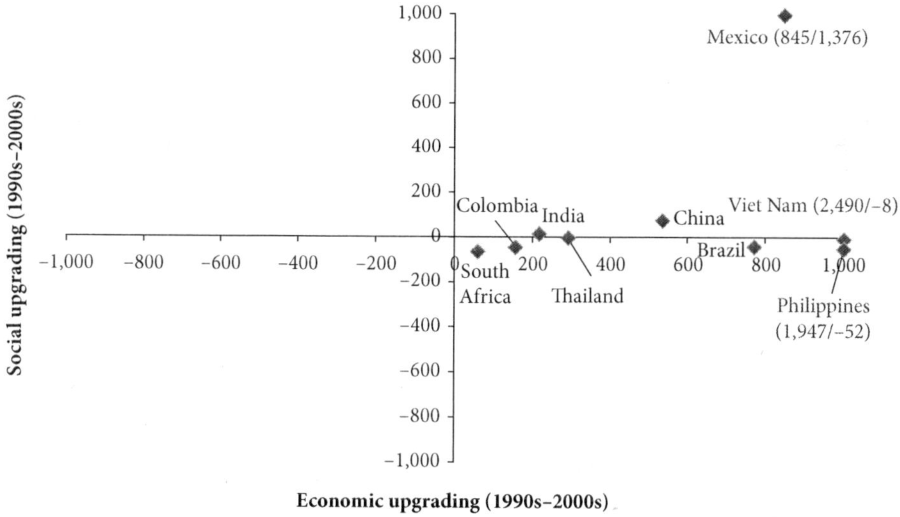

FIGURE 20.6 Economic and social upgrading and downgrading in mobile telecom, 1990s to 2000s.

Source: Authors' own illustration based on data from UNIDO's INDSTAT4 (2010) and the IMF's IFS databases.

two South American countries in our sample, Brazil and Colombia, in turn, have experienced quite decent total economic upgrading but also quite pronounced total social downgrading. By far the worst performer has been the only African country in our sample, South Africa. Recording the smallest improvements in economic terms and the largest deteriorations in social terms, South Africa actually performed worst on *both* fronts.

In the **tourism** sector, developments have been the inverse to those seen in the mobile telecom sector: While there has been widespread social upgrading (experienced by *all* of the countries in our sample for which data were available), there has been somewhat less economic upgrading. In Figure 20.7, all the countries are situated above the horizontal axis, signaling that they have registered social upgrading. Among them, three (China, Costa Rica, and India) have also experienced economic upgrading so that we observe three instances of overall upgrading in the tourism sector. China has been the premier performer with remarkable economic upgrading but even more impressive social upgrading. In Costa Rica, the pattern (economic upgrading combined with even more social upgrading) has been the same, albeit at a smaller scale. In fact, this pattern—with the social performance trumping the economic performance—can also be observed for the two intermediate cases, Brazil and Jordan. These two countries have recorded social upgrading but economic downgrading. The only exception to the pattern described above is India, the third overall upgrader, which is the only country in our sample whose economic performance in tourism has been better than its social performance. There is thus no plain overall downgrader in the tourism sector, as indicated by the empty southwestern quadrant in Figure 20.7.

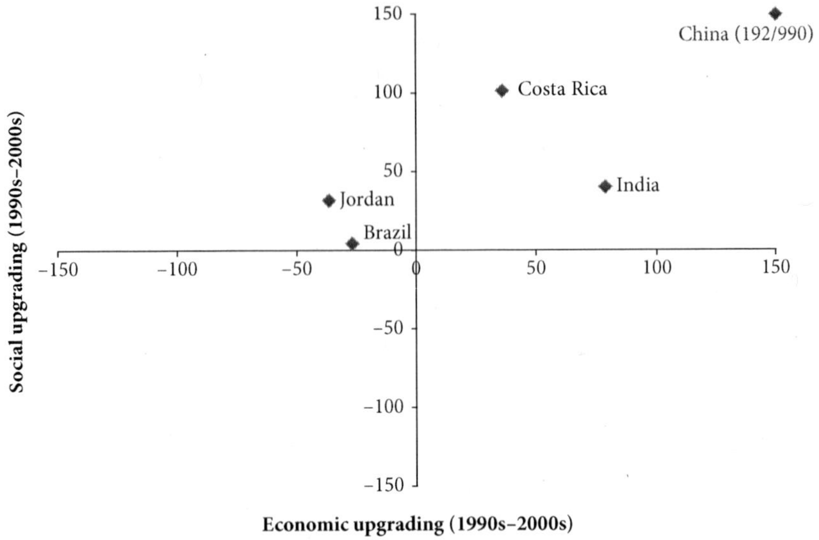

FIGURE 20.7 Economic and social upgrading and downgrading in tourism, 1990s to 2000s.

Source: Authors' own illustration based on data from UNCTAD's *Handbook of Statistics* 2009, as well as WTTC, ILO's LABORSTA and KILM, and the IMF's IFS databases.

5.2 Robustness tests

One problem with our method of calculating economic or social upgrading is that outcomes have a lower bound of –100 percent but an upper bound of infinity. To be sure, none of the indicators can fall below zero—which would correspond to a decrease of –100 percent from the initial level. On the other hand, countries can—and did, as we saw in the last two sections—register increases on any of the indicators that go far beyond +100 percent, especially with very low initial values. This introduces a certain pro-upgrading bias in our method. To assess the robustness of the findings based on this method, we introduce two alternative algorithms for determining upgrading/downgrading. Here we summarize the three measures (beginning with method 1 adopted above), and then discuss how the findings change when the other methods are used.

Method 1: Symmetric composite index

In the first method (used in the previous section) all four underlying indicators enter symmetrically, that is they are given equal weight. This method gives unambiguous results in those cases where both underlying indicators within one sphere (i.e., economic or social) have the same sign: If both indicators are positive, or if both are negative, so will be the composite index, respectively. For ambiguous cases, the sign of the "composite index" depends on the absolute values of the two underlying indicators. If the absolute value in the increase of one indicator is higher than the absolute value in the decrease of the other indicator, the composite index will have a positive sign. It can be argued that this is a reasonable result as it makes sense to characterize a country's sector as having experienced economic or social upgrading as long as the positive development in one indicator *outweighs* the negative development in the other indicator.

Method 2: Asymmetric composite index

The second metric addresses the problem of the existence of a lower bound (-100 percent) in the absence of an upper bound. The underlying formulas for method 2 are:

Economic Upgrading = [(1 + change in market share) × (1 + change in unit value)] − 1

Social Upgrading = [(1 + change in employment) × (1 + change in real wage)] − 1

As with method 1, this second metric also delivers unequivocal results in those cases where both underlying indicators within one area (i.e., economic or social) have the same sign. For the intermediate cases, in turn, it is important to note that the bias towards upgrading does not vanish altogether (because there is still a lower bound for each of the four underlying indicators while there is still no upper bound). Yet, this second metric "penalizes" a decrease in one of the two indicators (within one sphere) in the following sense: the more one of the indicators declines, the more the other indicator has to increase to yield upgrading as a result. In other words, pronounced decreases on one front have to be "compensated" by an even higher increase on the other front for total upgrading to be the result. On the other hand, this method "rewards" countries that perform well on both fronts. For example, if a country has experienced high increases on both of the two indicators for upgrading within one sphere (economic or social), this metric will—because of its multiplicative form—yield a value of total upgrading that is higher than the symmetric "composite index" of method 1.

Method 3: Narrow definition

The second method is stricter than the first in the sense that it will categorize fewer countries as upgraders. This is so because, as we have seen, a country sector that experiences a decline in one of the two indicators in either the economic or the social sphere has to record a bigger increase in the other indicator to still give a result of economic or social upgrading. Yet it is still possible with the second metric (as it is with the first metric) for a country to qualify as economic or social upgrader even if one of the indicators has a negative sign. This might be disputed on the basis of a very narrow interpretation of our definitions of economic and social upgrading presented in section 2 above. A very strict reading of these definitions would imply that a country can be said to have experienced economic or social upgrading in a sector *if and only if both* indicators have positive signs. This is the method adopted by Kaplinsky and Readman (2005). Using this method there are no intermediate cases. Any country that experiences a decline in any of the indicators automatically disqualifies as an upgrader and is instead rated as a downgrader. In other words, method 3 only ranks those countries as *overall* upgraders where *all* four indicators have a nonnegative sign.

We turn now to a brief analysis of the robustness of the results presented in the previous section in light of the two other calculation methods proposed. In the horticulture sector, overall upgrading was found to be widespread with method 1 and this finding is robust to the other two methods.[22] In fact, the only difference between methods 1 and 2 is that the latter classifies Mexico as intermediate case (and not an overall upgrader). The reason for this is that Mexico's gains in export market share (+43 percent) have not been sufficient to outweigh its decrease in export unit values (−31 percent) when using the second metric to calculate economic upgrading. By contrast, application of method 3 yields dramatically different outcomes. According to this approach, only Bangladesh qualifies as real overall upgrader in the horticulture sector while all the other countries have to be called downgraders (see Table 20.9). Belize's outstanding performance in this sector is also confirmed if we use method 2, but Belize does not qualify as overall upgrader if we apply method 3 because of a decline in its export unit values. This was swamped by a much higher increase (in absolute terms) in its export market share which allowed it to qualify as upgrader according to both methods 1 and 2. This reveals that all of the countries in our sample, with the exception of Bangladesh, have registered a decrease in at least one of their indicators.

Meanwhile, the apparel sector has also witnessed quite a lot of overall upgrading as judged according to method 1, and this finding is again supported with method 2. The number of overall upgraders is the same in both cases. However, the number of overall downgraders increases by one as South Africa is a plain downgrader according to method 2, not an intermediate case as under method 1. This difference in the assessment of South Africa's performance is rooted in the fact that the growth of its export unit values (+83 percent) has not been enough to outweigh its loss of export market share (−67 percent), making South Africa an economic downgrader according to the arithmetic of method 2. Given that South Africa has also experienced total social downgrading, classifying it as economic downgrader reinforces the overall impression of a positive correlation between economic upgrading and social upgrading in the apparel sector.

While methods 1 and 2 yield exactly the same categorization of countries (except, as noted, for South Africa), method 3 leads to a significantly different diagnosis. In fact, according to method 3, only Cambodia and China qualify as full-fledged overall upgraders in the apparel sector. By contrast, the remaining six countries in our sample are classified as overall downgraders, disclosing that they have not managed to progress on *all four* indicators (see Table 20.9).

The mobile telecom sector has experienced widespread economic upgrading but very little social upgrading. This is corroborated by applying method 2. Actually, methods 1 and 2 lead to exactly the same classification of countries with only minor differences in the numerical values of the composite economic and social indicators but no differences in their signs. By contrast, method 3 yields a distinct assessment and identifies only China as a full-fledged overall upgrader in the mobile telecom sector. The remaining eight countries in our sample, in turn, are all classified as overall downgraders. Even Mexico, the outstanding performer according to methods 1 and 2, does not qualify as overall upgrader when evaluated through the strict lenses of method 3. The reason is

Table 20.9 Upgraders and Downgraders according to the different approaches (1990s–2000s)

	HORTICULTURE							APPAREL					
	Method 1		Method 2		Method 3			Method 1		Method 2		Method 3	
Countries	EU	SU	EU	SU	EU	SU	Countries	EU	SU	EU	SU	EU	SU
Bangladesh	+	+	+	+	+	+	Cambodia	+	+	+	+	+	+
Belize	+	+	+	+	–	+	China	+	+	+	+	+	+
Brazil	+	+	+	+	–	+	India	+	–	+	–	+	–
Costa Rica	–	+	–	+	–	+	Lesotho	+	+	+	+	–	–
El Salvador	+	+	+	+	–	+	Mauritius	+	–	–	–	–	–
Honduras	–	–	–	–	–	–	Mexico	+	+	+	+	+	–
Mexico	+	+	–	+	–	+	South Africa	+	–	–	–	–	–
Nicaragua	+	–	+	–	–	–	Viet Nam	+	+	+	+	+	–

	MOBILE TELECOM							TOURISM					
	Method 1		Method 2		Method 3			Method 1		Method 2		Method 3	
Countries	EU	SU	EU	SU	EU	SU	Countries	EU	SU	EU	SU	EU	SU
Brazil	+	–	+	–	+	–	Brazil	–	+	–	+	–	–
China	+	+	+	+	+	+	China	+	+	+	+	+	+
Colombia	+	–	+	–	+	–	Costa Rica	+	+	+	+	+	+
India	+	+	+	+	+	–	India	+	–	+	–	+	–
Mexico	+	+	+	+	+	–	Jordan	–	+	–	+	–	–
Philippines	+	–	+	–	+	–							
South Africa	+	–	+	–	–	–							
Thailand	+	–	+	–	–	–							
Viet Nam	+	–	+	–	+	–							

Note: EU denotes Economic Up-/Downgrading and SU denotes Social Up-/Downgrading. A "+" indicates (economic or social) upgrading according to the respective method while a "–" indicates downgrading.

that one of its social performance indicators (namely the change in real wages) has a negative sign—a feature that it shares with all the other countries in our sample (with the exception of China, as noted). As a result, overall upgrading has been very scarce when judged by method 3, with China—the only country that has succeeded in registering improvements on *all four* indicators—as solitary upgrader (see Table 20.9).

In the tourism sector, developments were broadly the opposite of those in the mobile telecom sector with widespread social upgrading and less economic upgrading. This is also true for method 2 which, by the way, leads to an identical categorization of countries in terms of their overall up- and downgrading performance. Again, differences between the results of methods 1 and 2 are minor and pertain only to the numerical values of the composite indexes. In terms of the larger picture, however, both methods lead to the same conclusion, namely that the tourism sector has experienced quite some social upgrading with less economic upgrading. As with the other sectors, application of method 3 yields a somewhat different result. Of course, all the intermediate cases of methods 1 and 2 are classified as plain downgraders by method 3. China, Costa Rica, and India, however, are recognized as full-fledged overall upgraders also by method 3. This means that, with a share of overall upgraders in the entire sample of 60 percent, the tourism sector has been the sector with the highest number of overall success stories when judged according to method 3 (see Table 20.9).

Visual inspection of the scatter plots for the four sectors (which were based on calculations using method 1) revealed a variety of patterns across sectors in the relation between economic and social upgrading. In the apparel and horticulture sectors, there seems to have been a positive correlation between economic upgrading and social upgrading. The mobile telecom sector, in turn, seems to have experienced economic upgrading without much social upgrading. Finally, the tourism sector seems to have seen quite some social upgrading with less economic upgrading. These findings were confirmed by using method 2 which led to almost identical outcomes as method 1.[23] Application of method 3, on the other hand, yields outcomes in terms of classification that are substantially different from those of methods 1 and 2. Table 20.9 gives an overview of how the different countries in our sample fared in the four sectors in terms of both economic and social up- and downgrading according to the three methods of assessment. This helps us in our attempt to draw conclusions about a possible relationship (or lack thereof) between a sector's economic performance and its social performance.

5.3 Connecting economic and social upgrading

While we have framed our analysis in terms of upgrading in global value chains, our analysis has implications also for economic theory relating productivity growth (economic upgrading) and wages (social upgrading). Referring to the marginal productivity theory of wages (or returns to factors of production more generally), economists often claim that higher productivity also leads to higher compensation or remuneration.[24] In the context of our analysis, this view would translate into saying that economic upgrading should lead to social upgrading.

Our framework does not allow for a direct test of this relation; however, the results cast doubt on the theory. A first indication of this discordance is provided by the scatter plots presented above, most notably by Figures 20.6 and 20.7 for the mobile telecom and tourism sectors, where no clear pattern emerges. A second piece of evidence can be drawn from Table 20.9. If the claim that economic upgrading is accompanied by social upgrading were true, then the signs that enter the economic up-/downgrading (EU) and social up-/downgrading (SU) columns for a given country and a given sector should be identical. However, the number of countries for which the signs for EU and SU are the same is rather low according to all three methods: Across countries and sectors, we have a total of 30 data points or data pairs for economic up/downgrading and social up/downgrading; according to method 1, only sixteen of these thirty data pairs have the same sign for economic up/downgrading and social up/downgrading while the sign of social up-/downgrading corresponds to the sign of economic up-/downgrading in just seventeen and fifteen out of thirty cases when we use methods 2 and 3 respectively.[25] Overall, this does not make a compelling case for the proposition that social upgrading goes hand in hand with economic upgrading.

We should emphasize that all that these exercises can at best indicate is a *correlation* between developments in the economic and social spheres. They tell us nothing about the *direction of causality* between the two. Causality may plausibly run in either direction, and there is empirical evidence on both sides. Flanagan (2005) presumes that the wage growth in the apparel sector in a large sample of developing countries over 1995–2000 is driven by productivity growth. On the other side, Robertson, Dehejia, and Brown (2011) find that Cambodian apparel firms that complied with labor standards under the ILO "Better Work" program also saw improved performance in terms of productivity and exports. Kucera and Sarna (2004) study inward FDI and find it unaffected by higher labor standards.

6 Conclusion

Our analysis of economic and social upgrading provided a parsimonious and operational definition of these terms and applied it to the analysis of horticulture, apparel, tourism, and mobile telecom in about twelve developing countries over the period 1990–2009. Our main findings can be summarized as follows.

Regarding economic upgrading, we find that in all sectors except for apparel, positive growth in world export market share is generally associated with economic upgrading. However, export market share growth was generally associated with less-than-proportional growth or even declines in export unit values. As for social upgrading, the general pattern was of employment growth and considerably less growth of real wages.

Contrary to the spirit of much case study literature on global value chains, our analysis using published data and an admittedly parsimonious definition of upgrading shows that economic downgrading and social downgrading are both fairly regular occurrences, with social downgrading more common, primarily due to stagnant real wages.

Standard economic theory predicts a direct connection between productivity growth and wage growth. In contrast, in our analysis, we find that there is a variety in the patterns observed across GVCs in the relation between economic and social upgrading: In apparel and horticulture we generally find a positive correlation between economic upgrading and social upgrading. In mobile telecom there is widespread economic upgrading without social upgrading. In tourism we found many cases of social upgrading with less economic upgrading. Overall, economic and social upgrading occurred together in fifteen to seventeen out of thirty cases, depending on the measurement technique adopted. These results were found to be generally robust across a few alternative techniques for measuring upgrading and downgrading. In sum, we can say that our evidence shows that economic upgrading does not automatically translate into social upgrading. Equally interesting, however, is that in all sectors except tourism (with the exception of Costa Rica in horticulture), there is no social upgrading without economic upgrading in our sample (see Table 20.9).

Throughout this chapter, we have tried to emphasize that our findings must be interpreted with caution, due to limitations of the published data. For one, our effort to give some precision to the measurement of economic and social upgrading suffered from considerable problems of data availability. Data gaps are particularly severe for social upgrading indicators as well as for export quantities (which are necessary for the calculation of export unit values). Comparability of data was hampered when different product categorization schemes were used in the different databases. This made it difficult to apply one single sector definition across all the indicators.[26] An implication of all these data shortcomings is that, given the new geography of trade characterized by the increasing international fragmentation of production and its organization in global production networks and value chains, we need to ask whether the current way of categorizing and collecting data is still appropriate. We support the ongoing discussions at the UN, WTO, OECD, and elsewhere that seek to rethink trade and related data collection and presentation.[27]

Future research on economic and social upgrading in global value chains will assess the robustness of the current findings by considering different weighting schemes for the different components of economic and social upgrading and also analyze different time periods (including subperiods of the time period studied here). More important will be to advance our understanding of the direction of causality between economic and social change.

It is important to stress that the present study must be taken only as part of a broader research effort that also involves considerable fieldwork in each of the four sectors. Our aim was to provide insights into the dynamics of global value chains, providing a broader context for case studies and fieldwork in the different sectors. This contextualization is crucial in grasping the strengths and limits of the work presented here in terms of contributing to the understanding of economic and social upgrading dynamics and their connection in global value chains.[28] The goal of such combined research is to answer the central research question of the "Capturing the Gains" project: what are the conditions under which economic and social upgrading are positively correlated?

Notes

1. PhD candidate and Professor of Economics at the Department of Economics of the New School for Social Research. This chapter draws on Bernhardt and Milberg (2011) and was done as part of a research program entitled "Capturing the Gains: Economic and Social Upgrading in Global Production Networks and Trade." We are grateful to Ashok Bardhan, Stephanie Barrientos, Barbara Evers, Gary Gereffi, Dwight Jaffee, Cynthia Kroll, Malte

Luebker, John Pickles, and Cornelia Staritz for valuable comments on a previous draft, and to the UK Department for International Development for financial support of this research.
2. For a review, see Milberg and Winkler (2011).
3. See Pickles et al. (2006) on the apparel sector in Central and Eastern Europe, for example.
4. For a discussion of the dynamics and the changing nature of the international division of labor, see Feenstra (1998), Hummels, Rapoport, and Yi (1998, 2001), Yeats (1998), and Yi (2003), for example.
5. For an overview of the project, see Barrientos, Gereffi, and Rossi (2011) and the project website at www.capturingthegains.org.
6. See Kaplinsky and Readman (2005) and Amighini (2006) for similar approaches.
7. Evgeniev and Gereffi (2008: 23).
8. Li and Song (2011: 77).
9. Our definition of social upgrading borrows to some extent from the International Labor Organization's "decent work" framework which emphasizes not only the protection of rights at work, the promotion of social dialogue and the extension of social coverage but also the generation of employment and the provision of adequate remuneration (see, for example, ILO 1999).
10. For recent studies of the global apparel value chain, see Morris and Barnes (2009), Frederick and Gereffi (2011), or Staritz (2011), for example.
11. For analyses of the mobile phone supply chain, see works by Dedrick, Kraemer, and Linden (2010), Xing and Detert (2010), Ali-Yrkkö (2010), Ali-Yrkkö, Rouvinen, Seppälä and Ylä-Anttila (2011) or Kraemer, Linden, and Dedrick (2011).
12. See Lessmeister (2009) or Christian (2011), for example.
13. China is not in the sample because of a lack of wage data, but on economic upgrading experienced a rise in world export market share of 57 percent and a decline in export unit value of 30 percent over the 1990–2009 period.
14. For details on the exact figures for all countries for 2000–2009, see Bernhardt and Milberg (2011: Appendix Table A.3.4).
15. On "conflict coltan" and the mobile phone supply chain, see Nathan and Sarkar (2011).
16. Due to data limitations, unit values of exports of HS code 8523 ("Discs, tapes, solid-state non-volatile storage devices, 'smart cards' and other media for the recording of sound or of other phenomena") were taken as a proxy for sector-wide developments.
17. The years in parentheses also indicate the latest years for which data are available.
18. Dussel Peters (2008: 18) confirms this pattern of Mexico's social upgrading performance in the yarn-textile-garment sector. Interestingly, this pattern also resembles the experience of the Mexican mobile telecom sector, as discussed below.
19. All wages reported here are nominal; they were taken from the ILO KILM and LABORSTA databases and converted into US$ using annual average exchange rates as reported in the IMF's International Financial Statistics (IFS) database.
20. The wage data in this section are drawn from the ILO KILM and LABORSTA databases and converted into US$ using exchange rates as reported in the IMF's IFS database. All wages reported here are nominal.
21. Below we present three methods for measuring upgrading and downgrading, one of which does not allow for "intermediate cases" but instead categorizes every country as upgrader or downgrader in any given sector.
22. Note that as we do not have employment data for the horticulture sector, we simply use wage data (i.e., the percentage change in real wages) as proxy for social upgrading.

23. For details, see Bernhardt and Milberg (2011), appendix tables and figures.
24. For a textbook presentation of this idea, see Mas-Colell, Whinston, and Green (1995) or Varian (1992). For recent empirical tests for developing countries, see Flanagan (2005) and Van Biesebrock (2011).
25. Among the sixteen cases where the signs of total economic up-/downgrading and social up-/downgrading correspond according to method 1, fifteen are overall upgraders while we have only one case of overall downgrading. Among the seventeen cases with consonant signs according to method 2, in turn, fourteen are overall upgraders and three are overall downgraders. Finally, among the fifteen cases where the signs of total economic up/downgrading and social up-/downgrading coincide according to method 3, only six are overall upgraders while nine are overall downgraders. These figures highlight a fact already emphasized above, namely that method 1 is indeed the least rigorous in terms of classifying countries as overall upgraders while method 3 is the strictest.
26. For an overview of sector definitions, see Appendix 2.
27. See, for example, the "Made in the World" initiative at the WTO or the "Global Forum on Trade Statistics" organized jointly by the United Nations Statistics Division (UNSD), the Statistical Office of the European Communities (Eurostat), the WTO, and UNCTAD.
28. While the fieldwork studies corresponding to our analysis have not yet been completed, it is a clear objective of the Capturing the Gains project to carefully link this analysis to the fieldwork in a series of papers and books that will be completed by the end of 2012. See www.capturingthegains.org for updates.

References

Aiginger, K. 1997. "The Use of Unit Values to Discriminate between Price and Quality Competition" *Cambridge Journal of Economics* 21 (5): 571–592.

Ali-Yrkkö, J. 2010. "The Value Creation of Mobile Phones: The Case of Nokia N95." In *Nokia and Finland in a Sea of Change*, edited by J. Ali-Yrkkö, 91–106. Helsinki: ETLA, Research Institute of the Finnish Economy.

Ali-Yrkkö, J., P. Rouvinen, T. Seppälä , and P. Ylä-Anttila 2011. "Who Captures Value in Global Supply Chains? Case Nokia N95 Smartphone." *Journal of Industry, Competition and Trade* 11 (3): 263–278.

Amighini, A. 2006. "Upgrading in International Trade: Methods and Evidence from Selected Sectors." In *Upgrading to Compete: Global Value Chains, Clusters, and SMEs in Latin America*, edited by C. Pietrobelli and R. Rabelloti, 221–250. Washington, DC: Inter-American Development Bank.

Barrientos, S., G. Gereffi, and A. Rossi. 2011. "Economic and Social Upgrading in Global Production Networks: A New Paradigm for a Changing World." *International Labor Review* 150 (3–4): 319–340.

Bernhardt, T., and W. Milberg. 2011. "Economic and Social Upgrading in Global Value Chains: Analysis of Horticulture, Apparel, Tourism and Mobile Telephones," Capturing the Gains Working Paper 2011/06, Brooks World Poverty Institute, University of Manchester.

Christian, M. 2011. "A Gendered Tourism Global Value Chain: Economic Upgrading Lessons from Kenya," Paper presented at the Better Work Conference, October 27, 2011, Washington, DC.

Dedrick, J., K. L. Kraemer, and G. Linden. 2011. "The Distribution of Value in the Mobile Phone Supply Chain." *Telecommunications Policy* 35 (6): 505–521.

Dolan, C., and J. Humphrey. 2004. "Changing Governance Patterns in the Trade in Fresh Vegetables between Africa and the United Kingdom." *Environment and Planning A* 36 (3): 491–509.

Dussel Peters, E. 2008. "GCCs and Development: A Conceptual and Empirical Review." *Competition & Change* 12 (1): 11–27.

Evgeniev, E., and G. Gereffi. 2008. "Textile and Apparel Firms in Turkey and Bulgaria: Exports, Local Upgrading and Dependency," *Economic Studies* 17 (3): 148–179.

Feenstra, R. 1998. "Integration of Trade and Disintegration of Production in the Global Economy." *Journal of Economic Perspectives* 12 (4): 31–50.

Flanagan, R. J. 2005. *Globalization and Labor Conditions: Working Conditions and Worker Rights in a Global Economy*. New York: Oxford University Press.

Frederick, S. and G. Gereffi 2011. "Upgrading and Restructuring in the Global Apparel Value Chain: why China and Asia are outperforming Mexico and Central America." *International Journal of Technological Learning, Innovation and Development* 4 (1/2/3): 67–95.

Gereffi, G. 1994. "The Organization of Buyer-Driven Global Commodity Chains: How US Retailers Shape Overseas Production Networks." In *Commodity Chains and Global Capitalism*, edited by G. Gereffi and M. Korzeniewicz, 95–122. Westport, CT: Greenwood.

———. 2005. "The Global Economy: Organization, Governance and Development." In *Handbook of Economic Sociology*, edited by N. J. Smelser and R. Swedberg, 160–182. Princeton: Princeton University Press and Russell Sage Foundation.

Gereffi, G., J. Humphrey, and T. Sturgeon. 2005. "The Governance of Global Value Chains." *Review of International Political Economy* 12 (1): 78–104.

Hummels, D., D. Rapoport, and K.-M. Yi. 1998. "Vertical Specialization and the Changing Nature of World Trade." *FRBNY Economic Policy Review* 4 (2): 79–99.

———. 2001. "The Nature and Growth of Vertical Specialization in World Trade." *Journal of International Economics* 54 (1): 75–96.

Humphrey, J. 2004. "Upgrading in Global Value Chains." ILO Working Paper, no. 28.

Humphrey, J., and H. Schmitz. 2002. "How Does Insertion in Global Value Chains Affect Upgrading in Industrial Clusters?" *Regional Studies* 36 (9): 1017–1027.

ILO (International Labour Organization). 1999. "Decent Work." Geneva: Report of the Director-General to the 89th Session of the International Labour Conference.

IMF (International Monetary Fund), ILO (International Labour Organization), OECD (Organisation for Economic Co-operation and Development), Eurostat (Statistical Office of the European Communities), United Nations Economic Commission for Europe, and World Bank. 2009. *Export and Import Price Index Manual: Theory and Practice*. Washington, DC: IMF.

Kaplinsky, R., and J. Readman. 2005. "Globalization and Upgrading: wHat Can (and Cannot) Be Learnt from International Trade Statistics in the Wood Furniture Sector?" *Industrial and Corporate Change* 14 (4): 679–703.

Kraemer, K. L., G. Linden, and J. Dedrick. 2011. "Capturing Value in Global Networks: Apple's iPod and iPhone." University of California, Irvine: UC Irvine Personal Computing Industry Center.

Kucera, D., and R. Sarna. 2006. "Trade Union Rights, Democracy and Exports: A Gravity Model Approach." *Review of International Economics* 14 (5): 859–882.

Lessmeister, R. 2009. "Why Selling Dreams Brings Power, but Making Dreams Come True Does Not: Governance, Power and Coordination in Special Tourism Value Chains." *Journal für Entwicklungspolitik* [Austrian Journal of Development Studies] 25 (2): 129–149.

Li, K., and L. Song. 2011. "The Technological Content of Chinese Exports and the Need for Upgrading." In *Rising China: Global Challenges and Opportunities*, edited by J. Golley and L. Song, 69–83. Canberra: Australian National University E Press.

Mas-Colell, A., M. Whinston, and J. Green. 1995. *Microeconomic Theory*. New York: Oxford University Press.

Milberg, W., and D. Winkler. 2011. "Economic and Social Upgrading in Global Production Networks: Problems of Theory and Measurement." *International Labor Review* 150 (3–4): 341–365.

Morris, M., and J. Barnes. 2009. "Globalization, the Changed Global Dynamics of the Clothing and Textile Value Chains and the Impact on Sub-Saharan Africa." UNIDO Research and Statistics Branch Working Paper 10/2008. Vienna: United Nations Industrial Development Organization.

Nathan, D., and A. Sarkar. 2011. "Blood on Your Mobile Phones? Capturing the Gains for Artisanal Miners, Poor Workers and Women." Capturing the Gains Briefing Note No. 2, February.

Pickles, J., et al. 2006. "Upgrading, Changing Competitive Pressure and Diverse Practices in the East and Central European Apparel Industry." *Environment and Planning A* 38 (12): 2305–2324.

Robertson, R., R. Dehejia, and D. Brown. 2011. "Working Conditions and Factory Survival: Evidence from Better Factories Cambodia." Mimeograph, Macalester College, October 20.

Sen, A. 1999. *Development as Freedom*, Oxford: Oxford University Press.

———. 2000. "Work and Rights." *International Labour Review* 139 (2): 119–128.

Staritz, C. 2011. *Making the Cut? Low-income Countries and the Global Clothing Value Chain in a Post-quota and Post-crisis World*. Washington, DC: World Bank.

Sturgeon, T. J., and G. Gereffi. 2009. "Measuring Success in the Global Economy: International Trade, Industrial Upgrading, and Business Function Outsourcing in Global Value Chains." *Transnational Corporations* 18 (2): 1–35.

UNIDO (United Nations Industrial Development Organization). 2011. *Industrial Value Chain Diagnostics: An Integrated Tool*. Vienna: UNIDO.

Van Biesebrock, J. 2011. "Wages Equal Productivity. Fact or Fiction? Evidence from Sub-Saharan Africa." *World Development* 39 (8): 1333–1346.

Varian, H. 1992. *Microeconomic Analysis*. New York: Norton.

Xing, Y., and N. Detert. 2010. "How iPhone Widens the US Trade Deficits with PRC." National Graduate Institute for Policy Studies, Discussion Paper, no. 10-21, Tokyo.

Yeats, A. J. 1998. "Just How Big Is Global Production Sharing?" Policy Research Working Paper, no. 1871. Washington, DC: World Bank.

Yi, K.-M. 2003. "Can Vertical Specialization Explain the Growth of World Trade?" *Journal of Political Economy* 111 (1): 52–102.

Appendix Table 20.A1 Country samples for the four sectors.

Horticulture	Apparel	Telecom	Tourism
Africa: Ethiopia, Kenya, Tanzania, Uganda **Asia**: Bangladesh, Thailand, Viet Nam **Latin America & the Caribbean**: Brazil, Chile, Colombia, Ecuador, all Central America	**Africa**: Kenya, Lesotho, Mauritius, South Africa **Asia**: Bangladesh, Cambodia, China, India, Sri Lanka, Viet Nam **Latin America & the Caribbean**: Dominican Rep., El Salvador, Guatemala, Haiti, Mexico, Nicaragua	**Africa**: Congo (Dem. Rep.), Ethiopia, Ghana, Kenya, Mozambique, Nigeria, Rwanda, South Africa, Tanzania, Uganda **Asia**: Bangladesh, China, India, Pakistan, Philippines, Sri Lanka, Thailand, Viet Nam **Latin America & the Caribbean**: Brazil, Colombia, Costa Rica, El Salvador, Guatemala, Haiti, Honduras, Mexico, Nicaragua, Paraguay, Peru	**Africa**: Kenya, South Africa, Uganda **Asia**: China, India, Indonesia, Jordan, Nepal, Viet Nam **Latin America & the Caribbean**: Brazil, Costa Rica, Jamaica

Appendix Table 20.A2 Sector and product definitions

Indicator	Horticulture	Apparel	Mobile telecom	Tourism
Export value & market share	**Sum of HS 06 + HS 07 + HS 08** (HS 06: "Live trees and other plants; bulbs, roots and the like; cut flowers and ornamental foliage"; HS 07: "Edible vegetables and certain roots and tubers"; HS 08: "Edible fruit and nuts; peel of citrus fruit or melons")	**Sum of HS 61 + HS 62** (HS 61: "Articles of apparel and clothing accessories, knitted or crocheted," HS 62: "Articles of apparel and clothing accessories, not knitted or crocheted")	**Sum of HS 851712 + HS 851761 + HS 851770 + HS 8523** (HS 851712: "Telephones for cellular networks or for other wireless networks"; HS 851761: "Base stations"; HS 851770: "Parts"; HS 8523: "Discs, tapes, solid-state non-volatile storage devices, "smart cards" and other media for the recording of sound or of other phenomena")	"Travel expenditures excluding transport": (from the Balance of Payments, as reported by UNCTAD)
Export unit value	**Weighted average of unit values of HS 0603 + 0709 + 0710 + 0803 + 0805 + 0806 + 0807 + 0808 + 0809 + 0810** (HS 0603: Cut flowers, dried flowers for bouquets, etc.; 0709: Vegetables nes, fresh or chilled; 0710: Vegetables (uncooked, steamed, boiled) frozen; 0803: Bananas, including plantains, fresh or dried; 0805: Citrus fruit, fresh or dried; 0806: Grapes, fresh/dried; 0807: Melons, watermelons and papaws/papayas, fresh; 0808: Apples, pears and quinces, fresh; 0809: Stone fruit, fresh (apricot, cherry, plum, peach, etc.); 0810: Fruits nes, fresh)	**Weighted average of each country's top-10 export products at the 4-digit level**	**Due to data limitations: Unit value of HS 8523 exports as proxy**	"Travel expenditures excluding transport" divided by "Number of visitors" (Leading to unit value indicator: Travel expenditures per visitor)

Employment	-	**ISIC code 1810:** "Manufacture of wearing apparel, except fur apparel"	**Sum of ISIC codes 3220 + 3230** (ISIC 3220: "TV/radio transmitters; line comm. apparatus"; ISIC 3230: "TV and radio receivers and associated goods")	"Travel & Tourism Direct Industry Employment" (as reported by WTTC)
Remuneration/ Wages	**Occupational groups as proxies:** Farm supervisor Field crop farm worker Plantation supervisor Plantation worker	**ISIC code 1810:** "Manufacture of wearing apparel, except fur apparel"	**Sum of ISIC codes 3220 + 3230** (ISIC 3220: "TV/radio transmitters; line comm. apparatus"; ISIC 3230: "TV and radio receivers and associated goods")	**Occupational groups as proxies:** Hotel receptionist Room attendant or chambermaid Cook Waiter

21

Regional Competitiveness in the Latin America Offshore Services Value Chain

KARINA FERNANDEZ-STARK,[A] PENNY BAMBER,[B] AND GARY GEREFFI[C]

1 Introduction

Historically, services were considered nontradable and offshoring was confined to the manufacturing sector. However, the evolution and diffusion of information and communications technologies (ICT) at the turn of the twenty-first century increased the potential for sourcing services globally, thereby creating an offshore services industry (Gereffi and Fernandez-Stark 2010b: 1).[1] Face-to-face contact between the client and the provider in traditional service trade began to be replaced by remote centers in the new knowledge era. To provide these services, firms began to search for new locations in the developing world, where talent was relatively cheaper and more abundant than in developed countries. This provided an important opportunity for emerging nations across the globe to enter the services industry, previously the exclusive domain of industrialized countries.

While a relative latecomer to the industry, Latin America emerged as a key region in the provision of offshore services in the early 2000s, due to its global geographic location and cheap labor costs. The growth of the sector was further driven by the industrial policies of numerous countries in the region, extensive new telecommunications infrastructure, and the availability of educated human capital. By 2013, the region had become an important participant in the offshore services trade, exporting services to countries all around the globe.

This chapter analyzes the region's participation in the industry and its contribution to global service trade by using the global value chain (GVC) framework, examining the structure of the industry, the business models driving the lead firms in the sector, and the favorable factors of its different countries. The GVC framework allows one to understand how this global industry is organized by examining the structure and dynamics of different actors involved. This framework also is a useful tool to trace the shifting patterns of global demand and supply, to link geographically dispersed activities and actors, and to determine the roles they play in developed and developing countries alike. The GVC methodology focuses on the sequences of value-added within an industry, from conception to production and end use. It examines the job descriptions, technologies, standards, regulations, products, processes, and markets in specific industries and places, thus providing a holistic view of this global industry from both the top down and the bottom up and facilitating an understanding for firms and policy makers in developing countries to drive growth.

2 Offshore Services Evolution in the Global Context

"Offshore services" specifically referred to services conducted in one country and consumed in another, that is, service exports. Structural changes in the global economy precipitated by ICT revolution transformed the way companies do business by lowering transaction costs and by significantly reducing the cost and time required to generate, process, store and transmit information from remote locations (Lopez et al. 2008). This allowed for the separation of production and consumption of services (Sako 2005) and permitted emerging nations to contribute significantly to the world's services industry for the first time (Fernandez-Stark et al. 2011b).

Multinational corporations (MNC) began by offshoring basic service activities to India in the early 1990s, but by the 2010s, increasingly sophisticated services were being performed for these firms by operations centers in a growing number of developing countries. Offshore service functions expanded rapidly beyond those in information technology (IT), to include human resources, finance and accounting, and research and development (R&D), among others, that were previously considered core activities of the firm.

Businesses began procuring services abroad not only to improve their efficiency levels in the global economy, but also to enter new markets and gain access to "strategic assets" in other countries (Lopez et al. 2008). They were attracted to developing countries by competitive advantages, including low labor costs, technological skills, and language proficiency (A. T. Kearney 2007c), as well as by similar time zones and geographical and cultural proximity to major markets (ECLAC 2008b). In addition, as more sophisticated, knowledge-intensive activities began to be performed abroad, the supply of scientific, engineering, and analytical talent offered by developing countries became much more important (Duke Offshoring Research Network & Booz & Co. 2007).

The potential socioeconomic impact of the industry in developed as well as developing countries attracted the attention of both analysts and the media around the world (Aron and Singh 2005; Aspray 2010; Batt et al. 2009; Dossani and Kenney 2007; Fernandez-Stark et al. 2011b; Gereffi and Fernandez-Stark 2010b; Mankiw and Swagel 2006; Mullan et al. 2008a). In the new knowledge era, developing countries play a significant role in the international division of labor as they supply a cheaper yet talented and educated workforce to serve customers in developed countries. India and the Philippines, in particular, emerged as key service suppliers. By 2009, four of the world's twenty leading global service providers were the well-known Indian firms Genpact, Infosys, Tata Consultancy Services, and Wipro, while the Philippines had become the global headquarters for call centers (Gereffi and Fernandez-Stark 2010a).

Offshoring services allowed these countries to increase their employment in the better-paid service sector (ECLAC 2008a). By 2008, in India alone, the offshore services industry had created 2.2 million direct jobs (NASSCOM 2009), and employment reached 2.5 million in 2010 (NASSCOM 2011).[2] Yet, despite this growth, the vast majority of the industry's potential still remained largely untapped at the end of the decade. The McKinsey Global Institute labor supply report (2009) estimated that up to 161 million jobs could be performed remotely, stating that "any task that requires no physical or complex interaction between an employee and customers or colleagues, and requires little or no local knowledge, can be performed anywhere in the world by a suitable qualified person." That global employment in offshore services had reached only 4.1 million by 2008 suggested that the employment potential for developing countries around the world remained substantial.

This potential for employment had important implications for emerging countries seeking to become destinations in the industry, especially those with the adequate infrastructure and human capital. However, the characteristics of the industry and the rapid development of IT infrastructure systems around the world meant that countries faced global, rather than local or regional, competition. Country success in the industry began to be determined by two key factors: low cost and industry expertise. Successful countries either competed for low-cost services due to abundant labor with inferior wages or they focused on pursuing higher-value services in specific niche sectors based on expertise and innovation potential. India was one of the few countries that was able to compete on both bases (Fernandez-Stark et al. 2011b).

The evolution of the sector was characterized by a dynamism rarely seen in other economic activities. By 2006, estimates of compound annual growth rate (CAGR) for the years 2005–2010 were as high as 43.2 percent, while estimates of global revenues in the industry ranged from \$101 billion to \$157 billion in 2008 (NASSCOM 2009; OECD 2008; Boston Consulting Group 2007). A more recent industry estimate published at the International Offshoring Forum in Santiago, Chile, placed the size of the industry in

2010 at US$300 billion (InvestChile CORFO 2011b). The 2008–9 economic crisis demonstrated the resilience of the industry as demand for basic offshore services increased rather than subsided, buoyed by new requests from client firms looking to further reduce their costs in order to survive the global downturn (Gereffi and Fernandez-Stark 2010b).

2.1 The offshore services global value chain

As the industry evolved, an increasing number of services were incorporated into the value chain. However, the earliest services to be offshored in the industry were general business services that can be provided across all industries, such as payroll and finance and accounting support. As buyers gained confidence in the offshoring business model, an increasing number of industry-specific activities were also included. In general, low-value services were the first to be offshored, gradually followed by services of higher and higher value (Gereffi and Fernandez-Stark 2010a).

General business services support generic business functions and include three main segments:

- **Information technology outsourcing (ITO)** is the basic building block for the offshore services value chain and is centered on the production and use of software. It encompasses services such as network management, applications development, IT consulting, and software R&D. ITO services span the low-, middle-, and high-value segments of the chain;
- **Business process outsourcing (BPO)** is a highly diverse category that contains activities related to the management of enterprise resources (ERM), human resources (HRM), and customer relationships (CRM). Specific BPO services including call centers, payroll, finance and accounting, and human resources activities are present in the low- and middle-value segments;
- **Knowledge process outsourcing (KPO)** refers to specialized activities that often require professional licensing (such as in the legal and accounting fields). KPO services include market intelligence, business analytics, and legal services, which are the high value-added general segment of the chain.

Industry-specific offshoring services include activities that are not related to general business functions and that require specific industry knowledge. This might include pharmaceutical R&D, industrial engineering, telecommunications equipment testing, and medical transcription, among others. These services may have limited applicability in other industries (Gereffi and Fernandez-Stark 2010a).

Continuous evolution of the industry has made efforts at categorization challenging. Despite these complexities, a fairly comprehensive, yet flexible, classification of the industry has emerged that employs the GVC framework (Gereffi and Fernandez-Stark 2010a), using firm-level analysis to determine the different stages of production of a good or service and the value of each component (Gereffi and Kaplinsky 2001). For manufacturing and extractive industries based on goods, value-added is determined by the difference between the cost of the inputs and outputs at each stage of the chain. In the case of the offshore services industry, measuring value is complicated by the lack of reliable company-level data and trade statistics for services (Sturgeon and Gereffi 2009).

To partially address this problem, the value of different services in the offshore services value chain can be related to skill levels and work experience, that is to say, the human capital inputs of offshore services. Human capital accounts for approximately 70–80 percent of the total cost of the industry (Morris et al. 2009) and has been found to be a key determinant of value creation and success in service exports from developing countries (Nyahoho 2010; Saez and Grover Goswami 2010).[3] The visual representation of the offshore services value chain presented in Figure 21.1 is thus based on the available proxy for value-added in human capital: wages paid to employees for different activities within industry segments. These relative wages, in turn, reflect required employee education and experience levels (Gereffi and Fernandez-Stark 2010a) and provide the best indication of "low" and "high" value-added activities. As a result, low-wage activities, requiring less education and experience, appear lower on the value chain map, while

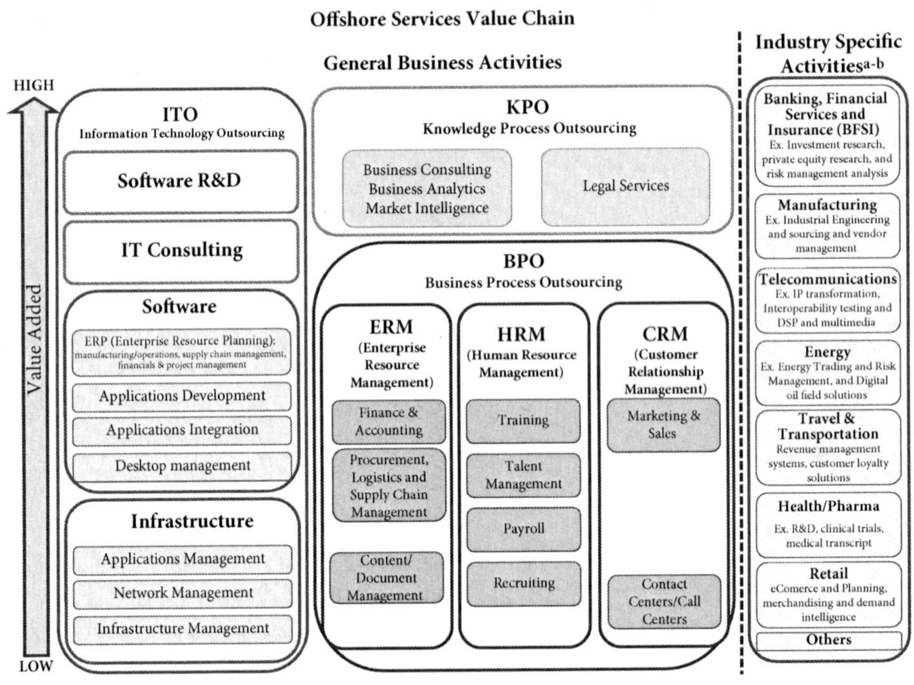

FIGURE 21.1 The offshore services industry global value chain.

Notes: [a] Industry specific: Each industry has its own value chain. Within each of these chains, there are associated services that can be offshored. This diagram captures the industries with the highest demand for offshore services.

[b] This graphical depiction of industry specific services does not imply value levels. Each industry may include ITO, BPO, and advanced activities.

Source: Gereffi and Fernandez-Stark 2010a.

Table 21.1 Employment, revenue and salary information, selected segments of the offshore services industry in a middle-income country, 2008

Segment	Activities	Most populous position within segment	Average education level for employees	Average revenue per employee[a] (US$)	Median salary per employee[a] (US$)
BPO	Call centers	Call center agents and technicians	High school/ bachelors degree	19,720	17,280
ITO	IT infrastructure	Computer technician	High school/technical institute	20,704	16,932
	Software development	Programmers	Bachelors/masters degree	36,788	28,065
	IT consulting	Systems analysts	Bachelors/masters Degree	55,956	45,455
KPO	Business and financial services	Financial analyst	Bachelors degree in business administration	127,081	47,150
Vertical activities	Engineering services	Engineer	Bachelors degree	103,844	53,514

Note: [a] This data is drawn from a confidential study published by Mercer 2008 for a specific country in Latin America. This information is for a middle-income country with a relatively small population. Due to a more limited labor supply, salaries are higher than in a low-income, populous country such as India or the Philippines.

Sources: Fernandez-Stark et al. (2011a); IDC Latin America (2009); Meller and Brunner (2009); Mercer (2008); Wadhwa et al. (2008).

higher-wage activities requiring employees with more formal education and experience appear in the upper section.[4]

Table 21.1 shows how both competitive salary and revenue data for different segments of the offshore services value chain in a middle-income country increase from segment to segment. As can be seen, employees in activities located in the lower part of the value chain have less preparation, particularly with respect to specialized skills, and earn lower wages, while the employees in the upper section of the value chain have more specialized skills and more years of experience and therefore command higher wages.

3 Participation of Latin America in the Industry

As the industry continued to expand, based on cheap yet educated labor forces around the world, there was great potential for Latin America to emerge as an important player.

This would allow countries in the region to leverage their growing workforce and would provide them with the opportunity to reduce their traditional dependence on natural resources and manufacturing-based economies and move into the knowledge economy.

During the first decade of the twenty-first century, Latin America's participation in the offshore services market increased substantially due to two key forces. First, there were a large number of global companies seeking to leverage the continent's various competitive advantages, particularly with respect to language skills and time zone positioning. Second, Latin American governments took on an active role in attracting offshore operations to use their countries as platforms to export services. (See section 5.1 for a discussion on these incentives.)

As a result of these combined forces, the industry grew exponentially in the region. In 2010, the size of the IT-BPO industry in Latin America had reached US$8 billion, compared to US$5 billion in Eastern Europe, despite its having entered the industry almost a decade later (Tucci 2011). This growth was driven to a large degree by foreign direct investment (FDI) projects established on the continent to serve mainly Spain and the Hispanic communities in the United States.[5]

The patterns of global industry development and the emerging role of Latin America thus were shaped by the business decisions of the leading global firms in the industry. Two key business approaches employed by these firms were particularly important in facilitating the region's entry into the industry: The emergence of the global delivery system (GDS) and the rise of nearshoring. The GDS consists of a global headquarters together with delivery centers in different regions around the world, located to allow the firm to provide twenty-four-hour service. These delivery centers served both global and regional clients and were supported by customer offices in the client countries (Gereffi and Fernandez-Stark 2010a). Nearshoring, on the other hand, leveraged geographic and cultural proximity, and delivery centers were located in the same time zone as the client (Abbot and Jones 2002; Carmel and Abbot 2007).

The emergence of the GDS is best explained by the emergence of the first generation of Indian entrepreneurs in the early 1990s. These firms were headquartered in India, and made the sector global by aggressively leveraging the interest in offshore services in new regions, such as the Philippines, Central and Eastern Europe, and Central and South America and the Caribbean, to provide their clients with round-the-clock attention. Due to their competitive cost advantages over the United States, Latin America and the Caribbean were the natural location selections for the Americas time zone. During the 2000s, Tata Consultancy Services (TCS), the largest Indian offshore services company, opened operations in Argentina, Brazil, Chile, Colombia, Mexico, and Uruguay; Wipro opened in Brazil; and Infosys opened in Brazil and Mexico, not only to serve the local market but also to export services (Gereffi et al. 2009). This innovative service delivery model was then slowly adopted by developed country third-party providers such as IBM and Accenture.

The rise of nearshoring was based on two key factors that emerged as the industry evolved: first, serving clients from bases with cultural proximity to and language capabilities with major markets offers important advantages for managing service quality; and second, operating in the same time zone was found to facilitate connections between countries, optimizing time and accelerating decision making (Carmel and Abbot 2007; Carmel and Prikladnicki 2010).

The recognition of these two factors was particularly important for the emergence of Latin American countries. Cultural affinity, geographic proximity, and similar time zones to the United States, combined with bilingual capabilities (English and Spanish) and a well-educated workforce (A. T. Kearney 2007a; Mullan et al. 2008b), opened the door for Latin America to take on an important role in providing services for the United States (Mullan et al. 2008b), the world's largest customer for offshore services (Boston Consulting Group 2007).

4 Business models of the industry in Latin America

GDS and nearshoring approaches provided a strong value proposition for establishing service centers in Latin America, and a range of different business models emerged across the region. Strategic decisions of client firms regarding the degree of control required over their service provider dictated whether this would be provided internally or externally (Holcomb and Hitt 2007; Sako 2005). These strategies were dynamic as external service providers developed expertise and clients gain confidence in their capabilities (Fernandez-Stark et al. 2011b). By 2010, services such as call centers and routine BPO, which were noncomplex services that could be easily codified, standardized, and transferred, had largely become commodified (Couto et al. 2007). Buyers simply expected access to low-cost labor and thus selected their services from multiple providers principally based on cost. The supplier was expected to provide the required competencies to fulfill the service obligations (Fernandez-Stark et al. 2011b). As a result, these service segments came to be dominated by external or third-party providers.

On the other hand, where the client was concerned about intellectual property, trade secrets, or the potential capabilities of external suppliers to adequately provide a service, they tended to maintain control over those operations by establishing in-house offshore centers, commonly known as "captive centers." By 2010, this had become a common business model for the offshoring of high-value R&D and innovation practices. These knowledge services were unique, nonrepetitive, and complex in nature, and required a high degree of coordination between the two parties (Couto et al. 2007; Lewin and Cuoto 2007; Thursby and Thursby 2006).

4.1 Four offshore services business models in Latin America

This section discusses the specific business models employed in the Latin American offshoring market. These are divided into four categories: (1) MNC captive centers; (2) third-party provider firms from developed nations; (3) third-party provider firms from India;

and (4) domestic firms from regional countries. This categorization is based on the framework developed by Mullan et al. (2008b). While their framework was limited to IT-based services companies, here it has been extended across the entire offshore services industry.

MNC captive centers in Latin America

MNCs established "captive centers" in developing countries in the early 1990s, as they offshored their business activities abroad in order to find lower-cost and appropriately skilled workers but to still maintain their operations' internal control. Captive centers, also named "shared service centers," allowed these MNCs to keep service operations in-house by opening subsidiaries in developing countries. In Latin American, these centers were concentrated in few countries, including Argentina, Brazil, Chile, Colombia, Costa Rica, and Mexico (see Table 21.2). These six countries received 50 percent to 75 percent of all captive centers operations in Latin America in the first decade of the twenty-first century (Neves 2009).

However, toward the end of the 2000s, many MNCs decided to sell these operations to third-party providers to further reduce costs. The decline of these captive centers, which were mostly focused on low-value BPO activities, gave way to the division of the market into two groups of large firms that came to dominate the supply of offshore services: third-party service providers from developed nations and those from India.

Third-party service providers from developed nations in Latin America

Third-party service providers are companies that set up operations in specific countries of the region to export services for clients based around the globe using the GDS model. Most of these firms have a long history in Latin America and were initially attracted by large internal markets. Later, these firms modified their business models and began to use Latin America as a platform for exporting ITO and BPO services in addition to serving

Table 21.2 MNC captive centers in Latin America

Country	Captive centers-company
Argentina	America Online, Cisco, Exxon, HP, IBM, Motorola, Microsoft, Oracle, palmOne, P&G, SAP, Walt Disney
Brazil	IBM, Exxon Mobil, Motorola, DELL, Johnson & Johnson, HSBC, EDS, Citigroup, GM, BASF, Shell, Roche, JPMorgan, Ambev, Ford, Google, Rhodia, Avaya, Dupont, Bosch, Caterpillar, Philips, Alcatel, GE, Gerdau, Pirelli, Ford, C.E.S.A.R., L&G. Nestlé, Alcoa, Cargill, Godyear
Chile	ABB, Accenture, Air France, Citigroup, Collexis, Delta Airlines, Equifax, Everis, Intersystems, JP Morgan, Monsanto, Oracle, Pioneer, Sandvik, Shell, Syngenta, Synopsys, Wise Ocean Systems, Yahoo
Colombia	Citibank, Motorola, SAP, HP, IBM
Costa Rica	Astra Zeneca SS, Baxter Americas, British American Tobacco, Chiquita Brands, Citi Business Services, DHL, Dole SS, Hellmann Logistic, Intel SS, Lyon Resources (Publicis), Oracle, Procter & Gamble GBS
Mexico	Compucom, CSC, GE Aeroespacial, HP, HSBC, IBM, Infosys, Patni, Perot System, Pearson Evaluation Centers, Tsystems

Source: Gereffi et al., 2009.

domestic businesses. These companies operated delivery centers in numerous countries within the region, although many of them concentrated their operations in Mexico and Brazil. Examples of these include Affiliated Computer Services (ACS), which exported BPO services such as human resource management, finance and accounting, and call center services from Mexico and Jamaica; Teleperformance, Convergys, and Sitel also provided BPO services such as call and contact centers with a particular emphasis on Central America. Twenty-three percent of Teleperformance employees were located in Latin America, distributed between Argentina, Brazil, Chile, Dominican Republic, El Salvador, Jamaica, and Mexico.

Third-party service providers from India in Latin America

Numerous leading Indian services providers set up operations in Latin America, establishing delivery centers in the 2000s both as nearshoring centers to serve the United States market and as a strategic location in the GDS model. These firms selected the region because it has the same time zone and has a cultural affinity with the United States, in addition to offering skilled and cheap labor. Firms such as Tata Consultancy Services (TCS) chose to develop a major regional presence, with delivery centers in Argentina, Brazil, Chile, Colombia, Ecuador, Mexico, and Uruguay. By 2010, of TCS's US$5.5 billion in revenues, 4.8 percent come from Latin America and the company's Chilean delivery center was the firm's largest outside of India, accounting for 13 percent of the company's non-Indian labor force in 2010 (*Times of India* 2010). Other firms were more attracted to the potential of the internal Brazilian market. Cognizant, HCL Technologies, Infosys, and Wipro all established service centers in Brazil to cater to both local and regional clients.

Domestic firms in Latin America

Domestic firms refer to the internal Latin American firms. These providers initially offered IT services and later moved into BPO services within their countries. In the late 1990s and early 2000s, these firms entered the offshore services trade when they began to export services not only to other countries in the region, but also to the entire world. However, significant market power of the lead global firms in the offshore services sector made it difficult for these local companies to compete worldwide. The large global providers could leverage economies of scale and organizational learning to provide services at lower costs and with lower risk to the client than local firms (Laughlin and Camino 2010).

In Latin America, nonetheless, several large firms maintained their competitiveness in service exports by focusing on regional strategies and niche industry services. Chilean ITO and BPO giant Sonda established offices across Latin America, leveraging the specific local expertise of each country to export services regionally. Sonda's Brazilian office specialized in SAP services, the Colombian operations provided healthcare-related services, while the Chilean headquarters was tasked with the provision of services that required high levels of innovation and product integration (Peña 2009).

5 Latin American participation in the industry: advantages and opportunities

5.1 Main advantages of Latin America in the industry.

During the 2000s, Latin America was identified as one of the locations with the highest potential for development in the offshoring sector. According to the A. T. Kearney Global Services Location Index (2009), eight Latin American countries, including Argentina, Brazil, Chile, Costa Rica, and Mexico, were among the top fifty most competitive international locations for offshoring services. Other countries such as Colombia, Guatemala, Peru, and Uruguay were identified as important "countries to watch" (Gartner 2009). This was the result of a combination of favorable factors, including improved economic and political stability, cost structure, availability of qualified human resources, and government support (see Table 21.3).

5.2 Industrial policy

Most countries in Latin America and the Caribbean adopted policies to attempt to improve their cost competitiveness and capture a share of the offshore services market. These measures varied slightly from country to country; however, they focused on three key areas: tax-related instruments, infrastructure-related benefits, and skills development (ECLAC 2008a). All countries launched promotional initiatives through economic development agencies or institutions focused on attracting foreign direct investment (Gereffi et al. 2009). The following gives an overview of the policies that were implemented in Latin America to promote the development of the offshore services industry.

Tax-related instruments: Tax incentives and exemptions were applied in a number of different ways in all countries, at national as well as at local state level. Argentina, Brazil, and Uruguay directed tax incentives to develop of the ITO segment and offered tax relief for investments in R&D and IT (ApexBrasil 2009; Gereffi et al. 2009); Colombia offered tax exemptions for BPO companies establishing operations anywhere in the country. In addition, Colombia, along with Costa Rica, El Salvador, and Uruguay, established free-trade zones for the industry that included exemptions on equipment, exports, and repatriation of profits (CEI–RD 2009; CINDE 2009; PROESA 2009; ProExport Colombia 2009; Uruguay XXI 2009). El Salvador also offered exemptions on value-added tax (VAT) for service exports (PROESA 2009). Chile was unusual as the only tax exemption offered for the industry development was for VAT, and this was available for all service exports from the country (CORFO 2009).

Table 21.3 Factors of attraction for Latin American offshoring locations

Factors/Countries	Argentina	Brazil	Chile	Mexico	Colombia	Costa Rica
Cost	●	◕	◑	◑	●	◑
Political and economic scenario	◔	◑	●	◑	○	●
Government incentives to support IT-related activities	◑	◔	●	◔	◔	●
Cultural compatibility	◕	◑	◕	◕	◔	◕
Language	◕	◑	◔	◕	◔	◑
Education system (availability of skilled labor force)	◕	◕	◑	◕	◔	◕
Total attractiveness	◕	◕	◑	◑	◔	◑

(Continued)

Table 21.3 (Continued)

Factors/Countries	Argentina	Brazil	Chile	Mexico	Colombia	Costa Rica
Key highlights	Lowest wages for skilled in the region. Political and economic stability for a relatively short time compared to neighboring countries.	Significantly outnumbers country peers in call center and ITO industries, though it has a strong domestic focus. Limited number of English and Spanish speakers.	Remarkable stability of political and business environment. Limited availability of professionals fluent in English.	Closest to the United States. Most developed market for BPO in the region, especially in finance and accounting. Key costs (salary, real estate) are higher than most peers.	Stable economy with available labor. Reputation impact: although crime rates in Bogota are lower than in Sao Paulo, the country's reputation reduces the inflow of investment.	Very good bilingual skills. Strong presence of large international (captive) service centers and vendors. Limited workforce availability given population size and potential saturation.

Notes: ● Excellent; ◕ Very good; ◑ Good; ◔ Fair; ○ Poor.
Source: Gereffi et al. (2009).

Infrastructure-related benefits: The provision of infrastructure benefits was a widely adopted strategy across the region. Argentina, Brazil, Chile, and Mexico all offered a variety of infrastructure support. In Argentina, Brazil, and Mexico, this was offered through local state subsidies focused on attracting industry development to their particular regions, while in Chile, subsidies from the national government were used to cofinance long-term infrastructure leases, as well as for office space in a newly constructed state-of-the-art technology park (ApexBrasil 2009; CORFO 2009; Gereffi et al. 2009; Gereffi and Fernandez-Stark 2010a).

Training benefits: Well-prepared human capital was considered one of the key bottlenecks of the establishment of the industry in Latin America (ECLAC 2008a), and thus governments initiated a broad range of training programs and subsidies across the region. In particular, there was a strong emphasis on English language training and certifications in most countries (CEI–RD 2009; CINDE 2010; Fernandez-Stark et al. 2011a; PROESA 2009). In Central America and Colombia, training focused on building skills specifically for the BPO industry. Chile offered very attractive training benefits for all segments of the value chain, although the most attractive benefits were those offered to firms in high-value segments of the chain (Fernandez-Stark et al. 2011a). These included both generous on-the-job and specialized training subsidies of up to 50 percent of annual salaries for new employees, and specialized training and recruitment for experts covering up to 50 percent of the training or recruitment costs up to a total of US$100,000 (CORFO 2009). English training programs for technicians and engineers complemented these incentives (CORFO 2009). Public-private partnerships were also formed to encourage workforce development. For example in Chile, the government, the private sector, and educational institutions joined forces in order to raise the quantity and quality of workers according to the industry needs (Fernandez-Stark et al. 2011a).

Promotional initiatives: Promotional agencies involved included ProsperAr (Argentina), Apex-Brazil, the Chilean Foreign Investment Committee (CIE), ProChile and CORFO (Chile), Proexport Colombia, CINDE (Costa Rica), CEI-RD (Dominican Republic), BANCOMEXT-Mexico, PROESA (El Salvador), and Uruguay XXI. These organizations were invited together on several occasions by international development organizations to align promotional policies and focus on establishing complementary rather than competitive approaches to development of the industry regionally (ECLAC 2008a; Gereffi et al. 2009; Gereffi and Fernandez-Stark 2008). In particular, the goal of this strategy was to foster competitiveness by focusing on niche areas in which countries could leverage particular expertise in an effort to avoid a costly and unsustainable "race to the bottom" (Gereffi et al. 2009). While no official strategy has yet been developed with respect to specific services offered, region-wide infrastructure projects were already underway by December 2011 to further integrate regional initiatives and improve both the cost and the speed of broadband internet to ensure the Latin American countries can compete effectively in the service export sector (Palma 2011).

6 Latin America countries in the global value chain in 2010: industry growth and upgrading trajectories

Despite similarities in industrial policy, value chain entry and upgrading[6] patterns in the offshore services industry differed across the region as a result of its heterogeneous set of countries and their varying sources of competitive advantage. Four broad categories can be identified of countries presenting similarities in industry development: (1) Countries with large domestic markets (Brazil and Mexico); (2) Spanish-speaking South American countries (Argentina, Chile, Colombia, and Peru); (3) Central American countries and the Dominican Republic; and (4) English-speaking Caribbean countries (ECLAC 2009). The evolution of offshore services in each of these categories is described below and the main suppliers are identified.

6.1 Countries with large domestic markets

The development of offshore services in Latin America began in Brazil and Mexico in the late 1990s in the IT sector. Between 2003 and 2009, approximately half of the BPO and KPO projects established in Latin America were in Brazil and Mexico by, among others, the leading Indian service firms TCS (2003), Infosys (2008), and Wipro (2006). According to estimates, in 2007 the export of offshore services (ITO–BPO) from Mexico was valued at US$1.3 billion (*Business News America* 2009) and Brazil reached US$800,000 in the same year (KPMG International 2008). The rapid growth of the industry in these two Latin American giants can largely be attributed to three factors: the presence of manufacturing and electronics production offshoring in the 1990s, their geographical proximity to the United States (especially Mexico), and their large domestic markets. Indeed, these two countries differ slightly in their appeal for third-party providers. While the rest of Latin America's new service centers were focused principally on exports, in these two countries, due to large potential domestic demand, service centers in both local and FDI operations typically served both domestic and international projects.

At the end of the 1990s, with the relocation of manufacturing industries to China, important hardware companies with a presence in Brazil and Mexico, such as IBM, HP, and EDS (Mullan et al. 2008a), began to transform their manufacturing plants into service centers, taking advantage of the available infrastructure and qualified human resources. This transition was accompanied by the arrival of large North American and European ITO and BPO suppliers that began to explore locations close to the US market. They installed low-value-added service centers, including transaction processing and data entry facilities. This was followed by the arrival of the Indian firms looking to take advantage of both nearshoring opportunities to serve their US clients as well as to tap into Brazil's and Mexico's large internal markets. By 2010, the majority of the world's leading ITO and BPO suppliers had established operations in these two countries (Gereffi and Fernandez-Stark 2010a).

6.2 Spanish-speaking South American countries

Entry into the offshore services industry in Spanish-speaking countries in South America began after the year 2000. Development was disparate and driven to a large extent by the arrival of foreign firms, rather than by the growth of domestic providers. The installation of a large number of operations centers across the region was fueled by trade and investment liberalization measures, the availability of qualified human resources at competitive prices, and promotion strategies implemented by their governments.

Growth in the offshore services industry in **Argentina** began in the early 2000s, driven by the devaluation of the peso in 2002 and an aggressive government policy implemented in 2004 to develop the software industry (ECLAC 2009; Mullan et al. 2008a). These two developments allowed multinationals to tap into the vast wealth of qualified human resources in Argentina at highly competitive prices. In particular, cities such as Buenos Aires, Córdoba, and Rosario, with extensive networks of higher-education institutions, were promoted as key locations for establishing offshoring centers through location-specific tax breaks (ECLAC 2009). In addition, Argentina was the first Latin American country to receive recognition from the European Commission for adequate protection of personal data (European Union 2003). This provided impetus for the strengthening of the country's position as a destination for call and contact center firms such as Teleperformance, Convergys, Atento, and TeleTech (ECLAC 2009), and the call center sector alone employed 24,000 people by 2008. That same year, Argentina's IT services exports were estimated at around US$422 million (CESSI 2008).

Chile combines capacities in different segments of the offshore services value chain, with competitive advantages found in its economic stability, quality of human resources, and moderate costs. Chile entered the offshore industry with a mixed approach into both ITO and BPO services and quickly upgraded into niche industry services in the engineering and financial sectors (Fernandez-Stark et al. 2010a). In 2008, Chile's exports of ITO, BPO, and KPO services totaled an estimated US$200 million, US$170 million, and US$470 million respectively (IDC Latin America 2009b), while by 2010 the industry revenue had reached US$1 billion and the sector employed 21,000 people (InvestChile CORFO 2011b). In the case of KPO, the most significant exports leveraged the country's expertise in the financial services industry in all segments of the value chain. At the beginning of 2010s, due to high labor costs within the country the industry moved into higher-value-added services, such as engineering services which accounted for one third of all offshore exports (IDC Latin America 2009b), reducing its participation in low-value-added services such as call centers.

Colombia's entry into the industry was fostered by increased political stability and aggressive promotional campaigns by the government during the latter part of the 2000s to change the negative international perception of the country. Entry into the industry began with voice and data services for call and contact centers and the BPO segment. Upgrading into niche services in engineering was driven by the lowest labor costs in Latin America for well-educated engineers (Fernandez-Stark et al. 2010b). The main global service providers in the early stages of development were Convergys, Sitel, Atento, Digitex, and EDS. In addition, captive centers such as that of Citigroup were established to serve their Latin American operations. By 2008, offshoring exports totaled $744 million, accounting for 0.3 percent of the national gross domestic product (Opertti 2010), and the sector employed 50,000.

Uruguay entered the market specifically to develop software exports in the 1990s. At first, it developed a local software industry with a clear export focus supported by the government through the exemption of software and IT services from export taxes. Several important Uruguayan companies emerged, including Quanam, Urudata, and Infocorp. Uruguayan offshore operations exported approximately US$200 million to destinations in Latin America, North America, and Europe in 2007 and employed 10,000 people. By 2010, a further 1,700 jobs had been created (Presidencia República Oriental del Uruguay 2010). Despite its small population of just under 3.5 million, Uruguay successfully created favorable conditions for the attraction of international providers. These included TCS, which established operations in 2003 and by 2010 employed over 800 people (Gonzalez 2008).

Peru was a late entrant into offshore services in Latin America and entered into the call center segment to serve Spain, the United States, and Chile. Entry was fostered particularly by low-cost, qualified human resources and several firms in CRM services moved their operations from Chile to Peru to take advantage of these assets (*El Mercurio* 2010). Labor in Peru is up to 25 percent cheaper than in Chile and 5 percent cheaper than in Colombia (Ramírez 2010). During the last years of the 2000s, the call center sector in Peru grew annually at 30 percent, creating 40,000 jobs by 2010. The passing of the Data Protection Act in April 2011 was expected to further drive growth (Asociación Peruana de Centros de Contacto 2012).

6.3 Central America and the Dominican Republic

Entry into the offshore services industry in Central American countries was focused principally on call center services that leveraged comparative advantages for nearshoring to the United States. Nearshoring was built on the significant availability of cheap, bilingual human resources, which increased following the displacement of manufacturing activities associated with duty-free systems to China (ECLAC 2009). This was also supported by favorable government policies. By 2010, there were over 150 offshoring centers in the region, employing more than 75,000 people (Casiano 2010; Dominican Republic Export and Investment Center 2010; ECLAC 2008a; Frost & Sullivan 2010; Gereffi et al. 2009; Invest in Guatemala 2010; PROESA 2010). However, despite this success in call center operations, the region remained in this low-value portion of the value chain and at the time of publication, with the exception of Costa Rica, most countries were yet to upgrade into higher services (Fernandez-Stark et al. 2011a).

Costa Rica experienced the greatest level of development in offshore services among the Central American countries. This process began in the 1990s with the attraction of internationally important ITO and BPO centers. Foreign direct investment was actively courted and promoted by the Costa Rica development agency, CINDE. The most emblematic of these investments was the installation of the Intel plant in 1998 (MIGA 2006). This was followed by the establishment of shared service centers by Procter & Gamble, Western Union, DHL, British American Tobacco, and AstraZenaca (Gibson 2008), as well as offshoring centers for companies such as HP and IBM (ECLAC 2009). In 2008, the offshore services industry employed approximately 23,500 workers (Gibson 2008), which increased to 31,747 by 2010 (CINDE 2012).

Panama, **El Salvador**, and the **Dominican Republic** made strong initial entries into the offshore services value chain, followed by developments in **Guatemala**, **Nicaragua**, and **Honduras**. By 2010, the Dominican Republic had 25,000 workers and more than 65 centers exporting business services, while El Salvador's sector employed 9,000 people (Fernandez-Stark et al. 2011a). Much of this activity focused on the lower end of the value chain with the installation of call centers (Fernandez-Stark et al. 2011a). Dell, Sykes, and Teleperformance set up call centers in El Salvador; Sitel established operations in Nicaragua; HP and Caterpiller set up their contact centers in Panama, attracted by the tax exemption provided by the government for those services; while Guatemala hosted Exxon Mobil, Capgemini, ACS, and 24/7 Customer (Everest Research Institute 2008).

6.4 English-speaking Caribbean countries

A number of small nations in the Caribbean also forayed into offshore services, supported by investment agencies targeting the numerous benefits the industry had bestowed upon other developing countries around the world. The growth of the offshore services industry was important for the English-speaking Caribbean because it provided the region with an alternative income source to tourism, which is highly cyclical (ECLAC 2009). The region began its offshoring activities in the 1980s, offering call centers and data entry for English-speaking markets (primarily the United States). Beginning in 2005, the industry was revived, particularly in Jamaica, where 10,000 workers were employed. In 2009, the country was host to the only service center with over 1,000 employees in the Caribbean (ECLAC 2008a). Other companies with operations in Jamaica include Teleperformance and ACS. As with the rest of the Caribbean, upgrading was challenging for the region. Barbados, for example, attempted to enter the medical transcription services segment by offering a range of incentives, including low corporate tax rates, free training of employees, and cheap office accommodation (Gereffi et al. 2009). However, it experienced difficulties in attracting and sustaining companies in the sector.

7 Employment, Workforce Development, and Upgrading

During the first decade of Latin America's entry into the offshore services industry, over 225,000 direct jobs[7] were created across the region, excluding those created in Brazil and Mexico. These positions in the service sector were considered notably better than those in production sectors. Service jobs were typically better paid, the hires came from groups that often experience high unemployment rates (youth and women), they could be geographically dispersed within a country, brain drain was reduced by providing employment opportunities at home, and they established a culture based on learning and continuous development (ECLAC 2008a). It was also estimated that for every job created in the offshore services industry, a further three to four indirect jobs were created (ECLAC 2008a).

The significant wage arbitrage opportunity offered by Latin America over other parts of the world combined with a supply of qualified human capital made the region as a whole an attractive destination. According to a 2011 Wipro study, Latin America offered employees at 30 percent lower costs compared to the United States and Western Europe (Wipro 2011).[8] Low attrition rates, between 8 to 20 percent in Latin America compared to rates as high as 35 percent in India, also helped to improve the cost competitiveness of the region's labor (Laughlin 2011).

However, within the region there were observable differences in cost structure, with some countries offering 25 percent cheaper wages, leading to noticeable shifts in early employment patterns across the region as lower-cost countries entered the industry. As wage inflation led to increases in labor costs in certain countries of the region, commodified services reliant on cheap labor tended to shift toward second-tier cities and countries. This led to a degree of decentralization across the industry, with lower-value service jobs being located in less developed countries in the region. Countries with rising labor costs were required to focus on offering high-value services to remain competitive (Fernandez-Stark et al. 2010a; Tucci 2011).

Countries with larger populations or a low-cost labor force, such as Colombia, were particularly successful in creating jobs in the lower segments of the value chain, such as in the call center segment. In Chile, however, high wages meant that the country's main centers were not competitive in that segment of the value chain, and they were forced to rely on higher-value services such as engineering, which earned considerably more revenue, but employment creation was much lower. Employment growth rates for countries seeking higher value-added showed a smaller increase, since these services demand a smaller number of specialized workers.

Different educational profiles were required for each of the segments of the value chain and the industry thus provided opportunities at all ends of the employment scale. Call centers or routine BPO activities in some countries were performed by university students, as in Chile and Argentina, while in others, including Colombia and several

Central American countries, agents were initially required to have a minimum of a bachelor's degree, but toward the end of the decade this began to shift lower, with high school graduates being accepted into in-house training programs. Market research or business intelligence was typically carried out by employees with a minimum of a bachelor's degree if not a more advanced one, while the highest-level research and analysis was performed by employees holding specialized masters degrees or PhDs. While the higher-value segments of the industry hired mostly workers with tertiary education, the minimum educational level required to provide the most basic services was the equivalent of a high school diploma combined with specific industry training (Fernandez-Stark et al. 2011a; Wadhwa et al. 2008).

7.1 Workforce development and upgrading

As the main input of the industry is human capital, workforce development is a key component to its continued growth and development (Fernandez-Stark et al. 2011a). Best practices across the industry saw a number of different initiatives emerge in the region to feed the labor pipeline required to sustain the rapid growth profiles that characterized firms in the industry and to sustain their competitiveness. Lower ends of the value chain required efficient training to produce large numbers of employees, while moving up the value chain, the need for quantity is surpassed by the demand for quality and the industry required fewer but more highly qualified personnel (Fernandez-Stark et al. 2011a). The availability of appropriate numbers of adequately trained staff thus limited the competitiveness of different countries across Latin America and to a large degree was the key factor that determined potential upgrading trajectories in the industry for each country.

Upgrading was an important goal for developing country governments because it brought about higher wages and greater export earnings.[9] Upgrading into higher-value services also provided more stable employment, with companies competing for limited talent. Comparatively, while the lower segments of the value chain, such as BPO, employed large numbers of workers, the nature of this work was temporary, turnover was high, and employment often targeted university students or recent graduates.

Several countries thus focused on creating workforce development initiatives to drive upgrading in which different institutions played different roles. Mechanisms for training included direct opportunities through private training programs, scholarships, public private initiatives, and collaborations between private firms and universities. For example, many private-sector firms in offshore services had representatives on the board of DuocUC, one of Chile's most prestigious technical educational institutions, to facilitate information sharing about the needs of the private sector (Fernandez-Stark et al. 2011a).

Workforce development efforts in English skills facilitated the successful entry of numerous low- to medium-income countries into the value chain. In 2008, the Colombian government created a new English training program ("Talk to the World") for 10,000 students in high school and technical institutions to increase the size of the labor pool available to serve the industry (Everest Research Institute 2009).[10] In 2010, the Guatemalan government offered 2,000 scholarships to workers of members of the Call Center Commission to study English (Fernandez-Stark et al. 2011a).

In light of the relatively mediocre education systems in the region (Holm-Nielsen et al. 2005), firms have noted particular success in workforce development when it has been tightly linked to demand, with staff trained in specific skills required to meet customer needs and with international performance standards (Fernandez-Stark et al. 2011a). Policy interventions, including facilitating coordination between educational institutions and the private sector and providing subsidies for training, scholarships for industry-specific training programs, grants for R&D, and seminars and consultations led by foreign experts amongst others, were also implemented. Amongst these initiatives, the private sector was the most effective in raising the standards of the labor force. The large and growing Guatemalan firm Transactel created an in-house university that provides courses in English, accounting, and finance, as well as leadership and management. In 2010, 200 employees opted to pursue an in-house bachelor's degree in business, while twenty-two enrolled in the company's MBA program (Fernandez-Stark et al. 2011a).

8 Offshore services: the case of Chile

In 2001, the Chilean economic development agency, Corporación de Fomento de la Producción (CORFO), began promoting Chile as a service platform. The industry grew impressively and by 2010, Chile was recognized as a leading offshore services destination in Latin America. The development of the offshore services sector within Chile illustrated a similar trajectory to industry development at a global level (Gereffi et al. 2009). The country began offering services in IT, followed by the provision of back office business services and then upgraded by beginning to export knowledge processes and high-value-added services across different industry segments (Fernandez-Stark et al. 2010a).

BPOs served an important role for Chile in the offshore services industry, establishing the country as a credible offshore destination (Mongillo and Tasner 2009) and helping it become better known internationally as a destination for operations centers (A. T. Kearney 2007b; Gereffi et al. 2009; McKinsey 2007). However, BPO services in Chile were focused on the lower end of the offshore services value chain. The revenue generated per employee was lower in this segment than in all other segments of the Chilean offshore services value chain (IDC Latin America 2009a), and increased demand led to inflationary pressure on wages. The emergence of Colombia and Peru as cheaper locations promoting offshore services also impacted Chile's competitiveness in this segment.[11] In order to retain call center services, CORFO began promoting the emergence of second-tier cities, Concepción and Valdivia, which are also university hubs (Au 2011).

Chile's competitive advantages in highly qualified workforce availability, smooth immigration policies, tax treaties, and economic and political stability made it an attractive destination compared to other regional alternatives for higher-value service exports in KPO and the equivalent high-value segments of individual industry value chains. These were the fastest-growing, most dynamic sectors of the offshore services market (Gereffi and Fernandez-Stark 2010a). Given its talented labor pool, Chile showed potential to become an important player in this R&D and engineering market. While domestic R&D spending was traditionally very low, progress was made in establishing an effective national system of innovation through the creation of both institutional capacity and funding opportunities (Ministerio de Economía 2009), and by 2009, the country was highlighted as one of the world's new innovation hotspots (Kao 2009).

Where Chile already presented significant expertise and human capital were those specific industries at the core of the country's economy: mining, agrifoods and forestry, retail, aquaculture, and financial services (Fernandez-Stark et al. 2010a). As the country began upgrading, successful initiatives leveraged this expertise into the development of new offshore R&D centers and other high-value-added services. In addition to available human resources, these sectors already had established regulatory frameworks to support the growth of exports of both products and services. In general, firms in these segments first entered the Chilean market to address local demand, then gained experience and developed knowledge and expertise either through technology transfer or by creating local solutions before beginning to export these services (Badilla 2009; Campos and Schlechter 2009; Jessen et al. 2009; Pino 2009).

8.1 Leveraging success in mining for offshore services in engineering

Chile had long been a center of mining operations, and by 2010, the country had also emerged as one of the leading centers of engineering focused on the mining industry (Fernandez-Stark et al. 2010b). As the international mining companies moved into Chile to tap into the country's tremendous mineral wealth, their large engineering partners began to set up operations in the country (Arze 2009; Sanchez and Boolan 2009). These firms, including Hatch, Fluor, SNC-Lavalin, Bechtel, SKM-Minmetals, and Ara Worley Parsons, established a significant presence in Chile in the 2000s (Arze 2009). Having started providing lower-value design drawings in Chile, by the end of the decade, five of these firms had established global "centers for excellence" for the copper industry based in Chile.[12] These centers served as the lead offices in the development of all copper projects around the globe. Together, the firms employed over 3,500 engineers and in 2008, at the height of the copper boom (Fernandez-Stark et al. 2010b), engineering services related to mining alone exported an estimated US$275.3 million, making them the largest offshore services export in the country for that time (IDC Latin America 2009a). The annual revenue per employee for service exports was thus almost $80,000, making it four times that of call centers.

While the economic crisis without doubt slowed the exports of these companies, with service exports declining to US$120 million in 2009, the positive upward trend of copper and mineral prices at the end of the decade led to strong demand for engineering services once again (Badilla 2009; Julio 2009; Pino 2009). Service exports reached US$170 million in 2010 and were expected to reach precrisis levels in 2011 (Cavallo 2011).

Chile emerged as a leader in this field, but the country continued to face several challenges, specifically in terms of costs, to remain competitive versus others countries such as Colombia and South Africa that had growing competencies in this field (Fernandez-Stark et al. 2010b; Julio 2009; Merino 2009; Sanchez and Boolan 2009). The government placed significant emphasis on supporting the export of Chilean engineering services and sponsored a variety of projects in this area. Milestone events such as the earthquake magnitude 8.8, in which just ten buildings were severely damaged, and the rescue of thirty-three miners who were trapped 700 meters below the surface, were also leveraged by the government to promote and portray the quality of local engineers (InvestChile CORFO 2011a) Additionally the government invested close to US$1 million on a branding and promotional project for Chilean engineering services in Canada (Au 2011).

In 2010, Chile established a new goal to export US$5 billion in offshore services by 2015. With policy makers keenly aware that the country could not compete on costs in lower segments of the value chain, a key challenge ahead for the country to achieve this goal was to ensure the supply of highly qualified, English-speaking professionals to attract operations centers at the highest levels of the value chain.

9 Conclusion

The offshore services industry presented a new opportunity for developing countries to enter the knowledge economy, particularly in Latin America, which had traditionally been highly dependent on natural resources. The industry grew quickly in the region between 2000 and 2010, offering employment to a large number of university students and graduates and encouraging young people to pursue higher education. Importantly, the diverse range of positions available in low-, medium-, and high-value services provided opportunities at all ends of the employment scale through both direct and indirect job creation.

The GVC methodology employed in this chapter helps to demonstrate that, while in general, Latin America had been offering low-value-added, labor-intensive services, such as call centers, the continent's focus was on value chain entry and seeking rapid upgrading into higher-value services. Initially, low-cost labor facilitated the region's entry into the value chain, and the growth of the sector fostered significant employment in better-paying service jobs. However, perhaps more importantly for the long term is that the region began to realize both the need and its potential to offer more than just low-cost workers. For example, to remain competitive in the industry, certain countries such as Chile also successfully leveraged existing areas of expertise to upgrade in the chain to offer higher-value-added engineering services.

The industrial policy and commitment to workforce development across the region, as well as the emergent coordination amongst Latin American countries, indicated both determination and foresight to continue fostering growth and to promote upgrading into less vulnerable, higher-value service segments. If the region continues to maintain this momentum throughout this decade, it has the potential to become a central player in the offshore services sector and to make advances toward transforming local economies into important service providers to the world.

Notes

A. Karina Fernandez-Stark is a senior research analyst at the Center on Globalization, Governance & Competitiveness, Duke University.

B. Penny Bamber is research associate at the Center on Globalization Governance & Competitiveness, Duke University

C. Gary Gereffi is professor, Department of Sociology, and director, Center on Globalization, Governance & Competitiveness, Duke University.

1. The offshore services "industry" refers to all services *conducted* in one country and *consumed* in another. These include a wide range of low-, mid-, and high-value services such as call centers, back office finance and accounting functions, and highly sophisticated research and development services. They serve client firms in multiple sectors, from finance and telecommunications to pharmaceuticals. Global services can be disaggregated along two dimensions, offshoring and outsourcing, which distinguish location and control over the organization contracted to perform the tasks. *Offshoring* is a location-based dimension in which all services provided by the host country are exported. *Outsourcing*, on the other hand, refers to contracting an external firm to perform the functions. While outsourcing contributes significantly to gross domestic product in developed countries, it requires internal or domestic demand to drive it. Most developing countries do not have sufficient demand for these internal services to be relevant factors in economic development. This chapter focuses on offshore services.
2. Services firms in the country were further bolstered by growing local demand.
3. Saez and Grover Goswami (2010) find positive and significant correlation between human capital and service exports after controlling for institutional variables and electronic infrastructure. In addition, research by Nyahoho (2010) on the importance of factor intensity as a determinant of trade also finds that human capital is clearly related to exports of information services, while Shingal (2010) finds that human capital is one of three key variables that have the biggest impact on bilateral service trade.
4. This classification was developed based on a series of interviews of leading firms in the industry in India and in Chile carried out between 2007 and 2009, compiling comprehensive employee, service, and client information, and complemented by secondary sources, including industry reports and 10 country case studies.
5. Between 2003 and 2009, 5% of all global offshoring projects in BPO and KPO were set up in Latin America (OCO Global & fDi markets, 2009).
6. In the GVC literature, movement within this value chain to provide new services is known as upgrading. Upgrading specifically refers to a "process of improving the ability of a firm or an economy to move to a more profitable and/or technologically sophisticated and skills-intensive economic niche" (Gereffi 1999: 51). In the case of the offshore services industry, upgrading has been driven in the private sector on the demand side by clients seeking more advanced services, as well as on the supply side by entrepreneurs and large

firms alike looking to exploit new, innovative opportunities within the industry (Athreye and Hobday 2010; Fernandez-Stark et al. 2011b; Wadhwa 2010).

7. Based on authors' calculations.
8. Although Asia presented cheaper labor costs than Latin America, higher wage inflation in the region meant that labor costs were estimated to soon align with those of Latin American countries
9. See Table KFS-1 for a summary of wage and export earnings for the industry.
10. By the end of 2011, 10,937 people had completed the second level of this program, achieving 110 percent of the 2008–2011 target (Invest in Bogota 2012).
11. In Chile, the majority of call center agents were university students seeking supplemental income, thus there were limited repercussions in the labor market following the withdrawal of these operations.
12. These are Fluor, SNC-Lavalin, Ara Worley Parsons, Bechtel, and SKM-Minmetals (based on a review of each of the company websites and interviews with company representatives).

References

Abbot, P. Y., and M. R. Jones. 2002. "The Importance of Being Nearest: Nearshore Software Outsourcing and Globalization Discourse." In *IFIP TC8/WG 8.2 Working Conference on Global and Organizational Discourse about Information Technology*, edited by E. A. Wynn, M. D. Whitley, and J. I. DeGross, 375–397. Barcelona: Kluwer Academic Publishers.

ApexBrasil. 2009. "Export Promotion." http://www.apexbrasil.com.br/portal_apex/publicacao/engine.wsp?tmp.area=145 [accessed August 11, 2009].

Aron, R. and J. V. Singh. 2005. "Getting Offshoring Right." *Harvard Business Review* 83 (12): 135–143.

Arze, E. 2009. Chile Interview Series: Ara Worley Parsons S.A. Personal communication with K. Fernandez-Stark and G. Gereffi. January 27.

Asociación Peruana de Centros de Contacto. 2012. "Noticias." http://www.apecco.org [accessed July 2012].

Aspray, W. 2010. "IT Offshoring and American Labor." *American Behavioral Scientist* 53 (7): 962–982.

A. T. Kearney. 2007a. *Destination Latin America: A Near-Shore Alternative*. Chicago: A.T. Kearney. http://www.atkearney.com/shared_res/pdf/Near-Shore_Latin_America_S.pdf [accessed December 6, 2012].

———. 2007b. *Exploring Chile as a Global Services Platform*. Chicago: A.T. Kearney.

———. 2007c. *Offshoring for Long-Term Advantage: The 2007 A.T. Kearney Global Services Location Index*. Chicago: A.T. Kearney.

———. 2009. *The Shifting Geography of Offshoring*. Chicago: A.T. Kearney.

Athreye, S., and M. Hobday. 2010. "Overcoming Development Adversity: How Entrepreneurs Led Software Development in India." *International Journal of Technological Learning, Innovation and Development* 3 (1): 36–46.

Au, R. 2011. Gerencia de Inversión y Desarrollo CORFO. Personal communication with K. Fernandez. December.

Badilla, R. 2009. Chile Interview Series: Biosigma S.A. Personal communication with K. Fernandez-Stark and P. Bamber. September 25.

Batt, R., D. Holman and U. Holtgrewe. 2009. "The Globalization of Service Work: Comparative Institutional Perspectives on Call Centeres." *Industrial & Labor Relations Review* 62 (4): 453–488.

Boston Consulting Group. 2007. "Estudios de Competitividad en Clusters de la Economía Chilena." Documento de Referencia Offshoring. May 18.

Business News America. 2009. "BPO Markets Expands 25% in 2008-Mexico." May 22. http://www.bnamericas.com/news/technology/BPO_market_expands_25*_in_2008.

Campos, H., and I. Schlechter. 2009. Chile Interview Series: Monsanto S.A. Personal communication with P. Bamber. November 13.

Carmel, E., and P. Abbot. 2007. "Why Nearshore Means that Distance Matters." *Communications of the ACM* 50 (10): 40–46.

Carmel, E., and R. Prikladnicki. 2010. "Does Time Zone Proximity Matter for Brazil? A Study of the Brazilian I.T. Industry." Working Paper Series. *SSRN eLibrary*. July 22. http://dx.doi.org/10.2139/ssrn.1647305.

Casiano, V. 2010. "El Salvador: On the Right Path." *Nearshore Americas*. April 10. http://www.nearshoreamericas.com/el-salvador-bpo-opportunities-on-the-right-path/

Cavallo, R. 2011. "Asociación de Empresas Consultoras de Ingeneria de Chile." Personal communication with K. Fernandez-Stark. December 22.

CEI–RD. 2009. Normas e Incentivos.
http://www.cei-rd.gov.do/ceird/normaseincentivos.aspx [retrieved August 11, 2009].

CESSI. 2008. *Situacion y Perspectivas de la PyME del Sector de Software y Servicios Informaticos en la Argentina*. Buenos Aires: Cessi Argentina.

CINDE. 2009. "Incentives and Costs of Investing in Costa Rica." http://www.cinde.org/en/incentives-and-costs [accessed October 19, 2012].

———. 2010. "Investing in Costa Rica: Free Trade Zone Regime in Costa Rica: Department of Investment Intelligence." http://www.cinde.org/attachments/073_029_Free Trade Zone Regime in Costa Rica.pdf.

———. 2012. "Services Sector." http://www.cinde.org/index.php/en/services-sector [accessed October 19, 2012].

CORFO. 2009. "Incentives and Services." http://www.hightechchile.com/incentives_and_services [accessed August 11, 2009, but since taken down].

Couto, V., A. Y. Lewin, M. Mani, S. Manning, V. Sehgal, and J. W. Russell. 2007. "Offshoring 2.0: Contracting Knowledge and Innovation to Expand Global Capabilities: Booz & Company and Offshoring Research Network." Durham: Duke Fuqua School of Business.

Dominican Republic Export and Investment Center. 2010. "Invest in the Dominican Republic." http://www.investinthedr.com/investment.asp [accessed December 7, 2012].

Dossani, R., and M. Kenney. 2007. "The Next Wave of Globalization: Relocating Service Provision to India." *World Development* 35 (5): 772–791.

Duke Offshoring Research Network & Booz & Co. 2007. "Offshoring 2.0: Contracting Knowledge and Innovation to Expand Global Capabilities." Durham: ORN. http://www.fuqua.duke.edu/offshoring/documents/pdf/research/previous-provider-surveys/ps_2007_survey_report.

ECLAC (Economic Commission for Latin America and the Caribbean). 2008a. *Foreign Direct Investment in Latin America and the Caribbean*. Santiago: Economic Commission for Latin America and the Caribbean.

———. 2008b. "Offshore Corporate Services in Latin America and the Caribbean." Paper presented at the Offshore Corporate Services in Latin America and the Caribbean. Santiago, Chile. November 18, 2008.

———. 2009. *Foreign Direct Investment in Latin American and the Caribbean.* Santiago: Economic Commission for Latin America and the Caribbean.

European Union. 2003. "Data Protection: Commission Recognizes that Argentina Provides Adequate Protection for Personal Data." July 2. http://europa.eu/rapid/pressReleasesAction.do?reference=IP/03/932&format=HTML&aged=0&language=EN&guiLanguage=en.

Everest Research Institute. 2008. *Central America: The Latest Entrant to the Global Sourcing Bandwagon.* Dallas: Everest Research Institute.

———. 2009. *Bogota's Potential as a Delivery Location for Offshoring and Outsourcing Services: Perspective and Value Proposition.* Dallas: Everest Research Institute.

Fernandez-Stark, K., P. Bamber, and G. Gereffi. 2010a. *The Chilean Offshore Services Industry: A Global Value Chain Approach.* Durham: Duke University, Center on Globalization Governance and Competitiveness. (Commisioned by CORFO.)

———. 2010b. *Engineering Services in the Americas.* Durham: Duke University, Center on Globalization, Governance and Competitiveness.

———. 2010c. *Workforce Development in Chile's Offshore Services Industry.* Durham: Duke University, Center on Globalization Governance and Competitiveness. (Commissioned by CORFO.)

———. 2011a. *The Offshore Services Global Value Chain: Economic Upgrading and Workforce Development.* Durham: Duke University, Center on Globalization, Governance and Competitiveness. http://www.cggc.duke.edu/gvc/workforce-development/index.php [accessed December 6, 2012].

———. 2011b. "The Offshore Services Value Chain: Upgrading Trajectories in Developing Countries." *International Journal of Technological Learning, Innovation and Development* 4 (1/2/3): 206–234.

Frost & Sullivan. 2010. "El Salvador in Motion: From Call Center to BPO: What is the Salvadorian outsourcing industry doing to diversify in a competed Market?" May 20. http://www.frost.com/prod/servlet/market-insight-top.pag?Src=RSS&docid=202261041.

Gartner. 2009. "Gartner Outsourcing & Vendor Management Summit 2009, Post Event Brief." May 4–6. Las Vegas: Gartner.

Gereffi, G. 1999. "International Trade and Industrial Upgrading in the Apparel Commodity Chain." *Journal of International Economics* 48 (1): 37–70.

Gereffi, G., M. Castillo, and K. Fernandez-Stark. 2009. *The Offshore Services Industry: A New Opportunity for Latin America.* Durham: Duke University, Center on Globalization Governance and Competitiveness. Report for the Inter-American Development Bank. Policy Brief #IDB-PB-101. http://idbdocs.iadb.org/wsdocs/getdocument.aspx?docnum=35030707.

Gereffi, G., and K. Fernandez-Stark. 2008. "Global Services Offshoring: Trends and Impact in Latin America and the Caribbean." Conference: Inversión Extranjera en Servicios Corporativos Offshore en América Latina, Santiago, Chile. November 18.

———. 2010a. *The Offshore Services Industry: A Global Value Chain Approach.* Durham: Duke University, Center on Globalization Governance and Competitiveness. (Commisioned by CORFO.) http://www.cggc.duke.edu/pdfs/CGGC-CORFO_The_Offshore_Services_Global_Value_Chain_March_1_2010.pdf.

———. 2010b. "The Offshore Services Value Chain: Developing Countries and the Crisis." In *Global Value Chains in a Postcrisis World*, edited by O. Cattaneo, G. Gereffi, and C. Staritz. Washington, DC: World Bank.

Gereffi, G., and R. Kaplinsky. 2001. (Eds). "The Value of Value Chains: Spreading the Gains from Globalisation." *IDS Bulletin* 32 (3).

Gibson, V. 2008. "Invirtiendo en Costa Rica." Conference: Seminar on Offshore Corporate Services in Latin America and the Caribbean, Santiago, Chile. November 18.

Gonzalez, I. 2008. "La industria Uruguaya de TI." Conference: Seminar on Offshore Corporate Services in Latin America and the Caribbean, Santiago, Chile. November 18.

Holcomb, T. R., and M. A. Hitt. 2007. "Toward a Model of Strategic Outsourcing." *Journal of Operations Management* 25 (2): 464–481.

Holm-Nielsen, L. B., K. Thorn, J. J. Brunner, and J. Balán. 2005. "Regional and International Challenges to Higher Education in Latin America." In *Higher Education in Latin America*, edited by H. De Wit, I. C. Jaramillo, J. Gacel-Ávila, and J. Knight, 39–70. Washington, DC: World Bank.

IDC Latin America. 2009a. *La Industria de Servicios Globales en Chile: Estudio Cluster de Servicios Globales*. Santiago: CORFO.

———. 2009b. *Observatorio de la Industria de Servicios Globales en Chile: Cuarto Informe de Avance*. Santiago: IDC Latin America.

Invest in Bogota. 2012. "Talk to the World." http://www.investinbogota.org/t2w [accessed October 19, 2012].

Invest in Guatemala. 2010. "Educación." http://www.investinguatemala.org/index.php?option=com_content&task=view&id=18&Itemid=21&lang=espanol [accessed October 19, 2012].

InvestChile CORFO. 2011a. Engineering Services. http://www.investchile.com/opportunities/offshoring/engineering_services [accessed October 19, 2012].

———. 2011b. "More Than USD 100 Million in Investment Committed in the International Offshoring Forum." November 15, 2011. http://www.investchile.com/corfo_det_20111115120925.aspx.

Jessen, A. E., J. Steffens, L. P. Araya, A. Diaz, and M. Levia. 2009. Chile Interview Series: SGS Chile S.A. Personal communication with P. Bamber and K. Fernandez-Stark. September 25.

Julio, E. 2009. Chile Interview Series: Fluor S.A. Personal communication with P. Bamber and K. Fernandez-Stark. October 7.

Kao, John. 2009. "Tapping the World's Innovation Hot Spots." *Harvard Business Review* 87 (3): 109–114.

KPMG International. 2008. *Exploring Global Frontiers, The New Emerging Destinations*. Amstelveen, Netherlands: KPMG.

Laughlin, K. 2011. "Continental Shift: What's Driving the Rise of Nearshoring?" Conference: International Offshoring Forum, Santiago, Chile. November 15.

Laughlin, K., and A. Camino. 2010. "Latin America as a Global Sourcing Destination: Lessons learned and the Road Ahead for Nearshore Delivery" Webinar. November 2, 2010.

Lewin, A., and V. Cuoto. 2007. *Next Generation Offshoring: The Globalization of Innovation*. Durham: Duke Offshoring Research Network.

Lopez, A., D. Ramos, and I. Torre. 2008. *Las Exportaciones de Servicios de América Latina y su Integración en las Cadenas de Valor*. Buenos Aires: CENIT: Documento realizado para la Comisión Económica para América Latina y el Caribe (CEPAL).

Mankiw, G. and P. Swagel. 2006. "The Politics and Economics of Offshore Outsourcing." *Journal of Monetary Economics* 53 (5): 1027–1056.

McKinsey. 2007. "How Chile Can Win from Offshoring." *Mckinsey Quarterly*, March. http://www.mckinsey.com/insights/mgi/research/labor_markets/how_chile_can_win_from_offshoring.

McKinsey Global Institute. D. Farrell, D., M. Laboissiére, R. Pascal, C. de Segundo, J. Rosenfeld, S. Stürze, and F. Umezawa 2009. "The Emerging Global Labor Market." McKinsey Global

Institute. June 2005. http://www.mckinsey.com/insights/mgi/research/labor_markets/the_emerging_global_labor_market.

Meller, P., and J. J. Brunner. 2009. "Futuro Laboral 2009/2010: Profesionales y Técnicos en Chile." Santiago: Government of Chile, Ministry of Education, CPCE Diego Portales University, and Industrial Engineering Faculty, University of Chile.

Mercer. 2008. *Comparative Salary Study about Professionals and Technicians in Latin America, US and India in IT, BPO and KPO functions (Finance and Biotech). August.* Santiago. Prepared for the Chilean Economic Development Agency (CORFO).

El Mercurio. 2010. "Miles de Trabajadores Pierden Empleos en Call Centers por Falta de Competitividad de Industria." April 8. http://www.mer.cl/modulos/catalogo/Paginas/2010/04/08/MERSTEB002BB0804.htm?idnoticia=C34445520100408.

Merino, M. 2009. "Chile Interview Series: SNC-Lavalin." Personal communication with K. Fernandez-Stark and G. Gereffi. January 29.

MIGA. 2006. *The Impact of Intel in Costa Rica: Nine Years After the Decision to Invest.* Washington, DC: Multilateral Investment Guarantee Agency, World Bank Group.

Ministerio de Economía. 2009. *Política Nacional de Innovación Para La Competitividad.* Santiago: Ministerio de Economía.

Mongillo, L., and G. Tasner. 2009. Chile Interview Series: Capgemini S.A. Personal communication with K. Fernandez-Stark and P. Bamber. October 6.

Morris, E., A. Ancajima, C. Chiri, J. Galindo, C. Guido, and E. Mejía. 2009. *Servicios de Contact Center Basados en Offshore Outsourcing.* Lima: Esan Ediciones.

Mullan, J., M. Kenney, and R. Dossani. 2008a. "Mexico and the Globalization of Services: Outflanked Once Again?" *Economía Mexicana Nueva Época* 17 (2): 171–202.

———. 2008b. "Offshoring IT-Based Services to Latin America: The Current State and Future Prospects." Davis: Inter-American Development Bank.

NASSCOM. 2009. "Indian IT-BPO Industry Factsheet." March. Bangalore: NASSCOM.

———. 2011. *The IT-BPO Sector in India: Strategic Review 2011.* Bangalore: NASSCOM. http://www.nasscom.org/sites/default/files/researchreports/Exec Summary_0.pdf.

Neves, R. 2009. "Roundtable: Shared Services & Outsourcing In Latin America." March 5. http://www.articlesbase.com/business-articles/roundtable-shared-services-outsourcing-in-latin-america-803191.html.

Nyahoho, E. 2010. "Determinants of Comparative Advantage in the International Trade of Services: An Empirical Study of the Hecksher-Ohlin Approach." *Global Economy Journal* 10 (1): 1–22.

OCO Global and fDi markets. 2009. FDI opportunities for Chile in the BPO sector. Santiago: CORFO.

OECD. 2008. *Europe Regional Investment Strategy Key Findings of the Sector Specific Study.* Sarajevo: OECD Private Sector Development Division.

Opertti, F. 2010. *El Mercado Mundial de Servicios Globales y las Oportunidades para Colombia.* Bogotá: Banco InterAmericano de Desarrollo. http://www.icesi.edu.co/imgs/offshoring_marzo_2010.pdf.

Palma, J. A. 2011. "Banda Ancha y Sociedad del Conocimiento Interconectando América del Sur." *Newsletter ELAC2015* 17.

Peña, R. 2009. Chile Interview Series: Sonda S.A. Personal communication with P. Bamber and K. Fernandez-Stark. October 2.

Pino, R. 2009. Chile Interview Series: Hatch S.A. Personal communication with P. Bamber and K. Fernandez-Stark. September 28.

Presidencia República Oriental del Uruguay. 2010. "Se Lanzó Consejo de las TICS." July 15. http://archivo.presidencia.gub.uy/sci/noticias/2010/07/2010071509.htm.

PROESA. 2009. "Incentivos Gubernamentales." http://www.proesa.gov.sv/ [accessed August 11, 2009].

———. 2010. "Oportunidades de Inversión." http://inversiones.proesa.gob.sv/ [accessed August 12, 2010].

ProExport Colombia. 2009. "Free Trade Zones and Other Incentives." http://www.investincolombia.com.co/investment-incentives.html [accessed August 11, 2009].

Ramírez, A. 2010, June 15. "Una industria con proyección de exportar." *El Comercio*. Economia. http://elcomercio.pe/impresa/notas/industria-proyeccion-exportar/20100618/496821.

Saez, S., and A. Grover Goswami. 2010. "Uncovering Developing Countries' Performance in Trade in Services." *Economic Premise* 39: 1–5.

Sako, M. 2005. "Outsourcing and Offshoring: Key Trends and Issues." Paper presented at the Emerging Markets Forum, Oxford, November. http://www.sbs.ox.ac.uk/research/people/Documents/Mari%20Sako/EMFOutsourcingNov095.doc [accessed October 19, 2012].

Sanchez, J., and H. Boolan. 2009. Chile Interview Series: Bechtel S.A. Personal communication with K. Fernandez-Stark and G. Gereffi. January 29.

Shingal, A. 2010. "How Much Do Agreements Matter for Services Trade?" Working Paper Series. Bern: World Trade Institute.

Sturgeon, T., and G. Gereffi. 2009. "Measuring Success in the Global Economy: International Trade, Industrial Upgrading, and Business Function Outsourcing in Global Value Chains." *Transnational Corporations* 18 (2): 1–35.

Thursby, J., and M. Thursby. 2006. *Here or There? A Survey of Factors in Multinational R&D Location*. Washington, DC: National Academies Press. Report to the Government-University-Industry Research Roundtable. http://www.nap.edu/catalog/11675.html.

Times of India. 2010. "10 Little-known Facts about the TCS Workforce." October 29, 2010. http://timesofindia.indiatimes.com/tech/itslideshow/6828840.cms.

Tucci, M. 2011. "The Future of Latin America's IT Services Sector." Conference on International Offshoring Forum, Santiago, Chile. November 15.

Uruguay XXI. 2009. "Incentivos para la Exportación." Retrieved August 11, 2009, from http://www.uruguayxxi.gub.uy/inversiones/incentivos-al-inversor/.

Wadhwa, V. 2010. "Indian Technology's Fourth Wave." *Business Week*. December 8. http://www.businessweek.com/technology/content/dec2010/tc20101128_116888.htm.

Wadhwa, V., U. K. De Vitton, and G. Gereffi. 2008. "How the Disciple Became the Guru: Is it Time for the U.S. to Learn Workforce Development from Former Discipline India?" Durham: Duke University and the Kauffman Foundation. http://www.soc.duke.edu/GlobalEngineering/papers_disciple.php.

Wipro. 2011. "A New World Option for Offshoring: Latin American Countries can Offer European Business Competitive Benefits." Wipro Consulting Services. http://www.wipro.com/documents/latinAmerica_final_online_2_17_11.pdf.

CHAPTER 22

Are NAFTA and Export-oriented Industrialization Passé for Mexico's Economy? Global Lessons

ENRIQUE DUSSEL PETERS

Like few other socioeconomies in the last thirty years, Mexico has engaged in a rapid and profound process of export-oriented industrialization (EOI) since the late 1980s. Until the beginning of this millenium, Mexico was considered to be one of the most successful socioeconomic cases for globalization: as the result of a coherent group of macroeconomic and regional policies—including the North American Free Trade Agreement (NAFTA)—Mexico was a symbol for most of Latin America, other parts of the world, and regional and multilateral institutions such as the Bank for Interamerican Development (IADB), the International Monetary Fund (IMF), and the World Trade Organization (WTO), among many others. Macroeconomic structural reform and macroeconomic stability, in addition to "horizontal" policies in other fields of Mexico's socioeconomy, were the main catchwords for the public sector since then and until 2011. Mexico's experience—if compared with its own performance and from an international perspective—has, however, been twofold. While experiencing some success in several macroeconomic variables, as well as positive results in export specialization, productivity, employment, and wage improvements in these sectors, the same sectors display few linkages with the rest of Mexico's economy. Since 2000, in addition, even these sectors have been deeply questioned by other countries, particularly Asia and China. Thus, the "King of Free Trade Agreements" (FTAs) for the first time explicitly cancelled the option to sign one with China, at least in the short and medium run.

Based on the analysis of GDP, employment, wage, and trade, this chapter will be divided into four sections. The first examines the theoretical and policy proposal of the current EOI developed in Mexico since the late 1980s, also relevant for the implementation of NAFTA in January of 1994. The second part analyzes the general trends in the mentioned variables since the EOI strategies took place, and particularly for its most export-oriented sector, manufacturing. In this general context the third section discusses the structural changes of a specific sector, the yarn–textile–garment (YTG) commodity chain, in order to understand the conditions and challenges of a concrete sector. This chain will also be useful to understand the specificities of EOI to the United States and the characteristics of Mexican exports in terms of linkages, inputs, and learning processes. The last section outlines conclusions and proposals for Mexico's socioeconomy in the current context of an open and globalized economy.

1 Mexico's Current Development Model: Export-Oriented Industrialization and NAFTA

Over the course of the 1980s, the new orthodoxy of export-oriented industrialization was widely adopted by policy makers in Latin America. The lessons of the East Asian miracle, famously summarized by the World Bank in its 1993 report, combined with influential analyses of the "rent-seeking" pathologies associated with earlier import-substituting industrialization (ISI) regimes in Latin America (Krueger 1978, 1997), led to a categorical rejection of development strategies throughout much of the region and an embrace of export-oriented policies as the key to growth and development. Convinced that creating a market-friendly environment was the best way to generate foreign direct investment (FDI), policy makers eschewed targeted industrial policy in favor of a neutral or horizontal approach,[1] and macroeconomic stabilization became the highest priority of governments that attached great importance to the task of getting the macroeconomic fundamentals right.

The argument in favor of EOI builds on the positive association between exports and economic growth or development. Contrary to ISI, EOI stresses that the global economy, through exports, is the point of reference for any economic unit (firm, region, nation, group of nations, etc.). Exports, in general, reflect efficiency; that is nonexporting economic units are not efficient from this perspective. It emphasizes neutral or export-oriented production of manufactures to maximize the efficient allocation of factors of production and specialization among nations according to their respective comparative cost advantages (Balassa 1981). Moreover, it underlines the central role of manufacturing in economies of the periphery, even though the theoretical justification for doing so has not been sufficiently developed to date. Contrary to structural restrictions or bottlenecks imposed by industrialization—as stressed by some ISI authors—this "intuitive Darwinian rationale for free trade" (Bhagwati 1991: 17) argues that the degree and the structure of protection in the periphery under ISI had a significant negative impact on the allocation of resources, and subsequently on exports and overall economic structure.

Probably the strongest argument of EOI supporters against ISI's infant-industry protection and the overall policy of state interventions is the rent-seeking behavior it generates. As a result of market intervention under ISI—such as import licenses, tariffs, but in general any form of market intervention—economic units in general, including firms and countries, generate perverse (or nonmarket-conforming) results in this environment: excess capacity to obtain rents provided by the state, overutilization of promotional instruments, and, in general, an economic structure aimed at reaping the incentives provided by the state. In parallel, these mechanisms generate perverse social incentives and structures, as in most of the cases incentives are not taken by the initially expected groups (potential modern or industrial groups), but rather by rent-seeking and corrupt groups, which do not have an incentive to modernize or industrialize. The ubiquitousness of rent-seeking from this perspective, is one of the most significant obstacles for development (Krueger 1997).

The proposed alternative to interventionist economic management, from this perspective, is for the government to place the establishment of the appropriate macroeconomic conditions for development—or the generation of a market-friendly environment—at the center of economic policy. Opening the economy by abolishing tariff and nontariff barriers to trade and investment and combating inflation by means of restrictive monetary and fiscal policies are the main macroeconomic goals of EOI. In this approach the state is minimalist, while the private sector is conceived as the motor for future development and industrialization.

It is in this international and national economic context that the major pillars and guidelines of liberalization strategy in Mexico since the 1980s, in contrast to import-substitution industrialization, have developed as follows (Aspe Armella 1993; Dussel Peters 2000; Salinas de Gortari 2000, 2004; Sojo Garza-Aldape 2005):

1. Macroeconomic stabilization was to "induce" the process of microeconomic and sectoral growth and development, that is, all sectorial subsidies and specific policies were to be abolished in favor of neutral or horizontal policies.
2. As an extension of point 1, the main priority of the government was to stabilize the macroeconomy. Since 1988, the government has viewed controlling inflation rates (or relative prices) and the fiscal deficit, as well as attracting foreign investments, as the main financing source of the new strategy, since oil revenues and massive foreign credits were not available and/or sufficient to be the main priorities of the new development strategy. The macroeconomic priorities of the liberalization strategy were backed by restrictive money and the credit policies of the Mexican central bank.

3. The nominal and real exchange rates are a result of the control of the inflation rate (the nominal exchange rate as an anti-inflationary anchor), that is, since the control of the inflation rate is the macroeconomic priority of the liberalization strategy, the government will not allow for devaluation, the latter resulting in increasing inflation rates because of imported inputs (Ibarra 1999). Additionally, a stable and overvalued real exchange rate will also incentivize foreign direct investments, particularly those in the financial sector.
4. Supported by the reprivatization of the banking system beginning in the mid-1980s and the massive privatization of state-owned industries, the Mexican private sector was to lead Mexico's economy out of the "lost decade" of the 1980s through exports. The massive import liberalization process, initiated at the end of 1985, was supposed to support the private manufacturing sector in order to orient it toward exports, as a result of cheaper international imports.
5. Finally, government policies toward labor unions were of utmost significance. As reflected in the respective *Pactos Económicos* (or economic pacts between the public and private sectors, as well as with trade unions) since 1987, only a few (government-friendly) labor unions were deemed acceptable to negotiate inside firms and with the government, while the rest were declared illegal. This process, which has included violent disruptions of independent labor unions, has made national wage negotiations possible in Mexico within the framework of the respective economic pacts and with the objective to control real wage growth.

Up to 2011, the Mexican government has continued, with few exceptions, with a consistent liberalization strategy (PND 2007). NAFTA's implementation in 1994 is of fundamental relevance for the liberalization strategy. In a best-case scenario, and allowing for a significant structural change towards exports in the Mexican economy, the Mexican economy required an outlet and welcoming market for the commodities and products resulting from Mexico's structural change. This outlet was to be Mexico's main trading partner, the United States. Otherwise, let us try to imagine a successful export orientation without a market in which to sell these commodities.[2]

The latter issues are relevant for understanding Mexico's macroeconomic and policy perspective in 2011. Additionally, and to understand the coherence and dogmatism of macroeconomic policies until today, at least two policies stand out. On the one hand, and even in the international and domestic crisis since 2008, the Mexican government explicitly rejected any kind of anticyclical policies, and ran contrary to massive fiscal and sectorial programs in countries such as China, Japan, the United States, and the European Union (Banxico 2010). On the other hand, the secretary of the economy continued even in December of 2008 with his unilateral liberalization of tariffs for the manufacturing sector, in the middle of the worst crisis since the 1990s.[3]

2 General GDP, employment, and trade conditions and trends for 1993–2010

What has been Mexico's socioeconomic performance since EOI and specifically regarding its manufacturing sector?

Two general issues stand out for Mexico's economy. First, Table 22.1 reflects that Mexico's GDP per capita growth—as well as its GDP growth—for the period between 1980 and 1990 has been far below levels since 1960. In addition, GDP per capita growth for 1990–2009 has been five times lower if compared to other countries such as China and below the Latin American average. When comparing the period 1980–2009, China's GDP growth per capita was fifteen times higher than Mexico's.

Second, Table 22.2 shows that labour productivity growth in Mexico has been very low during 1995–2010 and even below the average of OECD countries. Rather surprisingly, even in the period after NAFTA (1995–2000), labour productivity growth in Mexico was only 1.9 percent and below the performance of the United States, France, Germany, and Japan, among others. Thus, the historical productivity growth gap (Moreno-Brid and Ros 2009) has not closed, but widened.

In order to understand the former tendencies and the causes for such a disappointing performance since EOI, several additional domestic economic issues have to be analyzed in depth.[4]

First, and from a macroeconomic perspective, at least two issues stand out. First, there has been the systematic and continuous overvaluation of the real exchange rate, coherent with the liberalization strategy to control inflation ("the real exchange rate as an anchor for the control of inflation"), that is, the inflation rate has been below two-digit levels since the 1990s—with the exception of the effects of the 1994–1995 crisis—also as a result of this exchange-rate policy. This constant overvaluation of the exchange rate (see Figure 22.1) also incentivizes cheaper imports—with positive effects on the control

Table 22.1 GDP per capita: Mexico and several other countries (annual average growth rate, constant 2000 $US)

	1960–1980	1980–2009	1990–2000	1990–2009
Argentina	1.8	0.9	3.2	3.0
Brazil	4.6	0.8	1.0	1.5
East Asia	4.9	2.5	1.9	2.3
China	2.9	8.9	9.3	9.5
Latin America	2.9	0.8	1.7	1.7
Mexico	3.5	0.6	1.8	1.1
United States	2.4	1.7	2.0	1.4
OECD	3.4	1.8	1.9	1.4

Source: own elaboration based on WB (2011).

Table 22.2 Labour productivity growth in the total economy: Mexico and several other countries (1995–2010)

	1995–2000	2001–2007	2007–2009	2009–2010
France	2	1.4	-1.1	0.8
Germany	2	1.4	-1.2	1
Italy	0.9	0	-1.4	1.7
Japan	2.1	2.1	-0.9	3.2
Korea	5.5	4.6	2.8	6.6
Mexico	1.9	0.9	-2.4	1.9
Spain	0.2	0.9	1.7	1.6
United States	2.4	2	2	2.9
OECD Total	–	1.9	0.1	2.1

Source: Author's elaboration based on OECD (2011).

of the inflation rate—and disincentivizes exports, since income in US$ obtains fewer Mexican pesos.

In addition, another significant characteristic of Mexico's development model since EOI has been the lack of financing to the economy and particularly to its productive and private sector. In spite of Mexico's profound privatization and internationalization process since the late 1980s (Avalos and Hernández Trillo 2006)—as a result, today more than 90 percent of the banking capital is property of foreign banks—the performance in terms of credits has been very disappointing: Figure 22. 2 reflects not only that the levels of domestic credit to the private sector over GDP have remained relatively stable throughout 1960–2009, never achieving levels above 35 percent, but also accounts for a fall of the variable since EOI at the end of the 1980s. Additionally, credit levels compared with other countries such as China and Latin America's average were six and two times lower respectively.

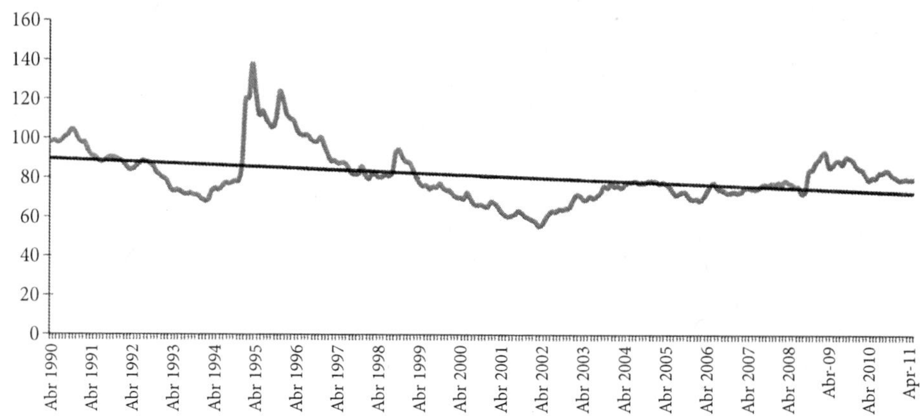

FIGURE 22.1 Mexico: real exchange rate (1990–2011/05) (1990 = 100).

Source: Author's elaboration basedon on Banxico (2011).

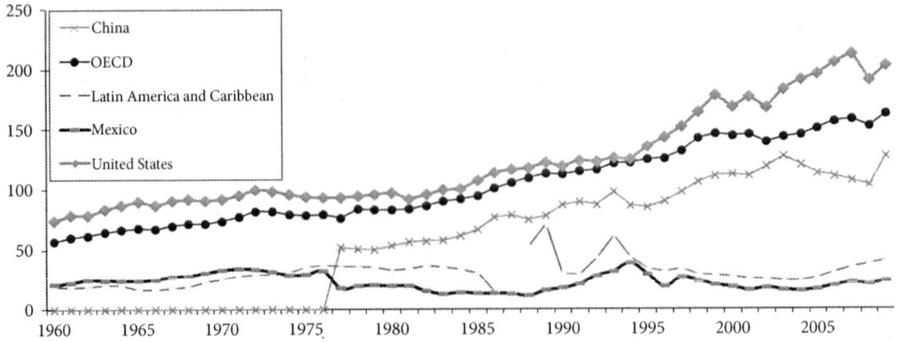

FIGURE 22.2 Domestic credit to private sector (as a percentage of GDP) (1960–2009).

Source: Author's elaboration based on WB (2011).

Both macroeconomic variables are very significant in understanding Mexico's socioeconomic performance since EOI, as the strategy generated important incentives against the productive sector.

Analyzing in more depth Mexico's EOI and the structural changes of Mexico's socioeconomy, four topics have to be looked at in detail: Mexico's overall and manufacturing trade, total and manufacturing employment, real wages, and GDP performance. These structures elucidate Mexico's EOI and its contradictions.

As a result of EOI, Mexico's export performance has been successful in increasing substantially over total GDP, from levels below 20 percent of GDP at the end of the 1980s to more than 30 percent since then. Table 22.3 shows the main structures of Mexico's trade and respective shifts in the last two decades: a period of strong growth, until 2000, with an AAGR for 1993–2000 of 18.1 percent, and a second period of higher global uncertainty, strong competition in the US market, a loss of market share in the United States mainly against Asia and China, as well as the increasing disintegration of NAFTA.[5] In addition, Mexico's overall trade since 2000 has shifted increasingly towards Asia and particularly China against the United States: in particular, imports from the United States fell dramatically—from levels above 75 percent in the 1990s to below 50 percent since 2007—and total trade with the United States fell from 81.03 percent of total trade in 1999 to 63.95 percent in 2010. These general trends are related to the increasing trade with Asia and China, and specifically their exports to Mexico: the share of China over Mexico's imports and total trade increased during 1993–2010 by more than twenty-six and twenty-three times respectively. These trade tendencies also account for an additional characteristic of Mexico's trade: the United States is Mexico main, and practically only, source of trade surplus, accounting for more than $85 billion in 2010, while Asia and particularly China are the main sources of Mexico's increasing trade deficit: in 2010 the import–export relationship with China was 11:1.

Mexico trade presents three important additional features to understand its overall socioeconomic performance.

Table 22.3 Mexico: main trade structures (1993–2010)

	exports						imports					
	TOTAL	UNITED STATES	EUROPEAN UNION	ASIA	CHINA	OTHER	TOTAL	UNITED STATES	EUROPEAN UNION	ASIA	CHINA	OTHER
	MILLION $US											
1993	51,886	42,912	2,704	1,348	45	4,923	65,367	45,295	7,908	7,373	386	4,791
1994	60,882	51,619	2,875	1,544	42	4,844	79,346	54,834	9,199	9,464	500	5,848
1995	79,542	66,274	3,372	2,044	37	7,852	72,453	53,902	6,830	7,699	521	4,022
1996	96,000	80,570	3,570	2,601	38	9,258	89,469	67,536	7,874	8,998	760	5,061
1997	110,431	94,377	4,072	2,392	46	9,590	109,808	82,002	10,156	11,315	1,247	6,334
1998	117,539	103,002	4,018	2,201	106	8,318	125,373	93,258	11,994	12,840	1,617	7,280
1999	136,362	120,262	5,484	2,124	126	8,492	141,975	105,267	13,180	15,129	1,921	8,399
2000	166,121	147,400	5,743	2,158	204	10,819	174,458	127,534	15,329	20,271	2,880	11,323
2001	158,780	140,564	5,419	2,223	282	10,574	168,396	113,767	16,841	25,345	4,027	12,444
2002	161,046	141,898	5,630	3,310	654	10,209	168,679	106,557	17,136	31,360	6,274	13,626
2003	164,766	144,293	6,216	3,683	974	10,574	170,546	105,361	18,645	31,854	9,401	14,687
2004	187,999	164,522	6,825	3,942	986	12,710	196,810	110,827	21,793	44,400	14,374	19,790
2005	214,233	183,563	9,144	4,779	1,136	16,747	221,820	118,547	25,982	53,654	17,696	23,636
2006	249,925	211,799	11,009	6,386	1,688	20,731	256,058	130,311	29,012	68,893	24,438	27,842
2007	271,875	223,133	14,554	7,613	1,895	26,575	281,949	139,473	33,822	79,451	29,744	29,203
2008	291,343	233,523	17,288	8,626	2,045	31,906	308,603	151,335	39,183	86,211	34,690	31,874
2009	229,783	185,181	11,626	7,561	2,208	25,416	234,385	112,434	27,226	72,158	32,529	22,568
2010	298,473	238,684	14,432	10,704	4,183	34,653	301,482	145,007	32,497	95,918	45,608	28,059
	GROWTH RATE											
1993	–	–	–	–	–	–	–	–	–	–	–	–
1994	17.3	20.3	6.3	14.6	−5.8	−1.6	21.4	21.1	16.3	28.4	29.3	22.1
1995	30.6	28.4	17.3	32.3	−12.2	62.1	−8.7	−1.7	−25.8	−18.7	4.2	−31.2

(Continued)

Table 22.3 (Continued)

	exports						imports					
	TOTAL	UNITED STATES	EUROPEAN UNION	ASIA	CHINA	OTHER	TOTAL	UNITED STATES	EUROPEAN UNION	ASIA	CHINA	OTHER
1996	20.7	21.6	5.9	27.3	3.4	17.9	23.5	25.3	15.3	16.9	45.9	25.8
1997	15.0	17.1	14.0	−8.0	19.9	3.6	22.7	21.4	29.0	25.8	64.2	25.2
1998	6.4	9.1	−1.3	−8.0	131.0	−13.3	14.2	13.7	18.1	13.5	29.6	14.9
1999	16.0	16.8	36.5	−3.5	19.2	2.1	13.2	12.9	9.9	17.8	18.8	15.4
2000	21.8	22.6	4.7	1.6	61.1	27.4	22.9	21.2	16.3	34.0	49.9	34.8
2001	−4.4	−4.6	−5.6	3.0	38.4	−2.3	−3.5	−10.8	9.9	25.0	39.9	9.9
2002	1.4	0.9	3.9	48.9	132.1	−3.5	0.2	−6.3	1.8	23.7	55.8	9.5
2003	2.3	1.7	10.4	11.3	49.0	3.6	1.1	−1.1	8.8	1.6	49.8	7.8
2004	14.1	14.0	9.8	7.0	1.2	20.2	15.4	5.2	16.9	39.4	52.9	34.7
2005	14.0	11.6	34.0	21.2	15.1	31.8	12.7	7.0	19.2	20.8	23.1	19.4
2006	16.7	15.4	20.4	33.6	48.7	23.8	15.4	9.9	11.7	28.4	38.1	17.8
2007	8.8	5.4	32.2	19.2	12.3	28.2	10.1	7.0	16.6	15.3	21.7	4.9
2008	7.2	4.7	18.8	13.3	7.9	20.1	9.5	8.5	15.9	8.5	16.6	9.1
2009	−21.1	−20.7	−32.8	−12.3	8.0	−20.3	−24.0	−25.7	−30.5	−16.3	−6.2	−29.2
2010	29.9	28.9	24.1	41.6	89.5	36.3	28.6	29.0	19.4	32.9	40.2	24.3
1993–2000	18.1	19.3	11.4	7.0	24.2	11.9	15.1	15.9	9.9	15.5	33.2	13.1
2000–2010	6.0	4.9	9.7	17.4	35.3	12.3	5.6	1.3	7.8	16.8	31.8	9.5
					SHARE OVER TOTAL (percentage)							
1993	100.00	82.70	5.21	2.60	0.09	9.49	100.00	69.29	12.10	11.28	0.59	7.33
1994	100.00	84.78	4.72	2.54	0.07	7.96	100.00	69.11	11.59	11.93	0.63	7.37
1995	100.00	83.32	4.24	2.57	0.05	9.87	100.00	74.40	9.43	10.63	0.72	5.55
1996	100.00	83.93	3.72	2.71	0.04	9.64	100.00	75.49	8.80	10.06	0.85	5.66

1997	100.00	85.46	3.69	2.17	0.04	8.68	100.00	74.68	9.25	10.30	1.14	5.77
1998	100.00	87.63	3.42	1.87	0.09	7.08	100.00	74.38	9.57	10.24	1.29	5.81
1999	100.00	88.19	4.02	1.56	0.09	6.23	100.00	74.15	9.28	10.66	1.35	5.92
2000	100.00	88.73	3.46	1.30	0.12	6.51	100.00	73.10	8.79	11.62	1.65	6.49
2001	100.00	88.53	3.41	1.40	0.18	6.66	100.00	67.56	10.00	15.05	2.39	7.39
2002	100.00	88.11	3.50	2.06	0.41	6.34	100.00	63.17	10.16	18.59	3.72	8.08
2003	100.00	87.57	3.77	2.24	0.59	6.42	100.00	61.78	10.93	18.68	5.51	8.61
2004	100.00	87.51	3.63	2.10	0.52	6.76	100.00	56.31	11.07	22.56	7.30	10.06
2005	100.00	85.68	4.27	2.23	0.53	7.82	100.00	53.44	11.71	24.19	7.98	10.66
2006	100.00	84.75	4.40	2.55	0.68	8.30	100.00	50.89	11.33	26.91	9.54	10.87
2007	100.00	82.07	5.35	2.80	0.70	9.77	100.00	49.47	12.00	28.18	10.55	10.36
2008	100.00	80.15	5.93	2.96	0.70	10.95	100.00	49.04	12.70	27.94	11.24	10.33
2009	100.00	80.59	5.06	3.29	0.96	11.06	100.00	47.97	11.62	30.79	13.88	9.63
2010	100.00	79.97	4.84	3.59	1.40	11.61	100.00	48.10	10.78	31.82	15.13	9.31
			TRADE BALANCE						SHARE OVER TOTAL TRADE			
1993	−13,481	−2,383	−5,204	−6,025	−342	132	100. 00	75. 23	9.05	7.44	0.37	8.28
1994	−18,464	−3,216	−6,324	−7,920	−457	−1,005	100.00	75.91	8.61	7.85	0.39	7.62
1995	7,088	12,371	−3,458	−5,655	−484	3,830	100.00	79.07	6.71	6.41	0.37	7.81
1996	6,531	13,034	−4,303	−6,397	−721	4,197	100.00	79.86	6.17	6.25	0.43	7.72
1997	623	12,375	−6,084	−8,923	−1,201	3,256	100.00	80.09	6.46	6.22	0.59	7.23
1998	−7,834	9,743	−7,976	−10,639	−1,511	1,037	100.00	80.79	6.59	6.19	0.71	6.42
1999	−5,613	14,995	−7,696	−13,005	−1,795	94	100.00	81.03	6.71	6.20	0.74	6.07
2000	−8,337	19,865	−9,586	−18,113	−2,676	−504	100.00	80.73	6.19	6.59	0.91	6.50
2001	−9,617	26,798	−11,423	−23,122	−3,745	−1,870	100.00	77.74	6.80	8.43	1.32	7.04
2002	−7,633	35,341	−11,506	−28,050	−5,620	−3,418	100.00	75.35	6.90	10.51	2.10	7.23
2003	−5,779	38,933	−12,428	−28,171	−8,426	−4,113	100.00	74.45	7.41	10.60	3.09	7.53
2004	−8,811	53,695	−14,968	−40,459	−13,388	−7,079	100.00	71.55	7.44	12.56	3.99	8.45
2005	−7,587	65,016	−16,838	−48,875	−16,561	−6,889	100.00	69.28	8.06	13.40	4.32	9.26
2006	−6,133	81,488	−18,003	−62,508	−22,750	−7,110	100.00	67.61	7.91	14.88	5.16	9.60

(Continued)

Table 22.3 (Continued)

	exports						imports					
	TOTAL	UNITED STATES	EUROPEAN UNION	ASIA	CHINA	OTHER	TOTAL	UNITED STATES	EUROPEAN UNION	ASIA	CHINA	OTHER
2007	−10,074	83,660	−19,268	−71,838	−27,848	−2,628	100.00	65.47	8.73	15.72	5.71	10.07
2008	−17,261	82,188	−21,895	−77,586	−32,646	32	100.00	64.15	9.41	15.81	6.12	10.63
2009	−4,602	72,747	−15,600	−64,596	−30,321	2,848	100.00	64.12	8.37	17.17	7.48	10.34
2010	−2,902	85,911	−16,636	−78,310	−38,027	6,133	100.00	63.95	7.82	17.77	8.30	10.45

Source: Author's elaboration based on Banxico (2011).

First, the successful shift in the composition of Mexico's exports towards manufacturing. That is, while at the beginning of the 1980s oil accounted for more than 80 percent of Mexico's exports, since the 1990s manufacturing's share—and particularly autoparts and automobiles, electronics and the yarn–textile–garments—was above 85 percent of Mexico's exports. This shift was according to the EOI strategy and the increasing integration of Mexico's trade with the United States and through NAFTA.

Second, and allowing for an analysis of processes versus products, Mexican exports since the late 1980s increasingly depended on temporary imports to be exported (TIE), with important incentives from EOI in terms of value-added and income taxes, as well as tariffs; that is, the main incentives are to import parts and components to allow for fast transformation processes in Mexico and its export (mainly to the United States).[6] Figure 22.3 shows this composition of Mexico's exports by process for 1993–2010, highlighting that exports are highly dependent on TIE and oil, accounting for almost 85 percent of total exports during the period.[7]

As a result of the former trends, EOI has incentivized a highly dynamic and export-oriented manufacturing sector, based on TIE and ever-increasing trade deficits. As shown in Figure 22.4, the coefficient of the trade deficit against GDP reflects that particularly in periods of growth the coefficient increases and falls but is constant in periods of crisis, such as during the 1994–1995 crisis. From this perspective, one of the most relevant results of the EOI strategy has been the creation of an industrial-organization

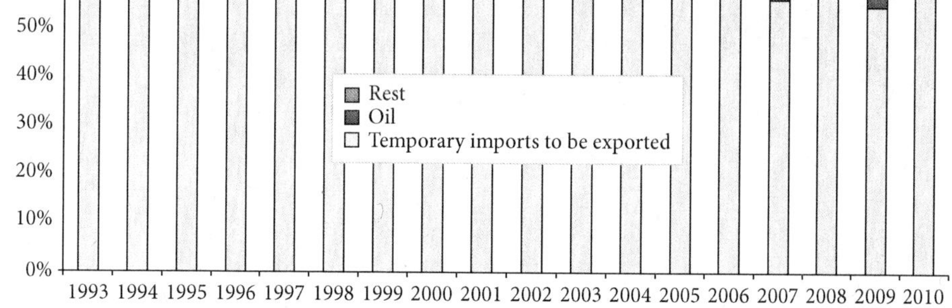

FIGURE 22.3 Mexico: export structure by type of process (percentage over total trade) (1993–2010).

Source: Author's elaboration based on INEGI (2011).

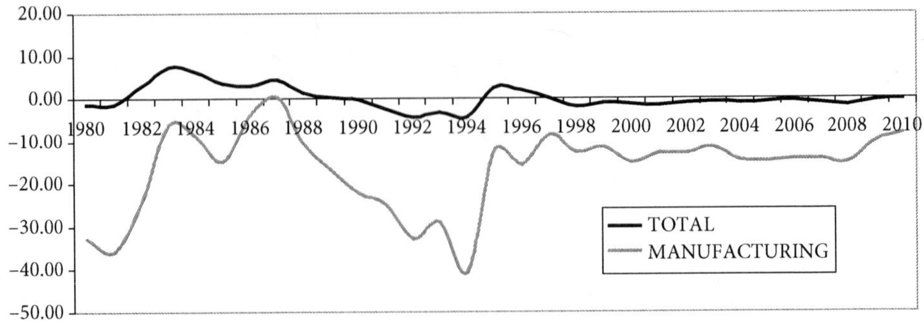

FIGURE 22.4 Trade balance/GDP (1980–2010) (percentage).

Source: Author's elaboration based on INEGI (2011).

structure that specializes in exports but requires ever-increasing imports in order to keep up with this dynamism. This industrial organization could also be defined as an "import-oriented industrialization" (Dussel Peters 2000), and contrary to EOI's premises.

To finalize the analysis of Mexico EOI, Mexico's manufacturing sector presents two additional features:

1. There has been a profound process of crisis between the end of the 1990s and beginning of the 2010s, both in terms of GDP growth and massive loss of employment. In terms of GDP, manufacturing—the engine of growth of Mexico's economy and the sector which was supposed to close gaps in terms of productivity, GDP, employment and real wages in the integration process of NAFTA—lost 5 percent in its share of the GDP of Mexico's economy during 1988–2010 (Figure 22.5). This process of deindustrialization in the process of export specialization was even deeper in terms of employment: as with GDP, employment in manufacturing increased its share over the total economy until the end of 1990s and lost more than 10 percent until 2010; in absolute values between October 2000 and January 2010 manufacturing lost 1.04 million jobs, or 24.5 percent.
2. Since the implementation of NAFTA in 1994, real wages have also presented difficulties for workers: real minimum wages have declined by more than 20 percent in these sixteen years, while real manufacturing wages fell after the crisis of 1994–1995 and have recovered slightly since then, but are still practically at the same level as sixteen years ago. This is one of the main reasons for the lack of growth of the domestic market: a lack of employment generation and, in the case of new jobs, with little growth in real wages.

FIGURE 22.5 Manufacturing: share over total GDP and employment (1988–2011).

Source: Author's elaboration based on INEGI (2011).

3 The Case of the Yarn–Textile–Garment Value-Added Chain

The yarn–textile–garment value-added chain (YTG) has been historically and globally one of the fastest changing in the last decades. In the last decade the increasing saturation of garments in developed countries, the deepening of full packaging processes in which suppliers are increasingly responsible for costs in manufacturing (from buying all required inputs to financing these inputs), but also in the service sector (such as transportation, customs, logistics, and the coordination and distribution of goods in the final consumer market), the increasing product differentiation (including those with ethical and ecological standards), the growing significance and control of the chain by retailers, as well as dramatic shortening of production and delivery time and impressive global competition affecting prices, are some of the characteristics of current YTG. As a result, the existence and strengthening of a local supplier system is critical for facing these challenges (Dussel Peters 2010). At the beginning of the twenty-first century, the chain, which is controlled by its buyers and clients, seems to find itself in a more liberal period compared with recent decades, considering the end of the Multifiber Agreement (MFA) in 2005 (Gelb 2003), the strong reduction of measures of public intervention—in terms of tariff, nontariff barriers and government subsidy—and the concentration of support instruments in the textile and accessories industry, and to a lesser degree in the clothing industry (Frederick and Gereffi 2009).

In addition to these trends, there has been a rapid "reorientatation" of the YTG chain. While China, India, Bangladesh, and Pakistan, among other countries, have substantially increased their share in global production and trade in the first decade of the twenty-first century, developed countries have witnessed a continuous fall in production and trade since the 1980s. In the case of the United States, for example, textiles and apparel still accounted for 1.1 million jobs in 2000, fell by more than half in 2008 and are expected to fall by 22.6 percent until 2016 (BLS 2009).

In Mexico the YTG chain is one of the symbols for global and NAFTA integration and of EOI as discussed in the first part of this document. Based on the last input-output Matrix of Mexico's economy for 2003 (Dussel Peters 2010), the YTG shows several features. On the one hand, the chain shows marked differences between the segments that make use of the inbond or maquiladora industry and the rest. The chain accounts for imported input/total input levels above those of the rest of manufacturing; these are 33.1 percent for the full YTG chain and 38.2 percent for the textile segment; in 2003 foreign trade accounted for 51 percent of production and 60 percent for the full YTG chain and the apparel segment respectively. Despite the high level of integration into the world market, the chain shows a profound structural weakness: its high component of net imports. In the case of the maquiladora industry, the domestic content for the entire economy, manufacturing, the YTG chain and the textile segment was 0.3 percent, 3.1 percent, 4.7 percent and 15.7 percent respectively. This structure is the result of a complex structure of incentives linked to TIE (see section 2). On the other hand, the YTG chain stands out for paying taxes—in relation to production—that are 45 percent higher than the entire Mexican economy (in apparel, taxes were 63 percent higher), for payments per employee 23 percent lower than the total economy with the exception of the textile segment, and for being particularly sensitive in the generation of employment as a result of import substitution: if final demand increased 10 percent via import substitution, the YTG chain would generate 17,000 jobs, particularly in the garment segment. Out of seventy-five activities of Mexico's economy in 2003, only five in the entire economy would generate more employment than the YTG chain.

Considering the YTG chain's growing orientation toward foreign trade, what are its main features in terms of production, employment, trade, and integration?

First, the YTG chain accounted for 0.9 percent and 5 percent of Mexico's total and manufacturing's gross value-added in 2009. Table 22.4 reflects the strong cyclical movement of the chain for the first NAFTA period until 2000 and the fall of gross domestic product (GDP) and employment indicators since then. In terms of GDP, while manufacturing has only slowly recovered since 2005 (in ten years its GDP grew by only 7 percent), the YTG GDP level is lower than prior to NAFTA and has lost more than a quarter in 2010 compared to 2000. This performance—also as a result of productivity growth and new forms of industrial organization—is more profound for employment: while Mexico's manufacturing sector as a whole has lost almost a million jobs during 2000–2010 (or a quarter of manufacturing employment), the YTG chain has lost almost half of its employment since 2000, contrary to initial gains for the period 1994–2000. These losses have been particularly profound in the garment segment and are also the result of competition in the domestic market and in foreign markets with Asian and Chinese producers.[8] The full chain still accounted for more than half a million jobs in 2009 (INEGI 2010).

Table 22.4 Mexico: GDP and employment trends in manufacturing and YTG (1994–2010)

	1994	1995	1996	1997	1998	1999	2000	2001	2002	2003	2004	2005	2006	2007	2008	2009	2010
GDP (2000 = 100)	72.77	68.77	75.94	83.90	89.93	93.90	100.00	96.13	95.10	93.75	97.44	100.91	106.89	108.74	107.95	97.38	107.03
Manufacturing																	
YTG	76.42	71.51	82.33	89.44	92.54	96.63	100.00	90.15	84.46	78.58	79.68	77.61	78.07	75.10	73.83	69.11	74.04
Employment (2000 = 100)																	
Manufacturing	71.84	70.07	74.97	83.48	88.54	93.95	100.00	95.99	90.84	87.20	86.86	87.24	88.60	88.83	85.88	77.30	80.70
YTG	94.34	85.38	90.99	96.38	98.26	98.85	100.00	90.91	83.65	77.27	71.67	68.65	66.52	64.52	60.11	54.86	55.47
Garment	91.34	81.02	86.98	92.05	100.30	101.45	100.00	91.74	83.56	77.60	71.97	67.15	66.07	63.74	58.68	53.27	52.75

Source: Author's calculations based on INEGI, EIM and SCN (2011).

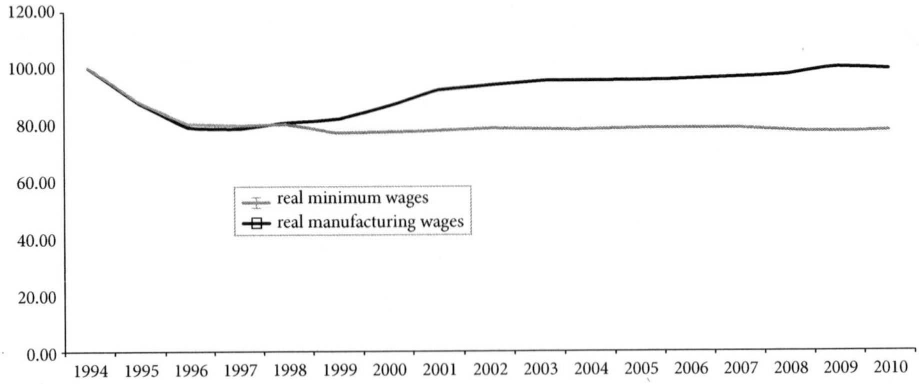

FIGURE 22.6 Mexico: real minimum and manufacturing wages (1994 = 100) (1994–2010).

Source: Author's elaboration based on INEGI (2011).

Second, during 1995–2008, 74.79 percent of Mexican exports from the YTG chain were in the apparel segment, followed by textiles (11.36 percent), yarn (5.49 percent), and other accessories (8.41 percent). Figure 22.7 reflects Mexico's differentiated dynamics of YTG before and after 2000, with an average annual growth rate (AAGR) of exports of 23.7 percent and –5.6 percent for 1995–2000 and 2000–2009 respectively. For the period 1995–2009 the United States covered 90.76 percent of Mexico's YTG chain exports. This differentiated performance is particularly profound for the garment segment (Figure 22.7). Rather surprisingly, Mexico's

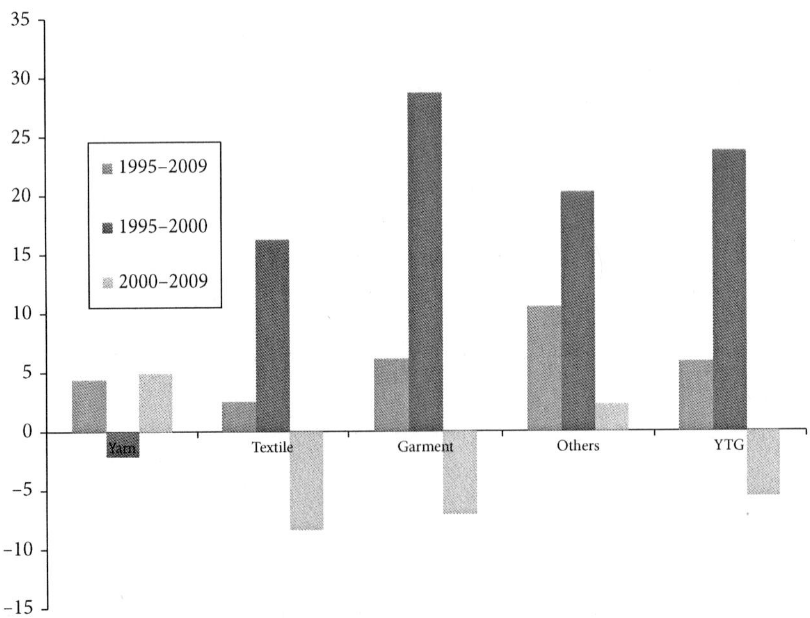

FIGURE 22.7 Mexico: YTG exports by segment (1995–2009) (average annual growth rate).

Source: Author's calculations based on USITC (2010).

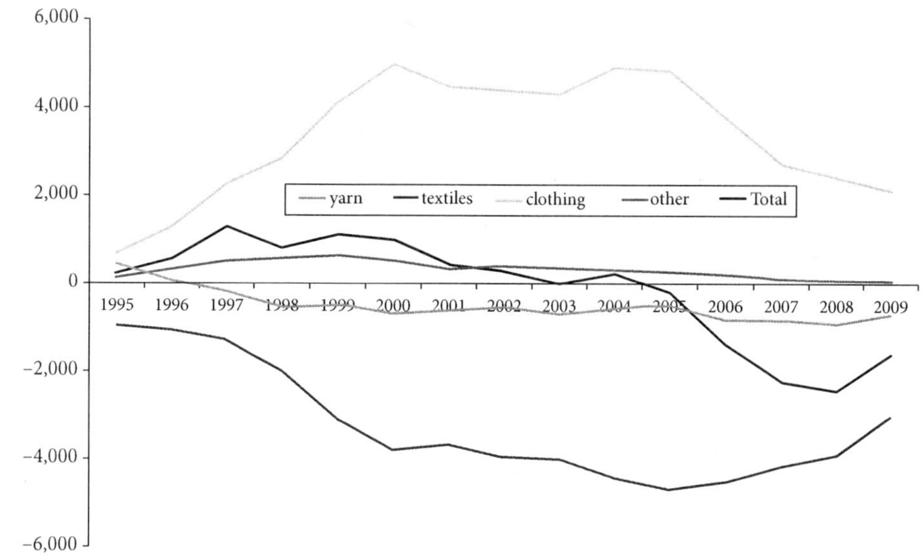

FIGURE 22.8 Mexico: trade balance of the YTG chain by segment (1995–2009) ($US million).

Source: Author's calculations based on USITC (2010).

trade balance in the YTG chain turned negative in 2006 (Figure 22.8) as a result of a drop in apparel exports since 2001 and the increasing import of the chains inputs.

Third, considering the high concentration of Mexican YTG chain exports to the United States, several issues highlight the increasing disintegration of the YTG industrial organization in the NAFTA region. Table 22.5 shows that Mexico's YTG exports to the United States increased substantially during 1990–2000 and declined again since then, with an AAGR of 30.7 percent and –8.8 percent for 1990–2000 and 2000–2009 respectively. Mexico accounted for its highest share over total US imports of the YTG chain in 1999 with 13.27 percent and it fell continuously up to 5.14 percent in 2009, while China's share increased from 12.41 percent to 40.41 percent. Two other aspects are important: a. the import/export coefficient of the United States –a proxy also for measuring the US content in US imports reflects that Mexico and Central America are major consumers of the US YTG chain, in contrast with the rest of the world and China; that is, Mexico is not only a major exporter to the United States, but also the country with the highest US value-added in its exports, which reflects an important degree of regional integration. Also as a result of NAFTA, Mexico still benefits from massive tariff incentives, paying in 2000–2009 only 4.99 percent of tariffs paid by all US YTG imports; tariffs in this chain are important and still account for 11.19 percent in 2009.

Finally, and in qualitative terms, business organizations (Dussel Peters 2010) in Mexico have outspokenly demanded the modernization of NAFTA, since after more than seventeen years NAFTA's regional integration framework is outdated. NAFTA was developed at the beginning of the 1990s and was based on an industrial organization of the late 1980s that does not exist today, since most of the textile and accessories

Table 22.5 United States: imports of the YTG chain (1990–2009)

	1990	2000	2009	1990–2000	2000–2009
		Share over total imports			
China	11.44	12.02	40.41	13.07	25.47
Vietnam	0.00	0.06	6.25	0.04	3.11
México	2.98	13.22	5.14	9.34	8.67
India	3.17	3.85	5.44	3.77	4.71
Indonesia	2.64	3.11	4.73	2.97	3.55
Total imports	100.00	100.00	100.00	100.00	100.00
		Import/export coefficient			
China	54.98	205.18	360.08	196.93	100.70
Vietnam	–	60.93	1219.33	774.10	30.43
México	3.09	7.54	6.22	7.03	6.74
India	103.98	254.42	282.49	220.41	143.23
Indonesia	160.05	282.43	823.74	285.10	177.29
Total imports	12.89	17.74	32.80	19.97	15.13
		Tariffs for imports (total = 100)			
China	92.66	105.24	118.18	99.23	112.76
Vietnam	–	371.40	152.72	99.23	161.22
México	85.76	3.38	18.68	14.26	4.99
India	86.12	109.69	101.52	101.99	108.92
Indonesia	124.88	159.46	144.33	147.27	168.94
Total imports	100.00	100.00	100.00	100.00	100.00

Source: Author's elaboration based on USITC (2010).

producers have left the region and Asia has become the main global producer. In addition, the United States has granted significant benefits to other FTA-signing countries that go further than NAFTA. Thus, from this business perspective, the rules of origin and other legal requirements are increasingly useless and impossible to fulfill in the NAFTA region—including in the United States—and the United States has developed a number of annual instruments to overcome these regional burdens. However, the current NAFTA framework and these annual incentives to ease and endure rules of origin of products that would otherwise fail to comply with these rules have weakened the regional and Mexican YTG chain, since firms cannot depend on monthly and annual decision making for long-term business and strategies.[9]

4 Conclusions and Proposals

What are the reasons for Mexico's disappointing socioeconomic performance and particularly of its export-oriented sectors and regions and what are the implications of these results?

On the one hand, it is relevant to stress that Mexico's EOI strategy, while of academic and policy interest in the 1980s and the first part of the 1990s, has become increasingly dogmatic and primitive at least since the last decade. Particularly in the light of several Asian countries and China—with a much better performance in terms of growth and other socioeconomic indicators, as discussed section 1—Mexico's EOI strategy has become academically, and from a policy perspective, outdated. Debates since the 1980s on endogeneous growth and market imperfections, analysis, and policy proposals by authors such as Paul Krugman, Joseph Stiglitz, and particularly Dani Rodrik, show however that, in the best of the cases, EOI proposals are too superficial and simplistic in light of these academic and policy experiences. Export performance should also be evaluated in terms of its structure and dynamism in terms of technology, financing, employment and wages, among other variables.

Mexico's experience since the late 1980s is also relevant from several perspectives. First, and in spite of Mexico's overall and profound deregulation and opening—in terms of trade and respective import tariffs, foreign direct investment, labor and an overall decreasing presence of the public sector—since the end of the 1980s Mexico has generated important monopolistic structures, in sectors such as telecommunications and the financial sector, that have not allowed for a convergence with other industrialized countries (World Bank 2006). This topic has not been discussed at all in the EOI literature or by policy makers. Second, Mexico's GDP and GDP per capita growth performance have been below its historical and potential levels as a result of low investment growth: Mexico's exports have not allowed for increasing investments and particularly in terms of technological development, productivity spillovers and human capital formation, that is, a process of technological upgrading, climbing up the value-added chain, has occurred only in a very limited scale. Large income disparities have deepened this problem (Moreno-Brid and Ros 2009). Third, Mexico's growth motor since the end of the 1980s—Mexico's export-oriented manufacturing sector—has been the cause of its increasing polarization process and the lack of linkages and growth: growth has been limited to an extremely small group of firms, households, branches, sectors, and territories in Mexico and has lacked an overall "learning process" for the rest of the socioeconomy (Dussel Peters 2000). Rather surprisingly, EOI has resulted in an ever-increasing dependence on imports as a result of the incentives offered by Mexico's federal government and executive. In times of growth of the economy and of exports, imports surge, since these processes lack any kind of "territorial endogeneity" but generate current account and balance of payment difficulties. Additionally, the levels of employment and linked real wages have also been disappointing and, since 2000, there has been a massive loss of employment in Mexico's export-oriented firms and sectors. The lack of incentives to integrate to the rest of the economy shows that this is the main structural problem of Mexico's economy and the reason for such poor results of Mexico's EOI in the last decades.

In general terms the Mexican experience of EOI since the late 1980s shows that the country's process of polarization accounts for increasing weaknesses in its socioeconomy: as a result of few linkages, the quality of employment does not improve, and neither do wages and the relevance of the domestic market. Additionally, the learning processes between export-oriented specialization and the rest of the economy are very limited and it cannot be expected that upgrading and innovation will occur under these conditions. Mexico's manufacturing sector accounts for most of these structural weaknesses: highly dynamic in terms of exports, but very weak in terms of high levels of imports and an expulsion of labor power. And while Mexico's manufacturing sector was able to deeply integrate to NAFTA during 1994–2000, since then it has not been able to stop its disintegration. The yarn–textile–garment value-added chain is a good example of the limitations of this form of EOI. Primitive EOI based on the assembly of imported goods had a positive performance only until 2000 and has not been able to compete either with Asian or with Central American firms. Mexico's EOI strategy since 2000, from this perspective, is not an attractive policy to follow vis-à-vis other global competitors.

Mexico's performance is however particularly disappointing from a policy perspective. The Mexican case is a "good bad case" where macroeconomists have been responsible for overall economic policy, and with little experience beyond macroeconomic development. Macroeconomic stability and export-specialization, from this perspective, is not only not sufficient from an economic policy stance, but neither are "horizontal" industrial policies and the dismantling of trade, R&D and financing instruments, among others. When comparing, however, the simplicity and primitiveness of macroeconomic stability and its assumed effects at the micro and meso levels with the complexity of public and private policies for a group of sectors and territories in the short, medium, and long terms in countries such as China (Jenkins and Dussel Peters 2009), Mexico's EOI policies reflect, as with NAFTA, that they require modernization and updating in the current process of globalization and competition, since the times of deep ideological debates—for free trade, liberalization, and against any kind of regulation of the market—are *passé*, and economic policies require much more precise goals and instruments that are not fulfilled by this initial and primitive version of EOI.

In addition, the export-oriented sectors in Mexico have been challenged in NAFTA since 2001 by Asia and in particular by China in terms of market share and a much more dynamic upgrading process in high-tech value-added chains such as autoparts, automobiles, and electronics, among others. That is, these developments since 2000 additionally challenge Mexico's EOI in terms of results, domestically and in terms of exports, and do not allow Mexico, or other Latin American countries, to continue with the initial and primitive version of EOI.

This set of results and contradictions shows that countries such as Mexico require, for a start, a new conceptual development framework beyond EOI. This process, however, would also require a political process of self-criticism, responsibility for the last two decades, and the need for socioeconomic and political change. Finally, Mexico would require a much better understanding of its socioeconomic challenges—at the micro, meso, and macro levels—and beyond a strict and dogmatic macroeconomic perspective to allow for a learning process at these different levels of analysis and with other countries and regions. So far, these processes have not started.

Notes

1. Neutral or horizontal policies—concepts that are well known in Latin America and particularly in Mexico for the last two decades—refer to a set of policies that attempt to affect firms, sectors and regions, for example, without any particular destinction and contrary to ISI-policies that priorized firms, sector and specific regions under chriterias such as import-substitution, value-added and/or innovation and technology, among others.
2. At the end of the 1980s, this was not merely a hypothetical possibility. Politicians such as Ross Perot and Patrick J. Buchanan in the United States presented strong criticisms of imports from Mexico. Stepped-up protectionism would have acted against an export orientation in Mexico and EOI in general.
3. By decree on December 25, 2008, the executive sector in Mexico liberalized unilaterally more than 8,000 items (Dussel Peters 2009). As a result, the average tariff fell from 11.5 percent in 2008 to 6.9 percent in 2010 (PEF 2010: 208).
4. Some authors (IMF 2006; WB 2006) have stated that Mexico's mediocre productivity and growth performance has also been a result of private and public monopolies, a topic that was not considered in the liberalization strategy by the same institutions that twenty years earlier proposed implemented these policies in Latin America and Mexico.
5. For a full discussion on this topic, also with an analysis of intraindustrial trade and an examination of specific value-added chains between China, Mexico and the United States, see: Cárdenas Castro and Dussel Peters (2011).
6. For a full discussion, see: Dussel Peters (2003) and Katz and Dussel Peters (2006).
7. TIE, for example, include typically processes in which parts and components -from electronics to automobiles and agriculture- are temporarily imported to be exported, oil is not a TIE since it does not require temporary imports. While there are no specific statistics on the value-added of TIE, in general, domestic inputs/total inputs have been between 2 and 4 percent until 2011.
8. Particularly in the mid- to late-1990s several US firms invested in a strategy to integrate regionally the YTG chain. Firms such as Parkdale Mills, Dan River, Guilford Mills, and Burlington Industries, among many others, saw Mexico as an ideal place for expanding capacity. However, most of these new plants were closed again in the beginnig of the 2000s, abandonning the effort to offer full-package services and filing for Chapter 11 protection and failing to offer a competitive strategy vis-à-vis Asian and Chinese competitors (Bair and Dussel Peters 2006).
9. For a full discussion on the issue of NAFTA and proposals for its modernization from a regional perspective, see Gallagher and Wise (2009).

References

Aspe Armella, P. 1993. *El camino mexicano de la transformación económica*. México: Fondo de Cultura Económica.

Avalos, M., and F. H. Trillo. 2006. "Competencia bancaria en México." *Estudios y perspectivas* (CEPAL) 62: 1–93.

Bair, J., and E. Dussel Peters. 2006. "Global Commodity Chains and Endogeneous Growth: Export Dynamism and Development in Mexico and Honduras." *World Development* 34 (2): 203–221.

Banxico (Banco de México). 2010. *Informe anual 2009*. México: Banxico.

Bhagwati, J. 1991. "Is Free Trade Passe After All?" In *International Trade and Global Development*, edited by A. Koekkoek and L. B. M. Mennes, 10–42. London: Routledge.

Balassa, B. 1981. *The Newly Industrializing Countries in the World Economy*. New York: Pergamon.

BLS (Bureau of Labor Statistics). 2009. http://data.bls.gov/PDQ/outside.jsp?survey=ip [accessed July 2010].

Cárdenas C., L. Dussel Peters, and E. Dussel Peters. "El comercio intraindustrial en México: un comparative entre China y Estados Unidos." *Comercio Exterior* 61 (4): 1–15.

Dussel Peters, E. 2000. *Polarizing Mexico. The Impact of Liberalization Strategy*. Boulder and London: Lynne Rienner.

———. 2009. "La manufactura mexicana: ¿opciones de recuperación?." *Economía Informa* 357: 41–52.

———. 2010. "Policies and Instruments Intended to Deepen Regional Integration in the NAFTA Region's Clothing Industry." Cámara Nacional de la Industria del Vestido/Cechimex-UNAM, 1–33.

Frederick, S., and G. Gereffi. 2009. "Review and Analysis of Protectionist Actions in the Textile and Apparel Industries." Paper prepared for World Bank and Center for Economic Policy Research.

Gallagher, K., and T. Wise (eds.). 2009. *The Future of North American Trade Policy. Lessons from NAFTA*. Cambridge, MA: Boston University, Frederick S. Pardee Center for the Study of the Longer-Range Future.

Gelb, B. A. 2003. "Textile and Apparel Rules of Origin in International Trade." CRS Report for Congress.

Gereffi, G. 2006. "Modelos de desarrollo y escalamiento industrial en China y en México: el papel del comercio internacional y de la inversión extranjera directa." In *Oportunidades en la relación económica y comercial entre China y México*, edited by E. Dussel Peters, 279–305. México: Cechimex-UNAM, CEPAL and SRE.

Jenkins, Rhys and Enrique Dussel Peters (coords.). 2009. China and Latin America. Economic Relations in the Twenty-First Century. DIE, CECHIMEX/UNAM, México.

Katz, J., and E. Dussel Peters. 2006. "Diferentes estrategias en el Nuevo Modelo Latinoamericano: importaciones temporales para su reexportación y transformación de materias primas." In *La industria maquiladora de exportación: ensamble, manufactura y desarrollo económico*, edited by K. J. Middlebrook and E. Z. Miramontes, 49–103. México: Universidad Autónoma Metropolitana.

Krueger, A. 1978. *Liberalization Attempts and Consequences*. Cambridge, MA: Ballinger.

———. 1997. "Trade Policy and Economic Development: How We Learn." *American Economic Review* 87 (1): 1–22.

Ibarra, D. 1999. *Política y economía. Semblanzas y ensayos*. México: Miguel Ángel Porrúa.

IMF (International Monetary Fund). 2006. *Mexico: Selected Issues*. Washington, DC: IMF.

INEGI (Instituto Nacional de Estadística y Geografía). 2009. *La industria textil y del vestido en 2008*. México: INEGI.

———. 2011. http://www.inegi.org.mx. México: INEGI.

Levy, S., and M. Walton (eds.). 2009. *Inequality, Interests and Competition in Mexico*. Washington, DC: World Bank.

Moreno-Brid, J. C., and J. Ros. 2009. *Development and Growth in the Mexican Economy*. Oxford: Oxford University Press.

OECD (Organisation for Economic Co-Operation and Development). 2011. *OECD.StatExtracts.* Paris: OECD.

PEF (Poder Ejecutivo Federal). 2010. *Informe Presidencial. Anexo Estadísitico.* México: PEF.

PND (Plan Nacional de Desarrollo). 2007. Plan Nacional de Desarrollo 2007–2012. *Presidencia de la República,* México.

Salinas de Gortari, Carlos. 2000. México. Un paso difícil a la modernidad. Plaza y Janés, México.

Salinas de Gortari. 2004. "Una agenda comercial para el largo plazo". *Foreign Affairs en Español* 4(1): 2–16.

Sojo Garza-Aldape, E. 2005. *De la alternancia al desarrollo. Políticas públicas del gobierno del cambio.* México: Fondo de Cultura Económica.

World Bank. 2011. *World Development Indicators.* Washington, DC: World Bank.

——. 2006. *Mexico's Competitiveness: Reaching its Potential.* Washington, DC: World Bank.

CHAPTER 23

Kenya's IT-Enabled Services and Employment Consequences of Offshore Linkages

BOB BELL

Introduction

Inspired by the successes of India and the Philippines, Kenya has embarked on a road to develop its own information technology (IT)-enabled services sector in contact centers, business process outsourcing, and software development.[1] This technology-based sector represents a future for Kenya, which has historically relied on agriculture and tourism as sources of economic rents. These opportunities in IT-enabled services provide a potential for diversifying economic activities through "smart exports" and creating jobs for its unemployed youth.

In this chapter I ask descriptively and analytically how Kenya's IT-enabled services cluster emerged in the first decade. This chapter starts by mapping out concepts from clusters to understand the regional context. It then provides a short history of Kenya's nascent IT-enabled services cluster, focusing on early firm formation, and government support of the sector and key recent developments. The chapter then focuses on constraints for sector growth with respect to labor, telecommunications infrastructure, integrating into offshore markets, policies and incentives, funding, and domestic and global exogenous developments. The chapter ends with lessons learned in the first decade of this nascent cluster. First, the perceived potential of the sector along with challenges faced in growing its firms led to institutional creation and reform. Second, weak offshore linkages created an opportunity for the sector to diversify into domestic and near-shore markets, potentially averting enclave economic effects.

Concepts

When analyzing the emergence of Kenya's ITES sector, there is a need to address it from analytic concepts that focus on the regional context (clusters) that connect the global marketplace to the region. Firms are integrated in clusters—a spatial and sectoral concentration of firms (including associated suppliers) and non-market institutions (e.g., universities, business and trade associations, relevant government agencies, etc.) (Bresnahan et al. 2005: 114, Goldstein 2005: 135; Porter 1998). Schmitz introduced the concept of collective efficiency to capture competitive advantage derived from the externalities (or local external economies) and joint actions (among local actors) emanating from clusters (Schmitz 1995; Pietrobelli and Rabellotti 2006: 6; Giuliani et al. 2005: 2). Based on the work of Alfred Marshall, external economies are economies external to the firm but internal to the cluster (Schmitz 2004: 2; Marshall 1920). That is, these are the (positive) externalities a firm receives when it locates within a cluster, including a market for specialized labor; the emergence of a market for specialized suppliers, inputs, machinery, and services; market access, where firms within the cluster attract (domestic and foreign) buyers and have better information about markets; and information or knowledge spillovers (McCormick 2007: 32; Pietrobelli and Rabellotti,2006: 6–7; Goldstein 2005: 137). Joint action is the deliberate, action-oriented aspect of collective efficiency.

As a cluster develops, there will be a growth in the cluster's firms, and not just in the number of firms in the cluster.[2] Around these growing firms, it is expected that the manifestations of collective efficiency will occur—emerging specialized suppliers, local training and research institutions, information accumulation and dissemination—and that cluster prestige will grow. This process takes time and depends on a number of factors, including the strength of the local environment for business formation, attraction of cluster participants from other states/nations, and forging ties with developed country market(s) (e.g., the United States) for customers and technology (Bresnahan et al. 2005: 119, 125; Porter 1998: 240–242). Clustering allows businesspeople to take "riskable steps" within their local environments, but without the trade networks, their products will not reach the appropriate markets (McCormick 2007: 33–34).

Though cluster literature explores characteristics of functioning clusters, rarely does it address how clusters actually emerge (Bresnahan et al. 2005: 116). Based on a model of cluster formation from the Washington, DC, Capitol Hill region along with an examination of other clusters, it appears that entrepreneurs in furthering their own business interests are critical for the institution building that shape cluster development (Feldman et al. 2005; Feldman and Francis 2004). The early entrepreneurs in a nascent cluster draw on existing resources and add new resources to the cluster that ultimately manifest as joint actions (e.g., business associations) and external economies (e.g., external markets for specialized labor), and so on. Feldman acknowledges that her model of cluster genesis may be specific for innovative, technology-intensive entrepreneurial clusters and that the literature would be enhanced with comparative case studies that consider cluster genesis with nuanced typologies of the variations of cluster formation (Feldman et al. 2005: 131). This chapter responds to Feldman's work with a case study of a nascent IT-enabled services cluster in a developing country. It is hoped that this case will illuminate the dynamics of cluster genesis in such a context.

Methods

The study uses the qualitative case method to unpack the processes within the institutional ecosystem supporting the Kenyan IT-enabled services sector. At the heart of the paper are forty in-depth field interviews and participant observation within the firm environments conducted in Kenya during the summer of 2009. I also conducted nine telephonic interviews with American firms using Kenyan vendors as well as members of the Kenyan Diaspora during summer 2010. The qualitative interview data is triangulated by follow-up with key stakeholders in the sector in 2011, document analysis of firm websites, marketing literature, internal business memos, media articles, conference call transcripts, and consulting and analyst reports. The qualitative case method was chosen because little is known about this phenomenon in this regional context, and this method allows the involved actors to share their narratives in a way that captures the diversity of their experiences. The goal of this case study approach is analytic generalization (Yin 1994: 10), that is applying this case to the theoretical and analytical frameworks mentioned beforehand (i.e., clusters). My approach is historically interpretive in a "restricted sense" by which I refer to a type of social science that "attempts to account for specific historical outcomes or sets of comparable outcomes or processes chosen for study because of their significance for current institutional arrangements" (Ragin 1989: 3).

Evolution of Kenya's nascent IT-enabled services sector, 2002–2011

Early firm formation

The beginnings of Kenya's IT-enabled services sector can be framed around the founding of three firms which pursued the opportunity to develop services primarily for the international market. Their firm-building efforts went hand-in-hand with institution-building for the emerging cluster.

Kenya's IT-enabled services sector starts with the founding of Preciss International. While giving a talk on her e-commerce business at a local convention of the United Nations in Nairobi in 2001, Mugure Mugo picked up a brochure which mentioned outsourcing. Following the meeting, she decided to start a BPO business in 2002 with another partner by initially offering online research services. Through her first contracts, she developed the capability to learn how to serve international clients. Over time, Preciss established a presence in the United Kingdom and built a firm providing nonvoice BPO work in transcription, captioning, and human resource outsourcing. By 2003, her company had developed a website to support one of the earliest country-level marketing efforts for Kenyan BPO firms (UNCTAD 2003).[3] In 2009, her firm had attracted private equity from Business Partners International-Kenya (a subsidiary of a South African investment fund) (Singer 2006).

Nicholas Nesbitt and Mugure Mugo both independently conceived the idea of an IT-enabled services firm around 2001.[4] Nesbitt, the founder of KenCall, decided to plan the creation of a call center after a distinguished career in the telecommunications industry in the United States. He started to plan it from his Denver apartment, raising money from his pension fund, friends, family, and later procuring debt funding from a Kenyan Bank that believed in the idea. The US$1.3 million investment started operations in November 2004 (Zavatta et al. 2008: 20). The firm faced many challenges early on. First, the company lost hundreds of thousands of dollars after being manipulated by a consulting firm that guaranteed international work for the call center. Second, it took almost two years and forty or fifty meetings with government officials and the Communications Commission of Kenya (CCK) for the call center to obtain the requisite licenses to operate a satellite and as a call center (Isenberg 2009). These developments facilitated the creation of new categories of CCK licenses for BPO and call center firms. After persevering through these difficulties and winning lucrative international contracts, by 2007 Thomas Friedman drew international attention to KenCall in the *New York Times*. Additionally, in 2008 KenCall won Non-European Call Center of the Year at the Birmingham Expo in the United Kingdom. The company built a reputation for servicing international clients and had become the poster child of Kenyan IT-enabled services, employing 500–600 call center agents.

Skyweb-Evans was established by Gilda Odera in 2005. In an effort to "liberate" Odera's internet service provider (ISP) Skyweb Technologies of bandwidth, she decided to move into the call center business. While at a World Information Technology and Services Alliance (WITSA) meeting, she met Ronald Evans from Canada who would eventually become her joint-venture partner. Odera managed the Kenyan operations and Evans pitched for work in Canada as well as facilitated training of the Kenyan agents in Canada.[5] This joint venture facilitated one of the longest contracts in the sector (up until recently)—three years. Odera formerly chaired the Public Computer Society of Kenya, a background that would enable her to found the Kenya BPO and Contact

Center Society (KBPOCCS) in 2007 and play a strategic role on the High-Level BPO/ ITES Working Group.

These entrepreneurs are presented not only because they played a pivotal role in Kenya's IT-enabled services sector but because they illustrate at least two things common to other successful entrepreneurs in the cluster. First, they leveraged previous related entrepreneurial experiences to transition into BPO. Mugo, Nesbitt, and Odera had experiences either in IT and/or the telecom sectors and through some combination of accident or opportunity recognition moved into BPO. Second, in growing their companies and addressing challenges to firm growth, these entrepreneurs began to build a set of institutions that not only benefited them but a growing and evolving cluster. For example, Mugo's website to attract investors to her firm and that of other BPO companies in 2003 would serve as a model for international marketing for the cluster. Nesbitt's need for CCK licensing singlehandedly created a category for BPO operators in the country. Odera created institutions for industry networking, call center training, and high-level government policy advice. Overall, these early cluster entrepreneurs created institutions that manifest themselves as joint actions (e.g., industry associations) or the formation of external economies (e.g., creation of labor supply) that would serve their needs and that of an evolving cluster (see Table 23.1). This cluster of firms would soon get the attention of the Kenyan government.

With the success of these early firms—and with more firms joining the IT-enabled services cluster—BPO and contact centers became a national priority and the government supported the development of this evolving cluster in BPO and call center services. In 2007, Kenya's Vision 2030 was launched, aiming to transform Kenya into a newly industrializing "middle-income country" by 2030. The vision was founded on economic, social, and political pillars. BPO was identified as one of the key economic sectors to drive economic growth of 10 percent per annum for twenty-five years. Within this sectoral focus, the overall goal was to be "the top BPO destination in Africa" by attracting global IT suppliers, large multinational company captives, and foreign BPO players and developing strong local firms. Kenya's Vision 2030 was to be implemented in five medium-term plans (MTPs). Within the first MTP (2008–2012), the goal was to create 7,500 direct BPO jobs with an additional GDP contribution of KSH 10 billion (US$149.7 million).[6] Specifically, this meant attracting at least five major leading IT suppliers, attracting ten large multinational captives and global players, and targeting five local players to develop as "local champions."[7] The strategy would entail a combination of marketing (in the United Kingdom, followed by the United States and Canada), training, incentives, improvement in telecommunications infrastructure, and the establishment of a BPO park (National Economic and Social Council 2007).[8]

In support of this strategy, the Kenya ICT Board was established as a state corporation by President Mwai Kibaki on February 19, 2007, and became operational in 2008 (Kenya ICT Board 2008).[9] In line with the medium-term goals of Vision 2030 for BPO, the board's marketing objectives were to develop and launch a brand, create BPO jobs, and become one of the top forty firms on A. T. Kearney's Global Services Location Index

Table 23.1 Key contact center/BPO operations[1]

Established[2]	Firm	Geographic Relationship	Type of Work[3]
April 2002	Preciss International[4]	Offshore	Call center services, Data processing and captioning, and subtitling services.
March 2004	Cascade Global	N/A[5]	BPO and Call Center Consultancy Services.
2005	KenCall	Onshore, Nearshore, Offshore	Level 1 Tech Support, Sales, Customer Information (CRM), Billing, Admin & Data Management.
2005	Skyweb-Evans	Onshore, Offshore	CRM Voice, Appointments, order taking, market research, event planning, telemarketing, customer care services, help desk, subscription services, and data conversion.
2006	G7 Systems	Offshore	Computer Programming, Rural ICT Infrastructure implementation, hosted Project Management Software [SaaS], and ERP [Enterprise Resource Planning] implementation and support.
2006	Andest Bites Ltd.	Onshore	Digital transcription, word processing, internet research, and data entry/digitization.
January 2006	eManage Africa	Onshore	Data management, data storage, and data protection.
Mid-2006	Oriak Digital	Offshore	Transcription and recruitment outsourcing.
October 2006	Techno-Brain BPO/ITES[6]	Onshore, Offshore	Customer Care, Finance & Accounting, Human Resources, Knowledge Services (Market Research, Data Mining, Lead Generation, etc), Order Management, and Web Services (Web Designing, Online Sales and Marketing).
December 2006	DaproIM	Offshore	Data entry, Form processing, Survey processing, Invoice Processing, Audio Transcription & Video Subtitling, and Web Design.
March 2007	Quest BPO	Onshore, Offshore	Call center services and back office.
April 2007	Northwest Offshore Ltd.	Onshore, Offshore	BPO and call center.
July 2007	Adept Technologies	Onshore, Offshore	CAD Services, Transcription Services, and Data Services (Data Capture, Internet Research, Data Processing).
October 2007	Beeline BPO and Call Center	Onshore, Offshore	Call Center and Data Processing.
2008	SimbaTech Direct Channel Kenya[7]	Onshore, Offshore	Outbound telemarketing, CRM, inbound call center services, field marketing distribution channel, debt collection & credit management, hosted platform and disaster recovery solutions, back-office fulfillment and admin services, and Contact center training.

(Continued)

Table 23.1 (Continued)

Established[2]	Firm	Geographic Relationship	Type of Work[3]
November 2007 (Started June 2008)	Call Center Solutions	Onshore, Offshore	Call center services and Business Center.
Incorporated October 2008 (Started June 2009)	Horizon Contact Centers	Onshore, Offshore	Customer Contact Services, Collections, Training and Content Solutions, Finance and Accounting, Procurement, HR and payroll services, Learning & Training Outsourcing, Analytics and Data Management, IT Services, Reengineering, Quality Assurance, and Workforce Management.
2010	Spanco Raps Kenya Ltd	Onshore	Call center operations (Voice, Non-Voice, and KPO), Building and managing call and data center infrastructure, and Global manpower outsourcing.
2011	Digital Divide Data	Onshore, Nearshore, Offshore	Digital Marketing—AdWords, Facebook, Mobile Ads, Data Entry & Conversion, Digital Publishing & e-books, Digital Libraries, Records Management, and Administrative Back-office Functions.

Source: Author.

[1] Not exhaustive but illustrative.

[2] Established means actual operations and not just date of incorporation.

[3] Work descriptions rely on firm self-descriptions.

[4] Initially called PrecissPatrol.

[5] Consulting to both domestic firms who want to setup BPO/Call center firms as well as to prospective investors.

[6] Formerly KenTech Data. Name change to Techno-Brain BPO/ITES effective January 1, 2011.

[7] Joint venture with South African-based Direct Channel Holdings and Kenyan-based Simba Technologies.

by 2012. Its five-point plan, which resembled Vision 2030, consisted of local and international marketing, capacity support, skills and standards intervention, bandwidth support, and research and benchmarking (Kenya ICT Board 2008: 8). To its credit, the board engaged the World Bank to fund local BPO and call center operators with a US$7 million telecommunications subsidy to offset the costs they were paying to access internet through expensive satellite while they were waiting to be connected via undersea fiber-optic cables. The board also commissioned McKinsey & Company to develop a value proposition and go-to-market strategy for the sector in 2009. And in 2011, they hired consultants from IBM to advise the government on data security and privacy law.

Recent developments

There was reported excitement surrounding the IT-enabled services sector around 2005–6, with numerous conferences, a mushrooming of call centers and BPOs, and advance discussions with foreign investors to locate offshore operations in Kenya. In the wake of the global economic recession, paired with Kenya's post-election violence in early 2008, Kenya's BPO and contact center firms that focused on international contracts increasingly began to engage in domestic outsourcing opportunities. These firms looked to outsourced work from the international NGO and intergovernmental industry (e.g., IT shared services for United Nations agencies) in the greater Nairobi area as well as public-sector (e.g., digitization projects for the Ministry of Lands) and private-sector (e.g., Telkom Kenya) entities. In 2009 and 2010, the rollout of two undersea fiber-optic cables along with terrestrial infrastructure (in mostly urban areas) have rejuvenated interest and potential growth in the sector. There have been new entrants into the sector through start-up (Horizon Contact Centers), joint venture (Direct Channel Simba Tech Kenya and Spanco Raps Kenya Ltd), acquisition (Techno-Brain BPO acquiring KenTech Data), or foreign direct investment (Digital Divide Data). Accenture Development Partnerships piloted an IT Shared Services Helpdesk in Nairobi (2009) and General Electric created an offshore captive servicing its internal clients and the entire Central and East African region with a centralized back office function (Kariuki 2010). In 2011, the government unveiled its plans for Konza Technology City, the US$7 billion 2000-hectare "e-city," 60 km outside of Nairobi, that aims to create 100,000 jobs, the majority of which will be in BPO.[10] This project is Kenya's largest development project in its history as a nation and it will host the BPO Park proposed in Vision 2030.

The evolving cluster, supported by both public and private efforts, has undergone a series of institutional developments to make Kenya an attractive destination for BPO and contact center services (Table 23.2). The job-creation targets set by Vision 2030, as well as the recent value proposition process, helped position Kenya's emerging cluster at the lower end of the services value chain, delivering basic data and voice services to Anglophone markets (i.e., the United States and United Kingdom). Entrepreneurs have played a role in creating a set of institutions that eventually received government attention and support.

Table 23.2 Institutional developments in support of BPO.[1]

Year	Period	Institutional Development(s)	Role in Industry	Public/ Private
2003	-	Mugure Mugo (PrecissPatrol) establishes first country-level marketing site	International Marketing	Private
	April	Export Processing Zone (EPZA) invites a number of firms involved in BPO to discuss how the EPZA could help them	Incentives	Public
2004	July	First BPO license/gateway (CCK) & EPZ license is granted to KenCall	Telecom Infrastructure	Public
2005	-	Sessional Paper No. 1 of 2005 on Policy Framework for Education, Training and Research aims to develop a national ICT education policy and strategy and also facilitate the formation of a National ICT coordination mechanism with sectoral committees to address specific sector training needs	Skills Development	Public
2006	-	Computer Society of Kenya conducts an ICT skills survey	Skills Development	Private
	March	Kenya National ICT Policy is launched	Policy	Public
	July	Ministry of Information and Communications commissions process to develop a strategy plan for BPO's	BPO Strategy Development	Public
2007	-	Kenya Transparency and Communication Infrastructure Project begins with assistance from the World Bank	Telecom Infrastructure	Public
	-	Freedom of Information Act, 2007 is passed by Parliament with provisions for data privacy and security	Policy Framework	Public
	-	Government starts process of constructing Submarine and Terrestrial fibre optic cable networks, The East African Marine Cable Systems (TEAMS) and the National Optic Fibre Backbone Infrastructure (NOFBI), respectively.	Telecom Infrastructure	Public
	-	Ministry of Education—KSH 600 million budget to ICT training in 2007/08, working with public/private providers.	Skills Development	Public
2008	Jan	CCK reduces BPO license fee from KSh 100,000 to 10,000	Incentives	Public
	Feb	Kenya ICT Board is established	Policy and BPO Strategy	Public
	March	Kenya BPO and Contact Centre Society is founded	Industry Mobilization	Private
	June	Augustana College launches Call Center Training	Skills Development	Private
	July	World Bank Bandwidth Incentive Scheme is launched	Telecom Infrastructure, Incentives	Public/ Private
		Government of Kenya allocates US$14.5 million to establish a modern BPO park, which will provide tax incentives to investors, while offering accessible, reliable, and affordable ICT services	Infrastructure, Incentives	Public
	Sept	University of Nairobi/IDRC commences study on BPO/call center sector	Policy and BPO Strategy	Public/ Private
	Oct	BPO becomes economic pillar of Vision 2030	Policy	Public
	Nov	Multimedia University College of Kenya is established under Legal Notice No. 155 of 2008 to provide industry-specific training for the country	Skills Development	Public

2009	-	Skills taskforce is set up by the Permanent secretary of the Ministry of Information and Communications to address any BPO/ITES skills gaps	Skills Development	Public
	May	Cabinet approves Special Economic Zones Policy (which includes special provision for BPO)	Incentives	Public
	June	Kenyan Government-sponsored TEAMS cable lands	Telecom Infrastructure	Public
	Summer-Fall	McKinsey & Company and the University of Nairobi/IDRC Study Teams commission and complete studies on the nascent sector	Policy and BPO Strategy	Public/ Private
	August	ICT Board officially launches its "Kenyan BPO Value Proposition"	International Marketing	Public
	Late 2009	African BPO Academy launches for skills development	Skills Development	Private
	Dec	High Level BPO/ITES Working Group is established	Policy and BPO Strategy	Public
2010	March	Kenya ICT Board launches Center of Excellence initiative to address skills gaps and employability in BPO/ ITES	Skills Development	Public
	June	International Institute for Outsource Management establishes its Africa charter and opens a Kenya office, offering Global Star Certification	Quality Assessment	Private
	Nov	Export Promotion Council launches strategic plan and strategy for Export Promotion of professional services in Kenya, including BPO	International Marketing	Public
2011	-	Pending Data Protection (Amendment) Bill in Cabinet and awaiting passage to Parliament	Policy	Public
	Early 2011	Kenya Methodist University in collaboration with the BPO Certifications Institute BCI USA launches courses in BPO, through the establishment of East Africa's very first International Centre for Outsourcing Studies (ICOS)	Skills Development	Private
	Jan	Jomo Kenyatta University of Agriculture and Technology (JKUAT) signs deal with Direct Channel Simba Tech Kenya to offer BPO and call center training	Skills Development	Public/ Private
	Feb	Konza Technology City funding is approved by Government	Incentives	Public
	Sept	NASSCOM signs MOU with Kenya ICT Board to cooperate on capacity development, ICT investment and trade promotion, Promote Innovation and Research	Industry Mobilization	Public

Source: Author.[2]

[1] This table is illustrative not exhaustive.

[2] The source for some institutional events is Mureithi (2007).

Challenges for Growing the Sector's Offshore Employment

In spite of the cluster's developments, Kenya's IT-enabled services cluster is very small in terms of employment. In 2007, it accounted for less than 0.01 percent of GDP, 500 seats and 1,000 employees (Office of the Prime Minister 2008: 78). According to the Kenya ICT Board, by 2011 there were an estimated 10,000 direct and indirect workers in IT-enabled services with 4,000 workers in BPO, contact centers, and software, including animation.[11] There are twenty-five BPO companies registered with CCK, though the actual number of BPO and contact center firms could be higher.[12] Most BPO and call center firms are 5–50-seat operations (Kariuki 2010: 5) (See Figure 23.1). In 2009–10, the sector created 619 direct BPO jobs and 4,168 jobs indirect jobs, only 8.3 percent of its Vision 2030 targets for the 2009–10 period (Ministry of State for Planning National Development and Vision 2030 2011: 77). In this section, the challenges to growing Kenya's IT-enabled services sector will be analyzed.

Labor

Labor is probably the greatest input to BPO or call center work. Kenya's quality and quantity of labor currently constrains its employment prospects and has led to a series of institutional developments for training in the sector. With respect to the *quantity* of its labor force, Kenya is at a disadvantage relative to other offshoring locations that com-

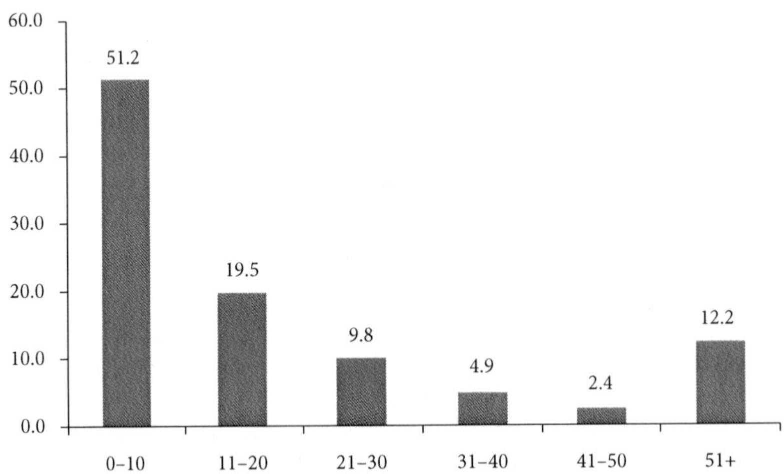

FIGURE 23.1 Percentages of Kenyan IT-enabled services firms at various seat capacities.

Source: Kenya ICT Board.[13]

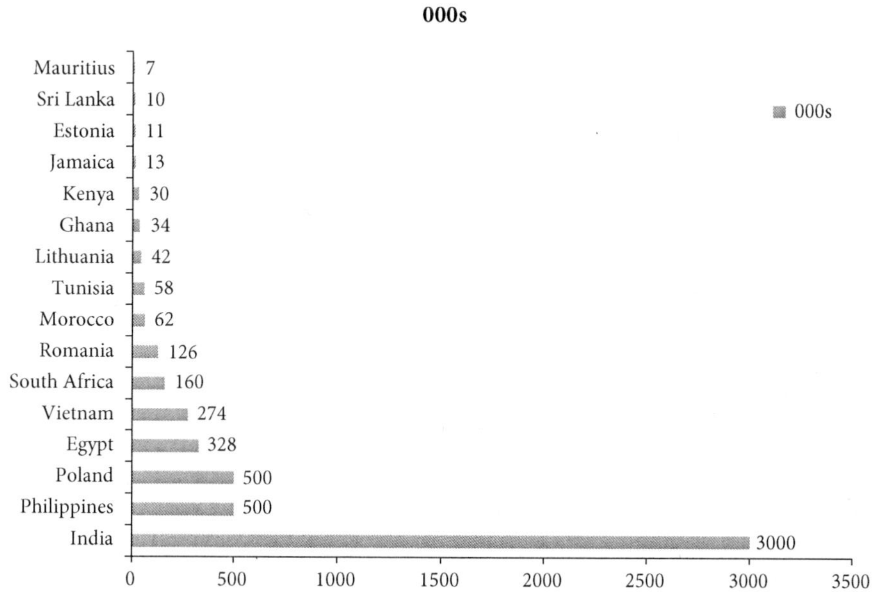

FIGURE 23.2 Annual tertiary education labor pool estimates by country (2009).

Source: Adapted from (Everest Research Institute, 2009:1).

pete for English language BPO and contact center work. In Figures 23.2 and 23.3, Kenya has significantly less labor than other locations in general and at the managerial levels.

Not just the *quantity*, but the *quality* of the labor force able to work in international BPO is critical. As part of McKinsey & Company's Value Proposition engagement for the Kenya ICT Board in 2009, they assessed how many out of the 30,000 university graduates (and 250,000 high school leavers) at the time were "ready to hire" for multinationals. According to the report at the time, only 5,000 graduates were suitable for employment in the industry (World Bank 2010: 31).[15] Kenya was constrained with respect to both

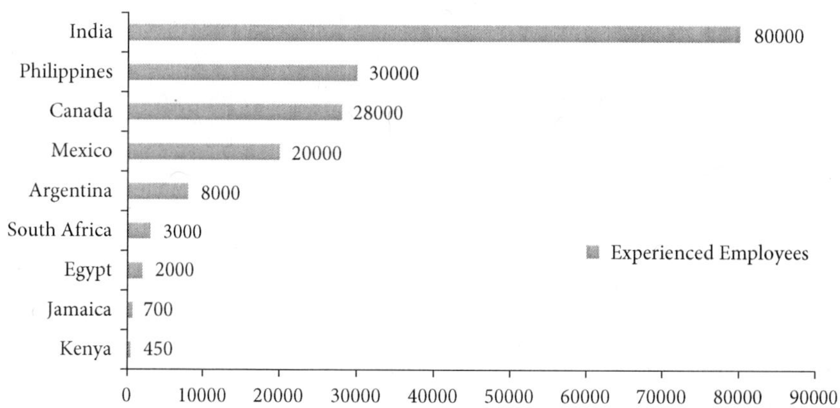

FIGURE 23.3 Experienced talent pool in BPO (2008).[14]

Source: (Everest Group and Letsema Consulting, 2008, p. 124).

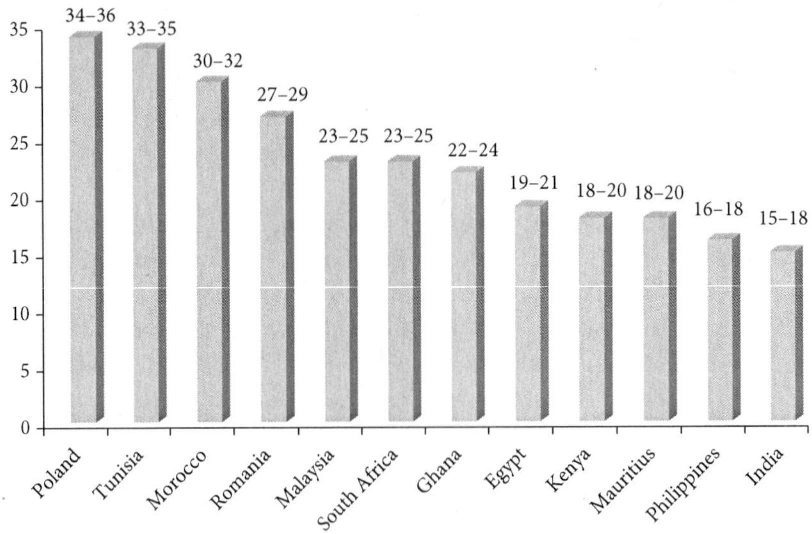

FIGURE 23.4 Direct operating cost per full-time employee (FTE) for transactional finance and accounting (F&A) (2009; US$ thousand per annum per FTE).

Source: Everest Research Institute (2009: 2).

population and talent, relegating it to lower-end services offshoring work like basic data and voice processing services (Sudan et al. 2010: 54, 59; Gathara 2010). But from a labor-cost arbitrage perspective, Kenya is relatively competitive. In both Figure 23.4 and Table 23.3, Kenya is shown to be relatively cost competitive, especially at the lower end of the services value chain. Kenya's challenge is in creating the scale of labor that is needed to attract multinationals as planned in Vision 2030.

In efforts to address Kenya's human resource quantity and quality constraints, various training programs have been launched. According to the 2010 Kenya ICT Board Survey, 73.5 percent of IT-enabled services firms facilitate their own in-house training, with huge costs for the BPO operators. For example, KenCall spends on average Sh10 million (US$133,802)[16] annually on in-house training (Juma 2009). As a result, the following

Table 23.3 Labor cost per hour per full-time equivalent for data processing (in US$)

Country	Data Processing	Voice Services	Knowledge	IT Services
United States	23.67	25.25	45.67	46.32
India	5.34	6.55	14.02	8.78
Indonesia	6.03	6.03	9.74	5.27
Kenya	4.41	4.85	12.73	7.50

Source: (Sudan et al. 2010: 64) based on McKinsey & Company 2008 Consultancy Inputs.

institutions have begun to offer BPO skills training: Multimedia University College of Kenya (industry-specific college established by the government for ICT skills development), Jomo Kenyatta University of Agriculture and Technology (JKUAT), Augustana College, Cambridge BPO training center, Horizon Call Centers, Direct Channel Call Centers, and Wisemen Trainers and Consultants (Kariuki 2010: 7). According to the Vision 2030 Medium Term Plan Progress Report, JKUAT trained 1,341 youth trained in BPO and entrepreneurship skills (Ministry of State for Planning National Development and Vision 2030 2011: 78). Other developments include the creation of the African BPO Academy by Gilda Odera, in partnership with the BPO Certification Institute (BCI), an international firm offering BPO standards, consultancy, and certification services.[17] The Kenya ICT Board is also planning the creation of a BPO Centre of Excellence to standardize BPO curricula and certification across the industry (Gathara 2010).

Telecommunications infrastructure

Like labor, telecommunications infrastructure is another critical input for the IT-enabled services cluster. A significant, if not overwhelming, portion of the expense of connecting to the internet from Africa is the cost of linking to distant international networks. Up until 2009, East Africa was the most poorly connected large region of the world (see Figure 23.5). In an effort to address East Africa's bandwidth poverty, several undersea fiber-optic cable projects were commenced, with the TEAMS (governments of Kenya and the United Arab Emirates) and SEACOM (privately funded) slated for arrival in mid to late 2009. Kenya developed a National Optic Fibre Backbone Infrastructure (NOFBI) project to facilitate access to affordable and reliable international telecommunication connectivity from the cable systems as well. Until the fiber infrastructure came, the World Bank provided a subsidy to BPO and call center firms relying on the outdated satellite infrastructure.[18]

With respect to the companies in the emerging sector, there were four general categories of responses to the arrival of the impending broadband infrastructure in 2009. The first response was that the rollout of the undersea fiber-optic cable (along with terrestrial fiber) would radically change the face of their businesses—both in terms of the range of services that could be delivered as well as the volume of work that could be done. Most BPO and contact center firms could not do voice work because of the quality (latency) and price (costs) of dialing over a satellite connection. Thus, the fiber represented an opportunity for Kenyan companies to truly exploit what they thought was their competitive advantage—voice. The second response was that fiber would not change the services the company offered but rather the volume of work they could perform. Several companies shared stories of how long it took to download multimedia files for transcription. Theoretically, if they were able to download more files in a shorter amount of time, they could get more business and thus employ more people. Therefore some managers saw bandwidth constraints as a bottleneck for business expansion and employment creation.

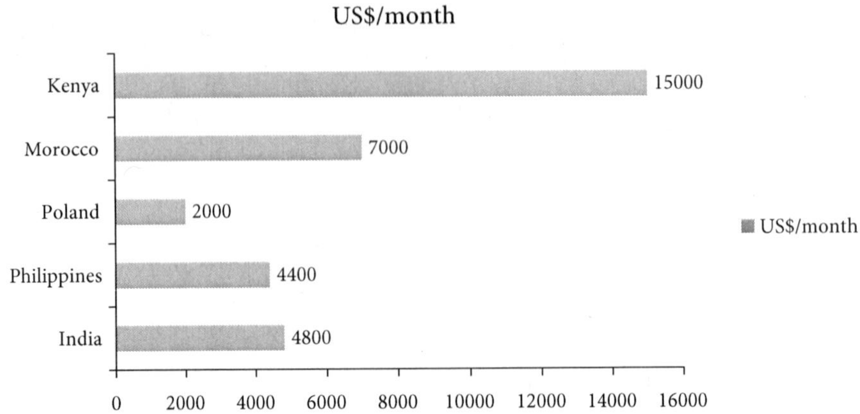

FIGURE 23.5 Telecom bandwidth cost for 2Mbps international leased line.[19]

Source: Kenya Ministry of Information and Communication, Telegeography, World Bank as cited in National Economic and Social Council (2007: 79).

The third response was that the presence of the undersea fiber-optic cables would help make Kenya a more attractive offsourcing destination. One of the consultants to the industry mentioned that some investors (interested in setting up a massive call center) would not locate their operations to a location without the presence of two or three undersea fiber-optic cables. Therefore, the fiber would essentially put Kenya on the global offshoring map. The fourth response (and one of the most interesting) is that fiber-optic cable developments would marginally, if at all, improve business processes, profitability, and expansion. They thought that ICT infrastructure was not the constraining factor for firm strategy but efficiency, the ability to secure contracts, and the track record of delivering projects on time and to the specification of the client(s).

Since 2009, the introduction of undersea fiber-optic cables has not led to the expected price reductions in the local market as promised. The wholesale international bandwidth was sold to local internet service providers, but in trying to recoup their investments they sold expensive broadband to the consumers. It has only been recently that the Kenyan market has experienced some price reductions (e.g., Kenya Data Networks announced a 30 percent price reduction in wholesale broadband prices in October 2010) (BMI 2011a: 39–41). There have been anecdotal reports of price reductions within some call centers (e.g., KenCall's operation pays US$600 per month instead of US$6,000 per month) (Southwood 2010). However, one senior manager within the industry commented (in January 2010) that the arrival of fiber had not led to a "commensurate increase in the amount of seats" (Kinyanjui 2010). Perhaps two things were overstated, first the contribution of telecommunications costs to a BPO operation (Table 23.4). The second thing that might have been overlooked is not just the physical infrastructure but the relational infrastructure that allows firms to integrate into the services offshore markets and procure the work.

Table 23.4 Typical percentage breakdown of the total cost of offshore

Cost Component	% cost for BPO	% cost for ITO
Wage rate	42	46
Communication system	5	3
Physical infrastructure and support	17	18
Transition and governance	8	7
Resource redeployment	3	4
Resource redundancy	2	1
Training and productivity	10	9
Disaster recovery & business continuity	5	3
Advisory services	2	4
Travel costs	3	3
Exchange-rate changes	2	3

Adapted from (Vashistha and Vashistha 2006).

Connecting to offshore markets

The relational infrastructure, not just the technical infrastructure, plays a significant role in the work that these firms are able to attract. Based on fieldwork and secondary research, Kenyan firms are integrated into the offshore services markets through at least seven ways (Figure 23.6). The first arrangement is through overseas sales agents. Early in the industry's origins and through 2009 during my fieldwork, I heard anecdotal reports that Kenyan companies hired brokers to match their firms with clients in offshore markets. Though not all narratives shared were negative, some brokers took advantage of the inexperience in the Kenyan market to get work done without

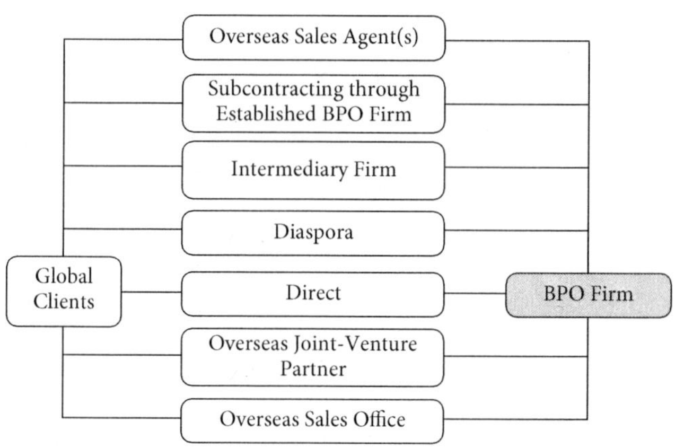

FIGURE 23.6 Linkages to offshore services markets.

Source: Author.

remitting payment (Mark 2007; Isenberg 2009: 3–4). In follow-up with several respondents within the industry, there is still reliance on the broker model as a primary source of business for some BPO operators. These "middle men" that generate business may extract the majority of rents from contracts, inhibiting growth for the Kenyan firms. The second model, the subcontractor model, is where more established BPO firms exclusively subcontract work to a smaller BPO venture in Kenya. An example of this is Paradigm Express in Kenya, which subcontracts work from Paradigm Infotech in India (Monitor Inclusive Markets 2011: 24).

The third way is through an intermediary firm based in the country of the prospective client market country or countries. Intermediary firms, like Samasource (and more recently Digital Divide Data), do marketing and client acquisition and relations, allowing the Kenyan firms to focus on service delivery. The fourth way that was cited by interview respondents is the Kenyan diaspora. One BPO manager said, "So we started to leverage on the networks of University X in the US. Also there is a fair number of Kenyans abroad who actually either went to University X or have one connection with University X and we tried to contact them and find out whether we could do something in this space." Later in the interview, he discussed how someone in his university network connected him to a senior employee of a company in the United States, helping them to procure their first BPO contract. In a similar way, a publicly available transcript published by Kenya's ICT Board on emerging players in the BPO Industry and members of the Kenyan diaspora in New York offers the following:

> In the role that I have with my employer, I was responsible for an operation that was channeling a fair amount of business probably in the range of $4 million to $5 million a year to outsourcing vendors, primarily in India, some South Africa and some Philippines. Over the last two years I have been able to move probably about 10 per cent of that business to operations in Kenya where people are doing between $500,000 and $750,000 in contracts with some Kenyan operations. It has been immensely satisfying for me on a personal level because I am Kenyan.

The fifth method is direct telemarketing (e.g., email, phone, web) channels to generate new sources of business. The sixth means is an overseas joint-venture partner where the joint-venture partner is usually located in a prospective client market abroad and focuses on marketing and sales while the Kenyan partner manages operations. This was the model that Gilda Odera used with the founding of Skyweb-Evans.

Seventh and finally, firms address the issue of getting clients by setting up marketing or other offices in target markets. According to the Kenya BPO Guidebook, Northwest Offshore Ltd had three marketing offices in Connecticut, Massachusetts, and Texas. Newbry, a BPO and call center firm had headquarters in Washington, DC, with offices in Nairobi. Arch-Link Consultants, a Kenyan architectural practice, had associate offices in the United States and Italy. SSI Kenya had teams in the United States and Kenya. And according to one of my interviewees, Preciss International, one of the first BPO firms in Kenya, has a representative based in the United Kingdom for marketing and sales while KenCall reportedly opened a London office in 2009 (Pflanz 2009).

According to many respondents and industry officials, overreliance on a number of these models has led to short-term contracts.[20] Some of the biggest and/or longest offshore contracts in the sector by local BPO and contact center firms have been forged through the intermediary (e.g., Samasource brokering a deal with TechnoBrain BPO for six months at 22.5 million KSh) and joint-venture models (Skyweb-Evans three-year contract). Other models do not appear to generate long-term offshore services contracts. However, there were exceptions. For example, Mugure Mugo sent unsolicited emails to her first clients for BPO work in 2002. Some of her clients have remained loyal for years and through to this day. This trust that she has built is what has made her a model of a firm in the emerging cluster and is the trust that the emerging cluster hopes to build through each of the seven models delineated.

Policies and incentives

Apart from Vision 2030, Kenya's policy framework for BPO also has roots in the ICT policy of 2006 which aimed to generate employment and promote entrepreneurship through IT, encourage investments in IT-enabled services, and provide adequate infrastructure. The Kenya Communications (Amendment) Bill, which was passed by parliament in December 2008 and signed by the president in January 2009, included a key section on e-transactions under Part VII, supporting the use of electronic records, electronic contracts, and digital signatures, as well as various dimensions of ICT and cyber crimes. One of the pending issues is that of data protection and privacy laws. Kenya's IT-enabled services sector has hitherto been constrained, from a policy perspective, by the lack of a framework protecting data transfers, especially from European Union member countries (Waema 2009: 24; TMG 2008: 43; Sudan et al. 2010: 69). Kenya has a Draft Data Protection Bill (2010), which was in the cabinet in early 2011 and awaited passage to parliament for enactment. With respect to incentives, BPO firms (like KenCall) are able to benefit from locating in export processing zones (EPZs) and will benefit from the special economic zones (SEZs), approved by cabinet in 2009, which will encourage both local and foreign investments and production of goods and services for both export and domestic markets (Kenya Ministry of Trade 2009).

Funding

Kenya's IT-enabled services firms are largely resource constrained from a start-up perspective. The majority of firms I spoke with started their firms from personal funds. Some of the small BPO and call center firms were unable to acquire loans because their intellectual assets did not qualify as collateral with the local banks. Some of the respondents mentioned that banks wanted land as collateral, making it difficult for some of them to start out. At the 2009 Nairobi Outsourcing and Shared Services Forum, there was a suggestion for government to develop more flexible policies for allowing SMEs to acquire bank loans for these information-based firms. However, I did find several exceptions. In one case, a bank supplied debt funding (early in the firm's formation) which was combined with money from family members, business partners, and overseas friends. And in a couple of other cases, the call center/BPO companies acquired equity financing. However, those companies received that funding five to seven years after those firms had been established.

My findings are corroborated by a study that identified a financing gap for ICT and ICT-enabled firms in Kenya seeking funding in the range of US$50,000–$500,000. Factors contributing to this gap include: (1) financing policies (banks hardly lend to SMEs and start-ups); (2) limited diffusion alternatives (where credit-guarantee schemes are available for agribusiness but not for IT-enabled services firms); (3) constraints on the demand side (entrepreneurs unfamiliar with equity instruments); and (4) understanding of ICT (bankers uncomfortable with new business models). On top of these factors, the initial investment in call centers tends to be more sizeable than for other IT-related ventures because of seat counts (e.g., 30–40+) and training costs (Zavatta et al. 2008: 1, 9). Typically, only large firms (like KenCall and Horizon Contact Centers) have access to sources of external start-up finance, including medium- and long-term finance (from African commercial banks), offshore borrowing, outside equity financing, venture capital, and equity (e.g., TBL Mirror Fund) (Fafchamps 2004: 434–436, 445–447). This financing gap means that the (few) firms that have access to significant cash up front in the start-up phase are able to build larger operations with more seat counts.[21]

Post-election violence and global economic recession

The confluence of post-election violence (2007–8) and the global economic recession reportedly slowed the sector and weakened offshore linkages. Kenya's image as the bastion of peace in East Africa was marred by the wave of violence throughout the country following the disputed presidential elections in December 2007. The violence which cost more than 1,000 lives ended in February 2008 when President Mwai Kibaki and Raila Odinga agreed to the creation of a coalition government. Most firm managers and industry stakeholders I spoke with shared a sober story about the role that post-election violence played in their companies and the industry at that time. Many companies shut down during the height of post-election violence, while prospective deals with transnational clients were tabled or canceled. In August 2010, Kenyans voted in favor of a new constitution addressing ethnic tensions, devolving power from the center and curbing executive and leadership powers. However, international investors may be deterred for some time because of this ethnic and political instability (Commonwealth Business Council and Cybermedia India 2009: 265; BMI 2011b: 8, 21; Sowinski 2010).

As the sector was faced with the political fallout, it was reportedly suffering from the global effects of the economic recession as well. Though some representatives in

Table 23.5 Summary of key cluster challenges

Issue	Challenge	Cluster Interventions
Labor	Quantity and quality of labor force	Creation of BPO training programs
Telecommunications Infrastructure	Lack of affordable and reliable undersea and terrestrial telecommunications connectivity	Commissioning of NOFBI and TEAMS projects, connecting with SEACOM, and World Bank subsidy assistance
Integrating into Offshore Services Markets	Lack of robust linkages to key client markets (US/UK)	In addition to direct marketing efforts, reaching offshore clients through overseas sales agent(s), subcontracting, intermediaries, diaspora, overseas joint venture partners, and overseas sales offices.
Policies and Incentives	Need for policy and incentive framework to support growing call centers and BPO	Vision 2030 Framework for BPO, ICT Policy 2006, Kenya Communications Amendment Bill, Draft Data Protection Bill, Draft Special Economic Zones Policy
Funding	Funding gap for BPO and call center firms	Commercial bank, venture capital, and private equity streams for more established BPO firms
Post-election violence and Global Financial crisis	These exogenous factors may have affected demand for IT-enabled services	Kenyan firms start to diversify geographically into domestic and near-shore (East African) markets

Source: Author.

the Kenyan IT-enabled services sector hoped the crisis would lead to more offshoring, the reality for some firms was exactly the opposite. One respondent mentioned, "If not for the financial service meltdown, we would be growing in leaps and bounds. Only a month ago Company A [US Financial Services Firm] told us they were going to reduce their head count with Company B [IT services company base in India] and increase ours in Kenya. All of that changed a week ago, when they announced they were closing their branch network [which is the unit we support from an IT perspective]."

Another recounted how, in light of the recession, potential offshoring contracts (through an intermediary) were canceled for onshore (US) service where tax incentives were offered to bring jobs back to America. Kenya (and many other developing countries) probably experienced the two effects of the economic recession: a general contraction in demand from existing customers as well as a substitution effect where new services were moved from developed economies to emerging economies. However, because this substitution effect was relegated to large developing-nation providers like India and the Philippines, more nascent services sectors like Kenya did not benefit from the substitution effect and as a result experienced weakened offshore linkages (Gereffi and Fernandez-Stark 2010). This confluence of political instability, global contraction of demand, and a nascent sector from a global perspective would lead the sector to look onshore (and nearshore) for market opportunities.

Shift to Domestic Outsourcing and Near-Shoring, 2009 to the Present

Kenya inherited the Indian export-oriented model as the archetype of an IT-enabled services sector. In fact, in 2007 (before post-election violence and effects of the global financial crisis), BPO had the highest export percentage turnover (90 percent) relative to other professional services sectors (e.g., legal services, accounting, insurance services, shipping and freight, banking, etc.) (Gicho and Kashangaki 2010: 13). Interviews with respondents and presentations by industry representatives revealed an export bias and a largely unexploited domestic market at the time.[22] However, the challenge of procuring contracts internationally led some operators to consider forging linkages onshore as well as nearshore with the East African economies (see Table 23.6). Northwest Offshore, which gathered data for fund managers on Wall Street, shifted its business to the local Kenyan market providing data management solutions (Kinyanjui 2010). KenCall and TechnoBrain-BPO began to penetrate the domestic insurance, nonprofit, and media sectors to remain afloat.[23] For example, TechnoBrain-BPO started offering an emergency helpline service for children and youth under the Department of Children Services while KenCall began managing a famine-relief campaign to help the government dispatch food to affected drought areas throughout the country (Mark 2011; Maalim and Were 2011). KenCall had also started to manage customer service for telecommunications firms in Tanzania (Riungu 2010).[24]

Within the domestic sector, some of the most significant outsourcing deals have been within the mobile telecommunications market. ICT has unarguably driven Kenya's economic growth over the past decade, growing on average by 20 percent annually and outperforming all other sectors (Figure 23.7) and there has been phenomenal growth in the growth of mobile phone subscriptions (Figure 23.8). The growing market has led to new market entrants and a price war where average revenue per user (ARPU) has fallen to amongst the lowest in Africa (BMI 2011b). The mobile competition has led new market entrants to cut costs by outsourcing noncore functions, including customer care. As a result, KenCall and Horizon Contact Centers have started to do customer service for Orange (formerly Telkom) Kenya, Horizon Contact Centers (formerly Aegis Services Kenya) does customer service for Essar Telecom Kenya Limited (yu), and Spanco Raps Kenya Ltd does customer service and back office work for Airtel Africa (across Kenya, Tanzania, Burkina Faso, Chad, Niger, and part of Nigeria) (Southwood 2010; Isenberg 2009: 8; Ochieng 2010; Nyabiage 2011; Kimutai 2011). Kenya's ICT revolution, especially in mobile, is not disconnected from the growth of domestic BPO opportunities in the area of customer care.

Despite the opportunities in mobile, there are challenges to growing the domestic segment of local BPO operators' portfolios. First, representatives in the BPO sector cite a lack of trust and data privacy as a potential barrier for local outsourcing, particularly in the banking, financial services, and insurance segment. In a recent study

Table 23.6 Respondents' views concerning international and domestic outsourcing.

	International	Domestic
Opportunities and Benefits	• Higher Margins • Credibility and World-Class Service that can be leveraged for Domestic Outsourcing • Foreign Companies understand outsourcing concept • Opportunity to Build Kenya as Global Brand for Offshoring • Attraction of FDI into the country can employ thousands of Kenyans, esp. youth	• Opportunity to gain experience and develop capacity to outsource • Credibility for International Outsourcing • Opportunity to deliver shared services to public sector and international NGO Sector based in Nairobi • Does not require accent neutralization • Potential clients are a car ride away, not a plane ride away • Domestic contracts are not necessarily cancelled because of international events (e.g., global economic recession, American political backlash to offshoring) • Legal recourse for due payment within territorial borders
Challenges, Disadvantages, and Risks	• Intense competition from India, Philippines, and the rest of the world • Stringent SLAs to meet, esp. strict infrastructural and human resource requirements • Intermediary company or broker may not pay for work rendered • International bandwidth very expensive and unreliable (dropped calls) • US (Obama) administration does not like offshoring • International market wants to know that you have a domestic track record • Need for legal incorporation (and/or) onshore presence in client country(ies) • Steep learning curve • Global Economic Recession contracts demand for offshoring	• Lower margins than international contract • Outsourcing is a new concept—private sector is agnostic or antagonistic towards the concept • Domestic Market Takes a long time to sell • Payment in domestic market is slow • Fear about information confidentiality—information could be passed on to a competitor • Lack of confidence in local operators

Source: Author.

of outsourcing in Kenya's commercial banks, customer account processing was the least outsourced function in the sector, with no banks outsourcing the function at the time (2008). The author of the research article explained that it had to do with the principle of confidentiality and explained that Kenya's banks associated outsourcing with "high reputational, operational, strategic and contractual risks" (Barako and Gatere 2008: 37). Second, the recent growth of local captive (or in-house) contact center operations (e.g., Safaricom Jambo Contact Centre, Kenya Commercial Bank, Barclays Bank, Co-operative Bank of Kenya) was viewed as a sign that local

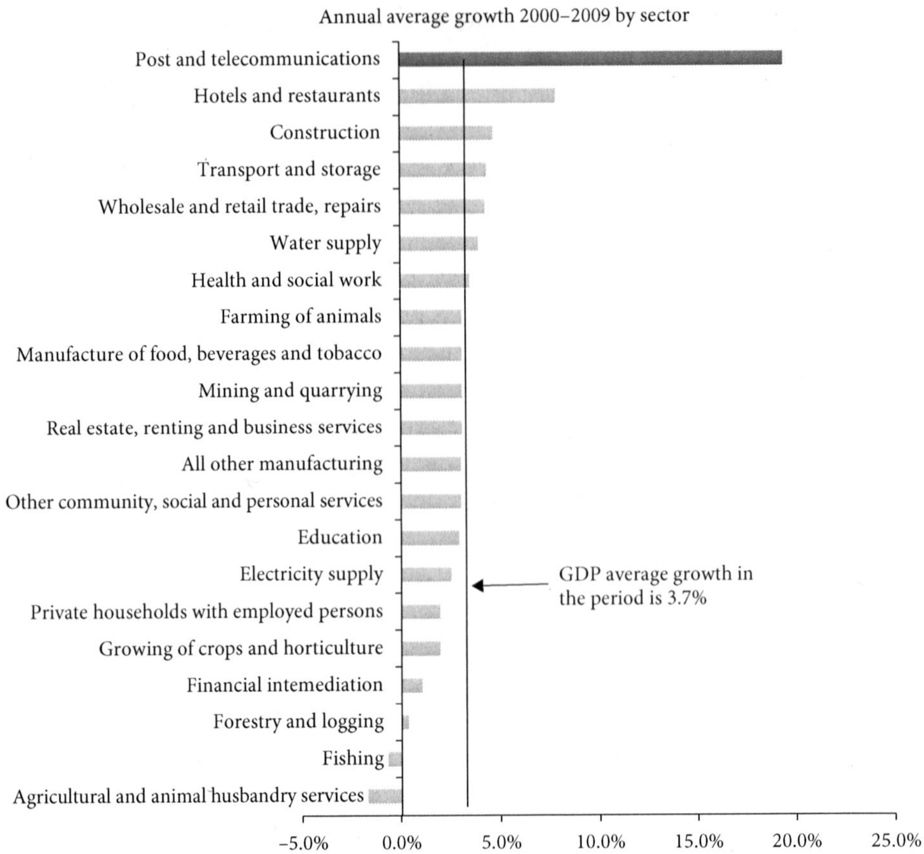

FIGURE 23.7 Since 2000, the telecom sector outperformed all sectors in the economy.

Source: Kenyan National Bureau of Statistics and World Bank staff estimates (World Bank 2010: 13).

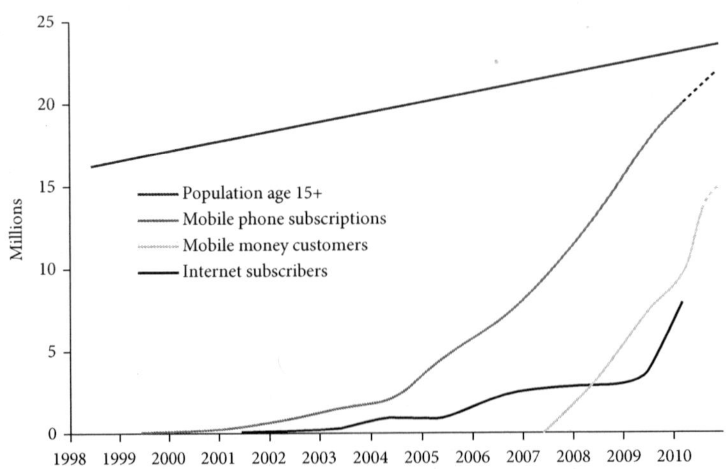

FIGURE 23.8 Growth of mobile and Internet in Kenya.

Source: International Telecommunications Union, KNBS, World Bank Projections (World Bank 2010: vi).

operators did not have the capacity to deliver customer service functions for these large local blue-chip firms (Bohnstedt 2009; Ouma 2009).[25] It will undoubtedly take time before local BPO and call center operators overcome—if they do—these challenges with respect to confidentiality, data security, and overall capacity to serve the local sector.

Discussion: What IT-Enabled Services Has Contributed in Spite of Low Employment

Offshore services, institutional creation, and cluster development

The Vision 2030 Medium Term Progress Report documented that the Kenyan IT-enabled services sector created 619 jobs in 2009–10, only 8.3 percent of the projected target in the first medium-term plan. Based on this progress, it is unlikely that the sector will achieve its employment targets in the short term. However, the promise of massive employment through offshore linkages has catalyzed a process of institutional creation and reform. The institutional developments are driven by the need to make Kenya a more attractive location for offshoring by building the stock of human resources, addressing the country's telecommunications constraints, supporting local BPO operators, and creating an enabling environment for offshored work. Nicholas Nesbitt's forty to fifty meetings with the Kenyan Government and the Communication Commission of Kenya would eventually create a new license category for BPO operators in the country. Gilda Odera's leadership, in helping form the Kenya BPO and Contact Center Society, would serve as a body promoting external economies of market information as well as joint action for lobbying government and creating draft industry standards. The human capital constraints would lead existing colleges and industry representatives to start training programs for BPO-specific skills. In line with Vision 2030, the government has also created bodies with strong support for BPO, including the Kenya ICT Board and the High-Level BPO/ITES Working Group. Key entrepreneurs and policy makers have played a role in developing the policy framework conducive for the sector, from transitioning the export processing zones policy to special economic zones to lobbying and assisting in the processes for the Data Protection Bill and Kenya Communications (Amendment) Bill. The confluence of high unemployment (40 percent in 2008) and US$250 million market opportunity in basic data and voice services (according to McKinsey & Company estimates) were contributing factors to this institution-building. Whether Kenya achieves its job targets or not is unknown. But what are empirically known are these institutional creations.

This process has been driven by a small constellation of actors—entrepreneurs—that while acting in their own interests are building the foundations of institutions that constitute the IT-enabled services cluster. The individual actions of entrepreneurs led to the creation of an evolving cluster which was manifest as joint action and external economies. Joint action and external economies were in response to challenges entrepreneurs faced in building either their firms or the cluster at large. The impediments to growing the firm and/or the cluster led the entrepreneurs to work together with others in the cluster (joint action) to create and build the necessary resources, institutions, and interventions in the cluster to meet their needs (external economies), whether it be a supply of labor, telecommunications, incentives, etc. What is unique about this case with respect to other examples of cluster genesis in high-technology sectors is that these entrepreneurs played a role not only in the creation of cluster-specific institutions but also in the roll-out of quasi-public goods like telecommunications infrastructure and educational organizations. A resource-constrained context like Kenya means that entrepreneurs building a cluster may not only build institutions addressing their cluster-specific needs but also broader constraints in the economy. The effectiveness of these institutions remains to be seen but this institutional creation answers, in part, a question of how clusters emerge. It begins to answer how nonmarket institutions for labor supply, policy and incentive creation, and telecommunications development develop in response to perceived and/or empirical challenges.

Weak offshore linkages as an opportunity to escape export enclavity

Kenya's limited success (as measured by its ability to reach its midterm Vision 2030 targets) in the offshore market created an opportunity for it to forge links with the domestic economy and overcome potential enclave economic effects. Local operators redeployed offshore competencies of customer care and BPO into the local market for the telecommunications, government, and non-profit sectors. In some ways, exogenous events like the global economic recession, post-election violence, and Kenya's telecommunications price war redirected the course of the sector early on such that it is not as outward-facing as the Indian sector it sought to emulate. India's export-oriented software sector, with limited links with the domestic economy, is spatially concentrated and has limited interindustry links (Arora and Athreye 2002: 272; Commander 2005: 23). Kenya's IT-enabled services sector, like the India software sector, did not really grow out of links with related sectors that served as sources of competency or demand like other countries (Ireland, Israel, Brazil, China) (Arora and Gambardella 2005: 7). However, at the end of its first decade it is establishing links with the telecommunications sector in particular because of Africa's mobile revolution. And as the sector is developing, it is resembling call center industries across the world which—unlike India—"serve a domestic market and in which large, outsourced call centers are the exception, rather than the rule" (Benner et al. 2007: 7). The inability to forge strong offshore linkages may be an opportunity to "reach for the nearest leaf," as one respondent remarked in the course of fieldwork.

Conclusion

If there is any discernible success in the nascent sector, it is in its ability to create institutions and redirect its market strategy. The institutions created thus far have laid a foundation which could support this emerging sector but have the potential to aid other sectors that could benefit from telecommunications infrastructure, the enabling policy frameworks put in place, and the capacity-building programs which can prepare Kenyans for a number of other careers as well.

Notes

1. Kenya's IT-enabled services (ITES) sector includes business process outsourcing (BPO), call center, and software development firms. I focus on BPO and call center firms because it is the segment of the ITES sector I studied in the context of fieldwork as well as the aspect of the ITES sector with the most market intelligence. Up until recently, this was the dimension of the ITES sector that has received, and to some extent still receives, the most attention in the Kenyan context.
2. Growing firms means creating sustained sources of economic rents and not just registering new companies. Examples of this growth in output include growth in revenue, thereby impacting employment (e.g., call center seat count).
3. www.outsourcetokenya.biz
4. Mureithi (2007).
5. This was through a Canadian International Development Agency (CIDA) grant. Some of the agents trained in that program have gone on to lead and manage major BPO and call center operations throughout the nascent cluster.
6. Assuming Exchange rate of 1USD = 66.78103KSh (2007 Yearly Average).
7. To put this FDI strategy in perspective, South Africa had 79,000 call center workers (captive and outsourced) in 2002 and managed to attract 9 major multinationals in the period 2003–2009 according to its latest BPO value proposition (i.e., 9 major MNCs in 6 years). Kenya by comparison had no more than 1,000 workers (captive and outsourced) in 2007 and intended to attract 10 multinationals in 4 years.
8. This strategy (developed by McKinsey & Company) for the Government of Kenya, would largely set the institutional agenda for the Kenya ICT (Information and Communication Technology) Board that would later be formed.
9. Personal Communication with Eunice Kariuki, Marketing Officer, Kenya ICT Board, June 21, 2011.
10. www.konzacity.co.ke.
11. This figure includes BPO and contact center operators as well as captive (in-house) operations by local blue-chip firms (e.g., Safaricom and Kenya Commercial Bank). No formal market sizing, skills audit or registry has been conducted in Kenya. Source: Personal Communication with Eunice Kariuki, Marketing Director for Kenya ICT Board, June 21, 2011.
12. KBPOCCS firm registration, recent presentations by and personal communication with industry representatives put the number of BPO firms at 50–60 rather than 25. Source: P. Were, 2010, "A Case Study of the ITES Industry in Kenya" 2nd Pan Commonwealth

Conference on Services Trade—Mauritius and Paul Kukubo, CEO, Kenya ICT Board, e-mail communication, March 26, 2009. Also, T. M. Waema, "Development of a Business Process Outsourcing Industry in Kenya: Critical Success Factors," 2009.

13. The results are from an online survey of the BPO industry organized by the Kenya ICT Board August–October 2010. Fifty-six firms were represented in the survey. Source: Personal Communication with Andrew Lewela Mwanyota, Project Manager, BPO/IT-Enabled Service, Kenya ICT Board (June 15, 2011) and Prof. Timothy Waema, University of Nairobi (June 13, 2011).
14. Includes supervisors/teams leads and managers in services (suppliers and offshore captives).
15. While in Kenya, there was considerable controversy over these findings which significantly discounted the labor pool for multinationals. However, by comparison, research by McKinsey Global Institute established that only 13 percent of university graduates from twenty-eight low-wage nations are suitable for multinationals. Factors limiting the talent pool include lack of practical skills, insufficient English proficiency, suitable talent not residing in major international hubs, and lack of cultural fit with multinational norms. The low-wage nations are Argentina, Brazil, Bulgaria, Chile, China, Colombia, Croatia, Czech Republic, Estonia, Hungary, India, Indonesia, Latvia, Lithuania, Malaysia, Mexico, Philippines, Poland, Romania, Russia, Slovakia, Slovenia, South Africa, Thailand, Turkey, Ukraine, Venezuela, and Vietnam. Furthermore, in India, the suitability of Indian grads for multinationals ranges from 10 to 25 percent. Farrell and McKinsey Globa Institute (2006).
16. Assumes US$1 = 74.73711 (2009 yearly rate).
17. http://www.africanbpoacademy.com.
18. In the first installment of the subsidy scheme (July 2007 to February 2009), only seven out of twenty-three companies that applied for the subsidy qualified to receive it. The combination of stringent criteria for the firms and the lack of price reductions five months following the arrival of the fiber optic cables systems would lead to only $508, 937.29 of the budgeted $7 million subsidy being disbursed in this first phase. The subsidy program was extended, based on the same set of criteria, and according to the Vision 2030 Mid-Term Report, thirty-eight BPO operators received the subsidy T. M. Waema, 2009, *Development of a Business Process Outsourcing Industry in Kenya: Critical Success Factors*, Mark (2010). Nairobi, Ministry of State for Planning National Development and Vision 2030 (2011) *Second Annual Progress Report on the Implementation of the First Medium Term Plan (2008–2012) of Kenya Vision 2030*. Nairobi: Government of the Republic of Kenya.
19. Based on an E1 connection (2Mbps) to the United Kingdom.
20. Paul Kukubo, CEO, Kenya ICT Board, e-mail communication, March 26 2009.
21. KenCall and Horizon Contact Centers, the largest BPO operations in Kenya, both started with multi-million dollar investments. Horizon Contact Centers reportedly started with an estimated investment of US$6 million. Nesbitt raised $470,000 from his personal network while convincing a Kenyan bank to lend him $1 million in debt. Source: Isenberg (2009).
22. T. Waema, "Introduction and Preliminary Observations." Mid-term Presentation for Development of BPO Industry in Kenya, "Critical Success Factors," December 10, 2008; P. Were, "BPO Trends, SWOT, Niche Areas," Stakeholder's Workshop Presentation for

Development of BPO Industry in Kenya, "Critical Success Factors," Kenyatta International Conference Centre, July 1, 2009.

23. According to Nicholas Nesbitt, 30 percent of his work is offshore. (personal communication, June 13, 2011)
24. KenCall reportedly hired 100 people from Mombasa, Kenya's coastal region, to serve Tanzania's Swahili-speaking market for Zain Tanzania. Mombasa residents speak with a Swahili intonation and fluency that is similar to the Tanzanian accent. KenCall had reportedly served Tigo Tanzania (telecom firm) as well.
25. Another industry view is that the creation of captive contact centers is for the purpose of developing in-house standards. Over time, mature customer service functions can be outsourced to local operators.

References

Arora, A., and S. Athreye. 2002. "The Software Industry and India's Economic Development." *Information Economics and Policy* 14: 253–273.

Arora, A., and A. Gambardella. 2005. "The Globalization of the Software Industry: Perspectives and Opportunities for Developed and Developing Countries." *Innovation Policy and the Economy* 5: 1–32.

Barako, D. G., and P. K. Gatere. 2008. Outsourcing practices of the Kenyan banking sector. *African Journal of Accounting, Economics, Finance and Banking Research* 2: 37–50.

Benner, C., C. Lewis, and R. Omar. 2007. "The South African Call Centre Industry: A Study of Strategy, Human Resource Practices and Performance." Part of the Global Call Centre Industry Project.

BMI. 2011a. *Kenya Telecommunications Report Q2 2011*. London: Business Monitor International.

———. 2011b. *Kenya Telecommunications Report Q3 2011*. London: Business Monitor International.

Bohnstedt, A. 2009. "KenCall Leads Call-centre Charge." *African Business*.

Bresnahan, T., Gambardella, A., and Saxenian, A. 2005. "'Old Economy' Inputs for 'New Economy' Outcomes: Cluster Formation in the New Silicon Valleys." In *Clusters, Networks, and Innovation,* edited by S. Breschi and F. Malerba. Oxford and New York: Oxford University Press.

Commander, S. 2005. "What Explains the Growth of a Software Industry in Some Emerging Emerging Markets." In *The Software Industry in Emerging Markets,* edited by S. Commander. Cheltenham, UK, and Northhampton, MA: Edward Elgar.

Commonwealth Business Council and Cybermedia India. 2009. "Country report for Kenya." *Outsourcing to Africa: A Relative Ranking of 15 Country Locations*. London: Commonwealth Business Council.

Everest Group and Letsema Consulting. 2008. "Ready to Compete: South Africa's BPO Capabilities in the Financial Services Sector."

Everest Research Institute 2009. *Curtain Raiser: Offshoring to Africa*. Dallas: Everest Research Institute.

Fafchamps, M. 2004. *Market Institutions in Sub-Saharan Africa: Theory and Evidence.* Cambridge, MA: MIT Press.

Farrell, D., and McKinsey Global Institute. 2006. *Offshoring: Understanding the Emerging Global Labor Market* Boston, MA: Harvard Business School Press.

Feldman, M. P., and J. L. Francis. 2004. "Homegrown Solutions: Fostering Cluster Formation." *Economic Development Quarterly* 18: 127–137.

Feldman, M., J. L. Francis, and J. Bercovitz. 2005. "Creating a Cluster While Building a Firm: Entrepreneurs and the Formation of Industrial Clusters." *Regional Studies* 39: 129–141.

Gathara, P. 2010. "As Kenya Gears up for Looming BPO Market, Its Vital Not to Dumb Down." *East African*. Nairobi.

Gereffi, G., and K. Fernandez-Stark. 2010. *The Offshore Services Value Chain: Developing Countries and the Crisis*. Washington, DC: World Bank.

Gicho, R., and Kashangaki, J. 2010. *Assessment of Kenya's export potential and supply capacities in selected professional service sectors*. Nairobi: World Bank, Export Promotion Council.

Giuliani, E., R. Rabellotti, and M. P. V. Dijk. 2005. Introduction. In *Clusters Facing Competition: The Importance of External Linkages*, edited by E. Giuliani, R. Rabellotti, and M. P. V. Dijk. Aldershot, UK, and Burlington, VT: Ashgate.

Goldstein, A. 2005. "Lead Firms and Clusters in the North and in the South: A Comparison of the Aerospace Industry in Montreal and São José dos Campos." In *Clusters Facing Competition: The Importance of External Linkages*, edited by E. Giuliani, R. Rabellotti, and M. P. V. Dijk. Aldershot, UK, and Burlington, VT: Ashgate.

Isenberg, D. 2009. *KenCall: Can Nik Nesbitt's Venture Succeed in Kenya?* Boston: Harvard Business School Press.

Juma, V. 2009. "Colleges Rush to Plug Skills Gap in Sector." *Business Daily Africa*. Nairobi.

Kariuki, E. 2010. "Progress Report: Implementation of the McKinsey BPO/ITES Study Recommendations." Nairobi.

Kenya ICT Board 2008. *Our Service Charter*. Nairobi: Kenya ICT Board.

Kenya Ministry of Trade 2009. *Draft Policy on Special Economic Zones*. Nairobi: Ministry of Trade.

Kimutai, C. 2011. "Spanco Eyes Kenya's Lucrative BPO Sector." *BiztechAfrica*.

Kinyanjui, K. 2010. "Two Faces of BPO Sector Linked to Lack of Vision." *Business Daily Africa*. Nairobi.

Maalim, A. & Were, E. 2011. "Toll-free Line for People in Need of Food Launched." *Nairobi Star*. Nairobi.

Mark, O. 2007. "Conmen Invade Call Centres With Vague Deals." *Business Daily*. Nairobi.

———. 2010. "Boost for BPO Firms As Subsidy Deal is Extended." *Business Daily Africa*. Nairobi.

———. 2011. "Kenyan BPOs Diversify as Foreign Rivals Turn Up the Heat." *Business Daily Africa*. Nairobi.

Marshall, A. 1920. *Principles of Economics: An Introductory Volume*, London: Macmillan.

McCormick, D. 2007. "Industrialization through Cluster Upgrading: Theoretical Perspectives." In *Industrial clusters and innovation systems in Africa: institutions, markets and policy*, edited by B. Oyelaran-Oyeyinka and D. McCormick. Tokyo and New York: United Nations University Press.

Ministry of State for Planning National Development and Vision 2030. 2011. *Second Annual Progress Report on the Implementation of the First Medium Term Plan (2008–2012) of Kenya Vision 2030*. Nairobi: Government of the Republic of Kenya.

Monitor Inclusive Markets. 2011. *Job Creation through Building the Field of Impact Sourcing.* New York: Rockefeller Foundation.

Mureithi, M. 2007. "Kenya at the Tipping Point: Business Process Outsourcing Set for Growth." In *ICT Sector Competitiveness—Negotiating Business Process Outsourcing: Case Studies From Africa Presentations.* (March).

National Economic and Social Council. 2007. *Kenya Vision 2030: A Globally Competitive and Prosperous Kenya.* Nairobi: Government of the Republic of Kenya.

Nyabiage, J. 2011. "Essar Kenya Gets New CEO." *The Nation.* Nairobi.

Ochieng, Z. 2010. "Taking Outsourcing to the Horizon." *CIO East Africa.* Nairobi.

Office of the Prime Minister (Kenya). 2008. *Kenya Vision 2030: First Medium Term Plan (MTP) 2008–2012.* Nairobi: Government of the Republic of Kenya.

Ouma, M. 2009. "Outsource Our Jobs? Why Firms Are Afraid of BPOs." *East African.* Nairobi.

Pflanz, M. 2009. Kenya joins outsourcing fast track Belated broadband connection threatens India's grip on call centres. *The Daily Telegraph.* London, Telegraph Group Limited.

Pietrobelli, C., and R. Rabellotti. 2006. "Clusters and Value Chains in Latin America: In Search of an Integrated Approach." In *Upgrading to Compete: Global Value Chains, Clusters, and SMEs in Latin America,* edited by C. Pietrobelli and R. Rabellotti. Washington, DC: Inter-American Development Bank.

Porter, M. E. 1998. "Clusters and Competition: New Agendas for Companies, Governments, and Institutions." In *On Competition,* edited by M. E. Porter. Boston, MA: Harvard Businesss School Press.

Ragin, C. C. 1989. *The Comparative Method: Moving beyond Qualitative and Quantative Strategies.* Berkeley: University of California Press.

Riungu, C. 2010. "Service Sector to Drive Kenya's Economy: Report." *East African.* Nairobi.

Schmitz, H. 1995. "Small Shoemakers and Fordist Giants: Tale of a Supercluster." *World Development* 23: 9–28.

———. 2004. "Globalized Localities: Introduction." In *Local Enterprises in the Global Economy: Issues of Governance and Upgrading,* edited by H. Schmitz. Cheltenham, UK, and Northhampton, MA: Edward Elgar.

Singer, B. 2006. "Start-Up Vies for Outsourcing Pie." *The Nation.* Nairobi.

Southwood, R. 2010. "KenCall Sees the Growth of New Local Outsourcing Opportunities." *Balancing Act Africa.*

Sowinski, L. L. 2010. "The Rebirth of a Nation." *World Trade,* 23.

Sudan, R., S. Ayers, P.Dongier, A. Muente-Kunigami, and C. Z.-W. Qiang. 2010. *The Global Opportunity in IT-based Services: Assessing and Enhancing Country Competitiveness.* Washington, DC: International Bank for Reconstruction and Development, World Bank.

TMG. 2008. *Trade in Information and Communication Services: Opportunities for East and Southern Africa: Final Report on Kenya, Tanzania and Uganda.* Telecommunications Management Group.

UNCTAD (United Nations Conference on Trade and Development). 2003. *E-Commerce and Development Report 2003.* New York and Geneva: UNCTAD.

Vashistha, A., and A. Vashistha. 2006. *The Offshore Nation: Strategies for Success in Global Outsourcing and Offshoring.* New York: McGraw-Hill.

Waema, T. M. 2009. Development of a Business Process Outsourcing Industry in Kenya: Critical Success Factors.

World Bank. 2010. *Kenya Economic Update: Kenya at the Tipping Point? With a Special Focus on the ICT Revolution and Mobile Money.* Nairobi: World Bank.

Yin, R. K. 1994. *Case Study Research: Design and Methods*. Thousand Oaks: Sage.

Zavatta, R., Economisti Associati SRL, Zernike Group BV, and Meta Group SRL. 2008. *Financing Technology Entrepreneurs & SMEs in Developing Countries: Challenges and Opportunities.* Washington, DC: World Bank.

CHAPTER 24

Industrial Strategy, Offshoring, and Employment Promotion in South Africa

MIRIAM ALTMAN[1]

Abbreviations

BFSI	banking, financial services, and insurance
BPA/P	Business Processing Association of the Philippines
BPeSA	Business Process Enabling South Africa
BPO	business process outsourcing
BPO&O	business process outsourcing and offshoring
DTI	Department of Trade and Industry, South Africa
FAO	finance and accounting outsourcing
FDI	foreign direct investment
GAS	Government Assistance and Support program, South Africa
GDP	gross domestic product
HRO	human resources outsourcing
ICT	information communication technologies
IPAP	Industrial Policy Action Plan, South Africa
ITES	information technology-enabled services
IT/ITO	information technology/information technology outsourcing
KPO	knowledge process outsourcing
MNC	multinational corporation
NASSCOM	National Association of Software Services Companies, India
O&O	offshoring and outsourcing
R&D	research and development
SACCCOM	South African Contact Centre Community
SETA	Sector Education and Training Authority

1 Introduction

South Africa has an extremely high rate of unemployment, in a middle-income country with substantial capability in service industries. Business process outsourcing and offshoring (BPO&O) presents as one of the few rapidly expanding global opportunities in which South Africa might generate large numbers of jobs in traded activities. BPO&O is essentially a new activity, enabled by the diffusion of broadband and internet services over the 2000s. Yet, to date, India and the Philippines are the only developing countries to have positioned effectively to the result of generating large employment numbers.

This chapter reviews the global positioning of South Africa for BPO&O industrial expansion. BPO&O is first defined and a review of global context considered. Since India and the Philippines are the market leaders, explanations for their success are presented. The chapter then considers the experience of one emergent entrant to BPO&O, namely South Africa, and its attempts to gain a greater share of this market.

2 Patterns of business process outsourcing and offshoring

2.1 Definitions and classifications

Historically, business services would have been undertaken mostly within firms or in face-to-face interactions with others. The increased penetration of broadband internet has enabled the emergence of extended relationships outside firms and across borders. This explains the rapid expansion and growing sophistication of business process outsourcing (BPO) over the past decade.

Understanding and measuring BPO and BPO&O activity are challenges. Data are poor on ITES offshoring and outsourcing (Gereffi and Fernandez-Stark 2010a, 2010b; Kierkegaard 2008). As the industry expands, existing statistical classifications are proving inadequate for measuring relevant trends (Sako 2005). While offshored services are captured through foreign direct investment (FDI) data (inward FDI flows) and through trade-in-services data, the data are neither consistent nor complete. There is no standard industrial classification that captures BPO&O activity statistically. The representation of trends often relies on nonscientific measures offered by business associations, sector-based consulting firms, or the press. This makes scrutiny of data near impossible. Moreover, reports may mix definitions, so it is not always clear what is included or excluded in any representation.

Business process *outsourcing* refers to service functions that are information intensive and that are transferred outside a company to a third party. Sometimes BPO data include captive services, where, for example, a company operates a call center as a separate cost or profit center for its own operations. Business process *offshoring* refers to a shift of service operations and functions beyond a nation's borders. *Captive offshoring* occurs where a company establishes BPO outside its country border in the form of a subsidiary primarily for its own purposes.

The various outsourced and offshored functions are often categorized as all falling under the umbrella of BPO&O. However, strictly speaking, this is not a correct assignment. There are three main categories: knowledge process outsourcing (KPO), information technology outsourcing (ITO), and business process outsourcing (BPO).

BPO specifically refers to activities such as customer relationship management, human resource management, and enterprise resource management. Although BPO encompasses the widest range of skills, from call centers often requiring only a high-school diploma to complex financial services, it mostly falls into the low- to middle-skills range. ITO, as the name suggests, refers to outsourcing of IT services such as software development. The range of ITO services can require low- to high-skill personnel. KPO encompasses specialist activities that are knowledge intensive, such as research and development (R&D), market intelligence, and legal services, and are considered to be at the high-skill end of the spectrum.

ITO, KPO, and BPO are "horizontal activities" that are generic to different industries. "Vertical activities" are specific to industries. The sectors with the highest demand for offshore services are banking, financial services, and insurance (BFSI), manufacturing, telecommunications, energy, travel and transportation, health and pharmaceuticals, and retail. For example, a company in the BFSI sector might be active in finance and accounting outsourcing (FAO), ITO, KPO, it might run a contact center and/or be engaged in some other horizontal activity. The telecommunications sector might likewise outsource any of these activities.

While the diffusion of internet and telecommunications services has facilitated the expansion of the industry, not all of these activities take place online. Voice-based activities, such as contact centers, take place online and therefore the quality and cost of telecommunications are key competitive factors. Call centers are the lowest end of BPO and therefore also compete on labor cost. However, most other functions can take place with intermittent online activity, as information can be downloaded and processed offline. In such cases, the country will compete on skill and capability.

2.2 Global expansion of BPO&O

Offshore services have grown dramatically over the past decade. Conservative estimates put this expansion at about 26 percent annually between 2005 and 2010. Contact centers account for about 10 percent of the global BPO market, and ITO remains dominant at about 60 percent of the global offshore service market (Everest Group 2009b). Conservative estimates are that ITO will continue growing at 6–9 percent per year, and will be overtaken by BPO, which is expected to continue growing by 10–15 percent per year (Gereffi and Fernandez-Stark 2010b; Oshri et al. 2009: 12, 31). While contact centers tend to be the focus of policy attention due to their employment intensity, they are amongst the slowest-growing subsectors of offshore BPO opportunities. Internationally, estimates put the value of the offshore services market at between US$100 billion and US$157 billion before the 2008 economic crisis, with the value of BPO varying between US$30 billion and US$140 billion (Gereffi and Fernandez-Stark 2010a: 6–7; Bartels and Lederer 2009; Oshri et al. 2009: 1).

It is difficult to assess the validity of prospects for future growth put forward by consulting firms in the sector. In 2005, Africa Analysis and Z-Coms (2005: 24–25) projected that only 60 percent of the global market would be tapped by 2008. This potential was linked to the possible creation of three million new direct jobs in offshored activities. Gereffi and Fernandez-Stark (2010a: 7) believe that BPO&O has achieved only 10 percent of its global potential. Smith (2006) and the BPO Partnership (2009) contend that financial services BPO has a potential value of US$250 billion. Projections are made on the assumption that BPO&O growth will be driven by further cost-reduction benefits, as well as by growing capabilities and an expanding range of products.

The demand for outsourcing primarily emanates from a handful of countries with high labor costs, namely the USA and the UK, which account for up to 80 percent of all offshored service activities, and the Netherlands (Sako 2005). India, China and the Philippines have joined the group of outsourcers over the past decade (Bartels and Lederer 2009).

In the early 2000s, US offshoring was dominated by IT and followed by FAO. Contact centers were the third-largest component of their offshored services. The activity was stimulated by Indian software experts who had worked in the United States and then returned home to set up their own firms to provide services to the US market. At that time, over 50 percent of large US multinationals stated their intention to offshore these activities, with a preference to outsource to a third party rather than to captives (Oshri et al. 2009: 5). BFSI firms have become leading consumers of offshore services, and financial services now account for 40–45 percent of all offshoring activities (BPO Partnership 2009). Generally, IT and contact centers offshored by US firms have been outsourced, while finance and accounting have followed a captive model of offshoring in almost 70 percent of cases (Oshri et al. 2009).

Two countries dominate amongst BPO&O suppliers: India and the Philippines. India accounted for about 40 percent of the global BPO market prior to the 2008 crisis, down, however, from a share of 65 percent in 2001. The Philippines accounts for 15 percent of the global BPO market (Philippines Congress, 2009: 1). However the two countries have experienced distinct trajectories, which are discussed below. Canada and Ireland accounted for 27 percent and 5 percent respectively of global market share in 2007.

All other suppliers are emerging off a much smaller base. By 2007, China had a 3.3 percent share of the global market but this was growing by 30 percent per annum. Newcomers in Central Europe met growing demand from neighboring countries such as Germany and Austria. Mexico held 5 percent of global market share, providing low-end services in Spanish to the United States, Spain, and South America. Emerging African players include South Africa, Mauritius, Egypt, and Kenya (Frost and Sullivan

2009). Common amongst the emerging suppliers is the critical support given by government to take-off and expansion.

The BPO&O sector was not diminished by the global economic crisis from 2008. Gereffi and Fernandez-Stark (2010a) and ITC (2010) assert that the global economic downturn may stimulate rather than dampen demand for offshored services, especially in the drive to cut costs. In 2008 and 2009, growth rates in the offshore service industry as a whole remained positive, in excess of 15 percent. BPO&O clients are increasingly concerned with cost considerations: for 74 percent of firms that offshore services, labor cost savings have become more important as a result of the crisis. Competition to improve service and reduce costs intensifies with a rising number of supplying countries.

2.3 Potential gains for buyers

Outsourcing and offshoring of manufacturing processes, and the separation of production and consumption, have long been features of the global economy. BPO&O growth is associated with the development of technologies that enhance the tradability of services and the unbundling of corporate functions in pursuit of cost reductions, risk mitigation, and process improvements (Sako 2005). In the process, competition is created in service markets, and firms emerge to provide services to buyer firms (Sako 2005: 12). Fragmentation in consumer markets and rising labor costs in high-income economies, even once adjusted for productivity, are further contributors to this (Bartels and Lederer 2009: 3).

Outsourcing and offshoring business services are mainly motivated by the search for cost savings, as well as the aim of externalizing business cycle risks (see Mehta et al. 2006; Oshri et al. 2009). Cost reduction arises as a result of a combination of lower-cost country conditions, specialization and learning, and economies of scale. Offshoring may also extend the production cycle by making it possible to add shifts across different time zones.

There are risks entailed in outsourcing and offshoring. Typically, there are gaps between outcomes and expectations, related to the assessment of the expertise of the vendor, the quality of the delivery, and the expected cost reduction. The more standardized a process, the lower the risk. This potential mismatch raises the attraction of outsourcing domestically, in a nearby country, to a captive offshore entity, or to firms in countries where there are well established capabilities and similar cultures and legal frameworks (see Lacity et al. 2009; Oshri et al. 2009; Willcocks and Lacity 2009).

Country comparisons are only indicative of savings to be had and they depend on what is being outsourced (and offshored), as well as on the adoption by the vendor of new technologies and their potential benefits for the buyers of the improvements in the functions outsourced. The savings need to be substantial enough to outweigh the complexity and risk incurred in offshoring. Mattoo and Wunsch (2004: 6) suggest that productivity gains of the order of 15–25 percent are expected from outsourcing and it is thought that a minimum gain of 30 percent would be expected in a decision to offshore (ITC 2010).

2.4 Specialization and cluster development in host countries

For middle-income developing countries aiming to generate employment, the service sector and ITES offer important opportunities. There is growing evidence that, even in countries with expanding goods production, the proportion of employment in goods-producing sectors is falling and the share of services is rising. There is a turning point at certain levels of GDP per capita, where manufacturing employment becomes a smaller share of the total, and this turning point has fallen over time (Palma 2008). This turning point is lower, as is the share of manufacturing employment, in mineral-exporting countries like South Africa. Services accounted for at least 60–70 percent of net new employment growth during the high-growth phases of Malaysia, China, Korea, Chile, and Brazil (ILO, various). The more employment can be sourced from traded activity, the more opportunity there will be for expansion and for real-wage growth in the services sector. Offshored ITES offer an important opportunity for such growth.

BPO&O has emerged as a focus of interest in developing country industrial promotion efforts for a number of reasons. First, it is believed that BPO&O will continue to grow over a long period. Second, the diversity of BPO-related activities means that there is great scope for employment creation across skill categories, with a bias toward the employment of women (Sako 2005). Third, there is an implicit assumption that success is easily replicable: this remains to be proven, since no other countries have yet achieved near the scale of India or the Philippines. There are relatively low barriers to entry in respect of skills, technologies, managerial requirements, and domain knowledge for many BPO subsegments (ITC 2010: 1).

In the supplying country, BPO&O is seen to generate new employment, exports, and investment opportunities. Additional benefits also exist beyond the sector, such as potential improvements in the business culture through adherence to standards, IT and telecommunications development, and the stimulation of infrastructure investments (ITC 2010). In the Philippines and India, the mass expansion of ITES has contributed to keeping skilled employees in the country. Moreover, both countries have demonstrated substantial diversification in service offerings, subsector development, and technology spill-overs. Spin-offs may arise where BPO activity generates demand for other service sectors and for related manufacturing. Examples include linked activities as new products develop, increased demand for producer and personal services, property development, construction and materials, amongst others.

The benefits from outsourcing rely on the extent to which assimilation and creation of knowledge can be leveraged. However, this knowledge needs to be supported by sufficient organizational capital. Such capital, which relates to the skills required to manage work with teams and organizations, is acquired over time and through experience (ITC 2010: 11–12; Mattoo and Wunsch 2004).

ITC (2010: 9) notes that "[w]orking on offshore projects is a form of knowledge transfer from the wealthy nations to the developing world: the technical and domain knowledge gained through working for foreign clients can be re-channeled and used for domestic projects." The development and availability of a skills foundation for securing knowledge is critical to securing and maintaining offshore business (Oshri et al. 2009: 62).

2.5 Choice of location

There are essentially five main factors that influence choice of location for offshore BPO facilities (Farrell 2006) including:

- costs decomposed into labor, infrastructure, and set-up costs;
- availability of skills;
- infrastructure quality;
- risk profile, including macroeconomic, regulatory, and intellectual property rights risks;
- the attractiveness of the local market and access to nearby markets.

Labor costs typically amount to 50–60 percent of the total costs of a BPO unit, but there are variations depending on the skill intensity of the activity. In the Philippines, 50 percent of total BPO cost is salaries and wages, 20 percent is infrastructure, 15 percent is for training and another 10 percent goes to utilities and communication (Philippines Congress 2009). In South Africa, labor makes up 58 percent of the cost of a 1,000-seat call center, 13 percent is spent on telecommunication and 14 percent goes to start-up amortization (BPO Partnership 2009: 34). Cost variations reflect differences in labor usage across BPO subsectors.

Labor costs matter more at the lower value-added level of BPO service value chains and in standardized functions. Costs related to managing relationships with clients, accounting for 5–7 percent of a typical enterprise's outsourced and offshored project, increase with risks. Capability to manage these contracts and relationships effectively is an important competitive advantage (see Willcocks and Lacity 2009).

Countries seeking to attract outsourced call centers require low-cost labor. The higher the skill complement, the less the influence of labor price on location choice. Low-income developing countries enter the market at the level of call centers for a range of reasons: barriers to entry are low in this segment; set-up costs are low; and contact-center-related tasks are easily replicable due to standardization and limited knowledge requirements. While the global growth in this aspect of outsourcing is slower than for other more knowledge-intensive activities, the scope for call centers is wide because they are used in serving customer needs for a wide range of goods and services.

2.6 Sector specialization and employment potential

Middle-income countries' competitive advantage will be found in specialization and quality service. BFSI is the fastest-growing BPO&O opportunity and appropriate to South Africa's capabilities, as shown below.

Developing financial services BPO&O is unlikely to directly create large numbers of jobs relative to the scale of activity. In contact centers, the scale of operation will expand almost directly in line with the business activity. In asset-management BPO, suppliers are likely to begin with a large infrastructure and more staff than required. This is made possible by the higher profitability and scale of transaction. For example, a supplier may see "low volumes" as having assets under administration of less than $25 billion. Profitability is achieved through volumes, which would not involve proportionate increases in employment. Administering services to retail banking may be more labor absorbing by comparison.

While the cost differential must be sufficient to warrant outsourcing, the higher up the value chain one goes, the less emphasis there is on labor and other input costs. Other factors such as quality, risk management or risk diversification become more important. Van der Heijden (2005: 25) lays out five levels and the associated key factors for buyers in asset management and related industries, with level 3 being a threshold where this differentiation takes place. This is shown in Table 24.1.

The service activities at higher skill levels, 3 to 5, are more appropriate to an upper-middle-income country cost structure. This means the country attracts offshore

Table 24.1 Service levels and activities: asset management and related industries

Service level	Activities	Key factors for buyers
Level 1: Data capture	Entering the details of trades manually on a back office system	Cost of labour (it is the major input) Overall absolute cost Location risk
Level 2: Supervision and checking	Checking and signing off that trades are entered correctly.	Some track record in these areas Cost Location risk
Level 3: Execution of specialist processes	Drawing up monthly fund accounts using the core back office system and supporting technology.	Proven ability to manage similar products at low error rates Some cost differential Location risk Client must be able to have regular physical contact with the supplier through a local office
Level 4: Supervision and management	Checking and signing off final client statements.	Proven ability to be a strategic business partner Proven track record in complex products Some cost differential required Availability of staff and low staff turnover Ability to meet onerous regulatory and compliance requirements Location risk
Level 5: Process design and integration	Setting up the back office systems(s) and processes to automatically interface with the client's accounting system.	As above Proven track record of innovative solutions in similar environment Proven track record of innovative products Familiar with client systems and applications High risk weighting (assessment of the risk of the supplier and his location)

Source: Van der Heijden (2005: 25).

activity on the basis of sophisticated oversight, risk management, or process design capability. These create relatively fewer jobs, but the lower-level activities do tend to be drawn along. For example, even if a client keeps level 1 to 2 activities (such as data capture) in-house, the outsourcer will nevertheless have to implement them anyway to ensure data integrity (Van der Heijden 2005). This is an absolutely critical approach to thinking about employment creation in upper-middle- and high-income economies. The employment opportunities are mostly generated indirectly through supporting services, as well as linkages into office support and related personal and business services. This is evident in India's experience.

Upgrading in the form of customized solution improvements is focused on the ability of external business service providers to meet as well as to adjust to buyers' demand, as well as to control expectations. Business service suppliers benefit from achieving scale as, unlike call centers, back-office processing has a greater component of fixed cost and the addition of services does not necessarily result in one-to-one employment expansion. The ability of business service suppliers to take on new functions through improved process-related expertise is critical to this expansion. Growing complexities developed from within the activities allow movements up the BPO value chain. Capabilities expanded at the business service provider level reduce the risk element that affects buyers. The performance of some key large, efficient, and effective service providers country then helps a country to develop a reputation for BPO expertise. Knowledge dynamics (for instance in the form of a deeper understanding of particular clients) can generate a progressive expansion of the portfolio of activities of individual firms where risk perception is reduced. This in turn enables activities that have higher margins and value-added.

3 BPO&O development in India and the Philippines

India and the Philippines are the global developing country BPO&O leaders, so their stories are instructive to other emergent countries seeking a substantial share of this activity. This section provides background to the evolution of BPO&O in India and the Philippines, which are both lower-middle-income economies.

3.1 Diversification in India

Overview and business strategy

The Indian BPO industry has progressed rapidly since 2000 in terms of revenue, employment and sophistication. Many countries look to its case with hope, but whether this success can be reproduced is still an open question.

The story began with the substantial presence of Indian software engineers trained in the United States, servicing US and EU markets, coupled with a strong interest among foreign investors in establishing operations in India. It is estimated that by 1995, 100,000 Indian software programmers were involved in this industry (Dossani and Kenney 2007). The Y2K scare in 2000 was leveraged well by Indian vendors, who offered low-cost technical support to overseas clients. It coincided with Indian telecoms deregulation and a global increase in the digitization of documents. This was the start of back-office processing in India, mostly in ITO, which evolved into finance and customer relationship management. The bursting of the dot-com bubble encouraged firms to look for lower-cost locations and relationships with Indian vendors were already well established. By 2006, 1.25 million Indians were providing offshore ITES, and by 2010, 2.5 million were engaged in offshore and domestic BPO&O activities, out of a formal workforce of about 44 million (NASSCOM 2010). By 2008, back-office processing accounted for almost 60 percent of the offshore BPO market in India (Everest Group 2009b: 16) and for a substantial portion of its growing process management competence (Dossani and Kenney 2007).

So, the first step in establishing the Indian BPO&O industry involved the development of Indian software engineers trained and working in the United States. The second step involved those engineers returning to India to start up companies servicing the US and EU markets. The companies provided low-cost services from India, delivered on US and EU ground. The third step involved delivering ITES directly from the base in India, the phase with the greatest jobs impact.

Evolving sophistication

ITO is the dominant form of services offshored to India, generating US$45 billion in revenue, while BPO amounts to approximately US$15 billion in revenues, of which a third is generated by contact centers. India has a 55 percent share of the combined global BPO and ITO market.

These services have become increasingly sophisticated and diverse (Dossani and Kenney 2007). The profile of services offshored to India transitioned from ITO to BPO between 2000 and 2006 (Dossani and Kenney 2007; Mehta et al. 2006: 335). Dossani and Kenney (2007) review the development of activity types over the short period of time from 2000 to 2006 and show that there were initially larger numbers in IT-related services ranging from programming to coding. By 2006, the IT services had grown in scale and sophistication but a plethora of other services also emerged: call centers, data entry, document digitization, medical services, chip design, and R&D, amongst others. The authors map the progression from five types of services in 2000 to twelve main types of services in 2006.

MNCs are now assigning key strategic and research functions to their Indian offices (see Athreye 2005; Dossani and Kenney 2007; Gereffi and Fernandez-Stark 2010b; Oshri et al. 2009: 31; Sako 2009). Having established a scale in core BPO skill sets in the onshore market and having established standardized IT and communication protocols to derive what Oshri et al. (2009: 7) describe as "[efficiencies] of inter-organizational activities," India has steadily diversified into an array of vertical and horizontal activities, focusing on niche-type BPO activities.

Knowledge acquired abroad was combined with local knowledge, allowing some imitation and a virtuous circle of knowledge acquisition and innovation. Vertically, R&D development occurred directly through foreign firms or indirectly through collaboration. R&D done for foreign manufacturing firms by captives generated outsourcing spillovers for Indian firms in some cases (see Mehta et al. 2006; Oshri et al. 2009). In Bangalore, horizontal and vertical collaboration in a cluster generated beneficial agglomeration effects, dynamic efficiencies through learning, and innovation (Basant 2006).

Table 24.2 shows that employment in ITES exports expanded substantially faster than the domestic BPO market. About 54 percent of the 430,000 BPO&O workers serviced the overseas market in 2000. By 2010, this figure had risen to 78 percent of the 2.5 million BP&O workers. IT services exports generated almost a million jobs, as compared to 765,000 in BPO exports and 361,000 through expanded domestic BPO services (NASSCOM 2010).

Indian companies contribute the largest share of IT services export employment. Indian companies account for 85 percent of ITES and 35 percent of BPO export revenue, with foreign multinationals contributing the rest. In 2008, Indian BPO companies had export revenues of US$10 billion, as compared to US$4.5 billion for MNCs. The MNCs tend to take their IT services offshore, while MNC BPO activity tends to be captive to non-IT MNCs (Kierkegaard 2008: 404). The big four Indian IT firms—Infosys, Tata Consulting Systems, Satyam, and Wipro—play an important role.

Labor and skills

India has done remarkably well in generating the range of skills needed to support this burgeoning sector, including high-level management, technical, and entrepreneurial capabilities. The sector also generates employment for middle- and lower-skill workers. It shows the possibility of making this leap, even in a low-income economy characterized by weak literacy.

A critical success factor was the presence of an educated workforce early in the cycle of transformation that supported the new investments in software-related activities (Basant 2006).

Table 24.2 Employment in India's BPO&O industry, 2000, 2005, and 2010

	2000	2005	2010
IT services exports	162 000	513 000	1 145 000
BPO exports	70 000	415 000	835 000
IT BPO domestic	198 114	365 000	560 000
	430 114	1 293 000	2 540 000

Source: Calculated from NASSCOM (2010).

The rapid pace of expansion has contributed to rising labor costs and, in some cases, shortages of college graduates to staff the industry. This may provide the space for competitors to emerge in other countries (see Sheth and Sharma 2006). Alternatively, the quality of Indian service suppliers and their tight and effective relationships with customers in the United States mean that they are still able to command a higher premium for their services than other providers.

Labor turnover is a critical concern in this industry globally and India is no exception, with rates reported to be in excess of 100 percent. NASSCOM and the government have been paying attention to this issue since 2005.

Numerous skills development programs target the range of industry jobs from entry to management level. Efforts have been directed toward securing a common assessment of skills and of expertise, so that certification is accepted as a national standard. There is a particular shortage of graduate engineers. A plethora of training schemes is in place at institutions such as colleges, complemented by a database of all IT and BPO employees to facilitate matching labor supply with demand.

Government support and industry associations

Two key packages of incentives drove the establishment and operation of foreign firms in India. These were "special economic zones," developed in 2000 in the least developed parts of the country, and "software technology parks" (BPO parks with incentives secured through lobbying by the National Association of Software Services Companies, NASSCOM) (see Bhatnagar 2006). Investors in software technology parks, including wholly foreign-owned firms, are exempted from tax for ten years from establishment. These incentives have been criticized for failing to optimize tax revenues. The problem of limited revenues secured through O&O activities has been exacerbated by the marked growth of captives from the late 1990s. In 1999, 100 percent foreign-owned firms were allowed into the country for the first time. In 2000, 44 Forbes 500 companies had captive centers in India. This rose steadily to 71 in 2003, 110 in 2006, and 500 in 2008. This growth has taken place in software, retail, and financial services (Infosys 2006).

NASSCOM was established in 1988 to represent the sector. It has strategically influenced the Indian government in all areas pertaining to ITES (and to BPO within it). Keeping its consultative and market analysis functions, it supports the development of new service exports focused on ITES/BPO. Also of note has been its role in two areas: information security—NASSCOM guided the development of the IT Act of 2000 and its subsequent changes—and skills development.

3.2 BPO and BPO&O in the Philippines

Overview and business strategy

The growth of BPO&O in the Philippines began in the mid-2000s. Between 2000 and 2008, the contribution of business services outsourcing to GDP in the Philippines increased from 0.1 percent to 3.6 percent (Philippines Congress 2009: 1). Overall, employment grew by an annual average of 68 percent and quadrupled from 100,500 in 2004 to 442,164 by 2009, in a formal urban workforce of about 9.5 million.

In 2008, two-thirds of professional service exports were in call centers, and call-center-agent employment in the Philippines matched that of India by 2010. Asia is a notable consumer of BPO services from the Philippines, accounting for 25 percent of all BPO services exports from that country. The Philippines also serves clients in the United States, the United Kingdom, and Australia. As in India, the BPO&O sector is highly concentrated in urban areas, especially in Manila, which is now the "world's largest city destination for BPO activities" (Gereffi and Fernandez Stark 2010a: 18)

Call centers generated US$2.7 billion in 2006 and employed 160,000 agents, about 76 percent of all BPO revenues and 68 percent of employment. By 2008, employment in call centers had risen to 198,000. These jobs are largely concentrated in a few large firms, including foreign-owned ones such as Convergys US.

The Philippines is the leading global player in the voice segment and is also active in the nonvoice segment (with some activities around FAO, HRO, and procurement outsourcing, although the bulk remains transactional). This sets the country up as a potential competitor to India.

Limited growth in sophistication

Two thirds of all BPO employment is found in call centers, and this has not changed as the sector has grown, over the period from 2004 to 2009. By comparison, less than a third of all Indian BPO jobs are found in call centers. In the field of nonvoice activity, the biggest employment gains were found in back-office and transcription services. These figures are shown in Table 24.3 (BPA/P 2010).

ITO contributed over 9 percent of all IT-BPO revenues and over 9 percent of all IT-BPO employment in 2009 (BPA/P 2009). The Philippines also has a hardware industry, and skills in this area are documented through the fact that Costa Rica is importing skilled workers from this industry to boost its own BPO development program (see Oshri et al. 2009). Niche activities have expanded, with higher value-added BPO activities such as medical prescription, publishing, and legal services, as well as new types of animation services for foreign buyers (Tschang, n.d.).

Table 24.3 BPO&O employment in the Philippines, 2004 and 2009

	Contact centres	Back office	Transcription	Animation	IT	Engineering services	Digital content/game development	Total
2004	64 000	15 000	6 300	3 000	10 000	2 000	200	100 500
2009	280 000	86 000	35 300	12 000	20 224	8 000	640	442 164

Source: Calculated from BPA/P (2010).

Labor and Skills

Industry experts emphasize that, given comparable location performance indicators, the Philippines has a much lower rate of labor turnover than India. Philippines Congress (2009: 2) reports that the rate of attrition in BPO is 62 percent, compared to 102 percent in India. By comparison, the attrition rate is 15–20 percent per annum in South Africa (BPO Partnership 2009: 23).

Scalability is a concern in the Philippines, with constraints on labor resources or human capital, particularly with regard to the more complex processes; the size of new BPO entrants remains small.

Roadmap 2010, a framework document guiding national developments and efforts around BPO, has deployed strong marketing efforts that led to substantial increases in investment in the BPO&O in the Philippines. It supports education through scholarships and skills development (through subsidies of up to 50 percent of training costs) and the development of individuals with middle management skills. The Special Programme for the Employment of Students targets poor students with a minimum level of education, to complement the focus on training and on employing college drop-outs.

The Philippines improved its BPO&O competitiveness between 2007 and 2009 (A. T. Kearney 2009) due to the quality of the education system: the country produces more college graduates than India. However, it is facing certain labor constraints (Sibal 2006). As is the case in India, there are problems with the quality of jobs (see Mehta et al. 2006). Furthermore, there is a lack of managers and, at least in the mid-2000s, there was a mismatch between available skills and industry demand. Although ICT skills are being developed, certifications are expensive and attrition rates are relatively high.

Government incentives and industry association

Government catalyzed the growth of BPO in the Philippines through focusing on software development, contact centers, BPO, animation, and medical transcription. Labor costs are still seen as a critical competitive advantage. The Philippines is expanding its BPO platform around the success of call centers. This dominant segment is still supported by policymakers and key BPO institutions.

Scalability may be constrained by current policy approaches. Many captives operate in the Philippines (Tschang, n.d.; ITC 2010); concern has been expressed that investment incentives which are sector specified by the Board of Investment are subject to renewal and are therefore uncertain. As is the case in India, substantial tax revenues are thought to have been lost through the tax-holiday status of a large proportion of BPO investment driven by foreign firms. Another concern is that BPO has been found to have generally displayed limited forward and backward linkages (Ramos et al. 2007).

The national Business Processing Association of the Philippines (BPA/P), an umbrella association set up in 2001, markets and provides support to the industry. Policy efforts intensified from 2007 with the introduction of Roadmap 2010. The Philippines government has provided incentives to attract offshore BPO investments and Roadmap 2010 intensified efforts in respect of human resource development, including at the higher management level, to address an issue that had arisen in the early 2000s (Tschang, n.d.):

the expansion of space available for BPO&O operations in cities and other support to the industry for expansion. A concern of Roadmap 2010 is to rapidly create direct as well as indirect jobs in and around the sector. The targets were aimed at doubling the country's global market share from 5 percent in 2007 to 10 percent for BPO by 2010 (equivalent to an 8.5 percent contribution to GDP) (Ramos et al. 2007).

4 BPO&O in South Africa

Unemployment in South Africa, an upper-middle-income economy, is extremely high and especially severe for young people. Only 41 percent of its working-age population was employed, and the strict unemployment rate was 25 percent in 2010. In the same year, youth unemployment was 51 percent in the age group 15–24 years and 29 percent for those aged 25–34 (NPC 2011). The majority of unemployed are black African. Countries like India and the Philippines have larger populations, with low unemployment but very large informal sectors. They have managed to generate sufficient skills and capability, even in the context of relatively small modern sectors. In South Africa, more than 70 percent of workers are in the formal sector, and there is substantial sophistication to enable industrial diversification. However, this hides extreme inequality and exclusion. BPO&O provides one of the few global opportunities for mass formal sector employment creation for young high school and college graduates.

The services sector has been the most important source of employment growth in South Africa, and especially after 1997. The share of services in employment grew from about 63 percent to 70 percent between 1995 and 2009 (Quantec). The share of financial services rose from just over 6 percent of GDP to just over 12 percent over the same period. Business services also account for about 12 percent of GDP. This expansion has stimulated both high- and low-skill employment. BPO activity, whether captive or not, has expanded considerably as part of this mix; the offshore component of this has also expanded, but is still very limited.

There is much debate in South Africa about an appropriate industrial policy that can enable a shift to a more employment-oriented growth path. BPO&O, with an emphasis on offshoring, has been identified as a possible opportunity for large-scale employment creation. Indeed, the majority of global employment is now sourced from services, and it is therefore imperative that developing countries devote greater industrial policy attention to services trade (see Altman 2010). There is no other industry that might achieve this pace of job creation: in India and the Philippines, employment grew at over 30 percent annually in the decade starting in 2000. There is also evidence that only a fraction of global market potential has been realized. This is especially the case in activities where South Africa has competitive advantage, such as financial services.

South Africa's approach to deepening its position in the global BPO&O market offers an interesting case study in whether and how an upper-middle-income economy can effectively compete in, and garner significant employment gains from, this trade. As the discussions above of India and the Philippines indicate, BPO&O can generate direct employment opportunities in call-center and back-office processing, as well as other services. Indirect opportunities may also arise through sector spillovers and multipliers which, for a middle-income economy, may be the main sources of new employment growth. While policymakers tend to focus on niches that might generate direct employment, a middle-income economy will likely be less competitive where there is a reliance on low labor costs. More potential might exist in competing in medium and higher-skill, but less employment-intensive niches that could potentially generate employment multipliers.

Reporting accurately on the BPO sector in South Africa is a challenge, as there are no official statistics and insights are gleaned from a number of primary and secondary sources. As with the international literature, there is substantial reliance on consulting reports, and no peer-reviewed scientific studies have been published. Some of the central reports include those produced by McKinsey & Co. (2005), Everest Group (2008), Frost and Sullivan (2009), and the BPO Partnership (2009) to support strategy building for provincial and national governments.

There are no official statistics for BPO&O. It is really a range of activities that could be categorized in different locations within the statistics—for example, one could ask whether an outsourced service administering payroll for a retailer should be categorized as "trade" or as other business services.

This case study begins by reviewing some key features of BPO&O in South Africa before turning to government's approach to positioning the sector.

4.1 Overview of BPO&O in South Africa

South Africa's BPO&O activities amount to less than 0.5 percent of the global BPO market, although they have been growing. In 2006, it was estimated that the outsourcing industry had 9,500 staff, 5,000 of whom serviced domestic clients and 4,500 of whom serviced offshore clients. Captive call centers, where companies run an in-house service, are a much larger employment sector. By 2007, it was estimated that there were about 80,000 contact-center agents in captive services, of whom only 33,000 were in outsourced services including offshore captives, with revenues of US$885.2 million (BPO Partnership 2009: 22; Frost and Sullivan 2009). This was in a formal nonagricultural workforce of 9.5 million. The BPO Partnership (2009) estimates that employment in offshore BPO rose from 7,732 in 2007 to 21,752 by 2009.

Call centers grew by 9 percent per annum prior to the 2008 crisis. This can be compared to leading BPO centers that have grown by compound annual growth rates of 30 percent or more, such as India and the Philippines. Of the 33,000 BPO workers in 2007, 24,156 were call-center agents, 3,630 worked in ITO, 2,310 in FAO, 1,320 in KPO, and 990 in HRO. There do not appear to be more recent figures available. There is a tendency for South African companies to offshore their ITO services to India, and to outsource HRO and FAO onshore (Frost and Sullivan 2009).

Call centers dominate BPO activity in South Africa, and are the focus of policy attention due to their labor intensity. About 90 percent of BPO seats are in call centers, but only 13.5 percent of this activity is outsourced. This means that companies are mainly running their own call centers. There is a domestic capability in voice, business processes, and ITES, but limited development of South African companies that can attract offshore ITES business in a meaningful way.

The BPO sector is not highly diversified. One country, the United Kingdom, dominates the base of South African offshore customers; it accounted for 70 percent of offshore customer services in 2005, falling to 60 percent by 2007. South Africa had not yet succeeded in attracting significant outsourced business from the United States or the Netherlands, despite the former being the largest outsourcing nation and the language synergies with both countries. In 2007, only 1,056 BPO South African workers serviced the US offshore market, with most of the US business going to India and the Philippines. In the same year, only 370 BPO workers serviced the Netherlands. There had been hope that the similarity between Afrikaans and Dutch would attract the Netherlands but this was not realized, potentially due to preference for onshore or near-shore providers. The investment that has taken place has been through captives. For example, Royal Dutch Shell established a call center in Cape Town in 2008 to service its customers in Belgium, the Netherlands, and Luxembourg. South Africa also provides services to Australia, Ireland, Germany, and the rest of Africa (634 workers in 2007) (Frost and Sullivan 2009).

Geographically, BPO activity is concentrated in particular urban areas. One region, Gauteng (covering Johannesburg and Pretoria), absorbs about 70 percent of all BPO employees, while the Western Cape (Cape Town) accounts for 20 percent of BPO employment.

The distribution of BPO employment across vertical segments in 2007 was concentrated in BFSI, retail, and telecoms. A total of 10,980 BPO workers serviced 240 clients in BFSI, of which 55 percent were front-office and 45 percent back-office. Three-quarters of this activity was for the domestic market, and one-quarter for offshore clients (2,745). Most offshore business is in front-office activity. There is limited domestic outsourcing growth, as firms reported having had "bad experiences" and reintegrating services as a result. It is estimated that about 75,000 workers were in captive financial services in 2007 (Frost and Sullivan 2009). Foreign businesses tend to offshore call-center activity, especially those from the United States. While this is typically seen as more labor intensive, there have been moves since 2006 to automate this low end. It is more difficult to automate the higher end, where discretion is needed. However, firms also tend to prefer to keep higher-skill, more sensitive services in-house or in offshore captives.

In telecoms, there were 9,240 BPO workers, with 65 percent in back-office, and 95 percent oriented to the domestic market. The call centers were generally managed in-house through captive services (Frost and Sullivan 2009). A total of 4,290 BPO workers serviced the retail sector, with 60 percent in back office and 90 percent domestic. This business is often regionally located near the main stores in small centers. The public sector generated demand for only 660 workers, often in very small centers of 50 seats or less.

4.2 Assessing competitive advantage and employment potential

In the decade starting in 2000, South African efforts at promoting BPO have concentrated on trying to attract new offshore activities on the basis of generic capabilities. However, new entrants are able to copy or improve on generic capabilities and so this is becoming a poor differentiator. Specialized niches and demonstrated capabilities are increasingly becoming important to attracting BPO&O activity (Frost and Sullivan 2009; BPeSA 2011).

South African BPO companies tend to lack sufficient global presence to attract offshore business, but the country has the advantage of the presence of leading MNC BPO providers such as IBM, Hewlett Packard, Accenture, and EDS. Dimension Data is a South African company that has developed a global presence through acquisitions, including that of Merchants. In turn, partnerships have developed to strengthen domestic capability, such as that between Merchants and Adcorp, a labor placement company. Offshoring expanded particularly with the entry of MNC captives from 2005 onward. By 2009, the BPO Partnership reported that larger players had generated R1.5 billion (US$214 million) of new foreign investment. This included IBM, Teleperformance (UK), Teletech (UK), Accenture, TCS, and the Budget Group, all starting between 2005 and 2007. There is a growing presence of Indian outsourcers such as Genpact, Aegis, and an alliance between Channel Holdings Ltd. and Mahindra Satyan BPO. Frost and Sullivan (2009) contend that future growth will depend considerably on near-shore servicing of African markets. South African companies have a comparative advantage in Africa with more sophisticated back-office skills, via pan-African operators such as Dimension Data, MTN, Standard Bank, and South African Airways. Some UK companies such as Fujitsu, Carphone Warehouse, and Virgin Mobile have directly outsourced to Gauteng Province, benefiting from relatively lower costs and cultural and language affinity (Frost and Sullivan 2009).

South Africa competes with mature destinations such as India and the Philippines, and with emerging offshore destinations such as Kenya, the Czech Republic, Mexico, and China. According to Everest Group, Johannesburg and Cape Town are about 50 percent cheaper than the United Kingdom and the United States respectively for front- and back-office work in financial services, 10 percent cheaper than some East European destinations such as Prague, but about 12 percent more expensive than Manila or Bangalore. Given the considerable gap in labor and telecommunications costs, it is surprising that the gap between South Africa and India is not greater. For example, an inbound agent in Manila and Bangalore is paid 32 percent and 70 percent less, respectively, than one in Johannesburg. By 2007, telecom costs were US$8,000, US$12,500, and US$17,500 per megabit per second per year in India, the Philippines, and South Africa respectively. This gap should have closed to some extent since then, with the laying of undersea cable and introduction of greater competition and discount rates for some BPO investors. In addition, it is known that the telecommunications parastatal Telkom has negotiated special rates with individual investors on a case-by-case basis (BPO Partnership 2009: 18). The costs of facilities and of real estate are central advantages in South Africa, at about half the costs in Manila and about 30 percent less than in Bangalore.

Quality improvements and further reductions in telecommunication costs are needed to counteract the cost gap between South Africa and India. As such, the BPO Partnership (2009) sees that a 30–35 percent reduction in telecommunication costs, combined with growing economies of scale, efficiency improvements, and a more favourable exchange rate, would allow South Africa to become 1.2 times more expensive than India compared to 1.8 times more expensive in 2009. In the context of the financial crisis, exchange rates between the Rand and the US dollar and pound sterling have been unfavorable to South African service exports. This is a long-run challenge for the country, with its commodity export profile and a highly traded currency linked to commodity prices. However, it is expected that South Africa will become increasingly attractive relative to India due to inflation differentials.

On generic capabilities, South Africa is considered to have adequate to very good infrastructure, connectivity, English proficiency, and overall education levels (see Everest Group 2009a; Gartner Research 2008). There are stated challenges in telecommunications costs and infrastructure, but these are also faced by many of the emerging countries such as Kenya. Telecommunication costs are declining and the services are improving. However, South Africa is falling behind on the ITU Development Index and the World Economic Forum e-Readiness index (see GCR 2010, Gillwald 2011). South Africa was 40th on the ITU ratings in 1995, and fell to 72nd in 2002 and to 92nd by 2008 (Gillwald 2011).

Competitive positioning in BFSI

There is growing interest in shifting from generic approaches to BPO promotion toward an emphasis on strategic sectors. South African BPO&O was, before the global crisis, assessed to have the most potential growth in BFSI, retail, and telecommunications, servicing the United Kingdom, the United States, and the Netherlands (Frost and Sullivan 2009). These opportunities were assessed on the basis of source country intentions to outsource and offshore, as well as South Africa's capabilities. These are scalable activities servicing large industries with deep business process needs. These industries would outsource or offshore FAO, IT services, HRO, KPO, or customer contact centers (Frost and Sullivan 2009).

By 2008, employment generated through BFSI O&O was very small. There were only 11,000 employees in South Africa's financial services BPO, as compared to India and the Philippines which respectively had about 380,000 and 130,000 employees. The scale of South Africa's financial services BPO employment was similar to that achieved by Argentina, Malaysia, or Romania.

Special attention to financial and insurance services has arisen since 2008 (BPO Partnership 2009). The South African market has a mature and economically sound financial sector, having been resilient to the global financial crisis through a prudent and conservative regulatory regime. Finance and business services accounted for 38 percent of gross value added and 15 percent of employment in 2010 (Quantec various).

Although the World Competitiveness Report ranked South Africa 54th out of 139 countries in 2010, the finance sector sophistication was ranked 9th (GCR 2010). Already a third of BPO employment is found in financial services, particularly in offshore captives (see Gelb et al. 2005; ITC 2010). The products on offer and regulations in place are similar to those found in the United Kingdom. South African companies have the advantage of being compliant with a range of standardized national codes of practice and quality standards required by offshore clients. These include Basel II, FSA 70 certification, ISO, Six Sigma, and Sarbanes Oxley (Frost and Sullivan 2009). Globally, there is a trend toward financial services offshoring and the intention is to target foreign financial services and BPO investors (Everest 2008). There is a growing presence of South African banks in global markets and foreign banks have engaged in mergers and acquisitions in South Africa.

There are specific advantages to expanding FAO&O for the South African economy. These enable a diversification into high-value-addition segments—in the area of back-office functions and new KPO opportunities—and in terms of leveraging technology. The latter is important, in the sense that technology is more advanced in financial services than in other sectors.

In BFSI, FAO offshore activity from the United Kingdom tends to be concentrated in lower-skill activities (such as accounts payable), with an apparent reluctance to offshore high-end riskier activities. There is significant pressure to prove data security. KPO activity, such as hedge funds or asset management, is generally offshored to captives (Frost and Sullivan 2009). This speaks to the necessity of attracting MNCs or encouraging MNCs already in South Africa to attract this business. It is less likely that South African firms will be sufficiently attractive, unless their global presence and therefore quality control are clearly recognized. Van der Heijden (2005: 14) and Oshri et al. (2009) argue that companies lacking global presence will have to become "suppliers of suppliers," where they indirectly provide service through well-known MNCs.

4.3 Labor and skills

South Africa promotes itself as a location where large numbers of English-speaking high-school and college graduates every year enter the market, which expands by about half a million annually. The country has emerged from a history of extreme exclusion, where only a very small proportion of the black population completed a high-school education. South Africa now has near universal high-school attendance and illiteracy is rare amongst young people (Sheppard 2009). However, the quality of high-school output is such that reading comprehension and numeracy are weak. There is also limited work readiness, particularly as many young people live in communities with high unemployment and are poorly prepared through family or peer networks for the world of work (Altman 2010). This limits labor availability at the level of both agent and manager. It is a challenge faced across the economy, but especially in labor-intensive activities. Since 1996, there have been concerted efforts to expand industrial training, with an overhaul of the entire system to introduce a new qualifications framework, enhanced funding—where firms pay a levy of 1 percent of payroll—and new training oversight bodies called "sector education and training authorities" (SETAs). While there have been mixed experiences, the SETA attuned to the BPO sector, namely the Services SETA, has been one of the more successful training authorities and has played an important role in generating a skills pipeline into the BPO sector. The higher-education system has substantial capacity, and the challenge for South Africa will be to expand its throughput rates so that a greater proportion of enrolled students complete their education and expand the pool of skilled labor (Sheppard 2009). A set of dedicated initiatives has been set up at national and local levels. At the national level, policies to address skills supply issues have been implemented, albeit unevenly. Accredited learnerships and standard bursaries in specific areas—such as accounting—are available. South Africa offers a series of incentives to foreign and local investors in BPO&O. The DTI's GAS program ran from 2007 until 2010. This provided support for investors who did not displace existing jobs and for a maximum period of three years (DTI 2007a). Equity requirements were imposed, where 85 percent and 54 percent of those supported would be black and female respectively (DTI 2007b: 6).

A long-term strategy will fundamentally rely on the development of a broader skills base. In terms of skills development, noncost characteristics that pertain to the quality as well as the availability of labor at the relevant level of skills are important to generate new contracts with higher-value-added service activities. Dossani and Kenney (2007: 788) present education as a central element for tapping service-related prospects as follows: "Perhaps, the most important policy conclusion from our research is that countries that do not educate their populations will have no opportunity to participate in the globalization of services. The service sector is infinitely rich in opportunities." It is the basic supply of skilled personnel (in technology, mathematics, statistics, and related fields), as well as specially accredited trainees, that signals the availability of a base of work-ready entrants.

Everest Group (2008) identifies two main dimensions critical to the expansion of financial services BPO, namely availability of skilled labor and existence of domain expertise. Within the skill category, South Africa has a key strength in the number of actuarial and certified analysts in the country, in absolute as well as relative terms. Financial services BPO is well suited to South Africa, especially in knowledge-intensive services where there is less cost competition, as shown in the study by Van der Heijden (2005) of two financial services subsectors, namely asset management and related financial services.

In sheer numbers of generic skills, South Africa falls short of its main competitors. South Africa produces 90,000 university graduates annually, as compared to 300,000 in Egypt, 480,000 in the Philippines and 3 million in India. A further 35,000 post-school diplomas are awarded annually in South Africa. The pool of experienced BPO supervisors and managers is very small, with only 3,000 in 2008, as compared to 20,000 in Mexico, 30,000 in the Philippines, and 80,000 in India. In more specialized expertise, South Africa has competitive skills supply. For example, in urban areas where BPO is concentrated, similar numbers of commerce graduates are produced annually in Johannesburg (12,000), Manila (16,000) and Mumbai (28,000). South Africa has a stock of about 850 chartered financial analysts (CFAs), 770 actuaries, and 26,000 chartered accountants (CAs). India has 4,000 CFAs, 225 actuaries, and 90,000 CAs. The Philippines has 75 CFAs, 65 actuaries, and 15,000 CAs (Everest 2008).

4.4 BPO&O support in South Africa

BPO&O began receiving focused policy attention in South Africa from the early 2000s in the hope that BPO&O offered opportunities for job creation. Call centers were the initial focus of attention, and from 2006 more attention was devoted to specific niches such as BFSI.

The DTI (2010: 87) claims that "[t]here is the potential to create 56,000 direct sustainable jobs over 10 years in business process services with an increase in foreign earnings from the 'exportable' services sector." This assumes a growth of employment in BPO of about 11 percent per year (as calculated by Everest Group, see BPO Partnership 2009). Frost and Sullivan (2009) contend that the limited amount of outsourced ITES to date reflects a potential for future expansion of BPO. Their report expresses the view that domestic outsourcing (rather than offshoring) is likely to be the biggest growth opportunity. In the context of the global opportunity, growth rates seen in some other developing countries, and South African capability, this seems unambitious.

For South Africa, demonstrated capability would originate through domestic outsourcing that could form a platform on which offshore activity can be performed. Frost and Sullivan (2009) propose that government should seek ways to raise the return on investment from domestic outsourcing to encourage its expansion. However, a strategy of building on domestic outsourcing is constrained by the extent to which firms are maintaining ITES such as customer care in-house (Frost and Sullivan 2009). Some domestic captives may choose to generate new revenue streams by attracting offshore business. Otherwise, offshore activity could arise only through captive multinational investment.

South Africa is an emerging international BPO provider, entering the competitive fray as a relative latecomer and with the cost structure of a middle-income country. It would typically not succeed in competition on the basis of cost alone, but it could compete on the basis of product quality, customer relationships, or some other differentiator. Policies have largely focused on promoting call-center activities, a particular BPO subsector, with relatively limited attention paid to value-added products in a range of activities such as back-office processing or to new service and industry sectors where there could be substantial competitive strength. More generally, the logic of policymakers has been to promote the most directly labor-intensive aspects of the BPO&O industry in a context of high unemployment at low levels of skills. However, this has been done on a comparatively small scale. The concomitant investments in telecommunications, skills, and specialized ITES have not been pursued at the scale or intensity needed to meaningfully position the country in the competitive fray.

South Africa's success is likely to be built on capabilities in certain niches. However, a review of marketing material might indicate otherwise. Promotional material and global presentations on South African BPO still express a generic approach to attracting investment (see BPeSA 2011; BPO Partnership 2009)

Other efforts are aimed at the development of a code of conduct to signal that South Africa is a quality BPO-supplying market for foreign buyers and investors.

The public policy approach has treated BPO as a stand-alone industry, rather than as a service integrally linked to other industries. The Human Sciences Research Council (Van der Heijden 2005) and Frost and Sullivan (2009) have shown that BPO&O arises through careful insertion into specific vertical industries (such as retail, BFSI or telecoms) and competitive advantage in certain horizontal activities (such as segments of FAO, ITO, KPO, HRO or call centers). This is over and above the generic requirements of competitive cost, regulation and standards, competitive telecommunications, or human resource supply. Hence, industrial policy should support both the outsource capability and the horizontal and vertical activities, many of which are found in service sectors. Yet services industries have been low on the industry and trade policy radar; most attention has been devoted to the expansion of tourism, with sometimes reference to "other services" or "high value services" in the Industrial Policy Action Plan (IPAP), which is the DTI's central communication of intention. The first IPAP was published in 2007 and IPAP 2 in 2010. The main contributions to service-industry support and development have been related to strong regulation and oversight of the finance sector and relatively weak oversight and regulation of telecommunications.

The 2007 IPAP identified BPO&O as a priority for a number of reasons, including its potential as an export growth sector and its potential for job creation. Industrial policy support has focused on investment promotion, training, and marketing. The orientation of South African industrial policy is such that contributions to learning, technology, and productivity are underplayed and yet these would be the factors that would be essential to South Africa becoming a premier BPO&O destination.

In 2006, the cabinet approved a substantial set of assistance and support measures to stimulate BPO under the Government Assistance and Support (GAS) program, with special focus on offshoring. This emphasis on offshoring, and not on outsourcing, was due to concern that the latter would displace jobs rather than create them. Given the investment approach globally requiring demonstrated capability, this will mean that South Africa will largely limit itself to trying to attract MNC-captive BPO activity, and will be less successful at attracting offshore business to South African third-party vendors. Everest Group (2008) identified limited vendor landscape and poor technology infrastructure as constraints. However, the policy approach does little to address them.

The incentive program for BPO operations was expanded in 2011, which pays investors for each full-time job created and maintained over a period of three years. It is estimated that this will reduce the cost of BPO operations by up to 20 percent. A "graduated bonus incentive" of 20–30 percent is also offered where 400 to 800 jobs are created, and it is intended to cover 50–60 percent of the capital investment per seat. Based on known information about cost differentials in 2007, this incentive would make South Africa cost-competitive with other major destinations such as Manila or Bangalore.

Insofar as MNC captives are attracted to South Africa, restrictions on the movement of people across borders will need to be eased. For example, in the early stages of US offshore captive investments, 35–50 percent of staff are American (Frost and Sullivan 2009).

The industry promotion agency was strengthened with the establishment in 2006 of Business Process Enabling South Africa or BPeSA to replace the former South African Contact Centre Community (SACCCOM) that was set up in 2004. The mandate of BPeSA was enlarged to encompass more than call centers, extending to ITO, FAO, and HRO. However, BPeSA represents only 30 percent of South Africa's agent base. It represents the regional bodies and works in partnership with government (especially the DTI) and business.

5 Conclusion

ITES and BPO offshoring are largely new activities, having emerged over the past decade. India and the Philippines have taken the lion's share of the market, albeit with very different strategies. New countries have entered the competitive fray, most notably China, the Czech Republic, Malaysia, Mauritius, and South Africa, amongst others. South Africa is a small provider with potential in a context of high unemployment. BPO is a sector with rapid compound growth potential, expanding by a third annually in successful countries.

It is surprising that the cost differential between South Africa and lower-income economies is not great, and investment incentives should make up for the gap in the first three years of a project. South Africa is a middle-income economy with considerable capability in some key activities such as financial services. Its competitive edge will need to rely on specialist rather than generic skills, which are easily copied and some of which are increasingly being automated.

Some have argued that South Africa should promote the expansion of domestic outsourcing to enable the attraction of offshore business into local third-party vendors. By the end of the 2000s, it was still common for firms to maintain ITES such as contact centers in-house rather than outsourcing. Encouraging firms to outsource domestically, with the aim of strengthening the sophistication of vendors, may be politically sensitive in a context of high unemployment, as it may be seen as replacing "good jobs" in larger firms with "bad jobs" in smaller outsourced firms. Policymakers have therefore chosen to focus on attracting offshore business to MNCs. MNCs often prefer to offshore into captive services. A more targeted approach will therefore be needed to attract this business. Special support, such as easier movement of foreign personnel, will become essential.

Although the strategy for expanding BPO&O explicitly recognizes the need to offer niche products, promotional efforts continue to emphasize generics. There is little attention paid in government industrial policy statements to the development of niche service industries, nor is there any apparent marketing that takes advantage of these niches.

Little attention has been paid in South Africa to attracting BPO&O business in sectors that have competitive advantage. An expansion of outsourcing necessitates an understanding not only of BPO, but also of how sector-specific dynamics influence the outsourcing of particular service functions. Some research attention has been devoted to BFSI, but it has not found its way strategically into sector promotion activities. Linking to areas of competitive capability offers greater possibility for technology spillovers and the stimulation of new industrial activities.

To achieve employment creation benefits, it will be essential that there are spillovers and linkages arising from the more skill-intensive activities that can be attracted and sustained.

The presence of an educated labor platform will be essential for the absorption and transformation of this knowledge for the purpose of BPO expansion and of movements up the value chain, both horizontally and vertically.

The generic approach, with emphasis on low-end contact services, and the slow pace of human capital development will impose high opportunity costs for South Africa. ITES may prove to be one of the few fast employment creators in global trade, that South Africa can ill-afford to squander.

Note

1. Distinguished research fellow, Human Sciences Research Council, Pretoria, South Africa, and Commissioner, National Planning Commission, The Presidency, South Africa. Mailing address: Private Bag X41, Pretoria 0001, South Africa. Email: maltman@hsrc.ac.za and miriamaltman2@gmail.com.

References

Africa Analysis and Z-Coms. 2005. "South African BPO and Contract Centre Industry, 2005: Market Overview and Value Proposition Analysis." Version 1, Report Release 1, prepared by A. Will, D. Pater and I. King. http://donar.messe.de/exhibitor/cebit/2011/I24229/south-african-software-industry-report-release-eng-130521.pdf [accessed October 19, 2012].

Altman, M. 2010. "Youth Labour Market Challenges in South Africa." In *Human Capital Trends*, edited by I. Boninelli and T. Meyer. KnowRes Publishers, Johannesburg.

Athreye, S.S. 2005. "The Indian Software Industry and Its Evolving Service Capability." *Industrial and Corporate Change* 14 (3): 393–418.

A. T. Kearney. 2009. "The Shifting Geography of Offshoring: The 2009 A. T. Kearney Global Service Location Index." http://www.atkearney.com/documents/10192/fda82529-b60a-4fae-8d92-22cfd69b95b3 [accessed October 19, 2012].

Bartels, F. L., and S. Lederer. 2009. "Outsourcing Markets in Services: International Business Trends, Patterns and Emerging Issues, and the Role of China and India." Working

Chapter 03/2009, Research and Statistics Branch, United Nations Industrial Development Organization, Vienna.

Basant, R. 2006. "Bangalore Cluster: Evolution, Growth and Challenges." Indian Institute of Management Working Paper WP 2006-05-02.

Bhatnagar, S. 2006. "India's Software Industry." In *Technology, Adaptation and Exports—How Some Developing Countries Got it Right*, edited by V. Chandra, 49–82. Washington, DC: World Bank.

BPA/P (Business Processing Association of the Philippines). 2009. "Philippines IT-BPO Industry on the World Stage." Paper submitted to the Asia Pacific Economic Cooperation, 2009/CTI2/GOS/SEM/007 for the Seminar on Commercial Realities of Cross-Border Services Trade, APEC 2009 Singapore, May 20.

———. 2010. "Product Market Study Matrade Manila (1/2010): Business Process Outsourcing in the Philippines: Trends and Opportunities." Technopreneurs Association of Malaysia, October 24. http://www.slideshare.net/teamcouncil/product-market-study-on-philippines-bpo-industry-oct-2010 [accessed October 19, 2012].

BPeSA (Business Process Enabling South Africa). 2011. "South Africa: The Gateway to Africa." Presentation to the NASSCOM India Leadership Forum 2011. Mumbai, February 8–11. http://www.offshoringsouthafrica.com/wp-content/uploads/downloads/2011/02/SA_Country-Session_20110209_vf-_NASSCOM.pdf [accessed October 19, 2012].

BPO Partnership. 2009. *Developing the BPO Sector: Report to Stakeholders 2009*. http://www.btrust.org.za/fileadmin/pdf/BPO_Stakeholder_Report_2009_Final.pdf [accessed October 19, 2012].

Dossani, R., and M. Kenney. 2007. "The Next Wave of Globalization: Relocating Service Provision to India." *World Development* 35 (5): 772–791.

DTI (Department of Trade and Industry, South Africa). 2007a. *Programme Guidelines: BPO&O Investment Incentives, March 2007*. Pretoria: Department of Trade and Industry, Enterprise Organisation.

———. 2007b. *Programme Guidelines: BPO&O Investment Incentives Training Support grant, February 2007*. Pretoria: Department of Trade and Industry, Enterprise Organisation.

———. 2010. *Industrial Policy Action Plan (IPAP2) 2010/11–2012/13*. Pretoria: Department of Trade and Industry.

Everest Group. 2008. "Ready To Compete—South Africa's Capabilities in the Financial Services Sector." December. http://research.everestgrp.com/Product/10531.

———. 2009a. "Impact of Global Crisis on Offshore BPO Market and Implications for South Africa, 27 March 2009." Research report commissioned by the BPO Partnership.

———. 2009b. "Mauritius as an Emerging Location for Delivery of Offshore Services." September. http://www.gov.mu/portal/sites/ictexport/Doc/Mauritius%20Emerging%20Offshore%20Services%20Location%20-%20Everest%202009.pdf [accessed October 19, 2012].

Farrell, D. 2006. "Smarter Offshoring." *Harvard Business Review* 84 (6): 84–92.

Frost and Sullivan. 2009. "Gauteng BPO Marketing Strategy." Report commissioned by the Gauteng Province Department of Economic Development, June.

Gartner Research. 2008. "Analysis of South Africa as an Offshore Services Location." Research note prepared by S Karisson, and I. Marriott.

GCR. 2010. "Global Competitiveness Report, 2010–2011." World Economic Forum. Geneva.

Gelb, S., L. Keeton, and C. Malikane. 2005. "Financial Services Second Chapter: Policy Recommendations and Interventions." Chapter prepared by the Edge Institute for the Department of Economic Development and Tourism, Western Cape Provincial Government.

http://www.westerncape.gov.za/other/2005/11/final_second_paper_fin_services_printing.pdf [accessed October 19, 2012].

Gereffi, G., and K. Fernandez-Stark. 2010a. "The Offshore Services Value Chain: Developing Countries and the Crisis." In *Global Value Chains in a Postcrisis World*, edited by O. Cattaneo, G. Gereffi, and C. Staritz, 335–372. Washington, DC: World Bank.

Gereffi, G., and K. Fernandez-Stark. 2010b. "The Offshore Services Global Value Chain." Chapter commissioned from the Centre on Globalization, Governance and Competitiveness, Duke University, by the Chilean Agency for Economic Development (CORFO).

Gillwald, A. 2011. "SA Telecoms: Still a Way to Go." ee publishers. http://eepublishers.co.za/article/research-act-africa.html [accessed October 19, 2012].

ILO (International Labour Organization). (various) *Yearbook of Labour Statistics*. Geneva: ILO. http://www.ilo.org/stat/Publications/Yearbook/lang–en/index.htm.

Infosys. 2006. "Win in the Flat World—Captives in India: A Research Study." Report prepared by M. Subraminian and B. Atri, February 2006. Accessed November 18, 2011. http://www.infosys.com.

———. 2008. "Win in the Flat World—Trends in BPO in Shipping and Logistics Domain." Report prepared by S. Gaikwad. http://www.infosysbpo.com/bpo-journal/Documents/future-forward.pdf [accessed October 19, 2012].

ITC (International Trade Centre). 2010. "Business Process Outsourcing: Key Lessons for Developing Countries." http://www.docstoc.com/docs/70738298/BUSINESS-PROCESS-OUTSOURCINGpdf [accessed October 19, 2012].

Kirkegaard, J. 2008. "Offshoring, Outsourcing and Production Relocations—Labor Market Effects in the OECD and Developing Asia." *Singapore Economic Review* 53 (3): 371–418.

Lacity, M., R. Hirschheim, and L.P. Willcocks. 2009. "Realizing Outsourcing Expectations: Incredible Promises, Credible Outcomes." In *The Practice of Outsourcing: From Information Systems to BPO and Offshoring*, edited by L. P. Willcocks, and M. Lacity, 37–58. Basingstoke: Palgrave Macmillan.

Mattoo, A., and S. Wunsch. 2004. "Pre-Empting Protectionism in Services: The WTO and Outsourcing." World Bank Policy Research Working Chapter 3237. Washington, DC: World Bank.

McKinsey & Co. 2005. "Creating Employment and Economic Wealth Through Developing the South African BPO&O Sector." Headline Report. http://www.tips.org.za/node/389.

Mehta, A., A. Armenakis, N. Mehta, and F. Irani. 2006. "Challenges and Opportunities of Business Process Outsourcing in India." *Journal of Labour Research* 27 (3): 323–338.

NASSCOM (National Association of Software Services). 2010. "Indian IT-BPO industry FY2011 performance & future trends." Slideshow posted on the NASSCOM Emerge Forum, February 4, 2011. http://emerge.nasscom.in/2011/02/indian-it-bpo-industry-fy2011-performance-future-trends/ [accessed October 19, 2012].

NPC. 2011. "Diagnostic Overview." National Planning Commission. Presidency, Republic of South Africa, Pretoria.

Oshri, I., J. Kotlarsky, and L. P. Willcocks (eds.). 2009. *The Handbook of Global Outsourcing and Offshoring*. Basingstoke: Palgrave Macmillan.

Palma, José Gabriel. 2008. "De-industrialization, 'Premature' De-industrialization and the Dutch Disease." *The New Palgrave Dictionary of Economics*, edited by S. N. Durlauf and L. E. Blume. 2nd ed. Palgrave Macmillan.

Philippines Congress. 2009. "Facts in Figures, No. 4." Congressional Planning and Budget Department House of Representatives, February.

Quantec. (various). http://www.quantec.co.za/

Ramos, N. M., G. Estrada, and J. Felipe. 2007. "An Analysis of the Philippine Business Process Outsourcing Industry." Working Chapter, no. 93, Economics and Research Department, Asian Development Bank, Manila.

Sako, M. 2005. "Outsourcing & Offshoring: Key Trends and Issues." Background chapter prepared by the Saïd Business School, University of Oxford, for the Emerging Markets Forum, November.

———. 2006. "Outsourcing and Offshoring: Implications for Productivity of Business Services." *Oxford Business Review* 22 (4): 499–512.

———. 2009. "Evalueserve: Globalizing the Business of Giving Insight?" Paper for the Saïd Business School, University of Oxford.

Sheppard, C. 2009. "The State of Youth in South Africa: Trends in Education Attainment." Working paper prepared for the Centre of Poverty Employment and Growth, Human Sciences Research Council, Pretoria. http://www.hsrc.ac.za/Research_Publication-21642.phtml [accessed October 19, 2012].

Sheth, J., and A. Sharma. 2006. "India as a Global Supplier of Products and Services: Expectations and Emerging Challenges." *Journal of Asia Pacific Business* 7 (3): 5–22.

Sibal, J. V. 2006. "Strengthening Offshoring in the Philippines: Issues and Concerns." *The Forum* 12 (3). http://www.up.edu.ph/upforum2.php?i=67&pg=99&pgidx=1&pgmax=7&issue=42 [accessed October 19, 2012].

Smith, D. 2006. "Offshoring: Political Myths and Economic Reality." *World Economy* 29 (3): 249–256.

Tschang, T. n.d. "The Philippines' IT-Enabled Services Industry." http://siteresources.worldbank.org/INTPHILIPPINES/Resources/Tschang-word.pdf [accessed October 19, 2012].

Van der Heijden, T. 2005. "Business Process Outsourcing in Identified Financial Services Sub-sectors." Pretoria: Human Sciences Research Council Employment Growth and Development Initiative, August. http://www.hsrc.ac.za/research/output/outputDocuments/4228_VanderHeijden_Businessprocess.pdf [accessed October 19, 2012].

Willcocks, L. P., and M. Lacity (eds.). 2009. *The Practice of Outsourcing: From Information Systems to BPO and Offshoring*. Basingstoke: Palgrave Macmillan.

Index